THE RECKO

Winner of the James Tait Memorial Prize and the Crime Writers' Association 'Gold Dagger' Award for non-fiction.

Charles Nicholl has written several books of biography, history and travel, including *A Cup of News*, *The Fruit Palace* and *The Creature in the Map*. His account of the French poet Arthur Rimbaud's years in Africa *Somebody Else*, won the 1998 Hawthornden Prize. selection of his articles and essays, *Screaming in Castle*, was published in 2000. He lives in Italy.

ALSO BY CHARLES NICHOLL

The Chemical Theatre
A Cup of News: The Life of Thomas Nashe
The Fruit Palace
Borderlines
The Creature in the Map: A Journey to El Dorado
Somebody Else: Arthur Rimbaud in Africa
Journeys (Anthology)
Screaming in the Castle (shorter pieces)

Charles Nicholl

THE RECKONING

THE MURDER OF CHRISTOPHER MARLOWE

VINTAGE BOOKS
London

Revised Edition published by Vintage 2002

10

Copyright © Charles Nicholl 1992

Revised Edition copyright © Charles Nicholl 2002

First published in Great Britain in 1992 by Jonathan Cape Ltd

Cover: detail from putative portrait of Christopher Marlowe reproduced
courtesy of The Master and Fellows of Corpus Christi College, Cambridge;
detail from Map of London and the River Thames, Sloane 2596 f.52 from
the British Library, London (photo: Bridgeman Library)

Vintage
Random House, 20 Vauxhall Bridge Road,
London SW1V 2SA

www.vintage-books.co.uk

Addresses for companies within The Random House Group Limited
can be found at:
www.randomhouse.co.uk/offices.htm

The Random House Group Limited Reg. No. 954009

A CIP catalogue record for this book is available from the British Library

ISBN 9780099437475

The Random House Group Limited supports The Forest Stewardship
Council® (FSC®), the leading international forest-certification organisation.
Our books carrying the FSC label are printed on FSC®-certified paper.
FSC is the only forest-certification scheme supported by the leading
environmental organisations, including Greenpeace. Our
paper procurement policy can be found at
www.randomhouse.co.uk/environment

Typeset by SX Composing DTP, Rayleigh, Essex
Printed and bound in Great Britain by Clays Ltd, St Ives PLC

For my Mother and Father

'I find the matter as in a labyrinth: easier to enter into it
than to go out.'
Lord Burghley, 1593

'Espionage is the secret theatre of our society.'
John Le Carré, 1989

CONTENTS

Introduction: A torch turning downward   1

Part One: The Killing

1 Deptford, 1593   13
2 The Official Story   18
3 The Witnesses   24
4 Widow Bull   40
5 Libels and Heresies   44

Part Two: Reactions

6 The First Epitaphs   59
7 The 'Goggle-eyed Sonnet'   70
8 Independent Accounts   77
9 Touchstone's Riddle   85
10 Vaughan and the Perrots   91
11 The Questions   97

Part Three: The Intelligence Connection

12 Faithful Dealing   109
13 The Elizabethan Secret Service   122
14 Thomas Walsingham   138
15 Shaking the Foundation   145
16 Robert Poley   156
17 The Babington Plot   173

Part Four: Poets and Spies

18 'Our Best for Plotting'   199

19 Thomas Watson   209

20 Fictions and Knaveries   219

21 The Wizard Earl   227

22 The 'Priest of the Sun'   241

Part Five: The Low Countries

23 New Masters   261

24 Lord Strange   268

25 The Dutch Shilling   278

26 Marlowe and Poole   286

27 Poley's Network   299

28 Roydon and the King of Scots   308

Part Six: The Frame

29 Texts of Atheism   317

30 The Damnable Crew   328

31 Placards and Fragments   346

32 The Target   356

33 'By My Only Means Set Down'   370

34 Drury Revealed   385

35 Marlowe's Liberty   400

36 The Reckoning   409

Epilogue   418

Appendix 1: False Trails   425

Appendix 2: Supplement to the Second Edition   435

Notes   462

Sources   539

Index   549

ILLUSTRATIONS

1 Coroner's inquest on the death of Christopher Marlowe, 1 June 1593
2 Signatures of Christopher Marlowe, Ingram Frizer, Nicholas Skeres and Robert Poley
3 Deptford Strand from a sketch-map of 1623
4 Extract from Richard Baines's 'Note containing the opinion of one Christopher Marly'
5 Thomas Nashe in leg-irons
6 The ghost of Robert Greene
7 Dr Gabriel Harvey
8 Edward Alleyn as Dr Faustus
9 Thomas Hariot, mathematician and 'conjuror'
10 The Queen's spymaster, Sir Francis Walsingham
11 Memorandum of the Privy Council's certificate for Christopher Marlowe, 29 June 1587
12 Part of Robert Poley's report on the Babington plot
13 Henry Percy, 9th Earl of Northumberland
14 The Dutch port of Flushing, from an atlas of 1576
15 Official docket relating to Marlowe's deportation from Flushing, 26 January 1592
16 Ferdinando Stanley, Lord Strange
17 Sir Robert Cecil
18 Poley's cypher-key and letter-drops for Low Countries intelligence
19 Informer's report on Richard Cholmeley
20 Robert Devereux, 2nd Earl of Essex
21 Sir Walter Ralegh, poet, explorer and reputed atheist
22 Interrogation of the playwright Thomas Kyd at Bridewell, 12 May 1593
23 Alterations to the scribal copy of Richard Baines's 'Note'

ACKNOWLEDGMENTS

For help in my research I am grateful to Adrian Meerman at the Gemeente Archief, Vlissingen; Karl Harrison at the Lewisham Local History Centre; and staff at the Public Record Office, British Library, London Library, Lambeth Palace Library, and Corpus Christi College, Cambridge. My thanks also to Alan Haynes, Adrian While, Josephine Nicholl, Betty Gilbert, Paul Murray, Jacqueline Korn and David Godwin; to Professor John Hazard for permission to use the unpublished work of the late Eugénie de Kalb; and of course to my wife Sally and my children, who lived with this book for longer than they might have wished.

To these acknowledgments of ten years ago, I wish to add the names of various scholars, researchers and friends who have provided or inspired new material in the second edition: David Riggs, Alan Nelson, John Bossy, Lisa Hopkins, Matt Steggle, Patrick Cheney, Mo Godman, Mark Thornton-Burnett, Peter Roberts, and Dympna Callaghan. Thanks also to my Vintage editor, Marcella Edwards. And greetings to David More of the Marlowe Lives! Association: keeper of the flame on which roasts the old chestnut of Marlowe's authorship of Shakespeare.

In the first edition I remembered two great Elizabethan scholars, Frances Yates and Muriel St Clare Byrne, and a great Shakespearean enthusiast, Ivor Davies, who had then recently died. To these I must now add Dorothy Wraight of the Marlowe Society, who died shortly before this edition went to press: she was the author of a fine biography, *In Search of Christopher Marlowe* (1965), and also of a fearsome pamphlet to 'set aright' what she regarded as wrong in

The Reckoning. My father Michael, who is one of the book's dedicatees, died in 2001: his interest in the spy's mentality was a source of my own, and thus of this book.

A Note on Dating: Elizabethan documents are frequently (but not always) dated according to the 'Old Style' new year, 25 March. Where necessary, I have amended dates to 'New Style' (e.g. a date written 1 February 1592 is here given as 1 February 1593). Another anomaly is due to the calendar reforms adopted on the continent in the late sixteenth century. Continental dating (also referred to as 'New Style') was ten days later than English dating. I have amended continental dates to English reckoning.

A Note on Prices: It is difficult to give precise modern equivalents for sums of money mentioned in the text. On the basis of the retail index, it is estimated that in 1600 £1 had the equivalent purchasing power of £133.81 today. However, this is an overal figure and does not necessarily provide good parallels: for instance, a pint of beer cost a halfpenny in 1600, but costs a good deal more than 28 new pence today. A usefully realistic coversion factor for the 1590s seems to be around 250 – in other words a penny (1d) was worth the equivalent of about £1 today. Other rounded equivalents: 1 shilling (1s) = £12, 1 noble (6s 8d) = £80, 1 angel (10s) = £120, £1 = £250. In the 1590s a meal would set you back 6d at a tavern, and 18d at a fashionable 'ordinary'. Falstaff's bill after a protracted dinner in East Cheap came to 10s 4d: this was for a capon with sauce, some anchovies and bread, and an 'intolerable deal of sack' (Spanish white wine) at around 4½d a pint. A shilling would buy you a ready-made shirt with a cut-work band, or an ounce of middle-grade tobacco, or half a dozen lemons, or a first edition of *Romeo and Juliet* in a leather binding. It would also buy you a serviceable dagger of the kind that killed Christopher Marlowe. A jobbing stonemason earned 10d a day, a writer sold a pamphlet to a publisher for £2 ('forty shillings and an odd pottle of wine') and perhaps got the same again for a dedication fee. After the death of the Earl of Leicester, his widow had an income of £3000 a year, and held capital assets worth twice that.

PREFACE TO THE SECOND EDITION

In the ten years since *The Reckoning* was published I have kept my 'Marlowe file' (in reality a collection of cardboard boxes) very much open. New material on the case has emerged, some of it in print and some in the form of personal communication, and I have pursued some new trails of my own when time has permitted. I have tried to incorporate as much of this material as possible into the second edition.

Minor additions and alterations have been inserted silently into the text, or into the 'Notes & Sources' section. More substantial additions are collected together in a new appendix (Appendix 2: Supplement to the Second Edition). These provide new information about various people and events in the book; they add to, but do not basically alter, the arguments presented in the text. The longest concerns the early career of the informer Richard Baines, further to the researches of Roy Kendall. Also included is a brief account of the life of one John Meere or Meeres, whom I suspect of some peripheral involvement in the affair, but as I cannot quite 'nail' him he must remain an appendix.

The major change concerns the final part of the book: I have completely redrafted the last section ('The Frame'). This change has been occasioned by some important discoveries – highly specific but radical in their implications – about some of the characters involved in the immediate circumstances of Marlowe's death. Among these are new documents found by Paul Hammer relating to the spy Richard Cholmeley; an important letter from Lord Buckhurst discovered by David Riggs; and my own new findings about the shadowy Thomas Drury.

This new material – and perhaps also the passage of time – has led to me to rethink the conclusions I came to about the case. Coming to any conclusion was difficult enough: I felt happier asking questions than coming up with a single over-arching answer, but after several hundred pages of questions I felt the reader was owed something approximating to an answer. My instinct now is to draw back from a schematic model of political or courtly conspiracy. (Or to draw back further from it, for in giving my 'conspiracy theory' in the first edition, I tried also to convey my sense of its limitations.) One thinks now more about what it must have been really like: these strange and deadly games you were caught up in. It is still a valid question to ask of these men clustered around Marlowe (as I asked rather exhaustively in the first edition): 'Who were they working for?' But what this question really means, within the realities of their world, is not 'Who is giving them orders?', which implies some specific and purposeful connection before the event, but 'Whose interests do they think or hope they are serving?' In other words, the keynote is not conspiracy but opportunism, and it is the foreground players, the spies and stool-pigeons, whom I tend to see as the villains, rather than any of those high-up courtly figures who may be glimpsed in the shadows behind them. Of course, the skill of these opportunists – these 'servants' – depended on them gauging correctly what their paymasters might want; and the skill of those masters depended on them getting what they wanted without any discernible proximity to a smoking gun, or in this case a bloodied blade. Deniability, one might say, is a pretty good option four hundred years after the event.

The sub-title of the book remains the same. We are talking, I still believe, about the *murder* of Christopher Marlowe: about who did it and why, and about how it came to be explained away as a 'tavern brawl'. It is a messy story, full of contradictions and uncertainties, but as Dashiell Hammett's detective says in *The Thin Man*: 'When murders are commit-ted by mathematics, you can solve them by mathematics. Most of them aren't and this one wasn't'.

INTRODUCTION

A TORCH TURNING DOWNWARD

Is THIS A true story?

Yes, in the sense that it is fact rather than fiction. The people in it are real people, the events I describe really happened, the quotations are taken verbatim from documents or books of the period. Where there is dialogue I have reconstructed it from reported speech. I have not invented anything.

Yet these true things are only part of the story, pieces of a jigsaw. Many other pieces are missing, lost between then and now. Much of this book is an attempt to fill in the spaces: with new facts, with new ways of seeing old facts, with probabilities and speculations and sometimes with guesswork. In this sense I am not telling a story but presenting a complex and rather painstaking argument. I am trying to get some meaning out of what remains, to reconnect it. It is as true as I can make it.

It all happened a long time ago, but I believe it was a case of murder, and an unsolved murder does not really age. It continues to require our attention, our questions, our unease. We owe the dead man something, and these are what we have to offer. We may never find the truth, but we can dig away some of the lies, and perhaps find beneath them a faint preserved outline where the truth once lay.

Much about the case is obscure – some things, perhaps, deliberately obscured – but the man himself is well-known. Though he had not turned thirty when he was killed,

Christopher Marlowe is still remembered. He is remembered first as a poet and playwright, as the author of *Dr Faustus* and *The Jew of Malta* and half a dozen other plays written in the late 1580s and early 1590s. A couple of his lines have passed into literary folklore: one of rapture ('Was this the face that launched a thousand ships?') and one of cruelty ('Holla, ye pampered jades of Asia').

In his brief heyday, Marlowe was probably the most popular dramatist in England. He packed them in at the famous London playhouses like the Theatre and the Rose, and at the makeshift auditoria of the provincial circuit. On one level, his success was shrewdly commercial. He gave people what they wanted: a spectacular action, exotic locations, patriotic sentiments, plenty of violence. He thrilled them with poetry – his 'high astounding terms', as he put it – and he fascinated them with a series of charismatic heroes who were usually more villain than hero. But for part of his audience, there was always something more than this *grand guignol*. They heard other, more complex messages, that layer of doubt and debate which lies beneath the surface, which at a time of rigorous state censorship had to be beneath the surface. They admired Marlowe, as we do today, for those cool sub-texts of irony and disaffection.

Words are what remain of Christopher Marlowe: words on a page, words echoing in a theatre – but other words also. He is remembered not just as a writer, but as an atheist and blasphemer, a dissolute homosexual, an Elizabethan 'roaring boy' who lived fast and died young. His famous quip – 'All they that love not tobacco and boys are fools' – has its place in the folklore too.

This side of Marlowe is to be found not in his plays, but in the reports of snoops and spies, in Privy Council papers and criminal charge-sheets. These, rather than the plays, are the texts that concern me here. I am interested in what they say about Marlowe, and in why they say it, and in what kind of truth they tell. Above all, I am interested in the strange political underworld out of which these allegations emerge. It is known that Marlowe himself was mixed up in some sort of espionage, that he found employment in the shadier strata of 'government service', but no-one has really investigated this. New evidence has emerged in the last twenty years, and more will come out in the course of this book.

The conventional wisdom is that Marlowe died in a 'tavern brawl', but we shall find that neither of these words is really accurate. The story is more complex, 'as in a labyrinth'. To find the truth about his death – or if not the truth, then at least some meaning in it – we have to go into some of the darker corners of Elizabethan politics, into that underworld to which he himself somehow belonged.

This is not a book about Marlowe the poet: there have been many of those. It is not a biography, indeed it is partly motivated by the complacency of many of his biographers on the subject of his death. Quite often it is not about Marlowe at all, but about the bad company that he kept.

Words are what remain, but there is also a portrait. It shows a striking young man: twenty-one years old, self-assured, a bit flashy. He stands with his arms folded, right over left. The stance is confident; it requires no props. It serves also to show off the rows of bossed golden buttons sewn down the sleeves of his doublet, fourteen on each arm.

The doublet is superb. In shape it is typical of the time: close-fitting, with big padded sleeves tapering to a narrow wrist. The material, black or deep brown, has the look of velvet. The zig-zag pattern is made of small slashes in the material, showing the lining underneath. You can see the jagged pattern of the tailor's pinking-shears. The lining is a peachy orange: a 'flame-coloured taffeta', perhaps, like a tart's petticoat. The doublet is so good he can offset it with casualness. He wears no ruff, no fussy ornamental pickadils, just a shirt of the fine linen called 'cobweb lawn', the collar falling over the top of the doublet, an inch of cuff at the wrist. His brown hair is long, brushed up and back. A stray curl catches on his collar. His cheeks are smooth, with just a thin tracing of beard along the jawline. The neat moustache is shaved in the dint of the upper lip.

This is the young man's statement. It is what he has made of himself, for this moment. The statement is one of prestige, of courtliness. It shows him as a young man with money to spend – not just the doublet, which even second-hand would have cost him thirty shillings or more; not just the rows of golden buttons like so many counterfeit coins; but the very fact of the portrait, which is itself a luxury.

Other parts of the statement are harder to read. The lips especially are difficult. You cannot say if he is smiling: if he is, it is not a warm smile, not a smile of complicity. He looks back out at the artist, at the world, with a quizzical gaze. The smile seems ready to mock us. We have been taken in so easily: it is only a portrait, a game he is playing.

To be scrupulous about it, we do not *know* who this young Elizabethan is. The portrait is unidentified. Its history is a blank between the year 1585, when it was painted, and the year 1953, when it was discovered by chance at Corpus Christi College, Cambridge. The Master's lodge was being refurbished for a new incumbent, Sir George Thomson. A passer-by noticed two pieces of wood protruding from a pile of builder's rubble. They proved to be two sections of an old portrait, measuring 24 × 18 inches. It was badly damaged: the colours were faded, the surface scored. It had lain for some days in the rain. It was sent to the National Portrait Gallery, where it was authenticated as a genuine Elizabethan portrait. Restored by the London art-dealers, W. Holder & Sons, it now hangs in the dining hall at Corpus Christi.

In 1955, the Canadian scholar Calvin Hoffman put forward the suggestion that the young Elizabethan in the portrait was Christopher Marlowe. The inscribed dating – '*Anno Dni 1585, Aetatis suae* 21' – is exactly correct. Marlowe was born in February 1564, and was therefore twenty-one in 1585. The provenance of the portrait is another factor, for Corpus Christi was Marlowe's own college. At the time of the portrait he was beginning his MA studies, having graduated BA in April 1584. The circumstances of its discovery suggest that the painting had been in the college for some time, concealed or forgotten, though it is unlikely to have been there continuously since 1585. It is known that the college had a small gallery of Tudor and Stuart panel-portraits, but these featured the kind of dignitaries one might expect – ten of them are listed in a catalogue prepared by the Fitzwilliam Museum in 1884; among them are portraits of Sir Thomas More, Sir Robert Cecil, John Foxe the martyrologist, and two of Archbishop Matthew Parker, himself a former Master of Corpus. There is no reason to assume that the college would have had anything to do with the commissioning of a picture of Marlowe, or would have had any wish to include the portrait of a mere student in its gallery. Marlowe was not even a particularly excellent student – in the *ordo senioritatis* of BA's in 1584 he is 199th out of 231 candidates. It is, however, entirely possible that a portrait known or believed to be of Marlowe was acquired by someone at Corpus sometime later, perhaps centuries later.

The identification is now widely accepted – at least in the sense that just about any book about Marlowe, including this one, features it on the cover. Objectors might say that this dandified young man does not look like a student, but this is not quite true. More accurately, he does not look how a student was *supposed* to look. The correct scholar's attire, as laid down in the university statutes, was an ankle-length gown and a hood. The gown should be woollen, 'of black, puke, London brown, or other sad colour'. Hair was to be worn short: 'polled, knotted or rounded'. But students and statutes do not always agree, and despite the threat of fines, there were many who flouted the regulations. They wore velvets and silks, 'excessive ruffs', 'hoses of unseemly greatness', 'deformed long locks'. In 1576, Stephen Lakes of Trinity was hauled up before the provost for wearing a 'cut taffeta doublet of the fashion', much like the young man in the portrait. He was punished with 'short commons' for a week. Another flashy undergraduate was Robert Greene, later to be Marlowe's literary rival in London. Looking back at his time at Cambridge in the 1580s, Greene recalled a mood of Bohemian bravado: 'I ruffled out in my silks, in the habit of malcontent, and seemed so discontent that no place would please me to abide in.'

In 1585 the regulations were further tightened up. The young man in the portrait disobeys most of them. In a sense, he looks exactly like a student: the kind of student that the regulations were aimed at. He identifies with the new Elizabethan mood, this explosion of colour amid the academic fustian, which was also a philosophical gesture, 'the habit of malcontent'. His imagination runs with Dr Faustus, who wished to 'fill the public schools with silk'.

There are many reproductions, but you need to see the portrait: see it for itself and for its setting. Roger, the head-porter at Corpus, greets my request with jocular disapproval. 'Christopher Marlowe? You don't want to see him. He died in a drunken brawl!'

'So they say.'

The portrait is in the panelled dining hall that Marlowe himself knew. It hangs among worthy prelates and forgotten dons, and yet not among them, for the portrait is in a corner, next to a service-door, on its own. Still, despite the acknowledgments of posterity, he does not quite belong here.

The reproductions are usually cropped. The actual portrait goes nearly down to the waist. I get a physical impression: someone quite tall, perhaps. I start to wonder about his left hand, which is concealed, perhaps under the right sleeve, more probably *in* it, in the pocket which they often had in their sleeve. What is he hiding from us? A purse, a dagger, some close-printed text in octavo? After all these years almost everything is hidden, but even if we could stand there in front of him, on a day in 1585, we still might not know what he was hiding from us.

The most striking difference in the portrait is the colouring. The book-cover reproductions give him a glamorous, rather feminine tone: the hair auburn, the lips pink, a faint blush on the cheek. Perhaps this is to do with Marlowe's supposed sexuality, or perhaps it is just the gloss we give to history. This is not the feeling of the portrait itself. It is altogether starker.

The face is pale, a sort of chalky, greyish tone. The hair is mousy brown, not auburn at all. He is less glamorous, more an intellectual. He is bookish and a bit unhealthy: too many late nights, too many dangerous trains of thought.

All this, of course, is just another layer of gloss. The colouring of the portrait is not original. It is informed artistic guesswork by a picture-restorer, Mr Vallence of Holder & Sons. He is now dead, and the only photographs of the portrait before restoration are black and white, so we do not know how much original colouring remained for him to work from. None the less, it is one step closer than a photograph, and it is as near to this young man as we will get.

We cannot know that he is Marlowe. The authorities at Corpus Christi insist on the portrait being referred to as 'putative' or 'apocryphal'. This is entirely correct, but is probably fighting a losing battle. There is a toe-hold of evidence in favour of the identification, and our need to put faces to names does the rest. In this matter, as in much that follows, we have to live with the uncertainty, with the absence of final proof. This portrait is a small pristine gift from the past. I cannot now envisage Kit Marlowe except with this boyish face, this sardonic air, this wary poise in a half-lit room.

There is also the motto, inscribed in the top left-hand corner of the portrait: '*Quod me nutrit me destruit*'. That which nourishes me also destroys me.

This is a popular Elizabethan motto, more usually written '*Quod me alit me extinguit*'. In the emblem-books of the day the device or *impresa* associated with it was a burning torch turned upside-down:

An amorous gentleman of Milan bare in his standard a torch figured burning and turning downward, whereby the melting wax, falling in great abundance, quencheth the flame; with this posy thereunto: *Quod me alit me extinguit.*

This particular description appears in Samuel Daniel's

emblem-book, *The Worthy Tract of Paulus Jovius*, which was published in 1585, the year the portrait was painted. The motto has this 'amorous', courtly meaning – the consuming passion of unrequited love – but it has many other applications: metaphysical, mystical and indeed political.

This 'posy' of doomed brilliance gives the portrait a strange biographical resonance. It seems so entirely apt for Marlowe. In 1585 he is a young man on the rise. The son of a Canterbury cobbler, the scholarship boy at Cambridge, he now stands on the threshold of a dazzling career. But the future which promises such nourishment – literary fame, government service, aristocratic friendships – also contains, as inextricably as the motto suggests, his destruction. Already he is running out of time. The torch is turning downward. In a few years he will be dead: a 'sudden & fearful end' at the age of twenty-nine.

So from his picture to his death, which is the subject of this book. What really happened? Who was responsible? And – looking at this handsome, aspiring young man in velvet and gold – what went wrong? These are the questions we owe the dead man. To begin to answer them we must first return, in the time-honoured manner, to the scene of the crime: to Deptford in the year 1593.

PART ONE

THE KILLING

I

DEPTFORD, 1593

THERE WERE OSIER-BEDS by Deptford Creek, and fishing boats drawn up along the gravelled beaches of the Thames, but already this seemed an image of Deptford's past, a memory of how it was.

What greeted you now were the sights and sounds of the great shipyards. They lay west of the creek: the Private Dock for merchant ships, the Royal Dock for the navy, and between them the sheds and warehouses of Her Majesty's Stores. Founded fifty years before, they were now working at peak capacity to supply the maritime needs of war, trade, exploration and piracy. Timber came in to Deptford by the thousand tons – English oak from the forests of Kent and Sussex, Russian spruce shipped in from Danzig – and sailed out again a few months later in the form of the *Swiftsure*, the *Peppercorn*, the *Scourge of Malice*, and dozens of others.

This was Deptford in 1593: a little Elizabethan boom-town. The expansion meant jobs and prosperity for some, high prices and racked rents for others. Local shipwrights like Peter Pett and John Addey became rich men. When Addey died in 1606 he left £200 a year for the poor of the parish, those whom jobs and prosperity had not touched.

Most of all, the expansion meant people. The parish registers, extant from 1590, suggest that for every person who died in Deptford there were ten who came into the parish to get employment or to marry – perhaps as many as 4,000 incomers during the last decade of the century, most of them living in the riverfront area known as Deptford Strand. The

13

ship-industry brought joiners and chandlers, caulkers and hemp-dressers, the clerks of the Stores and the cadets of the naval college at Trinity House. It brought a transient, rowdy population of sailors, with their tales of tropical voyages: 'nothing but eating tallow and young blackamoors', and 'five to a rat in every mess', and everyone 'lamentable sick of the scurvies'. It also brought some celebrated naval figures. The Admiral of the Fleet, Lord Howard of Effingham, had a house on the edge of Deptford Green. Another local figure was Sir John Hawkyns, the former slave-trader knighted for his services against the Armada. As Treasurer of the Navy he lived in the Treasurer's House beside the Royal Docks. He fretted to be away to sea again – 'I cannot end my life in better cause: I am out of debt and have no children to care for.' He got his wish in 1595, and died that year in Puerto Rico.

Other factors helped to crowd Deptford's tenements and lodging-houses. Less than a mile downriver, just the other side of the creek, lay the royal palace of Greenwich, the Queen's favourite residence and frequently the meeting-place of her cabinet, the Privy Council. Deptford took the overspill, provided the lodgings for minor courtiers, officials and suitors: the downmarket fringe of the court. Foreign musicians, who performed in the Queen's consorts and in the choir of the Chapel Royal, lived here – a French trumpeter, Pierre Rossel; a German singer, Dente Natrige; a Welsh chorister, Wenfayd Royce. You could hear many languages in the streets of Deptford.

Still others came from London, because in this year of 1593, with the city gripped by the 'ragingest fury' of bubonic plague, anywhere was better to be than London.

The city was close – you could take a boat up the Thames to London Bridge, or travel inland and pick up the highway – but Deptford was decidedly not London. It was in the county of Kent, in the diocese of the Bishop of Rochester, and beneath the new industrial surface it remained a village at heart. Events were still local events, the parameters were as they had always been: the riverfront, the village green, the parish church and the manor house.

The manor of Deptford was Sayes Court, a three-gabled house looking west, turned away from the winds that blow in across the marshes of Erith. There was a walled garden, with plum, apricot and cherry trees *en espalier*, and a summer-house with a 'settle round about', and beyond that a 'rude orchard' and expanses of pasture. The lord of the manor was Christopher Browne. Like his predecessors at Sayes Court, he held the picturesque title of Clerk of the Green Cloth. This made him responsible for the finances of the Royal Household, and also for the provision of meat for the court when the Queen was in residence at Greenwich. There were slaughter-yards near the manor house, and a butchers' row along the waterfront. The street-names of Deptford still recall this: Oxestalls Road, Bow Ditch, Borthwick (formerly Butcher) Road. In 1593 local residents were complaining to the Commissioners for Sewers about the state of the slaughter-house. The walls and banks adjoining it were 'in great ruin and decay, and needful to be coped'.

Inland from Sayes Court a road called Butt Lane (now Deptford High Street) ran back up towards the main London highway. The land was fertile: small rectangular fields, apple orchards, plots of woad and madder. New market-gardens were being planted, the soil enriched with manure brought in by barge from the London stockyards. Further south lay the wilderness of Lewisham and Blackheath, royal hunting-grounds. The Queen's buck-hounds howled in their kennels in Deptford.

If you looked downriver from Deptford Strand you could see the turrets and pennants of Greenwich Palace, but if you looked across the river your eye met the swampy wastes of the Isle of Dogs, a haunt of fugitives and criminals, a depository of sewage and detritus washed downriver from London. Deptford looked both ways, to the heights and the depths of Elizabethan society.

There was a day that the people of Deptford cherished in their memory, when Francis Drake was knighted aboard the *Golden Hind*. Drake and his crew returned from their three-year circumnavigation in September 1580: it was a Sunday when they entered Plymouth Sound but, there being no International Date Line, they thought it was Monday. A few weeks later Drake coasted round to the Thames, docked at Deptford, and entered London in triumph. He was mobbed in the streets, the toast of the balladeers. The Queen maintained a discreet distance from Drake's freebooting activities, but she was soon softened by estimates of the *Hind*'s cargo – over £300,000 worth of jewels and bullion, much of it plundered from the Spanish galleon *Nuestra Señora de la Concepcion*, vulgarly known as the *Cacafuego*, the 'Fire-shitter' – and on 4 April 1581 she journeyed in state to visit Drake aboard the *Hind* in Deptford.

It was one of those magnetic events around which the folklore instantly clusters: the richness of the banquet, the radiance of the Queen, the press of the crowd that caused the gangway to crack and deposit a hundred people in the mud below, though on this auspicious day not one of them was injured.

When the feast was done – the story goes – the Queen had Drake kneel before her. She said that the King of Spain had demanded his head. 'Now,' she joked, 'I have a golden sword to strike it off.'

She did not actually knight Drake herself, but handed the sword to her guest, Monsieur de Mondoucet, the ambassador from her long-time suitor, the Duke of Anjou. It was he that conferred the knighthood, the scene bathed in a symbolic glow of Anglo-French amity. The Queen then 'consecrated' the ship and ordered for it to be laid up at Deptford, in dry-dock, as a monument to the first Englishman to have 'circuited round the whole earth'. She gave her famous speech about the freedom of the sea: 'that the use of the sea, as of the air, is common to all, and that the public necessity permits not it should be possessed.' Fine words, though also politic ones: a charter for plunderers and freebooters like her 'little pirate' Drake.

The *Hind* remained at Deptford, a tourist attraction, suffering from souvenir-hunters who hacked bits off to take home. Few who were on the waterfront that day in 1581 can have forgotten the stirring spectacle. They were meant to see and remember it: the ceremony was performed out on deck, in the full spate of royal razzmatazz.

Twelve years later, in 1593, there was this other event in Deptford. It was not a sumptuous public spectacle like the knighting of Drake, but a shabby affair, performed in privacy and tidied away in haste. It featured a twelvepenny dagger rather than a golden sword. If the victim had not been a poet of genius it would now be long forgotten.

This is a story of the underside of Elizabethan politics, not the glittering propagandist surface. It is part of the unauthorised version. It has the feel of history in the raw, history as it suddenly happens. A man is walking in a garden in Deptford on a summer afternoon. The smell of the garden is sweet, but a breath of river-breeze takes the sweetness away, and there is the familiar stink: fish, pitch and sewage, the dung-boats and the dog-kennels, the slaughter-yards busy for some stately banquet, the blood running down Bow Ditch and into the river.

2

THE OFFICIAL STORY

CHRISTOPHER MARLOWE WAS stabbed to death in Deptford on the evening of Wednesday 30 May 1593. The coroner's inquest, held two days later, gives a brief but detailed account of the killing. It may not be an entirely true account, but it is the one we must begin with.

At about 10 o'clock that morning, four men met at a house in Deptford Strand. They were Ingram Frizer, Nicholas Skeres, Robert Poley and Christopher Marlowe. The house where they met belonged to a widow named Eleanor Bull. In a certain room there, they spent the morning together in conversation. The room contained a bed, a table, a bench: these are the only furnishings we hear of in the inquest. The four men took lunch together, and afterwards walked in the garden. Their mood was 'quiet'. The meeting has an air of privacy.

At about six o'clock in the evening, they came in from the garden, to the same room, and had supper. After supper Marlowe lay down on the bed. The other three were sitting at the table, in a row, with Ingram Frizer in the middle. According to a later account they were playing 'tables' – backgammon – but this is not mentioned by the coroner.

An argument flared up. Marlowe and Frizer spoke 'malicious words' to one another. They were quarrelling about the bill, the 'sum of pence owed' for the day's food and drink. The word used in the inquest is the 'recknynge', or reckoning.

Frizer was sitting at the table with his back to Marlowe. He had Skeres and Poley either side of him, in such a way that he 'could in no wise take flight'. Marlowe, 'moved with anger', leapt from the bed. He snatched up Frizer's dagger from its sheath, and struck him twice about the head with it. The wounds on Frizer's head, measured afterwards, were two inches long and a quarter of an inch deep. They were flesh-wounds, slashes more than stabs. One inference is that they were inflicted with the hilt rather than the blade of the dagger. This was a recognised form of attack: to 'pummel' means literally to strike someone with the hilt or 'pommel' of a dagger.

Frizer, still hemmed in by Skeres and Poley, struggled with Marlowe to get the dagger off him. 'And so it befell, in that affray, that the said Ingram, in defence of his life, with the dagger aforesaid of the value of twelve pence, gave the said Christopher a mortal wound above his right eye, of the depth of two inches and of the width of one inch.' From this wound, Christopher Marlowe 'then & there instantly died'.

Judging from this description, the point of the dagger went in just above the right eye-ball, penetrated the superior orbital fissure at the back of the eye-socket, and entered Marlowe's brain. On its way the blade would have sliced through a major blood-vessel, the internal carotid artery. The actual cause of death was probably a massive haemorrhage into the brain, or possibly an embolism from the inrush of air along the track of the wound. [See Appendix 2.1]

Such details are not recorded by the coroner. Nor does he mention Marlowe's 'brains coming out at the dagger's point' when the blade was extracted, nor that Marlowe 'died swearing'. These appear in later accounts: they must be considered dramatic rather than factual, though they may well be right. The blood and the scream are not the coroner's concern. He simply notes that Marlowe died 'instantly'.

The document has little else to tell us. In the immediate after-math of the event, the only thing considered worthy of record is the behaviour of Ingram Frizer. He 'neither fled nor withdrew himself'. The crime of homicide brought automatic imprisonment on a charge of felony. He would face the death-penalty unless he could prove he had killed in self-defence. He stood his ground, however, and he was present, along with Skeres and Poley, when the inquest opened on the morning of Friday 1 June, thirty-six hours after the killing.

The man in charge of the inquest was William Danby, Coroner to the Royal Household. Such an important official would not usually be involved in a routine stabbing incident, but Danby's position charged him with all legal investigations 'within the verge'. The 'verge' was defined as the area within a twelve-mile radius of the body of the Queen. The house of Eleanor Bull at Deptford lay less than a mile from Greenwich Palace.

Sixteen jurors were assembled, good men and true: gentlemen and yeomen, land-owners and wharf-owners, two bakers, a grocer, a miller. Most were local men. The miller, Robert Baldwin, kept Brook Mill, spanning the creek on the road between Deptford and Greenwich. The bakers, George Halfpenny and Henry Dabyns, both held tenements in Deptford. William Curry owned profitable pasture in Deptford Strand: the sixteen-acre New Dross Field, and three closes called Longlands, Brookshottes and Brome Close. He took in his rents twice yearly in the north porch of the parish church, St Nicholas's.

As far as it went, the inquest was thorough and efficient. It was held at the site of the crime, and upon view of the victim's body. The various cuts and wounds were measured, the lay-out of the room noted, the weapon priced, the testimonies taken. Coroner Danby was an experienced official: he had begun his legal studies at the Inns of Court half a century ago, and had been coroner for the last four years. The finding of the inquest was that Ingram Frizer had killed Marlowe 'in the defence and saving of his own life'.

Later that day the poet's body was carried from Mistress Bull's house, through the dockyard streets, to the church of St Nicholas on the edge of Deptford Green. There he was buried, in an unmarked grave. According to local tradition it was near the North tower, the only part of the church that remains as it was in Elizabethan times. It is possible that news of his death had reached his friends, and that some were at the graveside on that June afternoon. Five years later, the publisher Edward Blount issued the first edition of Marlowe's poem, *Hero and Leander*. He dedicated it to a former patron of Marlowe's, Thomas Walsingham. 'Sir,' he wrote,

> We think not ourselves discharged of the duty we owe to our friend when we have brought the breathless body to the earth. For albeit the eye there taketh his ever-farewell of that beloved object, yet the impression of the man that hath been dear unto us, living an afterlife in our memory, there putteth us in mind of farther obsequies due unto the deceased.

This may be an actual memory shared, and it may be that Blount, Walsingham and others were present to take an 'ever-farewell' of Marlowe.

The vicar of St Nicholas's, Thomas Macander, noted the burial in the parish register. The entry reads: 'Christopher Marlow slaine by ffrauncis ffrezer'. The vicar's error – writing Francis instead of Ingram – was no doubt innocent, but it began a trail of misinformation that persisted for centuries.

Ingram Frizer probably remained in custody while the legal wheels turned. He would also have petitioned the Lord Chancellor for his case to be heard, though this document has not been found. On 15 June, a writ of *certiorari* was issued, summoning the case into the Chancery court, and Coroner Danby was ordered to submit his inquest to the court officials. On Thursday 28 June, just four weeks after Marlowe was buried, the Queen issued a formal pardon. This was a remarkably quick outcome by Elizabethan standards: some have thought it suspiciously quick. Ingram Frizer had killed his man in self-defence, and the case was therefore closed.

This may be called the official story of Marlowe's death: a trifling quarrel, a tragic mishap, a thorough investigation, a decent burial, a sensible verdict. The tenor of the official story is that here is nothing out of the ordinary. If Coroner Danby knew anything about the dead man, or about the three witnesses, or about the web of association that brought them together in Deptford – if he knew anything at all out of the ordinary about the case – he made no mention of it in his report. This was routine business: another casual, sordid Elizabethan death. In a month when the plague killed nearly two thousand people in London alone, death was certainly routine.

There were other accounts of the killing, some of them eventually finding their way into print. They add a few stray details to the story, which we will look at later, but they are mostly based on hearsay, and animated more by moral disapproval of Marlowe than by a desire for facts. Any investigation of Marlowe's death has to begin with the inquest: with what it says and with what it does not say.

It gives us certain indisputable facts, but we must be clear which those are. It is undoubtedly true that those four men met at the house in Deptford, that Marlowe died in their company that evening, that the cause of his death was a stab wound above the right eye, and that the wound was inflicted by the twelvepenny dagger of Ingram Frizer. These were facts that could be corroborated by other witnesses, or determined from the physical evidence. There is no reason to suppose that the coroner and his jurors were mistaken, or in any way misrepresented the evidence presented to them. These, and these only, are the facts of which we can be sure.

The major flaw in the inquest is the lack of any independent witness *inside* the room where Marlowe died. For an account of the actual 'affray' – the most crucial evidence of all – the inquest had to rely on the testimony of Skeres and Poley. They, together with the defendant Frizer, were the only people who actually knew what had happened. They are not quite independent witnesses, because they were physically involved in the fight, and – in the case of Skeres – because he was a known accomplice of the defendant's (known as such to some, but possibly not to the coroner and his jurors). The precise sequence of events inside that room, and the

22

immediate motive cause of the killing – the argument over the 'reckoning' – are not established facts enshrined in the legal record. They are part of a story, told by Nicholas Skeres and Robert Poley.

Their account is plausible: Marlowe had been involved in knife-fights before, one in Canterbury just a few months previously. It is also convenient: certainly convenient for Ingram Frizer, perhaps for others too. But what is plausible and convenient is not necessarily true. And if Frizer, Skeres and Poley were lying about what happened, then the official story – for all its thoroughness, for all its nearness to the event – is also a lie.

Of the many questions to be asked about Marlowe's death, the first concerns these three men, the companions of his last hours and the witnesses of his killing. What the inquest tells us about them can be summed up in a sentence. They are all three '*generosi*' – gentlemen – and residents of London. But what kind of men were they, and how much can we trust their version of events?

3

THE WITNESSES

IN THE SUMMER of 1598 a bill of complaint was lodged in the Chancery court by Drew Woodleff of Aylesbury, Buckinghamshire, and his mother Anne. They complain about the underhand dealings of a pair of loan-sharks who had tricked Drew out of the sum of £34. The events they describe took place 'about five years now last past', in other words in mid-1593, around the time of Marlowe's death. The two fraudsters, working together to 'undermine and deceive' young Drew Woodleff, were Ingram Frizer and Nicholas Skeres.

The story, such as it can be reconstructed, is as follows. Robert Woodleff, Drew's father, died in January 1593, and within a few months Drew was in dire financial straits. He 'made request unto' Nicholas Skeres for assistance. Skeres was, he says, a man he held in some 'affection'. Skeres said he was unable to help: he had no ready cash by virtue of 'employing his money to usury'. Instead he introduced Woodleff to Ingram Frizer. Frizer promised Woodleff £60 'against his time of need'. He persuaded Woodleff to sign a bond – an IOU – to him for that sum. He then told Woodleff that he too had no ready money, and offered him instead a 'commodity'.

Frizer was playing a familiar extortioner's game. Marlowe's friend Thomas Nashe, a perennial debtor, complained about the 'notorious cosenage and villainy' that is 'shrouded under this seventy-fold usury of commodities'. Since the statute on usury of 1572, money-lenders were

24

bound to a maximum interest-rate of 10 per cent. They got round this by offering, instead of cash, a 'commodity' – goods represented as being worth the sum in question, but invariably worth far less. They were often the kind of goods that were almost impossible for the debtor to convert into cash except by selling them back to the lender, or to some accomplice of his, at a reduced rate. A popular commodity was lute-strings, another grey paper. In Greene and Lodge's play, *A Looking Glass for London*, a debtor complains:

I pray you, sir, consider that my loss was great by the commodity I took up. You know, sir, I borrowed of you forty pound, whereof I had ten pounds in money, and thirty pounds in lute-strings, which when I came to sell again, I could get but five pounds for them, so I had, sir, but fifteen pounds for my forty.

Marlowe too speaks of these 'tricks belonging unto brokery'. They have 'filled the jails with bankrouts', and 'every moon made some or other mad, and now and then one hang himself for grief.'

The commodity which Frizer offered to Drew Woodleff was 'a certain number of guns or great iron pieces' which he had stored on Tower Hill. Woodleff agreed, and asked Frizer to help him sell them. This Frizer did, or pretended to do. He then gave Woodleff only £30, which he claimed was all he could get for them. The net result was that Frizer – who had never offered the guns for sale anyway – had lent him £30, and had a signed bond to receive £60: a loan at 100 per cent interest.

Despite this, Woodleff continued to deal with Skeres and Frizer, and there followed a further piece of chicanery, in which they once more 'combined' to defraud the gullible young heir. Skeres claimed that he owed Frizer twenty marks (£4), and he persuaded Woodleff to help him out by signing a bond to Frizer for this sum. Woodleff, 'in his then unwary age', consented to this. By now he was in debt to Frizer for a total of £64. In order to cover the debt, he was forced to enter still deeper into hock, and sign a 'statute staple' for £200 to a certain 'gent of good worship'. This statute – a particular kind of bond which allowed the seizure of the debtor's land in case of default – is dated 29 June 1593. It was entered the day after Frizer received the Queen's pardon for the killing of Marlowe. Frizer was probably in custody throughout June, so it looks like he and Skeres were at work on Woodleff in about April or May.

The Woodleff case provides two connections not mentioned in the coroner's inquest on Marlowe's death. The first is the connection between Frizer and Skeres: they were accomplices, business-partners of a sort. The second is the connection between Frizer and Marlowe, for the 'gent of good worship', the beneficiary of Woodleff's statute, was Thomas Walsingham of Chislehurst, a young cousin of the great spymaster Sir Francis Walsingham. According to the Woodleffs, Thomas Walsingham was at this time Frizer's 'master'. Other documents bear this out, linking Frizer with the family – particularly with Thomas's wife, Audrey Walsingham – well into the next century. And Thomas Walsingham was also Marlowe's 'master', or patron, at this time. Marlowe was himself at Scadbury, Walsingham's country house near Chislehurst, in the weeks before his death. A government messenger, despatched to find him on 18 May, was directed 'to repair to the house of Mr Tho: Walsingham in Kent'. It may have been at Scadbury that Marlowe wrote *Hero and Leander*, unfinished at his death, and later dedicated to Walsingham by the publisher, Edward Blount.

These connections start to flesh out the meeting at Deptford. The Woodleff case also tells us something of the type and character of two of Marlowe's companions that day. They were sharps, wheeler-dealers, real life 'conny-catchers' of the kind exposed in underworld pamphlets of the time. They operated on the edge of the law while never seeming quite to overstep it.

Virtually all we know about Ingram Frizer comes from documents of this sort. He was an Elizabethan businessman:

no better, but not much worse, than most. Nothing is known of his birth and origins. The earliest record of him is a transaction, in Basingstoke, in the autumn of 1589. On 9 October he purchased the Angel Inn for £120. Two months later he sold it again, 'for a competent sum', to a wealthy local man, James Deane. There may be a family connection here, for nearly twenty years later Deane included Frizer in his will. He bequeathed him £20, and 'so much black cloth as will make him a cloak'. He also – figuring perhaps that a lifetime was long enough to keep trying – 'forgave' Frizer a debt of £5. Deane's sister Margery married into another prominent Hampshire family, the Chamberlains of Kingsclere. Her son, Andrew Chamberlain, made a similar bequest to Frizer in his will. Both Deane and Chamberlain are described as 'citizen and draper of London'. [See Appendix 2.2]

Frizer was a man with disposable capital. Having paid out £120 to purchase the Angel Inn, he was still in a position to offer further cash, in the form of a loan, to one of the vendors, Thomas Bostock. How much he loaned depends on what his credit rate was: the bond Bostock signed bound him to repay Frizer the sum of £240. Bostock failed to discharge the debt, and Frizer sued. His suit was heard in the Exchequer in June 1591: the court proceedings describe him as a 'yeoman' of London. In the Easter Term of 1592 he won his case, and received the sum owed, plus £4 costs.

A couple of years later he was in the courts again. On 28 June 1594, exactly a year after he received the Queen's pardon for killing Marlowe, he took out a three-year lease on a house in Southwark, close to the Rose theatre where Marlowe's plays had often been performed. He took possession immediately, but three days later a man called Ballard entered the house and 'drove him out'. Again Frizer sued, and again he won. He was a man who knew how to use the law, who trusted it, as he did that night in Deptford when he 'neither fled nor withdrew himself'.

This is Ingram Frizer as one might know him in the year 1593: a property speculator, a commodity broker, a fixer for gentlemen of good worship, a friend to the citizen-drapers, a racker of young fools like Woodleff. His métier is money: the power of capital, the price of everything. In the Exchequer court in 1591 he was a 'yeoman'. A couple of years later, at the Deptford inquest, he is a 'gentleman'. These terms are not clear-cut, but they counted for a lot: they describe an impression as much as an exact status. We could call Frizer 'upwardly mobile', with the brittleness and effort which that term suggests.

He was something to Marlowe but we do not know what: a friend, a contact, a creditor. According to a later account of the killing, it was Frizer that invited Marlowe to Deptford, 'for a feast'. According to another, Marlowe attacked Frizer because 'he ought a grudge' against him. The only link between them that we know for sure is that they shared the same 'master', Thomas Walsingham. They were fellow hangers-on at Scadbury House: the poet and the financial adviser. They are linked in dependence, and then in violence.

Nicholas Skeres, an accomplice in the gulling of Woodleff and a companion at Mistress Bull's in Deptford, steps out of the same world. Even more than Frizer, he belongs quite unequivocally down the shady end of it.

He was born in March 1563: he was thirty years old at the time of the Deptford affray, a year older than Marlowe. He was a Londoner, though the family traced itself back to the Skyeres of Skyeres Hall, near Wentworth in Yorkshire. His father, Nicholas Skeres senior, was a merchant-tailor. An uncle, Ralph, was a draper. The family belongs to the same citizen milieu as Frizer. They lived in the parish of Allhallows-the-Less, down near the river between Dowgate and Coldharbour. Skeres senior died in 1566, leaving his estate to his wife, Audrey, and his two sons, Jerome and Nicholas. The estate included lands in Yorkshire and Surrey, as well as the London property. Nicholas was three years old when his father died.

While still a teenager, Skeres fell in – partly as a debtor, partly as an accomplice – with certain notables in the money-lending racket: men like Richard Parradine, whom he first met in a tavern in the year 1576; and John Wolfall of Silver Street, a skinner by trade. Skeres's long association with Wolfall led eventually to a law-suit, filed by one of their victims, John Smith. In April 1593 – just a month before the meeting at Deptford – Skeres was questioned at length in Star Chamber. The charges, and his answers, show that the gulling of Drew Woodleff was entirely typical of his dealings. Over the last ten or twelve years, he says, he has been used by Wolfall as an 'instrument' to 'draw young gents into bonds'. For this winding-in service, Wolfall would pay him a small commission, 'xl shillings, or some suchlike petty sum'. Skeres probably had the same kind of arrangement with Ingram Frizer.

Skeres's deposition in Star Chamber was excavated from the Public Record Office stacks in the 1940s but none of Marlowe's biographers has since mentioned it. Through a veil of legal opacities we glimpse Skeres in his element. We are at his lodgings in fashionable Blackfriars. His mark, John Smith, arrives there with a friend, expecting to sign a bond and leave with £70. He does not know that Skeres is working on behalf of Wolfall. As Skeres gives his spiel, Smith's friend grows suspicious about the terms of the deal:

> You [Skeres] told the plaintiff [Smith] that he and you should seal a bond of £120 . . . whereupon the plaintiff's friend spake to him in his ear, which you perceiving, withdrew the plaintiff into a chamber adjoining, where a scrivener's man was, with the bond ready engrossed, and there willed the plaintiff not to grow jealous of your dealing, protesting you meant honestly, and would faithfully perform what you had promised.

Smith is persuaded, the bond is signed, but Skeres does not, after all, have the cash. New arrangements are made: Smith must come to a scrivener's house in Ludgate, by 2 o'clock that afternoon, to receive the money. Thus begin the delays and recriminations, the ducking and weaving, and by the time the case comes to court Smith has still not received 'one penny of money or pennyworth of wares in lieu of the said bond'.

Skeres's answers to the charges sound confident enough. The bond in question, he claims, has been 'cancelled and defaced': everything is above board. He makes no effort to deny his general role as a usurer's tout. He is, he says, a victim himself. He is deeply in debt to Wolfall, and has been forced to work for him by 'threats' and 'fair promises', in the 'hope of clearing such old arrearages'. Once, when he refused to follow instructions, Wolfall 'did threat, and say he would make England too hot for him'.

In the early 1580s, Skeres was resident at Furnival's Inn in Holborn, perhaps as a student of law. Furnival's was one of the Inns of Chancery (as opposed to the Inns of Court). Here he could learn yet more about the legal niceties of money. During his time there, Skeres knew another young law-student, the poet Matthew Roydon, who was enrolled at Thavies Inn. In January 1582, Roydon signed a bond for £40 to a London goldsmith. His co-signatories in the bond were Nicholas Skeres and his brother Jerome. It is very likely that Skeres was playing his usual tout's role in this. It is one of his techniques, as described in the Star Chamber deposition: having drawn his 'young gents' to the money-lender, he would then be 'joined with them' in the bond. Whatever the outcome of this particular transaction, Matthew Roydon continued to deal with Skeres, and he was duly enticed by him into the Wolfall web. By 1593, he and two others were bound to Wolfall in the considerable sum of £150. At this time, Skeres tells us, Roydon 'makes his abode in the Blackfriars, at a shoemaker's house there'.

This is another unspoken connection behind the Deptford meeting: Skeres knows Roydon, and Roydon is – as we shall see – a close friend and associate of Marlowe's. Another writer, well-known to both Marlowe and Roydon, was George Chapman, author of *The Shadow of Night* and later the famous translator of Homer who inspired Keats. He too was caught up in the snares of John Wolfall the skinner in the early 1580s. There is a strong supposition that Skeres and Marlowe knew one another through such mutual connections. Skeres, at any rate, is a figure on the edges of this literary set: a plausible, predatory young man, a purveyor of breakable promises. He is your bounden friend until the ink is dry, and then his countenance changes.

Another of Skeres's sidelines comes to light in a report compiled by William Fleetwood, Recorder of London. In July 1585, Fleetwood wrote to Lord Burghley about a 'number of masterless men & cutpurses, whose practice is to rob gentlemen's chambers and artificers' shops in and about London'. There are forty-five names listed, some of them known only by underworld nicknames like 'Staring Robyn' and 'Welsh Dick'. One of the names on the list is Nicholas Skeres. He was by no means a 'masterless man' (an unemployed vagrant), nor probably was he a cut-purse, but thieves need contacts for the disposing of stolen goods, and what we know of Skeres fits him well enough for this job.

Fleetwood's report names the various haunts and 'harbouring houses' of this light-fingered crew: inns mostly – the Crown at Bishopsgate, the Maidenhead by the Town Ditch, the Bear and Ragged Staff at Charing Cross, the Pressing Iron at Southwark – but also some private dwellings. At a house in Smart's Key, there are 'divers posies' written 'in a table'. One of these goes: '*Si spie sporte, si non spie tunc steale*' (which means, I suppose: if someone's watching, play it cool; if not, then steal). Another exhorts the company to 'foist, nip, lift, shave & spare not'. Fleetwood helpfully glosses: to 'foist' is to pick a pocket, to 'nip' is to cut a purse, to 'lift' is to rob a shop or gentleman's chamber, and to 'shave' is 'to filch a cloak, a sword, a silver spoon or suchlike, that is negligently looked unto'. This is the arcane jargon that Robert Greene later publicised in his 'conny-catching' pamphlets.

There is no record that Skeres was prosecuted over this matter, and no mention is made of it in the Star Chamber examination. It is an allegation, rather than a proven fact, but I find it convincing enough. He has been seen in these dives, seen in the company of known criminals. Perhaps he is just a dodgy young gentleman with a taste for the underworld. More likely he is turning a profit. To John Wolfall the skinner, whose fingers smell faintly of rancid blood, he brings sometimes a poet in need, and sometimes a tasty trinket filched by Staring Robin.

The border between the criminal world and the secret world is a shifting one, and a year after this Skeres surfaces on the fringes of government intelligence work. And so the meeting at Deptford takes another twist.

In the summer of 1586, the net was drawing in around the Catholic conspiracy now known as the 'Babington plot'. The aim of the conspirators was nothing less than the assassination of Queen Elizabeth and the liberation of the imprisoned Mary Stuart, to rule as a Catholic monarch of England. The Queen's spymaster, Sir Francis Walsingham, had staked out the conspiracy from its inception, and was now ready to make arrests. On the morning of 3 August 1586, one of his assistants, Francis Milles, received information that Anthony Babington, 'with others like himself', had taken new lodgings near Bishopsgate. A watch was put on the premises. Later that day Milles reported the names of two of Babington's 'crew' who had been seen there: 'Dunn' and 'Skyeres'. Dunn is Henry Dunne, who was among those executed the following month. 'Skyeres' – a spelling he uses in his signature – is almost certainly Nicholas Skeres.

It looks like he was there as a government plant. He was recognised by Walsingham's watchers, and was named without further comment in Milles's report. His name does not figure among those later arrested. He quietly drops from the story, almost certainly because he was Walsingham's man all along. If so, he was one of many such infiltrators and 'false brothers' involved in the Babington plot. This was the tone of the times. The military threat from Spain and the Papal alliance was being aided and compounded by the subversive threat of Catholic loyalists at home, the 'enemy within': that, at any rate, was the view of anti-Catholic hard-liners like Walsingham. It was a time of crisis management, of suspicion and surveillance, of special powers of investigation to 'make windows in men's souls'. Spies and tale-tellers were everywhere, gaining and selling confidences. Thus Nicholas Skeres, glimpsed in the company of Anthony Babington in a not so safe house in Bishopsgate. The terms people used about him in his financial dealings – 'undermining and deceiving', 'entrapping young gents' – suggest his aptitude for this kind of political work.

The next we hear of Skeres is three years later, and his career is prospering. In July 1589, he carried confidential letters to court from the Earl of Essex, who was then at Exeter. He received official payment for this service, under a warrant signed by Sir Francis Walsingham, and was despatched back to the Earl with answers. This was just after Essex's return from the 'Portingale voyage', an abortive English expedition on behalf of the Portuguese pretender, Don Antonio. Essex had incurred the Queen's disfavour by joining the voyage without her permission – she wrote demanding his return, to explain his 'strange actions' and 'undutiful departure' – so it may be that Skeres was carrying letters of some delicacy from the wayward Earl.

This suggests that Skeres was already in Essex's service by 1589. He certainly was a couple of years later, for in the course of the evidence he gave in Star Chamber concerning his dealings with Wolfall the skinner, he mentions that he 'went into France' with the Earl in the summer of 1591. He describes Essex as his 'Lord and Master'. This statement, recorded in the semi-legible scrawl of the Star Chamber clerk, is quite unequivocal. As far as I know, it has never been noticed before. It is yet another item of information not contained in the Deptford inquest. Skeres is a servant of the Earl of Essex, as Frizer is of Thomas Walsingham. Essex was the charismatic young star of the court, the Queen's latest 'minion'. He attracted a motley crew of opportunists and adventurers: Skeres is not the only one we shall come across in this story.

Skeres's going 'into France' with Essex would have been as part of the English expedition sent to assist Protestant French troops against Spanish incursion from the Netherlands. It was Essex's first military command. He landed at Dieppe in

August 1591, at the head of a troop of 4,000, and promptly set off – again disobeying the Queen's instructions – to rendezvous with Henri of Navarre at Compiègne. He entered Henri's battle-camp in style: a troop of a hundred horsemen, six pages mounted on charges, six trumpets sounding before him, and a personal entourage of 'twelve tall body-squires'. He wore a jewelled velvet cloak and his charger wore matching accessories. An observer nimbly calculated that 'his dress and the furniture of his horse alone were worth 60,000 crowns'. Among this troop, perhaps, sporting the Earl's tangerine and white livery, was Nicholas Skeres. The campaign was indecisive, and within a few months Essex's force was down to a thousand. In the atrocious conditions of the battle-camp, more died from dysentery than from enemy action. By the end of the year Essex was preparing to pull out. He 'sent away with passport as many as were able to creep towards Dieppe on their feet', and on 8 January 1592 he handed over command to Sir Roger Williams. Soon afterwards he embarked for England. Skeres was in service in France for the full duration, for he states that he 'did not return back into England until Shrovetide' – mid-February 1592.

The following year there came the case in Star Chamber, and the milking of Drew Woodleff, and then that unpleasant business at Deptford. Skeres remained in the Essex circle, for in 1595 he is described in police records at a 'servant' of Essex. It is almost the last we hear of him, and the circumstances are once again unsavoury.

At five o'clock on the afternoon of 13 March 1595, 'Nicholas Kyrse, alias Skeers' was arrested by the officers of Sir Richard Martin, Alderman of London. He was one of thirteen men and two women – 'a very dangerous company, and very well provided of weapons' – found at the house of Edmund Williamson in Philip Lane, near Cripplegate. The house was raided in connection with Williamson's brother, Nicholas, a captured Catholic who was under interrogation at the Gatehouse prison.

Skeres was committed close prisoner, along with the others,

in the Counter in Wood Street. The following day they were examined by Alderman Martin. With some disappointment the alderman finds reasonable cause for their presence at Williamson's house. Williamson is 'a most notable broker, to help young men to money upon all kinds of wares upon excessive loss' – in other words, a commodity-broker like Ingram Frizer, John Wolfall and the rest. In their search of Williamson's house, the officers had found 'nothing but wares and bills of contract' and other papers relating to his 'evil bargains'. It is decided to 'discharge all the persons committed that gave us good account of their dealings'. Skeres was among those released, for only Edmund Williamson and another brother, James, were further detained. [See Appendix 2.3]

Nicholas Skeres belongs with Ingram Frizer in this world of 'notable brokers' and their 'evil bargains', but his career also touches on the shadier edges of politics. This brings us to the third of the witnesses to Marlowe's death: Robert Poley.

If Skeres was a minor cog in the entrapment of Babington in 1586, he is likely to have known Poley, for Poley was one of the major players in the government's counter-moves against the conspiracy. He shuttled between Babington and Walsingham, embraced by both, fully trusted by neither. Among his tasks was to provide lodgings and entertainment for the conspirators. On the evening of 2 August, one of Walsingham's watchers 'found Babington to be in town, and was directed where he and a whole knot might have been taken at supper in Poley's garden'. This 'knot' of Babington's accomplices probably included Skeres – identified as one of Babington's company the following day – so we have here a strange premonitory glimpse of the Deptford meeting: Poley and Skeres at a supper party on a summer's evening. On that earlier occasion the atmosphere was heavy with tension and mistrust. The conspirators were not taken that night, but one of the ring-leaders was arrested at Poley's lodgings two days later. As he prepared to flee from London, Babington wrote a last poignant letter to Poley: 'Farewell sweet Robyn, if as I take thee true to me. If not, adieu *omnium bipedum nequissimus.*' Of all two-footed creatures the worst. That must have been Babington's final verdict, when his doubts about Poley proved to be well-founded.

Of the three men present at the stabbing of Marlowe, Robert Poley is the most complex, perhaps the most sinister. His career as a government agent can be traced over two decades. It took him to Denmark, France, Scotland and the Netherlands, as well as into the Tower and the Marshalsea, the political prisons of Elizabethan London. He was notorious among Catholics as a double-dealer, informer, *agent provocateur*, and – according to some accusations – poisoner. He has been called 'the very genius of the Elizabethan underworld'.

On the day of Marlowe's death Poley had recently returned from one of his confidential missions to the Netherlands. Two weeks later, on 12 June 1593, he received payment of £30 for this work, on a warrant signed by Sir Thomas Heneage, who disbursed such payments in his office as Treasurer of the Chamber. According to this warrant, Poley was paid

> for carrying of letters in post for Her Majesty's special and secret affairs of great importance, from the Court at Croydon the viijth of May 1593 into the Low Countries to the town of the Hague in Holland, and for returning back again with letters of answer to the Court at Nonsuch the viijth of June 1593, being in Her Majesty's service all the aforesaid time.

This chronology is interesting. Poley was despatched from court – then being held at Archbishop Whitgift's manor-house in Croydon – on 8 May, and returned to court, by then removed to Nonesuch Palace, exactly a month later, on 8 June. As we know from the Deptford inquest, he was actually back in England by the morning of 30 May at the latest. There is, in other words, a period of about ten days during which Poley was involved in some other kind of business than the transmission of intelligence between the court and the Low

Countries. This other business apparently detains him for a week *after* the killing at Deptford, for it is not until 8 June that he presents himself and his 'letters of great importance' at Nonesuch.

The last phrase in the warrant is also interesting: 'being in Her Majesty's service all the aforesaid time'. There are twenty-six payments to Poley recorded in the Chamber accounts. They stretch over nearly thirteen years, from 1588 to 1601. This is the only entry to contain this covering phrase. It is an exculpation, an avoidance of awkward questions, natural enough in the circumstances. None the less it should be noted. Technically speaking, Poley was on government business that day at Mrs Bull's house.

If there is an 'unofficial story' to the death of Marlowe, this very unofficial gentleman may well be a part of it. He was a man of great charm – 'Sweet Robyn' – and great danger. The keeper of the Marshalsea prison, who had reason to know him well, warned: 'he will beguile you of your wife or of your life.' Others described him as a 'very bad fellow', and a 'notable knave with no trust in him'. According to the Jesuit poet Robert Southwell, he was – like Marlowe – 'either an atheist or an heretic, or both'. And a serving-man called Thomas Wenden, involved in an uprising at Colchester in 1596, was looking forward to nothing so much in the coming revolution as the chance 'to cut Poley's throat'.

Even more than Frizer and Skeres, Poley's reputation undermines the reliability of the evidence given at the Deptford inquest. His slipperiness under questioning was well-known. He bragged of it. He even claimed that he had outwitted Sir Francis Walsingham, whose skills as an interrogator were legendary. Poley told a London cutler, William Yeomans, how he had been examined by Walsingham about his possession of a copy of the banned Catholic tract, *Leicester's Commonwealth*.

'Mr Secretary' – as Walsingham was known – 'did use me very cruelly,' he recalled, 'yet would I never confess it.' Walsingham was put into such a 'heat' by Poley's obstinacy, that 'he looked out of his window and grinned like a dog'.

Yeomans asked Poley how he dared to deny possessing the book, when 'he very well knew' that he had it.

'Marry,' said Poley. 'It is no matter. For I will swear and forswear myself, rather than I will accuse myself to do me any harm.'

Another account of Poley under examination, not published before, confirms this picture of craft and composure. In September 1593, just a few months after the Deptford affray, he was arrested while on government business in the Netherlands. He was examined by the Dutch authorities, the States General, further to accusations made against him by another English agent, Roger Walton. The accusations were serious, amounting to treason, but after a couple of weeks he was released without charge. The States General found 'no subject to detain Poley any longer, nor stuff to examine him upon'. Throughout the examination he 'carried himself carefully and discretely, so as none could find just cause to confirm the conceit they had'.

The man who made Walsingham grin like a dog with exasperation, and who negotiated his way so 'carefully and discretely' round the Dutch authorities, would not find it difficult to mislead Coroner Danby and his jury. We have his own assertion that if he had to, he would willingly perjure himself, rather than say anything that would do him 'harm'.

These are the three companions of Marlowe's last day: Frizer, Skeres and Poley. Just scratch the surface of this meeting at Deptford and you find yourself down among sharks and spies. Already, the brisk, normalising tone of the coroner's inquest seems to be dispersing – like those sweet scents in the garden where they walked – to reveal another mood entirely. There is a kind of community between these three men. They belong, in slightly different ways, to the same semi-legitimate world. They deal in the perennial currency of that world: bargains, tricks, betrayals, lies. Their paths intersect, part, join again. It is no great surprise to find them meeting up on a summer's morning in Deptford Strand.

The puzzling thing is the presence of the fourth man. What

is their business with Christopher Marlowe, and his with them? What is Marlowe *doing* down there?

These are questions I will try to answer. For now, the important point concerns the reliability of the inquest, the 'official story'. Our knowledge of Marlowe's death – of exactly how and exactly why it happened – depends on this profoundly slippery trio. The account given in the coroner's report is to be trusted precisely as much as they are.

4

WIDOW BULL

ALTHOUGH FRIZER, SKERES and Poley were the only people present when Marlowe was killed, there is another figure in the immediate landscape of his death: Mrs Eleanor Bull of Deptford, the owner of the house where he died.

It is often said that Marlowe died in a tavern, but there is no evidence for this. It is an interpolation from the fact that there was a bill or 'reckoning' over which Frizer and Marlowe allegedly argued. There was no lack of taverns in naval Deptford, but there is nothing to link Mrs Bull with any of them, and if her house had been known by a sign it is likely that the inquest would have said so.

More probably she ran a lodging-house or victualling-house, a private establishment which offered accommodation and food, rather than a public 'place of resort'. It was common for home-owners to have their house licensed for this purpose. Marlowe's own father did just that in Canterbury in 1604, and was licensed to 'keep common victualling in his now dwelling-house'. The will of a London widow living near Fleet Street speaks of her receiving money from certain gentlemen 'for their commons', and of her 'allowing to the said gentlemen meat for their said money'. This is more like Widow Bull at Deptford Strand, and the four gentlemen who lunched and dined at her house, and passed the day in 'quiet mood', and were expected to pay a 'sum of pence' for what they had consumed.

Precisely where her house was is impossible to say. Deptford Strand covered an area which ran up along the river from Sayes Court to Deptford Creek, and inland from the river as far as the through-road from Greenwich to Rotherhithe (now called Evelyn Street, after the diarist John Evelyn, who lived at Sayes Court in the seventeenth century). It is not a big area, perhaps a quarter of a square mile, much of that taken up with the shipyards and storehouses, and the great swathe of the 'Common Green'.

In a map of Deptford Strand drawn in 1623 (Plate 3), the houses are clearly marked, about a hundred dwellings all told, straggling along the dirt roads that lead up from the riverside and loop around the Green. Most of the buildings looking on to the Green are substantial, detached houses. Elsewhere, especially in the dock-side alley between Middle and Lower Watergate, there are close-packed little tenements. Virtually all the houses give on to open ground of some sort, so the fact that Mrs Bull's property had a garden does not help to identify it.

We can guess, at least, that it was one of the bigger houses, because Eleanor Bull was a woman of substance, well-born and well-connected, not at all the shabby old ale-house keeper she is often portrayed as.

She was born Eleanor Whitney, a member of an ancient border-country family whose seat was at Whitney-on-Wye, near Hereford. The Whitneys' history can be traced back to the thirteenth century. They provided generations of county knights, MPs and sheriffs. A generation before Eleanor, James Whitney held minor court office as a Server of the Chamber to Henry VIII.

The Whitneys were related to another prominent local family, the Parrys of Bacton. In her will of 1589, Blanche Parry, Chief Gentlewoman of the Privy Chamber and long-time confidante of Queen Elizabeth, made several bequests to the Whitneys, including her god-daughter, Blanche Whitney, and her 'cousin' Eleanor *née* Whitney, now Mrs Bull of Deptford. Eleanor's legacy was a handsome £100, though it took the inconvenient form of a debt recoverable from a third party, a Mr Montague. This was probably James Montague, who later became Dean of the Chapel Royal, and lived just downriver at Greenwich.

'Cousin' is a loose term, but an important one. In the extended tribalism of Elizabethan society it means something that Eleanor Bull could call a courtly lady like Blanche Parry her 'cousin'. Another of Blanche Parry's cousins was the great Elizabethan magus and mathematician, Dr John Dee: she was godmother to his son Arthur, as she was to one of the Whitney girls. Yet another who called her 'cousin' was the great Lord Burghley. He was, like Eleanor, a beneficiary of Blanche's will: there is a draft of it, still extant, in his own handwriting.

There is a point at which family connections grow tenuous, but technically speaking Eleanor Bull was related to Lord Burghley, the Lord Treasurer of England and still, in his last ailing years, the Queen's chief political adviser.

Like most well-breeched country families the Whitneys had London connections. Eleanor's uncle, John Whitney, lived at Lambeth, and she herself was married in London. Her husband was Richard Bull. They were married at the church of St Mary-le-Bow, on 14 October 1571. The next that is heard of them, they are in Deptford. There Richard Bull held the post of sub-bailiff at Sayes Court, the manor-house at Deptford. His immediate boss, the bailiff, was Sir George Howard, probably a kinsman of the Lord Admiral who lived across the way on Deptford Green. As a local manor-official, Richard Bull would have been well-known to some of the jurors at the Marlowe inquest. To Henry Anger, for instance, who leased his house from Sayes Court; or to Robert Baldwin, the local miller, who supplied the manor-house bakery. They, and other jurors, would have known his widow, Eleanor Bull. [See Appendix 2.4]

Richard Bull died in Deptford in the spring of 1590. He was buried on 9 April at St Nicholas's, where Marlowe would be buried in 1593. In the parish register, the vicar styles him 'gentleman'. Less than three years after the Marlowe affair, Eleanor herself died. She was buried, in the same little churchyard, on 19 March 1596. If she and her husband had any children they did not survive her. The beneficiary of her estate was George Bull, a yeoman of Harlow, Essex, who is described as her next-of-kin. He cannot have been her son: any child of her marriage to Richard would have been less than twenty-five years old in 1596, and could not have had – as George Bull did – a married daughter. He may have been her stepson, or else some close family relation of her husband's. George Bull's bondsmen in his claim on Eleanor's estate were two London tradesmen, a clothworker and an ironmonger.

The truth about Eleanor Bull – what little we know of it – helps us reconstruct something of the tone of that day in Deptford. It takes us beyond the blandness of the official story, beyond the obscuring mythology. Marlowe died not in a tavern or bawdy-house, but in the house of a local official's widow. His hostess was a woman of standing, both by birth and marriage. She was someone who could call on court connections if she needed, someone who might serve court connections if they needed.

5

LIBELS AND HERESIES

THE CORONER'S REPORT has even less to say about Marlowe than it does about his three companions. Neither his social status nor his place of residence is indicated. He was now beyond such concerns. There is certainly nothing from the coroner to indicate that the dead man lying before him was perhaps the most popular, certainly the most talked-about dramatist of the day. This was no place for literary considerations, and anyway dramatist – or as they would have put it, 'playmaker' – was barely considered an occupation at all, at least not a separate occupation from the general rabble of popular entertainers: players, tumblers, balladeers, and so on. The only contemporary document which mentions Marlowe's profession describes him as a 'scholar'.

Marlowe's fame as a writer is not immediately relevant to his death, but it is bound up with another kind of fame. He was a man who held highly controversial – most would have said heretical – opinions about religion, and about the political uses and misuses of religion. He did not express such unorthodox views in his plays, at least not openly, but he was known to hold them. Jibes about his 'atheism' had appeared in print, vague but damaging, and were busily enlarged on in reports prepared by government informers.

In the weeks preceding his death, Marlowe's 'monstruous opinions' were under investigation. He was, at the time of his death, reporting daily to the Privy Council. No charges had actually been brought against him, but they may have been in the offing. This adds yet another dimension to the meeting at

Deptford, and perhaps to the killing. It is one more crucial aspect of the inquest's limitations. It seems likely that a court official like Coroner Danby would have known something of this. Possibly he considered it outside the scope of the inquest. He may also have felt it safer, more convenient, not to mention it. These were edgy times, as the events of the last few weeks had made very clear.

It was a time of plague and war – the long, draining conflict in the Low Countries, the renewed threat of Spanish invasion, political divisions, savage executions. Unemployment and inflation were widespread. The mood in London was ugly.

In these times people look for scapegoats, and chief among these were the city's immigrant traders – Dutch, Belgian, French: Protestant refugees from the battle-grounds of Europe. 'The common people do rage against them,' wrote one observer, 'as though for their sakes so many taxes, such decay of traffic, and their being embrandled in so many wars, did ensue.' London's traders and shopkeepers felt particularly threatened. The foreigners, they protested, 'contented not themselves with manufactures and warehouses, but would keep shops, and retail all manner of goods.' As well as taking business from the locals, the immigrants had a reputation for stinginess. Thirty years ago, wrote John Stow, the parish of Billingsgate levied £27 per annum 'for help of the poor'. Now the area is full of 'Netherlanders', and 'since they came so plentifully thither, there cannot be gathered above £11, for the stranger will not contribute to such charges as other citizens do'.

Several petitions were signed against the 'strangers', but these seem to have been ignored. The official line was that the immigrants were *bona fide* refugees and Protestant allies, and that they benefited the economy. On 21 March 1593 the House of Commons voted to extend the privileges of resident aliens. A lone voice of dissent came from Sir Walter Ralegh. 'I see no reason that so much respect should be given unto them,' he said. 'In the whole cause I see no matter of honour, no matter of charity, no profit in relieving them.'

On the streets, more militant action began. Some time shortly before Easter Day, 15 April 1593, a 'placard' was nailed up, threatening that the apprentices of London would soon 'attempt some violence on the strangers'. On Easter Monday, the Privy Council met at St James's Palace, and drew up a letter to the Lord Mayor of London, Sir Cuthbert Buckle, expressing their concern about this 'vile ticket or placard'. They understood that an arrest had already been made. The suspect should be examined about his 'meaning and purpose' in the writing. He should be 'punished by torture', if necessary, to make him talk.

The Council feared that more was to come – 'oftentimes it doth fall out of such lewd beginnings that further mischief doth ensue' – and so it proved. During the following week, further 'libels' were posted up. One of these was addressed to the 'beastly brutes the Belgians', the 'faint-hearted Flemings', and the 'fraudulent Father Frenchmen'. It accuses them of 'cowardly flight' from their home countries, of 'hypocrisy and counterfeit shew of religion'. It complains that the Queen allows them 'to live here in better case and more freedom than her own people'. It demands that they quit the country within three months. If not,

There shall be many a sore stripe. Apprentices will rise to the number of 2336, and all the apprentices and journeymen will down with the Flemings and Strangers.

The Queen was informed, and on 22 April the Council set up a special five-man commission under Dr Julius Caesar. Caesar, the son of an Italian physician, was Master of the Court of Requests: a trusted legal figure. The commission's brief was to 'examine by secret means who may be authors of the said libels'. The emphasis was on a more covert, 'secret' approach. Two of the commissioners – William Waad and Thomas Phelippes – were old hands from the Walsingham intelligence service.

The authorities also ordered a 'strict account' to be taken of the immigrant population in London. The certificates, returned on 4 May, show the number of foreigners in London, including children and servants, to be 4,300. Of these 237 were 'denizens' (property-owning foreigners granted certain rights). Overall the immigrants represented little more than 2 per cent of the city's population, though in some areas considerably more. Many were now planning to leave, terrified by this violent 'commotion' against them.

On the night of Saturday 5 May, between eleven o'clock and midnight, a new and particularly virulent libel appeared. It was 'set upon the wall of the Dutch Churchyard' in Broad Street. There it was 'found by some of the inhabitants of the place, and brought to the Constable and the rest of the watch'. It is this document which brings Marlowe into the affair.

The 'Dutch Church libel' survives in a manuscript copy made in about 1600. It is a doggerel poem, fifty-three lines long. It is in four verses, each rounded off with a catch-phrase. This is a ballad format, and it may have been intended to be sung or chanted as the anti-Dutch mob went about its business. This document is signed 'Tamburlaine'.

Whoever 'Tamburlaine' was, he was an admirer of Marlowe's plays. His pseudonym is that of the Scythian warrior whose remorseless conquests are chronicled in Marlowe's two-part play, *Tamburlaine the Great*, first performed in 1587. But this is not the only reference to Marlowe. Here are the libeller's lines about the foreigners' stranglehold on the London economy:

> Your Machiavellian Merchant spoils the state,
> Your usury doth leave us all for dead,
> Your artifex & craftsman works our fate,
> And like the Jews you eat us up as bread.

This is suggestive of Marlowe's *Jew of Malta*, which had played at the Rose theatre the previous year. The political theories of Machiavelli were controversial at this time, and Marlowe's *Jew* was explicitly a study of Machiavellianism in action. It opens with a prologue spoken by the ghost of 'Machevill' himself, who makes it clear that the eponymous Jew is a true follower of his principles. 'I come', he says,

> to present the tragedy of a Jew,
> Who smiles to see how full his bags are crammed,
> Which money was not got without my means.

Marlowe's tragi-comic villain, a 'stranger' himself in Malta, was certainly in the libeller's mind when he penned those lines about Machiavellian merchants and predatory Jews.

After rehearsing the usual grievances, the libel moves into crude incitement, and here it mentions another Marlowe play:

> Since words nor threats nor any other thing
> Can make you to avoid this certain ill,
> We'll cut your throats, in your temples praying,
> Not Paris massacre so much blood did spill.

'Paris massacre' refers to the slaughter of French Protestants in Paris on St Bartholomew's Eve 1572, but the phrasing particularly suggests *The Massacre at Paris*, Marlowe's lurid reworking of the atrocity. This was premièred, at the Rose, in late January 1593, just a few months before these troubles began. The takings that day were £3 14s, the highest of the season. Shortly afterwards the playhouses were closed, due to plague, so this latest piece by Marlowe was one of the last plays to have been seen in London. It was a natural allusion in the circumstances. As the libeller imagines the butchering of immigrants in their 'temples' – in other words in the Dutch church itself, or in the French and Italian churches hard by – he recalls the scenes of blood-letting in churches and monasteries that are represented on-stage in the *Massacre*.

Any one of these allusions might be fortuitous: common currency. All three together add up to something more. As this rabid document passed from hand to hand, from constables to commissioners to Privy Councillors, someone must have recognised the allusions, and wondered about

Marlowe's connection, witting or otherwise, with this mysterious 'Tamburlaine'. It is perhaps unlikely that he was suspected as an actual author of the libel – he would hardly have signalled himself so clearly, and anyway he was out of town, with Thomas Walsingham in Scadbury: an alibi of sorts – but the connection was there.

The Council deliberated *in camera*: an air of urgency and secrecy. The city authorities were summoned, not by 'open notification' but by 'private admonition only, to the mayor and discreetest aldermen, and they not to know the cause of their sending for'. A wide-ranging investigation of the city's traders and apprentices was ordered: 'the subsidy-books for London and the suburbs to be seen; how many masters and how many men, and of what trades, and if they use double-trades; and such as be of no church to be avoided hence.' On 10 May a proclamation was read at Guildhall, offering 100 crowns reward for information about the libels. The following day the Privy Council issued its own directive. It spoke of 'divers lewd and malicious libels', but it was particularly concerned with the one 'set upon the wall of the Dutch Churchyard, that doth exceed the rest in lewdness'. Officers were ordered to 'apprehend every person so to be suspected' and to 'search in any of the chambers, studies, chests or other like places, for all manner of writing and papers that may give you light for the discovery of the libellers'. If suspects refused to talk, 'you shall by authority hereof put them to the torture in Bridewell, and by the extremity thereof draw them to discover their knowledge.' These are – not for the last time in this story – the raw tones of the Elizabethan police-state.

Among those brought in under these wide-ranging powers was the dramatist Thomas Kyd, the author of the hugely popular *Spanish Tragedy*, and of some Italian translations, and perhaps of a lost early version of *Hamlet*. He was a known associate of Marlowe's. They had shared a chamber together in 1591: they were then writing for the same company of players, Lord Strange's Men. A fellow playwright and 'familiar friend' of Marlowe's – perhaps this was enough to put the unfortunate Kyd in the frame as 'Tamburlaine': a panicky, literal-minded arrest. There may have been other reasons, too.

The Council's directive was issued on 11 May. Kyd was perhaps arrested that night. By the following day, at any rate, he was 'Thos Kydd, prisoner'. He was charged as the author of the Dutch Church libel, a charge he vehemently denied. He was interrogated and – as the Council had recommended – tortured. Later, writing to the Lord Keeper, Sir John Puckering, he speaks of the 'pains and undeserved tortures' he has undergone. There is no reason to think he is speaking figuratively. He appeared before the commissioners, assured them of his 'reverend meaning to the state', protested his innocence. He repeats his forlorn protestations in the letter to Puckering, written when he was free again but still under a cloud: 'As for the libel laid unto my charge, I am resolved with receiving of ye sacrament to satisfy your Lordships & the world, that I was neither agent nor consenting thereunto.' He swears that if he could name any involved in this 'mutinous sedition toward the State', he would. He believes he is the victim of an informer, 'some outcast Ismael' who has 'incensed your Lordships to suspect me'. Given the hundred-crown reward for information, this is plausible. At first Kyd speaks of one informer, then of many. He hopes they will themselves be brought forward and questioned, to 'break open their lewd designs and see into the truth'. Their lives, he says, should be 'examined & ripped up effectually'. There are echoes of the torture chamber in his choice of words.

The questioning of Thomas Kyd quickly led to a charge both vaguer and graver than the libelling itself: the charge of atheism. When he was arrested his papers were seized, and among them was found a theological manuscript, three pages long, written in a neat italic hand. Kyd described it, accurately enough, as 'some fragments of a disputation', but his interrogators took a harsher view. On 12 May, in a dark scratchy hand, one of them endorsed the document with these words:

Vile hereticall conceipts denyinge the deity of Jhesus Christ our Savior, founde amongest the papers of Thos Kydd, prisoner.

Then, in a different ink, he added: 'wch he affirmeth that he had ffrom Marlowe'. First the theatrical allusions in the Dutch Church libel, and now this. For the second time in a week the investigation throws up Marlowe's name.

The heretical document is rather milder than the endorsement suggests, though its overall thrust is indeed to deny the deity of Christ. The views it contains are Unitarian, rather than atheistic, and this particular expression of them had been in circulation for over forty years. In 1549 a parish priest called John Assheton was accused of the Unitarian heresy: he 'denied Christ divinity and equality with God the Father, affirming that he but a mere creature, and a passable man only, not God'. By order of the Archbishop of Canterbury, Assheton made a written declaration of his views. Copies of this were circulated, and later that year a theologian named John Proctour published a counter-blast, *The Fall of the Late Arian* (an 'Arian' was a follower of the fourth-century Alexandrian Arius, an early Unitarian). In this book, as was conventional, Proctour quoted large chunks of the heresy he was rebutting.

This is the provenance of the document found in Kyd's lodgings. It was an Elizabethan transcript, with a few omissions and variations, of Assheton's Arian views, as quoted in Proctour's book. Hence Kyd's description of it as part of a 'disputation'. Kyd affirmed that the document was Marlowe's – that it belonged to him, not that it was by him. He claimed, or anyway surmised, that it had got 'shuffled' with his own papers, 'by some occasion of our writing in one chamber two years since'.

It is all a question of context. Housed in Proctour's book, the tenets of Arianism could be read with impunity. Marlowe may have read them when he was a schoolboy at King's, Canterbury: there was a copy of the book in the headmaster's library. Extracted, copied, and found among the papers of a suspected libeller, they spelt 'atheism' – at least inasfar as this word covered all forms of religious dissent that were not specifically Catholic or Puritan.

Of course, this was not the first time that Marlowe's name was associated with heresy. Less than a year before this, he had been accused of atheism in print by his old rival, the pamphleteer and playwright Robert Greene. As Greene lay dying in Dowgate in the summer of 1592, he dashed off a series of fraught confessions, complaints and reminiscences. In one of these – *Greene's Groatsworth of Wit Bought with a Million of Repentance*, published posthumously in September 1592 – he addressed some words to three playwrights, his 'fellow scholars about this city'. The first of these was Marlowe. He is not actually named, but everyone knew who was meant when Greene addressed the 'famous gracer of tragedians', just as they recognised the identity of the other two writers addressed, Thomas Nashe and George Peele. Greene urges Marlowe to turn aside from 'diabolical atheism' and 'pestilent Machiavilian policy'. Greene was once, like Marlowe, a scoffer at religion – he 'hath said, with thee, like the fool in his heart: There is no God' – but now he has repented. He warns Marlowe to repent while there is still time, for – a strangely prophetic note – 'little knowest thou how in the end thou shalt be visited'.

Greene's public incrimination was vague, but it was amply confirmed by professional informers and rumour-mongers, and by the depositions made against Marlowe by Kyd. Of special interest to the government was an informer's report about a strange man called Richard Cholmeley, in which Cholmeley is quoted as saying 'that one Marlowe is able to show more sound reasons for atheism than any divine in England is able to give to prove divinity'. He also asserted that Marlowe had 'read the atheist lecture to Sir Walter Ralegh & others'.

Richard Cholmeley is one of the keys to this story. He is an ambiguous character: he served the government as an anti-Catholic agent, yet he himself professed wildly seditious and atheistic views. But there is nothing ambiguous about his reported statement concerning Marlowe. It amounts to a charge much more pointed than Greene's: not just that Marlowe held 'atheistic' views, but that he was an active propagandist of them. This document was in the government's hands in May, and this talk of Marlowe giving an atheist 'lecture' may have connected in their minds with the heretical 'disputation' found in Kyd's rooms. Later accounts, perhaps conflating the two, speak of an actual 'book' that Marlowe had written 'against the Trinity'.

Kyd, desperate to save his own neck, doubtless made matters worse. His charges against Marlowe were only written down after Marlowe's death, but they probably echo what he told his interrogators in the days following his arrest. He confirmed the picture of Marlowe as a propagandist against religion. 'It was his custom,' he says, 'in table talk or otherwise, to jest at the divine scriptures, jibe at prayers, & strive in argument to frustrate & confute what hath been spoke or writ by prophets & such holy men.' And he gave instances of the 'monstruous opinions' that Marlowe held. One of these is genuinely provocative: 'he would report St John to be Our Saviour's Alexis', in other words, 'that Christ did love him with an extraordinary love'. Others seem mild enough. Kyd recalled a time when he told Marlowe he was intending to write a poem about the conversion of St Paul. Marlowe replied that St Paul was a 'juggler', and that Kyd might as well 'go write a book of fast & loose' – a book, in other words, about the tricks of con-men. Another comment of Marlowe's retailed by Kyd: 'that the Prodigal Child's portion was but four nobles' – a trifling amount – because 'he held his purse so near the bottom in all pictures'. It is so desperately unheretical: a throwaway remark of Marlowe's, now dredged up by a frightened man under arrest.

On 18 May, the Privy Council issued a warrant for Marlowe to be apprehended. They commanded one of the Queen's Messengers, Henry Maunder,

to repair to the house of Mr Tho: Walsingham in Kent, or

53

to any other place where he shall understand Christofer Marlow to be remaining, and by virtue hereof to apprehend and bring him to the Court in his company. And in case of need to require aid.

This is conventional phrasing for a warrant, and does not indicate special powers. Maunder found his man and brought him in. On 20 May Marlowe appeared before the Council. The clerk wrote:

This day Christofer Marley of London, gent, being sent for by warrant from their Lordships, hath entered his appearance accordingly for his indemnity herein, and is commanded to give his daily attendance on their Lordships, until he shall be licensed to the contrary.

He was not, at this stage anyway, under arrest. He was on bail (the 'indemnity') and under orders to remain at the Council's disposal.

Meanwhile, further evidence against him was being prepared by another informer, Richard Baines. Baines entitled his report 'A note containing the opinion of one Christopher Marly, concerning his damnable judgment of religion and scorn of God's word.' Again it gives a picture of a man recklessly eager to broadcast his dangerous views. 'Almost into every company he cometh, he persuades men to atheism, willing them not to be afeard of bugbears and hobgoblins.' Many of Marlowe's comments, as recorded by Baines, are brief and trenchant: that 'all protestants are hypocritical asses'; that 'the first beginning of religion was only to keep men in awe'; that holy communion 'would have been much better being administered in a tobacco pipe'; and – the same homosexual blasphemy which Kyd reported – that 'St John the Evangelist was bedfellow to Christ, and used him as the sinners of Sodoma'.

Baines lists these and other heresies for a page and a half, then concludes darkly: 'I think all men in Christianity ought to endeavour that the mouth of so dangerous a member may be stopped.'

According to an official annotation, Baines handed his 'Note' in to the authorities three days before Marlowe's death: in other words, on Sunday 27 May. Confusingly, the same annotation also states that it was 'delivered on Whitsun Eve'. This fell on Saturday 2 June, three days *after* Marlowe was killed. This is another of those maddening lapses – like the mistake over Frizer's name in the Deptford church register – which had helped to obscure the reality of Marlowe's death. The earlier date is more probable, but either way the baleful words of Richard Baines haunt the last few days of Marlowe's life.

All this is a backdrop to the Deptford killing: libels and heresies, arrests and interrogations, accusers and informers and their recommendations that dangerous characters like Marlowe should have their mouths stopped. This is part of what the inquest does not say, part of the 'unofficial' story of Marlowe's death. Two of the men involved here – Richard Cholmeley and Richard Baines – are mixed up in the intelligence business. They belong in the same shady stratum of government service as two of Marlowe's companions at Deptford, Robert Poley and Nicholas Skeres. Once again, as we look behind the scenes of the killing, we find ourselves drawn down into the Elizabethan secret world.

PART TWO

REACTIONS

6

THE FIRST EPITAPHS

THE QUESTIONS WE are asking about Marlowe's death –
about the character and status of the witnesses, about
Marlowe's parlous situation at the time, about the whiff of
secret politics hanging over the event – must also have been
asked by people at the time. Another way of getting beyond
the confines of the 'official story' is to look at some of the
public reaction to the news of Marlowe's death.

What did people think about this event? What, indeed, did
people *know* about it?

The earliest notices are to be found in the writings of two
of Marlowe's literary colleagues, George Peele and Thomas
Nashe. These were men who personally knew Marlowe: they
are the two 'fellow scholars' addressed, along with Marlowe,
in Greene's *Groatsworth of Wit*. The works they were writing
at the time contain traces – explicit in Peele, more veiled in
Nashe – of Marlowe's death.

In June 1593, George Peele completed *The Honour of the
Garter*, a long 'poem gratulatory' about the Order of the
Garter. He dedicated it to Henry Percy, 9th Earl of
Northumberland, one of the five men installed that year as
Knights of the Garter. The Garter ceremony was performed,
at Windsor Castle, on 26 June. Peele had probably presented
the poem to Northumberland a few days before this, for on
23 June the Earl's account-books record the payment of a £3
'liberality' to 'one Geo: Peele, a poet'.

Peele's poem, completed about three weeks after Marlowe's
death, contains the earliest known reference, outside the

inquest, to the fact that Marlowe was dead. Peele pays tribute to his – and Marlowe's – friend Thomas Watson, who had died the previous September, and then to Marlowe himself:

> . . . To Watson, worthy many epitaphs
> For his sweet poesy, for Amyntas' tears
> And joys so well set down. And after thee
> Why hie they not, unhappy in thine end,
> Marley, the Muses' darling, for thy verse
> Fit to write passions for the souls below.

There is admiration and warmth in this, but the only thing Peele actually says *about* Marlowe's death is that it was an 'unhappy' end. The adjective had a more specific meaning then – it carried the idea of evil chance, of mishap, as well as the idea of sadness – but it tells us only that Marlowe died suddenly and, even by Elizabethan standards, too young.

Though it was published later in the year, Peele's brief tribute to Marlowe was initially made within the context of a private poem, addressed to a young nobleman who had actually known Marlowe. Northumberland – nicknamed the 'Wizard Earl' because of his occultist interests – was a close associate of Sir Walter Ralegh. He was part of that free-thinking, philosophical clique, centred on Ralegh, which some historians call the 'Durham House Set' (after Ralegh's town-house in the Strand) and some the 'School of Night' (after a supposed allusion in Shakespeare's *Love's Labour's Lost*). Marlowe was certainly connected with this group – according to Richard Cholmeley, he read his 'atheist lecture' to it. Fortunately, we do not have to rely on Cholmeley's word alone. Marlowe himself said, in early 1592, that he was 'very well known' to Northumberland, and there is other evidence of the connection.

The context of this first epitaph is a safe one: a private poem for a sympathetic audience. Marlowe's associations with Northumberland and Ralegh, and their coterie of philosophers and poets, is something I will return to later – another, very important piece of the jigsaw.

*

Another early epitaph, seldom mentioned by the biographers, appears in the poem *Narcissus* by Thomas Edwards. This was not published until 1595, but it was circulating in manuscript by the autumn of 1593, when the publisher John Wolfe secured the copyright on it. It was entered to Wolfe on the Stationers' Register on 22 October. Wolfe had a few weeks earlier purchased the copyright on Marlowe's *Hero and Leander*, though this too was not published till later.

Like Peele, Edwards links the death of Marlowe with that of his friend Thomas Watson. He refers to them both by the names of their most popular poetic creations:

> Amyntas and Leander's gone,
>   Oh dear sons of stately kings,
> Blessed be your nimble throats
>   That so amorously could sing.

I first came across Thomas Edwards in the *Penguin Book of Elizabethan Verse*, where his biographical note consists of a single sentence: 'About Edwards nothing is known except his name.' This is quite untrue. He was born in Shropshire in 1567; he was (like Nicholas Skeres) a resident of Furnival's Inn in the mid-1580s; he later shared a chamber at Lincoln's Inn with John Donne's friend Christopher Brooke; and he was at the time of Marlowe's death a 'servant' of Sir John Wolley, the Queen's Latin secretary. He need not reside in total oblivion, but his epitaph on Marlowe tells us nothing except that he admired him as a poet, and that he knew *Hero and Leander* in manuscript. These we would guess anyway from his frequent filching of phrases from that poem.

The pamphleteer Thomas Nashe, meanwhile, was putting the finishing touches to his picaresque story *The Unfortunate Traveller*. He completed the manuscript on Wednesday 27 June 1593, exactly four weeks after the killing of Marlowe.

The two men undoubtedly knew each other well, though Nashe did not share his friend's extremist religious views.

Nashe was quarrelsome and satirical, and he had a journalist's eye for abuses, but he held essentially orthodox views about society and religion. He was nearly four years Marlowe's junior: a small, skinny, volatile young man, known for his boyish looks and his funny 'gag-teeth'. They had first met at Cambridge, where they were both undergraduates in the early 1580s, Marlowe at Corpus, Nashe at St John's. They shared, among other tastes, a cordial dislike of the Harveys: the poetic don Dr Gabriel Harvey, and his brother Richard. This probably took shape at Cambridge, where the Harveys were prominent and controversial. Nashe later quoted Marlowe's scoff about Richard Harvey: 'Kit Marloe was wont to say he was an ass, and fit to preach only of the Iron Age.' By the end of the 80s both were embarked on a literary career in London. The fact that Nashe was also a friend and collaborator of Marlowe's rival Robert Greene may have strained relations for a time, but such rivalries were skin-deep anyway, a repartee of quips and scoffs which was all part of the image of these 'University Wits'. Certainly Nashe's open references to Marlowe – all made some while after Marlowe's death – are warm ones. In the summer of 1594, he defended 'poor deceased Kit Marlowe' from the slanders of Gabriel Harvey. Later, when things were going badly for him, he recalled Marlowe as one who had 'used me as a friend'.

People would be expecting some comment from Nashe in the aftermath of Marlowe's death, but they would also expect it to be well-camouflaged. Nashe was a topical, gossipy writer, and he suffered much from the curse of so-called 'interpreters', those 'mice-eyed decipherers' who would comb each new pamphlet for suspicious political allusions, and 'run over all the peers of the land in peevish moralizing and anatomizing it'. He had long since developed ways of identifying people without actually naming them. When he spoke of someone behaving like 'the Kid' in Aesop's Fables, it was a reference to Thomas Kyd. When he starts off a story, 'Not far from Chester I knew an odd foul-mouthed knave called Charles the Friar', he is in fact embarking on a rather risky anecdote about an imprisoned Catholic named Charles Chester. Other allusions are more complex, like his political fable about the 'Bear and the Fox' in *Pierce Penniless*.

In *The Unfortunate Traveller*, Nashe sets his story back in time, a couple of generations ago, 'in the time of King Henry the 8, the only true subject of chronicles', and makes his comments not through puns or 'fables', but through historical parallels. Thus the Anabaptists of Münster reflect the militant tendency in Elizabethan Puritanism, episodes at the sieges of Tournai and Térouanne relate to current English exploits in France, the Roman plague of 1522 is the plague in London in 1593, and so on.

In this way Nashe's tribute to the great Italian dramatist, Pietro Aretino, proves to be a sidelong epitaph for Christopher Marlowe. Aretino, like Machiavelli, was controversial among Elizabethans: a bogey-man or a hero, according to taste. He was known as an outspoken political satirist, but also as a pornographer and an atheist. His works, written half a century earlier, were still not available in English.

In making this connection between Aretino and Marlowe, Nashe is trading on a comparison already made by the disapproving Gabriel Harvey. In the course of his *Four Letters*, written in September 1592, Harvey had attacked two contemporary writers for their swaggering behaviour and questionable opinions. They 'domineer taverns and stationers' shops' and 'scare multitudes of plain folk' with their satirical 'scoffing and girding'. He nicknames these two writers 'the Devil's Orator' and 'Aretine'. The 'Devil's Orator' is Nashe himself, whose pamphlet *Pierce Penniless* took the form of a jocular 'supplication to the devil'. 'Aretine' is Nashe's friend and fellow-scoffer, Marlowe. The identification trades, of course, on Aretino's twin reputation as a dramatist and an atheist. In a later work – dated April 1593, though not published until after Marlowe's death – Harvey renews the attack, and makes the connection with atheism quite plain. 'Aretine and the Devil's Orator', he writes, neither fear Goodman Satan, nor Master Beelzebub, nor Sir Reverence, nor my Lord Government himself. O wretched atheism! Hell but a scarecrow and heaven but a wonder-clout in their doctrine.

The phrasing is intended to echo Marlowe, both his words spoken on stage – Faustus's famous challenge, 'Come, I think Hell's a fable' – and his alleged table-talk, urging people 'not to be afeard of bug-bears and scarecrows'.

The readers of the 1590s lapped up these literary dog-fights, this 'civil war of wits', and they would have no problem in identifying Nashe's true subject when he breaks off the narrative of *The Unfortunate Traveller* to 'speak a word or two of this Aretine'. It is the tribute to Marlowe they were expecting.

It is a fine one, both in itself and because there is some courage in making it. The opening words come from the heart – his dead friend was 'one of the wittiest knaves that ever God made': an unguarded moment of fondness – but then he collects himself into more tribute-like order.

He first touches on Marlowe's literary greatness, his huge impact as a poet:

His pen was sharp-pointed like a poignard. No leaf he wrote on but was like a burning-glass to set on fire all his readers. With more than musket-shot did he charge his quill where he meant to inveigh.

Having run through a hasty gamut of metaphors on this sub-ject, Nashe moves on to a more specific point about Marlowe: his reckless outspokenness. Nashe the satirist, conscious of the limits and dangers of political comment, champions this:

He was no timorous servile flatterer of the commonwealth wherein he lived. His tongue & his invention were foreborn: what they thought they would confidently utter. Princes he spared not, that in the least point transgressed.

And then, a sentence that echoes in the mind of this aftermath of the killing: 'His life he contemned in comparison of the liberty of speech.'

Next Nashe turns to Aretino's reputation for atheism, and so to a defence of Marlowe on this score. He says: 'Some dull-brained maligners of his accuse him of that treatise, *De Tribus Impostoribus Mundi*.' This anonymous atheist tract – denouncing the three 'imposters of the world', Moses, Christ and Mohammad – was often fathered on to Aretino. Dr Harvey had referred to it in one of his attacks on 'Aretine' quoted above: 'Whom durst he not impeach, revile and blaspheme, that forged the abominable book in the world, *De Tribus Impostoribus Mundi*?' Since 'Aretine' in that passage is intended to suggest Marlowe, it seems that Harvey is glancing at the rumours of Marlowe's anti-religious writings: the 'atheist lecture', the supposed 'book against the Trinity', and so on. Nashe makes the same connection in reverse. In denying Aretino's authorship of the *De Tribus Impostoribus* – 'I am verily persuaded it was none of his, and of my mind are a number of judicial Italians' – he is making a specific rebuttal of these rumours about Marlowe. This business about an atheistic 'book' is nonsense, Nashe says, and sensible people know that it is.

Such 'judicial' tolerance, Nashe recognised, was more than Marlowe's name could now hope for. The 'dull-brained maligners' will have their say. His tribute closes on a bitter, bidding note:

> Puritans, spew forth the venom of your dull inventions. A toad swells with thick troubled poison: you swell with poisonous perturbations. Your malice hath not a clear dram of any inspired disposition.

It was an accurate enough forecast of the Puritan propaganda against Marlowe that was to come.

The Unfortunate Traveller was 'under the printer's hands' in September 1593, but for various reasons did not appear until the spring of 1594. The earliest work of Nashe's actually to be published after Marlowe's death was very different: the long, brooding and largely unreadable religious invective entitled *Christ's Tears over Jerusalem*. This was written in the summer of 1593, entered on the Stationers' Register on 8 September, and probably published in late September or early October.

Death haunts *Christ's Tears* like a refrain. To Nashe himself this meant actual deaths: of Marlowe, of Greene and Watson the previous year, of many other unrecorded acquaintances in the plague:

> We see great men die, strong men die, witty men die, fools die, rich merchants, poor artificers, ploughmen, gentlemen, high men, low men, wearish men, gross men and the fairest complexioned men die.

In a sense, the whole subject-matter of *Christ's Tears* may be a response to Marlowe's demise. Its startling religiosity, quite unexpected from Nashe's previous brash writing, seems that of a man keen to show off his religious probity, anxious to ward off any implication in those dangerous speculations which had got Marlowe and Kyd into such trouble.

To the informed reader of 1593, Nashe's passage on the evils of atheism would inevitably summon Marlowe to mind. He speaks of 'blasphemies and Scripture-scorning ironies'; of the Arian heresy about 'the Trinity's unexistence'; of those who deny damnation and say 'that there is no Hell'. These are all views and attitudes associated with Marlowe. Another atheist slander, according to Nashe, is that Moses was a crafty illusionist, and that he struck the water out of the rock 'not by any supernatural work of God, but by watching to what part the wild asses repaired for drink'. Again this accords with Marlowe's views, as reported by Richard Baines: that Moses 'was but a juggler', and was skilled 'in all the arts of the Egyptians' (in other words, conjuring tricks). And then there is the 'pre-Adamitic' heresy. According to Nashe, today's atheists 'impudently' claim that 'the late discovered Indians are able to shew antiquities thousands before Adam'. This was considered an affront to orthodox Biblical chronology. It is precisely the first of Marlowe's heresies reported by Richard Baines: that 'the Indians and many authors of antiquity have assuredly written above 16 thousand years agone, whereas Adam is proved to have lived within 6 thousand years'.

Some of these parallels can be explained as mere convention. They are the terms and ideas people associated with atheists: common stock. I am not saying they are peculiar to Marlowe, and I am not saying it is certain that Marlowe really held these views. But he was certainly believed to hold them: in the popular imagination he was the supreme topical instance of the 'scripture-scorning' atheist. I think it is clear that Nashe's readers would think of Marlowe when they read this passage, and that Nashe is intentionally distancing himself from his friend's unorthodoxy.

We find in Nashe, perhaps typically, a divided response to Marlowe's death. In *The Unfortunate Traveller* he celebrates him, under the cloak of Aretino, as a poet of immense power, a reckless and radical critic, one who valued 'the liberty of speech' above his very life. This is the first, more heartfelt reaction. In *Christ's Tears* a few weeks later, he seems to turn against him, to become one of those 'dull-brained maligners' he had earlier scorned. He is now protecting himself from that taint of atheism and sedition which surrounds Marlowe in this long hot summer of 1593. [See Appendix 2.5]

It is an understandable move, but you feel it cost him a lot. The tone of *Christ's Tears* is one of stress and breakdown. There is a bitterness in the very act of writing it:

I that have poured out mine eyes upon books, & well-nigh spit out my brain at my tongue's end this morning, am dumpish, drowsy, & wish myself dead.

I would not say that Nashe deserted Marlowe, though readers of *Christ's Tears* in the autumn of 1593 may have felt he had, since they had not yet read the tribute in the *Unfortunate Traveller*, which remained unpublished for another six months. In fact Nashe continued to champion Marlowe's name, at least in its literary aspects. In 1594 the first edition of Marlowe's early play *Dido, Queen of Carthage* was published, and Nashe's name appeared alongside Marlowe's on the title-page. The play probably dates from under-graduate days: Nashe may have had some connection with it then, more probably he prepared and edited it for publication. In the front of this – in certain copies, anyway – was an 'elegy' on Marlowe by Nashe.

Sadly this is now lost. There are four extant copies of the 1594 *Dido* – in the Bodleian and Huntington libraries, and two in the Folger library – but none of them contains the elegy. It was last seen in the eighteenth century. Bishop Tanner writes of Nashe praising Marlowe in 'Carmine Elegiaco tragediae Didonis praefixo in obitum Christoph. Marlovii' (an elegiac song on the death of Christopher Marlowe, prefixed to the tragedy of *Dido*). Since Tanner is writing in Latin anyway, it is not clear whether Nashe's piece was in Latin or English. Of its contents Tanner says little: only that it mentions five of Marlowe's tragedies, and that it 'utters many things in commendation' of him.

Another sighting was made by the bibliophile Thomas Warton, who saw Nashe's poem in a copy of *Dido* on sale at Osborne's bookshop in 1754. He describes it as an elegy 'on Marlowe's untimely death', and says it was 'inserted immediately after the title page'. It is just possible that it was a manuscript addition (in other words, that Tanner and Warton were describing the same unique copy of *Dido*) but more likely it was a printed single-leaf insertion in certain copies. It would be a good selling-point for the book, but the publisher – Thomas Woodcock, trading at the sign of the Black Bear in Paul's Churchyard – might have cause to be wary of it.

Like Peele, Nashe makes no comment about the actual manner and cause of Marlowe's death. They leave us with vague hints only: an 'unhappy end', an 'untimely death'. Nashe's statement that Marlowe valued 'liberty of speech' above his life is unsettling. One recalls the recommendation of the informer Richard Baines: that 'the mouth of so dangerous a member should be stopped'. But even if Nashe is really trailing that idea – that Marlowe was killed in order to silence him – we do not know if this is just a session of fraught guesswork on his part, or because of something he actually knows about the case. There is little to be gained, anyway, from advancing the idea that Marlowe was killed *because* of his outspoken attacks on religion and government. The upholders of religion and government, as Nashe well knew, had many legitimate means of silencing critics, including the gallows and the prisons. They did not need to resort to daggers in a back-room. If there is a connection between Marlowe's heresies and his death, it is a more complex one.

The only definite information about the death of Marlowe that can be retrieved from these first epitaphs is the fact that it was known about. We have Edward Blount's description, in the preface to *Hero and Leander*, of Marlowe's 'breathless body' being laid to rest. This *may* mean that he and other friends were at the graveside on 1 June, but the words might equally be metaphorical: we cannot be sure. Peele's tribute gives us a definite time-span. He is writing some time before 23 June. He is aware that Marlowe is dead. He feels free to mention the fact, and to express his regret.

There was, then, no attempt to hush up the fact of Marlowe's death. But as to how it happened, and why, there was as yet no public comment.

7

THE 'GOGGLE-EYED SONNET'

THE FIRST WRITER to comment on the actual manner of Marlowe's death – or so it is generally supposed – was Dr Gabriel Harvey. In October 1593, four months after Marlowe died, Harvey's latest work appeared on the bookstalls. It was entitled *Pierce's Supererogation*. It was another salvo in that 'civil war of wits' between Harvey and Tom Nashe. The 'Pierce' of the title alludes to Nashe's chosen nickname, 'Pierce Penniless'.

Most of the *Supererogation* was written in London during the early part of 1593 – the date at the end of it is 27 April – and though it mentions Marlowe (both by name and as 'Aretine') it obviously contains nothing about his death a month later. In mid-September, now back in his native Saffron Walden, Harvey wrote a short additional piece, the *New Letter of Notable Contents*, addressed to his publisher John Wolfe. Wolfe had this printed up with the *Supererogation*, and the two works were issued together in October. At the end of the *New Letter*, Harvey appended a poem called 'Gorgon', subtitled 'The Wonderful Year'. It is this – the 'goggle-eyed sonnet of Gorgon', as Nashe calls it – that contains the material on Marlowe's death. It is extremely puzzling, because Harvey seems to think that Marlowe had died of the plague.

The poem is in four parts: an opening sonnet, a 'stanza declarative', a 'postscript' and a 'gloss'. In among these are various tags and 'envoys' (short rhyming verses: from the French *envoi*). Nashe describes the closing envoy as 'like a fart after a good stool', which more or less sums up the literary quality of the poem.

The style is opaque and difficult, which is Harvey's way. The drift of the poem, as it is conventionally understood, is as follows. It opens with a reference to some great event of 1588, probably the Armada, the 'wonderment of *Eighty Eight*'. This amounted to nothing: 'the wonder was no wonder fell that year.' By contrast, he says, 'the fatal year of years is *Ninety Three*'. He refers to various momentous political events – the death of the Duke of Parma, the conversion of Henri of Navarre – and then to the death of Marlowe: 'Weep Powles, thy Tamburlaine vouchsafes to die'. 'Powles' is St Paul's Churchyard, the city's book-market and the hub of London literary life. 'Tamburlaine', of course, is Marlowe's famous hero. This now proves to be the main point of the poem. Marlowe's death is taken as an example of bragging pride brought low. The great poet, the 'Gargantua mind', has been silenced:

> Is it a dream? Or is the highest mind
> That ever haunted Powles, or hunted wind,
> Bereft of that sky-surmounting breath,
> That breath that taught the tympany to swell?

Naturally enough, Harvey also rehearses the by-now familiar charge of Marlowe as an atheistic scoffer:

> He that nor feared God, nor dreaded Devil,
> Nor aught admired but his wondrous self,
> Like Juno's gawdy bird, that proudly stares
> On glittering fan of his triumphant tail.

So far, there would be nothing surprising about this. We know Harvey's attitude to Marlowe, and this accords with it. The poem is intended as a warning to his adversary Nashe. Marlowe is dead, but his fellow swaggerer, 'the second Shakerley of Powles', is still alive:

The hugest miracle remains behind:
The second Shakerley Rash-swash to bind.

This 'second Shakerley' is obviously Nashe. (I will return later to the meaning of this curious phrase.)

It is in the final verse, the 'gloss', that Harvey makes his curious assertion about the actual nature of Marlowe's death:

He and the Plague contended for the game:
The haughty man extols his hideous thoughts,
And gloriously insults upon poor souls . . .
The grand Disease disdain'd his toad conceit.
And smiling at his Tamburlaine contempt,
Sternly struck home the peremptory stroke.

This seems quite unequivocal. Harvey is saying that Marlowe died as a victim of the bubonic plague then rampant in London.

Marlowe's biographers have all noted the allusion, scratched their heads a little, and passed on. Why does Harvey make this blunder? Was he misinformed about the facts, or was he deliberately misrepresenting them?

The idea that he just got it wrong is difficult to swallow. If anyone was in a position to know the facts, it was the meddlesome Dr Harvey. Consider his treatment of the death of Robert Greene, less than a year previously. Greene was another of Harvey's *bêtes noires*, and Harvey came up to London with the purpose of suing him for libel. But Greene was a sick man, and on the evening of 3 September 1592, in a cobbler's house in Dowgate, he died. This denied Harvey the pleasure of litigation, but afforded him excellent copy. The following day he was there at the funeral, gathering up the gossip, battening on Greene's landlady, Mrs Isam. He quickly penned an account of Greene's pitiful death, and by the end of the week this was out on the bookstalls, a six-leaf 'butterfly pamphlet'. It is lurid but highly factual. It gives names, times, locations. It reproduces the text of one of

Greene's last letters, to his estranged wife, Doll. It describes his mistress – a 'ragged quean', sister to a cutpurse – and his bastard son, Fortunatus. It records the cost of the funeral, 10s 4d.

Whatever you feel about Harvey's gloating treatment of Greene's death, there is no disputing his acumen. It was the sort of thing on which he prided himself: a man with a finger on the pulse of literary London. So when he comes to write in public about the death of Marlowe, you would expect him to be informed on the subject. He was almost certainly in London when it happened, billeted at John Wolfe's printing-shop in St Paul's Churchyard, perfectly placed to pick up the gossip. According to Nashe, he spent 'three quarters of a year' lodged with Wolfe, 'ink-squittering and printing against me'. He was there in April 1593, when he completed the text of *Pierce's Supererogation*, and there in July when he signed a prefatory letter for the book, so he was presumably there in early June, when the news of Marlowe's death was circulating.

He would have had another source of information, too. His younger brother, Richard, was at this time rector of St Nicholas's, Chislehurst. This was the parish church of Thomas Walsingham – Marlowe's patron, Frizer's master – and his family, who lived at nearby Scadbury. Richard Harvey was a little man 'no bigger than a tailor's pressing-iron', but he was a mighty controversialist. He had already tangled in print with Nashe, and he would have known and disliked Marlowe as well. Their paths had first crossed at Cambridge, and perhaps again in Chislehurst, when Marlowe was a guest of Mr Walsingham. Marlowe's comment that Dick Harvey was fit only 'to preach of the Iron Age' may recall some sermon he had to sit through at St Nicholas's.

Richard Harvey is therefore close to a local concentration of interest in the killing: both Marlowe and Frizer are known to people down here. He has, like brother Gabriel, the motivations of malice and polemic to make him curious about it. We know he corresponded with Gabriel, and that their letters touch on literary matters.

All the auspices for Gabriel Harvey's information on the matter are good, and yet he gets it *totally wrong*.

Faced with this puzzle, which no-one has tried to solve, I began to think that there was clear evidence here of some kind of cover-up: that the only plausible explanation of Harvey's belief that Marlowe died of the plague was that it was disinformation, a false set of 'facts' deliberately put about. Either Harvey was taken in by this disinformation, or he was going along with it.

But there is another explanation. A single entry in a London church register provides the clue, and a careful re-reading of 'Gorgon' confirms it. It solves the puzzle at a stroke. Gabriel Harvey's 'goggle-eyed sonnet' is not about the death of Christopher Marlowe at all. It is about the death of a man called Shakerley, whose name actually appears twice in the poem, when Nashe is described as the 'second Shakerley'.

Peter Shakerley was one of those self-publicising Elizabethan oddballs who found their way into the popular imagination. There were others: an absurdly dressy Italian called Monarcho, the loquacious barber Tom Tooley, old Mother Livers of Stoke Newington, and so on. They were a bit crazy, and people laughed at them and talked about them, and their names remain like curious fossils in the pamphlets and ballads of the day. Peter Shakerley was particularly associated with a style of fantastical, bragging oratory. In his popular miscellany, *Palladis Tamia*, Francis Meres writes of 'proud and haughty persons' who 'walk stroutingly and Shakerleyan-like'. Describing men who 'gape after' praise and applause, he instances Herostratus among the ancients, 'and in our age, Peter Shakerley of Paul's'.

As an habitué of St Paul's, and a noted eccentric, this man was known to both Nashe and Harvey. According to Nashe the 'house of the Shakerleys' had for its coat of arms 'three dog turds reeking'. In *Strange News*, written in the autumn of 1592, Nashe made a hit at Harvey by comparing him with Shakerley:

Now do I mean to present him and Shakerley to the Queen's fool-taker for coach-horses: for two that draw more equally in one oratorical yoke of vainglory there is not under heaven.

In *Pierce's Supererogation* Harvey returns the insult. Nashe's writings, he says, are 'lighter than Tarlton's toy' – a piece of business by the famous clown Dick Tarlton – 'and vainer than Shakerley's conceit.'

Peter Shakerley, gent, died in September 1593, and was buried in the churchyard of St Gregory-by-St-Paul's. His funeral took place on 18 September. We can now add, I think, that he died from the plague. It was Shakerley's death, not Marlowe's, which occasioned Harvey's poem. It was Shakerley that Harvey described, in comic hyperbole, as 'the highest mind that ever haunted Powles', as the strutting 'Tamburlaine' who now 'vouchsafes to die'. The poem *uses* Marlowe as a reference-point, is in part written in a cod-Marlovian style. He is present in the poem not as its subject, but as part of its lumbering irony.

Everything in Harvey's poem makes sense when it is read this way: as a mock-oratorical funeral elegy for Peter Shakerley of St Paul's, and an admonition to Nashe, the 'second Shakerley', to watch his step. The timing also makes sense. Marlowe had been dead nearly four months when Harvey wrote this piece. In the topical world of the pamphleteers – 'New herrings new, we must cry, every time we make ourselves public' – interest in the matter was staling. The death of Shakerley, on the other hand, was piping hot. The date of Harvey's *New Letter*, which includes 'Gorgon', is 16 September. He wrote it, in Saffron Walden, in reply to a letter he had received from his publisher, John Wolfe. Shakerley was buried on 18th, but would have died a few days earlier: the grave-diggers were busy this plague summer. I think it likely that Wolfe's letter contained the news of Shakerley's death – Wolfe himself lived in St Paul's. The good Doctor's first thought was to make some literary capital out of it.

This tasteless *bagatelle* of Harvey's can now be dumped, as Nashe recommends, into the 'dry-fat of oblivion'. It adds a fragment of information about the eccentric Mr Shakerley, but in the case of Christopher Marlowe it is just another red herring on the trail.

8

INDEPENDENT ACCOUNTS

THERE ARE IMMEDIATE reactions to Marlowe's death, tributes from his friends, but on the actual circumstances of his killing there is silence. We cannot be certain that nothing was published. So much Elizabethan writing has simply disappeared: there is this element of randomness in what we now know. We have a glimpse of one lost piece about Marlowe, Nashe's 'elegy', spotted in a copy of *Dido* in the eighteenth century. There could have been others. But nothing remains. With the jettisoning of Harvey's 'Gorgon', we are left only with this silence.

It lasts, in fact, for about four years. Then, in 1597, the first independent account of Marlowe's death is published. It appears in a book called *The Theatre of God's Judgements* by a young Puritan divine, Dr Thomas Beard. Beard had been a junior contemporary of Marlowe's at Cambridge, and was shortly to become the rector of Hengreave in Suffolk. He was later headmaster at Huntingdon grammar-school, where he taught – and, according to tradition, flogged – the young Oliver Cromwell. The *Theatre of God's Judgements* was his first book, a thunderous collection of 'histories' illustrating God's punishment of the 'transgressors of His commandments'. In a chapter entitled 'Of Epicures and Atheists', Beard turns to the case of Christopher Marlowe, and invites us to 'see what a hook the Lord put in the nostrils of this barking dog'.

After rehearsing the usual charges about Marlowe's 'atheism and impiety', Beard goes on to describe the manner of his death:

It so fell out that in London streets, as he purposed to stab one whom he ought a grudge unto with his dagger, the other party perceiving, so avoided the stroke that withal catching hold of his wrist, he stabbed his own dagger into his own head, in such sort that notwithstanding all the means of surgery that could be wrought, he shortly after died thereof.

This 'terrible' death was, he needs hardly add, a 'manifest sign of God's judgement'.

The book is crude Puritan propaganda, but this is our first gauge of current knowledge about Marlowe's killing. Four years have elapsed, but Beard still considers it 'of fresh and late memory'. It shows that the basic scenario of Marlowe's death was known about: he died in a knife-fight. It also shows that Marlowe was held to blame in the matter. Beard's account accepts the findings of the coroner and the Chancery court: that Marlowe was the aggressor, and that his killer acted in self-defence. This does not mean that everyone accepted this: only that Dr Beard, a despiser of Marlowe, is happy to do so.

Beard's version also shows what was *not* known about the case: the facts which had changed as the story circulated. The most significant inaccuracy is that Beard places the event 'in London streets'. This is not just an error of location. It alters the whole topography of the killing, takes it out of its claustrophobic interior context – the room, the meeting, the air of privacy – and makes it a common street-fight. (It has been suggested that 'streets' is a printer's error for 'streete', and that Beard is actually placing the event in London Street in East Greenwich: not quite Deptford but very nearly so. I think this is unlikely. There were scores of roads called London Street in the outlying villages of Kent, Surrey and Middlesex, and Beard could not have expected the reader to know which one he meant.)

There are other less important divergences from the 'official story'. Beard says that Marlowe was killed with his own dagger. This agrees in one sense with the inquest – that in this fight there was only one dagger – but gets it wrong as to whose dagger it was: it was actually Frizer's blade that dealt the death-blow. Beard's version suits his polemical purpose, accords with the notion of Marlowe's *self*-destruction: that 'his own hand, which had written those blasphemies' was the 'instrument to punish him'. Another minor discrepancy is that according to the coroner's report Marlowe died 'instantly'. Beard has him lingering a while, amid the efforts of 'surgery', then dying 'shortly after'. Again this may be an interpolation. It allows Marlowe a respite, a few dramatic minutes to repent his ways. This, according to Dr Beard, he refused to do. 'He even cursed and blasphemed to his last gasp, and together with his breath an oath flew out of his mouth.'

The next person to comment on the case of Marlowe's death was a literary gadfly named Francis Meres. He was, like Beard, a Cambridge man. His career overlapped with Marlowe's for three or four years: he graduated BA at Pembroke College in 1587, the year Marlowe left Cambridge. There seems, understandably, to be a concentration of interest in the case at Marlowe's old university. It was perhaps at this time of Puritan tub-thumping that Marlowe's portrait was removed from the gallery at Corpus.

In the autumn of 1598, a year after the appearance of Beard's *Theatre*, Meres published a miscellany – a 'wit's treasury', as he put it – entitled *Palladis Tamia*. This portmanteau of quotes, jottings and gossip has indeed proved a 'treasury' for literary historians. It contains, for instance, the earliest list of Shakespeare's plays (twelve of them, including the enigmatic *Love's Labour's Won*) and the first reference to his 'sugared sonnets', then circulating 'among his private friends'.

One of the most informative parts of Meres's book is a series of comparisons between classical and contemporary authors. Thomas Nashe, who had been forced to leave London after the suppression of his stage comedy *The Isle of Dogs*, is compared to Ovid in exile among the Getes. In less complimentary vein we learn that 'as Anacreon died of the pot, so George Peele died of the pox'. Thus, five years on, Marlowe's friends are dispersing.

It is in this section of the book, and in this form, that Francis Meres makes two separate allusions to the matter of Marlowe's death. The first is this:

> As Jodelle, a French tragical poet, being an epicure and an atheist, made a pitiful end, so our tragical poet Marlowe for his epicurism and atheism had a tragical death.

This is unhelpful. It is merely an echo of Dr Beard's published account. Meres acknowledges this, and refers the reader to the relevant chapter of the *Theatre*, where 'you may read of this Marlowe more at large'. A few pages on, however, he has something more to say, and this adds a new dimension to the story:

> As the poet Lycophron was shot to death by a certain rival of his, so Christopher Marlowe was stabbed to death by a bawdy serving-man, a rival of his in his lewd love.

This rich morsel of gossip introduces two new elements into the story, elements that every story needs: the who and the why. It does not disagree with Beard's version, it adds to it. Marlowe's antagonist, faceless in Beard's account, is fleshed out: a 'bawdy serving-man'. And the cause of the quarrel, an unidentified 'grudge' in Beard, is now the perennial one of a love-triangle. Meres was certainly no Puritan, but he was, like Beard, destined for the church: he was rector of Wing, in Rutland, for over forty years. His opinion of Marlowe's character, one infers, was not high, however much he admired his poetry. This account of Marlowe's death is not openly hostile, but it is demeaning and dismissive.

Meres's version, like Beard's, is an index of current rumour on the subject. In one aspect it is completely at variance with the official evidence: according to the inquest it was money, not love, that caused the fatal fight. In another aspect it is misleading: 'serving-man' is technically correct to describe

Ingram Frizer – he 'served' Thomas Walsingham – but the term suggests a menial status which is quite inaccurate. Frizer was a gentleman, a property owner, and he was employed by the Walsinghams as a financial agent, not some kind of pantry-man. Whether Frizer was 'bawdy' or not we don't know. The word could just imply loose morals, or it could mean he was a 'bawd' or pimp. I think it likely that Meres is trailing another, more specific meaning: that this serving-man was, like Marlowe, a homosexual, and that the cause of the fight, the object of their 'lewd love', was another man.

As with Beard's version, it is the ambience of the event that has got altered. The core of truth is there – Marlowe was stabbed to death – but it has been relocated into this folklorique setting, this 'low life' world of bawdy men and sixpenny love-affairs. This is the way hearsay works. It is collective. It neutralises the particularity of events.

These stories are in themselves only hearsay, but once enshrined on the printed page they become something more. Five years after his death, the consensus view on Christopher Marlowe – unless you happened to know otherwise – was that he had died on the streets of London in a fight over some rent-boy.

If there were those who knew otherwise, they seem to have kept their counsel. But Marlowe's detractors did not have it all their own way. In this same year, 1598, there appeared the first edition of Marlowe's unfinished poem, *Hero and Leander*, with its poignant dedication by the publisher, Edward Blount. He speaks of his personal memory of Marlowe: 'the impression of the man that hath been dear to us, living an after-life in our memory'. His publishing of the poem, commercial motives aside, is a 'duty' he owes to the 'unhappily deceased author'. The dedication is addressed to Thomas (now Sir Thomas) Walsingham, Marlowe's former patron, and seeks his allegiance in the defence of Marlowe. The poet once enjoyed the 'gentle air of your liking', and 'in his lifetime you bestowed many kind favours, entertaining the parts of reckoning and worth which you found in him.' The wording is careful – there were, it is implied, other 'parts' of Marlowe which Walsingham had nothing to do with – but the determination overall is to honour the dead man, and to do whatever 'we may judge shall make to his living credit'.

Edward Blount – or Ned Blunt, as his fellow-booksellers called him – is a voice in Marlowe's favour at a time when other voices were dragging his name through the mud. This is a publisher defending his author, a man defending his friend: Thomas Kyd had mentioned certain 'stationers in St Paul's' as being among Marlowe's familiar friends, 'such as he conversed withal', and Blount was doubtless one of them.

Later in the same year, a second edition of *Hero* appeared. As well as a reprint of Marlowe's lines, it contains a long sequel by George Chapman. Like Blount, Chapman is a former associate of Marlowe, now ready to make public his affection and admiration for the man. In one highly charged passage he speaks of his longing to reach the realm of 'spirits immortal', there to 'confer' with the soul of his dead friend:

> Now, as swift as time
> Doth follow motion, find th'eternal clime
> Of his free soul, whose living subject stood
> Up to the chin in the Pierian flood.

Also like Blount, Chapman looked to the Walsingham family for patronage, and dedicated his sequel to Lady Audrey Walsingham, wife of Sir Thomas.

Thomas Nashe, meanwhile, living in 'discontented exile' in Great Yarmouth, was also writing a version of the story of Hero and Leander. It appears in *Lenten Stuff*, published in 1599. He notes the sudden ubiquity of the poem – here is a story that 'every apprentice in Paul's churchyard will tell you for your love and sell you for your money' – and acknowledges its authors: 'divine Musaeus' and 'a diviner muse than him, Kit Marlowe'. Here is another friend of Marlowe's speaking up. His choice of adjective to describe Marlowe, 'divine', sounds like a casual superlative, but given the theological elements in the controversy about Marlowe, it is actually quite provocative.

In 1600, another of Marlowe's poems made its first appearance: his translation of Lucan's *Pharsalia*, published by Thomas Thorpe. Once again, Blount is involved, for Thorpe dedicated the book to him, his fellow-publisher and 'true friend'.

> Blount, I purpose to be blunt with you, and out of my dullness to encounter you with a dedication in the memory of that pure elemental wit, Christopher Marlow, whose ghost or genius is to be seen walk in the Churchyard in at the least three or four sheets.

Thorpe is also referring to this sudden printed effusion of Marlowe's work. His 'ghost' (his poetry) walks in the 'churchyard' (the book-mart of St Paul's) in different 'sheets' (the various editions of *Hero*, with a pun on winding-sheets and sheets of paper). In this more humorous vein, Thorpe conveys the sense of Marlowe's continued *presence*.

One other volume of Marlowe poetry deserves mention here: his superb translation of Ovid's *Elegies*, also known as the *Amores*. This had appeared earlier, perhaps during his lifetime, but it was in the news at this time. On 1 June 1599, Archbishop John Whitgift issued a series of 'commandments' in his capacity as chief censor. He ordered the immediate calling-in of various 'unseemly satires and epigrams', and top of the list was Marlowe's Ovid. On 4 June, various books 'presently thereupon were burnt' in the yard of Stationers' Hall. The banning of the *Elegies* relates solely to their erotic content, but it adds one more note to this controversy about Marlowe which flares up in the later 1590s. The writer who suffered worst in this edict was Nashe. It was decreed that all his books 'be taken wheresoever they may be found', and that none 'be ever printed hereafter'. This marks the end of his pamphleteering. He was dead two years later, at the age of thirty-three.

*

There is a clear polarising of opinion about Marlowe. In one corner we have Beard and Meres, with their contempt for the man and all he stands for: a blasphemous 'barking dog', a 'lewd' fellow stabbed in a tiff. In the other corner there is this little pro-Marlowe grouping of publishers and authors – Blount and Thorpe, Chapman and Nashe – and their patrons, the Walsinghams.

For the antagonists, Marlowe's violent death is a matter of punishment. It is just desserts and good riddance. Beard actually says this, and Meres implies it. If those who wished to damn Marlowe found in the 'official story' something convenient for their purpose, what about those who wished to defend him? What was their version, their reconstruction of the event?

We do not know, because they do not tell us. In this sense the silence continued, even after it was broken by the strident sound of Dr Beard's Puritan propaganda.

9

TOUCHSTONE'S RIDDLE

THIS NEW FLURRY of controversy about Christopher Marlowe was noted by another author, one very conscious of his literary debt to Marlowe. References to *Hero and Leander* appear in the play he was writing at the time, and these in turn lead into some veiled allusions to Marlowe's death. They are difficult to interpret, but they suggest that the versions of Marlowe's death provided by Beard and Meres were not the *only* versions in circulation at the time.

The author was Shakespeare, and the play *As You Like It*. It was written in about 1599. It was unknown to Francis Meres when he compiled his list of Shakespeare's plays in 1598, but it was certainly completed before August 1600, when it was entered on the Stationers' Register. With its outlaw duke and its forest setting, it was probably inspired by the two Robin Hood plays, written by Anthony Munday and Henry Chettle, which were pulling in the crowds at the Rose in 1598. *As You Like It* was the Globe's rival production: a bandwagon job.

In the middle of the play comes a totally unexpected window on to the case we are investigating. The line is spoken by Touchstone, the play's 'wise fool'. It is a single sentence: 'It strikes a man more dead than a great reckoning in a little room.' It sounds like a riddle, and it is generally agreed that the clue to the riddle is Marlowe's death. In this strange, resonant line Shakespeare seems to describe, in a kind of vivid shorthand, the circumstances of Marlowe's death as given in the coroner's inquest. He was struck down, in a fight over the reckoning, in a little room. Another point to note is that Touchstone's words echo a famous phrase from Marlowe's *Jew of Malta*: 'infinite riches in a little room'.

To understand Touchstone's riddle a little better, we must first look at the play's other allusions to Marlowe, and at the question of how and why Marlowe comes into the play at all.

Shakespeare had echoed Marlowe before, particularly in *Henry IV* – Pistol's 'hollow pampered jades of Asia' – and in *The Merchant of Venice*, which has obvious links with Marlowe's *Jew*. *As You Like It* goes further. Marlowe is actually addressed by one of the characters:

> Dead shepherd, now I find your saw of might:
> Whoever loved, that loved not at first sight?

The dead poet – 'shepherd' in the spoof pastoral language of Arden – is Marlowe, and his 'saw', or saying, is a famous line from *Hero and Leander*. It would be instantly recognisable to the audience, as familiar as a line from a classic pop-song. This is the only occasion in all Shakespeare's plays when he quotes and acknowledges – rather than just quietly borrowing – a line by a contemporary author.

There is another reference to *Hero and Leander* later in the play, when Rosalind pours scorn on the romantic common-place of people dying for love:

> The poor world is almost six thousand years old, and in all this time there was not any man died in his own person, *videlicet* in a love-cause. Troilus had his brains dashed out with a Grecian club, yet he did what he could to die before, and he is one of the patterns of love. Leander, he would have lived many a fair year though Hero had turned nun, if it had not been for a hot midsummer night; for, good youth, he went but forth to wash him in the Hellespont, and being taken with the cramp was drowned, and the foolish chroniclers of that age found it was Hero of Sestos.

But these are all lies: men have died from time to time, and worms have eaten them, but not for love.

This second allusion to *Hero and Leander* brings Marlowe once more to mind, and I think it does so in a rather special context. The point of this speech, from first to last, is the absurdity of the idea of dying for love. This was precisely the current rumour, courtesy of Francis Meres, about Marlowe: that he had died fighting over a 'lewd love'. In Rosalind's dismissal of these romantic legends, I hear also a dismissal of Meres's allegations about Marlowe: 'These are all lies.' Marlowe died, but not for love.

So here – not noticed before, as far as I know – is another allusion to the matter of Marlowe's death to set beside the Touchstone text.

Meres had been highly complimentary to Shakespeare in *Palladis Tamia*. There is no suggestion of any ill-will between them. If Shakespeare is making this point about the cause of Marlowe's death, he is doing so out of a concern for accuracy. He may have simply considered Meres's story preposterous. He may, on the other hand, have *known* it was untrue. Shakespeare had known Marlowe personally. They were both writing for Lord Strange's company in the early 1590s: there is evidence of their collaboration in parts of the *Henry VI* trilogy, performed at the Rose theatre in 1592. He was probably in London during the early summer of 1593, when Marlowe was killed: his poem *Venus and Adonis*, registered at the end of April, was then being printed at Richard Field's shop in Blackfriars. At the least, he would have been as curious about the killing as any of Marlowe's other associates.

It is interesting that Rosalind's speech begins with the observation that 'the poor world is almost six thousand years old'. It is an innocent remark, but – in the context of the controversy about Marlowe – curiously reminiscent. It recalls one of Marlowe's supposed heresies. According to the informer Baines it was Marlowe's contention that

the Indians and many authors of antiquity have assuredly

written above 16 thousand years agone, whereas Adam is proved to have lived within 6 thousand years.

This questioning of Biblical chronology is not peculiar to Marlowe, but it was one of the heresies attributed to him at the time of his death. Nashe knew about it, and mentions it in *Christ's Tears*, in a context suggestive of Marlowe. Rosalind's words recall this known Marlovian heresy, and a connection is made between the current rumours about Marlowe's death, and those other rumours of his atheism and heresy. Whether Shakespeare thought that these too were 'all lies' I cannot say.

The exiled Duke's court in Arden is a kind of miniature society, and one of the ideas explored in *As You Like It* is the social role of satire and political comment. The melancholy Jaques, casting a mordant eye over the 'fat greasy citizens', is Arden's satirist. He demands complete freedom of expression:

> I must have liberty
> Withal, as large a charter as the wind
> To blow on whom I please, for so fools have.
> And they that are most galled with my folly,
> They most must laugh . . . Give me leave
> To speak my mind, and I will through and through
> Cleanse the foul body of th' infected world.

It is generally agreed that this interest in the boundaries of satirical comment reflects topically on the book-burning edict of June 1599, with its blanket suppression of 'unseemly satires and epigrams'. This is another channel through which Marlowe, one of the banned authors, enters into the play. It is, in fact, the backdrop of Touchstone's enigmatic line about the 'great reckoning'.

Freshly landed in rustic Arden, Touchstone compares himself to the poet Ovid in exile: 'I am here with thee and thy goats, as the most capricious poet, honest Ovid, was among the Goths.' There is a triple pun here – 'goats', 'capricious' (literally meaning goat-like) and 'Goths' – the point of which is to undercut the innocence of 'honest Ovid' ('honest' meaning chaste) with the more popular perception of him as a lecherous old goat and writer of erotic poetry, notably those 'wanton' elegies, or *Amores*, consigned to the bonfire by the Archbishop's decree. In this way Touchstone's line links with the play's sub-text about literary freedom, and summons Marlowe – the translator of the banned elegies – into the audience's mind once more.

Touchstone now continues, still apparently on the subject of Ovid's banishment among barbarians:

> When a man's verses cannot be understood, nor a man's good wit seconded with the forward child understanding, it strikes a man more dead than a great reckoning in a little room.

Shakespeare's allusion to Marlowe's death flows quite naturally out of the context. He is thinking – as he does elsewhere in the play – about all the fuss now surrounding Marlowe: the perturbations of the Puritans, the lies of Meres, the banning of the *Elegies*. Through the wise fool Touchstone he is saying that when a dead poet's reputation is mishandled and his work misunderstood, as Marlowe's now is, it is like a kind of second death for him; a death even worse than his first, physical death in that little room in Deptford.

This is not the *only* interpretation of Touchstone's words about the great reckoning. Although no-one seems to have explained it this way, the line has another coherent meaning: a bawdy one. This depends on sexual meanings in Elizabethan usage of the words 'dead' and 'room'. 'Dead' meaning detumescent is part of a subterranean literary imagery in which 'spirit' means semen, and 'death' – a yielding up of the spirit – means ejaculation. These meanings are found in Shakespeare's guilt-ridden sonnets ('The expense of spirit in a waste of shame', where 'waste' is also 'waist' or womb); and in John Donne's love poetry ('When I died last, and dear I die as often as from thee I go . . .'). 'Room', rather less subtly, is the vagina. An instance of this occurs in Marlowe's *Massacre*, where Mugeroun is accused of dallying with the Duchess of Guise:

> Now, sir, to you, that dares make a duke a cuckold, and use a counterfeit key to his privy chamber. Though you take out none but your own treasure, yet you put in that displeases him, and fill up his room that he should occupy.

Touchstone's 'great reckoning in a little room' can therefore be read to mean an ejaculation. The overall meaning of the lines would be that the poor reception of a poet's work is more dismal to him than post-coital *tristesse*.

The sexual reading is doubtless there, carrying on from the business about Ovid as goatish poet. There are guffaws in the Globe, but for others there is another meaning behind this, connected with Marlowe, the 'dead shepherd' who quite definitely did not 'die for love'.

10

VAUGHAN AND THE PERROTS

ANOTHER WHO KNEW more on the subject of Marlowe's death than either Beard or Meres was a Welshman named William Vaughan. His is the most interesting of the independent accounts of the killing. It appears in his book *The Golden Grove*, published in 1600.

The context, as in Beard, is punitive. Vaughan is writing about atheists, and showing the 'extraordinary punishments of God' on this 'damnable opinion'. He instances the deaths of Diogenes in Athens, and of Pliny at Pompeii, then moves to a more topical example:

> Not inferior to these was one Christopher Marlow, by profession a playmaker, who, as it is reported, about 7 years ago wrote a book against the Trinity. But see the effects of God's justice: so it happened, that at Detford, a little village about three miles distant from London, as he meant to stab with his poignard one named Ingram, that had invited him thither to a feast, and was then playing at tables, he quickly perceiving it, so avoided the thrust, that withall drawing out his own dagger for his defence, he stabbed this Marlowe into the eye, in such sort that his brains coming out at the dagger's point, he shortly after died. Thus did God, the true executioner of divine justice, work the end of impious atheists.

Vaughan gets much closer to the facts than any of the previous commentators. He places the killing correctly, both

91

in time ('about 7 years ago' in 1600) and in location (at 'Detford'). He is the first to identify Marlowe's killer, 'one named Ingram'. And he is the first to be precise about the fatal struggle: that it was this Ingram whose dagger struck the blow (Beard says it was Marlowe's dagger), and that Marlowe was stabbed 'into the eye' (Beard has the less specific stabbing into his head). In all of this Vaughan reflects the official story as contained in the coroner's inquest. His only divergence is that, like both Beard and Meres, he claims that Marlowe first drew his *own* dagger.

Since so much of Vaughan's account in *The Golden Grove* is corroborated by the official evidence, this gives weight to other statements he makes, which are not corroborated elsewhere. Perhaps he is right about these, too. One adds a stray human detail: that Ingram Frizer was playing back-gammon ('tables') when Marlowe lunged at him. The other is more significant: that is was Frizer himself who had invited Marlowe to Deptford. If true, this is an important piece of additional evidence, the first that tells us anything about *why* this meeting took place. Vaughan also identifies the purpose of the meeting: a 'feast'. The word is less formal than it sounds: it means simply that it was a social occasion, a bit of a party.

These are important additions to the story, but none of Marlowe's biographers has investigated Vaughan, or asked how he might have acquired this information. With a little digging, it is possible to pinpoint his sources with reasonable certainty, and to say that it is very likely he was right.

Born in 1577, William Vaughan was the second son of Walter Vaughan of Golden Grove, Carmarthenshire. The title of his book is a reference to the family home, a huge estate comprising 50,000 acres, twenty-five lordships, and six castles. He studied at Westminster and Jesus College, Oxford, graduating MA in 1597. His first literary work was published that year: a selection of religious verses mainly based on the Psalms. Two further volumes of verse followed in 1598. One of these, *Poematum Libellus*, was dedicated to the Earl of Essex. In

1600, as well as *The Golden Grove*, Vaughan published a medical handbook, *Natural and Artificial Directions for Health*. This proved very popular, and went through seven editions in his lifetime.

So far there seems little to connect him with Marlowe or his circle. At the time of Marlowe's demise Vaughan was a somewhat over-serious teenager in his second year at Oxford. His bent was religious, philosophical and medical: a conventional, rather melancholic Welshman. All this might explain his disapproval of Marlowe, but not his knowledge of the facts of his killing.

It is a family connection which provides the clue. When Vaughan's mother Katherine died, his father took a second wife: Letitia (or Lettice) Perrot. She was the daughter of the swashbuckling Welsh soldier Sir John Perrot, who was popularly reputed to be the bastard son of Henry VIII. Perrot had four children: Thomas, by his first wife; James, an illegitimate son born to Mrs Sybil Jones of Radnorshire; and William and Lettice, by his second wife.

When Lettice Perrot became the second Mrs Vaughan, she brought not only Pembrokeshire lands and money, but a range of important connections. In 1583, her half-brother Sir Thomas, heir to the Perrot estates, had made a very fortunate marriage. The circumstances of the wedding were well-known: Perrot and his bride arriving at a secluded church in Hertfordshire; the church surrounded by a gang of Perrot's men; the vicar forced at swordpoint to marry the couple without any banns being posted. The identity of the bride explains this violent haste: she was Dorothy Devereux, the younger sister of the Earl of Essex. Essex was the new star at court, and the Queen viewed this marriage as quite unsuitable for the noble Dorothy. Sir Thomas was duly despatched to the Fleet prison for his presumption, but the marriage stood, and soon produced a daughter.

Lettice Vaughan was therefore sister-in-law to Dorothy *née* Devereux, the sister of the Earl of Essex. It sounds a bit tenuous on paper, but in the dynastic world of the Elizabethans this was very good for the Vaughans. Dorothy became their 'cousin', in the loose Elizabethan usage, and they would have plenty of occasion to meet her when she visited the Perrot estates at Traventi, just a few miles from Golden Grove. Through her beckoned the magic of the Essex circle.

For the young Vaughan brothers, now embarking on their careers, it was a golden opportunity, and they reached out for it with both hands. In 1598, William Vaughan, the scholar of the family, dedicates his latest volume of poems to the Earl of Essex. He includes a fulsome 'ode' in celebration of the Earl. At about the same time, his brother John, more the man of action, enlists under the Earl's banner in Ireland, and in 1599 he is knighted by him. Both are here calling on their family connection, via their stepmother Lettice and their 'cousin' Dorothy, with the Earl of Essex.

Another Perrot – Lettice's illegitimate half-brother, James – was a close associate of William Vaughan. Like Vaughan, he was a student at Jesus College, Oxford, and an author of philosophic bent. His first work was *A Discovery of Discontented Minds*, an anti-Catholic broadside published in Oxford in 1596. This too was dedicated to the Earl of Essex, exploiting the same Perrot-Devereux connection. In 1600, Perrot published *The Consideration of Human Condition*, a book which offers, in his own words, 'the moral consideration of a man's self'. It can hardly be coincidence that Perrot's *Consideration* and Vaughan's *Golden Grove* are so similar. They are two edifying works of moral philosophy, both written at Oxford, and both published in the same year. The two authors are related to one another, and share the same aspirations towards the Essex circle. To confirm that this closeness is a matter of friendship, rather than competition, the *Golden Grove* contains a poem by Perrot, warmly commending his 'loving cousin', Vaughan.

For both William Vaughan and James Perrot, the fulcrum of their aspirations towards the Earl of Essex was Dorothy Perrot, the Earl's sister. This is where we cross back to the question of the Marlowe material in *The Golden Grove*. For by the time Vaughan was writing this book, Dorothy Perrot was no longer Dorothy Perrot. Her husband Sir Thomas had died in 1593, and the following year she had married again. This time the wedding was blessed by the Queen: an altogether more suitable, noble match for Essex's sister. Her new husband was Henry Percy, Earl of Northumberland, popularly known as the 'Wizard Earl'.

This is a connection which strongly validates Vaughan's statements about Marlowe's death. As already mentioned, the Earl of Northumberland was one of Marlowe's patrons. By 1591, and probably earlier, Marlowe was (in his own words) 'very well known' to the Earl. Three of his close friends – the poet Matthew Roydon, and the scientists Thomas Hariot and Walter Warner – were also part of the Northumberland circle. It was for Northumberland that George Peele wrote *The Honour of the Garter*, containing the earliest of the epitaphs on Marlowe. So unlike Beard and Meres, Vaughan's knowledge has identifiable sources. It comes from his *entrée* into the Northumberland household. Through his noble kinswoman Dorothy Devereux, now the Countess of Northumberland, Vaughan was in contact with people who had known Marlowe personally, and who were close to the events surrounding his death.

Some of those people would have been friends of Marlowe's, others less enamoured. Vaughan's portrait of Marlowe in *The Golden Grove* is an unflattering one. This may be linked to factions in the Northumberland household. The Countess was 'closely tied' to the cause of her brother Essex, while Northumberland himself was a close friend of Essex's rival, Sir Walter Ralegh. There was marital friction, divided loyalties. We can see Vaughan as connected with this little Essex faction *within* the Northumberland circle. Essex himself was an implacable enemy of all kinds of 'atheism', so this is a faction that would disapprove of the speculations that went on under Northumberland's protection, a faction that would enjoy Vaughan's presentation of Marlowe's death as a lesson to all 'impious atheists'.

Whatever his opinions about Marlowe, Vaughan's account of the killing is highly factual – unusually so, by Elizabethan standards. He knows where and when it happened, and he knows the name of the killer. My identification of his probable sources helps to explain his inside knowledge of the case. Perhaps more important, it gives further weight to those statements he makes which cannot be cross-checked. They are hearsay, but informed hearsay. When he says it was Ingram Frizer who 'invited' Marlowe to the meeting at Deptford, we should take him seriously.

II

THE QUESTIONS

THE PUBLIC REACTION to Marlowe's death adds almost nothing to our knowledge of the event. We are dealing with a few scattered fragments of reaction: epitaphs from his friends, propaganda from his enemies, a morsel of gossip from Meres, a puzzling comment from a clown in a playhouse. Four years passed before the first circumstantial accounts appeared in print. The broad scenario of the killing – the knife-fight, the stab to the head – was common currency, but much had been obscured in the transmission. It is thought of as a street fight, a quarrel between rival, probably homosexual, lovers. Shakespeare, writing in 1599, seems to dismiss this as a lie, and to show some knowledge of the official account in the coroner's inquest. A year later, Vaughan provides the first accurate synopsis of the event, though he makes no comment about the actual cause of the fight. In most details he reflects the official version, but he has acquired other information, probably through his association with the Countess of Northumberland. He states that it was Marlowe's killer who had initiated the meeting in the first place. This is the nearest we come to a new, independent fact about the killing. Other than that there are only those unsettling nuances – a life valued less than 'the liberty of speech', a 'great reckoning in a little room' – and the sense they bring, as much by their veiledness as by what they say, of other facts, other versions, that remained unspoken.

The accounts given by Beard, Meres and Vaughan swiftly became accepted lore. Far more than the 'official story', they were the basis for people's knowledge of Marlowe's death. In a documentary sense, the official story was simply not available: it lay gathering dust in the stacks of the Chancery Court, and whatever had come out at the time was subsumed into the hearsay. In the following century there is only repetition. Beard's tirade is repeated, with minor variations, in Edward Rudierde's *Thunderbolt of God's Wrath* (1618), and Anthony à Wood draws on both Beard and Meres when he retells the story in *Athenae Oxonienses* (1691). Already the folklore has grown new layers. According to Wood, Marlowe was 'deeply in love with a certain woman', and took it as a 'high affront' that his rival was only 'a bawdy serving man, one rather fit to be a pimp than an ingenious *amoretto* as Marlowe conceived himself to be'. Marlowe therefore 'rushed in upon' the man and attacked him with his dagger. This seems to take snobbery as a major cause of the affray.

The first attempt at a more scientific enquiry into Marlowe's death only succeeded in clouding the issue further. In 1820, the historian James Broughton – noting Vaughan's mention of Deptford as the scene of the killing – decided to write to the vicar of St Nicholas's, to ask if any record of Marlowe's burial remained. The vicar, the Reverend Jones, consulted the parish registers, and there found the entry, dated 1 June 1593. As we have seen, this entry was already inaccurate: it gave the name of Marlowe's killer as Francis Frezer. Rev. Jones now compounded the confusion by misreading 'Frezer' as 'Archer', and so out of a double clerical error there emerged this chimerical assassin, 'Francis Archer'.

Francis Archer did not have it all his own way. Also taking the field was the equally illusory Francis Ingram, a hybrid formed out of the burial entry and Vaughan's 'one Ingram'. Later in the century, the Deptford registers were re-examined, and the misreading corrected back to Francis Frezer, but he was no more substantial than the others. Throughout the Victorian period, one or other of these Francises sported with increasing freedom through a series of lurid romantic scenarios. He was variously called a 'villain', a 'lackey', and in one case Marlowe's own 'valet'. With each version the object of their rivalry was painted an inch thicker, and the scene of the killing sank by degrees from tavern to ale-house to brothel. By the beginning of this century there was serious historical material being gathered about Marlowe, but on the matter of his death this gutter-level vignette held sway.

This is a cautionary tale for all investigators, historical or otherwise. Beware Francis Archer, that poultergeist of mis-information who will one day wreck your neatly constructed theories.

So it proved in 1925, when a brilliant young Harvard scholar, Leslie Hotson, was working through the calendar of Elizabethan close-rolls at the Public Record Office in London. There he chanced, in a reference to a property-deal, upon the name Ingram Frizer. Well-versed in the Marlowe story (as it then stood), Hotson immediately guessed the truth: that Vaughan's 'one Ingram' was, in the typical Elizabethan way, a reference to the man's forename; and that the 'Francis' in the Deptford register had been an error all along. The poulter-geists vanished upon the instant, and Ingram Frizer moved into the frame. Armed with this new clue, Hotson tracked down a reference to Frizer's pardon in the patent-rolls for 1593. This in turn led him to the coroner's inquest, and to the seemingly pristine story of Marlowe's death as it was told on 1 June 1593, upon testimony of eye-witnesses and upon view of the dead poet's body.

The discovery was a piece of archival genius by Hotson, and not surprisingly he thought that it settled the matter once and for all. After three hundred years of rumour, here were the historical facts about Marlowe's death. Others since have felt less certain that the discovery of the inquest really closes the case. It gives us the real people, in the real landscape, but does it also give us the truth? There are those nagging doubts about it, a sense of its severe limitations. This is partly its narrowness of scope: so much is omitted. More, it is a question of its unreliability, its dependence on that dodgy, delusive trio – Poley, Skeres and Frizer – for the crux of the story.

*

Once again we are drawn back to the inquest: to what it says, to what it does not say. We look at the story told to Coroner Danby and his sixteen stout jurors, and we wonder about it. How well does it hang together? At some point on the evening of 30 May 1593, after a long 'quiet' day together in Deptford, Frizer and Marlowe start to argue about who should pay the 'sum of pence' owed to Mistress Bull. There is nothing implausible about this – one can see the components: the money-maker's stinginess, the poet's quick temper – but there is nothing certain about it either. The only evidence for it is the testimony of a pair of professional deceivers, Nicholas Skeres and Robert Poley. This argument may never have happened.

Then comes the fight. Marlowe climbs off the bed, whips out Frizer's dagger and strikes him. He attacks from behind, 'on a sudden', with surprise on his side. Frizer is sitting on a bench, 'with the front part of his body towards the table'. He is hemmed in tight by Poley and Skeres either side of him. The advantage is clearly Marlowe's, but despite this Frizer receives only a couple of minor scalp-wounds, and manages to drive the dagger into Marlowe's face with such force that it penetrates his brain to a depth of two inches.

What are Skeres and Poley up to while this happens? They are, we are told, sitting either side of Frizer in such a way that he 'could in no wise take flight'. They are there as the two men argue, as Marlowe clambers to his feet, as the dagger is drawn, as Frizer is wounded, as the fighters wrestle for control of the knife, and *still* they are tight in there, so that at the very moment when Frizer makes the fatal thrust, he is still physically unable to 'get away from' Marlowe. The coroner is quite clear about this: it is a vital point in Frizer's plea of self-defence. Skeres and Poley are oddly motionless figures during the last moments of Marlowe's life. No strangers to violence, a soldier for Essex and a spy for the Queen, they prove inept in this particular crisis. They seem to have made no effort to restrain or separate the fighters. They are close enough to impede, but not to intervene.

This kind of questioning will never get an answer, never recover the logic of that moment. We can only listen to the coroner's narrative, the story given by the witnesses, and say once again that what actually happened might have been different – or indeed that it might have been the same except for one vital thing: *it was the other way round*. It was not Marlowe who was the aggressor, but Frizer. It was not Frizer who was pinioned between Skeres and Poley, so that he could not 'get away', but Marlowe. The shallow slashes on Frizer's head were not inflicted by a man standing over him, but by a victim flailing and lunging for his life. The killing of Christopher Marlowe was not self-defence but murder.

All the physical evidence could point to this, just as well as it could point to the story told in the coroner's inquest. In some senses, it is a better deduction from the evidence. There was only one knife used in the affray at Mistress Bull's house: the twelvepenny dagger of Ingram Frizer. This is, *prima facie*, an awkward point in his plea of self-defence. Frizer needs this story, this particular reconstruction of the event, to explain away a more obvious deduction. He has killed an unarmed man with his dagger, but by virtue of this story it is not his fault.

It is sometimes said, in defence of the inquest's account, that the wound Marlowe received is more suggestive of a chaotic struggle than a planned attack, but I do not think this is so. The face, and particularly the eye, was regarded as a prime target. The manuals of swordsmanship described the thrust *alla revolta*, whose precise purpose was to skewer your opponent's eye-ball. Nashe transfers this to mental combat: Harvey's style is an unwieldy 'two-hand sword', and he cannot 'make one straight thrust at his enemy's face'. In another fight, another inquest, we hear of the actor Gabriel Spenser driving his rapier, scabbard and all, into the face of a man called Feake. The blade went 'between the pupil of the right eye and the eyebrows, penetrating to the brain'. Like Frizer, Spenser claimed he stabbed in self-defence, but in one famous case a man was murdered in this way. This was Thomas Arden, killed by two men in his house at

Faversham in 1551. A contemporary account describes the attack:

> Black Will stepped forth and cast a towel about his neck, so to stop his breath and strangle him. Then Mosby, having at his girdle a pressing-iron of 14 pound weight, struck him on the head with the same, so that he fell down and gave a great groan, insomuch that they thought he had been killed. Then they bare him away to lay him in the counting-house, and as they were about to lay him down, the pangs of death coming on him, he gave a great groan and stretched himself. And then Black Will gave him a great gash in the face, and so killed him out of hand.

In this case too, the *coup de grâce* is a 'gash in the face'. It is not a premeditated stroke, exactly, but it is the one chosen for its effectiveness: to kill him 'out of hand'.

Another frequent statement about the inquest version is that it agrees with what we already know, from other sources, about Marlowe's physical aggressiveness. One of the chief sources cited is Thomas Kyd, who describes Marlowe as 'intemperate', and speaks of his 'rashness in attempting sudden privy injuries to men'. This is always taken to mean that Marlowe physically attacked people, but again I am unsure about this. In Elizabethan usage to 'injure' almost always means to insult, to abuse verbally. This is closer to the root-meaning of the word, which is connected with injustice, and it is the invariable meaning of modern French *injurier*. This contemporary sense is exemplified in Florio's 1603 edition of Montaigne: 'he began to rail upon them with a thousand injuries'. Kyd's particular phrase, 'privy injuries', is similar to a term in Puttenham's influential *Art of English Poesy*, published in 1589, where a certain kind of insult is called the 'privy nip'. From Puttenham's definition, it sounds like what we call sarcasm: 'when ye give a mock under smooth and lowly words,' he says, 'we may call it the privy nip, or a mild and appeasing mockery'. Kyd is not being quite so specific, but I am sure that his general meaning is to do with

Marlowe as a scoffer, not as a brawler. This certainly is the context in which the phrase appears. Kyd is writing about Marlowe's dreadful blasphemies and dangerous opinions. He mentions this 'rashness' against people because it is part of the same general accusation. He is talking about the violence of language, not of the dagger.

This does not, of course, mean that Marlowe is innocent of the charge, only that Kyd was not actually making it when he wrote those words. There is plenty of independent evidence that Marlowe was as quick on the draw as any other young Elizabethan. In 1589 he was imprisoned after a swordfight in Shoreditch which resulted in the death of William Bradley, an innkeeper's son. In 1592, again in Shoreditch, he was bound over by the local constabulary to 'keep the peace'. A few months later, on a street corner in Canterbury, he fought a tailor named Corkine 'with a staff and a dagger'. These are part of the lurid side of Marlowe's reputation, but what really do they show?

They show that he was no stranger to violence, but they do not prove much about him as an *aggressor*. There is no evidence that he started the fight with Bradley. In fact, he did not actually inflict any wound on Bradley at all – Bradley was killed by another man – and he was bailed and acquitted shortly afterwards. His later breach of the peace in Shoreditch may well be another case of verbal rather than physical rowdiness. His attack on the tailor Corkine is, on the face of it, a clear instance of aggression (and quite possibly entailed the embarrassing situation of being arrested by his father, who was then serving as a constable) but once again there are extenuating factors. When Corkine sued him for assault, Marlowe's response was to file a counter-suit, claiming that it was not he but Corkine who was the assailant. The tailor had 'beat, wounded and maltreated' him to his 'grave damage'. What the truth was we do not know. By the time it came to court the two men had patched up their differences, and the case was dismissed. Twenty years later, a William Corkine published a lute accompaniment to Marlowe's famous lyric 'Come Live With Me'. This was almost certainly the tailor's son.

On the basis of Marlowe's police record – perhaps known to the coroner, perhaps not – we can say that he had twice been involved in violent clashes, in public, though in neither case can we be sure that he was the aggressor, and in neither case was he subsequently charged with any crime. The story of his assault on Ingram Frizer is plausible – we know that anyway – but these earlier events do not really add weight to it, as they are usually thought to, and the 'privy injuries' mentioned by Kyd add nothing at all.

I am not the first to doubt the 'official story' of Marlowe's death. Most of his biographers have expressed some unease with it, but they have ended up accepting it for lack of any provable alternative. The inquest is granted precedence: too authentic, too close to the event, to be overturned. The witnesses are untrustworthy, the story unsatisfactory, the circumstances shady, but for all that the document is 'quite unassailable'. These magisterial decisions filter down into the potted biographies, the ongoing hearsay. Marlowe died in a 'tavern brawl'.

I think this is complacent. The story of the 'reckoning' is not true by virtue of its immediacy. How long does it take to tell a lie? We have seen how the story of Marlowe's death has changed over the centuries, but perhaps the most significant change occurred during the first thirty-six hours, in the period between the killing and the inquest.

And perhaps those areas of doubt about the inquest have always been there. In the hearsay accounts of Beard, Meres and Vaughan, there are interesting points of disagreement – disagreement with the official evidence, and also with one another. The first is the business about the dagger. The inquest says Marlowe drew Frizer's dagger and was stabbed with it; Beard says Marlowe drew his own dagger and was stabbed with it; Vaughan says Marlowe drew his own dagger but was stabbed with Frizer's. This is a minor point – they all agree that Marlowe was the aggressor – but the variations suggest uncertainty about this aspect of the event. The second disagreement concerns the cause of the killing. According to the inquest, it was an argument over the bill; according to Beard it was a flaring up of some previous grudge; according to Meres it was a squabble between rival lovers. These shifting values in the story occur at just those points where the inquest itself seems weakest. The exact sequence of the fight, and the exact cause of it: this is where the inquest depends entirely on the word of Skeres, Poley and Frizer, and this is where the independent versions are uncertain.

In this sense the public reactions to Marlowe's death are valuable not for any answers they give us, but for the questions they continue to raise: how and why was Marlowe killed? The first question, barring any major new discovery of evidence, cannot be answered. To explore the second question, to find some coherent motive for the killing of Marlowe, is now my purpose in this book.

PART THREE

THE INTELLIGENCE
CONNECTION

I2

FAITHFUL DEALING

IN THOSE POTTED biographies of Marlowe which tell you he died in a 'tavern brawl', you will also often read that he was a 'spy'. Exactly what he did as a spy, and for whom he did it, is not specified, because no-one has fully investigated the subject. Yet it is vital to the whole question of Marlowe's death. Two of the men with whom he met at Deptford – Poley and Skeres – were involved in intelligence work. The third, Frizer, has no active record in intelligence, but he was a servant of Thomas Walsingham, who had been employed in secret service by his cousin Sir Francis. Other figures from the shadow-world, notably the informers Richard Baines and Richard Cholmeley, cluster around the periphery of the affair. If Marlowe was himself a 'spy' – to stick with that loose term for a moment – this would seem to complete a remarkably consistent picture.

So now we pull back the focus a little, away from the moment of Marlowe's death, to consider the meeting which preceded it, which contained it. What is the meaning of that meeting at Deptford? Vaughan says it was a 'feast', a nice innocent term. The inquest gives a very different feel: a meeting that lasted over eight hours, in a private room, in 'quiet mood'. This sounds more like business.

To find the true meaning of the Deptford meeting, we must venture into the world of Elizabethan espionage, though conscious all the while that in the world of espionage true meanings are notoriously hard to come by.

*

The beginning of Marlowe's dealings with the Elizabethan intelligence service takes us back to his days at Cambridge in the mid-1580s, back to the time of the Corpus Christi portrait: that young man who seems to promise so much, yet also hides so much.

On 29 June 1587 the Privy Council met at St James's Palace in Westminster. Present were Archbishop Whitgift, Lord Burghley, Lord Hunsdon, Sir Christopher Hatton and 'Mr Comptroler', Sir James Crofts. Their business that morning included the drafting of a sharply-worded communiqué to the authorities of Cambridge University. It concerned a student named Christopher Morley, who was due to receive his MA degree the following month, but was being 'defamed' by certain people who wished to block his candidature.

The letter itself is no longer extant, but there is a full summary of it in the Council minutes:

> Whereas it was reported that Christopher Morley was determined to have gone beyond the seas to Reames and there to remain, their Lordships thought good to certify that he had no such intent, but that in all his actions he had behaved himself orderly and discretely, whereby he had done Her Majesty good service, & deserved to be rewarded for his faithful dealing. Their Lordships' request was that the rumour thereof should be allayed by all possible means, and that he should be furthered in the degree he was to take this next Commencement, because it was not Her Majesty's pleasure that anyone employed, as he had been, in matters touching the benefit of his country, should be defamed by those that are ignorant in th'affairs he went about.

Morley was, without any doubt, Christopher Marlowe of Corpus Christi College. The same spelling of his name is found in the inquest, and in other legal documents, and though there was another Christopher Morley at Cambridge, he had already received his MA the previous year. This is definitely Marlowe, and this certificate of good behaviour drawn up on a summer morning in 1587 is the earliest record of his involvement in confidential government work. He has been employed, says the Council, 'in matters touching the benefit of his country'. He has 'done her Majesty good service'. He deserves to be rewarded, not defamed, for his 'faithful dealing'.

The chief rumour against Marlowe, which the Council expressly refutes, was that he 'was determined to have gone beyond the seas to Reames and there to remain'. 'Reames' is Rheims, in Northern France, and in the 1580s going to Rheims meant one thing and one thing only. It meant turning your back on Queen and Country, and enlisting in the Catholic struggle against the established church and government. It meant, in a word, defection. Rheims was the home of the English College, one of the two chief Catholic seminaries for young Englishmen. (The other was at Rome, and a third would shortly be founded at Valladolid.) It was a rallying-point for English exiles, a centre for anti-government propaganda, and a training-centre for missionaries returning to convert the country back to the Old Faith. So the accusation against Marlowe in 1587 is a serious one: that he is a malcontent young Catholic, and that he plans to defect to the Catholic cause. The government's unequivocal answer is that he had 'no such intent', and that those who have broadcast these rumours are 'ignorant in th'affairs he went about'.

Here are two very different accounts of Marlowe's behaviour at Cambridge. According to one he is a potential traitor: according to the other he is a faithful servant of the Queen. The explanation of this is not hard to find. These opposites must be different layers of behaviour. On the surface Marlowe appears to be a Catholic sympathiser, but this is only a pose. In reality he is the government's man, working in some way against the Catholics. This seems the only possible interpretation of the Council's wording.

This document is, in effect, a retrospective 'warrant' from the Council. It exonerates Marlowe from suspicious or illegal behaviour because it was being done for the government's 'benefit'. Agents and informers needed this kind of protection, and preferably they got it before they ventured into undercover work. The veteran anti-Catholic spy Nicholas Berden insisted on such a 'warranty'. It should be 'set down in as large words as may be', for without it 'I am most fearful of my security'. Robert Poley also spoke of the need to get prior allowance from the Privy Council:

> If, at mine own election, without Her Honourable Council's consent and direction (for which consent and direction from Mr Secretary I have laboured a whole year), I should have insinuated the conversation of any, at home or abroad, suspected for religion or practice against the State, and not in convenient time (as often it must needs fall out) detected anything, then should I have been directly charged as a practiser with them, neither should my close intent have availed for excuse.

This danger – the anti-Catholic spy being charged 'as a practiser with them' – was illustrated in the case of William Parry, hanged for treason in 1585, and insisting to the last that he had been working as an *agent provocateur* for the government.

The actual text of one of these warrants survives. It was drawn up by the Council in 1590, on behalf of John Edge, a cavalry-officer serving in the Low Countries. Edge offered his services as an English 'espial' in the Spanish camp of the Duke of Parma. He would need to pretend to be a Catholic, and to consort with certain English outlaws in Parma's service. The Council accepted his offer and duly provided him with a 'certificate of allowance'. Should he 'incur some danger or reproof' for his actions, the Council promises to 'acquit him', and

> to preserve his credit against such as might maliciously, or ignorantly and for lack of knowledge of his intent to do such good service to her Majesty, condemn or reprove him.

This is not, however, an unqualified promise, for the Council adds that they will protect him if, and only if, he has provided 'something worthy of knowledge', or performed some 'action laudable and profitable for Her Majesty'. Results were required before the government gave its protection.

This document is very close in its wording to the Council's certificate for Marlowe, and broadly confirms the circumstance which required it. Marlowe has been acting like a renegade Catholic but is really a government 'espial' or agent. He has suffered 'reproof' from people ignorant of his true role, and the Council has intervened to 'preserve his credit'. We can infer that he must have been quite useful to them. The Council is prepared to stand by him and, judging from the Edge document, they would only do this if they felt he was worth it. The rumours against him are in themselves an index of his effectiveness. His Catholic pose – his cover – was good enough to take in the Cambridge authorities, who intended to withhold his degree as a result.

The Council's countermand – that the idle talk against Marlowe should be 'allayed by all possible means', and that he should be 'furthered in the degree he was to take' – proved effective, and he duly received his degree, and left Cambridge a Master of Arts.

It is sometimes said, on the strength of this document, that Marlowe actually went to Rheims. This seems unlikely. There certainly were infiltrators at the English College, but if you look through the very detailed college diaries for the mid-1580s, you will find no mention of Marlowe (or Morley, or Marley, or Marlin, or any other variant). A Christopher More catches the eye, but he has a legitimate life of his own, and is not Marlowe. It is possible he used an alias – as did many Catholics, genuine and otherwise – but I can find no pointer to this. The idea of Marlowe at Rheims is, anyway, a rather dubious deduction from the evidence. The Council officially denies his 'determination' to go there: this was, they say, an 'intent' which he did not have. If he did actually go to Rheims, the phrasing of the Council's denial seems all but meaningless.

Marlowe may well have travelled on those 'affairs he went about', and perhaps to France, but on the matter of Rheims the rumours against him remain at this level of his intention. He has the appearance of a man *about to* defect, and this seems to point to his behaviour at Cambridge itself, where the rumours originate.

There was a strong Catholic presence at the university, and the authorities were very concerned about it. Some of the students were Catholics because they had been brought up as such. They were from the many English families who continued as Catholics, or 'recusants', despite the increasing penalties this brought. They were allowed to study at Cambridge, but were barred from taking a degree. The recipient of a degree was obliged to swear to the Act of Supremacy, which a Catholic could not do (a 'recusant' literally means a 'refuser'). Among the young Catholics studying at Cambridge in the 1580s were the poets John Donne and Henry Constable.

Others were drawn to the Catholic side out of choice. For a young intellectual at Cambridge, there was something potent and seductive about Catholicism. To become a Catholic, or to voice sympathies in that direction, was a gesture of defiance and dissent. It appealed in particular to those students who deplored the spread of Puritanism in the university. There was a polarity between the forbidden, atmospheric aura of Catholicism, and the 'plain, simple, sullen, young, contemptuous' features of the Puritan faction now in the ascendant. Those words are John Donne's, but a hatred of Puritanism is constant among all these Cambridge-bred writers, and in some – Nashe, for instance – it shades into moments of Catholic sympathy.

It is not hard to imagine Christopher Marlowe involved in this sort of Catholicism: a gesture of opposition, a 'turd in the teeth' of the Puritans, a kind of faddish extremism. The rumours against him at Cambridge are rather plausible. Here is a restless young man who has grown up in the shadow of Canterbury Cathedral, in the heartland of Anglican orthodoxy. His father, John Marlowe the shoemaker, was church-warden of the parish: he possessed, on his death in 1605, no books by his son, only a copy of the Bible. As Marlowe

114

embarks on young adulthood at Cambridge, on the long journey which led to those 'monstruous' heresies, an emotional shift towards Catholicism would be an obvious first step. Some remnants of this can be found in the Baines 'Note', where among Marlowe's atheistic sentiments, there is also recorded this opinion:

> That if there be any God or any good religion, then it is to be found in the Papists, because the service of God is performed with more ceremonies, as elevation of the Mass, organs, singing men, shaven crowns, &c.

Baines also quotes Marlowe as saying that 'all Protestants are hypocritical asses'.

So the rumours against Marlowe at Cambridge may not have been as 'idle' as the Council pretended. He probably was – at some stage, at least – what he appeared to be: a young malcontent with fashionable papist sympathies. This would certainly figure in terms of Elizabethan spy-craft, for the turning of Catholics, through pressure or promises, was one of the government's standard policies. All of the chief anti-Catholic agents used by Walsingham – Berden, Aldred, Gifford, Barnes, Poley, Moody: we shall meet some of these later – were themselves Catholics before they became spies. Perhaps this is the case with Marlowe too. It is a favourite maxim of those in the deception business, that the truth is the best cover of all.

In some ways this pull towards Catholicism in the 1580s is similar to the flirtations with communism in Cambridge in the 1920s and 30s. It was a gesture of anti-orthodoxy, of going over to the enemy. At its outer reaches – Burgess, Philby, Blunt, etc. – lay a career of treason, but for most it was just a dilettante game. There are many differences – not least that Catholicism was nostalgic and reactionary, rather than new and radical – and these broad parallels can be misleading. Let us just say that this Elizabethan spy-story begins, as that later one did, in the chilly, idealistic air of Cambridge University.

*

115

We can pinpoint a little more clearly the kind of targets an anti-Catholic spy might have had at Cambridge in these years. The government kept tabs on Catholics of all sorts – in the 'interests of national security', as we now put it, and especially so after England's formal entry into war with Spain in 1585 – but their chief concern was not with the peaceable majority of recusants. They were concerned with the militants, the potential enemies of the State. At Cambridge this meant the young men who went to Rheims to train as missionaries, and even more, it meant those who encouraged and helped them to do so.

As early as 1581, during Marlowe's first year at Cambridge, the seminary had established a recruitment network at the university. This was one of the achievements of the first Jesuit mission to England, spearheaded by Edmund Campion and Robert Persons. In September 1581, Persons reported to Claudius Acquaviva, the General of the Jesuits at Rome:

At Cambridge I have at length insinuated a certain priest into the very university, under the guise of a scholar or a gentleman commoner, and have procured him help not far from the town. Within a few months he has sent over to Rheims seven very fit youths.

Who this Catholic agent was is not known. He was wealthy enough, perhaps out of Jesuit funds, to be a 'gentleman commoner' (a student who paid for his own 'commons'). The back-up he received from someone 'not far from the town' may refer to Sawston Hall, home of a distinguished Catholic family, the Huddlestones, though the lists of Cambridgeshire recusants mention many local gentlemen – Ferdinando Parris of Linton, Thomas Caldecott of Orwell, John Rackwood of Great Shelford, Richard Johnson of Tadlow – any one of whom might have been prepared to assist the Jesuits' talent-spotter at Cambridge. He would have also been assisted by the more militant Catholics within the university, students like Robert Sayer of Caius College, who was accused of having 'laboured to pervert divers scholars' by 'secret conference'. Sayer was also involved in dispersing clandestine Catholic literature: he 'used to gather together papistical books, and to convey them secretly into the country'.

Sayer was himself one of the scores of 'fit youths' sent over from Cambridge to Rheims. Two others from Caius College were John Ballard and John Fingelow. Ballard later returned to England under the alias of Captain Fortescue, became the prime-mover of the Babington plot, and was executed in 1586. Fingelow – 'a pernicious papist', according to the college authorities – also returned to England, as a missionary priest. He too was hanged in that year. The route from Cambridge to Rheims led them, and many others, to the gallows.

It was this area of covert recruitment and conversion that worried the authorities most of all: this invisible, undermining Catholic presence in Cambridge. The openly rebellious Catholics, who 'bewrayed themselves' by their 'malicious and violent speeches', were easy enough to deal with, but the 'other kind of papists', these invisible Catholics, were not. They 'come to church', outwardly conforming, but in secret they 'do much harm in corrupting of youth'. They 'lurk in colleges, more in number and more dangerous than is commonly thought'. This was still accounted a problem in the early 1590s, when these words were written in a letter to Lord Burghley. It would have been of particular concern to the government in 1586, after the discovery of John Ballard's conspiratorial plans, which had their genesis at Cambridge and Rheims. We do not know if the Jesuit recruiter installed by Persons was still active by then, but there were undoubtedly others. In January 1587, from the pulpit of St Mary's, the university preacher warned students about certain 'members of the university' who were 'spying' on behalf of the seminaries of Rheims and Rome. These Catholic cells would be the targets of government surveillance and infiltration, and judging from the Council's certificate, issued in the summer of 1587, Marlowe was among the snoops. He is moving among these potential defectors to Rheims, he appears to be one of them, in a part of his heart he probably *is* one of them, but he is also working against them, for the 'benefit of his country', and perhaps more particularly for those financial rewards which the Council says he has 'deserved'.

The Privy Council certificate is retrospective. It relates solely to the dispute over Marlowe's MA, and gives no indication of *when* Marlowe was recruited to government service, or for how long he had been performing the 'actions' for which the government was now expressing its gratitude.

For this we need to go to other sources. There are various university records relating to Marlowe. Some deal solely with his academic progress – steady and unremarkable, until the controversy over his MA – but others give a more detailed picture of his movements during the Cambridge years. One of these is the record of his scholarship payments. Marlowe was a Parker scholar at Corpus Christi. According to the conditions of Archbishop Parker's bequest, a scholar received one shilling for each week of residence. If he remained in residence throughout any given term, he received 13s (14s for the Michaelmas term): a total of £2 13s per annum. During periods of absence this payment was docked, on a weekly basis. Marlowe's scholarship payments run from the Lent term of 1581 to the Easter term of 1587: they are missing for one year (1585–6), but the rest are still preserved.

Another interesting record is Marlowe's account at the college buttery, where the students paid for what they ate and drank in the panelled refectory where his portrait now hangs. His first entry in the Corpus buttery books is in December 1580. This probably marks his arrival at Cambridge, on about 10 December, at the end of a long cold journey from Canterbury. He spent 1d – a farthingworth of beef, perhaps; some porridge of oatmeal and beef-broth; a couple of 'cews' of beer – and took up his residence, with three other Parker scholars, in a converted store-room in the corner of what is now the Old Court at Corpus. Thereafter the buttery books log his weekly consumption of food and drink, though as with the scholarship payments, not all of them are extant.

Between them these two records provide the broad outline of Marlowe's physical presence at the university. More significantly, they show unusually long periods of absence. A student was expected to attend university right through the year, with a permitted annual leave of up to four weeks. As with other regulations – dress, for instance, judging by the Corpus portrait – Marlowe goes well beyond the permitted norm.

Between his arrival in December 1580 and his graduation as Bachelor of Arts in April 1584, he was in residence almost continuously. There are two periods of absence of about six weeks each: more than the permitted leave, but not unusual. It is during his fourth year at Cambridge that his career begins to take on a more fragmentary aspect. During that academic year, 1584–5, Marlowe received only 19s 6d in scholarship payments. This is less than half the due sum. Some of this money may have been docked for reasons other than non-attendance, but by cross-referring to the weekly entries in the buttery books we can pinpoint two prolonged periods of absence in mid-1585. The first lasted eight weeks: he left Cambridge about the middle of April and did not return until mid-June. After his return he remained in residence for about a month, and then was away again for nine weeks, July to September. He returned to Cambridge in late September, and was in residence for the last couple of weeks of the Trinity Term.

The scholarship accounts for the next academic year (1585–6) have also disappeared, so the only evidence is the buttery books. These show he was absent for two weeks in early November 1585, but on this occasion he was visiting his family in Canterbury. On a Sunday morning he walked with his father, uncle, and brother-in-law to the house of their neighbour, Mistress Benchkin of Stour Street. There he witnessed the drafting of her will, and read the text out to the assembled company. He spoke 'plainly and distinctly'. This will, discovered in the Canterbury archives in 1939, contains the only known specimen of his signature.

The next notable spell of absence from Cambridge was in

the Easter term of 1586, when he was missing from the buttery for nine weeks, between April and June. Early the following year he was on the move again. During the Lent term of 1587 he received only 5s 6d in scholarship payments, indicating seven or eight weeks' absence.

By the end of this term, 25 March 1587, he had received his allotted six years' worth of scholarship payments, and his name does not appear in the accounts after this. As the buttery books are not available either, there is no way of knowing if he was at Cambridge at all after the end of March 1587. By the summer *Tamburlaine* was on-stage in London, and Marlowe was launched on his career as a 'playmaker', one of the new 'alchemists of eloquence'. His successor to the Parker scholarship, Jacob Bridgeman, paid his 3s 4d entry fee, and on 10 November 1587 he was formally elected '*in locum domini* Marley'. There were doubtless some at Cambridge who breathed a good riddance to Master Marley.

In this chronology of Marlowe's movements at Cambridge we find that after a period of conventional time-keeping during his 'bachelor years', he becomes suddenly mobile in the spring of 1585. From then on, his attendance is irregular, and punctuated by lengthy absences. It is strongly suggested that this reflects his entry into government service: that he was recruited in early 1585, and that the subsequent absences were missions of some sort, missions which added both to his ill-fame at Cambridge and to his favour with the Privy Council.

This timing would tie in with another kind of evidence in the Corpus buttery books. In 1585 Marlowe's actual spending at the buttery leapt from a customary few pennies to lavish weekly sums of 18d and 21d. So here again is the cross-over: this new source of money and status in the year 1585.

Here too is a reason for the snazzy doublet and the smirk of achievement we see in the Corpus portrait, painted some time in this year. It is hard to reconcile with a Cambridge student, scraping along on his shilling-a-week scholarship, but not with a young man in the first flush of courtly payment for certain services rendered. The portrait may in itself commemorate this turning-point in Marlowe's career, this moment he catches so acutely in the words of young Spenser in *Edward II*:

> You must cast the scholar off,
> And learn to court it like a gentleman.
> 'Tis not a black coat and a little band,
> A velvet-caped cloak faced before with serge,
> And smelling to a nosegay all the day,
> Or holding of a napkin in your hand,
> Or saying a long grace at a table's end,
> Or making low legs to a nobleman,
> Or looking downward with your eyelids close
> And saying, 'Truly, an't may please Your Honour',
> Can get you any favour with great men.
> You must be proud, bold, pleasant, resolute,
> And now and then stab as occasion serves.

There is something of this in the portrait. The black coat has been cast aside, and with it the scholar's modest demeanour. The gaze is level, with eyelids open. The mood is 'resolute' but edgy.

The government described Marlowe's service as 'faithful dealing', but in the performance of it there must have been much deception, much unfaithful dealing towards people with whom he consorted day by day at Cambridge, people whose violent disaffection he in some measured shared. We do not know what kind of pressure he was under, or how deeply he damaged those he informed on, but in our estimation of Marlowe we have to take on board the elements of falsehood and coldness, the hidden left hand behind the velvet sleeve.

121

13

THE ELIZABETHAN SECRET SERVICE

FOR A YOUNG man of wit and political ambition, there were many routes to success, but all of them depended on a system of personal preferment and patronage. It was all a matter of who you knew. The 'court' was a notional centre, over which the Queen exerted a close and sometimes whimsical control, but the reality of political life was still highly factional. Success lay in 'service', in becoming part of the retinue of some important man or family. In the circles of courtiers and aristocrats, of civil servants and regional governors, of churchmen and gentlemen, you found your niche as a clerk, secretary, tutor or body-squire, or even as a poet writing 'private toys' for My Lord's pleasure. In these circles you might scrabble your way into the foothills of influence, but above them rose the three eminences of Elizabethan government in the 1580s: Lord Burghley, the Queen's Treasurer and chief adviser; the Earl of Leicester, the country's military supremo; and Sir Francis Walsingham, the Secretary of State.

It is usually assumed that Marlowe's involvement in covert work, as instanced by the Council certificate, means that he was working for Sir Francis Walsingham. This is probably true. It is not a foregone conclusion – both Burghley and Leicester had their spies in Catholic circles – but there is no doubt that Walsingham was the spymaster *par excellence*, and it is likely that when Marlowe entered government employment in about 1585, he was entering at least the outer fringes of the Walsingham secret service.

Walsingham comes down to us as an archetype of Machiavellian political cunning. This was the characterisation of his first biographers, all contemporaries or near-contemporaries. William Camden calls him a 'most subtle searcher of hidden secrets'. Robert Naunton says he 'had certain curiosities and secret ways of intelligence above the rest'. David Lloyd claims that he 'outdid the Jesuits in their own bow, and over-reached them in their own equivocation'. The portrait of him, attributed to the elder John de Critz, was painted in about 1585, the same year as the Corpus portrait of Marlowe. He was then in his mid-fifties: a keen-eyed, long-faced, dour-looking man, with a sharp *pic-à-devant* beard. The simple clothes and the skull-cap – everything black except the high, goffered ruff – suggest his Puritan leanings, his 'austerian embracements', as one biographer phrases it. His colouring is dark. The Queen, with her skittish fondness for nicknames, called him her 'Moor'. He suffered from ill-health and money troubles, and from an involvement in his work that bordered on obsession.

Like many committed Protestants, Walsingham left the country during the terror of the 1550s, when Mary Tudor ('Bloody Mary') tried to return the country to the Catholic fold. In Europe he acquired his famous skill in foreign languages, and the range of political contacts that would later form the basis of his foreign intelligence network. 'Books are but dead letters,' he once wrote to his nephew. 'It is the voice and conference of men that giveth them life, and shall engender in you true knowledge.' He returned to England with the accession of Elizabeth in 1558, and soon came to the notice of Sir William Cecil, later Lord Burghley. He supplied Burghley with information and advice on foreign affairs, and in 1569 he was Burghley's chief agent in breaking up the Ridolfi plot. The first of many conspiracies centred on Mary Queen of Scots, this involved the Catholic Duke of Norfolk and an Italian adventurer called Roberto Ridolfi. Walsingham's dealings with Ridolfi are an early instance of his technique of giving plotters enough rope to hang themselves and their accomplices. 'He would cherish a plot some years together,' wrote Lloyd, 'admitting the conspirators to his own and the Queen's presence familiarly, but dogging them out watchfully.' This was to be his policy in dealing with the Babington conspiracy, and among those who 'dogged out' that plot was Robert Poley, later a witness to the killing of Marlowe.

In the early 1570s Walsingham served as English ambassador in Paris. There he was involved in the frustrating delicacies of the Queen's marriage negotiations with the French king's brother (François, Duke of Anjou, usually referred to by Englishmen as 'Monsieur'). There too he witnessed the massacre of French Protestants on St Bartholomew's Eve 1572. This atrocity, committed by followers of the Duke of Guise, confirmed his pessimistic view of Catholic intentions in Europe. The following year the Queen recalled him from France, and created him Secretary of State, a post he was to hold for more than sixteen years, until his death in 1590.

During that time, 'Mr Secretary' was at the heart of English foreign policy, and of the defence of England against all Catholic designs: military, missionary, conspiratorial. In foreign policy he was part of the hawkish, pro-war faction which opposed the more cautious policies of Lord Burghley. In this he was allied with the Queen's current favourite, the Earl of Leicester. This alliance was strengthened by the marriage of Walsingham's only daughter, Frances, to Leicester's nephew, the poet Sir Philip Sidney. Walsingham held what was broadly speaking a 'domino theory': that England should check, sooner rather than later, the spread of Spain in Europe. This meant military support: in France, for the Protestant Huguenots against the pro-Spanish Guisards; and in the Netherlands, for the forces of William of Orange fighting the Spanish army of occupation. Timely support of William of Orange would, he promised, give the King of Spain 'such a bone to pick as would take him up twenty years at least, and break his teeth at last'.

Walsingham's view prevailed in 1585, when Elizabeth finally committed herself to military intervention in the Low Countries. The war with Spain and her allies would drag on for many years, on many fronts, indecisive and expensive. War, and its consequent political emergencies, is the backdrop throughout this story.

Walsingham had used spies of all sorts for years, but it was in the 1580s, with the country facing the twin threat of Catholic conspiracy and Spanish invasion, that he actually created his 'secret service', dedicated to the penetration and exposure of Catholic groupings at home and abroad.

It was, to begin with, a largely private affair. It was financed out of his own purse, and it depended in its day-to-day operations on men who were described as his 'servants' or 'followers'. As international tension increased, however, the Queen was persuaded to invest regular sums of public money in it. This, it is said, makes Walsingham's organisation the first official secret service in English history. The earliest subvention on record was in the summer of 1582, when a warrant under the Privy Seal granted him £750 per annum in quarterly instalments. In 1585, with the outbreak of war in the Netherlands, the payments rose to about £2000 a year, and continued at that level through the years of crisis. It is at this stage of increased funding and activity that Marlowe enters the lower ranks of the intelligence world.

The purpose of Walsingham's network was the invariable purpose of all espionage: to obtain information from the 'enemy', in this case the Catholics. His spies performed many other types of sabotage, but their basic task was to gather 'intelligence' (a word which acquired its connotations of espionage at about this time). It was one of the spymaster's favourite maxims, that 'knowledge is never too dear'.

The purpose is always the same, but the methods of intelligence were very different in those days. In modern espionage, the channels of transmission are various and fast – radio, camera, satellite, all the electronic paraphernalia of signals intelligence ('sig-int'). The beacons that relayed news of the Armada through the country in a matter of hours might be called an early form of 'sig-int', but generally speaking Elizabethan intelligence was confined to just two forms of transmission: the written word and the spoken word. Intelligence, like all forms of news, moved physically. Whether written down in letters, or coded in despatches, or committed to memory, it had to be actually carried from place to place. The fastest that intelligence could travel was the speed of a horse.

This made for a high incidence of interception, and various concealment devices were used to counter this. A Spanish courier passing into Scotland in the early 1580s posed as a dentist, and carried letters in a compartment in the back of his mirror. A spy called Bisley, bringing messages into England from the renegade Sir William Stanley, had them sewn into his buttons. Another English conspirator, Edmund Yorke, sent letters from France 'inside a blood-stone, that can be worked like paste, and made hard again, so that it cannot be broken but one way'.

Each of these failed – they were discovered, and that is why we know about them – and much intelligence travelled in the expectation of being intercepted. Hence the importance of codes. A skill in ciphering and 'secret writing' was an essential part of Elizabethan tradecraft. Every self-respecting spy had his copy of della Porta's book on codes, *De Furtivis Literarum Notis*, and some of them – notably Walsingham's right-hand man, Thomas Phelippes – built an entire career on this skill. Numerical or hieroglyphic codes were used, usually including 'nullities' (meaningless ciphers designed to confuse). Also, trading and business jargon with pre-arranged meanings: an agent with secrets to convey was told to 'make them up merchant-wise'. A letter to Sir Robert Cecil in 1591 about a cargo of wines – their vintage, their prices, their readiness for export – is actually a coded report on the disposition and intentions of the Spanish fleet. Invisible inks were another method: orange-juice and onion-juice, milk and urine.

What has also changed is the scope of intelligence. Much now lies outside the brief of espionage because it is already available. The secret world was larger and darker in Elizabethan days. Simply put, people knew less. Much of the 'intelligence' that flowed to Walsingham, particularly from abroad, was the sort of information that would now be in the public realm. The despatches which fill the red leather volumes of State Papers at the Public Record Office often read like newspaper reports. They were the government's only way of knowing what was going on. They come from merchants and factors and soldiers and diplomats. A list of 'sundry foreign places' from which Walsingham received 'advertisements' enumerates forty-five towns, spread through France, Germany, Italy, Spain, the Low Countries and Turkey. In all the major commercial centres, there was at least one English 'agent' in this non-covert sense: George Gilpin in The Hague, Thomas Jeffries in Calais, Stephen Paule in Venice, and so on. They were informed observers, honorary consuls, foreign correspondents, but not necessarily spies.

So there is, when we look at the Elizabethan secret service, this distinction to be made: between the intelligencer as reporter, filling much the same function as the information media today; and the intelligencer as spy, playing the perennial dirty game of penetration and betrayal. Thomas Nashe quibbles over this in one of his pamphlets against Dr Harvey. Harvey had called Thomas Bodley, the Queen's agent in the Netherlands, a 'curious intelligencer'. He meant nothing amiss: he used the word in its overt, reportorial sense. Nashe pretends to take it the other way, as a slur on Bodley. The 'hellish detested Judas name of intelligencer' has been 'thrown upon him'. He has been 'registered in print for such a flearing false brother or *ambodexter*'.

These roles overlap, of course – there is no clear point at which information-gathering becomes espionage – but one of the features of this period of crisis was a huge increase in this more treacherous, 'ambidextrous' type of intelligencer. Particularly in England itself, Walsingham came to depend on a sinister network of snoops and informers. This is the shabby side of his achievement: the great architect of Elizabethan foreign policy was also the chief of the Elizabethan secret police.

Walsingham's assistant in the daily running of the secret service was Thomas Phillips or (the spelling he used himself) Phelippes. In his zeal, his minuteness and his total lack of scruples, Phelippes was the ideal henchman. The devious counterplots of the Walsingham years may have been the product of the spymaster's peculiar genius, but always Phelippes is there, the busy chief of operations, processing the papers, handling the agents, disbursing the blood-money. He played a crucial role in the entrapment of Mary Queen of Scots, and was a familiar figure at Chartley, where she was held prisoner. She gives us this glimpse of him: 'a man of low stature, slender every way, dark yellow-haired on the head, clear yellow-bearded, erred in the face with small pocks.' She also notes his 'short sight': he probably wore spectacles.

'Young Phillips', the son of the customs inspector at Leadenhall, is first heard of as Walsingham's 'servant' in 1578. He was then in his early twenties. A couple of years later he was in Paris. There he dealt with an equally slippery fish: the Welsh Catholic Thomas Morgan, one of the busiest conspirators on behalf of Mary Queen of Scots. Phelippes later entertained his colleagues with impressions of the Welshman. 'In conversation,' one of them recalled, 'he could take off Morgan to the life.'

Morgan, it seems, had hopes that Phelippes could be turned to Mary's advantage. In a letter to one of her secretaries, dated October 1585, he wrote:

It is very like that one Phelippes hath great access to your host [i.e. Sir Amias Paulet, Mary's keeper] in this time, and peradventure hath some charge before him. It is the same Phelippes of whom I made mention before. If you do use him according to my former instructions, it may be that he may be recovered to your service. But try him long and in small matters before you use him, being a severe Huguenot, and all for that state, yet glorious and greedy of honour and profit, &c.

Morgan is probably right: if Phelippes had a weak point, it was not any shred of sympathy for the Catholics – he is 'all for' Protestantism – but a greed for 'honour and profit'. But there is no hint that Phelippes ever tried to play false with Walsingham, and anyway everything Morgan says has to be treated with caution. In Phelippes's dealings against Mary there is a ghoulish industry, an eagerness to destroy. When he sent up the fatal letter from Chartley in July 1586, supposedly containing Mary's assent to the Babington conspiracy, he sketched a cartoon of a gallows on the outside. This was a blunder. Walsingham wrote testily that some of the plotters were 'very inward with the post from London', and had seen and understood 'the gallows upon the packet'. This lapse was soon forgiven. Phelippes was recognised as a key figure in the break-up of the plot, and was awarded a royal pension of 100 marks a year. 'You will not believe', wrote Walsingham, 'in what good sort the Queen of England accepts your services.'

Phelippes's particular skill was in code-breaking. His scribbled deciphers can be seen in the margins of scores of intercepted despatches from Catholics. The Jesuit Robert Southwell refers to him simply as 'Phillips the decipherer'. His sidekick in the cypher department was 'ingenious' Arthur Gregory, a Dorset man, whose speciality was 'the art of forcing the seal of a letter, yet so invisibly that it still appeareth a virgin to the exactest beholder'. He is another regular in Mr Secretary's back-room entourage.

Phelippes continued to work closely with Walsingham until the latter's death in 1590. At this time many important secret service files disappeared. There are various suspects, but Phelippes must be chief among them. A year or so later he surfaces as part of a new intelligence network, set up under the aegis of the Earl of Essex.

Phelippes is a regular fixture: Walsingham's chief of operations. Others who feature regularly as Walsingham's 'servants' are Francis Milles and Nicholas Faunt. Milles is ubiquitous, brisk, colourless, but Faunt is a more sophisticated character: I will come back to him later. Two others, William Waad and Robert Beale, both described as 'Clerks of the Council', were also closely linked with Walsingham. The duties of these men are not clearly defined, but they were, like Phelippes, part of the management of the intelligence service. They were not spies themselves: they were the case-officers, the confidential messengers, the private secretaries.

Beneath them, and handled by them, was the shifting legion of freelancers who provided the raw material of anti-Catholic intelligence. Judging from the Privy Council certificate, Christopher Marlowe was one of them, and so these people become, to an unhealthy degree, a subject of this book.

The typical Elizabethan spy was a man of middling to low status. He might be a gentleman, more often he hoped to become one. He was often a former servant or page in some prominent Catholic household, who had turned, or had been turned, into an informer. His motivations, in the most part, boiled down to greed or fear, or a mix of the two, with the question of patriotism coming in a poor third. To the spymaster and his officers, of course, he would present himself as a zealous patriot. 'Though I am a spy, which is a profession odious though necessary, I prosecute the same not for gain, but for the safety of my native country.' So wrote Nicholas Berden in 1586, though his career of bribery and extortion makes this ring a bit hollow.

Their new masters on the whole considered these turncoats untrustworthy and rather contemptible. Sir Edward Stafford, English ambassador in Paris, comments drily about one of them, the elusive Scotsman Robert Bruce:

> There be no trust to a knave that will deceive them that trust him, yet such as he is must be entertained. For if there were no knaves, honest men should hardly come by the truth of any enterprise against them.

Salomon Aldred – a tailor by trade, a spy at the seminary at

Rome, and later one of Walsingham's agents in France – was similarly described:

> He is one in show simple, but better acquainted with Romish practices against England than any . . . He is unnatural, and of little honesty, yet he is one very worth the winning.

This is the typical tone, wary and weary. These were the supergrasses: men 'worth the winning' only in terms of cynical political strategy. Walsingham used scores of them. Throughout their careers there runs a querulous, servile note. They battled and wheedled to get money out of the privy coffers, and many were shuffled off without payment once they had served their purpose. With a few exceptions – like the £100-a-year salary awarded to Gilbert Gifford – these agents were not paid on a regular basis. They were freebooters. They got money *pro rata*, for specific assignments or for useful information.

In the matter of payment there is, once again, a distinction between different kinds of agent. For courier work and continental missions – the more respectable end of the business – agents were paid through the office of the Treasurer of the Queen's Chamber, Sir Thomas Heneage. Payments, anything between a few shillings and £30 depending on the assignment, were made on presentation of a warrant, signed by Walsingham, under such favoured formulae as 'carrying letters for Her Majesty's special and secret affairs', or 'employed in affairs of special importance'. The Chamber accounts are preserved at the Public Record Office, a musty roll of vellum the size and weight of a small carpet. They provide an intimate record of the comings and goings of Walsingham's agents, but they only tell part of the story. Many other, more covert payments, disbursed by the likes of Phelippes and Milles, went unrecorded. As a government clerk later noticed, as he trawled through the patchy records that remained:

Money was paid to such as Sir Francis Walsingham appointed, whose privy seal from time to time went without prest or account, and without showing the cause of the employment of the same, which were sometimes for French causes and otherwise, to us unknown as to the employment hereof.

For this sort of reason, none of the agents used to track and break the Babington conspiracy appears in the Chamber accounts at that time. These are the undercover operators, employed and furnished on a discreet, deniable basis. Marlowe's name does not appear in the Chamber accounts, either. Whatever reward he received for his work, he received it unofficially. The only record of his early activities as an intelligencer is the certificate supplied by the Privy Council, perhaps reluctantly, in response to the particular problem of his MA.

Another way of payment to the spy was in the form of permitted profiteering from his victims. Nicholas Berden is again typical. In 1586 he wrote to Phelippes about two imprisoned Catholic priests: 'If you can procure me the liberty of Ralph Bickley at his Honour's [Walsingham's] hands, it will be worth £20 to me; and the liberty of Sherwood, alias Carlisle, will be worth £30.' He was 'in extreme need' of the money. It grieved him, he cunningly added, 'to have to draw on his Honour's treasure, and if he will yield to some suits now and then at my request, I might be served out of the store of those traitors'.

This kind of bribery was doubly convenient to Berden, because it was actually part of his cover. As far as those priests were concerned, he was a man who had friends at court, and could buy their release with money. There was a thriving trade in this, and men like Berden and Phelippes profited greatly by it. They were like commodity-brokers, dealing not in lute-strings and grey paper, but in life and liberty. One of Marlowe's later associates, Richard Cholmeley, played the same game. Employed by the Privy Council 'for the apprehension of papists and other dangerous men', he used 'to take money of them, and let them pass in spite of the Council'.

Another notorious profiteer was Richard Topcliffe. In one particularly nasty deal he colluded with a rich young Catholic, Thomas Fitzherbert. He undertook to prosecute Fitzherbert's father and uncle to the death, so that Fitzherbert could inherit the family estates. Fitzherbert promised him £5000 for this, and signed bonds to that effect.

With Topcliffe we scrape the bottom of this barrel. He provided intelligence to Walsingham and others, but he was not primarily a spy. Topcliffe's métier was enforcement. He was the chief of the pursuivants, the government interrogator, Her Majesty's rackmaster. Details of his brutality to Catholic suspects would fill many pages: rackings and whippings and mutilations; the ingenuities of the 'iron gauntlets' and the 'scavenger's daughter'; the simple expedient of the manacles. A Catholic priest named White describes a session of the manacles at the Marshalsea prison in Southwark:

> I was hanged at the wall from the ground, my manacles fast locked into a staple as high as I could reach from the stool. The stool taken away, there I hanged from a little after 8 o'clock in the morning till after 4 in the afternoon, without any ease or comfort, saving that Topcliffe came in unto me, and told me that the Spaniards were come into Southwark by our means: 'For, lo, do you not hear the drums?' For then the drums played in honour of my Lord Mayor.

There are more physically harrowing accounts of Topcliffe's tortures, but this casualness is somehow worse: the sound of the procession drifting into the torture-room; the interrogator's cruel, rather banal joke.

In these ways Topcliffe 'digged into the hearts' of Catholic prisoners. It was known as 'scraping the conscience'. The physical effects were crippling: a man severely 'pinched' on the rack, often with a stone under his spine, was lucky if he walked again. Here is the Jesuit Edmund Campion recovering by stages from a racking:

Benumbed both of hand and foot, he likened himself to an elephant, which being down could not rise. When he could hold the bread he had to eat betwixt both his hands, he would compare himself to an ape.

We would call Topcliffe a sadist: a word they did not have. When he arrested the Jesuit Robert Southwell, he ran at him with his rapier drawn, and called him 'a priest and a traitor'. Southwell replied: 'It is neither priest nor treason that you seek for, but only blood.'

Topcliffe was not Walsingham's man. He had his own fiefdom of pursuit and persecution, and often he reported direct to the Queen. He said that 'he did not care for the Council, for that he had his authority from Her Majesty', and that 'when he pleaseth to speak with her, he may take her away from any company'. In a letter to the Queen he calls her his 'goddess'. In another he asks her permission – her 'pleasure' – to torture Southwell. He imagines the victim writhing as he hangs from the manacles: 'it will be as though he were dancing a trick or figure at trenchmore.' On a day in September 1591, in strangely overheated mood, he told another of his victims, the priest Thomas Pormont,

> that he was so great and familiar with Her Majesty that he many times putteth his hands between her breasts and paps, and in her neck; that he hath not only seen her legs and knees, but feeleth them with his hands above her knees; that he hath felt her belly, and said unto Her Majesty that she hath the softest belly of any womankind.

Pormont reported this to the Council, but Topcliffe seems to have escaped any consequence. Whatever the truth of these masturbatory claims, there is this unsettling hint of royal collusion in Topcliffe's activities.

He is not Walsingham's man, but he is part of the machinery of Elizabethan state security. The spies go about their business, 'odious though necessary', and this is where it often leads: to the interrogation rooms of the Tower, the

Marshalsea and Bridewell; to the dungeons known as Limbo, Little Ease and The Pit; and, for many, to the gallows at Tyburn. These horrors, like the war, are part of the backdrop of this story. They are part of what it was like to live in England at the end of the sixteenth century. They are particular to the time, but also perennial. You will find Master Topcliffe, many times over, in the files of Amnesty International.

There is nothing more real than physical torture, but I would end this brief survey of the Elizabethan secret service by saying that the keynote of it all is a curious sense of unreality. One of the effects of a system of paid informers is that it encourages people to *create* information, to see conspiracy where none exists. This is the secret police atmosphere of these years. There are watchers and listeners everywhere, ready to twist some innocent remark into sedition against the State. 'Get thee glass eyes and, like a scurvy politician, seem to see the things thou dost not.'

This added hugely to Walsingham's work-load, sifting out genuine intelligence from reams of malicious rumour. 'Be not too credulous,' advised his secretary Robert Beale. 'Hear all reports, but trust not all. Weigh them with time and deliberation, and be not too liberal of trifles. Observe them that deal on both hands, lest you be deceived.' Yet this whole element of make-believe was also something Walsingham used: he too created conspiracy where none existed. So often his spies are more than just informers. They are *agents provocateurs*, or – the more common term then – 'projectors'. They actively encourage conspiracy. They tout for sedition. This becomes the classic feature of Walsingham's tradecraft: at its most cynical, it takes the form of the 'sham plot', created *from the start* by Walsingham's projectors, and used as a means of drawing out genuine Catholics. John Le Carré calls espionage a 'secret theatre', and I find this applying, time after time, to Elizabethan espionage. So much was concocted, so much was unreal.

A few of these spies and projectors became regular

members of Walsingham's service, but they all went through long periods of probation. Many spent time in prison. This was partly for expediency – it preserved their cover, and released them into the useful role of prison-informer – but it was also because no-one was quite certain of their true allegiances. The better they were at their job, the harder it was to distinguish them from 'genuine' subversives. Even after years of service they remained ambiguous: used but never trusted, spied on even as they were spying.

We are in the familiar 'wilderness of mirrors' – another phrase from Cold War espionage that is entirely apt for the Elizabethans. A Catholic may be turned, but he is still a Catholic. Perhaps he is playing the double game, so that his role as informer is just another layer of cover. This was a problem for the spymaster, and it is a problem for anyone trying to investigate this business four hundred years later. These people have left behind a paper-chase of documents and records, but the things they did and said are always open to diametrically opposed interpretations. Is he a genuine conspirator or an *agent provocateur*? Is he a purveyor of information or disinformation?

Often the only workable answer is that he is both. These agents constantly played both ends against the middle, and fed information to both sides. In a sense they did not even know which side they were really working for. The political situation was volatile: the Spaniards were threatening to engulf Europe, the Queen was ageing, the question of the succession was unresolved. England had reverted to Catholicism a generation ago, under 'Bloody Mary', with attendant burnings, imprisonments and sequestrations. There was a real possibility of this happening again. The spy kept a foot in both camps, and was ready to jump either way. His commitment to Mr Secretary, to Protestantism, to Queen and Country would be cast off in a moment.

Investigating the secret world you learn to live with this ambiguity. There are no clear answers, only a juggling of different questions, an assortment of different masks. You have to take it as a kind of theatre, a political house of games in which everything is potentially different, potentially reversible. Friends change suddenly into enemies. Patriots are revealed as traitors, and then with a flick of the wrist they are patriots again, servants of Her Majesty.

So it is with Marlowe. A wild young Catholic bound for Rheims turns out to be a faithful dealer for the government. And a quarrel about the bill may yet prove to be another kind of 'reckoning' entirely.

14

THOMAS WALSINGHAM

RESULTS WERE DEMANDED in Sir Francis Walsingham's service. This was not the kind of retinue where well-bred young dilettantes coasted into court on the shoulders of Fortune. It was a government department. Its chief officers, Phelippes and Milles, were professional men: solid, industrious citizen class. Its covert operatives were a hotch-potch of desperate Catholics, disbanded soldiers, failed priests, moonlighting merchants, and gentlemen-adventurers of no fixed abode. Good breeding was not a requisite in Walsingham's service, and high style not an aim.

Yet among these there was one young gentleman who owed his position in the service to breeding, for he was himself a Walsingham. Thomas Walsingham was the youngest son of Thomas and Dorothy Walsingham of Chislehurst, and he was Sir Francis's second cousin. While still a teenager, he was employed as a confidential courier in France, and he rose through the ranks of the service to a position of some trust.

This is the first personal link between Christopher Marlowe and Sir Francis Walsingham's intelligence service. As we know, this younger Walsingham was to become one of Marlowe's patrons. Marlowe was actually staying at his house near Chislehurst as the storm-clouds gathered in May 1593, and – judging from Edward Blount's words in the preface to *Hero and Leander* – the relationship between them was friendly rather than formal. Thomas Walsingham was also Ingram Frizer's 'master' at that time. He is a shadowy figure, but he is there on the edges of the Deptford meeting, and he is here in the intelligence world of the mid-1580s.

Thomas Walsingham was born in 1563. He was a year older than Marlowe. His elder brother, Guldeford Walsingham, was employed in military intelligence during 1578, and Thomas soon followed him into the service. He is first heard of in October 1580, aged seventeen, bringing 'letters in post for Her Majesty's affairs' from the English ambassador in France. He travelled from Morette to the English court at Richmond, and a month later returned to France. He performed the same job several times the following year. In February he was at Blois with the English ambassador, Sir Henry Cobham, and in August he was in Paris with Sir Francis.

Thomas Walsingham's service in France was connected with the Queen's reluctant suitor, the Duke of Anjou ('Monsieur'), and this served him well, perhaps saved his life, when he ran into a troop of French soldiers on a road in Picardy. The incident was described by Ambassador Cobham, in a letter to Sir Francis, dated 12 November 1581:

> They stopped Walsingham and Paulo, my Italian, whom they seemed resolved to rob, but that he showed them Monsieur's packet. They spoiled another Englishman in his company, called Skeggs as I remember.

This Walsingham is undoubtedly Thomas. His travelling companion is Paolo Citolino, also frequently employed as a courier at this time. They flourish the packet of letters, the Anjou seal, and are allowed to pass. Also in their company is a certain 'Skeggs', who fares less well and is robbed by the soldiers. Cobham seems unsure about the name: could this possibly be Skeres rather than Skeggs?

This is quite unprovable, but it is a suggestion to bear in mind: that Nicholas Skeres, one of the witnesses of Marlowe's death, was also an associate of Thomas Walsingham's.

Walsingham continued to be based in France till about 1584. He posted to England with confidential despatches from the ambassador. He was involved in negotiations with the Catholic Archbishop of Glasgow, James Beaton, who was Mary Stuart's official ambassador in Paris. He was, in all this, a trusted servant of his cousin, Sir Francis: a link in the chain of foreign intelligence. He doubtless knew another of Mr Secretary's servants, little bespectacled Thomas Phelippes, who was also in Paris at this time.

In early 1584, Ambassador Cobham wrote requesting funds to pay Thomas Walsingham for his services as a 'messenger'. This seems to mark the end of Walsingham's days in France. He was now twenty-one years old. He had acquitted himself well: a probationary period. Shortly after this we find him in London, in circumstances that suggest some promotion. He is at Seething Lane. Sir Francis had a property here, at a 'fair and large' house built by a former Mayor. It was in effect his London office, conveniently close to the Tower. Here Thomas Walsingham is 'attended' by a government informer who wishes to have 'secret recourse to Mr Secretary'. He is now something more than a messenger. He has a position. He is a contact, a case-officer perhaps, someone you come to meet when you need 'recourse' to the spymaster.

This was some time in the latter half of 1584, and the informer who attended Thomas Walsingham at Seething Lane was none other than Robert Poley. And so the fourth of the four men at Deptford slips into view in connection with Thomas Walsingham.

This is not an isolated connection, for a couple of years later Poley and Thomas Walsingham were working together at the climax of the Babington plot. The two men met, at Poley's lodgings, on the morning of 4 August 1586. It was an operational meeting: Poley 'delivered' to Walsingham 'such speeches as Mr Secretary had commanded me the previous day'. At the same house, shortly after Walsingham left, the conspirator John Ballard was arrested. This was the government's first overt move against the plotters, and it marked Poley as a traitor in their midst. He describes the arrest, and Babington's reaction, as follows:

The messengers came and apprehended Ballard, which (being done in my lodging, a place where Ballard had not often been before; and for that Mr Thomas Walsingham was immediately departed from me, in their sight, before the pursuivants came) would be imputed, said Babington, directly to my charge.

It is clear from this – inasfar as Poley's bland, convoluted style is ever clear – that the plotters knew Thomas Walsingham by sight, that they associated him with official anti-Catholic business, and that they guessed his meeting with Poley was linked with the apprehension of Ballard.

The involvement of Thomas Walsingham at this point makes me think once more of Nicholas Skeres. As we saw earlier, Skeres was also mixed up in these last stages of the government operation against Babington. He was seen in Babington's company, a member of his 'crew', on 3 August, and he was probably present at the supper-party 'in Poley's garden' the previous evening. Everything points to his presence as a government plant. This makes him an accomplice of Poley, who was certainly a plant among the conspirators; and also of Thomas Walsingham, who has some undetermined logistical role in the affair. This connection is not exact (I do not know if 'accomplice' is the right word) but it seems to me pretty definite.

So Thomas Walsingham, a difficult figure in many ways, proves to be unexpectedly present at the Deptford meeting. He was not actually present, of course, but he was almost certainly known to all of the four men who were. That he was Marlowe's patron and Frizer's employer we already knew. We now have the other two connections. He had worked with Poley in secret affairs: Poley 'attended' on him at Seething Lane, and 'delivered' information to him about Babington. He had probably dealt with Skeres in the same circumstances, and may even have known him (the 'Englishman called Skeggs') in his early years in France.

What this tells us about the Deptford meeting I am not sure. It does *not* necessarily mean that Thomas Walsingham has some sinister, puppet-master connection with the killing. In certain fanciful versions of Marlowe's death he appears in this role, but this is often just a knee-jerk reaction to the name Walsingham. In fact his last known connection with the secret service was in early 1589, when he was employed for fifteen days 'about special services for Her Majesty, wherewith Her Highness was acquainted', and received £5 for his 'pains and charges'. In this year, following the death of his brother, he inherited the family estates at Scadbury. This new financial standing seems to mark his retirement from active political service, and of his career in the early 1590s we have hardly any knowledge.

It is too vague and easy to put him up as the schemer behind the scenes. It is possible, but there is no real evidence for it. The same goes for that other pleasant pipe-dream, which makes him Marlowe's lover.

Walsingham's connections with Poley and Skeres point back to the mid-1580s. They were professional connections within the intelligence world. It was at just this time, in about 1585, that Marlowe was entering this world. He was engaged in certain secret 'affairs', he did Her Majesty 'good service'. Who was he taking his orders from? Who was he reporting to? Not, of course, Her Majesty. Nor, directly, Sir Francis. He would have a contact, as these spies did: someone to 'attend' on for his 'recourse to Mr Secretary'.

If I were going to speculate about Thomas Walsingham and his relations with Marlowe, I would not say that he was the man who ordered Marlowe's death, nor that he was Marlowe's gay lover. I would say that he was Marlowe's friend and protector, as Edward Blount clearly thought he was, and that their friendship went back to the year 1585 or thereabouts, when he was one of Marlowe's contacts in the Elizabethan intelligence service.

This is rather more prosaic, but more likely to be true.

A couple of other names associated with the Walsingham service have possible connections with Marlowe. They do not lead very far, but they are worth mentioning. One is Nicholas

Faunt, a 'secretary' of Sir Francis's from about 1580, 'very honest and discrete', and much employed in France. Faunt is interesting because he is a university connection. He is the only one of Walsingham's regular officers to have attended Cambridge, and his college was the same as Marlowe's: Corpus Christi. His career there does not overlap with Marlowe's, but if Walsingham was looking for recruits at Cambridge in the mid-1580s, Faunt might well be involved as a talent-spotter, and his eye might well alight on this promising young scholar from his own college. In short, Faunt may have been the actual recruiter of Christopher Marlowe. In early 1587 Faunt was on a government mission in Paris, dealing with certain suspicious figures in the retinue of the English ambassador, Sir Edward Stafford. This was one of those periods when Marlowe was absent from Cambridge: it is possible that he travelled to France in Faunt's employ, and that this is reflected in the rumours about him later that year. [See Appendix 2.6]

All this is speculative: I have made some inroads into Faunt's correspondence but can find nothing definite to back it up. Faunt is at least, like Thomas Walsingham, someone who helps to define Marlowe's presence in this business. He is a scholar, an amateur author, a high flyer. His career, like Thomas Walsingham's, will prosper into the next century. These men give us – more than Phelippes, with his grim stable of snoops – the tone of Marlowe's government service.

Another figure is Paul Ive, or Ivy, a blacksmith's son from Limehouse who later rose to some eminence as a military and marine engineer. He had a chequered career in the Netherlands as a soldier and spy. In 1585 he was at Gravelines, apparently in the service of the pro-Spanish governor, la Motte, but also sending military intelligence to Walsingham via a courier named Bate. At the end of the year, his cover blown, he urged Walsingham to recall him: 'if Your Honour will command me home, I will lay such tumbling blocks in their way as I will devise, knowing their dealings as I do.' The following year he was paid, under Walsingham's warrant, for carrying despatches from 'Gravelinge', and he was in the Low Countries again, on government business, in July 1587. At about this time Christopher Marlowe was setting to work on his second *Tamburlaine* play, written at speed to capitalise on the success of the first. In this he includes a long, rather technical speech about fortifying a garrison. It is drawn, in parts verbatim, from a manual on the subject written by Paul Ive. Here, for instance, is Marlowe:

> It must have privy ditches, countermines
> And secret issuings to defend the ditch.
> It must have high argines and covered ways
> To keep the bulwark fronts from battery.

And here is Ive:

> It must also have countermines, privy ditches, secret issuings out to defend the ditch, casemates in the ditch, covered ways round about it, and an argine or bank to impeach the approach.

The borrowing is unmistakable, but what is interesting is that Ive's manual had not yet been published. It appeared in 1589, entitled *The Practice of Fortification*, dedicated to Sir Francis Walsingham. Marlowe must have used the work in manuscript. This does not prove he knew Paul Ive, but in 1587 he is somewhere where Ive's manuscript is available, and that somewhere is, almost certainly, the purlieus of the Walsingham intelligence service.

Nicholas Faunt and Paul Ive are hints, no more, of this hidden circle of Marlowe's in the 1580s: this network of contacts and activities that must lie behind the judicious wording of the Privy Council certificate. Thomas Walsingham is another, stronger hint of this circle: a young intelligence officer, cultivated and cosmopolitan. He becomes a patron of Marlowe and of other poets, he employs at various times at least two, if not all three, of Marlowe's companions at Deptford. He is the first link, though still a mysterious one, between Marlowe's early political dealings and the fatal events of 1593.

15

SHAKING THE FOUNDATION

VERY LITTLE IS known about Marlowe's government service at this time, but we do know that it was in some way connected with the English Catholic seminary at Rheims. His actions belong within a specific intelligence context. There were many groupings of English Catholic exiles in France, and many efforts by Walsingham to infiltrate and disable them, but throughout these years of conspiracy, the seminary at Rheims was a constant target.

The English College was founded at Douai, in Flanders, in 1568. Its first president was Dr (later Cardinal) William Allen. Douai was then under Spanish occupation, but ten years later the tides of war had changed, and the Protestants gained control of the town. The seminarists were forced out. They settled eventually at Rheims. There, protected by the Duke of Guise and partly financed by the Vatican, the College prospered. It became a rallying-point for Catholic Englishmen of all social strata, including – as we have seen – many 'fit youths' from Cambridge and Oxford. It was a centre for the printing of anti-government tracts and banned devotional works (including the 'Rheims Testament', issued in 1582), and it was a training-ground for militant Catholic missionaries who returned to succour or subvert, according to your view, the people of England.

Rheims was high on Walsingham's French agenda. The purpose of his operations against the seminary can be summed up as two-fold. The first was intelligence: to gather details of Catholic strategy, both military and political, and to get advance warning of priests intending to enter England. The second was sabotage: to sow faction and disunity in the very heart of the Catholic mission. When an English agent claimed that he had 'shaken the foundation of the English seminary at Rheims', he was exaggerating his particular claim, but expressing well enough the government's intention.

A contemporary account of the government's efforts to undermine the seminary is found in an 'epistle', written by certain English priests to Pope Clement VIII in July 1601. It is a biased account, but well-informed. 'When the Council of England did hear of this Seminary', it says, they resolved 'wholly to persecute the same'. To begin with, they used overt political methods: they set about 'egging underhand some other Catholics in England to mislike of it, as a thing that would exasperate the State and hinder their peace in England'. They appealed, in other words, to the more moderate Catholic majority, who lived in the hope of toleration. International pressure was also brought to bear, 'procuring the heretics and rebels of Flanders to drive the seminary out of their countries'. When the College migrated to Rheims, the government 'dealt effectually with the King [Henri III] to drive them also from thence'. In this they nearly succeeded, but Henri was swayed by the intercession of Pope Gregory, and by the powerful Guise faction.

When these methods failed, the government was forced into more undercover actions:

They resolved to begin another way of persecution, which was to put sedition among ourselves, by sending over spies and traitors to kindle and foster the same. Such a one was one Bayne, who besides other ill offices, was to poison also Dr Allen at that time in the seminary.

So here begins the covert operation: the infiltration of spies, traitors and poisoners. And the first of these that comes to mind is 'one Bayne'.

This man was not the most effective of Walsingham's agents at Rheims – he was discovered and imprisoned there –

but he was one of the earliest. His identity is of some significance to this story, because he is another link, a rather sinister one, between Marlowe's intelligence work in the 1580s and the circumstances of his death. This 'Bayne' was Richard Baines, the informer who later compiled the 'Baines Note' with its detailed list of Marlowe's heresies, and its suggestion that 'the mouth of so dangerous a member' should be 'stopped'.

The early career of Richard Baines is typical of the circles in which Marlowe was moving at Cambridge, though he was of an earlier academic generation. He came up to Cambridge in November 1568: a 'gentleman pensioner' at Christ's College. Some time after 1573 he moved to Caius, and there he received his MA in 1576. In this strongly Catholic college, he would have known the future conspirator John Ballard, and others like Fingelow and Sayer who defected to Rheims. It is possible that Baines was useful to the government at this stage of his career, like Marlowe a few years later, but there is no evidence of this.

In 1578, Baines himself left England to enrol at Rheims. From another Englishman's account – John Chapman, who migrated the following year – we have some details of a typical journey. Chapman sailed from Dover to Calais in the company of 'Frenchmen and English merchants'. His passage cost him two shillings. From Calais he walked to Rheims, via Ardres and Cambrai. This journey, about 150 miles, took him a week. He spoke no French along the way, only Latin. In Rheims he put up at a 'common inn' and 'enquired for Englishmen'. He was welcomed at the seminary by Dr Baily, the Vice President, delivered up a 'stock of money' (20s) to the college coffers, and was admitted 'without any ceremony or profession'.

Life at the seminary was frugal and scholarly: familiar enough to university men like Baines. The seminarists wore black gowns and tricorn hats, attended divinity lectures, subsisted on simple fare – dinner was a 'little broth, thickened merely with the commonest roots' – and contemplated the murals of blessed martyrdom painted on their chamber-walls. It was an intensely tight-knit community. These were young men a long way from home, surrounded by hostile locals, and steeped in a fanatical ideal of devotion and sacrifice: 'soldiers of Christ'.

Among them Richard Baines, proceeding in holy fashion to his ordination as a Catholic priest. He was made a sub-deacon on 25 March 1581, a deacon on 8 May, and a full priest on 21 September.

All this while, it later transpired, he was plotting against the seminary, and particularly against the President of the College, Dr William Allen. According to his later confession, he intended to return to England, and reveal Allen's secrets to the Privy Council. To this end he insinuated himself with senior figures in the College, 'undermining by art' those 'whom I thought knew somewhat of my superior's secrecy'. He 'fraudulently discovered certain points of secrecy, and set them down in writing, with intent to give the note of the same to the Council.' The penning of informative 'Notes' for the government seems to have been one of Baines's specialities.

He also pursued that policy of 'kindling' faction and disunity which was part of the government's game-plan against Rheims. 'I found means', he says, 'to insinuate myself to the familiarity of some of the younger sort, that methought might be easily carried into discontent.' He encouraged them 'to mislike of rule and discipline, and of subjection to their masters.' To this end, he 'used ordinarily some pretty scoffs against every of the elders of our house.'

His most dastardly stratagem was nothing less than mass-murder: 'how first the President might be made away, and if that missed, how the whole company might easily be poisoned.' His plan was to 'inject poison' into the college well, or the communal bath, and so take off the whole seminary in one fell swoop. In this he foreshadows Marlowe's Jew, who is said to 'go about to poison wells', and who does indeed succeed in poisoning an entire religious foundation: 'Here's a drench to poison a whole stable of Flanders mares: I'll carry it to the nuns with a powder.'

Some time in 1581 or early 1582, Baines was putting all these suggestions to a fellow-seminarist, unnamed. 'For a month's space, or thereabouts, I dealt with my said fellow boldly', and 'uttered to him my intention to go into England'. There he would 'preach heresy' and generally 'annoy the common cause of Christ's church [i.e. Catholicism] and especially this seminary.' He assured his confederate that Walsingham would pay them handsomely for information. He mentions the hugely optimistic sum of 3000 crowns (£750) each.

Unknown to Baines, this man 'uttered the whole matter' to the college authorities. They did not act immediately, but they had Baines's number. As Allen later wrote: 'while Baines was daily celebrating mass, believing himself unsuspected, his treachery and illicit dealings with the Privy Council had become known.'

At some point after his ordination, Baines asked for 'leave and journey-money' to travel to England as a Catholic missionary. Dr Allen, of course, knew his true intentions, and it was probably this that precipitated Baines's arrest. He was 'unmasked' – according to a letter from Allen to the Jesuit Agazzari – on 28 May 1582. The following day, 29 May, the College Diary records his imprisonment: 'Richardus Baynes presbyter in carcerem conjectus est.'

He remained in the Rheims town gaol for nearly a year, during which he made an oral confession, undated, in the presence of Allen and others. On 13 April 1583, unable to afford the expense of keeping him there, Allen had him transferred to a chamber (*cubiculum*) in the seminary. There, on 13 May, he made his signed confession, 'which I voluntarily make and subscribe with mine own hand', in the presence of three college officials.

The Marlowe scholar F.S. Boas first drew attention to this confession in the *Times Literary Supplement* in 1949. He had found the text of it in Latin, in John Bridgwater's Catholic collection *Concertatio Ecclesiae Catholicae in Anglia*. None of Marlowe's biographers since has troubled to read this confession, of which Boas only quoted a couple of snippets.

And no-one seems to have realised that there is a contemporary English version of it, in a book published at Rheims in 1583.

This book is an obscure little quarto called *A True Report of the Late Apprehension and Imprisonment of John Nicols*. There is a copy of it in the British Library, catalogued under Allen, who edited and introduced it. It mainly concerns Nicols, a seminarist from Rome who deserted to the government, but it includes statements and apologies from other priests who 'of fear or frailty have lately fallen'. One of these is the confession of Richard Baines. The last part of the book, Allen's 'Admonition to the Reader', is dated 1 June 1583. Printed at Rheims by Jean Foguy, the book was probably issued that month: topical Catholic polemic.

So this is Baines verbatim: six pages of confession, printed up within a few weeks of his uttering it. It describes his various stratagems against the seminary, including the scheme to poison its water-supply. I have already quoted it in this respect. But it offers something more: a glimpse into the mind of Richard Baines, his motivations, his mentality. This glimpse will be important when we come to look at Baines's contribution to the Marlowe affair of 1593.

Of course, much of what Baines says has to be viewed with caution. He describes his confession as a 'public writing', and it was probably intended for print all along. It is likely that it was part of a deal, that he wrote it in exchange for his release. The theme of Allen's little collection is that apostasy, deserting the Catholic faith, is a form of sin, and that these priests have suffered for it, repented it, and returned to the fold. Baines's confession describes this arc: a 'fall' into 'wickedness' followed by a heartfelt repentance. So there is this element of propaganda, or homily, in his account. It is a tampered version of the truth, a crafted presentation of himself – he was a spy, after all – but it is no less interesting for that.

He presents the two main motives of his treachery as ambition and greed. He spied for Walsingham and the Council out of a desperate desire for status: 'the preferment I hoped & gaped after so inordinately'. He speaks of this ambition as a 'devil' within him: he does not know 'how far this devil would have driven me, who now wholly occupied my heart in hope of advancement in England by these practices'. This desire for advancement was itself, he says, a form of greed: 'an immoderate desire of more ease, wealth and (which I specially also respected) of more delicacy of diet and carnal delights than this place of banishment was like to yield unto me.' This note of gluttony creeps in again, when he recalls 'calling for flesh pies or pasties on Fridays at night'.

This 'licentious' talk about flesh pies and carnal delights was one of Baines's methods of sowing discontent among the scholars at Rheims. It worked on their empty stomachs and sexual longings, as they shivered in their dormitory in the cold Champagne nights. It helped to break down discipline, to breed 'discontentment' and 'mislike of rule': this was one of Baines's purposes as an agent.

Perhaps most interesting is Baines's presentation of his actions against the seminary as a process of collapsing belief, a loss of faith, a moral and religious crack-up. At first there was an *ennui*, a period of intellectual rejection. The 'holy writers' he was supposed to be studying 'began daily to wax more and more tedious and loathsome'. Instead,

> I most delighted in profane writers, and the worst sort of them, such as either wrote against the truth, or had least taste of religion . . . I had a delight rather to fill my mouth and the auditors' ears with dainty, delicate, nice and ridiculous terms and phrases, than with wholesome, sound and sacred doctrine.

This literary touch is interesting, given his later association with Marlowe. He associates 'dainty' popular writing – romances, poems, perhaps plays too – with profanity. Together with this literary straying from the straight-and-narrow went a new temper of jesting and contempt, against the seminary and against the Catholic faith. He used 'pretty scoffs against every of the elders'. He spoke 'wicked words'.

He started 'omitting the divine service', and 'scoffing thereat before some of my companions'.

Suddenly the young Catholic stands before a doctrinal abyss of doubt and rejection. 'Proceeding farther and farther in wickedness', he 'began to mock at the lesser points of religion.' From there he went on to 'utter divers horrible blasphemies in plain terms against the principal points of religion.' In all this he tried to influence the other seminarists, 'by arguments and often communications'.

As to where all this was leading him, he had no doubt. 'The next step of this stair is atheism and no belief at all.' This is 'the highway to heresy, infidelity & atheism, as to my great danger I have experience in mine own case.'

There are elements of truth in this. Baines would have used his heretical talk, like his 'calling for flesh pies', to entice the waverers at the seminary. But since there is good evidence that he was a spy from the first, this narrative of theological breakdown is also something of a pose. It is part of the propagandist presentation to show Baines's apostasy as a 'fall' from grace, rather than as a mercenary undertaking by an English spy.

The extraordinary thing about this part of Baines's confession is its closeness to that other product of his pen, the 'Note' on Marlowe. What he says about his own behaviour in 1583 – the 'scoffing' at religion, the 'horrible blasphemies', the efforts to draw people to atheism – is the same as what he says about Marlowe's behaviour ten years later. This immediately throws new light on the Baines 'Note'. In one sense, it makes it more psychologically complex. His denouncing of Marlowe's blasphemy is not done in a mood of prim-mouthed disapproval, as is often implied. He was, on the evidence of the confession, far *closer* to Marlowe than we have realised. He has travelled down this 'highway to heresy'. Yet it also makes the 'Note' more questionable as an indictment of Marlowe. Baines has played this part of the scoffer and atheist himself. He has handled these terms before, used them to create an impression which is partly true and partly a charade. Perhaps this element of charade is the key point about

Baines's confession. He piously renounces his spying career: it was 'abominable perjury, dissimulation & fiction'. Yet there is 'dissimulation & fiction' involved in the confession itself, and these are words to bear in mind when we come to look more closely at his portrayal of Christopher Marlowe. [See Appendix 2.7.]

Baines's confession is the last we hear of him at Rheims. From the view of Walsingham back in England, he was a blown agent. His arrest had put an end to his usefulness as an *explorator* in the seminary. From the view of Dr Allen at Rheims, he was a burden and an embarrassment. The possible dangers of releasing him would soon be outweighed by the desire to be rid of him. In April 1583 he had been moved back to the seminary because the cost of keeping him in the town gaol was too high. In May he wrote his confession. He probably bought his freedom by giving Allen this public disavowal.

Back in England, despite his failure at Rheims, Baines would continue to be useful to Walsingham. There is no evidence that he continued in active service, but he would have a fund of intimate information about the seminarists, and from what we know of him we can guess he made full use of it. The Rheims confession and the 'Note' on Marlowe are his only writings to have survived, but perhaps one day other documents will surface.

In 1587, a Richard Baines was installed as the rector of Waltham, near Cleethorpes in Lincolnshire. He is described as a Cambridge man, and this is almost certainly our Baines. The wavering Catholic, the anti-Catholic spy, the Protestant minister: it is a plausible progression. But there is a more worldly aspect to consider too. A religious benefice was also a financial blessing: it brought property and stipend. It could be – it frequently was – a form of payment or reward. According to recently discovered documents, Baines procured this benefice through the financial assistance and patronage of a certain William Ballard of Southwell, Nottinghamshire. It is possible that this Ballard was a kinsman of John Ballard, the arch-conspirator of the Babington plot, who had been

Baines's contemporary both at Caius College, Cambridge, and at Rheims. This link is hard to interpret in detail, but one scenario would be that Baines had been useful to Walsingham in some by-way of the Babington affair, and that the following year he was rewarded, at the expense of Ballard's family, with the Waltham rectory.

That is conjecture, but whether it is true of Baines or not, the link between Rheims and the Babington plot is a real one. After Baines was grounded, Walsingham began to cultivate other, more subtle agents at Rheims. Chief among these was Gilbert Gifford, who was later a key figure in the government operation against Babington and his 'crew'.

When he first enrolled at the seminary in 1577, Gifford was described as '*clarus adolescens*': a youth of great promise. He was then sixteen, but there is this touch of boyish brilliance through his brief life: a young man of 'wit and learning', with piercing blue eyes and a beardless chin. After a chequered career at Rheims and Rome, and some mysterious 'vagabondizing' elsewhere, Gifford was finally ordained a deacon in the spring of 1585. He was by now, almost certainly, a covert agent of Walsingham. His particular sabotage at the seminary was the turning of his cousin, Dr William Gifford, who was Professor of Theology there. He had a sinister hold over the learned but malleable Doctor. 'He can hide nothing from me,' Gilbert assured Walsingham, 'I can know all his thoughts.' Another seminarist who fell under Gifford's spell was John Savage. At Rheims, some time in the middle of 1585, Gifford extracted from Savage a solemn 'oath' to kill Queen Elizabeth. This was a vital piece of provocation, for the following year Savage appears as one of the Babington conspirators. He was to be their 'instrument', the actual assassin of the Queen – the precise role for which Gifford first fitted him. With this seed planted at Rheims, Gifford returned to England in December 1585, to nurture it further towards full-blown conspiracy.

In this way Walsingham's moves against the English College at Rheims feed into the mainstream of his most important and most ruthless *coup*: the counter-plot against the Babington clique, and the consequent destruction of Mary Queen of Scots. Marlowe was some kind of cog in the operations against Rheims, and so his career brushes obliquely with these momentous events.

Richard Baines now disappears into the shadows for a while, presumably in the windy reaches of Lincolnshire. But he did not sever all links with the secret world, and he will reappear in this story, revealingly, in the year before Marlowe's death.

The point for now is how the paths of Baines and Marlowe come so close at this earlier stage, in the intelligence world of the 1580s. This has not been understood before. After leaving Cambridge, Baines goes to Rheims as an English government spy. Marlowe too is said to be intending to go to Rheims when he leaves Cambridge, and he too is working for the government. As part of his activities as a saboteur, Baines broadcasts heresies and blasphemies. Perhaps Marlowe was doing something similar in the Catholic circles he was moving in at Cambridge and elsewhere. The dating is broadly convenient: Marlowe comes into this world in about 1585, not long after Baines's return to England. I think it is likely that they met around this time, within this context of Walsingham's anti-Catholic operations. If so, Baines was the man of experience, Mr Secretary's former agent in Rheims, though there may also be an undertone of failure in him, since his activities there seem to have achieved little towards 'shaking the foundation' of the Catholic mission.

They are, strangely, men of the same stamp. Or perhaps they are different kinds of men caught in the same trap. There is this constriction in the world of espionage: it narrows people down, finds that common denominator of falsehood which is in them – which is in all of us – and rewards them for using it.

16

ROBERT POLEY

SIFTING THROUGH THE rosters of the Elizabethan secret service, we come upon two names that will later be associated with Marlowe during the last weeks of his life: Thomas Walsingham, his host at Scadbury and one of his literary patrons; and Richard Baines, who denounced him to the authorities as a seditious atheist. We have found, broadly speaking, one friend and one enemy of Marlowe's in 1593. Both these men were involved in Sir Francis Walsingham's French operations. Both returned to England shortly before Marlowe's entry into government service. Marlowe's activities also have a French aspect. Whatever he was up to, there is this suggestion of a professional connection which links him with both Walsingham and Baines in the mid-1580s, and which carries forward in some undetermined way to the events surrounding his death.

Amid all this there is another man. He too finds his niche in the secret world at this time. He serves Sir Francis Walsingham, he attends on Thomas Walsingham, he travels to France, he works with Gilbert Gifford in the toils of the Babington plot. He is a denizen of the same dingy corridors of government, and then he is there at Mrs Bull's house on the night of Marlowe's death, ostensibly on the sidelines of the fracas, a mere bystander, but also the one who brings, more than any other, the smell of secret politics into that room in Deptford.

Whether he was a friend or an enemy of Marlowe is one of the puzzles of this story. Even those who knew him found that sort of question hard to answer.

*

Robert Poley (also spelt, and probably pronounced, Pooley) was born some time in the mid-1550s, parentage unknown. He was about ten years older than Marlowe. The first we hear of him is as a student: he is yet another Cambridge man. He entered Clare College at Michaelmas 1568, and was therefore an exact contemporary of Richard Baines, who matriculated at Christ's a month or so later. Unlike Baines, who was a well-off 'pensioner', Poley entered Cambridge as a 'sizar'. The sizars were the lowliest of scholars, performing menial tasks – bed-making, chamber-sweeping, water-carrying, serving at table – in return for free 'sizes' or rations from the college buttery. By inference, Poley was not a man of inherited wealth. He would later be described as 'but a poor gentleman'. There is no record of his taking a degree at Cambridge. A ready explanation for this, borne out by other evidence, is that he was a Catholic.

In the late 1570s, there was a certain 'Pooley' in the service of Roger, Lord North, who lived at Kirtling, near Cambridge. It has been thought that this was Robert Poley, but on closer investigation I find that the man referred to is probably Sir John Poley of Badley, Suffolk. It is possible that our Poley belonged to some offshoot of this family (one of his close associates in secret affairs, Christopher Blount, was a nephew of Sir John Poley) but if so, the connection is a distant one. I have found an early genealogy of the Poleys of Badley at the British Library. It covers about twenty generations, from the fourteenth to the eighteenth century, but there is not a single Robert Poley among them.

This shadowy figure emerges into some kind of light, in London, in the early 1580s. Whatever he was up to in the interim, it had improved his fortunes. By now the humble Cambridge sizar has become a man of conspicuous con-sumption. On one occasion he is seen handing over a chest containing £110 of 'good gold'. This is a tremendous sum, the Elizabethan equivalent of a brief-case stuffed full of bank-notes. Another time he lavishes £40 on redecorating his new lodgings. Where he got this sort of money from, and to what extent it was *his* money, I do not know.

He was still, in outward form at least, a Catholic. We know this from a brief description of his marriage. The circumstances of this are unmistakably Catholic. It was a fugitive ceremony, held at a tailor's house, and conducted by a 'seminary priest'. The priest is unnamed, but we know a bit about the tailor. His name was Wood, he lived on Bow Lane, and he was involved in the dispersal of clandestine Catholic tracts like *The Treatise of Schism*.

Poley's wife is referred to only as 'one Watson's daughter': I will return to her later. The date of the marriage was about 1582. A daughter – their first and only child, it appears – was conceived some time over that Christmas, and born the following August. She was named Anne, and christened at the church of St Helen's, in Bishopsgate.

It is around this year, 1582, that we first hear of Poley's efforts to enter political service. In a letter written to the Earl of Leicester in early 1585, he refers to his 'three years past determination' to 'do Her Majesty and the State some special service'. He later extends this retrospective period: he has 'carried three or four years intent to serve the State'. Exactly how that 'intent' showed itself is not clear. It was presumably some kind of advance to Sir Francis Walsingham, offering himself as an informer or 'projector' against his fellow-Catholics.

The next we hear of him, however, he is in prison. Some time in 1583, on the orders of Walsingham himself, he was committed to the Marshalsea. For a while he was held there as a 'close prisoner', a dark and harrowing experience, but afterwards he was on a more relaxed régime, and had 'the liberty of the house'. It is very likely that his offer of service and his imprisonment are linked, and that Walsingham was using him, or at least trying him, in the shabby role of prison informer.

While in the Marshalsea, Poley refused to have anything to do with his wife, who tried often to see him. Instead, he was entertaining a lady named Joan Yeomans at 'fine bankets' in his chamber at the prison. She was the wife of William Yeomans, a London cutler. It was to her that Poley entrusted the mysterious chest full of 'good gold'. Their relationship was more than carnal: she was a contact or accomplice of some sort. She later said, 'I have dealt with him in matters of estate as far as my life does extend' – by 'estate' she means matters of State, not of property. Her husband was growing suspicious of them, but on his release from the Marshalsea, Poley sweetened him with the gift of a 'silver bowl of double gilt'. The date of his release was 10 May 1584.

Thus Poley up to about the age of thirty: a university man, a Catholic, a political suspect in the Marshalsea, a potential informer. In his cell he holds court, carouses with his mistress. He is a man with big money to hand; a certain dangerous charm. He has cheated on his wife, and he is ready to cheat on anyone foolish enough to trust him. He will build a career out of cheating, though all in the name of 'loyalty and behoveful service' to the State.

The Marshalsea was a dark fortress near the south bank of the Thames in Southwark, much the same in its essentials then as it was when Dickens described it in *Little Dorrit*. It was one of the chief holding-prisons for Catholics. The number of Catholics there in April 1584 – just before Poley's release – was forty-seven. Of these, seventeen were priests sent over from Rheims or Rome, and the remainder were 'temporal'. In the inner reaches of the prison were Topcliffe's interrogation rooms, and the cells of the 'close prisoners', but those who could afford it were allowed to move freely and receive visitors, and there was clandestine Catholic worship. Three chambers in the prison – Mr Shelley's, Mr Parpoynt's and Mr Denton's – were regularly used by 'mass-hearers', and had 'abominable relics' and 'vile books' in them.

Wherever Catholics concentrated, Walsingham listened. He had plants in all the major prisons where Catholics were held – at the Tower, at Wisbech Castle near Cambridge, at the port-of-entry prisons in Rye, Dover and Portsmouth – but because of its openness, the Marshalsea was a particularly rich source of information for him. In 1586 one of his agents, Maliverny Catlin, wrote to him from Portsmouth jail:

> It had been better to have spent some part of this time rather at the Marshalsea than here, as well for insinuating of myself amongst those men [i.e. Catholics], as also to have given the world a more apparent view of mine imprisonment.

Catlin was duly transferred to the Marshalsea, and reported information gleaned there from a priest named Jackson.

This is the kind of role that Poley was playing in the Marshalsea in 1584. He is himself a Catholic suspect, but he is keen to use his imprisonment to Walsingham's benefit, to 'insinuate of himself' into Catholic plots and projects. To Walsingham, of course, he is an unknown quantity. He has made an offer of service, but this is no guarantee. He is just another piece on the chess-board. Walsingham would use him for many years, but would never quite make up his mind about him. Even during the Babington operation, he told Phelippes he was 'loath' to 'lay himself open' to Poley.

One man whom Poley haunted at the Marshalsea was a priest named Richard Norris. Another seminarist from Rheims, Norris was arrested in late 1581. He was a fellow-prisoner throughout Poley's spell there. He ministered to the Catholic prisoners, and was reported for 'saying of mass' in the chamber of 'Mr Parpoynt' (Gervaise Pierrepoint). In his letter to the Earl of Leicester, Poley justified his dealings with this priest. His 'recourses to Norris in the Marshalsea' and his 'receiving and keeping a few purposeless books from the said Norris' were a blind. It was 'but coldly done, as seeming to favour their religion and cause'.

Early in 1584 Norris was one of nine priests indicted for treason. Some of them went to the scaffold, but Norris was luckier. His punishment was deportation. The following January he was on the prison-ship that carried forty 'Jesuits and seminaries' over to Normandy. One of the men escorting this cargo of exiles was Anthony Hall, who would be associated with Poley the following year. It was his house that Poley used as a base for his dealings with the Babington conspirators: they dined there, sometimes slept there, and one of them, Ballard, was arrested there. Hall is described as a 'citizen and skinner of London' – another of that unsavoury trade, like Nicholas Skeres's accomplice John Wolfall. He ran various errands for the government: a minor secret police-man. This is the milieu that Poley is entering. In July 1584, Norris's brother Silvester was arrested, 'intending to pass over into France'. He was perhaps a victim of Poley's information.

We might take Richard Norris to be the first of Poley's dupes: he got off more lightly than some. Poley was using him: for information to offer Walsingham, but more than that, for an *entrée* into deeper levels of Catholic conspiracy. He would later claim that his whole dealing with Norris was done with this purpose: to gain good 'opinion and report of me to Morgan'. In other words, Poley was already preparing the ground that would lead him to Thomas Morgan, the chief agent of Mary Queen of Scots in Paris. To this end, Poley actually wrote to Morgan, professing to offer his services. He received a promising reply. This letter Poley kept by him, 'as a testimony to be showed Mr Secretary' of his 'credit' with Morgan.

Following his release from the Marshalsea in May 1584, Poley began seriously to pursue his 'suit' to Walsingham for 'admittance and direction' into State service. Walsingham was still unconvinced. Poley describes the period as one of fruitless effort: he trailed to and fro – 'to Greenwich, to Oatlands, to St James's, to Seething Lane' – but all, he frankly admits, 'to lost labour'. It was at this time that he mentions attending on Thomas Walsingham for his 'secret recourse to Mr Secretary'.

All this while Poley continued his liaison with Joan Yeomans. He was lodged, conveniently for their purpose, at the house of Joan's widowed mother, Mistress Browne. In March 1585, 'on a Friday about Shrovetide', Mrs Browne told her neighbour Agnes Hollford, a hosier's wife, that 'one Mr Polley lay in her house', and that she had found her daughter, who had come over to dry clothes, 'sitting upon the said Polley's knees'. This sight, she said, 'did so strike to her heart that she should never recover it'. She 'prayed God to cut her off very quickly, or else she feared she should be a bawd unto her own daughter.' As it happened, the good lady died that very weekend, and when Mrs Hollford called on her the following Monday she found her 'ready to be carried to the church to be buried'. We cannot actually blame Poley for her death: he is on the sidelines, as always.

In early 1585, Poley was in trouble again. He was discovered in possession of certain seditious 'libels', and was accused of being a 'procurer' and disperser of them. These libels were copies of 'a book which was made against the Earl of Leicester'. This was undoubtedly the Catholic scandalsheet called *Leicester's Commonwealth*, also known, because of its green-tinted pages, as 'Father Persons's Greencoat'. This book – mainly the work of Charles Arundel, rather than Persons – was printed in Antwerp in 1584, and was now being smuggled into England. 'Books against Leicester' were 'found on one at Scarborough' in early 1585, and the three Catholics examined on 18 March as 'dispersers of traitorous books' were probably also handling the 'Greencoat'. The book's racy combination of scandal, satire and polemic won it a wide readership in England, including many nonCatholics, and the Privy Council had to issue a specific edict against it in June.

This was a serious charge against Poley, and Walsingham took personal charge of his interrogation. He questions Poley 'by the space of two hours', and 'did use him very cruelly', but Poley remained cool, and refused to confess to any knowledge about the libel.

The copy or copies of *Leicester's Commonwealth* were not the only seditious books found at Poley's lodgings at Mrs Browne's house. There were also those Catholic books that Poley had received from Norris. And then there was the letter from the arch-conspirator, Thomas Morgan. If, as Poley claimed, it was part of his ploy against Morgan, why had he not brought the letter to Walsingham when he first received it? Poley claimed he had intended to show it to Walsingham all along, but by now it was too late. His 'reserving of Morgan's letter' suggested concealment.

Shortly after his examination, at liberty but in 'distress', Poley wrote a long letter of exculpation and apology to the Earl of Leicester. He has been traduced by 'sinister reports or conceits', wrongfully accused as a Catholic libeller, hauled over the coals by Walsingham, when all along his only desire has been to 'serve the State'. He lards it on thick. He is all courtly abjection, so different from those snatches of his conversational style, which is sneering, witty and boastful. The letter covers three pages, in Poley's strange, drifting hand, but the nub of it is at the end. Rejected by Walsingham, he is now making a direct appeal to Leicester for employment in his service:

Here I most humbly beseech Your Honour, so far as may conform with your pleasure or wisdom, either to direct or licence me in some course of discovery and service, either abroad or at home. But rather I wish with Morgan, because my plat being laid that way, my credit is both enough with him, and also with some of them which were last sent over, as Norris the priest and the rest. And I in no whit mistrust, the grounds being secretly laid and so kept, but that in short time I shall accomplish something both worthy Her Majesty's and Your Honour's acceptance, and also sufficient to countervail and recompense any offences and misbehaviours of my youth past and lost.

It is clear from what followed that Poley's offer of service was accepted. This letter, written in March or April 1585, marks the true beginnings of his professional career as a spy. After years on the outlaw Catholic fringes, and months of attendance at the back-doors of the court, Poley now enters government service. The line is a fine one: a matter of accreditation. In every other respect, Poley continues to be Poley. As one Catholic priest later put it: 'Poley now liveth like himself: a notorious spy, and either an atheist or an heretic.' The same words will be used against Marlowe, who also entered government service in this year 1585.

*

163

In his letter to the Earl Poley claimed that his target for some while had been to get into the 'credit' of Thomas Morgan. His 'plat' – a scheme, a game-plan; also, in theatrical circles, the synopsis of a plot – 'lay that way', and Leicester's acceptance of his service was an invitation to pursue this further.

The 'plat' was against Morgan, but the true target was Morgan's royal mistress, Mary Queen of Scots. Mary was the great figurehead for English Catholics: the cousin of the Queen of England, the mother of the King of Scotland, the widow of a King of France, she was the charismatic Catholic Pretender, and her years of imprisonment in England had only increased her potent appeal. Among the many who worked on her behalf, none was busier than Thomas Morgan, another Rheims alumnus. He had begun as a 'cypher clerk' in the service of her official ambassador in France, James Beaton, but his influence had now far outgrown this. According to the Papal Nuncio, writing in March 1585, many of the Jesuits considered him a 'knave', but 'the Queen of Scots relies on him more than her own ambassador'. Working with other exiles in Paris – Charles Paget, Thomas Throckmorton, etc. – Morgan was at the hub of intrigue, overt and covert, in support of her cause. France was the natural centre for this. Mary was linked to the ruling Valois family through marriage, and to the Guisard faction through her mother, Marie of Guise. There was also her enormous 'French dowry': 30,000 crowns *per annum*. The Morgan clique had virtually gained control of these funds, and so – as Father Persons drily observed – 'were able to pleasure much their friends, and hinder their adversaries'.

A tireless, meddlesome man, Morgan brought discredit and confusion to most who dealt with him. It was later thought by Catholics that he was a double agent all along, a deliberate saboteur of Marian conspiracy, but for now we must take him as most did in 1585: a devotee of Mary's, working ceaselessly to keep her in touch with the dealings of the world beyond her prison walls.

Among the many Englishmen in touch with Morgan was a follower of the Earl of Leicester, Christopher Blount. As already noted, Blount's mother was a Poley – the sister of Sir John Poley of Badley – and Robert Poley may have been a distant kinsman. At any rate, we now find Poley working with Blount, under the aegis of Leicester, as the 'plat' against Morgan unfolds.

Christopher Blount was a tall, swarthy man in his late twenties. He was soon to be named Leicester's Master of Horse, and was later knighted by the Earl for his services in the Netherlands. A gentleman of good means, 'worth about £160 a year', his situation radically improved after his patron's death. In the summer of 1589, just eight months after Leicester died, Blount married his widow, Lettice. He was sixteen years younger, her third husband. The marriage brought him vast wealth, but also political advantage. Lettice was the mother, by her first husband, of the Earl of Essex. Blount became Essex's step-father and – being only seven years older than him – his 'very dear friend'. Thus neatly he steps from one power-centre to another. His fortunes rose thereafter with Essex's, and fell with them too. In March 1601 he was beheaded at Tower Hill for his part in the Essex rebellion. His adventurous marriage duly led him to the scaffold – another Elizabethan over-reacher: *Quod me nutrit me destruit*.

All this lay in the future. For now he was an ambitious young courtier, ready to turn his hand to a bit of 'projecting' against the Queen of Scots. He had himself been brought up a Catholic, and, like so many in these shifting times, he was turning his old allegiances to political profit.

Blount had met Thomas Morgan in Paris in the early 1580s. Morgan was 'well persuaded of his faith and honesty', and hoped he might 'serve some friendly turn' to the Catholic cause. Now, with Robert Poley at his elbow, Blount wrote to Morgan, offering his services on Queen Mary's behalf. Morgan responded swiftly. Mary was about to be moved to a harsher, more sequestered imprisonment at Tutbury Castle. Morgan was anxious to establish some kind of communication-link with her in her new fastness. This dangerous mission he now offered to Blount. It was eagerly accepted, and Blount was soon travelling down to Tutbury, to 'view the state of the country and the people thereabouts', and to 'frame intelligence' with the imprisoned Queen of Scots.

Soon after writing to Blount, however, events overtook Thomas Morgan in Paris. On the evening of 11 March 1585, a company of French guardsmen entered his lodgings and arrested him. On 15 March he was transferred to the Bastille. The arrest was a piece of Anglo-French co-operation. Morgan had been closely involved with another Welsh adventurer, William Parry, and was implicated in Parry's supposed plot to kill the Queen. For this reason – or under this pretext – the English government requested his arrest. Their next step was to extradite him for questioning, but this proved harder. The Queen asked, through diplomatic channels, to have him 'delivered to her hands'. She also sent over one of Walsingham's officers, William Waad, and he 'with great fury pressed the same'. But Morgan had powerful friends in France, and the request for extradition was refused. In early April Waad returned to England 'much discontented'.

Morgan remained in the Bastille, and this presented a problem for Christopher Blount. He was keen to strengthen the link he had established with Morgan. He needed to report back to him, to indicate that he had prepared a channel of communication to Mary in Tutbury. He wanted to get the intelligence flowing from Morgan to Mary, and thereby to Leicester and the government. But Morgan was in the Bastille, incommunicado.

About the middle of June 1585, Blount despatched a 'special messenger' to Paris. His task was to make contact with Morgan in the Bastille, and to deliver Blount's letter to him in person. The messenger was Robert Poley.

Poley arrived in Paris on about 26 June. There he 'rencontred' with an unnamed English exile, and told him he had 'some things of importance' to deliver to Morgan. News of Poley's approach soon reached Morgan in the Bastille. He sent word back that Poley should deliver his messages to Thomas Throckmorton. Throckmorton was one of Morgan's closest allies, and frequently features (under the code-name 'Barasino') in Morgan's despatches to Mary. This Poley refused to do, 'declaring that he would not deliver his charge to anyone living', until he had spoken with Morgan in person.

It was at this stage, a couple of days after his arrival in Paris, that Poley wrote certain letters back to Blount in England. We later hear, from Morgan, that these letters were 'intercepted at the port of England, and sent to the Council', and that both Blount and Poley were 'like to fall into trouble' as a result. Morgan's friend Charles Paget, writing to Mary on 18 July, refers to the same news:

> Poley on his first arrival here has committed an error in writing hence to Mr Christopher Blunt . . . Presuming that (by the credit he had by Blunt) it might safely have passed the ports, he sent it by an ordinary messenger, so that it was taken.

It is possible that this was not an 'error' on Poley's part, but an intended communiqué to the Privy Council.

Though they did not yet know about these intercepted letters, some of Morgan's friends were already suspicious of Poley's eagerness to deal directly with Morgan. As Morgan explained in a letter to Mary, their chief fear was that Poley 'was sent by England to practise my death in prison, by one means or other'. Despite their dissuasions, Morgan made arrangements to speak with Poley:

> I found the means to have him conducted as near as might be to the window of the chamber where I am prisoner, and through the window I spoke so much to him as satisfied him. At last he delivered the letters where I appointed [i.e. to Throckmorton], and so they came to my hands.

Poley, in turn, ingratiated himself with Morgan. He professed himself 'marvellously well pleased' that Morgan was alive and well, since there had been reports in England that he had been 'despatched away'. He also reassured Morgan that none of his papers, seized at his arrest, had been used to 'hurt any' back in England.

Morgan was too seasoned a conspirator to trust Poley with any secrets at this first meeting: 'I wrote not one line with him, but signified that Blunt should hear from me by some other means.' This was to be expected: operational caution. Of Poley's actual loyalty to the Catholic cause Morgan had no doubt:

> Upon conference and conclusion with the said Poley I found nothing but that he meant well, and a Catholic he shows himself to be, and much disposed to see some happy and speedy reformation in that state.

Even here, crouched against a grille in some backyard of the Bastille, Poley tells a plausible story.

These letters from Christopher Blount, delivered with such diligence by Robert Poley, cemented Blunt's link with Morgan. They contained, in Morgan's words, 'ample instructions of the state of England', and many further pledges of service to Mary, whom Blunt lavishly calls 'the only saint that he knows living upon the ground'. Blunt also sent via Poley an 'alphabet' to 'entertain a good intelligence' – in other words, a cypher-key to be used by Morgan and Mary.

The letters indicated to Morgan, in short, that this new line to the imprisoned Queen of Scots was now open. He communicated this 'with speed' to Ambassador Beaton and to Charles Paget, and ordered Paget to inform the Spanish ambassador in Paris, Don Bernadino de Mendoza. By about 10 July, Poley was on his way home, with thirty pistolets in his purse paid to him by Paget for his 'viage and charges'.

Morgan had swallowed the hook, and wrote confidently to Mary: 'I have no cause but to conceive both of Blunt, for the testimony of his dutiful care to your Majesty; and of Poley, for his pains taken.'

What Blunt and Poley had accomplished in the summer of 1585 was the establishing of a communications channel between Mary and her supporters in exile in France – a genuine channel, in that it would carry intelligence to and from Morgan; a phoney channel in that it was set up so that the English government could listen in on it. Blount had the 'alphabet', and any intelligence that passed between Tutbury and Paris would be deciphered by Blount, and handed to the Earl of Leicester.

In the event, it was another such device – a communications channel with a built-in 'bug' – that actually caused Mary's downfall. This, the notorious 'beer keg' post, was the work of one of Walsingham's most brilliant agents, Gilbert Gifford. But this was not even being considered before December, five months after Poley's mission to Paris. Poley is in there at the outset, and will continue to play a part in what now becomes the single, pressing priority of the secret service: the entrapment and elimination of Mary Queen of Scots.

Throughout the autumn of 1585, we watch him further establishing himself among Mary's followers. He haunts the French embassy in London. The new ambassador, Chateauneuf, a staunch supporter of Mary's cause, reports well of him to Morgan. Poley has, he says, done 'acceptable service'. But Poley is also reporting to Walsingham. He retails low-grade political intelligence gleaned from Chateauneuf: he 'dare not enter with him too boldly', he says, for fear of discovery. Leicester was now busy with preparations for war in the Netherlands, and with him Christopher Blount, his new Master of Horse. The secret operation against Mary is now in Walsingham's hands, and Poley has found a place in Mr Secretary's service at last.

Some time in late 1585, apparently due to the efforts of Christopher Blount, Poley entered the service of Sir Philip Sidney, the famous poet and soldier who was Leicester's nephew. Morgan refers to this in a letter to Mary: 'Blount has placed him to be Sir Philip Sidney's man, that he may more quietly live a Christian life under the said Sidney.' (By 'Christian' Morgan meant Catholic: Sidney was by no means a Catholic, but he was a man of tolerance and moderation.) More important to Morgan, this placed Poley close to the enemy's inner sanctum, for Sidney's wife was Frances Walsingham, the spymaster's only daughter. When Sidney left England for the Low Countries in November 1585, his wife remained behind, and with her Poley. A couple of months later, Morgan informs Mary that Poley is 'placed with the Lady Sidney, the daughter of Secretary Walsingham, & by that means ordinarily in his house'. He is 'thereby able to pick out many things to the information of your Majesty'. This he 'beginneth to do, to the disadvantage of the common enemies'.

From Morgan's point of view, Poley is physically close to Walsingham, with this household cover as a servant of Lady Sidney's. He is seen as a Catholic spy who has penetrated close to the heart of the English government. In reality – if the word can be used about him – he is Walsingham's man.

In January 1586, Morgan and Paget wrote direct to Poley from Paris. They asked him to organise the delivery of a packet of letters to Mary; to make contact with Lord Seton as a channel of communication to the Scottish king; and generally to ensure that the Catholic party in England 'be encouraged and put in hope'. They also sought news of England's 'employing' of Don Antonio, the Portuguese pretender, who had recently arrived in England. They wanted to know the details of Don Antonio's fleet: 'how many ships, of what burden, how furnished, who be the captains.' They then suggested that Poley should return to France to 'confer' with them, and then 'pass into Holland to Blount', who was by now fighting in the Low Countries with Leicester. Their hope was that Poley should persuade Blount to perform some sabotage there:

> that Blount be dealt with to practise deliverance of some important town in Holland to the King of Spain, or to undertake the conveying of some other notable enterprise touching the default of the Earl of Leicester.

It is a long shopping-list, and it testifies to their sense of Poley's value as an agent. Poley drew up a neat précis of their letters and delivered it to Thomas Phelippes, for the attention of Walsingham. A little later – in March or early April – Poley received further messages from Morgan and Paget, this time concerning a 'practice' for 'killing my Lord of Leicester'. This too Poley revealed, to Leicester, at the first opportunity, and on Leicester's instructions he wrote back to the conspirators with the intention of getting a 'full discovery' of this plan.

All the while Poley was busy trying to establish relations with Mary Stuart herself down at Tutbury. In late 1585, he was seen 'in the parks at Tutbury, where the Queen's horses are'. His purpose there, Morgan explained to Mary, was to find 'means to convey such letters as I commended to his care, to serve to make an intelligence with your Majesty'. Morgan continues to recommend Poley to his mistress. 'We have applied him this twelvemonth or thereabouts, and have found him to deal well & very willing to serve your Majesty.' For Mary herself, Poley was just another ambiguous, Catholic-seeming gentleman flitting around the edge of her beleaguered little retinue. He was a name in her head, a morsel of hope. There is no evidence that they actually met at Tutbury, and shortly afterwards – on Christmas Eve 1585 – Mary was on the move again, to Chartley Hall.

Another service Poley offered to the conspirators was to courier letters between Mary and her sympathisers in Scotland. In January 1586 Morgan was recommending Poley to Ambassador Chateauneuf as the 'fit man' to deliver a certain 'packet' to Scotland. He had been there before, and 'knoweth the best ways to pass into Scotland'. Poley was unavailable, perhaps at Chartley, and the packet remained at the embassy. It was still there two months later, for Thomas Phelippes refers to it in a memorandum to Walsingham, dated 19 March 1586. Chateauneuf has, says Phelippes,

> been anxious to find some apt means to send a packet into Scotland with some secret matters. I thought good to send Your Honour word hereof, to the end that if Poley be not attainable, you may think of some other who will deliver it . . . If Poley received it, do not think but that he will send it to you, for as appears from Morgan's last, he is

recommended as a fit man for that convoy of Scotland. Poley, I think, may be sent to the ambassador to see what he will offer touching the convoy of these letters, which if he commit to Poley, you shall either have it out-carried at their costs, or else know Poley thoroughly.

As always there is the question mark over Poley. He is now a key player in the government's counter-plots against the Marian faction. He is in regular contact with Morgan and Paget, he is employed as a courier by Chateauneuf, he haunts 'the parks at Tutbury', and all the while he supplies a steady stream of intelligence to Phelippes and Walsingham. For all that, they are still unsure. They have not yet managed to 'know him thoroughly'.

17

THE BABINGTON PLOT

POLEY'S SLIPPERY DEALINGS – with Morgan and Paget on one side, with Leicester and Walsingham on the other – lead us, as they led others, into the difficult and rather disturbing story of the 'Babington plot'. No account of the Elizabethan secret world, and certainly no account of Robert Poley, would be complete without a brief survey of these events.

It is hard to say exactly when the 'plot' took shape. In a sense it never did. There was a lot of wild talk – heads filled with wine, with dreams of Catholic rebellion, with an overheated, cultish devotion to the imprisoned Queen Mary – but what shape it had in terms of real action was largely provided by the government itself, whose agents infiltrated the conspiracy not so much to destroy it, as to encourage it. In the words of a priest named Davis, who was with Babington on the night before his capture, the plot was a 'tragedy', in which 'the chief actor and contriver' was Sir Francis Walsingham. This is a partisan view, but on the evidence it is true enough. The Babington affair was a classic piece of Walsingham 'projection': a piece of political theatre, conjured up for reasons of cynical expediency.

This drama has many prologues – Anthony Babington's first glimpse of Mary when he was a page-boy in the Earl of Shrewsbury's household; John Ballard's wanderings as an outlaw priest in England; John Savage at Rheims, swearing a solemn oath to kill Queen Elizabeth – but a useful opening scene is a convivial-seeming meeting at the Plough Inn, outside Temple Bar in London's legal district, in March 1586.

Present were Robert Barnwell, a tall and 'comely' Irishman, 'white-faced, flaxen-bearded, freckled and disfigured with the small pox'; Harry Dunne, a young Kentish gentleman, possibly a relative of the poet John Donne; Chidiock Tichbourne, now famous for his eve-of-execution poem, 'My prime of youth is but a frost of cares', and a couple of others. These were the bit players. The two men at the centre of the group at the Plough, and of the conspiracy itself, were Anthony Babington and John Ballard.

Babington was twenty-four years old: handsome, cultivated, impulsive, impressionable. He was a rich squire's son up from Derbyshire, a student at Lincoln's Inn, a young Elizabethan *boulevardier*. He was also, like those others, a Catholic born and raised, and he had been involved in a minor way in Catholic intrigue. In about 1580, travelling on the continent, he had met Morgan in Paris, and he had helped to courier letters to Mary when she was held by his former master, the Earl of Shrewsbury. He also assisted the movement of priests in the Catholic Midlands. But with Mary removed to the harsher régime at Tutbury, and the consequent closing down of communications with her – the breach into which Blount and Poley offered to step – Babington's role as a courier came to an end. Twice in early 1586 he received letters from France, destined for Mary, but in each case he declined to 'deal further in those affairs'. He was thinking of leaving England, becoming one of those rootless Catholic émigrés on the continent. He and a friend, the Welshman Thomas Salisbury, tried to get passports, but this was never easy without some powerful backing. They engaged the help of a sympathetic courtier, Sir Edward Fitton, but to no avail. 'By God's just judgement of our sins,' as Babington later put it, they remained in London, and he was here at the Plough Inn on this March day, surrounded as always by friends, talking and drinking and dreaming of sedition.

Babington was an amateur, and the plot bears his name not so much because he was its prime mover, but because he was its weak link. The real animus was the militant, somewhat megalomanic priest Father John Ballard. Ballard was part of the Plough group, though as a missionary Catholic from Rheims he had a price on his head, and to all outside the group he was not John Ballard but 'Captain Fortescue', a swashbuckling, courtly soldier. He wore a fine cape laced with gold, a cut satin doublet and silver buttons on his hat. A tall, dark-complexioned man, he was known as 'Black Foskew'. Ballard was different from the others there. He was a front-line Catholic: a life on the run, a life of commitment. He made the others feel like spoilt dilettantes.

With Ballard there was his inseparable companion, Barnard Maude, a quiet man with a chequered past. He was Ballard's fixer. He had recently procured false passports for them to cross over to France. They were to depart the following day.

In the terms of his cover, 'Captain Fortescue' was leaving on military business, and this was a party to send him off. In reality, as the men at the Plough Inn knew, Ballard's purpose in France was to confer with Morgan and Paget at the conspiracy-factory in Paris, and also with the Spanish ambassador there, Don Bernadino de Mendoza. Mendoza was a hard-line, old-style Spanish aristocrat, who nursed a particular resentment against England since his expulsion from the London embassy two years previously. The project they were to discuss in Paris – already in preparation, according to Ballard – was the long-awaited Catholic invasion of England.

One cannot say this was the beginning of the plot – Ballard had probably broached the others before this meeting – but in the confessions that followed it appears as the first purposive meeting of these young Catholics, the first sign of that inexact phenomenon, 'conspiracy'. And whatever was discussed over supper at the Plough, it would soon be known to Walsingham, for one of the men who met there that night – Ballard's fixer, Barnard Maude – was a government spy.

A couple of months later, towards the end of May 1586, Ballard returned from France. He went immediately to Babington's lodgings at Hern's Rents, Holborn. There, in a mood of intense excitement, he told Babington his news. The invasion of England was a reality: it would be accomplished that summer, by September at the latest. A strike force of 60,000 soldiers was in preparation: French troops under the Duke of Guise, Italian and Spanish under the Duke of Parma. What was now needed was some planning on the home front: an uprising of English Catholics to act in concert with the invasion force. It was towards this that Babington, with his wide range of Catholic contacts, must work. Ballard himself would travel to Scotland, with Maude, to sound out the Catholic gentry there, who were always considered ready for rebellion.

Babington was sceptical at first. The English state was too 'well settled', the Queen too much beloved, for any uprising to gain support.

'That difficulty will be taken away,' Ballard replied. 'The means are already laid. Her life can be no hindrance.'

So here the plan takes a major twist: it becomes an assassination plot. The 'remove of the Queen' was a precondition of the invasion. When Ballard said that the means for this were laid, he meant that he had an assassin ready. He told Babington who this was: 'The instrument is Savage, and he has vowed to perform it.'

Shortly after this John Savage himself visited Babington at Hern's Rents. He had returned to England from Rheims the previous autumn, and was now quietly reading law at Barnard's Inn. But he was still pledged to his vow to kill the Queen. He had, in fact, been reminded of it just recently, by the very man who had been instrumental in the vow in the first place: Gilbert Gifford. As Babington later put it, Gifford 'came over' to Savage, 'much miscontent that he had left to execute what he had vowed, and that he could not be discharged in conscience'.

This is Gifford in pure form as *provocateur*, urging Savage to screw his courage to the sticking-place. He cannot be discharged of his oath. He must 'execute' it. So here again the government, through its agent Gifford, is close to a key moment in the development of the conspiracy.

1 THE OFFICIAL STORY. Coroner's inquest on the death of Christopher Marlowe, held on 1 June 1593.

2 THE DEPTFORD FOUR. Signatures of Christopher Marlowe, Ingram Frizer, Nicholas Skeres and Robert Poley.

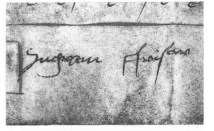

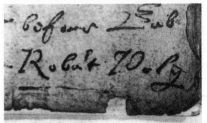

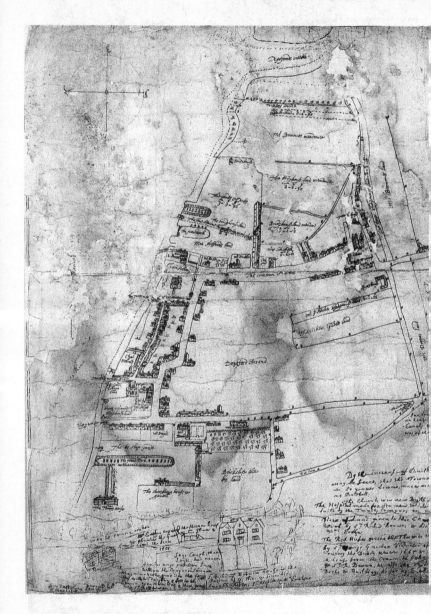

3 DEPTFORD STRAND. Detail from a sketch-map of Deptford drawn in 1623.

4 MARLOWE'S HERESIES. Extract from Richard Baines's 'Note containing the opinion of one Christopher Marly', delivered to the authorities in May 1593.

5-9 FRIENDS AND ENEMIES. (Clockwise, from top left) Thomas Nashe in leg-irons, 1597; the ghost of Robert Greene, 1598; Dr Gabriel Harvey, 'ready to let fly upon Ajax', 1596; Edward Alleyn as Dr Faustus (title-page of the 1624 edition). (Opposite) Thomas Hariot, mathematician and 'conjuror', 1602.

10 MR SECRETARY. The Queen's spymaster Sir Francis Walsingham, in a portrait attributed to John de Critz the elder, *c.* 1585.

11 MARLOWE'S WARRANTY. Memorandum of the Privy Council's certificate for Christopher 'Morley', 29 June 1587.

12 POLEY THE PROJECTOR. Part of his report on the Babington plot, written in the Tower of London, September 1586.

TANTI

13 THE WIZARD EARL. Henry Percy, 9th Earl of Northumberland. A miniature portrait by Nicholas Hilliard, *c.* 1595.

Babington is appalled, fascinated, self-heroising, but he is not yet a convinced conspirator. The case for the prosecution later contended that the conspiracy was a cohesive unit by the beginning of June, including a full-strength meeting on 7 June. The truth seems, as always, less neat. There was much discussion between Babington and his friends – Barnwell, Dunne, Tichbourne, Salisbury, and also two young Catholic courtiers, Charles Tilney and Edward Abingdon – but they were ambiguous in their responses. They were ready to pledge themselves to assist an uprising, but most considered the 'remove' of the Queen quite out of the question.

Also ambiguous is the fact that in early June Babington was renewing his efforts to get a passport to leave the country. It was probably his Welsh friend, Thomas Salisbury, who revived the idea. He was the least enthusiastic of the plotters, and wanted to draw Babington away from the dangerous magnetism of Ballard. Babington seems to be wavering at this point. He seems ready to quit the country, to disentangle himself from the web. It is possible, of course, that the passport was a ploy, a decoy for his regicidal intentions. It was no doubt presented to the others as such. The passport is a kind of cover, but it is also a genuine escape-route for Babington.

Babington and Salisbury had failed to get their passports when they tried before, through Sir Edward Fitton, but now they had hopes from elsewhere. An acquaintance of theirs by the name of Tindall knew someone: a man with contacts at court, a friend to Catholics. He was a member of the household of Lady Sidney, and thereby had access to her father, Sir Francis Walsingham. He was the ideal man to further Babington's 'suit' for a passport.

And so, at this point of hesitation and ambiguity, Robert Poley enters the stage. As he later describes it, in the clipped, bland tones of his report on the Babington affair: 'My first acquaintance with Mr Babington was about the middle of June last, the means Mr Tindall, the cause to procure a licence of five or three years travel for Babington and Salisbury.'

Babington undoubtedly knew something of Poley's double-edged reputation, but this came with the territory. He saw Poley as a contacts man, an influence-broker, someone with a few footholds in a slippery world. A man like that was bound to play on both sides. Babington had, anyway, no need to question Poley's motives at this point. He was offering a generous fee of £300 for the obtaining of a passport, and this was motive enough for anyone on the court circuit.

Poley duly 'moved' Babington's suit to Mr Secretary. He also suggested to Walsingham that if Babington was about to go to the continent, this was a good chance to plant someone on him: 'someone fit, at his Honour's appointment, might be enforced into Babington's service, who following him in his travel might do the State some good service.' Walsingham approved of this, and told Poley to 'put Babington in hope' about the passport. Back Poley toils to his friend Mr Tindall:

> I laboured with Tindall to procure for me with Babington, that I might accompany him between the condition of a servant and companion, being utterly unable to maintain myself in all this journey, thinking with myself that I should both better myself thereby, both in language and experience, and also do the State much better service in that course abroad than in that wherein I remained at home. Babington agreed to supply all my charges of travel, and to give me some yearly stipend at my return.

I like Poley's description of his status: someone halfway between 'a servant and a companion'. There is also a genuine note of need: he is 'utterly unable to maintain himself'. This should be remembered in estimations of people like Poley. They worked on the edge of destitution. They are knaves, but their knaveries are a form of survival.

In the last week of June 1586, Poley brought Babington to Greenwich for a personal interview with Walsingham. This was the first of three meetings between them: a curious *rapprochement*. The meeting was very civilised. Babington made, in his own words, 'general offers of service'. Walsingham replied with 'many honourable speeches'. He stretched out his hand to Babington and said, 'Come now, act with confidence, do not fear to converse freely amongst Catholics on the subject of our affairs, so as to escape observation.' He was pressing Babington, in other words, to play the informer. This was to be the pattern of their meetings: Babington professing to offer some anti-Catholic service, Walsingham professing to encourage him.

Poley's role in all this is a subtle one. It was part of his task simply to spy on Babington. At the time of their first acquaintance, in mid-June, the government still knew comparatively little about Babington himself. They had their man Barnard Maude fastened on to Ballard, and Gifford pressurising John Savage, and they also had an intercept of a letter from Morgan to Mary recommending her to get in touch with Babington. But they did not know his response to all this. Those critical meetings between Babington, Ballard and Savage in late May were conducted in privacy: we only know about them from later confessions. Babington was still a dark horse, and it was Poley's brief to 'sift' him. But he has a more delicate task: to keep things going, to further this illusory *rapprochement* between Walsingham and Babington. This is partly in the hope that Babington can be turned, but more it is to reassure him. By making him believe he could claim some immunity, some official 'warranty' for his actions, Walsingham was encouraging him to continue the conspiracy. Without that encouragement, he might well have turned his back on it.

So Poley becomes his confidant: 'sweet Robin'. He is the man at his shoulder, the politic adviser. He thrusts charmingly into Babington's circle and – this is Babington's own word – into his 'love'.

Babington asks him, 'What think you of Mr Secretary's disposition? How will he deal with me if I should open fully all my former dealings?'

Poley is quick to soothe him. 'He will deal with you most honourably, and in all according to promise.'

We cannot see Poley's face, but when he speaks I always see a certain kind of smile. I see in him something of another spy, the Russian agent George Blake, as described by a journalist who knew him: 'Very secretive but very charming. People liked him. Smiled a lot, smiled rather too much.' Poley is glib in this way: quick and genial, smiling too much, telling you everything except what really matters.

Things were now moving ahead fast, and on or about 6 July, Babington made the fatal step of writing to Queen Mary. The letter was long, and dangerously specific in its itemisation of the conspiracy's aims. First, to prepare the ground for the Catholic invasion force: 'ports to arrive at appointed, with a strong party at every place to join with them'. Second, the 'deliverance' of Mary from captivity. And third, 'the despatch of the usurping competitor', Elizabeth. For this last act, he writes, 'there be six noble gentlemen, all my private friends, who for the zeal they bear to the Catholic cause and your Majesty's service, will undertake that tragical execution.' (The 'six', in Babington's mind, would probably be Savage, Tichbourne, Barnwell, Salisbury, Tilney and Abingdon, though when later questioned he was vague: 'they were never named nor sounded, nor in my own determination resolved upon'. This statement was suppressed at his trial, as were others that tended to blur the image of these men as a die-hard confederacy.)

Babington's letter to Mary was a request for her assent, for legitimisation of the plot: 'forasmuch as delay is extreme dangerous, it may please your most excellent Majesty to direct us, and by your princely authority to enable such as may advance us.' It was also precisely what Walsingham was waiting for: the point at which this carefully nurtured treason actually touched the Queen of Scots.

It was now that Walsingham's 'listening device' came into its own. As we saw, Poley had been patiently working on this the previous year. It was the nub of his dealings with Morgan at the Bastille, and it was his purpose down at the 'parks' in Tutbury: to set up a line of secret communication between Mary and her agents which would also leak directly to the government. In fact it was Walsingham's other projector, bright-eyed Gilbert Gifford, who planted the bug that caused her downfall. This was the ingenious, notorious beer-keg post, set up by Gifford and Phelippes in early 1586, shortly after Mary's arrival at her new quarters at Chartley Hall.

Every Friday there was a delivery of beer at Chartley: fresh ale was loaded in, empty barrels sent out. Mary was led to believe that the brewer, a Burton man, had been suborned to her service, and could smuggle her despatches past the guards. Incoming letters were sealed in a waterproof pouch – *'une petite boite ou sac de cuir'*, as Mary describes it – and outgoing letters were sent out in the empty barrels. Actually the brewer, whom Gifford christened 'The Honest Man', was reporting directly to Mary's keeper, Sir Amias Paulet, who in turn reported to Gifford or Phelippes or some other government agent, according to the circumstance. In this way every secret despatch that passed to and from Mary was intercepted and deciphered before proceeding on its way – outwards to her clearing-house at the French embassy in London, or inwards to her chambers in a damp outbuilding at Chartley – and before it ever reached its destination, Walsingham had digested its contents.

It was along this very porous channel that Babington's letter to Mary was passed, in early July, and now Walsingham waited for Mary's reply.

Poley, well eased into his role as Babington's confidant, now begins to deepen his involvement with the conspirators. He is more than just a courtly go-between. He is adding his own impetus, egging Babington on to further thoughts of sedition. This does not appear in Poley's report on the affair, nor at the trial, but it is very plain from Babington's own statements:

Pooley said it was convenient for to take away my Lord of Leicester by poison or violence. I thought there were men, and he means, to do it. He named likewise my Lord

Treasurer and Mr Secretary, who might easily be taken away.

These words record Poley in the role of 'projector', urging his victim on to treason.

Even the naive Babington could not fail to see certain anomalies in Poley's position. In a postscript to his letter to Mary, he asks her secretary, Claude Nau, for advice about him:

> I would gladly understand what opinion you hold of one Robert Pooley, whom I find to have intelligence with Her Majesty's [i.e. Mary's] actions. I am private with the man, and by means thereof know somewhat, but I suspect more. I pray you, deliver your opinion of him.

Nau's reply, dated 13 July, was equivocal:

> There is great assurance given of Mr Poley's faithful serving of Her Majesty, and by his own letters hath vowed and promised the same. As yet Her Majesty's experience of him is not so great as I dare embolden you to trust him much.

In conclusion, Nau requests Babington: 'let me know plainly what you understand of him'. As so often with Poley, a question about him finds no hard answer, only another question.

Babington's doubts about Poley at this point seem to have been worrying the government. They feared that he would begin to distance himself from Poley. On 7 July Thomas Phelippes writes to Walsingham: 'I think Poley may yet last, if he begins first to charge Babington to Paget for a suspected person, for his readiness to offer you service.' That Poley should 'last' means that he should continue to be trusted by Babington. Phelippes's ingenious suggestion is for Poley to use his own link with the Morgan-Paget clique in Paris. By communicating to Paget these pretended doubts about Babington's

Catholic loyalty, he would further his own cover as a sincere Catholic.

One evening about 13 July, as they were rowed downriver to London, after another meeting with Walsingham at Barn Elms, Babington challenged him with his doubts.

'How is it,' he asks, 'that your credit grows with Mr Secretary?'

Poley replies, 'By my dealing with him in some business of my master, Sir Philip Sidney.'

Babington brushes this aside. He is tense, confused: he *wants* to trust Poley. He urges him to open up. Poley says, 'I am in a like course of doing service to the State as you yourself have undertaken.'

'That is impossible! I know that all men in England, being Catholics, have you in vehement suspicion.'

'I did it by an intelligence held with Morgan.'

'How can that be, considering how suspicious Morgan is?'

But Poley has had enough, and replies with his wafting smile: 'Such things are rather to be imagined, than questioned or resolved.'

In his quarters at Chartley, meanwhile, Thomas Phelippes was waiting anxiously for Mary's reply to Babington. On 14 July he sent up some intercepts to Walsingham, but 'the answer to B's letter' was not yet among them. It could only be a matter of time. 'We attend her very heart at the next.'

On the night of Sunday 17 July the fatal letter passed out of Chartley on the back of the brewer's cart. It was in Phelippes's hands the following day. Deciphered and resealed, it passed on towards Babington in London. The decipher went up to Walsingham. Mary's letter was just what Walsingham hoped: it answered Babington's proposals point by point, and therefore incriminated her in the conspiracy. On the outside of the packet, on a ghoulish impulse, Phelippes sketched three lines: ⌐‾⌐ This was what the letter represented: a gallows for the Queen of Scots.

This letter is controversial. Mary's defenders point out that, as with other key documents in the affair, the original letter has disappeared. All that remains is the cyphered version of the letter, as received by Babington, after it had been through Phelippes's hands. This, the *textus receptus*, may well be different from the original. There is clear evidence that the letter Babington received had been tampered with, and that a postscript, requesting the 'names and qualities of the six gentlemen' involved in the conspiracy, was added by Phelippes in order to obtain that information. It is certainly possible that there were more substantial forgeries in it. Mary's secretaries, Curll and Nau, authenticated the text, but they were in the process of saving their own necks. Mary denied she had ever written it. The truth depends on your view of her. Would the government *need* to forge this evidence against her? I think, by this stage, probably not. Walsingham had set the trap, but Mary stepped into it of her own desperate volition.

Phelippes clearly believed that Mary's answer was evidence enough to arrest Babington and wrap up the conspiracy. In his accompanying letter to Walsingham he writes:

> I look for Your Honour's speedy resolution touching his apprehension or otherwise. I think, under correction, that you have enough of him, unless you would discover more particularities of the confederates.

It would seem that Walsingham did not want to do this. It was not until about 29 July that Babington finally received the letter (or rather Phelippes's version of it, including the interpolated postscript) and it was not until early August that any arrests were made. He let the conspiracy run.

As the net closed around Babington and his accomplices, Poley was a ubiquitous presence among them. On about 23 July he is seen in Babington's company at the Three Tuns in Newgate Market. Five days later Poley, Babington and Savage are dining together at the Castle Inn near the Exchange. Another of their haunts was the Rose at Temple Bar.

On Tuesday 2 August Babington and a whole 'knot' of

conspirators – probably including 'Skyeres' or Nicholas Skeres – dined 'in Poley's garden'. These lodgings of Poley's were actually provided for him by the government. The house had been requisitioned from its owner, Anthony Hall, one of the Queen's messengers.

The following day, growing impatient, Walsingham wrote to Phelippes: 'I look to Poley, from whom I hope to receive some light.' That afternoon Poley came to Richmond to confer with Mr Secretary. Despite the part he has played in the entrapment, he is still an ambiguous quantity in Walsingham's eyes: 'I do not find but that Poley hath dealt honestly with me, yet I am loath to lay myself any way open to him.' Walsingham did not take Poley fully into his confidence at this meeting. He did not, for instance, tell him that arrests were imminent. He 'only delivered' to him 'such speeches as might work' on Babington, whom he still hoped to use as a weapon against other elements of the conspiracy, particularly the shadowy Ballard.

Poor Babington was becoming ever more reliant on Poley, yet also more uncertain about him. He even found Poley furtively copying the contents of his papers. As Poley relates it,

That same Tuesday afternoon [2 August] Babington showed me a sheet of paper of his own writing, which he said was the particulars of a letter written to him either by the Queen of Scots, else from someone near about her. And going abroad with Ballard and Savage he left it with me two or three hours, out of which paper before his return I had taken out certain principal notes.

Babington returned unexpectedly, and 'suddenly demanding the paper again all unawares, he saw the abstract I had taken'.

Poley makes light of it, rips up his copy: 'I rent it before his face, saying I would not keep any such papers.'

The game was nearly over now. Walsingham had kept Babington in play as long as he dared. The man was proving slippery. The risk that he might actually accomplish something – a risk implicit in every waiting-game – was growing. On 3 August, Walsingham instructed Phelippes: 'If your messenger receive not answer this day at Babington's hands, then it were not good to defer the apprehension of him, lest he should escape.' It was better, he had decided, 'to lack the answer than to lack the man'.

The following day, Thursday 4 August, John Ballard was arrested. Early that morning he arrived at Poley's 'garden house' to meet with Babington. The house was staked out by Walsingham's men. His trusty, Francis Milles, was in charge of the operation. He had a warrant for Ballard's arrest signed by the Lord Admiral: Walsingham was keen to distance himself as much as possible. The officer who would make the arrest was Mr Casey, deputy-alderman of Aldgate. The spy Nicholas Berden was there, also young Thomas Walsingham, seen conferring with Poley that morning.

They entered the house shortly before midday. Ballard went quietly. He was taken to the Counter prison in Wood Street. The whole matter, Milles wrote crisply to Walsingham, 'was handled so circumspectly that neither you nor any of yours need be known in the matter'.

At this turn of events Babington was, in Poley's words, 'much troubled and altered, both in hope and fear'. His immediate thought was to go personally to Walsingham, to pursue this fiction that he had intended all along to reveal Ballard's murderous intent. Poley thought this unwise: 'I counselled him rather to stay,' he says, 'whilst I went to court and signified Mr Secretary of him.' But what will Poley say to Walsingham? He will say, of course, that he was on the verge of getting Babington to reveal everything; that Ballard's arrest has compromised him, 'being done at my lodging'; and that Babington too would be compromised when the other conspirators learned of the arrest:

In fine I pursuaded him, for the better convey of his credit and mine, I would entreat Mr Secretary to remove Ballard secretly out of prison, as though he were discharged, as taken under a wrong name, and keep him unknown elsewhere for some five or six days.

In this 'unlikely hope' – Poley concludes laconically – 'I left him assured, and went to court.'

All this, I should add, is Poley's own account, in his later report to Walsingham. It is the only version of what passed between him and Babington at this moment of crisis.

That evening, when Poley failed to return to his lodgings, Babington feared the worst. He scrawled a last, despairing letter to Robin Poley, his affection for the man – perhaps even something more than affection – struggling with the doubts and forebodings that beset him:

Robyn—

Sollicitae non possunt cure mutare aranei stamina fusi! I am ready to endure whatsoever shall be inflicted, *et facere et paci Romanorum est.*

What my course has been towards Mr Secretary you can witness, what my love towards you, yourself best can tell. Proceedings at my lodgings have been very strange. I am the same I always pretended. I pray God you be, and ever so remain towards me.

Take heed of your own part, lest of these my misfortunes you bear the blame. *Est exilium inter malos vivere.*

Farewell, sweet Robyn, if as I take thee, true to me. If not, adieu, *omnium bipedum nequissimus.*

Return me thine answer for my satisfaction, and my diamond, and what else thou wilt. The furnace is prepared wherein our faith must be tried. Farewell till we meet, which God knows when.

Thine, how far thou knowest,

Anthony Babington

The conspirators scattered. Warrants were issued, watches put on the main roads out of London. Within a couple of days, Savage, Tichbourne and Tilney were taken, attempting to travel south. Babington headed northwards, with a couple of companions. They holed up in the wilderness of St John's Wood. There they were joined by Robert Barnwell and Harry Dunne. They lived wild in the wood for eight days. Half-starved and filthy they reached Uxendon, near Harrow, the home of a Catholic family, the Bellamys. Here they were given food and refuge. They were housed in a barn, like itinerant labourers. They put on rough smocks, cut their hair short, and stained their skins with walnut juice.

But there was talk, and suspicion, and on Sunday 14 August, the authorities raided Uxendon. The conspirators were arrested, together with their abettors, Bartholomew and Jeremy Bellamy. The following morning they were brought up to London. Order was given for the church bells to be rung in thanksgiving for the Queen's safe deliverance.

The interrogations then began, and the painstaking search into every nook and cranny of the conspiracy. Wives, mothers, servants, messengers, bystanders, and friends of friends were hauled in to give evidence. Reams of paper were filled with questions and answers, confessions and briefs. For all the exhaustive documentation, little is said about the duplex parts played by Barnard Maude and Robert Poley, and even less about Gilbert Gifford, now cooling his heels in Paris, far from suspicion.

On 13 September 1586, Babington, Ballard, Savage, Barnwell, Dunne, Tichbourne and Salisbury appeared before a commission of Oyer and Terminer at Westminster, charged with high treason. Ballard, who had suffered worst in the interrogations, was unable to walk. He was carried into court in a chair. Two days later seven others were charged as co-conspirators. Jeremy Bellamy, one of the harbourers at Uxendon, was charged as an accessory after the fact. His brother Bartholomew had died in the interim. Officially, he had 'strangled himself' in prison.

Guilt was a foregone conclusion, but the trial ground on through the all-important formalities. The prosecution, led by Sir Christopher Hatton, was the usual hectoring tirade that passed for judicial proceeding. By the evening of 16

September, the defendants had all been found guilty of treason, and condemned to death.

The sentence was carried out over two days, 20 and 21 September, at a specially constructed gallows on St Giles's Fields, close to Babington's chambers in Holborn. There were the usual preliminaries: the drawing of the men on 'sleds' through the streets, their speeches from the scaffold, exhortations from onlookers to repent their Popish ways.

During his speech, Charles Tilney was challenged on a point of doctrine by a Protestant minister, Dr White. He answered: 'I came hither to die, Doctor, not to argue.'

On the first day, Ballard, Babington, Savage, Barnwell, Tichbourne, Tilney and Abingdon were executed, in that order. The killing was done with maximum cruelty. Each man was left to hang for only a few moments after the cart was driven away. They were then cut down, fully conscious, to be butchered: first 'their privities cut off', then 'bowelled alive and seeing', then quartered. Savage, a big man, broke the rope on his first swing, and was disembowelled without even hanging.

The following day the executions were more humane. It was later explained:

> The Queen, being informed of the severity used in the executions the day before, and detesting such cruelty, gave express orders that these should be used more favourably.

They were therefore 'permitted' to hang until they were 'quite dead'. This royal intercession strikes one less as a tardy scrap of humanity, more as a small directorial adjustment to the playing of the final scene.

And what of Poley?

He was himself arrested during the round-up of the conspirators, and on 18 August – four days after the apprehension of Babington at Uxendon – he was committed to the Tower, 'charged to have dealt treacherously'. His imprisonment was, and is, widely held to be a bluff: an extension of his cover as Babington's confidant. Not to have arrested him would have been an admission of his role as the government's 'projector'.

It is also true to say that there were, as always, genuine doubts about Poley. Francis Milles was particularly suspicious. When he arrested Ballard at Poley's lodgings, he also confiscated from the house a packet of letters, 'sealed with Poley's seal'. These he forwarded to Walsingham later that day, and in a covering note he wrote: 'P. is a notable knave, with no trust in him.' (In the Calendar of State Papers, 'P' is glossed as Phelippes, but it is obviously Poley.) The spy Berden also doubted Poley's role in the later stages: by mid-July, he believed, Babington had 'long since discovered' Poley. For Walsingham, the same question mark as always hung over Poley's actions. He was giving intelligence to the government, but what was he giving to the other side? How much was he telling Babington? How much room was he giving him? There exists, in Walsingham's own hand, a list of 'Questions whereof Pooley is to be charged'. The first is this: 'That he had conference with Babington apart, a little before his departure.' This presumably refers to the conversation between Poley and Babington on 4 August, shortly after the arrest of Ballard. Did he tip Babington off, that all further dealing with Walsingham was hopeless?

Poley had been a useful piece in Mr Secretary's 'game at chess'. Hereafter it was convenient to consider him as a suspect, both for reasons of cover and because of these doubts.

Shortly after his arrival at the Tower Poley penned his 'confession' or report. It is twelve pages long, an extensive diary of his dealings with Babington from their first meeting in mid-June to their hurried farewell on the afternoon of 4 August. For all its volubility, it is a typical piece of Poleyesque elusiveness. It has little to say about his own motives, and it omits much that might be damaging to him or to Walsingham: there is no mention, for instance, of his provocations about the killing of Leicester, as recorded in Babington's confession. The whole narrative is a masterpiece of blandness: brisk in tone, tedious in detail. He was a go-between, no more: an honest broker. He was certainly not a conspirator, nor really a spy, just a 'true subject' trying to do everyone a good turn.

In these letters and reports that Poley has left us, we perhaps learn more about him from the frozen gesture of his handwriting, than we do from the words which he wrote. The hand is graceful, sinuous, light of touch, with tall showy loops and balloons. It is a strangely attenuated, disconnected script, of the type known to graphologists as 'thread-writing'. Individual letters are seldom joined: the pen has not flowed across the page, as it at first appears, but has made a series of minuscule jumps. In his signature, the roundel of the 'P' is millimetres away from the downstroke, hovering like a bee about to feed. Thus Poley left his mark: these flourishes of ink, and this emptiness between them.

The imprisoning of Poley fooled few Catholics. As news of the fall of the conspirators travelled through the country, with it went the word that Poley had been the traitor in their midst. On 19 September, one of Walsingham's agents, Maliverny Catlin, wrote to him with information gathered during a spell among the Catholics of the North:

> There is one Robert Poole alias Polley the Papists give out to be the broacher of the last treason. They rest persuaded that his committing to the Tower was but to blind the world after he had revealed Babington and his complices. He in troth consorted with them by the Council's direction.

The Jesuit Robert Southwell took an equally sceptical view of Poley's imprisonment. It was only 'for a fashion', he says: 'a little large imprisonment, more for policy than punishment'. This is, he claims, the only explanation of Poley's escape from any direr consequences, for he was

> as deeply to be touched in all things, and as much to be proved against him, as any that were executed. He was

191

continually with Babington and Ballard. He heard mass, confessed, and in all things feigned to be a Catholic.

For Southwell, there is no shadow of doubt that the government was responsible for the entire plot: 'the matter of Babington was wholly of their plotting and forging, of purpose to make Catholics odious and to cut off the Queen of Scots.' Babington and his accomplices were 'drawn blindfold to be the workers of their own overthrow'. This was why they were allowed to remain free so long: weeks before their apprehension, they were 'pointed at in the streets of London, and yet not touched until the matter was brought to that pass to which the Council would have it come'. He accuses Walsingham, Leicester and Burghley as the 'chief plotters', and Poley as the 'chief actor in it here in England':

It is known to all that Poolie, being Sir Francis Walsingham's man, and throughly seasoned to his master's tooth, was the chief instrument to contrive and prosecute the matter, and to draw into the net such green wits, as (partly fearing the general oppression, partly angled with golden hooks) might easily be overwrought by Master Secretary's subtle and sifting wit.

This was a Catholic's view of Poley's role, written five years after the event, but it was not a view confined to Catholics. William Camden's version, in his *Annals of England*, gives much the same leading role to Poley, or 'Poll', whom he describes as a 'most cunning counterfeiter and dissembler'.

Poley enters the grim portals of the Tower on 18 August 1586. He was there on that morning in September when Babington and the others were marched down from the death-cells, strapped to the hurdles in Tower Yard, and hauled off to execution. One can only guess – hardly even that – at his feelings as the men he had helped to betray were taken away.

On 25 September, Poley is one of the prisoners in the

Tower described as 'fit to be further examined'. There is uncertainty about his status: next to his name is written, 'the matter evident against him, but Mr Secretary to be conferred withal therein'. Mr Secretary decided it was best to hold him, and a list of prisoners in the Tower on 30 November, drawn up by Walsingham himself, includes 'Ro Pooley', and next to his name the words, 'to be continued'.

He remained in the Tower for a little over two years, in fact: a brief spell by Elizabethan standards. Southwell describes it as 'a little large imprisonment' – by 'large' he means that Poley was there under a relaxed régime, rather than 'close' or 'straight' imprisonment. While there, Southwell says, 'he had what he would'. The quarterly bills drawn up by the Lieutenant of the Tower, Sir Owen Hopton, show his fees as amounting to £1 2s 4d per week (13s 4d for board and lodging, 5s for a keeper, and 4s for 'fuel and candle').

While in the Tower, Poley resumed his old role of prison informer. In 1587 he wrote twice to Walsingham about a fellow-prisoner named Andrews or Anderson. He is still in touch with the spymaster, still full of glib airy promises of service. He also maintained contact with Christopher Blount, now knighted by Leicester, and fighting in Flanders. Letters from Blount were delivered to him by his old prison-flame, Joan Yeomans. She is still closely involved in Poley's affairs. Her husband describes how he once found her with one of these letters from Blount, and how she threw it on the fire rather than let him read it.

According to some, Poley's role in the Tower stepped beyond the work of an informer. The Jesuit Southwell claimed that he 'there poisoned the Bishop of Armacan with a piece of cheese that he sent him.' Richard Creagh, Archbishop of Armagh, had been a prisoner of the English for over twenty years. He was 'a dangerous man to be among the Irish, for the reverence that is by the nation borne unto him.' His last appearance in the Tower lists was on 30 November 1586. There is no evidence he was poisoned, but the rumour was widely believed, with Poley as the chief suspect. Many years later, a captured Catholic called Nicholas Williamson alleged that Poley had 'poisoned the Bishop of Divelinge' (i.e. Dublin). This is probably a garbled version of the same rumour.

Poley was not the only government man in the Tower at this time. There was also George Gifford, the cousin of Gilbert, who was committed 'upon suspicion for divers causes' in early August. His elegant carved graffiti can still be seen on the walls of the Beauchamp Tower: *Dolor patientia vincitur* ('Sorrow is conquered by patience') and – a tag for these paranoid times – *Mala conscientia facit ut tuta timeantur* ('A bad conscience makes what is safe seem fearful'). Another of these twilight operators was an Irishman named Michael Moody, imprisoned in the Tower in January 1587 for his part in the so-called 'Stafford Plot'. It was claimed that Moody had offered to kill the Queen, by placing a 'train of gunpowder' under her bed, and that the instigator of the plot was Monsieur des Trappes, chief secretary to the French ambassador, Chateauneuf. In fact this episode has all the markings of a Walsingham sham-plot, the chief purpose of which was to embarrass the French ambassador, and to render him incommunicado during the trial and execution of Mary Stuart, which was deeply deplored in France. The Stafford plot was little more than a brief epilogue to the 'tragedy' of the Babington plot: a last turn of the screw. Poley and Moody are men of the same stamp: players in the secret theatre, provokers of sedition, pledgers of false vows. They now had leisure, in the long Tower days of 1587, to get to know one another. Moody also struck up an acquaintance in the Tower with a Catholic prisoner named James Tipping. Four years later we will find Poley, Moody and Tipping all operating in the same intelligence network, in the Netherlands, in close proximity to Christopher Marlowe.

Poley was released from the Tower in September or October ('about Michaelmas') 1588. He immediately went to lodge with the Yeomans, and lavished '£40 at the least' furnishing his room there. William Yeomans, understandably, 'made very great moan that Poley was come to lodge'. His friend

Richard Ede, gate-keeper at the Marshalsea, commiserated. It were best to be rid of this man Poley, Ede advised. For if not, 'he will beguile you either of your wife, or of your life'.

Poley bragged to Yeomans about his release. 'Had not I good luck to get out of the Tower?' he said. 'Mr Secretary did deliver me out.'

'You are greatly beholding unto Mr Secretary.'

'Nay,' says Poley. 'He is more beholding unto me than I am unto him, for there are further matters between him and me than all the world shall know of.'

It is just another of Poley's brags, but there is truth in it, and from the time of his release Poley found regular employment in government service. In November or early December 1588, he received his first official commission from Walsingham. He journeyed to Denmark, and 'brought letters in post for Her Majesty's affairs from the King of Denmark to the Court at Richmond'. For this he was paid £15, on a warrant signed by Walsingham on 27 December. The following summer he was sent on a similar mission to the Netherlands. His career now enters a new, more secure phase of regular work as a 'messenger of the court' – a designation that covers a multitude of intelligence activities. Between 1588 and 1601, when he disappears from the record, he travelled on at least thirty separate missions. The Babington plot was the making of Robert Poley. Walsingham never grew to like him, I think, but he grew convinced of his expertise. It was one of the spymaster's maxims that 'knowledge is never too dear', and part of the price he paid was his dependence on knaves like Poley. As Sir Edward Stafford once put it: 'I am of a mind to use the Devil himself well, if he comes to me in the likeness of a man to serve the Queen withal.'

PART FOUR

POETS AND SPIES

18

'OUR BEST FOR PLOTTING'

RICHARD BAINES AND Robert Poley are the kind of men
Marlowe was mixing with when he entered the periphery of
Sir Francis Walsingham's intelligence service in about 1585.
There are others he might have known – Gilbert Gifford, for
instance – but these two stand out because of their involve-
ment, some eight years later, in the matter of his death.
(Gifford was himself dead by then: a sordid end in a prison in
Paris at the age of thirty.)

These are devious, predatory, deceitful men. There is – in
Poley and Gifford, at least – a certain brilliance of opportunism, a dangerous spark which I find alluring though I do not
wish to. But this does not alter the sense of their basic
nastiness. We are brought back to the same question that
hangs over the meeting at Deptford: why is Marlowe to be
found in this bad company?

One answer is easily made: Marlowe becomes mixed up in
this world because it is a way forward. It puts money in his
purse, gets him noticed, gives him *entrée* to influential circles.
The desire for 'advancement' – the 'devil' of ambition, as
Baines would have it – brings him here. This is one reason, but
not one that tells us much about Marlowe himself. There were
thousands of ambitious young men in England, but they did
not all become spies.

Another answer might be that Marlowe enters this devious,
predatory company because he was himself a devious,
predatory young man. This is possible but not provable.
Thomas Kyd said of him, 'he was intemperate & of a cruel

199

heart'. He spoke of Marlowe's 'rashness' in 'attempting sudden privy injuries to men'. This seems to chime in with the spy's mentality: this cruelty of heart, these secret woundings. But we know that Kyd's comments about Marlowe were uttered under pressure, in the shadow of the rack-house: he was saying what someone wanted him to say. His comments are, anyway, only one perception of Marlowe. They must be put alongside the words of others – Nashe, Peele, Chapman, Edward Blount – which testify to him as a friend. Kyd calls him cruel but another poet (identified only as 'J.M.': it may be John Marston or Jervis Markham) calls him 'kind Kit Marlowe'.

For all this, Kyd's words are troubling: a young man with a 'cruel heart'. A similar impression of Marlowe seeps in continuously from reading and watching his plays. They are 'cruel' in their frequent depiction of brutality, but more than that they have a certain mental ambience: sardonic and bleak. T.S. Eliot saw Marlowe's dramatic mode as not so much tragedy as a kind of 'serious, even savage' farce. Perhaps, in this chilliness that lies behind the often passionate lyricism of his poetry, we see something of the spy's *sang-froid*.

There is also an undercurrent of equivocation in his plays. Beneath their overt political message, which is orthodox and nationalistic, there are those other messages, a hidden agenda of irony. A good example is the *Massacre at Paris*. In its protagonist, the Duke of Guise, Marlowe raises up an historical bogeyman, the murderer of Protestants, and portrays him as a full-blown Machiavellian villain. In this sense the play is straight anti-Catholic propaganda, but it is full of contradictory signals which – particularly the equivocal portrait of the Protestant champion, Henri of Navarre – tend to blur the propaganda into a general dark comment about the cynical pragmatism of these religious wars. Given the prominence of the St Bartholomew's Eve atrocity in the Protestant imagination, this undertone is provocative. Marlowe's play was performed in January 1593. Henri of Navarre was by then King Henri IV of France, though it was not until July of that year that he renounced the Protestant cause for which he had fought, and was embraced into the Catholic church. In this case, Marlowe's covert ironies proved accurate enough.

Something similar goes on in *The Jew of Malta*, where Marlowe uses a racist stereotype of the Jew, but then applies its features of greed and predation to the Christians and the Muslim Turks who are the Jew's adversaries. Other Marlowe treatments – of Tamburlaine, of Dr Faustus, of Edward II – have this same ambiguity, this toying with the audience's expectations. Here is a brutal tyrant, a heretical magician, a besotted homosexual unfit to rule. And yet, and yet, there are these other ways of seeing them, these ambidextrous responses.

These plays are markers, nothing more, of Marlowe's mentality. A play is an artefact, not a personal manifesto. It is made to meet certain demands: formal, commercial, social. But it is not hard to envisage the man that wrote these plays also turning his hand – with some success, as it appears – to the 'secret theatre' of espionage.

How far Marlowe's intelligence activities actually provided material for his plays is difficult to say. His knowledge of French politics in *Massacre at Paris* is detailed and acute, but as much of it can be traced to the news-pamphlets of the day, it is not necessarily inside knowledge. On the whole, the idea of trawling Marlowe's playhouse work for matters of State seems to me of limited use. Or rather, it seems to ask the wrong kind of question about the relationship between Marlowe's work as a poet and his position as a government agent. There certainly *is* a relationship: the young man who was described in 1587 as working 'for the benefit of his country' was also the young man who had by then written his marvellous translations of Ovid and Lucan, and such early theatrical pieces as *Dido, Queen of Carthage*, the first part of *Tamburlaine*, and perhaps (though this is controversial) an early version of *Dr Faustus*. They are not separate people: they are one and the same Kit Marlowe.

The interesting question is not how much his political position influenced his work as a writer, but the opposite question, the one that no-one has asked: how much did his position as a writer influence his political work?

Marlowe was not the first nor the last writer to become entangled in the world of espionage. The roster – hardly a roll of honour – runs from Geoffrey Chaucer to the late Graham Greene, and includes Ben Jonson, Andrew Marvell, Daniel Defoe, Somerset Maugham, Erskine Childers, Rudyard Kipling and Ian Fleming. Marlowe's involvement in government service is in this sense just one instance of a frequent intersection of the literary world and the intelligence fraternity.

In the fast-expanding area of Elizabethan espionage, writers were an obvious source of recruits. They were intelligent, educated, observant young men. They knew the international language, Latin, and the literary tastes of the day gave them a good smattering of French and Italian. They were mobile people: geographically mobile – young men disposed to travel and see the world – but also socially mobile. In a class-ridden society, the literary *demi-monde* floated free, touching at once the back-streets of London and the heights of the nobility. They were also continually in need of cash. Authorship was becoming a recognisable profession, rather than a gentleman's pastime, but it was not one that paid much. A big name like Robert Greene might command a fee of 20 nobles (£6 13s 4d) for a play, but most scribbled for derisory rates. The standard payment for a pamphlet was 'forty shillings and an odd pottle of wine', with not a whiff of copyright thereafter.

With these aptitudes, and these needs, it is perhaps not surprising that a number of Elizabethan writers crop up in the files of the intelligence services, both foreign and domestic. They are remembered now as poets, pamphleteers and playwrights, but down there in the reality of their lives they had to profess other skills if they were to survive.

Some found employment as official couriers and clerks, like the poet Edmund Spenser, who carried diplomatic despatches from France in the autumn of 1569. He was at this time still a student at Cambridge, as was Marlowe when he entered government service. Another early example is George Gascoigne, a popular and innovative poet of the 1570s. He served as a soldier and intelligencer in the Low Countries, and was esteemed by the Prince of Orange. He was in Antwerp when the city fell to the Spanish in 1576. He witnessed the carnage at first hand, and spent three months in the occupied city: the famous stock-exchange was filled with dicing-tables, and the Spaniard 'jetted up and down the street with his harlot'. Gascoigne lived to tell his tale, and he told it in print. *The Spoil of Antwerp* – 'faithfully reported by a true Englishman, who was present at the same' – was published later that year. It is a crackling piece of front-line journalism. Among the various reasons for a writer entering this sort of world is the simple one of good copy.

Gascoigne died while Marlowe was still a schoolboy, and he is a rather different sort of intelligencer from the informers and projectors of the Walsingham world. He comes into the business from the military end, and though he was described as a spy, he is more in the mould of that respected Elizabethan type, the 'soldier-poet', whose motto was '*Tam Marti quam Mercurii*': as much for the god of war as for the god of eloquence.

A man much closer to Marlowe in time and circumstance was the poet Samuel Daniel, author of the influential sonnet-sequence *Delia*. In late 1585, having recently left Oxford without taking a degree, Daniel was 'licensed' by Sir Francis Walsingham to 'travel into France'. This was not a recruitment as such: Daniel's intention was, as he puts it, 'to study, to the end to render myself fit for the service of my country'. By 'study' he means to observe: he calls Paris 'the theatre of Europe', where 'may be descried the conduct and managing of this admirable time'. He wishes to be a political observer for Walsingham, an intelligencer in the non-covert sense. He hopes his 'slender ability' will be thought worthy of this. He took up lodgings at the sign of the Fleur de Lys, on Rue St Jacques – the same street where Gilbert Gifford sometimes lodged, at the sign of the Elephant. Later he was employed by

Sir Edward Stafford, the English ambassador in Paris, perhaps filling the post of embassy chaplain. He became a part of Stafford's retinue at just the time when the Ambassador – an extremely tricky character himself – was involved in Walsingham's moves against Rheims, and was dealing daily with people like Gifford, Morgan and Salomon Aldred. He is the poet on the sidelines of the plotting. On 20 May 1586, 'from my chamber in my Lord Ambassador's house in Paris', he wrote plaintively to Walsingham: he has received no reply to his previous letters, is uncertain if they have got through, or if they have been 'accepted *sereno fronte* or not, coming from the experience of a raw traveller'. He renews his offers of service, and sends further information about the 'affairs of this afflicted country', some of it rather faulty. The letter was, he adds apologetically, 'written in haste'. All this has the feel of a young man fishing for preferment, and Walsingham too busy even to notice him.

Daniel landed back in England, at Rye, on Sunday 4 September 1586. His return was duly noted by the Rye 'searcher', Henry Gaymer, whose job was to keep a 'register of men's names to and fro'. Daniel is described as a 'servant unto my Lord Stafford'. Gaymer was far more interested in one of the men travelling with him. This man went under the name of Julio Martino, an Italian, but 'it is said his name is Renney, and a poisoner'. He was, in fact, the assassin of the Queen of Navarre, usually called Renat or Renato, who had poisoned her 'with a venomed smell of a pair of perfumed gloves'. He appears in Marlowe's *Massacre at Paris* as the 'Pothecarie'. This is a moment of physical contact on that borderline between literature and politics: the mild-mannered poet and the Italian assassin on a pinnace bound for Rye.

Daniel received 20 marks (£5) for 'bringing letters in post for Her Majesty's affairs', and that is the last we hear of him in government affairs. His future lay with the Countess of Pembroke, in whose household at Wilton he lived for many years. On his death in 1619 Ben Jonson said of him, 'Samuel Daniel was a good honest man': hence perhaps his failure to prosper in Walsingham's service.

Both Gascoigne and Daniel were cogs in the Elizabethan intelligence machine, but they were not spies in the full sense of the word. One Elizabethan writer who certainly was a spy – and who certainly was not a 'good honest man' – is Anthony Munday. Munday was a prolific poet, romancer, balladeer and dramatist, whose published work spans over forty years. He was a hack, but a very popular one. Francis Meres called him 'our best for plotting', a facility which served him well in his other career.

Munday was, like the shady Nicholas Skeres, the son of a London draper. In his youth, according to a contemporary, he 'first was a stage player' and 'after an apprentice'. He was actually apprenticed on his sixteenth birthday, to the book-seller John Allde, so if this is correct he must have been treading the boards in his early teens: a boy-actor playing female roles, perhaps. In 1578, after two years of apprenticeship, he skipped his indenture and left for Europe. The following February, under the alias of 'Antonius Auleus', he enrolled at the English College at Rome.

Among those studying or employed at the Rome seminary in 1579 were Gilbert Gifford and Salomon Aldred, both later Walsingham agents, and Charles Sledd, the serving-man at the College, whose diary of Catholic activities on the continent proved particularly useful to the government. Whether any of these was already on Walsingham's pay-roll is a moot point, but they were showing promise in that direction, chiefly as promoters of the various factions and 'broils' that split the College at this time. Munday threw himself wholeheartedly into these, so much so that he was removed from the 'roll of scholars' and 'made to sleep in a cupboard in disgrace'. He is much the same kind of stirrer and enticer as Baines was at Rheims, who was also locked up in a *cubiculum* for his pains. Munday left Rome in the spring of 1579 and travelled to Paris. He was probably the 'young man called Anthony' who turned up at Rheims on 9 July. A few days later he returned to England.

Throughout the 1580s, Munday worked as an informer

and pursuivant. He was described by the rackmaster Topcliffe as a man 'who wants no sort of wit', and he was employed as one of the Messengers of the Queen's Chamber, a courtly title which belies their work as secret policemen. Among his colleagues was Anthony Hall, the skinner who provided Poley's lodgings during the Babington affair; and Henry Maunder, who brought Marlowe in from Scadbury in 1593.

Munday's earliest literary works are crude tracts of anti-Catholic propaganda. His account of the capture of the Jesuit Edmund Campion was on sale within a few days of the event itself (though according to George Elliot, the man who actually betrayed Campion, it was as far from the truth 'as an egg is contrary in likeness to an oyster'). At Campion's trial, both Munday and Charles Sledd gave evidence for the prosecution: they had known him personally at Rome. And when Campion was executed at Tyburn in December 1581, there was Munday at the gallows, note-book in hand. His *Discovery of Edmund Campion*, published shortly afterwards, gives an eye-witness account of those gruesome last rites. On the title-page of this book he signs himself 'A.M., sometime the Pope's scholar, allowed in the Seminary at Rome amongst them'. This was to give the impression that he was a Catholic who had seen the error of his ways. It was also a puff for his forthcoming book, a journalistic account of his experiences at the seminary, *The English Romayne Life*, published the following year.

In 1584, again at Tyburn, Munday was at hand for the execution of another priest he had known at Rome, George Haddock. As he stood with the noose round his neck, Haddock was urged by one of the sheriffs to confess and recant. Haddock spoke touchingly of his loyalty to the Queen: 'I have said this morning these many paternosters for her, and I pray God she may reign long Queen. If I had her in the wilderness I would not for all the world put a pin towards her with intent to hurt her.'

The sheriff broke in. 'There is since thy arraignment worse matter found against thee.'

At this point Anthony Munday was brought forward. He asked Haddock to recall a time when they had been 'walking together at Rome', and one of their company had uttered seditious words about 'wishing the heads' of three of the Privy Council. 'Whereupon you said, Mr Haddock, "To make up a mass, I would we had the head of the Queen."'

Haddock protested that he had never said these words, but he was in no position to argue. The sheriff cried, 'Away with the traitor!' After he had hanged for a few moments he was cut down, and when 'the tormentor was in pulling out of his bowels, Mr Haddock was in life'.

This stagey performance at Tyburn is probably the low point of my estimation of Anthony Munday.

In the later 1580s he turned his attentions to the other end of the religious spectrum, and worked for the government in tracking down Puritan extremists. In December 1588, in his capacity as the 'Archbishop's pursuivant', he arrested the Puritan preacher Giles Wiggington, and escorted him by boat to Lambeth Palace for questioning. During the journey he wheedled information out of Wiggington, which he promptly relayed to the Archbishop. Munday was part of the team which worked against the clandestine authors and printers of the 'Martin Marprelate' tracts – militant Puritan pamphlets which poked ribald fun at the Anglican hierarchy – and he was probably among the writers commissioned to answer these pamphlets 'after their own vein of writing'. Such anonymous pieces of anti-Martinist doggerel as *A Whip for an Ape* and *Mar-Martin* may be his.

In one of the Marprelate pamphlets, the author imagines the Archbishop exhorting his pursuivants, and exclaiming against Master Munday: 'Ah, thou Judas, thou that has betrayed the papists, I think thou meanest to betray us also.'

Munday's is an unsavoury career, but it is a fascinating instance of this cross-over between the world of the writer and the spy. All the while he was betraying and persecuting Catholics, he was entertaining the public with such popular romances as *Palmarin of England*, and volumes of poetry with sickly titles like *A Banquet of Dainty Conceits*. He was not much liked by other writers – Nashe is rude about him, and Ben Jonson ridicules him as Antonio Balladino in *The*

Case is Altered – but there is a troubling sort of parallel between his two careers. Topcliffe, the government torturer, commends his 'wit'. Meres, the man of letters, commends his 'plotting'. The writer and the spy perform in different arenas, but their skills are similar.

19

THOMAS WATSON

THOSE MEN ARE poets involved, like Marlowe, in some aspect of the Elizabethan intelligence service, yet none of them has any particular connection with him, and none of them sounds very like him. George Gascoigne is a hard-bitten soldier, not a callow young Cambridge scholar. Samuel Daniel is closer in time and type, and he is close to Walsingham's intrigues against Rheims, but he is on the sidelines. His service remains at the level of hopeful entreaty, and nothing he did, as far as I can see, would have merited the special intervention of the Privy Council, had he needed it. As for Anthony Munday, I can only state my belief that Marlowe was not this kind of government thug and gallows-hunter.

But there is another poet glimpsed in the secret world of the 1580s. He is an elusive and engaging figure, he was a close friend of Marlowe's, and he opens up some rather interesting connections.

Thomas Watson is best-known for his sonnet-sequence *Ekatompathia* (1582), and his Latin pastorals, *Amintas* (1585) and *Amintae Gaudia* (1592). The latter, published posthumously, appeared with an elegant Latin dedication to the Countess of Pembroke, signed by his friend, 'C.M.'. He is little read now, but he was one of the most admired poets of his time. When Shakespeare's narrative poems were published in the early 1590s, he was praised as 'Watson's heir'. He was an eclectic, cosmopolitan man: a scholar of the law, a writer on philosophy and science, a translator accomplished in French, Italian, Latin and Greek. Despite his learned output, he came to depend, as so many did, on writing for the popular stage. Francis Meres praises him for tragedy, but another implies comedy when he says of him: 'he could devise twenty fictions and knaveries in a play, which was his daily practice and his living.' None of his plays in English has survived.

'Witty Tom Watson' was a popular figure on the literary circuit. Among his friends were John Lyly, George Peele and Matthew Roydon, all of whom contributed verses to *Ekatompathia*. He in turn wrote Latin verses for Robert Greene, in the preface to Greene's love-pamphlet, *Ciceronis Amor*. Thomas Nashe was a great admirer: 'he was a man that I dearly loved and honoured,' Nashe wrote after Watson's death in 1592, 'and for all things hath left few his equals in England'. He recalled a night on the town with Watson, when they drank at the Nag's Head in Cheapside, and Watson entertained him with spurious tales and doggerel poems about the follies of Gabriel Harvey.

Watson's friendship with Marlowe probably goes back a while, but it steps into sharp physical focus on a day in September 1589. They are on the outskirts of London, on Hog Lane, a dirt road running west from Shoreditch to Finsbury Fields. These were the 'liberties': areas beyond the city walls, and therefore outside the city's jurisdiction. Here, among 'base tenements' and 'poor cottages' and 'alleys backward', the actors and playwrights of the day found cheap and convenient lodgings, close to London's first purpose-built playhouses, the Theatre and the Curtain. Both Marlowe and Watson lived close by, in the area just south of Shoreditch called Norton Folgate. They were neighbours, possibly roommates.

The incident that brings them into focus is one of violence, and death, and it is – as in the case of Marlowe's own death four years later – a coroner's inquest that tells the story.

On Hog Lane, between two and three o'clock on the afternoon of 18 September 1589, Marlowe was fighting with an innkeeper's son named William Bradley. It is not stated who started the fight, nor what weapons were being used. It may have been a deadly duel, or it may have been little more than a scuffle after an alcoholic lunch. As they fought, people in the street raised a 'clamour'.

Thomas Watson now appeared on the scene. Seeing the two men fighting, he drew his sword and intervened. He later claimed that he did so to 'separate' them, and to 'preserve the Queen's peace'. At this point Marlowe drew back and took no further part in the fight.

Bradley turned to Watson. He saw him with sword drawn. 'Art thou now come?' he shouted. 'Then I will have a bout with thee!'

Instantly he 'leapt upon' Watson, and 'then and there, with a sword and a dagger of iron and steel, he struck, wounded and maltreated the said Thomas Watson so that there was fear for his life.' Watson defended himself, but he was driven back, and retreated as far as the ditch that ran along the roadside. Still Bradley came at him. Watson, unable to retreat any further, then struck Bradley with his sword. The point of the sword penetrated six inches into the right side of Bradley's chest. From this wound, William Bradley 'then and there instantly died'.

Like Ingram Frizer at Deptford, Watson and Marlowe stood their ground. They were arrested by the constable of the precinct, Stephen Wyld, a tailor, and marched off to the nearest Justice. This was Sir Owen Hopton, Lieutenant of the Tower of London, whose home was at Norton Folgate.

Later that day they were led to Newgate prison, where they were committed, in the dog-Latin of a prison official, 'pro suspicione murdri'. Watson is styled generosus, a gentleman, while Marlowe is called 'yeoman'. Both are described as lately resident in Norton Folgate. If Newgate tradition then followed, the two poets were taken – as all those under a charge of felony were – to the dungeon called the Limboes, 'a dark, opace, wild room', illuminated by a single candle set on a black stone. Here they were left to sweat, among the rats and the straw and the moans of the gaol-fevered.

The following day the inquest was held at Finsbury, presided over by the Middlesex coroner, Mr Chalkhill. Twelve jurors, under the foremanship of Geoffrey Whitworth, a Shoreditch tallow-chandler, viewed the body of William Bradley, and heard the testimony of witnesses, presumably including Marlowe and Watson. The finding of the inquest – as in the later case of Ingram Frizer – was that Watson had killed his man in self-defence. They were then returned to Newgate. Marlowe, not touched with any crime, was now entitled to bail, though it took him nearly two weeks to arrange the necessary sureties. On 1 October 1589 he was bailed for £40 upon a promise to appear in person when the case came up at the next Sessions. His sureties were Richard Kitchen, attorney of Clifford's Inn, and Humphrey Rowland, horner.

Marlowe was now a free man, but Tom Watson remained in 'The Stink'. The case was heard at the Old Bailey on 3 December. The court found no cause to doubt the correctness of the coroner's verdict. Marlowe, who was there to satisfy his bond, was discharged. Watson was returned to Newgate to await 'the grace of the Queen'. This took a further two months, and it was not until 10 February 1590 that Watson at last received the pardon *se defendendo* that brought his freedom.

For Marlowe's biographers, the Hog Lane incident is a vivid, beautiful footnote. It takes us straight to Marlowe in his physical and social landscape: young men out in the shanty-town suburbs of London, poets with 'muses so mutinous, as every stanzo they pen after supper is sharp-pointed with a stab'. It takes us also to Thomas Watson, who proves to be another piece in this jigsaw of Marlowe's political career.

There is every indication that Watson was born and brought up a Catholic. He was a Londoner, born in the parish of St Helen's, Bishopsgate, but in 1567, at the age of eleven, he was sent to school in Winchester. This had a strong Catholic presence among the staff. An exact contemporary of his was Henry Garnett, who later became the chief representative of the Jesuits in England. According to his early biographers, Garnett was converted to Catholicism while at Winchester, and he later emigrated to Italy in the company of another Catholic Wykehamist, George Gallop. Another schoolfellow was Christopher Parkins, who also left England to become a Jesuit, though he was later turned, and worked for English intelligence.

Watson followed a similar course. He studied briefly at Oxford, then in 1570, aged thirteen or fourteen, he embarked for Europe. 'I devoted my early years to study,' he later wrote, 'and far from my native land I spent a *lustrum* and a half, learning to utter words of diverse sound'. A *lustrum* is five years, so Watson's travels on the continent lasted over seven years. He learned the 'language and manners' of Italy and France – this is reflected in his cosmopolitan poetry – and studied canon and civil law, though in France 'wars often hindered my study'. In 1576 Watson surfaces at the English College at Douai, in Flanders, the same Catholic seminary which later removed to Rheims. The College diaries do not mention his arrival, but record some of his later movements. On 15 October 1576, 'Dominus Watsonus went from here to Paris'. The following May he returned from Paris, and 'after some days was admitted into our community'. In July he left the College, and on 7 August 1577 embarked for England.

Two years later we find Watson lodging in Westminster, 'in a house of one Waller', where he 'did now and then lie with one Mr Beale, a preacher, & his acquaintance in Oxford before'. It may be around this time that Watson made the acquaintance of the historian William Camden, who was deputy headmaster at Westminster school. Camden contributed verses to Watson's *Antigone*. The poet Spenser was also living in Westminster at this time, and the literary group known as the Areopagus – featuring Spenser, Sir Philip Sidney, Edward Dyer, Gabriel Harvey and others – met there. Watson may have been loosely involved with these writers and their little 'senate'. He was also cultivating other literary friendships: with that 'dapper and deft companion' John Lyly, the famous author of *Euphues*; with George Peele and Matthew Roydon, both later friends of Marlowe; and with other minor poets like George Buc, Thomas Acheley and

Christopher Ocland. Out of this early grouping emerged the dominant literary set of the late 1580s, the so-called 'University Wits'.

Watson's early Catholic profile – the scholar at Winchester, the wandering émigré in Europe, the visitor to the seminary at Douai – becomes still clearer with the publication of his first book, a Latin version of *Antigone*, in 1581. This was dedicated to Philip Howard, Earl of Arundel. The Howards were the premier Catholic family in England. Young Arundel's father was Thomas Howard, 3rd Duke of Norfolk, who had been executed in 1572 for treasonable dealings with Mary Queen of Scots. His godfather was the King of Spain. He was also a former pupil of Gregory Martin, the Catholic scholar and translator of the Rheims Testament, whom Watson may have met at Douai.

The dedication was permissible – Arundel had not yet 'come out' as a Catholic – but it shows the drift of Watson's allegiances. Not surprisingly, these allegiances surface on to the official record. In June 1581, a list of 'strangers that go not to church' was drawn up by the authorities. It includes Thomas Watson, yeoman, of St Helen's, Bishopsgate. Given his association with this parish – he was born there, and he was living there in 1587 – this is almost certainly Thomas Watson the poet. This would explain how this very English name comes to be in a list of 'strangers'. Here is a young man who has spent seven formative years on the continent, who speaks several languages, who cultivates fashionable European airs, and who refuses to attend church: a 'stranger' in all but his birth.

I can find very little about the Watsons of Bishopsgate, but what there is strongly suggests that young Thomas was not the only Catholic in the family. According to a government informer, there was a Catholic priest named Watson who had 'an uncle or father dwelling in St Helen's, Bishopsgate'. This was some while later, after Thomas Watson was dead, but it is likely that this was the same family. The priest in question may have been William Watson. He enrolled at Rheims in 1581, had a colourful career as a missionary and propagandist, and was hanged in 1603 for his part in the so-called 'Bye Plot'.

Another member of the family appears briefly on the record. We do not know her Christian name, but we know that she was 'one Watson's daughter', and that her own daughter was christened at St Helen's, Bishopsgate. It is probable that she was the sister of Thomas Watson. She too was a Catholic, as the circumstances of her wedding make plain. It was performed by a seminary priest, at a tailor's house in Bow Lane. The marriage did not last. Her husband was arrested in the year their daughter was born. In prison he refused to see her, though she 'came often unto him'; he consorted instead with his mistress, a cutler's wife.

This caddish husband was none other than Robert Poley, the Walsingham spy and the witness of Marlowe's death.

This is one of the connections that Thomas Watson opens up. He was a kinsman of Robert Poley: probably his brother-in-law. This does not necessarily mean they were friends. Poley married Miss Watson some time in or before 1582, but by 1584 he had deserted her and was canoodling with Joan Yeomans in his chamber at the Marshalsea. He seems to have had nothing to do with her after his release. This shabby treatment can hardly have endeared him to the Watson family. As a personal relationship, we can only say that Poley and Thomas Watson knew one another in the early 1580s, and that whatever like or dislike there was between them to begin with, there were grounds for dislike after 1584.

What one can also retrieve from this is a sense of the similarity between Watson and Poley. They are much the same age, they are both Catholics, they are men of wit and education. More than this, they are both hovering on the edges of government service. Poley's long, mistrusted apprenticeship with Sir Francis Walsingham began in about 1582, which is just about the time he married into the Watson family. It is at this time too that we find the first record of Thomas Watson in official employment. This leads to another interesting connection, for the man Watson was working with was the young Thomas Walsingham, the cousin of Sir Francis and the future patron of Marlowe.

Evidence of Watson's involvement with the Walsinghams is found in his poem *Meliboeus*, published in 1590. This is an elegy for Sir Francis Walsingham, who died that April, and it is addressed and dedicated to Thomas Walsingham. The poem is framed as a pastoral dialogue between Watson ('Corydon') and Thomas Walsingham ('Tityrus'), and the whole tone of it, and of the dedication, is warm and affectionate. Watson is addressing a patron, but also speaking to a friend.

In the course of the poem Watson recalls the time of his first friendship with Thomas Walsingham, when they were both living 'by the banks of the Seine' in Paris. This takes us back to the early 1580s when, as we have seen, Thomas Walsingham was working in France as a confidential government messenger, being groomed for Sir Francis's service. He is first mentioned in France in 1580, carrying despatches for Sir Henry Norris. The following August he was attending on Sir Francis himself, who was in France to negotiate the Queen's marriage with Duke of Anjou and an Anglo-French treaty 'for the preventing and staying of the over-greatness of Spain'. In his diary for 1581, Lord Burghley records Sir Francis's movements: his landing at Boulogne on 27 July, his audiences with King Henri and Catherine de' Medici in August. He also records the arrival in England of couriers carrying despatches from Mr Secretary. Three of them arrived in the space of one week in August. One is 'young Walsingham', undoubtedly Thomas. Another is John Furriar, who would later deal with Poley in the Babington affair. The third is a man called Watson, who arrived at court on 13 August, bearing 'letters from Mr Sec. dated 10 August'. Watson is a common name, but given the evidence of *Meliboeus*, it is highly likely that this courier from France was Thomas Watson the poet.

An entirely separate allusion confirms that Watson was in France around this time. In an anonymous book called *Ulysses upon Ajax*, the author refers *en passant* to 'witty Tom

Watson's jests', and then adds, 'I heard them in Paris fourteen years ago.' This book was written towards the end of 1596, in response to Sir John Harington's scandalous *Metamorphosis of Ajax*, so the author seems to be stating quite clearly that Watson was in Paris in about 1582, and that he conversed with him – or at least heard him converse – there. This would again tie in with Thomas Walsingham's movements, who was in Paris at this time.

The Parisian friendship between Watson and Walsingham, fondly remembered in *Meliboeus*, can be dated with some precision to a period of about eighteen months between the summer of 1581 and the spring of 1583. Here, then, is a cross-over point. Tom Watson – the recusant 'stranger' of St Helen's, the former resident at Douai, the admirer of the Earl of Arundel – is carrying messages for Sir Francis Walsingham and consorting with 'young Walsingham' in Paris. He is another of these 'ambodexters', a man in both camps, a young Catholic gentleman pressed into government service. We know that Thomas Walsingham's work in Paris included the carrying of sensitive communications between the English Ambassador, Cobham, and Mary Stuart's ambassador, James Beaton. We can guess that he would have known those other, less official agents of Mary's, Thomas Morgan and Charles Paget, and also Sir Francis's young servant, Thomas Phelippes, who was in Paris at this time, consorting with Morgan.

It is also around this time, in about 1582, that Watson's brother-in-law, Robert Poley, is seeking a position in Sir Francis Walsingham's service: another Catholic gentleman with his eye on the main chance. In 1583, he is committed to the Marshalsea by Walsingham. There he is given the 'liberty of the house', and fastens on the priest Richard Norris. His purpose in doing so, he claims, is to get into credit with Thomas Morgan in Paris. The following year, after his release from the Marshalsea, he is attending on Thomas Walsingham. In 1585 he himself journeys to Paris, and converses with Morgan at the Bastille, in which conversation may be heard a faint anticipatory death-knell for Mary Queen of Scots.

Some of these links are speculative, but this is a powerful cluster of associations. Thomas Watson was a fellow-poet of Marlowe's, but he was also – to put it broadly – a fellow-spy. His career leads us straight back to the intelligence world, leads us to Thomas Walsingham and Robert Poley, and to this whole context of anti-Catholic intrigue in France in the 1580s. He is another link in this chain which seems to connect Marlowe's shadowy dealings in government service with the friendships of his later years, and – in the case of Poley – with the circumstances of his death.

20

FICTIONS AND KNAVERIES

TWO RATHER CURIOUS incidents throw more light on the mentality of tricky Tom Watson. In both episodes there is a strong element of fraud and deception. They suggest the man's relish for intrigue. There is cruelty in them, too: the intrigue has victims. The first of these episodes took place in 1579. We might call it 'The Case of the King of Spain's daughter'.

While lodging at Westminster, Watson made the acquaintance of Edward and Anne Burnell. Edward Burnell was a wealthy Nottinghamshire Catholic, the step-brother of the poet Barnaby Googe. He had recently done a spell in the Tower, and would be imprisoned again in the round-up of Catholics that followed the Babington plot in 1586. It may be that Watson was keeping an eye on this seditious Catholic, but in the event it was the eccentric Mrs Burnell that claimed his attention.

Born Anne Kirkall, a butcher's daughter from East Cheap, Mrs Burnell was strangely touched with the belief that she was the daughter of the King of Spain, and that various marks upon her body were 'tokens' of her hidden royalty. She had been told as much by a witch in Nottinghamshire, who said 'she was a Spaniard's bird, & that she had marks about her which would more appear hereafter.'

In her later testimony she describes her meeting with Watson in the autumn of 1579, when 'she came to London & did lie at Westminster' at the same house where he was lodging. She describes him as 'a gent that was said to be very well learned'. The plausible young scholar played along with her delusions, perhaps out of sport, perhaps because she might yield information, also probably to make something out of it.

'You are proud,' he told her, 'but if you knew yourself, you would be the proudest woman in the parish.'

She told him what the witch had said to her, and he answered that 'the best learned man in England could not say so much in twenty four hours study'. He also warned her that the witch 'had the devil about her'.

Some days later they spoke again. Mrs Burnell swore that if he explained to her the meaning of the witch's words, 'she would never reveal him'. This suggests something of the parlousness of the situation: soothsaying with political overtones. Watson now goes into the full routine. He tells her: 'The best Spaniard that ever came in England was your father' – meaning King Philip II – and then, playing to her dreams:

> You have marks about you that shall appear greater hereafter. You shall have a lock of hair like gold wire in your head, and a mark in the nape of your neck like the letter M, and three moles standing triangle upon your right shoulder, and upon the reins of your back you shall have a mark of the breadth of twopence, which in time shall grow to a greater compass.

On another occasion, a witness testified, she 'sent for' Watson, but he 'could not be found'. He 'should have told her fortune, if he had come.'

The lady's delusions were now well fuelled, and sure enough, looking in the mirror one day, she saw 'a red spot of the breadth of twopence' on her kidneys. This mark grew bigger, until it was 'the breadth of both her hands'. It seemed to her in the form of a 'rundell' – a roundel, or heraldic medallion – 'having on the one side a lion, & on the other side a dragon, & a crown on the top'.

One day she asked her husband to look at this, but he only laughed.

She asked him, 'Why do you laugh?'

'Because you are branded on the back like one of Queen's great horses is on the buttock.'

There the matter rested, but in 1587, with anti-Spanish paranoia at its height, Anne Burnell's beliefs about her royal origins were causing some concern. On one occasion, 'hearing that Sir Francis Drake had brought the ship called the *Philip of Spain*' – the carrack *San Felipe*, escorted into Plymouth in June 1587 – she said that the ship's master, meaning the King of Spain, 'would not be long after'. This was dangerous talk, and by the sort of whispered route we know so well, it came to the ears of the Privy Council.

On 8 August 1587, Mrs Burnell was examined by a Council officer, James Dalton. In the course of her examination, she told of the learned young gentleman at Westminster, but she had promised Watson she would not reveal him, and she kept her promise. Dalton records: 'she refuseth to tell his name, because she had made an oath to the contrary.' However, another deponent, Elizabeth Bradshaw, was able to identify him: it was 'one Watson, a wise man in St Helen's, that could tell strange things'. The term 'wise man' suggests both the scholar and – as scholars were frequently reputed to be – the magician or 'cunning man'.

On 12 August, Watson himself was summoned to be examined by Dalton. He confirms that he knows Mrs Burnell, that he first met her at Westminster some eight years previously, and that he remembers her talking of an old witch who had told her 'she was better born than she was taken'. That was as far as he was prepared to go. To this speech of hers, he claimed, he had 'said nothing'. He had never said, or heard her say, that she was the King of Spain's daughter, nor that she had 'the marks of England' upon her body.

Thus coolly Watson exculpates himself. It is his word against hers. No further trouble seems to have come his way, though he must share some of the reproof in Dalton's summary of the case: that the lady's 'melancholy' and 'phantastical imaginations' might prove dangerous 'if she should come among such evil people as would feed her humour, as among such it seemeth she hath been too much already'.

Anne Burnell persisted in her 'imaginations', and in 1592 she was examined again, this time by officers of the Lord Mayor. Her maid, Alice Digges, who also claimed to see these chimerical marks, was brought in as well. It was deemed that the two women were guilty of 'lewd and imposterous pretence', and that they should 'receive some public punishment'. A warrant was issued for them 'to be well whipped at the tail of a cart through the city', with placards to be placed 'on the hinder part of their heads' showing their crime.

Leniency was exercised on the 'young wench Alice Digges' (as Lord Burghley called her), but sentence on Mrs Burnell was carried out on 14 December 1592. It was recorded in John Stow's chronicles:

> a certain Gentlewoman by the Council's commandment was whipped through the City of London, for affirming herself to be the daughter of Philip, K. of Spain, as she had been persuaded by some accompted soothsayers, after proved liars.

A ballad about the whipping appeared a few days later. Watson was by then dead. Stow's summary of his role in the affair – a 'soothsayer' who turns out to be a liar – is a kind of covert epitaph, to set beside the literary epitaphs for 'sweet Amyntas' and his 'tears and joys so well set down'.

This is a story of an unscrupulous young man and an unfortunate old woman. Watson's actions are amusing on one level, a jape, but they have a hard edge. He trades on his learning, on the mystique it has for those who lack it. There is the overtone of charlatanism, of phoney magic and mumbojumbo. It is a piece of theatre, with Watson giving his best in the role of the 'soothsayer'. The whole thing plays like a comedy, but the comedy has a victim who ends up whipped at the cart's tail.

The second incident took place over ten years later, but

reveals much the same mentality. In this case the intrigue shades into outright fraud, and some of the actors in it were later imprisoned and prosecuted.

In the early 1590s Watson was adding to his income by working as a private tutor in the household of William Cornwallis. His pupil was Cornwallis's son, William junior: he 'read unto him daily'. The Cornwallis family were wealthy neighbours in the Bishopsgate area. They were also, like the Burnells, staunch Catholics, and it is probable that Watson was spying there, as well as imparting his deep learning to young William. Watson was by now a married man: his wedding to Anne Swift took place at St Antholin's, Watling Street, in September 1585. Two of his wife's brothers, Thomas and Hugh Swift, feature in this story.

Thomas Swift was another retainer in the household – as Cornwallis later put it, 'he never fed himself nor clad himself to this hour but out of my favour' – and in about 1591 he and Watson were involved in some complex trickery at the expense of their employer's elder daughter, Frances Cornwallis. There are two readings of this intrigue. One is that Swift had genuinely fallen in love with Frances, and was desperate to marry her; the other is that the whole thing was a con-trick from the beginning. Perhaps there are elements of both. Either way, it was a very dodgy business, with Tom Watson at the heart of it. Swift himself, when in prison, is said to have 'exclaimed against the said Watson as the cause of his woe, misery and undoing'. He later denied that he had said this, but he certainly did think that Watson had been a bad influence, and had 'done him much hurt, in that he did so deeply dissemble with his late master'.

The actual course of this intrigue is very tangled, and I can only give a summary. The first move was the drawing-up of a certain contract between Thomas Swift and Frances Cornwallis. The nub of the scam, it seems, was that this document appeared to be a straightforward bond, in which Frances promised to repay a sum of money to Swift, but that it was actually, in the fine print of it, a promise to marry him. The contract was drawn up by Thomas Swift's brother Hugh, an attorney. It was he who suggested some of the finer points: the gift of twelve angels to Frances, which 'might be to her instead of a ring to bind the contract', and the use of the word 'irrecoverable' in the contract, which was a 'natural and binding word'. So the Swifts were the perpetrators, but the whole thing (or so it was later claimed) was the brainchild of their brother-in-law Thomas Watson.

Frances was duly tricked into signing this contract, and was thus legally bound to marry her father's servant, Thomas Swift. Swift perhaps hoped that the family would be forced to accept this undesirable match, but – probably on Watson's advice – he did not broach the matter with Frances's father. Watson himself hoped to make other kinds of capital out of it, for the next thing we find, he is wheedling a letter of some sort out of Frances. What exactly was in this letter is not clear. Frances wrote it in the belief that Watson was her ally, because he promised her, in return for the letter, 'to get away the cozening paper' (the phoney marriage-contract) from Swift. On the other hand the letter, once signed by Frances, seems to become another compromising document against her, and when the case later came to court Swift was threatening to produce it as evidence. The go-between in all these dealings was Frances's brother, William. It was he who got her to write the letter in the first place, but in this and all else he did, he was urged on 'by the politique persuasion of Watson'.

The 'knavery' of this letter was the main charge levelled against Watson when the affair came to a head in March 1594. By this time Watson was dead, and Swift was in the Marshalsea, and William Cornwallis senior was writing furiously to Sir Thomas Heneage about Watson's role in the affair, which was in the end, he reflected, just what one would expect from a mere play-maker:

Sir, he that could devise twenty fictions and knaveries in a play, which was his daily practise and his living, could draw the lies and devices of this letter, which Sir, upon my life, was Watson's penning for the most part.

There was also the sinister hold which Watson had over his pupil, young William Cornwallis:

> My son, Sir, who knew this knavery of the writing a year before me, and concealed it by Watson's deep dissimuled advice, who read unto him daily and had gotten a young man's love, knows all this and much more manifesting lies, perjury and cozenage.

Another, quite separate charge against Watson is that he and Thomas Swift were conspiring to defraud some of Swift's relations 'of his mother's side', and had 'heretofore laid plats for their goods and lives'. There is no evidence to support this, but by now one would not be surprised.

We are not far here from the scams and stings of crooked brokers like Nicholas Skeres and Ingram Frizer: the fast talking and the fine print, the whisking away of the document before the ink has dried. We are not far, either, from the complex projections of spies like Robert Poley. These 'plats' and 'devices' of Watson's, his 'politique persuasion' and 'dissimuled advice', are the skills of the spy played out in another context: this is a domestic conspiracy, a backstairs intrigue.

Far more than those others like Samuel Daniel and Anthony Munday, Watson is a man close to Marlowe. They are friends, and they share other friends, and one guesses that they are rather similar in character and style. They are bracketed together in those first epitaphs of Marlowe by Peele and Edwards, and often thereafter. When Edwards praises them both for their 'nimble throats' he is speaking of their poetry, but I hear also a curious echo of their work in the political realms of intelligence, where such nimbleness of language is a requisite for survival.

What I like about these incidents is the way Watson bridges a kind of psychological gap. He is one of the most admired poets of his day; he is a small-time swindler and fixer. In this sort of way, as a glimpse into a certain mental atmosphere,

Thomas Watson helps me to understand Marlowe, and perhaps also to understand that grouping at Deptford, where a poet meets up with a trio of swindlers.

2 1

THE WIZARD EARL

THOMAS WATSON'S 'KNAVERY' in the Cornwallis household gives a psychological clue of sorts, but perhaps it has something more to tell us. It provides a certain kind of location in which to see the activities of the poet-spy. Earlier I said that the interesting question about Marlowe was how his position as a writer influenced his spying. Here is one answer: the writer was an ideal man to infiltrate into a household. As a poet *per se*, as a witty companion, as a tutor, clerk, secretary or entertainments manager, the successful writer of the day found his niche in the retinue of some noble patron or family: John Lyly with the Earl of Oxford, George Chapman with Sir Ralph Sadler, Samuel Daniel with the Countess of Pembroke, William Shakespeare with the Earl of Southampton, and so on. The poet has an *entrée*. He has a key to the door, and often to the intimate chambers, of the rich and the powerful, and it is precisely the rich and the powerful that the government is so keen to keep an eye on.

This is almost certainly the case with Watson and the Cornwallises: here is a wealthy, rather fractious family of Catholics, and here is Watson among them, the private tutor, a family daily presence in the house at Bishopsgate. He gets young William's 'love', he blackmails poor Frances, he gains and steals confidences, and whatever might be useful is fed back to the government. In his letter to Sir Thomas Heneage about Swift and Watson, William Cornwallis is aware that Heneage has been a supporter of Watson's widow Anne, 'who by your favour, I hear, is beholding to some of your servants'.

Heneage was by this time, as we shall see, a major figure in the English intelligence service. If Watson was reporting on the Cornwallises in about 1591, Heneage would be the kind of man to whom he could report. This would be an interesting connection, because one of Heneage's chief intelligence agents at that time was Watson's old acquaintance, Robert Poley.

That Walsingham had agents placed in key households is well-known. According to an early biographer, 'his spies waited on some men every hour for three years'. This is how I see the usefulness of a poet and scholar like Thomas Watson. He is a man on the inside, a listener in the entourage, a Rozencrantz or Guildenstern. For the poet-spy, one might say, poetry itself could be used as a kind of cover, as a means of infiltration. This is not to question their devotion to the muse, but to accept the perennial fact that the muse herself does not pay any wages. 'Learning and poverty will ever kiss', and this was one rather unsavoury way for a poet to struggle out of that embrace.

The general context of the poet as 'household spy' offers a new understanding of Marlowe's government service in the 1580s, and of how it might relate to the circumstances of his death. It is another of Tom Watson's connections that provides the key: his connection with the young Earl of Northumberland.

Watson dedicated two works to the Earl of Northumberland. One of these is a long Latin poem, *Helenae Raptus*, published in 1586. This is a translation from the Greek of Coluthus; its subject is the seizing of Helen of Troy and the resulting Trojan wars. The other piece he dedicated to Northumberland is an undated manuscript, now in the Bodleian. It is a translation from the French of Bernard Palessy, entitled 'Concerning Waters and Fountains, both Natural and Artificial'. This work does not seem to have been published: it is a private dedication to the Earl.

This association between Watson and Northumberland in the year 1586 is mentioned *en passant* by one of Marlowe's biographers and ignored by the rest. This is curious, because it is the earliest instance of a literary grouping around the Earl which includes – or comes to include – Marlowe himself, as well as Matthew Roydon, George Peele and George Chapman. All these writers were friends of Watson, and of one another. In terms of Elizabethan literary history, this is a definable, rather upmarket sub-group of the 'University Wits'. They were all poets with a philosophical bent, and it was as such that they sought, and received, Northumberland's patronage. The more harum-scarum, populist, prose-writing 'Wits' like Nashe and Greene have no known connection with Northumberland.

In the case of Marlowe, the earliest hard evidence of his involvement with the Earl dates from January 1592. Roydon, Peele and Chapman, similarly, are visible in Northumberland's circle in the early 1590s. So Watson's earlier presence in the Northumberland orbit cannot be taken as evidence that these other writers also knew the Earl at that time, but it is quite possible that some of them did. Friendships are hard to date: from Marlowe's statement that he was 'very well-known' to Northumberland in 1592 we learn only that the acquaintance must have begun before that. Whether a few months before, or several years, it does not tell us.

Marlowe is, in fact, tantalisingly associated with the very poem that Watson dedicated to Northumberland, *Helenae Raptus*. According to the eighteenth-century bibliographer Thomas Coxeter, Marlowe made a translation of it, 'into English rhyme', in the year 1587. No trace of this translation now remains. As with Nashe's lost elegy on Marlowe we are left with nothing but an old scholar's word. Coxeter does not have an impeccable reputation, but it seems an assertion too precise, too dependent on specialist biographical knowledge, to have been invented by him. And we have, perhaps, an inkling of the contents of this fugitive poem of Marlowe's. Some of the best-known lines he ever wrote were on just this subject: the vision of Helen of Troy in *Dr Faustus*—

> Was this the face that launched a thousand ships,
> And burnt the topless towers of Ilium?
> Sweet Helen, make me immortal with a kiss.
> Her lips suck forth my soul. See, where it flies!

A lost Elizabethan poem, last seen over two hundred and fifty years ago, is not enough to build any theories on, but it adds another hint to this speculation that Marlowe might have been known to Northumberland, as Watson certainly was, back in the mid-1580s.

Henry Percy, 9th Earl of Northumberland, was the Elizabethan nobleman-scholar *par excellence*. He was born in 1564, an exact contemporary of Marlowe, and succeeded to the Earldom at the age of twenty-one. He was quiet and reclusive: 'naturally a kind of inward and reserved man'. He had a stutter, and more than once used this as an excuse to refuse diplomatic appointments. He gazes languidly from a Hillyard miniature, stretched out on a grassy bank, propped up on one elbow, *distrait*, melancholy. His eye half-rests on the portraitist, as a young man on a drowsy picnic afternoon might look at someone taking his photograph. His black satin doublet is unbuttoned. Beside him lie his hat and a pair of gauntlets, and a thick leather-bound tome with the look of philosophy about it.

In his youth, the Earl said, he followed the pastimes of the day – 'hawks, hounds, horses, dice, cards, apparel, mistresses' – but these he soon forsook for 'private domestical pleasures', and the pursuit of 'this infinite, worthy mistress', knowledge. He later recalled his conversion to the abstruse pleasures of study. One day, tormented by an unhappy love-affair, 'giddy with thinking', he reached for some trifling love-pamphlet, 'for the *Arcadia* or books of like subject, whereby I might learn to utter my lethargious passions with their sweet flimflams.' In doing so, he knocked aside an ancient learned tome by the 'old Arabian', Alhazen. The book fell open, 'perhaps by reason of a stationer's thread uncut'. He was not a man to ignore such a portent: he was 'superstitious' that the page was revealed by 'a spirit that directed me, by hidden and unconceivable means, what was good for my purpose'. He read the page, and found it to be 'a demonstration of the colours of the rainbow, the cause of his arkedness'. (This book was probably the Latin edition of Alhazen's work on atmospheric refraction, published in 1572.) He later saw this moment of random revelation as a turning-point, a seductive glimpse of the world of knowledge.

At his principal home, Petworth in Sussex, the Earl amassed a huge library – estimated at approaching 2000 books: a major collection to rank with those of Dr John Dee, Sir Edward Coke and Lord Lumley. An inventory records fifty-two chests of books, with enough volumes piled up all around to 'fill twelve small chests besides'. The library was furnished with several 'wainscot stools', four tables, and a bed on which to throw yourself down when the mental labour giddied you. There were four globes – one of them the Molyneux globe of 1592, said to have been given him by Sir Walter Ralegh – and a cupboard full of mathematical instruments. On the walls hung prints depicting the labours of Hercules, and a series of twenty-four 'antic pictures of the Emperors of Rome', bought for £1 each in 1586.

He was a man of eclectic skills – a gardener, a chemist, a horseman, and on occasion an able military commander – but his chief bent was for science, mathematics and philosophy, which in the popular verdict meant 'magick', and earned him his nickname as the 'Wizard Earl'. In these pursuits he was assisted by his friend and chief scholar, Thomas Hariot, whom he kept on a handsome salary of £100, and provided with a house and laboratory. Hariot was a polymath in the late Renaissance mould: mathematician, astronomer, philosopher, geographer. He is an important figure in the history of science – he corresponded on optics with Kepler; he was a pioneer of the 'perspective trunk', or telescope; and he compiled the first thorough logarithmic tables – but he was also deeply imbued in Renaissance occultism. Another scientist in the Earl's retinue was Walter Warner, whose theories on the circulation of the blood predated the more famous William Harvey's. According to Aubrey, Warner's left hand was missing: 'he had only a stump with five warts upon it' and he 'wore a cuff on it, like a pocket'. Hariot and Warner, together with the geographer Robert Hues, came to be known as the Earl of Northumberland's 'three magi', and in his later years of imprisonment in the Tower they attended on him: a little 'academy of learning' within those bleak walls.

Both Thomas Hariot and Walter Warner were close associates of Marlowe. They were named by Thomas Kyd as Marlowe's familiar friends, 'such as he conversed withal'. Marlowe's involvement in the Northumberland coterie brings him into contact with these speculative minds: scientists or 'magi' according to view, really something of both. It probably also brought him into contact with the famous Dr John Dee. Dee was the grand old man of Elizabethan occultism. He was not a protégé of Northumberland, but he was associated with this group, and particularly with Hariot: some abstruse meetings between the two are recorded in Dee's diary.

Another important friendship of the Earl's – important to Marlowe's story – was with Sir Walter Ralegh. Ralegh, the great Elizabethan adventurer, courtier and poet, was an older man, and different in temper, but there was a marriage of minds between them, with an intermixing of mercenary motives: Northumberland was deeply wealthy, Ralegh more a charismatic freelancer. There is evidence of their growing friendship from the first years of Northumberland's accession to the Earldom in 1585. They exchanged gifts: jewels, paintings, shirts, a 'bed of cedar'. They gambled together – judging from the Earl's account-books, canny Sir Walter regularly cleaned up at the card-table. They smoked together, they rode out together with their horses caparisoned in the same 'straw-coloured velvet', and without a doubt they discussed and speculated together. As Ralegh found his courtly aspirations thwarted – particularly by the enmity of the new star, Essex – he turned more and more to the philosophical pursuits that eventually produced his monumental *History of the World*, as well as many fine poems in a melancholy vein of *contemptus mundi*:

Say to the court it glows
And shines like rotten wood.
Say to the church it shows
What's good, and doth no good.
If church and court reply,
Then give them both the lie.

It is certain that Marlowe and Ralegh knew one another, but how well we do not know. They are associated together as poets, Marlowe's famous lyric, 'Come Live With Me And Be My Love', being wittily and philosophically answered by Ralegh's 'If All The World And Love Were Young'. There is also the assertion of the mysterious Richard Cholmeley, made in 1593, that Marlowe had 'read the atheist lecture to Sir Walter Ralegh & others'. The two men belong together, as poets and 'atheists', in the popular imagination of the time, and whatever the truth of the relationship, this *reputed* closeness of Marlowe and Ralegh will later prove to be important.

This coterie of philosophers and poets, centred on Northumberland and Ralegh, is a classic expression of late Elizabethan occultism. The mood is sceptical, speculative, experimental: scientific in one sense, but still linked to the animistic precepts and mystical aspirations of Renaissance magic. Needless to say this group was highly controversial, and its activities attracted suspicion. As Aubrey writes, about one of Northumberland's followers, Thomas Allen:

> In those dark times, astrologer, mathematician and conjuror were accounted the same things, and the vulgar did verily believe him to be a conjuror. He had a great many mathematical instruments and glasses in his chamber, which did also confirm the ignorant in their opinion, and his servitor (to impose on freshmen and simple people) would tell them that sometimes he should meet the spirits, coming up his stairs like bees.

This is the 'vulgar' view: hostile and half-fearful. It is the view of the mob – the mob that ransacked Dr Dee's library and

233

laboratory at Mortlake; the mob that lynched the astrologer John Lambe in the streets of Southwark. It was also the view of certain anti-Ralegh propagandists, who described this coterie as no more than a 'school of atheism'. Cholmeley's assertion about Marlowe's 'atheist lecture' ties in with this, in fact the whole controversy about Marlowe's atheism, as we shall see, is linked to this Ralegh-Northumberland clique.

Though his occultist interests later earned him suspicion, in the mid-1580s the Earl of Northumberland was the object of a rather different kind of suspicion. He was a young nobleman with a profoundly Catholic pedigree. The Percys were one of England's premier Catholic families. Henry's grandfather, Sir Thomas Percy, was executed for his share in the Pilgrimage of Grace. His uncle Thomas, the 7th Earl, took part in the revolt of the Northern Earls and was executed in 1572. His father steered a more moderate course, but he too became ensnared in conspiracy, and died in the Tower. In this sense, the Wizard Earl was born into Catholic intrigue. Though brought up a good Protestant, and temperamentally unsuited to political conspiracy, he became a target, a figurehead, of Catholic aspirations.

As early as 1582, Lord Percy (as he then was) was the subject of machinations. He was eighteen years old, rounding off his education in Paris. There he fell in with the Catholic exile Charles Paget, the friend and fellow-intriguer of Thomas Morgan. The English ambassador, Sir Henry Cobham, wrote to Walsingham expressing his fear that Paget was trying to reconcile young Percy to the Old Faith. Paget also wrote to Walsingham, denying the charge. He said he had been asked by the old Earl, Percy's father, to keep an eye on the youngster's 'conversation and study', but that he had no Catholic designs on him: 'I have been careful not to touch on matters of religion, knowing that he would greatly dislike persuasion to alter that religion he has been bred up in.' He asked that 'there be no hard interpretation made of Lord Percy'. Cobham remained suspicious of them, and when Percy visited the embassy one day in March 1582, the ambassador turned him away with 'very passionate speeches'. A couple of weeks later, Percy wrote huffily to his father:

> I am sorry for your disquiet, through an advertisement of the Ambassador of England, that Mr Paget is about to alter me in religion, and practises with me in matters offensive to Her Majesty. Neither is true. Mr Paget has always carried himself dutifully (his private opinion in religion I speak not of) or I would not entertain his company.

Whatever Percy's innocence in the matter, there is independent evidence of these Catholic designs on him. Both Dr Allen at Rheims and Father Persons at Rome were eager to draw this young aristocrat back to the Catholic fold. They hoped 'to get the young Lord to stay abroad, and go to Italy, in the hope of his conversion there.' A certain Captain Pullen, who later became a priest, was sent over to England in the hope of getting the old Earl's backing for this plan.

So at this early stage, there are high Catholic hopes for Henry Percy, the future Earl of Northumberland, and the eyes of the English government are watching him carefully. This is made quite clear by Cobham, who justifies his actions in the affair as a matter of national security:

> As the young Lord is a principal personage of the realm, I was moved to write to you [Walsingham] and to my Lord Treasurer thereof, by whose letters my Lord Percy was recommended to my care.

'Care' is rather a euphemism. What Cobham meant is that Walsingham and Burghley wanted young Percy kept under surveillance.

In the autumn of 1583, a Catholic named Francis Throckmorton was arrested. Papers found in his study, and confessions extracted on the rack, furnished Walsingham with evidence of a planned Franco-Spanish invasion, and a list of English Catholics ready to assist them. Chief on this list was the old Earl of Northumberland, Percy's father. Further guilt by association was added by the dubious Paget, who had recently visited the Earl under a false name. The Earl was placed under house-arrest at Petworth, and later imprisoned. On 21 June 1585, he was found dead in the Tower, shot through the heart with a 'dag'. The official verdict was suicide, but there was no lack of other versions. Henry Percy was still in Paris when news came of his father's death. He returned to England immediately, and was installed to the Earldom of Northumberland.

With this elevation, Henry Percy's religious and political persuasions became even more interesting to Walsingham. He was now a rich, influential and potentially Catholic nobleman. He was also, by some computations, seventh in line to the throne, and this was to draw him, through no desire of his own, into the great unsolved equation of late Elizabethan politics: the succession. The childless Queen was visibly ageing, and the question of who might succeed her was already beginning to stir. Catholic hopes would cluster round various dark-horse claimants, one of which was Northumberland.

This was in the future – all Catholic hopes were now centred on Mary Queen of Scots – but from the moment of his succession in June 1585, Northumberland was a marked man. The following summer Walsingham received disquieting news. In July 1586, one of his most trusted agents, Maliverny Catlin, was working as a prison informer in the Marshalsea. There he fastened on a priest named Jackson: 'the keeper for want of stowage hath lodged him with me,' he reports, 'a thing provided by God, as the sequel will declare.' The 'sequel' was certain information about the Earl of Northumberland, whom Jackson had served in France. Catlin reports as follows:

He [Jackson] went out of this realm in the service of the Earl of Northumberland that now is, whom he knows to be as constant a Catholic as the time will allow, or so green years admit; not doubting when opportunity shall serve, he will help to revenge the untimely death of his father.

According to Jackson, Northumberland was a crypto-Catholic, and beneath the exterior of Anglican orthodoxy, he was plotting political 'revenge' for his father's death. Jackson further says – referring back to Northumberland's days with Paget in Paris – that 'the young Earl should have been reconciled at his being in France, but that it was suspected the same might be discovered, and so hinder a greater matter.' This 'greater matter', Catlin makes clear, is the imminent Catholic invasion of England. Jackson 'assured me,' he writes, 'that before harvest be ended, there will be a power sent from the Pope, assisted with some force out of France, with whom the Catholics of England will be ready to join, being no small number.'

This invasion force, so confidently predicted by Jackson in the summer of 1586, is the one which figured in the plots, or dreams, of the Babington conspirators: the one hatched up between Ballard, Morgan and Mendoza in Paris, and communicated by Babington to Mary Stuart in that fatal letter which began her downfall. So among Walsingham's many preoccupations, as he drew tight the strings of his counter-plot, was the allegiance of the young Earl of Northumberland. Was he, as Jackson stated, a covert Catholic? Was he, as Jackson certainly implied, involved in that 'greater matter' of Catholic invasion, as his father had allegedly been?

In mid-August Catlin was out of the Marshalsea, trailing round the northern counties, testing the mood in the wake of the Babington arrests. In the autumn he was back in London, and in November he wrote to Walsingham:

> I have within these four or five weeks used my best endeavour to pierce into the mind of a very great one of this realm, and have been with him these few hours, not doubting but to find his affections thoroughly, and then I will advertise you.

There are few people who would merit this high-flown title, a 'very great one of this realm'. The Earl of Northumberland certainly would, and I suspect that Catlin is here following up the trail he began at the Marshalsea, and attempting to insinuate himself as a spy into the Northumberland retinue. How successful he was is not recorded.

In the same year, 1586, that tricky character Thomas Watson enters Northumberland's literary orbit, with his dedication of *Helenae Raptus*. As I showed earlier, Thomas Watson had himself been in Paris in the years 1581–2. There he ran messages for Sir Francis Walsingham, and enjoyed the friendship of young Thomas Walsingham 'by the banks of the Seine'. The expatriate community in Paris was small, and it is very likely that Watson met the future Earl there, at that time when Cobham and Walsingham were worried about the young man's dealings with Charles Paget. A man of charm and learning and apparent Catholic leanings, 'witty Tom Watson' would press easily into Percy's Parisian circle, and so keep an eye on him for the government. It is the kind of work he was cut out for. Thomas Walsingham, employed by Cobham as a special messenger, may also have been involved with Percy in this double-edged way.

With or without this earlier connection, I think it is highly probable that Watson's presence in Northumberland's literary circle in 1586 contains this element of government surveillance: that the poet was also the spy at this time of renewed suspicion about the Earl's Catholic leanings. Whether he was very intimate with the Earl we do not know: the position of a poet in these entourages is hard to define, sometimes a real friend, sometimes just another employee on the 'check-roll'. Even if he was only on the periphery, Watson would be well-placed to observe, and to enter into, the currents of intrigue that were going on around the Earl. Of much of it Northumberland himself was probably innocent. He was at the card-table, or in the library, or brewing up some potent liqueur in his laboratory. But there is undoubtedly this shady Catholic dimension among his followers: men like Paget and Jackson in Paris, and others later like Thomas Hole, a tutor in the Earl's household, who is said in 1588 to be a 'chief agent' in plans to 'raise a Catholic party' in support of the Armada. And with this, hand and glove in these paranoid times, there are the government's men, the tale-bearers, the squeak of floorboards outside the door. Watson was one, Catlin perhaps another. A little later a man called Roger Walton surfaces in this role, reporting to Walsingham about the tutor Thomas Hole. Walton had himself been page-boy to the Earl's father; now he is selling information to the government. We have a vivid glimpse of this Walton, a young man about the same age as Marlowe: tall, clean-shaven, lean-faced and 'sallowish', wearing a 'doublet of black cark cut upon a dark reddish velvet'. We also hear of his unruly ways:

> To some he showeth himself a great Papist, to others a Protestant, but as they taketh him that haunteth him most, he hath neither God nor religion, a very evil condition, a swearer without measure, and tearer of God.

These are the kind of men you would meet in the shadier corners of the Northumberland retinue: Thomas Watson, poet and spy; Roger Walton, atheist and spy; and perhaps also Christopher Marlowe, a poet, a spy, and an atheist. We have no direct evidence of Marlowe's involvement with Northumberland before the early 1590s, but it is certainly possible this brilliant young poet had attracted himself to the Earl at this earlier stage, and that part of the 'good service' which earned the gratitude of the Privy Council in 1587 was his work as a government tale-bearer within the Northumberland retinue. He was still a student at Cambridge, of course. As we have seen, there was plenty of scope for an intelligencer at the university itself, and I do not doubt that Marlowe was used in this way. But he was also often absent from Cambridge during 1586 and early 1587, away for months at a time. These may mark the poet's first spells of attendance at Syon House or Petworth; his first meetings with the Earl and Sir Walter Ralegh, with his future friends Hariot and Warner, and perhaps with Thomas Watson himself.

If I could prove this, it would be a big step forward in this investigation. It would give some concrete shape to

239

Marlowe's intelligence work in the 1580s, placing him in this particular context of the Earl of Northumberland, and in this particular role of the poet-spy, using his literary *entrée* into a nobleman's household for ulterior ends. This has disturbing implications. It would open up Marlowe's literary relations to the tinge of betrayal: the poet's patron becomes, in some measure, his target as a spy. It would also open up a connection between Marlowe's intelligence work and his supposed 'atheism', which was connected in people's minds with his membership of the Northumberland-Ralegh coterie.

Proof is hard to come by at this distance, but I believe there are other traces to be found of this early connection between Marlowe and Northumberland, and of the 'atheism' they supposedly shared.

22

THE 'PRIEST OF THE SUN'

IN 1587, MARLOWE left Cambridge, trailing controversy, and almost immediately took the London theatrical world by storm with the exotic barbarities and 'high astounding terms' of *Tamburlaine the Great*. This was performed by the Lord Admiral's troupe, with Edward Alleyn in the title role, resplendent in a 'coat with copper lace' and 'breeches of crimson velvet'. He was an actor in the big, stentorian tradition: none of the 'admired tragedians' of antiquity, said Nashe, 'could ever perform more in action than famous Ned Allen'.

The success of *Tamburlaine* led – much as it does in Hollywood nowadays – to the swift cobbling up of a rather inferior sequel:

> The general welcome Tamburlaine receiv'd
> When he arrived last upon our stage,
> Hath made our poet pen his second part.

This sequel – *The Second Part of the Bloody Conquests of Mighty Tamburlaine* – was on-stage by the autumn of 1587, and acquired some extra publicity from an accident that occurred at a performance in early November. It was during the scene where the Governor of Baghdad is executed by firing-squad. By accident one of the 'calivers' used in this scene was loaded. Apparently realising this, the player 'swerved his piece' at the last moment, 'missed the fellow he aimed at, and killed a child and a woman great with child

241

forthwith'. Another member of the audience was wounded in the head 'very sore'. This incident was retailed by a young lawyer, Philip Gawdy, in a letter dated 16 November 1587. It is the earliest reference to a Marlowe play on-stage: an explosive début.

With the success comes controversy, and within a few months there is an attack on Marlowe in print. It comes from the pen of Robert Greene, the flamboyant red-bearded pamphleteer and playwright who jealously guarded his position as the popular star of Elizabethan letters (and who would later attack another upstart, William 'Shake-scene'). In the preface to his latest pamphlet – *Perimedes the Blacksmith*, registered at Stationers' Hall on 31 March 1588 – Greene sounds off against this new competitor. He has 'had it in derision', he says – in other words, he has been criticised—

for that I could not make my verses jet upon the stage in tragical buskins, every word filling the mouth like the fa-burden of Bow Bell, daring God out of heaven with that atheist Tamburlan, or blaspheming with the mad priest of the sun. But let me rather pocket up the ass at Diogenes's hand than wantonly set out such impious instances of intolerable poetry, such mad and scoffing poets that have prophetical spirits as bred of Merlin's race. If there be any in England that set the end of scholarism in an English blank verse, I think either it is the humour of a novice that tickles them with self-love, or so much frequenting the hothouse.

There are one or two obscurities about the passage, but the gist is clear. This is an attack on Marlowe, identified by the allusion to *Tamburlaine*, and by the pun on 'Merlin' and Marlowe. (The bridge of this pun is a variant spelling of Marlowe's name – Marlin or Merling – frequently used at Cambridge, where Greene first met him.) Greene attacks both the overblown style of Marlowe's poetry – booming like the Bow Bell – and its 'impious' contents. The motive cause of Greene's attack, the 'derision' he has suffered, probably refers to the poor reception of his own play, *Alphonsus, King of Aragon*, which closely imitated *Tamburlaine* in subject and style.

This squib of Greene's has an interest outside the narrow sphere of literary faction, for it is the first dateable reference to Marlowe's connection with 'atheism'.

It should not be taken too literally. Greene calls Tamburlaine, not the author of *Tamburlaine*, an atheist. The implication is there, because people tend to conflate the author and his fictions, but in itself it is not really an accusation about Marlowe to say that his character – an avowed enemy of Christianity – is an 'atheist'. Atheism is dramatically appropriate to *Tamburlaine*, and Greene must have recognised this. What Greene is complaining about, perhaps, is Marlowe's failure to condemn Tamburlaine: the absence of moral standpoint. In a later play, *The Tragical Reign of Selimus*, he presents a kind of riposte to this. Selimus is another exotic, 'atheist' warlord, and Greene thumps home the message that secular power – power divested of Christian ethics – becomes barbarous tyranny.

Greene is complaining about Marlowe's presentation of atheism, but not – at this stage, anyway – openly claiming that Marlowe *is* an atheist. What he actually calls Marlowe is a 'mad and scoffing' poet, with a 'prophetical' spirit 'as bred of Merlin's race'. If there is an accusation about Marlowe himself, it is that he is a dabbler in magic, and that his vaunted powers as a poet are the mumbo-jumbo of a latter-day Merlin.

As we know from *Dr Faustus* – which, however problematic in terms of its ultimate 'message' about magic, is clearly the product of a writer *interested* in the subject – this part of Greene's accusation is plausible.

Another, independent reference to the earlier stages of Marlowe's 'atheism' tells much the same story. This is found in the note-books of a country gentleman and minor *littérateur*, Henry Oxinden of Barham, Kent. His remarks about Marlowe were written down in the mid-seventeenth century, but they were based on Oxinden's conversations with a 'Mr Alderich' who had reason to know what he was talking about.

This 'Alderich' was Simon Aldrich. He was a Canterbury man, born in about 1580: his father was a registrar at the city's ecclesiastical court, and the family probably knew the Marlowes. He went up to Cambridge in about 1593, the year of Marlowe's death, and commenced MA in 1600. He was not a Corpus man, but he may have been related to the Norfolk Aldriches who were prominent at the college: Thomas Aldrich, who was Master of Corpus in the early 1570s, and his brother Henry, a college fellow who died in 1593, bequeathing £40 to buy charcoal 'to keep up the hall fire'.

Aldrich was thus a younger contemporary of Marlowe, in Canterbury and Cambridge, and he took a keen interest in this notorious literary figure who grew up in a house round the corner.

Half a century later, old 'Mr Alderich' is living with his daughter's family at a 'brick house' called Little Maydeken, on the estates of Henry Oxinden. His interest in Marlowe is undimmed, and on 10 February 1641, Oxinden notes down various details about Marlowe 'from Mr Ald.': that he was the son of a shoemaker in Canterbury, that he was an excellent scholar, that he was an atheist, and so on.

Part of the material Aldrich gave Oxinden is a very interesting anecdote about another local man, 'Mr Fineux of Dover', and his relationship with Marlowe. This was Thomas Fineux junior, the eldest son of Captain Thomas Fineux of Hougham, near Dover. He was born in 1574, and entered Corpus Christi, Cambridge, as a gentleman pensioner in the Easter term of 1587. There, it seems, he met and fell under the spell of Christopher Marlowe. Perhaps there were personal connections: Marlowe's mother was from a Dover family, the Arthurs. Marlowe was in his last months at the college. It was the time of the rumours about Rheims, of the dispute over his MA, of new horizons opening – *Tamburlaine* was ready, London beckoned. This is what Oxinden records about Fineux and Marlowe:

Mr Ald. said that Mr Fineux of Dover was an atheist, &
that he would go out at midnight into a wood, & fall down
upon his knees, & pray heartily that the devil would come,
that he might see him (for he did not believe that there was
a devil).

Mr Ald. said that he [Fineux] was a very good scholar, but
would never have above one book at a time, & when he
was perfect in it, he would sell it away & buy another. He
learned all Marlowe by heart, & divers other books.
Marlowe made him an atheist.

Here, again, this early glimpse of Marlowe's 'atheism' is
bound up with magic: Fineux out in some moonlit wood,
conjuring a devil that he does not – but half-wishes to –
believe in. This potent little cameo seems to come straight out
of the mental world of *Dr Faustus*:

> Come show me demonstrations magical,
> That I may conjure in some bushy grove,
> And have these joys in full possession.

This is anecdotal, but Aldrich is a good source, and the fact
that Marlowe and Fineux intersect at Cambridge supports it.
Greene's tirade in *Perimedes* and Fineux's woodland
conjurings both lead to the same conclusion, the same
emphasis. At this earlier stage – before the government
informers and the Puritan propagandists shaped our
conception – Marlowe's 'atheism' is primarily an involvement
in the dangerous terrain of magic. "Tis magick, magick that
hath ravisht me!'

To the orthodox, of course, magic *was* a kind of atheism,
but it is important to register this shift, to see that Marlowe
the atheist is in the first instance Marlowe the occultist, 'bred
of Merlin's race'.

Greene's attack on Marlowe in 1588 is another case – like
Harvey's absurd 'Gorgon' – where the biographers have

chosen to remain silent on a puzzling aspect. When Greene talks of Tamburlaine 'daring God out of heaven' he is obviously referring to Marlowe's play: the phrasing probably echoes the line in *Tamburlaine* 2, 'His looks do menace heaven and dare the Gods'. But what does he mean by the next phrase, where he talks of Marlowe 'blaspheming with the mad priest of the sun'? As far as I know, no-one has found anything in *Tamburlaine*, or in any other play current in 1588, to explain this allusion.

This 'mad priest of the sun' was not, I suggest, a theatrical character, but an actual living person – the famous Italian occultist, Giordano Bruno, whose fiery mystical pronouncements were one of the philosophical talking-points of the 1580s. Bruno spent two years propagandising in England. He disputed at Oxford in 1583, and held court at London *soirées* attended by the likes of Sir Philip Sidney, Fulke Greville and John Florio. He left England in the autumn of 1585, but he was still much talked about, and the works he had published here – *Spaccio della Bestia Trionfante* ('The Expulsion of the Triumphant Beast'), *Cena de le Ceneri* ('The Ash Wednesday Supper') and *De Gli Eroici Furori* ('The Heroic Frenzies') – were still highly controversial. His style was extravagant, to say the least. 'Behold now standing before you,' he wrote in 1585,

> the man who has pierced the air and penetrated the sky, wended his way amongst the stars and overpassed the margins of the world, who has broken down those imaginary divisions between spheres – the first, the eighth, the ninth, the tenth, what you will – which are described in the false mathematics of blind and popular philosophy.

All this was delivered with appropriate histrionics. An eyewitness at the Oxford disputes recalled him as a small man – 'that Italian didapper with a name longer than his body' – with immense presence. He stepped 'more boldly than wisely' to the lectern, and there, stripping up his sleeves like some juggler, and telling us much of *chentrum & chirculus & circumferenchia* (after the pronunciation of his country language), he undertook among very many other matters to set on foot the opinion of Copernicus, that the earth did go round and the heavens did stand still, whereas in truth it was his own head which rather did run round, & his brains did not stand still.

As this suggests, the idea that Bruno was 'mad', the epithet Greene uses, was no more than commonplace. Bruno himself complained that the *Cena*, the finest of his London dialogues, had been scoffed at as 'rabid and demented'.

As this account of him at Oxford also shows, Bruno was a champion of Copernicanism, and this is the clue to Greene's description of him as the 'priest of the sun'. Nicolas Copernicus revolutionised Renaissance cosmology by recognising the sun-centred structure of what we now call the solar system. This challenged the mediaeval assumption that the earth was the centre of the universe, and caused philosophical repercussions that are felt throughout the period. Bruno's interest in Copernicus, however, was not that of the astronomer, the 'scientist', but that of a magician imbued in all the currents of Renaissance occultism. His version of heliocentricity was mystical, emblematic: the sun as the divine light of truth and revelation towards which the magician aspired. Copernicus had, in Bruno's view, only *restated* an ancient magical truth. Other early Copernicans believed this too – Thomas Digges referred to heliocentricity as a 'most ancient doctrine of the Pythagoreans, lately revived by Copernicus' – but none expressed it with such fervour as Bruno. He was a kind of evangelist for occultism, and this symbolic reading of Copernican astronomy was at the core of his message. As the great Bruno scholar Frances Yates puts it: 'the sun-centred universe was a hieroglyph of Bruno's magical religion'.

This volatile, heretical Italian, with his sun-centred magical religion, is the man Greene describes as 'the mad priest of the sun'. To the reader of 1588, I think, the identification would be obvious. This riddling reference actually turns out to be part of this same association between Marlowe and magic. Marlowe is an admirer of the mad priest Bruno, just as he is a poet 'bred of Merlin's race'.

That Marlowe was intensely aware of Bruno can be gauged from *Dr Faustus*. Bruno contributes to Marlowe's overall presentation of Faustus as magician, though other magi of the time – Cornelius Agrippa, Paracelsus, Dr John Dee – are also present in his mind. These figures are at least as important as the actual historical prototype, Georg Faust of Heidelberg.

Bruno is especially present during Faustus's first, thrilling renunciation of orthodox scholarship in favour of the adventure of 'magick'. Both in his disputes at Oxford and in his London publications, Bruno poured contempt on the limitations of English university teaching. He criticised the 'rudeness and ignorance' of the Oxford doctors, mere 'grammarian pedants'. He pitied 'the poverty of this country, which is widowed of good learning in the fields of philosophy and pure mathematics'. In this 'good learning' – in other words, occult wisdom – 'all are so blind, that asses like these can pass themselves off as seers'.

This is the mood of Faustus the scholar, discovered in his study at night, ranging angrily through his books, dismissing the gamut of university learning: logic, medicine, law, divinity. These are 'servile and illiberal' arts: 'a greater subject fitteth Faustus's wit'. This 'greater subject' is the same as Bruno's 'good learning': magic. A particular *bête noire* of Bruno's was the rigid emphasis on Aristotelean studies at university. In the *Cena*, a character called Prudenzio is mocked as one of those scholars who 'wish to live and die for Aristotle' (*'voglion vivere e morire per Aristoteles'*). This is precisely echoed by Marlowe, when Faustus dismisses those who 'live and die in Aristotle's works'. Bruno says that the Aristoteleans are 'estranged from the truth', and that only those philosophers who are 'miraculous in magic' can 'purge all doubts and clear away all contradictions' (*'purga tutti i dubii e toglie via tutti le contradizioni'*). Faustus says the same. Aristotelean philosophy is 'odious and obscure': only magic will 'resolve me of all ambiguities'.

These parallels could be continued. They suggest Marlowe's knowledge of Bruno's London dialogue, the *Cena de le Ceneri*, and his appropriation of Bruno's rhapsodic occultism into the portrayal of Dr Faustus as he stands on the brink of heresy, and then steps over it:

> Divinity adieu!
> These necromantic books are heavenly:
> Lines, circles, scenes, letters and characters:
> Ay, these are those that Faustus most desires.

The link between Bruno and Faustus is also suggested by Marlowe's allusions to Wittenberg. Shortly after his return to Europe Bruno took up a post at Wittenberg University, in Saxony, and he remained there – in an atmosphere more congenial than he had found in England – until 1588. Marlowe's Faustus (unlike the historical Faust) is also a scholar of Wittenberg:

> I that have with subtle syllogisms
> Gravelled the pastors of the German church
> And made the flowering pride of Wittenberg
> Swarm to my problems, as the infernal spirits
> Of sweet Musaeus.

This bragging tone recalls Bruno, who might also claim to have 'gravelled' – pounded to pieces – his Protestant opponents in England, namely the 'pedants' who had disputed so poorly against him at Oxford in 1583.

In a later scene in the play, Faustus uses his magic to free a heretic called 'Saxon Bruno' from the inquisitorial clutches of the Pope. This is a scene often assigned to a rewriter, rather than to Marlowe himself. It seems to relate to Bruno's trial by the Inquisition in Rome: he was burned at the stake as a heretic, in the Campo dei Fiori, in 1600. This was long after Marlowe's death. The scene was probably the work of Samuel

Rowley or William Birde, who were paid for certain 'adiciones in Doctor Fostes' in 1602. Though not Marlowe's work, the scene suggests that these hacks were aware of Bruno's original presence in the play.

When Greene speaks of Marlowe 'blaspheming with the mad priest of the sun', he is ascribing to Marlowe the same interest in Bruno that emerges from a reading of *Dr Faustus* itself. Greene may have got this idea through personal knowledge – he knows Marlowe, and knows him to be an admirer of Bruno – or it may be that he had already seen *Dr Faustus* when he wrote his tirade in early 1588. The textual history of *Faustus* is a maze. There is conflicting evidence as to the date of composition, and much puzzling variation between the two printed texts of the play (1604 and 1616). There is a source-book which Marlowe used closely – *The Damnable Life of Dr John Faustus* – but we do not know when this was first published (only the second edition is extant), nor who wrote it (the author identifies himself only as 'P.F., gent'). The play's earliest recorded performance was at the Rose in September 1594, over a year after Marlowe's death, but it is unlikely this was the first. The dramatist Thomas Middleton mentions a performance 'when the old Theatre cracked and frighted the audience'. This probably refers to an earlier run, at the Theatre in Shoreditch, though there is no documentary record of this.

I would say that Greene's 'priest of the sun' allusion adds strength to the view that *Faustus* was an early work (or at least that there was an early version of it, only partially recoverable from the play as we now have it, which is textually corrupt and which may also have been subject to official censorship). There is another phrase in Greene's attack which suggests that he knew the play: he speaks of Marlowe's poetry striving 'to set the end of scholarism in an English blank verse'. This has general application to Marlowe as an exponent of the iambic pentameter form known as 'blank verse', but it would have a specific point if applied to Faustus's opening soliloquy, which is precisely a poetic rejection of orthodox 'scholarism'.

*

This reading of Greene's tirade throws light on the vexed dating of *Dr Faustus*, and I offer it up to the hungry hounds of literary history. For me it has other implications too, which lead back to the question of Marlowe's early involvement with the Earl of Northumberland.

By the time Greene wrote this, Bruno had been gone from England two years and more. He left in the autumn of 1585 when his patron, Mauvissière, handed over to the new French ambassador, Chateauneuf. He is no longer a presence, but – as Greene evidently believes – he is still an influence: a pernicious, blasphemous influence, even. There are various places one might look to find evidence of Bruno's continued influence in England. One would be the Sidney-Pembroke circle. Bruno had assiduously cultivated the company of Sir Philip Sidney, and had dedicated two of his London works to him. How warmly Sidney responded is not quite clear, but it is certainly true that the extraordinary 'emblematic' sonnets of Bruno's *Eroici Furori* had an influence on Sidney's own sonnet-sequence, *Astrophel and Stella*, and later on the work of poets like Samuel Daniel who are associated with Sidney's sister, the Countess of Pembroke. But this is a strictly literary influence, at most a dilution of Bruno's philosophy to an acceptably vague neo-Platonism. Much of what Bruno had to say, as a controversialist and as an occultist, was quite unacceptable to the strongly Protestant outlook of the Sidney circle, and it cannot be argued that Bruno's teachings as a whole prospered in that quarter.

There is only one definable intellectual group where Bruno's influence as a philosopher persists – the Northumberland circle. The Earl himself was an assiduous collector of Bruno texts. Six formerly owned by him remain in the Northumberland collections at Petworth House and Alnwick Castle. There were probably others, since dispersed. His copy of the *Eroici Furori* is closely annotated, and it has been shown that his reading of this work strongly influenced the composition of his own essay, variously called 'On Love' or 'On Friendship'. Interestingly, the *Furori* is the only one of

Bruno's London works in the collection: the others are all abstruse and serious Latin texts which articulate the more complex reaches of Brunian philosophy. The Earl, it is clear, was no dabbler in the showier side of Bruno.

The poet George Peele gives us a good impression of the philosophical mood of the Northumberland set, in his verse-dedication to the Earl in *The Honour of the Garter*, the same poem which contains the earliest epitaph on Marlowe. He describes the mood as one of intellectual adventure and exploration:

> Leaving our schoolmen's vulgar trodden paths
> And, following the ancient reverend steps
> Of Trismegistus and Pythagoras,
> Through uncouth ways and inaccessible
> Dost pass into the spacious pleasant fields
> Of divine science and philosophy.

This has the ambiance of Bruno, and indeed of *Dr Faustus*: the discarding of orthodox 'vulgar' scholarship in favour of occult Pythagorean and Hermetic studies ('Trismegistus' is Hermes Trismegistus, the apocryphal high-priest of Egyptian magic) which lead to 'divine' understanding. Another occult system that Peele mentions is 'mathesis': a kind of mystical mathematics. Northumberland is said to 'clothe mathesis in rich ornaments'. This again chimes in with Bruno, who described mathesis as one of the 'four guides in religion' (the others being love, art and magic).

None of this is exclusive to Bruno – the interest in 'mathesis' probably reflects the influence of Dr Dee as well – but at least one of Peele's phrases in this poem points directly to Bruno. He describes the Earl as one of the 'heroical spirits', who uphold true learning in these 'unhappy times'. In this context, the word 'heroical' sounds like a deliberate echo of Bruno's *Eroici Furori*, or 'Heroical Frenzies'. Bruno uses the word in just this sense of metaphysical adventure: the magician achieves 'divine and heroical frenzies, as the mystical and cabalistic doctors interpret'. We know that Northumberland studied the *Furori* closely, and obviously Peele knew this too.

The philosophical centre of the group was Marlowe's friend Thomas Hariot, and there is no doubt that he was familiar with Bruno's work. His correspondence with the astronomer Sir William Lower refers to their discussions of the 'opinion of Nolanus' – in other words Bruno, who came from Nola, near Naples – 'concerning the immensity of the sphere of the stars'. This is confirmed by a marginal annotation among Hariot's papers: 'Nolanus de immenso & mundi' (a shorthand reference to two of Bruno's works: *De Immenso* and *De L'Infinito, Universo e Mundi*).

Other, more controversial, opinions attributed to Hariot can be traced back to Bruno. Some of these are also attributed to Marlowe. This leads into a very complex area, where the whole charge of 'atheism' against Marlowe, brought by Richard Baines and others, can be seen as a deliberately tarnished version of certain occultist speculations suggestive of Bruno (though, again, not exclusive to him). The business about 'men before Adam', for instance – the first item in Baines's charge-sheet – is often connected with Hariot's knowledge of American Indian mythology, but it also echoes Bruno's speculations about pre-Adamitic races in the *Spaccio*.

By an entirely different route, we have arrived back at the same early connection between Marlowe and the Northumberland circle which I argued in the previous chapter. Robert Greene is writing in early 1588. He describes Marlowe as 'blaspheming with the priest of the sun': a follower of Giordano Bruno. The group which most clearly represents Bruno's type of esoteric knowledge, the group where his ideas prospered after his departure from England in 1585 – or at least where they were discussed and understood, rather than condemned – is the intellectual circle associated with the Earl of Northumberland and Sir Walter Ralegh.

Inevitably, Bruno's influence brings with it certain *political* considerations which take us back, once more, to the central question of Marlowe as spy. Bruno was a Catholic, and poured scorn on the 'asses' of Protestantism, but he was equally critical of the aggressive Catholicism of the Counter-Reformation, as represented by the Pope, Spain and the French Guisards. While working in France he was protected by King Henri III, a moderate Catholic with mystical leanings: he called Henri a 'lion of peace'. When he travelled to England in 1583, he carried letters from Henri to the French ambassador, Mauvissière, and it is thought by some that Bruno's occultist 'mission' in England was connected with Henri's efforts to create a political middle-ground between the extremes of Protestantism and Hispanic Catholicism. This is Yates's view: that Bruno was sent to England as a 'missionary of conciliation', hoping to influence the English government to a 'supra-national' policy of religious union; that he was advocating his own 'magical religion' as a new doctrine that would break the stalemate of sectarian conflict. Through his intensive cultivation of Sidney, it is argued, Bruno hoped to communicate his message to those political supremos of Elizabethan England, Sir Francis Walsingham and the Earl of Leicester, Sidney's father-in-law and uncle respectively. In one of the books he dedicated to Sidney, the *Spaccio della Bestia Trionfante*, Bruno addresses both Walsingham and Leicester by name, and offers many grand, cloudy hints about his mission of reconciliation.

This is one view. A new theory, compellingly argued by John Bossy, holds that Bruno was in touch with Walsingham in less elevated ways than this: that he was, in fact, used by Walsingham as a spy within the French embassy. It has long been known that Walsingham had a well-placed source in Mauvissière's embassy in the mid-1580s. His name, or code-name, was Henry Fagot. His reports – often in French, but full of errors no Frenchman would make – provided Walsingham with many useful tips and one major coup: it was Fagot's information about the clandestine visits of a 'Sieur Frocquemorton' that led directly to the exposure of the so-called Throckmorton Plot. Fagot, argues Bossy, was none other than the Francophone Italian Giordano Bruno, moon-lighting at the embassy all the while he was performing his more public antics as a controversialist. A 'philosopher-spy', in short, parallel in many ways to the 'poet-spy'.

I do not think that these views of Bruno are mutually exclusive. Bruno is keen to influence Walsingham with his philosophy of occult reformism; Walsingham cares nothing for the philosophy, but is keen to exploit the man and his position. Bruno's role as an informer in the French embassy is thus convenient to both.

I say that Walsingham cared nothing for Bruno's message. I would go further and say that he intensely distrusted it. For both Walsingham and Leicester, the architects of England's aggressive foreign policy, Bruno's arcane talk of religious harmony and conciliation would be seen as a threat, or at any rate a distraction: a potential weakening of Protestant resolve for the anti-Catholic crusade at just the time when the Queen had at last consented to the military option. Even before Bruno arrived in England, he merited a despatch from Ambassador Cobham to Walsingham: 'Doctor Jordano Bruno Nolano, a professor in philosophy, intends to pass into England, whose religion I cannot commend.' It is likely that Cobham's suspicions were as much political as theological, and that they relate to Bruno's purpose as a propagandist of Valois moderation. The barrage of hostility which greeted Bruno in England has this political aspect. The orthodox view – that he was a mad Italian blasphemer: Greene's view – was to some extent a cloak for the government's more particular, more cynical disapproval of his message of conciliation.

How much the political element of Bruno's message was carried on by the Earl of Northumberland and his philosophers – how much they regarded occultism as a kind of doctrinal solution to the politics of strife – is hard to say. But from the government's point of view there was this overtone to Bruno, and therefore to his occultist admirers.

So Walsingham's interest in the Northumberland coterie in the mid-1580s would have two aspects. There is his concern about the Catholic conspiratorial groupings around the Earl; and there is this other concern, about the political ramifications of Bruno's 'magical religion', its potential for subverting opinion among the intelligentsia in this time of war. And if this is something that concerns Walsingham, it is something of which his spies will be keeping him abreast.

It is significant, but perhaps not surprising, that our tricky friend Thomas Watson turns up again here, for he too reveals an interest in Bruno. When Watson was in Paris in the early 1580s, Bruno was himself a Parisian figure. He was lecturing at the Sorbonne, and producing works like *De Umbris Idearum* ('The Shadows of Ideas'), published in Paris in 1582. Northumberland, or Lord Percy as he then was, was also resident in Paris: we have no exact idea of when he forsook the 'flim-flam' pleasures of dicing and womanising for the pursuit of occult wisdom, but it is possible that his interest in Bruno dates from this time.

Watson's interest in Bruno is made clear in his own book on the art of memory. Mnemotechnology, or *ars memoriae*, was one of Bruno's specialities, part of his package of magical powers. He recommended the topographical method, where complex ideas are stored in 'places', typically the rooms of a house, and can be retrieved by an imagined progress from room to room. This is exactly Watson's subject in his book *Compendium Memoriae Localis*: 'The Compendium of Placed Memory'. He acknowledges Bruno as the master of this art, and modestly states that his own contribution is minor compared to that of 'Nolanus'.

Unfortunately, Watson's book is not dated, but it is dedicated to the courtier Henry Noel, so one pointer is the date of Watson's other dedication to Noel. This was his translation of Tasso's *Amintas*, which was published in 1585. Some time around this date, Watson is broadcasting Bruno's ideas on 'placed memory'. He is part of – or is jumping on the bandwagon of – the intense interest that Bruno aroused. One recalls the description of him as a 'wise man' and 'soothsayer' – words which convey an idea of occult wisdom – in the depositions concerning his dealings with Anne Burnell, the *soi-disant* daughter of the King of Spain. One recalls also that he was in this case only *playing* the soothsayer: that it was all just 'fiction and knavery'.

Once more there is a tantalising parallel between the

careers of Watson and Marlowe in the years before they shoulder into view together on that afternoon on Hog Lane. They share, on the separate evidence of the *Compendium* and of *Dr Faustus*, an interest in the teachings of Giordano Bruno. This helps to explain their association with the Northumberland circle, where Bruno's teachings were highly valued, yet it also links to their involvement with the Walsingham service, where Bruno's teachings were highly suspect.

We arrive at an unsettling idea: that Marlowe's involvement in 'magick', like his involvement in Catholicism, has this double edge, this dimension of government service which is also a dimension of betrayal. In Walsingham's intelligence network, as in all successful networks, there is specialisation. Particular problems require particular solutions, and we can now see a specialisation that fits Marlowe in 1587. This young man said to be a Catholic, said to be an occultist – a dangerous subversive on both counts – is actually working for the benefit of his country. One way he might be doing so is as a spy for Walsingham in the retinue of the Earl of Northumberland, where there are elements both of Catholic intrigue and of the political occultism associated with Bruno.

PART FIVE

THE LOW COUNTRIES

23

NEW MASTERS

THIS ENQUIRY INTO the nature and circumstances of Christopher Marlowe's 'government service' in the mid-1580s has produced few certainties and several rather disturbing possibilities: I will summarise these briefly before moving on.

On the basis of the Privy Council certificate of June 1587, it is fairly certain that Marlowe was involved in the kind of undercover activities on which the government depended for information and leverage against the perceived enemy of Catholicism. This work probably began in 1585: the year of his portrait, the year when his attendance at Cambridge becomes irregular and his spending at the college buttery suddenly rockets. It is possible that he was, like many of Walsingham's ferrets, a genuine Catholic sympathiser who turned, or was forced to turn, into an informer. His first targets were other Catholics at Cambridge, particularly the militant fringe of students who planned to defect to the seminary at Rheims. The rumour that he was himself intending to defect is actually a description of his cover as a government spy. So, at least, the Council believed, though in this game the line between treason and loyalty is a fine one.

This work, undertaken at Cambridge and elsewhere, brought Marlowe into the fringe of Walsingham's covert operations in France, which were focused on the seminary at Rheims, on émigré groups in Paris, and ultimately – so it proved – on the entrapment of Mary Queen of Scots. Certain 'plats' laid at Rheims and Paris blossomed into the Babington plot, which achieved that end. Also involved in this complex of intrigue we find various names associated with Marlowe's later career, and some associated with his death at Deptford in 1593. We find the sinister Richard Baines, an early Walsingham spy at Rheims. We find Robert Poley, a government 'projector' with Morgan in Paris and Babington in London. We find Nicholas Skeres, another government plant in the Babington camp. And we find Thomas Walsingham, the confidential courier in France, the case-officer of Poley and perhaps of Marlowe himself.

This is one of the disturbing elements: the way the intelligence game of the 1580s furnishes these key players in the events of 1593. There is a suggestion of continuity: that Marlowe's death involves these people because it is itself somehow part of the covert world which they all inhabit. There is a sense of closeness, a claustrophobia, in these repetitions and reappearances.

And then there is Tom Watson, the poet-spy who uses his literary and scholarly attainments as a way into Catholic households. He opens up a new dimension to Marlowe's intelligencing. Either during or shortly after his university career, I believe, Marlowe gained the acquaintance of the Earl of Northumberland. This brings him, somewhat earlier than the documentary evidence, into contact with Northumberland's intellectual circle, which includes Ralegh, Hariot and Warner, and perhaps those other poets like Peele and Roydon who are later associated with the Earl. Walsingham has his suspicions about this circle. Marlowe belongs to it as a poet and malcontent, takes part in its dangerous speculations and perhaps in its intrigues, but his presence – like Watson's – is ambiguous. He is one of Walsingham's listeners on the inside of this suspect clique. The 'good service' that the Council praised in 1587 may relate as much to this as to his activities, now past, at the university.

This too is disturbing: as a personal imputation about Marlowe, and as another kind of continuity to the events surrounding his death. In early 1588, Greene accuses Marlowe of 'atheism' and 'blasphemy': I would relate this to the occultist tendencies of the Northumberland circle, which could be – and frequently were – described as 'atheist'. Yet if Marlowe was in part a spy in the Northumberland circle, there is a double edge to his supposed atheism. It has an element of provocation, of projection. Like his Catholicism, it is sanctioned by his role as an informer. This may prove to be a new twist to the events of 1593.

At eleven o'clock on the night of 6 April 1590, Sir Francis Walsingham died, aged about sixty. According to the historian Camden, he died of a 'fleshy growth within the membrane [*tunicas*] of the testicles', though Camden adds that it was probably the 'violence' of the physicians' cures that actually did for him. Catholic gossip gave this account of his last hours:

> The Secretary Walsingham, a most violent prosecutor of Catholics, died never so much as naming God in his last extremities. And yet he had his speech, as he showed by telling the preacher that he heard him, and therefore he needed not to cry so loud – which were his last words. In the end, his urine came forth at his mouth and nose, with so odious a stench that none could endure to come near him.

He was buried quietly at St Paul's the following day.

Walsingham's death created a vacuum at the heart of the English intelligence service. He had succeeded in centralising the business, and in getting government money for it, but much of this was due to his own magnetic political skills, his compendious involvement in the network he had created. The disappearance of his files, in the days following his death, remains a mystery.

There followed a period of uncertainty, as rival factions jockeyed for control of the intelligence service and for the power that this brought, both in terms of hard political information and in terms of prestige with the Queen. All the major government figures had their own little network of contacts and place-men, but in the post-Walsingham era two power centres quickly emerged, two networks of intelligence-gathering at home and abroad. On the surface they co-operated, and pooled their intelligence, but there is plenty of evidence of competition, and at times outright hostility, between them.

The figureheads under which these two networks operated were Lord Burghley and the Earl of Essex. Each man saw himself as the natural successor to Walsingham. Burghley had been Walsingham's mentor back in the early days of Elizabeth's reign: he was the old dog who had taught Mr Secretary his tricks in the first place. Essex saw himself as the new generation, the inheritor of the aggressive, expansive Protestantism once represented by Leicester and Walsingham.

The Burghley faction was the stronger, because of his unchallenged position as the elder statesman of the Elizabethan government. He had a whole generation of political contacts; he had decades of experience; he had the Queen's unquestioning trust, however much his cautious pragmatism exasperated her. But he was an old man now, and his taste for the more drastic expediencies of the secret world was fading. It was his younger son, Robert Cecil, who shouldered the day-to-day burden of paperwork, and who took the operational decisions. A small, fastidious, complex man, 'bossive Robin' was physically deformed with a hunch-back, probably due to scoliosis, but he made up for his disability with a prodigious mental nimbleness and stamina. The Queen called him her 'elf'. He inherited his father's pragmatism, his ability to watch and wait in the shadows while others rushed into the dangerous limelight: *prudens qui patiens*. Cecil had served his political apprenticeship in France, where he consorted with the adventurer Parry and ran errands for the government. He was now being seriously groomed by his father for political office. In May 1591 he was knighted and incorporated into the Privy Council. It was rumoured that he would be made Secretary of State, in succession to Walsingham, but in fact the Queen kept the position vacant, and the candidates guessing, until 1596.

No less important within the Burghley aegis was Sir Thomas Heneage, the Queen's Vice-Chamberlain, and a Privy Councillor since 1587. Camden described him as a man 'born for the court', and praised 'his elegancy of life and pleasantness of discourse'. Sir William Pickering called him 'my well-beloved gossip'. Heneage was an 'avid office-seeker', and the first of the positions he acquired, back in 1570, was Treasurer of the Chamber. This brought him into daily contact with the couriers and informers of Walsingham's service, who received payment through this office. In June 1590, championed by Burghley, he took over the Chancellorship of the Duchy of Lancaster, previously held by Walsingham.

Increasingly Heneage appears as a central figure in English intelligence, often a liaison between the espionage world and the Privy Council. And chief among his operatives is Robert Poley. As we saw, Poley had fallen on his feet after his release from the Tower in 1588, and was employed by Mr Secretary as a 'messenger of the court'. Following Walsingham's death, he slid effortlessly into the service of Heneage: with one exception, Heneage expedited all Poley's secret service payments between 1590 and 1595 (when Heneage himself died). Poley now has senior status in the service: a section-head or case-officer. He reports directly to Heneage, relays instructions from him to other agents. In one letter, dated 1594, he is described as Heneage's 'man'. He is also in contact with Sir Robert Cecil. Lower down the scale, out in the field, worked the various Cecil agents, among them Michael Moody, Roger Walton, and Marlowe's shadowy associate Richard Cholmeley. We shall meet these characters in due course.

Burghley's tightness with government money was axiomatic, and the complaints of penniless agents punctuate the despatches. By late 1591, a new source of funds was beginning to attract them: the Earl of Essex. The chief figure in Essex's intelligence service, when it took proper shape the following year, was Anthony Bacon, the elder brother of Francis Bacon. He was also cousin to Sir Robert Cecil.

Physically, there are disconcerting similarities between these two rivals: the same pinched pallor, the same thin, over-refined features. Both had the brooding energy of the invalid, though in Bacon's case it was the gout that crippled him. The Bacon brothers were homosexual: Anthony was still technically wanted in France on a charge of buggery. Their private circle was gay, filled with dubious young dandies who were 'coach companion and bed companion': men like Tom Lawson and Harry Percy, a 'profane, costly fellow'. In the matter of intelligence, however, Anthony Bacon came to rely on a very different sort of man: that rather grim character Thomas Phelippes, Walsingham's old henchman. Phelippes had known the Bacons for years, so this was a personal allegiance, but it was also a coup for the Essex faction: no-one was more closely involved in the grass-roots of intelligence-gathering and code-breaking than Phelippes (and no-one, in my opinion, more likely to have squirrelled away those missing Walsingham files). A letter to Phelippes from Francis Bacon, dated early 1591, sounds like the beginnings of his service with Essex:

> I send you a copy of the letter I have written to the Earl, touching the matter proposed between us, wherein you will see how I have spoken of you. I advise you, in this beginning of intelligence, to spare no pains. The more plainly and frankly you deal with the Earl in this action, the better.

At about the same time, one of Phelippes's underlings was assuring people that there was no 'inwardness' between Phelippes and Lord Treasurer Burghley. Thus the new factions of the secret world take shape.

Phelippes brought with him a stable of experienced agents from the Walsingham days. Others, like Roger Walton, were soon persuaded to shift their allegiance from the Cecil camp. Another name to remember at this stage is Nicholas Skeres, a 'servant' of the Earl of Essex from about 1589, and a still unexplained presence on the day of Marlowe's death.

So this was the more fractured state of affairs in the early 1590s. Poley had fallen on his feet, found his niche in the service of Heneage and Cecil. Phelippes was hunched over his papers, in the service of Bacon and Essex. Both networks were hungry for intelligence, for leverage, for product.

Another change to be registered is the new importance of the Netherlands, or Low Countries, as an arena of English intelligence operations. Under Walsingham, the prime target had been Catholic groupings in France, but now – hovering like a cloud of insects over the indecisive progress of England's military campaign in the Netherlands – the spies and projectors are to be found not in Paris and Rheims, but in Brussels and Antwerp and Flushing. They haunt the shifting front-line of the war, they slip in and out of the Spanish battle-camps, and they mingle with the English exiles gathered around the court of the Duke of Parma, Spain's military commander in the Low Countries. This exile community, based in Brussels, is now the headquarters of Catholic conspiracy against England. Among them are names we have met before: the indefatigable Jesuit Robert Persons; and slippery Charles Paget, the former accomplice of Thomas Morgan in Paris.

This is now Poley's domain. His missions took him often to Scotland and France, but by far his most frequent area of operation is the Low Countries. In a little over seven years, between 1589 and 1597, he travelled there at least fourteen times. He is the Low Countries specialist within the Burghley network.

It is at this time, in the year 1591, and in this context of Low Countries intelligence, that we find new and curious evidence of Marlowe's continued involvement in the covert world.

24

LORD STRANGE

IN 1591 MARLOWE was sharing a room, probably in London, with Thomas Kyd. They were at this time both writing plays for the theatrical troupe of a certain 'Lord'. Kyd mentions this in his letter to Sir John Puckering, written not long after Marlowe's death. He does not name this Lord, but there is little doubt that it was Ferdinando Stanley, Lord Strange. In January 1592, in the same breath as he mentioned the Earl of Northumberland, Marlowe claimed also to be 'very well known' to Strange. In the same month Strange's company of players was performing *The Jew of Malta* at the Rose theatre – as far as we know, the play's first public run – and a year later they gave the première of *The Massacre at Paris*, also at the Rose.

Lord Strange's Men were the top company of the day. Their leading actor, following a merger with the Admiral's Men, was Edward Alleyn, the famous interpreter of Marlowe's tragic heroes. Their comic was Will Kemp, and they included a number of actors who would later form the Lord Chamberlain's Men, the company for which Shakespeare was to produce his greatest plays. Shakespeare himself wrote for Lord Strange's Men, and early works like *Titus Andronicus* and the *Henry VI* trilogy were first performed under Strange's theatrical patronage. This is Marlowe's circle as a dramatist – Alleyn and Kemp, Kyd and Shakespeare: the best of English theatre in the early 1590s.

Another member of Strange's literary set was Marlowe's friend Thomas Nashe. In *Pierce Penniless*, published in 1592,

Nashe lauds Strange as 'this renowned Lord, to whom I owe the utmost powers of my love and duty'. Strange is also the 'Lord S' to whom Nashe dedicated his dirty doggerel *The Choice of Valentines*, popularly known as 'Nashe's Dildo'. Other friends of Marlowe who enjoyed Strange's favour were Matthew Roydon, who praised him – along with the Earl of Northumberland – as an 'ingenious' scholar-nobleman whose generosity contributed 'to the vital warmth of freezing science'; and George Peele, who wrote of his dashing performance in the Accession Day Tilts of 1590. Edmund Spenser – a kinsman of Strange's wife, the foxy Alice Spenser – was another admirer. As well as a patron of poets, Strange was a talented poet in his own right who, as Spenser puts it, 'could pipe himself with passing skill'. Some of his efforts appear in the anthology *Belvedere* (1600).

Writing in 1593, after Marlowe's death, Kyd is at pains to stress that Marlowe's relations with Strange were purely professional. He writes:

> My first acquaintance with this Marlowe rose upon his bearing name to serve my Lord, although his Lordship never knew his service but in writing for his players, for never could my Lord endure his name or sight when he had heard of his conditions, nor would indeed the form of divine prayers used duly in his Lordship's house have quadred with such reprobates.

Kyd further claims that he 'left & did refrain' from Marlowe's company, both out of 'hatred of his life & thoughts', and 'as well by my Lord's commandment'.

Whether Kyd is reporting truthfully is not certain. It seems hard to believe that any patron of Marlowe's could be unaware of his reputation for holding dangerous opinions, so it is unlikely that these opinions alone would be enough suddenly to turn the patron against Marlowe. There may be some other reason for this falling-off of favour, or it may simply be that Kyd is anxious to distance Strange from the taint of Marlowe in 1593. Strange himself died the following year, a tragic early death in his mid-thirties, attributed at the time to either poisoning or witchcraft.

Both Marlowe and Matthew Roydon speak of Strange and Northumberland together, in the same sentence. This has led to the assumption that Strange was himself part of that intellectual, occultist coterie, centred on Northumberland and Ralegh. According to one well-known theory, Shakespeare alludes to this coterie as the 'school of night' in *Love's Labour's Lost*, and names Strange as a leading figure in it through various puns and concealed references. This theory has many opponents. There is actually no hard evidence that Strange even knew Northumberland, though it is very likely that he did. He is a more courtly figure than the reclusive Earl, but they are much the same kind of intellectual, free-thinking young aristocrat. They patronise the same poets, and they share an interest in those philosophical investigations which Roydon calls 'science' but which others called 'magic' or 'atheism'.

Another similarity between Strange and Northumberland leads straight back into the political world. It marks Strange with the same taint of Catholic intrigue, and it brings into his retinue spies as well as poets. Marlowe 'bore name to serve' Lord Strange as a play-maker, and the *Jew* and the *Massacre* are the fruits of this. But there was another, hidden piece of 'theatre' which he was involved in at this time, and I want to try and retrieve at least the bare outline of it.

The first clue lies in Strange's origins. He was the son and heir of Henry Stanley, 4th Earl of Derby. He grew up on the Stanley estates in Lancashire, centred on the great houses at Knowsley, Lathom and New Park. The family lived in 'princely style', entertaining with 'hospitality and magnificence'. The Derby retinue ran to about 140 servants and dependents. While the old Earl of Derby was never less than loyal to the Queen, and presided efficiently over the Council of the North, the family was of the kind viewed with some suspicion at court. They were classic 'Northern earl' stock, nostalgic for baronial autonomy and deeply tinged with the old religion.

Like Northumberland, Strange was born into a Catholic mould. He was not himself a Catholic, but he was surrounded by it. His brother, Sir Edward Stanley, was listed as a recusant and a 'dangerous person' in 1592. His cousins, Sir William and Sir Rowland Stanley, were both well-known Papists. Among his friends were Thomas Langton, the self-styled Baron of Walton, indicted in 1593 for 'harbouring seminary priests', and members of prominent Catholic families like the Heskeths and the Houghtons. Lancashire was a stronghold of Catholic reaction. In 1590 over seven hundred Lancastrians were charged with recusancy, and of the county's gentry only ten out of seventy-one were considered reliable Anglicans. It was here, among Strange's neighbours, that the Jesuit Campion had been sheltered.

Again like Northumberland, Strange's Catholic circumstance combined with his high standing in the order of succession. He was descended from blood royal on both sides: his father's great-uncle was Henry VII; his mother was the daughter of Henry VIII's niece, Eleanor Brandon. This made him the ideal royal figurehead for Catholic plotters. He comes to feature in their dreams of revolution: a Catholic King Ferdinand to rule when the Queen has died or, in the more extreme scenario, been 'removed'. Lord Strange shares with Northumberland this dubious distinction of Catholic figurehead, and their names are mentioned together not just by poets like Marlowe and Roydon, but also by informers like the apostate priest James Younger, who reports that 'Lords Strange and Percy [i.e. Northumberland] are talked of as much alienated by discontent', and that the 'rebels beyond sea' believe that both men would 'easily be moved by the Spaniard, who would promise to put them in places of authority if he should possess England'.

The first that is heard of this Catholic interest in Lord Strange comes from a captured priest named John Cycell. Like others in this story, Cycell was a university man who went to Rheims, and who was used there by Walsingham. In 1588, when he was Dr Allen's Latin secretary at Rheims, he was also in touch with Walsingham under the alias of 'Juan de Campo'. He has something of the profile of Richard Baines, but he was probably more of a waverer than an out-and-out saboteur at Rheims. In early 1591, Cycell was in Spain with Father Persons. From there he travelled to England with another priest, John Fixer. Their ship was seized in the Channel, and the priests were arrested. They were brought up to Lord Burghley, and with the usual stark choice before them, they threw in their lot with the government. This marks the real beginning of Cycell's long, accomplished career as a spy, agitator and propagandist.

Of particular interest to Lord Burghley was a letter that Cycell was carrying. It was from Father Persons, the most senior and most troublesome of the English Jesuits on the continent. Dated 3 April 1591, it contained various instructions for Cycell and Fixer, including the following:

I pray you both to have great care to advertise me by the first, and by as many ways as you can, either by Holland, Ireland, St Malo or Flanders, what you find in the man *my cousin*, whereof Mr Cycell and I talked so much . . .

The form in the which you may advertise me may be this, and I pray you note it: '*Your cousin the baker* is well-inclined and glad to hear of you, and meaneth not to give over his pretence to *the old bakehouse* you know of, but rather to put the same in suit when his ability shall serve . . .

I request you that *my cousin's* matter be dealt in secrecy, lest it may turn the poor man to hurt, but great desire have I to hear truly and particularly of his estate.

In the margin the code-words are deciphered: 'By his *cousin* is meant my Lord Strange', and 'by *baker* and *bakehouse* is understood my Lord Strange and the title they would have him pretend when Her Majesty dieth'. At the top of the letter Cycell has written: 'This letter I brought of purpose, that you might see it was no matter framed of mine own head that which they pretend of my Lord Strange.' The matter was passed on to Burghley's son, the intelligence specialist Sir

Robert Cecil. In early July, Cecil received further details from Cycell concerning Persons's intentions *in re* Lord Strange:

> The drift of his letter is charging us by means of John Garrat, a priest, to make trial of my L. Strange, and see how he was affected to that pretence of the Crown after Her Majesty's death. This matter he would not communicate to any but Garnet and Southwell, who are Jesuits at liberty in England. I brought this letter that my Lord [i.e. Burghley] might not think that what I told him of Lord Strange was a chimera.

Serious doubts have been raised about the Persons letter. It is not actually in his handwriting – 'by reason of my indisposition,' it begins, 'I cannot write this with my own hand' – and it could easily be a forgery by Cycell, purposely designed to discredit Lord Strange. Dr Allen hinted as much, when he alerted Persons to the arrest of Cycell and Fixer. 'They were with the Treasurer,' he writes, 'and were suspected to have discovered all they knew, and perhaps added somewhat of their own more than they knew.'

Whether forged or genuine, this letter opens up a chapter of deep uncertainty about Lord Strange. According to Cycell's information, there was a plan afoot in the spring of 1591, emanating from the English Jesuits on the continent, to sound out Lord Strange as a Catholic pretender to the throne. The 'Garrat' who was to be used is the Jesuit John Gerard, the son of Sir Thomas Gerard of Bryn. This Lancashire family was known to Strange, and Gerard was to use this as access to Strange. Lord Burghley knows of this plot shortly after Cycell's arrest in May 1591, and he has Sir Robert Cecil on the case.

Burghley and Cecil would also know who was behind this move to press Lord Strange on the subject of his 'claim'. They would know from Cycell that Sir William Stanley had been with Persons in Madrid in April 1591, and they would have guessed Stanley's involvement anyway. The code-word used in Persons's letter virtually gives it away – perhaps suspiciously so – for Stanley was indeed Lord Strange's cousin.

Of all the tarring by association which Strange suffered in the early 1590s, the blackest was his blood-relationship to Sir William Stanley. Stanley was a by-word for treachery, a bogey-man. He was a swashbuckling but oddly poignant figure. For years he fought loyally for the Queen in Ireland, where he was knighted but unrewarded. In the summer of 1586, he led his regiment across to the Low Countries to join the Earl of Leicester. He was in action at Zutphen, where Sir Philip Sidney was wounded, and at the taking of Deventer. Leicester said he was a man 'worth his weight in pearl', but a few weeks later this valuation changed. On 29 January 1587, while Leicester was back in England, Sir William Stanley and Sir Rowland Yorke handed the town of Deventer back to the Spanish. Of Stanley's troop of about nine hundred men, a third remained loyal to the Queen and were allowed to leave Deventer. The remainder proceeded, with Stanley, into Spanish service.

This was a huge blow to the English campaign in the Netherlands: militarily and, even more, in terms of morale. The Dutch placed a price on Stanley's head of 3000 florins. The English denounced him as a heretic and a traitor. A propaganda pamphlet, *A Short Admonition Upon the Detestable Treason*, was rushed out (printed by Richard Jones, who later printed the first edition of *Tamburlaine*). On the other side, Stanley was applauded by the Jesuits and defended in print by Dr Allen, but on the whole his defection caused him more hatred in England than love in Spain. King Philip was said to have commented: 'I like the treachery, but not the traitor.'

Stanley's 'English regiment' – something of a misnomer for this rag-bag of English, Irish, Italians, Burgundians and Walloons – saw action on various fronts in the Netherlands. In the summer of 1588 they were at Nieuport, some 700 strong, ready to go in behind the Armada. By 1591 they were in action near Nijmegen. The regiment was a magnet for mercenaries and spies, as well as genuine Catholics. Among their number was Iacomo Francisci, the notorious 'Captain

Jacques', who was Stanley's lieutenant-colonel; Richard Williams, later executed as a would-be assassin of the Queen; and the Jesuit Henry Walpole, one of the regiment's chaplains. A subaltern of Stanley's in later years was a young man called Guy Fawkes.

In the Low Countries Stanley was closely associated with the Catholics' chief intelligence-gatherer, Hugh Owen, a Welshman from the Lleyn peninsula who was described by Father Persons as a 'very active, diligent, faithful and secret solicitor'. Working from Brussels, Owen gathered intelligence from Catholic priests and agents in England, and passed it on to the Duke of Parma, or directly to the Spanish court in Madrid. He was highly valued by Spain, and received a salary of 60 escudos a month. Little escaped his sharp eye in the fractious world of the English exiles, and few of the spies set against him achieved much. He exposed them and outwitted them: some were handed over to Spanish interrogation, others were turned and played back against their English masters.

This is one of the inner circles of English Catholic conspiracy in Europe in the 1590s: Persons the Jesuit, Owen the intelligencer, and Stanley the military commander. These are the 'Spanish Elizabethans', who have taken their opposition to Queen and Country to its furthest point, and are now high-ranking figures in the service of the Old Enemy. Owen and Stanley have their headquarters in the Low Countries, but they are often in Spain, at the court of King Philip in Madrid, where Persons was mainly based at this time. One such occasion was in early 1591, when Stanley was with Persons in Madrid, trying to get Spanish backing for an expedition to seize Alderney, in the Channel Islands. It was on this occasion, if not before, that Stanley impressed on Persons the fitness of his noble young cousin, Lord Strange, as a pretender to the English crown.

In the event, the Alderney *empresa* never materialised, but this two-fold strategy becomes the typical Stanley plan against England: military advance, usually via Ireland or Scotland, combined with a domestic Catholic uprising centred on Lord Strange as pretender. Later, when Strange succeeded as the

Earl of Derby in the autumn of 1593, this dream of Stanley's becomes even stronger. In December 1593 Henry Walpole, a former chaplain in Stanley's regiment, embarked for England. Shortly before leaving, he received instructions from Stanley 'to deal with some priest that might get access to the Lord Strange, now Earl of Derby, to induce him to the Catholic religion'. Once again, the priest John Gerard is considered a 'fit man thereunto'. And a few months later, in Brussels, conversing with Edmund Yorke (the nephew of Sir Rowland Yorke, the fellow-betrayer of Deventer), the conversation turns once more on Strange: 'Sir Wm Stanley said if the Queen were dead, he would go to Scotland with his regiment, make it strong, and go to the Earl of Derby, as would all the English.'

These were the Catholic hopes heaped upon the shoulders of Lord Strange. Similar hopes had been foisted on the Earl of Northumberland. Northumberland had showed himself unwilling to dabble in these matters, but what of Strange's attitude?

The view of the torturer Topcliffe, voiced in 1592, was that 'all the Stanleys in England are traitors'. He would undoubtedly include Lord Strange in this blanket accusation, but the truth is less simple. Strange held the office of Lord Lieutenant of Lancashire, and on a level of local government he seems to have been no friend of the Catholics. His duties included the identifying and charging of recusants, and he performed this to the government's satisfaction. What is probably truer than Topcliffe's charge is the comment made at the time that Strange 'was of no religion'. This sounds like the tolerant, philosophical Lord who might patronise Marlowe, but on the other hand it does him no good in the eyes of the government, because a man of 'no religion' is, in their view, a man ready to belong to either religion. There were some also who spoke of Strange's rather haughty references to his supposed claim to the throne. The old Countess of Shrewsbury, hatchet-faced Bess of Hardwick, heard him bantering in 'foolish speeches' on the subject with

Sir Francis Hastings (the son of the Earl of Huntingdon, and another possible claimant). She reported Strange as 'saying that they two should one day fight for the Crown'. She also spoke of 'the show of his great will and haughty stomach, his making of himself so popular, and bearing himself so against my Lord of Essex.' All this, she said, in a fine display of hindsight after Strange's death, 'I thought would be his overthrow.'

In the end, Strange's own attitude to the plotters is not the point. He was, wittingly or otherwise, a magnet for Catholic conspiracy. This cell of militant exiles – Stanley, Persons, Owen – was busy in Brussels and Madrid. There was another nest of pro-Strange plotters in Prague, whose activities I will look at later. And there are Catholics around him here in England, particularly in his local fiefdom in Lancashire, but also in his more courtly circle at London.

So this is the situation in the summer of 1591, when the first intimations of these Catholic plans for Lord Strange reach the ears of Lord Burghley and Sir Robert Cecil. According to the nobbled priest John Cycell this was no 'chimera', but a very real plot. They had intercepted Cycell, but who else might be sent to 'sound' Strange, and what might his response be? It is at this point, perhaps, that their thoughts turn to Lord Strange's playwright, Christopher Marlowe, a man who has already proved his mettle in 'matters touching the benefit of his country', and who had perhaps served as a government listener in the Northumberland circle.

Thomas Kyd says the relationship between Marlowe and Strange was distant, merely professional. Marlowe, on the other hand, says he is 'very well known' to Strange. The truth may be somewhere in the middle. Let us say, at least, that in 1591 Marlowe is in a position to mingle with the conspiratorial elements around Lord Strange: to observe, to report, and perhaps, as is the Elizabethan way, to provoke.

25

THE DUTCH SHILLING

WE NOW COME to the most enigmatic episode in Marlowe's brief enigmatic career: his arrest in the Netherlands on a charge of 'coining', or counterfeiting money. This only came to light recently, in 1976, when a letter referring to it was discovered at the Public Record Office. It has been mentioned since in books on Marlowe, but it has not been properly examined or understood. It belongs, I believe, to this 'secret theatre' of Elizabethan espionage, and more particularly to this context of pro-Strange plotting.

In January 1592 – the seventh year of war in the Netherlands – Marlowe was lodging in a chamber with two other Englishmen in the little sea-port of Vlissingen, or Flushing, at the mouth of the Schelde river. Flushing was full of Englishmen – it was actually an English possession, a 'cautionary town' ceded by the Dutch in return for Elizabeth's military support against the Spanish invaders. There was an English governor, an English church, and a permanent garrison of English troops. The town was overcrowded and insanitary, the locals hostile. The traffic of war passed through, incessantly, chaotically – soldiers and supplies on their way to the front, the cashiered and the wounded on their way back home, and the usual wartime flotsam of profiteers, adventurers and spies, travelling in both directions and in neither.

Among the last group I would place the Christopher 'Marly' who was arrested there as a counterfeiter, and deported on 26 January 1592. Even without this ignominious conclusion one might guess that something was afoot in that chamber in Flushing, for one of Marlowe's 'chamber-fellows' was none other than Richard Baines, the former spy at Rheims and the future penner of the 'Note' concerning Marlowe's 'damnable judgement of religion'.

The governor of Flushing, Sir Robert Sidney – younger brother of the late Sir Philip – summed up what he knew of the case in a letter to Lord Burghley. It was carried across to England by Sidney's 'ancient', David Lloyd, who also had charge of the presumed coiner Marly or Marlowe. It was this letter that was rediscovered in 1976, by Professor Robert B. Wernham, as he worked through the uncatalogued recesses of SP84 – State Papers (Holland) – at the Public Record Office:

Right honourable,

Besides the prisoner Evan Flud, I have also given in charge to this bearer, my ancient, two other prisoners: the one named Christofer Marly, by his profession a scholar, and the other Gifford Gilbert, a goldsmith, taken here for coining, and their money I have sent over unto your Lordship.

The matter was revealed unto me the day after it was done, by one Ri: Baines, whom also my ancient shall bring unto your Lordship. He was their chamber-fellow and, fearing the success, made me acquainted withal. The men being examined apart never denied anything, only protesting that what was done was only to see the goldsmith's cunning, and truly I am of opinion that the poor man was only brought in under that colour, whatever intent the other two had at that time. And indeed they do one accuse another to have been the inducers of him, and to have intended to practise it hereafter, and have as it were justified him unto me.

But howsoever it happened, a Dutch shilling was uttered, and else not any piece. And indeed I do not think that they would have uttered many of them, for the metal is plain pewter and with half an eye to be discovered. Notwithstanding, I thought it fit to send them over unto your Lordship, to take their trial as you shall think best. For I will not stretch my commission to deal in such matters, and much less to put them at liberty and to deliver them into the town's hands. Being the Queen's subjects, and not required neither of this said town, I know not how it would have been liked, especially since part of that which they did counterfeit was Her Majesty's coin.

The goldsmith is an excellent workman, and if I should speak my conscience, had no intent hereunto. The scholar says himself to be very well known both to the Earl of Northumberland and my Lord Strange. Baines and he do also accuse one another of intent to go to the enemy, or to Rome, both as they say of malice to one another. Hereof I thought fit to advertise your Lordship, leaving the rest to their own confession, and my ancient's report. And so do humbly take my leave. At Flushing the 26 of January 1592.

Your Honour's very obedient to do you service,

R. Sydney

This letter is our only source of knowledge about Marlowe in the Low Countries. I have spent some time both in the town archive of Flushing, and at the *rijksarchief* of the provincial capital, Middelburg, and though I found some documentary traces of certain English spies like Roger Walton, I found none of Marlowe. In the town itself, his footsteps are long obscured, though the formidable, flinty bulk of the Gevangetoren, the town prison, still looms over the harbour; and the cobbled streets that ripple out from the church of St Jacob probably contain the site of his lodgings; and if I had to guess, or stick a pin into the map of Flushing drawn up by Robert Adams in 1585, it might perhaps point me to a certain little garage-like 'café' hard by the church, filled with loud music and the smell of hashish, where a lounging leather-jacketed group in the corner seemed for a moment – to a pair of archive-weary eyes unused to the darkness – like young men *wearing doublets*.

This brief visitation aside, I return to Sir Robert Sidney's letter, and to the skeletal narrative which can be reconstructed from it.

At some point in late 1591 or early 1592 Marlowe arrives in Flushing. Whether Flushing was his only destination, or whether he was *en route* to or from other places in the Netherlands, we do not know. By the middle of January 1592, he is sharing a chamber in the town with Richard Baines, the former Walsingham spy, and with Gifford Gilbert, a goldsmith and an 'excellent workman' in metals. I can find nothing about Gilbert. The fact that his name is another spy's name in reverse has to be taken as coincidence, though it could conceivably be some kind of cocky alias. A Bartholomew Gilbert, also a goldsmith, was imprisoned in the Wood Street Counter in 1594: he may be related to the Flushing goldsmith.

Persuaded by Marlowe – or so Baines claims – the goldsmith agrees to perform the criminal act of 'coining'. Various coins are produced, including some counterfeit English currency, but only one is actually issued, or 'uttered', in public. This is a Dutch shilling. The raw material used is pewter, probably given a silver wash. The counterfeit is poor: easily discernible. The following day Richard Baines slips down to the Lord Governor's house, standing on the west side of Flushing's inner haven, on what is now Molenstraat. There he informs Governor Sidney of the crime. He accuses Marlowe as the 'inducer' of the goldsmith. He says that Marlowe intends to learn the craft of counterfeiting himself, and to 'practise it hereafter'. He also claims that Marlowe is intending to go over 'to the enemy or to Rome'.

By the 'enemy', of course, Baines means the Catholics. The clear implication – though it is not actually stated in Sidney's summary of the case – is that Marlowe is intending to join up with the renegade English of the Low Countries: the exile community grouped around Hugh Owen in Brussels; the 'English regiment' under Sir William Stanley, currently based near Nijmegen. Another implication – also not stated by Sidney, probably because it was too obvious to need stating –

is that these two separate charges, of coining and of intending to defect, are connected with one another. The one thing that the Catholic exiles lacked – conspirators and soldiers alike – was money. They had cut themselves off from their own wealth and lands in England, and though they were exploited by Spain they were seldom rewarded. Their letters are filled with the frustrations of political under-investment, and with tales of hardship, hunger and sometimes death, as of the old campaigner Sir Thomas Markenfield, who lived in 'extreme want' at a 'miserable poor cottage' in Brussels, and who was found dead in the summer of 1592 'lying on the bare floor of his chamber, no creature being present at his death'. Anyone who brought money, whether it was real or counterfeit, would find the doors of the Brussels conspirators opening up in welcome. This is the undoubted logic of Baines's accusation about Marlowe.

Marlowe and Gilbert are duly arrested by officers of the Governor. They are probably held at the Governor's house, or in the English barracks, rather than in the town's Gevangetoren. Whatever their crime, they are the Queen's subjects, and Sidney does not wish to deliver them 'into the town's hands'.

Under examination, Marlowe claims that he was only testing out the goldsmith's skills: it was curiosity, nothing more. He throws Baines's accusations back at him: that Baines was as much the 'inducer' of the counterfeiting as he was; that Baines was the one who was intending to defect to the Catholics. There is 'malice' between the former chamber-fellows.

This retort of Marlowe's comes too late. Timing is an all-important factor in the protocol of the informer. Baines has revealed the matter first, and he is believed. As they assemble on the waterfront to take ship for England, it is Marlowe and Gilbert who are the prisoners. They are to be taken to Lord Burghley for further questioning, and 'to take their trial' as he thinks fit. Baines travels with them, but he is not under arrest. He is there as the informer, the furnisher of evidence: his métier. There is a third prisoner in the party, Evan Flud. He is probably the Mr Flood who is described elsewhere as a kinsman of Lord Lumley, and who was serving in Stanley's regiment the previous year.

The party embarks under the watchful eye of David Lloyd, Sidney's 'ancient' or ensign. Whatever Marlowe's mood and intent when he had left England, this is how he returns: a prisoner under escort, cold, scared, dying for a smoke. Arrest is always an undignified experience, yet it has also a certain foolish charisma. And so the little boat heads out into the winds of the Westerschelde.

Coining was an extremely serious charge. It was a criminal activity in the financial sense – the term 'coining' covers various abuses of the coinage, including adulterating and 'clipping' as well as counterfeiting – yet it had an overtone of sedition as well. English coins carried the image of the Queen, as well as various religious or nationalist devices. The names of the coins reflect this: sovereigns, crowns, nobles, angels. There is a talismanic aspect to coinage, and the act of counterfeiting is an offence at that level, as well as at the level of profiteering.

For this sort of reason, coining came under the broad heading of 'petty treason', which included various forms of insubordination to authority, such as the murder of a master by his servant, or of a husband by his wife, or even striking a Justice of the Peace. It was less heinous than 'high treason', but it too was punishable with death. The poet Thomas Lodge refers graphically to the fate of coiners in his satire, *A Fig for Momus*:

> When other subtle shifts do fail
> They fall to coining, & from thence by course
> Through hempen windows learn to shake their tail.

The 'hempen window' is, of course, the hangman's noose.

So if due process of law were to take place, Marlowe and Gilbert stood in danger of a traitor's death. Judging from the docket on the back of Sidney's letter, written by one of Lord

Burghley's secretaries, due process of law was expected. It describes Marlowe and Gilbert as 'taken for coinage', and says they have been sent over 'to be tried here for that fact'.

We know nothing of Marlowe's interview with Lord Burghley at the end of January 1592. It is likely to have been uncomfortable at the least. Whatever ulterior motives he might claim, Marlowe is on the carpet, with the plausible Baines to accuse him, and the bag of tinny coins sitting on the Treasurer's desk. Among the letters of the Dutch Catholic Richard Verstegan, there is a verbatim account of Burghley interrogating another Flushing suspect some months later. It gives us a hint of the crabbed tone of things. The culprit this time was a young Norfolk Catholic, Thomas Dawbney. On 23 December 1592 he was 'taken at Flushing as he would have passed into England' and, like Marlowe and Gilbert before him, he was 'sent prisoner thither unto the Lord Treasurer'. The following fragment of the examination is probably based on Dawbney's own account.

'Now, rogue,' says the Treasurer. 'Where hast thou been a-roguing?'

'I have been in Douai, my Lord, but nowhere a-roguing.'

'To whom is the letter that was taken about thee?'

'I know not other than the direction doth declare. A Dutchman gave it to me.'

'You can tell if you list.'

Burghley ordered Dawbney to be imprisoned in the Gatehouse, until such time as he could 'put in sureties for his reformation'. He also sent a tart message back to Lord Governor Sidney, saying that he did not wish to be troubled with small fry like this. 'When any more such rogues come thither,' Sidney should 'whip them, and send them back again from whence they came'.

This shows Burghley's rather severe style, and though he was not a punitive man, someone taken coining in Flushing would not be expecting leniency from him. So it is significant that Marlowe escapes any serious punishment for his crime. He was certainly free by May of 1592, for in that month he tangled with the local constabulary on Holywell Street in

Shoreditch. If he suffered any punishment for his efforts as a coiner in Flushing, it can have been no more than a few months' imprisonment.

The last reference to the affair on the official record is on 3 March 1592, when Burghley signed a warrant for the payment of £13 6s 8d to Sidney's ensign, David Lloyd, 'for bringing of letters from ye said Sir Robert Sidney, knight, importing Her Majesty's special service, together with three prisoners committed to his charge'. Thus Marlowe makes a brief, anonymous appearance on the rolls of the Chamber accounts, not as a confidential courier or a special servant, but as one of three prisoners under escort. This entry has not been noticed before, and can now be added to the small but growing body of extant documents about his life.

26

MARLOWE AND POOLE

THIS IS NOT quite the end of the affair, however, for when the informer Richard Baines came to compile his 'Note' of Marlowe's heresies in 1593, he included a couple of comments on the subject of coining. The first was that Marlowe believed 'that he had as good right to coin as the Queen of England'. This has the authenticity of the Flushing episode behind it, and probably echoes some remark of Marlowe's as he urged the goldsmith on to 'see his cunning'.

The second of Baines's statements on the subject is more precise, and it opens up certain connections behind the Flushing episode. Marlowe, says Baines,

> was acquainted with one Poole, a prisoner in Newgate, who hath great skill in mixture of metals, and having learned some things of him, he meant through help of a cunning stamp-maker, to coin French crowns, pistolets and English shillings.

It used to be thought that 'one Poole' was a reference, in variant spelling, to Robert Poley, but there is no record of Poley having done time in Newgate, nor any suggestion that he had metallurgical skills. There is a far more plausible candidate for Marlowe's tutor in the art of counterfeiting. His name was John Poole. He was a Cheshire gentleman, the son and heir of John Poole senior, of Poole Hall in the Wirrall. He fits the bill perfectly, because in about 1587 he was imprisoned in Newgate, and the crime he had committed was coining.

Poole remained in Newgate at least until 1590. Marlowe himself spent a couple of weeks there in 1589, alongside Tom Watson after the Hog Lane affray, and it was probably then that he made Poole's acquaintance. Either then or later he learned from Poole those 'things' about the working of metals which he was caught putting into practice in Flushing.

John Poole was himself a man under close surveillance. One night in July 1587, in the pitch-dark dungeon in Newgate known as the Limboes, he had conversed rather too freely with a man called Humphrey Gunson or Gunstone. He believed Gunson was a fellow-prisoner, but actually he was a prison informer. Gunson duly delivered a three-page account of Poole's treacherous sentiments to the authorities.

Though Gunson describes Poole as 'imprisoned upon suspicion of coining', this was only part of his crime. He was also known as a militant Catholic, and had once been 'apprehended for a seminary priest, for that the crown of his head was shaven'. Gunson's report gives instances of Poole's seditious Catholic sentiments and rumours:

> The Queen, he said, was betrothed to the Earl of Arundel before she came to the crown, & after she would not have him . . .

> The Queen doted upon Monsieur, he said, and how that she tumbled on a bed with him, but he could do nothing & so was fain to leave her . . .

> He saith there is a prophesy that the Rose & the White Bear shall flee in the Castle of Care (meaning the Queen & the Earl of Leicester) & never be seen after.

Poole was especially critical of the Earl of Leicester, whom he calls 'the common bull of the court'. He spoke darkly of Leicester's dealings – how 'his wife's neck was broken down a pair of stairs'; how he connived at the death of the old Earl of Essex in order to marry the widow; how he tried to marry his son to Arabella Stuart. All Leicester's dealings showed,

287

according to Poole, 'how desirous he hath been of a kingdom'. This picture of Leicester as a scheming Machiavellian is drawn wholesale from *Leicester's Commonwealth*, the Catholic pamphlet which got Poley into trouble, and which Poole here praises as a book full of 'most strange & rare matter'.

As well as these malcontent opinions, Gunson reports Poole's actual involvement in the smuggling in of priests and seminarists: 'he conveyed from Chichester one Poole that all the country was layen for' and 'he enquired of one Potter, a priest that came from Rome for him'. This namesake whom Poole smuggled out of Chichester was probably Geoffrey Poole of Lordington, the grandson of the famous Cardinal Pole, who was active at Rheims and Rome (though not himself a priest), and who later helped the seminary priest Thomas Pormont cross from Flushing into England. The 'Potter' who came from Rome is the priest George Stransham, who used the name Potter as an alias. He was another of the Cambridge-Rheims alumni. He graduated BA at Cambridge in 1580, was admitted to Rheims in 1583, and was ordained priest in 1585, the same year as Gilbert Gifford. In the spring of 1586 he and two others set out for England. When Gunson says Potter came 'for' Poole, he presumably means that Poole was to be his contact in England. In fact Potter and his companions were arrested on entry. They were taken 'a-shipboard' in Arundel Haven, and were committed to the Marshalsea on Walsingham's orders. Thomas Phelippes called him 'a shrewd fellow and obstinate', and the spy Berden said he was 'meet for the gallows or the galleys', but he was in fact despatched to the gulag of Wisbech Castle, where the government housed long-term Catholic prisoners.

So Marlowe's acquaintance John Poole was not just a coiner with 'great skill in mixture of metals'. He was also a man who held subversive Catholic views, a man involved in the conveyance and handling of seminary priests infiltrating the country. His connection with the Rheims priest, Stransham alias Potter, can be dated to 1586, which is just about the time that Marlowe was involved in his pseudo-

Rheims posture at Cambridge. Another man connected with
Poole in 1586 was Sir Edward Fitton: the two men were
involved together in land-deals in Ireland. The same Fitton
was in touch with Anthony Babington that year, trying
unsuccessfully to fix up a passport for him. Marlowe and
Poole were evidently part of the same little world, apparently
either side of a boundary – Marlowe the faithful dealer for the
government; Poole the genuine subversive – but the boundary
keeps shifting, and one cannot be sure where Poole stood, or
indeed Marlowe.

This is already an interesting new dimension to the Flushing
episode, and tends to confirm the strong political overtones
that are heard in Baines's original accusation: the idea that
Marlowe was coining for subversive Catholic ends, that he
intended to 'go to the enemy' with his purseful of blue money.
But even more interesting, and more precise in its implications
about the Flushing episode, is John Poole's connection with
the Stanley family. He was the husband of Mary Stanley, who
was daughter of Sir Rowland Stanley of Hooton in Cheshire.
In local dynastic terms this is a marriage between two
prominent Catholic families. A document of about 1580,
listing certain Cheshire gentlemen 'whose houses are greatly
infected with popery', includes side by side John Poole senior
of Poole, and Rowland Stanley of Hooton.

Through his marriage to Mary Stanley, John Poole was
brother-in-law to the traitor Sir William Stanley. It is very
likely he is the John Poole mentioned in a letter of Sir
William's, written from Ireland in about 1580. He may have
been in Stanley's service in Ireland. He certainly shows his
commitment to Stanley during his conversation with Gunson
the informer. Gunson, doubtless to draw him out, ventured
the orthodox opinion about 'what an unnatural act Sir
William Stanley had accomplished in the delivery of the town
of Deventer to the enemy, banishing himself thereby from the
favour of ye Queen.' Poole reacted to this with a spirited
'answer in Sir William's defence' – how he had fought
courageously for the Queen in Ireland and 'brought the

country in quiet', how he had been tricked of his rewards by his enemy Ralegh, and cast off 'altogether unrecompenced'. Poole's whole attack on Leicester and Ralegh as 'carpet knights' is made in the context of his defence of the soldierly Sir William Stanley. Stanley's treachery was still fresh in the memory – they were speaking six months after the yielding of Deventer – and Poole's pro-Stanley statements are given prime position in Gunson's report on him.

Linked by marriage to the Stanleys, John Poole was thus a kinsman of the most elevated members of the family – Henry Stanley, 4th Earl of Derby, and his son and heir, Lord Strange. The family was certainly known to Strange. In October 1587, just three months after Poole was shooting his mouth off in Newgate prison, John Poole senior and 'one other of the Pooles' dined with Strange and his father at Knowsley Castle.

It is no surprise, therefore, to find John Poole touching on the vexed question of the succession, and voicing the claim of Lord Strange. According to Gunson, he first argued that 'the Earl of Hertford's sons were base-born, & therefore could lay no right title to the Crown', and then he 'showed of' Lord Strange's claim. This is certainly consistent with a kinsman and devotee of Sir William Stanley, who was the chief plotter of Catholic coups centred on Lord Strange as pretender to the crown.

Though it was written in 1587, Gunson's report surfaces as part of a government investigation of Poole over three years later. On 14 October 1590, the Privy Council ordered four officials, including the recusant-hunter Justice Young, to 'resort to the prison of Newgate', and there 'to examine a matter concerning certain traitorous speeches uttered by one John Poole, contained in a writing sent herewith'. The text of Gunson's report on Poole as we have it is probably a copy made at this time. How long he remained in Newgate after this is not recorded. In 1593 a man was seen carrying two 'trunks full of plate' aboard a ship called the *Bray*, then lying near Erith. According to witnesses, 'the plate was church plate'. He also had 'a bag sealed up, as much as he could lift', which contained gold and silver. This dealer in stolen metal was a Cheshireman, referred to by witnesses as 'Captain Poole'. He was almost certainly John Poole the coiner, last heard of in Newgate in 1590, but now seemingly back to his old criminal 'skill', which required a ready supply of metals to work on.

Whatever they were like personally, John Poole and Christopher Marlowe have a curiously similar profile. Both men are arrested for coining, and both are charged with seditious Catholic allegiances: Poole by Gunson in Newgate, and Marlowe by Baines in Flushing. And both men are figures on the fringes of Lord Strange's circle: Poole as his relative by marriage, and Marlowe as a writer for his players. What would, in any case, be a close parallel between the two men is made into a concrete connection by Richard Baines, who says it was Poole who had actually instructed Marlowe in the art of coining.

To confirm the implications of this, I would like to leave Poole and Marlowe a moment, and bring on a man called Edward Bushell. My interest in Bushell is that he has *exactly* the same profile. He is a coiner dealing in stolen metal; he is a Catholic; and he is a servant of Lord Strange.

In about 1591 Bushell was involved, with others, in a major robbery at Winchester cathedral. The church 'plate' they stole was later 'melted and coined' at the chambers of Sir Griffin Markham in Gray's Inn. The metal was said to be worth £1800, a huge sum of money, and according to one of the participants, there were 'many gentlemen' that had 'shares' in this venture. It is possible that John Poole was one, and that the trunks full of church plate which he had at Erith were also part of the Winchester haul.

As well as being a sharer in the Winchester coining, Bushell was reported as saying that 'when his father was dead, he would make money of all he had, and go oversea'. To 'make money' is meant quite literally: the melting down of massy goods to turn them into counterfeit coin. This done he would 'go oversea' – to Sir William Stanley, I would guess – but whether or not he did go I cannot discover. When the warrants finally went out for the Winchester robbers in 1594, he was still associated with the Stanley family: no longer with Lord Strange himself, who was by then dead, but as a 'servant' of his widow Alice, Lady Strange.

Other members of the Winchester gang, though not specifically connected with Lord Strange, are in the same mould of Catholic malcontent. One of them, Henry Duffield, is glimpsed interestingly in the context of Ralegh and Northumberland. In early 1592, he was reported to Lord Burghley as 'a discontented man, and bitter in invectives against the State'. He was plotting, it was said, to sabotage the Queen's fleet at Chatham:

He proposes to go to Dunkirk, to the Prince of Parma, thence return with a galley of ten or twelve oars, come in an evening into Chatham river, and burn the ships as they lie at anchor with balls of wildfire. But as he requires many men to bring this to pass, he is gone with Sir Walter Ralegh this voyage, and means to select some desperate sailors for this purpose. He will not choose malcontent gentlemen at home, lest he be crossed in the height of his hope, as Babington was.

Further to this intelligence, Burghley wrote to Ralegh in May 1592: 'I, the Treasurer, am secretly informed, but with what truth I know not, that one Duffield, having charge under Sir John Borough, is a man much miscontent, and hath given his promise to do some special service to the Spaniard.' It is interesting that Duffield was serving under Sir John Borough, or Burgh, the Vice-Admiral of Ralegh's privateering fleet. Burgh was a particular friend of the Earl of Northumberland. In one of the Earl's 'breving books' (kitchen accounts), covering a ten-week period during autumn 1591, Sir John was a guest at Northumberland's table no less than nineteen times. The man who provided Burghley with the information about Duffield, a spy called Paul Crushe, had connections himself with the Northumberland household.

The ringleader of the Winchester robbery was the Welsh

Catholic Richard Williams. Shortly after the robbery, in August 1591, he left the country with Essex's expedition to France: he may have known Nicholas Skeres, who also went out with the Essex troop. Once on the continent, Williams deserted and joined up with Stanley's regiment at Nijmegen. He served with Stanley three years, and was 'very great' with Stanley's adjutant, the notorious 'Captain Jacques'. In 1594 Williams was planning an assassination attempt on the Queen, urged on by Sir William Stanley himself. He was captured on his return to England in August 1594, charged with treason and hanged. So in this case, the coining of money leads not only to the Low Countries, and to Sir William Stanley, but also to the gallows. Another participant in the Winchester robbery was a Captain Dyer. He too joined up with Stanley, and in 1594 he was described as one of Stanley's 'lieutenants'.

In the ramifications of the Winchester robbery, we find this nest of Catholic coiners with connections that lead into the circles of Lord Strange and the Earl of Northumberland, and into the revolutionary designs of Sir William Stanley in the Low Countries. This bolsters up this context of 'political coining' which I have applied to the main figures of this chapter, John Poole and Christopher Marlowe.

As so often in this story of the secret world, what the evidence seems to show and what it really shows are two different things. On the face of it, Sir Robert Sidney's letter from Flushing seems to show that Marlowe was a criminal. But as we trace through the circumstances behind the episode, there emerges a more complex reading: that this coining has a political overtone, that it is linked to seditious Catholic elements in the circle of Lord Strange – men like John Poole and Edward Bushell – and so with this whole element of succession-plotting centred on Strange's supposed claim to the English throne. Marlowe's presence in the Low Countries, intending to 'go to the enemy', brings him close to the leading pro-Strange plotters, Sir William Stanley and Hugh Owen. Or rather it would have done, if Baines had not stuck a spanner in the works.

By this train of thought we arrive at conspiracy, rather than simple criminality, as the main feature of the Flushing episode. From this it is only a short step – as we have seen time and again in this book – to 'projection': that particular type of conspiracy which was secretly encouraged by the government, as a means of infiltrating and sabotaging subversive Catholic groups. We know that Lord Burghley was aware of this pro-Strange intrigue in the early summer of 1591, further to the revelations of John Cycell. We can certainly assume that he – or more particularly, Sir Robert Cecil – wished to know more about it, and that the tried and trusted way to find out more would be to infiltrate spies. We know that Marlowe had worked as a spy: he had his credentials from the Walsingham days. I believe he is now at work again, a Cecil projector within the circle of Lord Strange, and that this is what breaks to the surface in Flushing in January 1592.

In this quirky way, the Sidney letter of 1592 becomes another record which relates to Marlowe's career in 'government service'. It leads us into the same kind of area as the Privy Council certificate five years earlier. The coiner in Flushing, like the defector to Rheims, is not really a criminal at all, but one working for the 'benefit of his country'. The fact that Marlowe escaped punishment for his coining would confirm that he was able to claim, as he had done in 1587, that his motives were loyal.

One question that arises is why did Marlowe not claim his status as an agent of the Cecils, in order to escape arrest at Flushing? Various answers present themselves. First, because he did not have the all-important warranty which would prove it. In this case, he is a cowboy, operating without licence in this dodgy area. The second answer tends the other way. He did not reveal his status as an English agent because his arrest and deportation were actually a reinforcement of his cover as a Catholic coiner: to the conspirators, arrest was a credential, a bona fide. A third answer might be that he considered it *more* dangerous to reveal himself as a spy than to take the consequences as a coiner. The English commanders at Flushing were heartily sick of spies and projectors, whether English or Catholic or, as most were, a motley of the two. Summary justice was sometimes executed, as in the case of Ralph Birkenshaw, sent by Burghley to Flushing in 1592 but while there denounced as a double-dealer. He was committed close prisoner by the Lieutenant Governor, Sir Edmund Udall, and his trunk of papers sealed up 'wherein were all such writings' relating to 'Her Majesty's service'. On Boxing Day 1592 he was brought, 'fast bound like a thief', to the marketplace near St Jacob's church. There his ears were nailed to a gibbet and sliced off. 'All the time the drums sounded, so that he should not be heard, in case he made the truth known to the soldiers.' He was then sent, 'all bleeding', out of the town.

Such a fate did not overtake Marlowe. He was escorted back to England, back to Burghley. His bluff pays off, and he escapes any punishment. This exoneration is another exercise in discreet governmental protection for a young man who was perhaps considered doubtful, even potentially dangerous, but who – more important in the priorities of Elizabethan *realpolitik* – was considered useful.

What exactly he was up to in this role as a Cecil projector is hard to say – the question is not really what he was up to, but what *would* he have been up to if he had succeeded in gaining the confidence of Stanley and Owen in Brussels. Perhaps the best answer is provided by the 'Hesketh plot' of 1593. This emanated from Prague rather than the Low Countries, but it is an insight into the kind of pro-Strange plotting that was going on, and into the kind of counter-moves that Cecil had in mind.

Prague, the capital of Bohemia and the court of the Holy Roman Emperor, Rudolf II, was one of the centres for English exiles, and among them were various Lancashire Catholics known personally to Lord Strange. One of these was a stout, 'yellow-haired' man, a merchant and a dabbler in alchemy, who arrived in Prague in 1589. His name was Richard Hesketh, and he has earned a place in the history books as the protagonist of the 'Hesketh plot'.

What happened can be briefly stated, though what lay behind it is more difficult. In the late summer of 1593, Hesketh travelled from Prague, via Hamburg, to England. He made his way up to Lancashire, and on about 27 September he presented himself at the household of Lord Strange, newly elevated as 5th Earl of Derby. There he delivered to Lord Strange a letter. This letter has since disappeared, but its gist is clear enough from the subsequent investigation. It was an offer emanating from those English Catholics at Prague, though also invoking the familiar name of Sir William Stanley. Its purpose was to broach Strange on the subject of his 'claim', and to seek his support for a Catholic *coup d'état* in his name. Strange's response was to turn Hesketh over to the authorities. He did not do so immediately – which caused some questions later – but by about 10 October he had personally informed the Queen, and Hesketh was 'under restraint'. Hesketh was interrogated, charged with conspiracy, and on 29 November – two months after his first overture to Strange – he was hanged and quartered at St Albans.

This much can be found in Camden's *Annals*, in the letters that flew to and fro about Hesketh (preserved in the Cecil papers at Hatfield House), and in most of the history books which mention the subject. But there is a different view of the Hesketh affair, which sees it as another of these 'sham-plots', an illusory conspiracy engineered by the government, and particularly by Sir Robert Cecil. Various Cecil agents can be glimpsed at key moments of the plot, and there is crucial evidence that the actual letter delivered by Hesketh was not penned by the Prague Catholics at all, but was given to Hesketh by a certain 'Mr Hickman'. Hickman was not, as Hesketh thought, a servant of the old Earl of Derby, but a government agent. And the letter was not, as Hesketh thought, some 'news of those that died in London', but a forged incitement to Catholic rebellion. Another document, supposedly showing Hesketh's dealings with Sir William Stanley in the Low Countries, is also thought to be a forgery, planted in Hesketh's lodgings at Prague by a Cecil agent, Samuel Lewknor.

Hesketh may have been a dupe, but he represented a genuine pro-Strange faction in Prague. The purpose of this government ploy is partly to discredit that faction, but more it is to test out Strange's loyalties, to answer those questions about him which had been hanging in Cecil's mind at least since the interception of Persons's letter to Cycell two years earlier. A more extreme interpretation would be that Cecil was deliberately trying to incriminate Strange, and there are aspects of his handling of the case after Hesketh's arrest which would support that idea. This was certainly the view of Catholics in the Low Countries. One, Richard Hopkins, writing to Cardinal Allen about the execution of Hesketh, says: 'it seemeth that they are afraid of this Earl of Derby [i.e. Strange], and do devise this rumour to colour the apprehension and destruction of him.'

Everything one knows about Cecil's opportunism suggests that both elements are present: the element of surveillance, which was justifiable, however unsavoury the methods used; and the element of antagonism, which saw political advantage in any dirt that might attach to Strange's name as a result of the affair. Cecil seems like an ally of Strange in the aftermath of Hesketh's arrest, but in the view of Christopher Devlin (who assembled much of this evidence, in a little-known study of the affair published in 1953) the whole thing was engineered as a 'campaign to eliminate him as a political factor'. It is not unlike the more famous Babington plot, which was a campaign to eliminate Mary Stuart. It has the same repertoire of stool-pigeons and forgeries, and the same twist whereby the protagonists of the plot turn out to be its victims.

All this happened after Marlowe was dead, but it helps to explain his activities the previous year. It brings to a head the kind of dodgy operation in which Marlowe was involved, briefly and unsuccessfully, at Flushing. It shows the unscrupulous methods Cecil was prepared to use, in the interests of 'national security', of course, but with an admixture of personal political advantage.

Thomas Kyd says that Lord Strange had turned against

Marlowe: 'never could my Lord endure his name or sight when he had heard of his conditions'. He implies, and perhaps really believed, that Marlowe's atheism was the reason for Strange's dislike of him. I suspect it was also, indeed primarily, Strange's knowledge of Marlowe's 'conditions' as a government projector that caused this tension between the play-maker and his patron.

27

POLEY'S NETWORK

THIS READING OF the Flushing episode opens up a connection that has not been suspected before: a connection, in this realm of secret politics, between Marlowe and the Cecils. It also brings Marlowe very close to another, more professional operator in the Cecil network: Robert Poley.

Poley's particular speciality was the Low Countries, to which he travelled frequently in these years. Just over a month after Marlowe's deportation, he was himself posting to Brussels about 'Her Majesty's special affairs'. The warrant for this trip was signed by Lord Burghley. He was not, primarily, a spy there: his Catholic cover had been blown after the Babington affair, and his name bruited about as a government agent. He was now in a more supervisory role: an operational chief or section head, running a small intelligence network in the Low Countries, and reporting to Vice-Chamberlain Heneage and the Cecils. His cypher-keys tell us something of his work. Three of these remain, the ink oxidised to a deep yellow, in the Public Record Office. The earliest, headed simply 'Po: Cypher', dates from about 1591. It provides the 'copy', or key, for a hieroglyphic cypher. There are five alternative symbols for each vowel, two for each consonant. There are also individual symbols for certain people. On the government side, Lord Burghley, Sir Robert Cecil, the Earl of Essex and Poley himself merit a cypher. On the Catholic side, there are ten names listed: all the principal conspirators in the Low Countries – Sir William Stanley, Hugh Owen, Charles Paget, Father Persons – together with various other Brussels-based exiles and politic Jesuits. These names show Poley's area of interest in the Low Countries: the groupings he wished to penetrate, in some cases to sabotage, in other cases to parley and entice. It is precisely the same area of interest that Marlowe's coining exploits have led us to.

Poley was in constant receipt of intelligence from the Low Countries. His cypher-key identifies the contact-points of his network:

Direction of letters to Ro: Pooly – Jacob Mynistrale, Italiano; Arnold Mulemake, jeweller.

Direction of letters from Ro: Po – Elizabeth Boogarde in den Lyllye in den Augustine Street, Antwerpen; Harman van der Myll, jeweller, op den Dame, Antwerpen.

Here are the letter-drops: two foreign merchants in London for incoming, two safe houses in Antwerp for the outgoing. Another of Poley's fronts in London was a broker named Robert Rutkin, and when Rutkin was himself under investigation, probably in the summer of 1592, he provided a brief but revealing glimpse of one part of Poley's Dutch network. 'The speech of Robert Rutkyn', as it is endorsed, runs as follows:

Robt Rutkin, broker, saith that the party who wrote the letters unto him by the name of Bar: Riche is Michael Moody, who lieth either at Brussels or Antwerp. The thing he promised him was brawn, sturgeon or oysters, which he promised him at his being there xii months past. The said Rutkin saith that his neighbour mentioned in the letter is one Robt Poolye, and that he delivereth him letters for Sir Thomas Henneage, & sendeth letters to him from Sir Thomas Henneage. Sometimes he writeth as he doth now (Yours in the way of honesty qd [i.e. quoth] Bar: Riche) but most commonly he writeth M.M. The said Robert Poolye lyeth in Shoreditch. He was at the post this time to look for letters from him, but had none, & receiveth no letters from him but that he acquainteth Sir Thomas Henneage withal. He was sent over by Sir Thomas Henneage with letters to divers persons about a year past.

There is the usual indiscriminate use of pronouns, but a careful reading produces the following set-up. Poley's agent in the Low Countries is Michael Moody. Moody, using the alias Riche, communicates with Rutkin on trading matters – brawn, sturgeon and oysters: staple imports from Holland. Using this mercantile cover, Moody also sends intelligence despatches, which Rutkin passes on to Robert Poley, his neighbour in Shoreditch. Poley delivers all of Moody's despatches to Sir Thomas Heneage, and conveys despatches back to Moody from Heneage.

Some of these despatches from Moody to Poley survive, probably only a fraction of what he wrote. The earliest dates from October 1591; the latest I can find is September 1594. As well as providing intelligence he also set things up for Poley's own visits to the Netherlands. A memorandum in his hand, listing various people at Antwerp, Douai and St Omer, is endorsed 'Moody's advice for Poley, for those to speak with and where'. In another letter from Antwerp Moody writes to Poley: 'I will pawn my life for your safe going and coming. You may come by those directions which I gave you.'

Michael Moody is one of those half-mad political meddlers whose double- and triple-dealings are the bane of anyone trying to make sense of Elizabethan intelligence operations. His letters are dark, scratchy thickets of words, but his signature – on the occasions when he uses his own name – is big and airy, with great looping curlicues pendant off the final 'y'. This seems to catch the spy's world: its suffocating closeness, its effortful empty façades.

We met the Irishman Moody briefly, when he entered the Tower in early 1587 in the wake of the 'Stafford plot', in which it was claimed that he planned to assassinate the Queen by placing a bag of gunpowder under her bed. This was an unlikely offer in an unlikely plot, whose main purpose was to embarrass the French ambassador, but this regicidal role is one Moody played well, and would play again in the Low Countries. The historian Camden calls him a 'notable hackster', a man 'forward of his hands' and 'resolute to dispatch any enterprise for money'. He shared the sombre walks of the Tower with Poley until the latter's release in September 1588. Like Poley he was probably used as an informer there. In prison lists he appears alongside a man called James Tipping, a minor figure in the Babington conspiracy. Tipping too becomes involved, with Moody and Poley, in Dutch affairs. These men constitute a little Tower academy of projectors. There is little to do in the Tower except talk. These are minds grown hyperactive, minds kept too long under lock and key.

Moody was released in late 1590, and the following May he was despatched as an undercover agent to the Low Countries. In Brussels he insinuated himself into the household of Hugh Owen, and began to feed back intercepts and 'advertisements'. Some of these were sent to Burghley, whom he code-named 'William White'; and some to Heneage, via Rutkin and Poley. Returning to England in August, he was debriefed personally by Heneage, probably with Poley in attendance. Having 'delivered the sum of all his good endeavours', he returned to the Low Countries. The next we hear of him, he is in Flushing.

Moody's ploys in Flushing bring him close, physically and politically, to Marlowe. He travelled there from Antwerp, in late September 1591, under one of his many aliases, 'Robert Cranston, Scotch merchant'. He immediately sought an interview with the Governor, Sir Robert Sidney, and made a startling 'offer of service'. This was nothing less than the turning of Hugh Owen, the Catholic spymaster in the Netherlands and the confrere of Sir William Stanley. Sidney listened with interest: Moody 'does not lack wit or ability to serve Her Majesty, if his affection be good'. To win Owen to the English cause would be the kind of intelligence coup that could earn Sidney huge esteem back home in England, esteem he felt he did not always enjoy. He accordingly wrote to Lord Burghley for advice as to how to proceed.

The Cecils already had their doubts about Moody. There is a list, in Sir Robert Cecil's hand, entitled 'Notes of Moody's bad proceedings'. This was based on information supplied by a companion of Moody's, John Ricroft, in August. So when Burghley heard of Moody's approach to Sidney he was deeply suspicious. On 12 October he wrote to Heneage:

He [Moody] has been at Flushing with Sir Robert Sidney, to whom he has declared how he is used on the Queen's behalf, to discover all such practices as are to be had about the Duke of Parma, and he has used my name to him, and gotten money of him, but how much as yet I know not.

He expresses to Heneage his doubts about the man: it is 'understood of late that this Moody has revealed to many there that he is sent thither by Her Majesty, and that they there do assure themselves to make him serve their purpose'. He also says he has 'read over Moody's writings sent to you', and finds the quality of the intelligence very poor, 'being things that come to every man that hearkens after news'.

As Moody's case-officer, Poley was called to give his account. Heneage asked him to draw up a digest of his recent communications with Moody. Poley did so, and it was sent to Burghley. It remains in the Cecil papers: a single page in Poley's hand, headed 'The particulars of that I wrote unto Moody under Your Honour's [Heneage's] mark'.

In Flushing, meanwhile, Sidney waited fretfully for some guidance from Burghley. Oddly, given all this coming and going about Moody in London, it seems that Burghley neglected to write to Sidney for some weeks. All the while Moody was working Sidney deeper into his snares. He persuaded him to write to Owen – indeed he brought the text ready-penned for Sidney to sign – and in early November he returned to Flushing with Owen's answer. Owen, who was doubtless using all this for ulterior ends, pledged his friendship to Sidney: 'I leave the unkindness between our superiors to be decided by the Almighty, but will love and serve you and your lady in anything I can.' He also sent some gifts for Lady Sidney: a pair of bracelets, a little case with scissors, and two 'writing tables' (note-books). Sidney in turn replied, on 8 November: he was ready to do Owen 'any pleasure, his duty to Her Majesty reserved'. Prudently he declined to accept the 'tokens' Owen had sent. He was 'not sure he could requite them', he said. (More likely he knew they could incriminate him later.) Moody was ever-present, urging Sidney on. Owen is 'the only Englishman in Flanders who is able to perform anything,' says Moody. He is ready to be hooked, though 'it must be no small bait that he will bite at'.

It was not until the end of November – two months after Moody's first overture to him – that Sidney at last received word from Burghley, ordering him to break off relations with Moody. Burghley's actual letter, dated 26 November, is lost, but judging from Sidney's reply the message was clear: the Queen disapproved of Moody, distrusted Owen, and was none too pleased with Sidney for entertaining them at all. Sidney replied contritely – 'I am sorry that the Queen thought so ill of my honesty and discretion as to imagine I would give Moody an occasion to glory' – and breathed a sigh of relief that he was 'delivered of that business'. He was not entirely delivered of Moody, however, who was in touch with him again in January 1592, demanding a passport to return to England with 'matters of great concern to Her Majesty'. In early February he was in Flushing, awaiting passage to England. He has 'become somewhat familiar to me', Sidney writes, but he remains an enigma: 'I know not what to say of Moody, who brags that he can do more than all those employed by the Queen.' Sidney cannot, he confesses, 'discover how his heart is framed'.

Moody continues his tricky ways in the Low Countries. The rumours proliferate about his treacheries – he is coming over to kill the Queen, he is conspiring with Charles Paget, he is writing letters 'in milk' to Stephen White, the Flushing merchant who was Paget's secret courier into England – but he continues to write to both Burghley and Heneage, and Poley continues as his case-officer. In May 1592 he is the subject of another little exchange between Burghley and Heneage. On 22 May the searchers at Sandwich found 'divers books of sedition and divers letters to Catholics' on the person of a Fleming. Among these was 'a bundle directed to one Rutkyn' – the broker Robert Rutkin who was one of Poley's fronts in London. The contents of this 'bundle' were sent forthwith to Lord Burghley. 'We find' – wrote Sir Robert Cecil to Heneage the following day – 'that they of Moore belong to you, and one to White which belongs to my Lord.' These were undoubtedly from Moody: 'Thomas Moore' is his code-name for Sir Thomas Heneage, and 'William White' for Lord Burghley. Burghley is once again put out by this, and Cecil writes, rather testily: 'My Lord doth desire to know who that Rutkyn is, and whether you can tell where Pooly is, that my Lord might speak to him.' Once again, Poley is being called in to explain Moody. It was probably on this occasion that Rutkin gave that deposition about Poley and Moody.

Three days later, Cecil writes again to Heneage:

The Queen is out of quiet, with her foreign foes and home broils. I have received your letter, and will show it as occasion may serve. I have spoken with Poley, and find him no fool, but I suspend all until our meeting, which I hope will be shortly. Meantime I am sorry that you are not here to participate vexations, which are good for nothing but to disquiet the Queen.

I sympathise with Cecil's weariness. This is all Moody will ever bring: broils, vexations, uncertainties. It is pointless to try and assess his true allegiance. He was working for all sides simultaneously: Heneage, Burghley, Sidney, Owen. He promises them political advantage. His promise has the hollow aplomb of a mountebank hawking some sovereign remedy, and it succeeds on the same small percentage of doubt: they do not believe it, but they dare not quite ignore it.

One can have a sneaking admiration for the sheer skill involved. Moody operates, and survives, in a political no-man's-land. He is hired by all and belongs to none. But there is also a draining sense of the meaninglessness of it all. This is the *reductio ad absurdum* of the intelligence world: self-perpetuating, self-referring. They live in and by the confusion they create. That is really their only allegiance.

The ploys of Michael Moody in Flushing are an intelligence backdrop to Marlowe's presence in the town at this time. Marlowe himself, it seems, is making a play towards the Stanley-Owen clique in Brussels. Through his contact with Lord Strange, through his dealings with the Catholic coiner John Poole, through his own act of illicit coinage, he places himself as an infiltrator into that grouping. The abortive comedy of the Dutch shilling remains as a marker of his efforts as a provocateur. This was precisely the circle in which Michael Moody was operating, as he shuttled between Owen and Sidney with his preposterous, veiled agenda of hooks and baits.

It is, at any rate, certain that Robert Poley knew a good deal about Marlowe's activities in Flushing in the winter of 1591-2. It was his patch. It was his business to know. Conversely, through his experience in Low Countries affairs, it is likely that Marlowe knew something about Poley's dealings there. Such knowledge, in certain circumstances, might prove dangerous. As always we cannot quite put the finger on Poley, and say exactly how or in what way he knew Marlowe. Throughout this story they are close in a circumstantial way. They are university men, living on their skills, nimble in many languages. Their paths cross in the 'skirts and outshifts' of the court, in the corridors of Walsingham's house on Seething Lane, in the tavern circle of Tom Watson. They share interests, and acquaintances, and perhaps also secrets. Now, in the winter of 1591–2, we find them linked again, in this particular stratum of political intrigue. Both are targeted on this cell of Catholic plotters in Brussels. Both are working under the protection of the Burghley network: the cold eyes of

Sir Robert Cecil are upon them. Marlowe is coining in Flushing, Moody is in and out of the town, carrying letters from Owen, writing letters to Poley: who is keeping an eye on whom?

28

ROYDON AND THE KING OF SCOTS

THE NAME OF Matthew Roydon has been mentioned in passing: a fellow-poet of Marlowe's, a shadowy but important figure. He wrote a poem in praise of Thomas Watson which appears in the forefront of Watson's sonnet-sequence, *Ekatompathia*, published in 1582. In the same year he was a co-signatory with Nicholas Skeres in a bond to repay £40 to a London goldsmith. Many years later he was still in Skeres's clutches, one of those 'young gents' that Skeres had ensnared on behalf of the skinner John Wolfall. A friend of Watson and a dealer with Skeres: this already presses Matthew Roydon into the kind of area with which we are concerned, this cross-over between the poets and the shady servants of government.

Very little of Roydon's poetry has survived. In 1586 he wrote a beautiful elegy for Sir Philip Sidney, 'A Friend's Passion For His Astrophel', from which one gathers he had been part of Sidney's literary circle. In 1589 Nashe praised him for his 'most absolute comic inventions': if these are plays they are, like Watson's, lost. He later appears as part of the literary set associated with both Lord Strange and the Earl of Northumberland. His praise of these two noblemen is recorded by George Chapman:

I remember, my good Mat, how joyfully oftentimes you reported unto me that most ingenious Derby [i.e. Lord Strange], deep-searching Northumberland and skill-embracing heir of Hunsdon [i.e. Sir George Carey] had

most profitably entertained learning in themselves, to the
vital warmth of freezing science, & to the admirable lustre
of their true nobility.

This appears in the preface to Chapman's occultist rhapsody,
The Shadow of Night, published in 1594. The work was
dedicated to 'sweet Matthew', his 'dear and most worthy
friend'.

Roydon is a part of this same coterie of poets and
philosophers, and he is named by Kyd as a familiar friend of
Marlowe, 'such as he conversed withal'. Kyd mentions him
alongside Northumberland's 'magi', Hariot and Warner, and
implies that they all three shared with Marlowe the 'viler
opinion' of atheism.

What has not been noticed, as far as I know, is Roydon's
association with Sir Edward Kelley, in Prague, in the year
1591. This takes us straight back into these intrigues
surrounding Lord Strange.

As we have seen, the Stanley-Owen clique in Brussels was not
the only centre of pro-Strange intrigue in the early 1590s.
There was also the Prague group of English Catholics, among
them Richard Hesketh, the protagonist of the Hesketh affair
of 1593. The leading figure in the group was the notorious Sir
Edward Kelley, the alchemist and spiritualist, and – according
to a typical contemporary judgment – 'the grand imposter of
the world'.

Like others in this group, Kelley had Lancashire connections, and he may well have known Lord Strange. In
Lancaster, in about 1580, he lost his ears in the pillory. His
crime was 'coining base money': he is another coiner in this
story. He was also in trouble for digging up corpses, doubtless
for necromantic purposes, in the churchyard at Walton-le-
Dale. The squire at Walton was Lord Strange's friend Thomas
Langton, the self-styled Baron of Walton. (It is possible that
this whole motif of 'political coining' in connection with
Strange has its origins in Kelley's early career as a gimcrack
magician up North: Marlowe 'learnt some things' about

coining from John Poole, and perhaps Poole learned them from Kelley. This is an attractive conjecture, nothing more.)

Shortly after this, in 1582, Kelley entered into a more famous association: with the Elizabethan magus John Dee. He was Dr Dee's 'scryer', or spirit-medium. His first arrival at Dee's house in Mortlake, under the assumed name of Talbot, has the ring of espionage about it, and it may be Kelley was planted on Dee. For five years they toured through Europe, performing 'angelic conferences' and alchemical trans-mutations. Dee returned to England in 1590, to a ransacked laboratory and a hostile atmosphere, but Kelley remained in Prague. There he was feted by the occultist Emperor, Rudolf II, who knighted him, incorporated him on to the Imperial Privy Council, and entailed on him 'lands in inheritance worth £1500 yearly'.

In this elevated position, Kelley became a natural centre for English exiles in Prague, and particularly for the group of Lancashire Catholics which included Richard Hesketh. Hesketh was himself an amateur alchemist, and an old acquaintance of Dr Dee. At the same time, Kelley was also – this no longer surprises me – in regular contact with Lord Burghley in England. Some of the correspondence between them concerned Kelley's vaunted powers as an alchemist and a healer. Burghley variously requests a smidgin of Kelley's gold-making 'tincture' in order to finance the war-effort against Spain; and a 'receipt' or recipe against another 'old enemy', the gout. But that is only part of the dialogue: Burghley was also using Kelley as a highly-placed asset in the court of Emperor Rudolf, and as a source of information about English plots in Prague.

There were many couriers between Kelley and Burghley. One was Sir Edward Dyer, poet and diplomat, an old friend of Sir Philip Sidney and an alchemical enthusiast. Another was Thomas Webbe, a busy Burghley agent who was himself charged with coining in 1593. A third was Matthew Roydon. In May 1591 Burghley wrote to Kelley:

I have cause to thank you, and so I do very heartily, for

310

your good, kind letter, sent to me by our countryman, Mr Roydon, who maketh such good report to you, as doth every other man that hath had a conversation with you.

Here is a new fragment of biography: Matthew Roydon – a friend of Marlowe, a poet associated with Lord Strange – was in Prague with Kelley in early 1591. He carried letters from Kelley to Burghley in England, and made 'good report' of the conversations he had had with him. This does not make Roydon a spy as such, but it makes him part of the Cecils' intelligence-network, in this particular context of Prague conspiracy which later surfaces as the 'Hesketh plot'. During his spell in Prague in 1591, Roydon would very likely have met Hesketh. Another of the English exiles there was a goldsmith, Richard Tankard, described as 'an Englishman who did divers times resort unto Sir Edward Kelley's house'. He may be connected with the Mr Tankard who in 1593 shared with Roydon a debt of £150 to John Wolfall the skinner. This is testified by Nicholas Skeres, in Star Chamber, a month before Marlowe's death.

It is a small world, suffocatingly so, and I think in 'sweet Matthew' we glimpse another of these poet-spies, using a literary connection with Lord Strange to gain entry into pro-Strange Catholic cliques on the continent. Roydon in Prague, Marlowe in Flushing: they are bit-players in the same complex and rather pointless intelligence-game which is being played around the reluctant Catholic pretender, their patron, Lord Strange. Roydon is reporting to the Cecils, as Marlowe almost certainly was a few months later.

There is a further broad hint of Roydon and Marlowe's involvement together, within the same intelligence context: one that takes us on in time towards 1593, and the events at Deptford.

In his deposition about Marlowe's 'monstruous opinions', written down shortly after Marlowe's death, Thomas Kyd included one item that sits rather oddly alongside the other allegations. It does not concern Marlowe's atheism, as all the others do. It occurs at the end of the document, and has the look of an afterthought.

> He would persuade with men of quality to go unto the K of Scots, whither I hear Roydon is gone, and where if he had lived, he told me when I saw him last, he meant to be.

According to Kyd, Marlowe was intending to go to Scotland, to 'be' there with Roydon. He was also urging certain 'men of quality' to 'go unto' King James. This is presented by Kyd as a recent development: 'when I saw him last'. We don't know when the two men last saw one another. In his letter to Puckering Kyd claimed he had decided to 'leave & refrain' Marlowe's company some time before, but their paths would have crossed among the book-stalls of St Paul's, and in the theatrical taverns and courtly ante-chambers of their lives, and it is likely that this information is quite fresh. It is worth pointing out that Nicholas Skeres, in his statement in the Star Chamber, says that Matthew Roydon 'makes his abode' at a shoemaker's house in the Blackfriars. This statement is dated 26 April 1593. Skeres is the kind of man who knows the whereabouts of his debtors, so we can be fairly sure that Roydon had not yet gone to Scotland. If he did go, as Kyd says he did, he went about a month, at the most, before Marlowe's death. This suggests the currency of this information about Marlowe: it probably belongs the last few weeks of his life.

What are we to make of this sudden access of Scottishness in Marlowe? It must be remembered that the context of Kyd's statement is one of disapproval. He is making a formal deposition about Marlowe's religious and personal bad habits. It is done to order, in the aftermath of torture. The statement would not be there unless it carried some bad implication. So this is no innocent jaunt to the Highlands. It has an overtone of sedition, and there is little doubt what that overtone is. It concerns the whole matter of the succession, the question that hung over all others in the political world at this time. We now know that, ten years after this, King James of Scotland succeeded to the English throne. In 1593, however, James was only one contender in the game. The canny backed him from the start, but as we have seen there were many other contenders. Throughout these years James played a game of *rapprochement*, holding out covert promises to the Catholics while maintaining a good Protestant front for the benefit of Elizabeth and Burghley. It was only after his succession that he made the famous brush-off, reneging on his promises of toleration: 'Nah, we'll no need the papists noo.' And so the scene is set for the Gunpowder Plot of 1605.

Kyd's allegation about Marlowe and Roydon is a political one: they are involved in this drift towards James, propagandising for it, persuading wealthy 'men of quality' to join the pro-Jacobean faction. This would not in itself be suspect – James was virtually the official candidate as successor – but Kyd seems to think it is, and what we know of Marlowe and Roydon tends to back him up. He is implying an element of adventurism in their involvement, probably a Catholic element. They are meddling in some way in this sensitive area of the succession.

It is an unsupported allegation, made in distressing circumstances, but it carries on quite convincingly from the political dealings I have been trying to uncover. Many of the Owen clique in Brussels – the group that Marlowe was trying to infiltrate in 1592 – were closely involved with Scottish intrigue: the Jesuits Holt and Crighton, Robert Bruce of Binnie, *et al.* Some were part of this covert Catholic *rapprochement* with King James, others had other interests. Catholic agents posted to and fro: they plotted and bargained in the Scottish court, they rallied the clusters of Catholic loyalism in the country, they laid the grounds for Sir William Stanley's long-planned invasion. And, of course, wherever there were Catholic agents, there were also Burghley agents, watching and listening and generally muddying the waters. Among Burghley's operatives North of the border was the turned priest, John Cycell, whose revelations first drew Lord Strange – and hence perhaps Marlowe – into this tangle of succession politics.

Kyd's allegation against Roydon and Marlowe, unsupported

though it is, makes sense. Both men have been employed by the Cecils in matters touching Lord Strange, and hence the succession. Now they are posting up to Scotland, going 'unto' the King of Scots. Roydon is already there, and Marlowe is ready to join him. But other events intervened, and Marlowe never made it there.

Once again Marlowe is brought close to Robert Poley, for the warrants of Poley's payments show a particular concentration of Scottish activity at this time. He was an old Scottish hand – back in the days of his dealings with Morgan he had been recommended as one who knows all the best secret ways into Scotland – but now he is especially busy there. On 1 June 1592 he set out from the court at Greenwich, and journeyed to Berwick-on-Tweed. The following October he travelled north once again, to deliver letters to the court of King James. On this occasion he remained in Scotland, 'riding in sundry places', for two months. He returned to Hampton Court on 14 December, and received payment of £43 two days later. Before the end of the month, he was riding to King James again. He was back at Hampton Court on 6 January 1593. A few weeks later he was over in the Low Countries, in Brussels, then in March he was once more in Scotland, carrying 'letters in post for Her Highness's special and secret affairs of great importance'. He returned on 23 March. Six weeks later, on 8 May 1593, he was despatched to the Netherlands, and the next we hear of him is at Mistress Bull's house, meeting up with Marlowe, Skeres and Frizer.

In less than a year Poley had visited the Scottish court four times, on one occasion staying there two months. There is no doubt this was connected with his work in the Low Countries, connected with the tentacles of Catholic intrigue that spread between Brussels and Scotland. And there is little doubt that Marlowe and Roydon were mixed up in the same business, in Prague, in Flushing, and now in these journeys 'unto the K of Scots' to which Kyd refers.

PART SIX

THE FRAME

29
TEXTS OF ATHEISM

WE NOW RETURN to the spring of 1593 and the events leading up to the killing of Christopher Marlowe. We do so with a new understanding of the continuity of secret politics as a factor in his life. He is remembered as a poet, 'the Muse's darling', and as a wild young blasphemer in an age of enforced devotion, but he was also a spy, as we have now come to understand that term: one of hundreds of such men, part of a maverick army of intelligencers and projectors on which the government of the day depended, sometimes out of a genuine need for information, but often in ways that relate more to political expediency, to courtly in-fighting, to police-state repression.

It is not a pretty view of the Golden Age of Elizabeth, and it is not a pretty view of Christopher Marlowe either. In these fragments which record his involvement in the secret world – the Privy Council certificate, the Sidney letter from Flushing, the Kyd deposition – there is a common thread of falsehood. They record his pretences, his masks. He is a militant Catholic 'determined to go to Rheims', he is a seditious coiner with 'intent to go to the enemy', he is a propagandist stirrer going 'unto the K of Scots', and yet we find he is really none of these things, that these appearances of commitment are only to cover – or as they said it, to 'colour' – his role as a spy, a deceiver, a politic meddler. This does not, of course, mean he was committed to the government side, or to Protestant conformity. The keynote of this kind of work is precisely non-commitment: to belong to both sides and to neither. It is a

317

world of gestures, of alterable meanings: the 'secret theatre'.

So we return to the circumstances of Marlowe's death armed with this perception of 'plats' and pretences, these forms of political gamesmanship which are such a feature of this world he belongs to. Marlowe's political career is not – as in the conventional literary biography – a separate and rather puzzling side-issue. It touches on so much else in his life: on his friendship with poets like Watson and Roydon; on his allegiance to patrons like Lord Strange and the Earl of Northumberland; on the very tone and temper of his plays. The leading question now is, how does his political career touch on his death?

One way in which it touches on his death is in the unsettling recurrence of men like Richard Baines and Robert Poley. The Flushing episode, hitherto unexamined, brings their previous involvement with Marlowe into closer focus. Baines is his 'chamber-fellow' at Flushing, first an accomplice and then an informer. Poley is a senior figure in Low Countries intelligence: he works, as Marlowe did, under the protection of the Cecils; he posts, as Marlowe intended, to Scotland. A third man in at the death, Nicholas Skeres, is also glimpsed in the covert world, but his allegiance lies not with the Cecils. He is a 'servant' of the Earl of Essex.

We cannot recover these men in their full likeness, only a patchy silhouette of circumstance, but what we have learned of them, and of Marlowe, seems to tell us how alike they all were. We find Marlowe in the company of spies and swindlers because, regrettably, he was one himself. Our regret has no real claim on him. Posterity prefers poets to spies, but this young man could not be so choosy. He lived on his wits or else went hungry, and he was probably rather better rewarded for spying than he was for the poetry we remember him by.

The events of April and May 1593 as they concern Christopher Marlowe must be looked at afresh: the anti-Dutch libels posted up in the streets, the arrest of Thomas Kyd, the discovery of Marlowe's heretical papers in Kyd's lodgings, the reports of government informers about Marlowe's atheism, the summons which brought him before the Privy Council. They are a chronological prelude to Marlowe's death, though how they might have contributed to it – how they might have caused it – has never been explained.

Charges of heresy and atheism against Marlowe filled the air at this time – or rather, they filled certain sheets of paper at this time. It is these, above all, that we must look at afresh: these texts which were circulating, in certain precise circles, in the weeks immediately before and after his death. They are mere bits of paper, unpublished and indeed unavailable for many years, but they are texts none the less: authored by certain individuals, aimed at a certain audience, conscious of the power of words to create an effect, one might almost say to create a truth, though one that is not necessarily *the* truth.

The subject of these texts is Marlowe: more precisely, Marlowe's dissident opinions on religion and politics. What we don't know, in the end, is how accurately they report his opinions. The exact proportion of truth and invention in them is very hard to gauge. This is due partly to the usual historical reasons about the limitations of evidence, and partly to a more particular problem. Of the three key texts of Marlowe's atheism – the Baines 'Note', the Kyd deposition, and the 'Remembrances' against Cholmeley – one was written by a man in the aftermath of torture, and the other two were written by professional informers ('professional' in a loose sense: the rewards they got for their information depended on its perceived usefulness.) And as we have found, time and again, informers have often a need to *create* information. They are 'projectors' who provoke or indeed invent dangerous sentiments in order to denounce them. They are 'politicians' in that pejorative Elizabethan sense, the sense in which Shakespeare means it when King Lear says, 'Get thee glass eyes and, like a scurvy politician, seem to see the things thou dost not'.

This is the particular problem with these texts of Marlowe's atheism. Did he really say what these people say he said? Or are they looking at him with those 'glass eyes', and pretending to see in him things that were not really there?

*

319

The most famous of these texts is the Baines 'Note', compiled
by Richard Baines, and entitled by him 'A Note containing the
opinion of one Christopher Marly concerning his damnable
judgment of religion and scorn of God's word'. This survives
in two separate manuscripts in the Harleian collection in the
British Library. One of these is almost certainly the original,
autograph 'Note'. It is a two-page document, the first page
densely written on both sides, the second having just the last
few lines of the text and the rest blank paper. The
handwriting is good, by the standards of these reports; an
educated hand, with italics for emphasis. The other
manuscript is a fairly exact scribal copy, with some interesting
annotations in another hand. This fair copy was apparently
prepared for the Queen herself, for the docket on the back of
it reads:

Copye of Marloes
blasphemyes
As sent to her H

The text of the 'Note' consists of nineteen separate
allegations: each of them an opinion or comment attributed to
Marlowe – 'that Christ was a bastard and his mother
dishonest', 'that all the New Testament is filthily written',
'that . . . the sacrament . . . would have been much better being
administered in a tobacco pipe', and so on. Most of them
concern doctrinal heresies but a few are of a more political
and personal nature (famously, 'that all they that love not
tobacco & boys were fools'). Baines implies that he has
personally heard Marlowe say these things, and promises to
produce other 'good & honest' witnesses to the same effect.
There are many such witnesses, we gather, because Marlowe
is a reckless broadcaster of these heresies: 'this Marlowe doth
not only hold them himself, but almost into every company he
cometh he persuades men to atheism'. The document is a
signed and sworn statement: 'as I Richard Baines will justify
and approve both by my oath and the testimony of many
honest men'. The whole thing has a competent air: an

experienced informer delivering the goods.

Whether it is also true has long been the vexed question of Marlovian biography. Attitudes have been struck, and cogently argued, at both ends of the spectrum. On the one hand, it is held that the 'Note' is a tissue of lies, and bears no relation whatever to Marlowe's beliefs; on the other hand, that the 'Note' is a genuine record of what Marlowe said, and may even contain, in somewhat garbled form, the actual text of his 'atheist lecture'. We are in a chicken-and-egg circle here, because either view can be argued from the same basic data. It has been shown, for instance, that the opinions which Baines attributes to Marlowe can be found in other contemporary sources, both printed and anecdotal. But these parallels can be interpreted either way: to refute the 'Note' (they show that it is no more than a digest of atheist clichés); or to validate it (they show that others held these views, so why not Marlowe?). Another, more particular parallel is between Baines's 'Note' and the other statements about Marlowe made by Cholmeley and Kyd. Once again this goes either way: it may back up the veracity of the 'Note', or it may suggest the suspicious neatness of an orchestrated campaign.

The 'Note' has the air of being a powerful document against Marlowe, both for what it contains and in the way it is presented, but there have always been doubts about it because of its shabby provenance (certainly since Boas's discoveries about Baines in the 1940s), and what we have learned about Baines in the course of this book has opened up further doubts. There is, first, the matter of his Rheims confession, made in 1583. This document, ten years earlier than the 'Note', shows that Baines had long been playing in these dubious doctrinal waters. In his confession, made to placate Dr Allen, he paints himself as a heretic and atheist, 'jesting and scoffing' at the scriptures, and striving by 'arguments' to draw his auditors into heresy – precisely what he accuses Marlowe of in the 'Note'. This does not actually tell us about the veracity or otherwise of Baines's allegations about Marlowe, but it places those allegations in a context. Baines has himself played this role: played it, furthermore, as part of his role as a government spy, an *explorator* among the seminarists at Rheims. Within the actual text of his confession there is an element of charade, of political motivation, a sense that his pronouncements contain something of the truth, but only so much as will gain a desired effect. This seems a perception one could transfer to the 'Note'.

Another context is the Flushing episode of 1592, where Baines and Marlowe are closeted together in a chamber, counterfeiting Dutch shillings, and where Baines proves to be the informer who runs to Governor Sidney and denounces Marlowe. This was a year and some months ago. Again, it does not disprove the 'Note', but it casts a personal shadow over it. Baines and Marlowe are at odds in Flushing: they speak against one another, says Sidney, out of 'malice'. The Flushing episode also raises the question as to *when* Baines is supposed to have heard Marlowe say these things. Their chamber at Flushing is itself a plausible location, though Baines makes no mention of these dangerous utterances when he turns Marlowe in to Sidney; perhaps he was storing them up for future use. It is unlikely Baines would have heard them at first hand after the Flushing incident, for by then Marlowe knew for certain that Baines was not to be trusted, and would be unlikely to broadcast these views in front of a man who had already betrayed him. Where there is genuine, first-hand reportage in the 'Note', therefore, it would seem to be a reporting of comments Marlowe had made at least sixteen months previously. The rest, which is not genuine reportage, would be second-hand accounts, hearsay or invention: the latter, we know, Baines would find easy enough, having played the blasphemer himself.

What we know of Baines – and we have more to learn as we look into the events of May 1593 – shows a man seasoned in deception and intrigue (though not necessarily very good at them). I have no doubt that there was genuine material for him to work on – in other words, that Marlowe genuinely held beliefs or non-beliefs highly questionable by the standards of 1593 – and I think it very likely that some of these comments are genuinely his (the 'tobacco & boys' *bon mot*, perhaps; the homosexual blasphemy about Jesus and John, which is echoed by Kyd; and others). But that Marlowe said *all* of these things, and that he said them to 'almost all men with whom he hath conversed', is surely too good – or rather too bad – to be true. This document, which has perplexed and scandalised Marlowe's biographers for centuries, tells us nothing for certain except that Richard Baines wished to accuse Marlowe of heresy. That is all we can be sure of: its motive, which is to incriminate, to make Marlowe a criminal. One has to take the 'Note' more as a performance than as a report. It is neither a lie, nor the truth, but a carefully tailored presentation: Marlowe as the pantomime atheist, spouting vile blasphemies; Baines as the dutiful reporter, backed up by 'good' but unspecified witnesses. It begins to sound like a 'shock horror' story in the *News of the World*, and perhaps that is not a bad analogy.

As mentioned, there was a copy made of the 'Note' for the perusal of the Queen. In itself this copy is a neat scribal version of the original 'Note'; there are a few minor variations in the text, but it is otherwise a verbatim copy. After the copy was made, however, someone went through it, writing in a fast, slapdash hand, making certain marginal comments and, more important, certain editorial changes to the text. These annotations, I can now reveal, are in the hand of Sir John Puckering, the Lord Keeper of the Privy Seal. This is a new fact, though hardly a surprising one. Puckering, together with another high-ranking court official and Privy Councillor, Lord Buckhurst, took a particular interest in what we might today call 'state security', and the two men played an important role in the investigation of Marlowe and his associates. It was to him that Thomas Kyd wrote his plaintive letter with its damnations of Marlowe, and the terms of the letter show that Puckering had been involved in, probably in charge of, Kyd's interrogation in mid-May.

Puckering's purview at this time covered a wide range of dissent: his papers (most of which survive in seventeenth century transcripts by Thomas Baker) include investigative material about troublesome Puritans as well as Catholics. He was involved in the prosecution of the 'separatists', Henry Barrow and John Greenwood, and the great Puritan propagandist John Penry. These three were all hanged at this time: Barrow and Greenwood at Tyburn on 6 April 1593, and Penry on 29 May, the day before Marlowe's death, and indeed just a few miles from Deptford, at St Thomas-a-Watering. What links these three men is not just their extremist religious position but their literary eloquence. They were propagandists of great power and skill: Penry is the supposed author of the audacious 'Marprelate' tracts, whose satirical brio so influenced the pamphleteers like Nashe who were called in to confute him. Therein lay their particular danger: as writers. Hence perhaps Sir John Puckering's interest in Kyd and Marlowe – it belongs within this broader political programme of silencing dangerously vocal dissidents. The 'Note' stresses precisely this element of Marlowe as broadcaster: 'almost into every company he cometh he persuades men to atheism'. It introduces also a soothing notion of silence: 'I think all men in Christianity ought to endeavour that the mouth of so dangerous a member may be stopped'. I have spoken of Baines's 'tailored' presentation of Marlowe as atheist: one could perhaps specify further, and say he has particularly tailored it to the interests of Lord Keeper Puckering, on whose desk a copy of the 'Note' duly lands, and is rather carefully processed before passing on to the Queen.

From Puckering's annotations to his copy we find out what he wanted to change in the text, presumably before 'Her H' got to read it (in which case, a further copy would have been made incorporating his corrections). There are both deletions and additions. Three passages are deleted entirely. The first is Marlowe's quip about loving tobacco and boys. The second is the paragraph about coining: Marlowe's statement about his 'right to coin' and about his acquaintance with Poole in Newgate. Thirdly, the whole of the last paragraph is deleted: this is Baines's conclusion, summarising Marlowe's attitude, promising to bring witnesses forward, and so on. The effect of the corrections seems to be to concentrate on the purely religious aspect of Marlowe's unorthodoxy. Related subversions – sexual, criminal – are no longer considered relevant. Puckering's editing has streamlined the 'Note' into a brisk itemisation of Marlovian blasphemies.

The oddest of his editorial activities concerns the title of the document, and it is here that the contradictory evidence arises about the dating of the 'Note'. The copyist had written:

A note contayninge the opinion of one Christopher Marlye concernynge his damnable opinion and Iudgment of Religioun and scorne of Gods worde.

This follows Baines's original more or less exactly, the only difference being the unnecessary repetition of the word 'opinion', which was probably a slip of the pen. This is now deemed inadequate, however, and with a series of insertions and deletions, Puckering changes the title to:

A note delivred on whitsun eve last of the most horrible blasphemes and damnable opinions utteryd by xtofer Marly who since whitsonday dyed a soden & vyolent deathe.

But still he is not satisfied, and he changes the text once more, so that the final clause instead reads:

. . . who within iij dayes after came to a soden & fearfull ende of his life.

Seeing that he is taking so much trouble over the title, it is curious that Puckering gets the facts wrong. First he says that Marlowe died 'since Whit Sunday'. In 1593, Whit Sunday fell on 3 June, whereas Marlowe actually died on 30 May, the Wednesday *before* Whit Sunday. Then he changes this, with an apparent concern for precision, so that it now says Marlowe died 'iii days after' Whitsun Eve, i.e. on 5 June. Certainly more precise, but still wrong.

There seem to be two alternative explanations for this. One is that Puckering is deliberately falsifying the date of Marlowe's death. This seems unlikely, or anyway risky: the Queen's coroner had presided over an inquest, the documents and writs were proceeding through Chancery. What can be gained from saying Marlowe died a week later than he actually did? The more plausible explanation is that it is a genuine error, though this too is curious when one considers how recent the events were. We can broadly gauge the date of Puckering's annotations from a marginal comment against the name of Richard Cholmeley, reading 'he is layd for'. Assuming the usual meaning of 'laid for' – staked out, under surveillance – this must have been written before the end of June: Cholmeley was arrested (and thus no longer 'laid for') on 28 June, and Puckering was alerted to this fact by a despatch from Justice Young written on 29 June. He was, therefore, redrafting the Baines 'Note' sometime in June, a few weeks at the most after Marlowe's death. An error, nonetheless, it probably is. But we still do not know where the error lies. Is Puckering wrong about Baines delivering the 'Note' on Whitsun Eve? Or is he wrong about Marlowe dying 'iii days after' the date of delivery? If this is a genuine error, I suppose he is more likely to be wrong about the dates than about the sequence of events. In this case the true part is that Marlowe died three days after the 'Note' was delivered. The date of delivery would therefore be Sunday 27 May; this was the Sunday before Whit, which in his haste Puckering erroneously called 'Whitsun Eve'.

This is just about plausible, but there remains a niggling suspicion that there is some kind of deliberate fudging going on. And what are we to make of Puckering's pains over his description of Marlowe's killing? What is wrong with his first description? It is adequate, and it is accurate: Marlowe 'died a sudden & violent death'. But no: a bit of quill-chewing, and a new phrase is inserted. Marlowe 'came to a sudden and fearful end of his life'. The alteration of 'violent' to 'fearful' is in the direction of blandness. Is the purpose to soften the event, to remove the bloody knife-blade from the equation? Is it, further, to introduce a note of admonition: that Marlowe's death shows the swift intervention of divine justice, a phenomenon which all right-minded people find 'fearful'? This idea was popular with later commentators like Thomas Beard, for whom Marlowe's death was 'terrible' in just this sense of transgression punished; we see it here, perhaps, as a first tweak of theological spin from the pen of Sir John Puckering. Not so much a violent death as a fearful ending of life.

We cannot be certain what is going on here, but I get a sense of effort. This is a troublesome business; the Queen is to be informed. It is important to strike the right tone – more important, it seems, than getting the facts of the matter right.

Even allowing for the earlier of the two possible dates, 27 May, the Baines 'Note' appears late on the scene: two weeks after Kyd's arrest, a week after Marlowe's summons before the Privy Council. It is the most detailed and virulent account of Marlowe's atheistic talk, and the chronology suggests it is a trump card in the case against him. In the short term perhaps it was, but the spy and part-time atheist Richard Baines is definitely not a 'good & honest witness' of what a man might have said or done, and one does not need glass eyes to see the marks of malicious exaggeration and ulterior motivation, of 'dissimulation & fiction', which strongly suggest that the card is false.

30

THE DAMNABLE CREW

ANOTHER IMPORTANT TEXT concerning Marlowe's atheism is less well known: it was circulating a little earlier than the 'Note', and it has interesting connections with it. This brings us to the elusive figure of Richard Cholmeley, whose name I have mentioned from time to time and whose career we must now carefully plumb. He has been oddly neglected by the biographers, but he fits into this story like a key into a lock. He was an anti-Catholic agent, he had connections with Lord Strange, he was used as a spy by Sir Robert Cecil, and he was an associate of Marlowe. This list of attributes calls to mind the Flushing episode of 1592, and one notes with interest that a certain William Cholmeley held a government post in that town. It is possible that Marlowe's association with Cholmeley – as with Baines – is traceable to that still shadowy affair in the Low Countries. There is no direct evidence that Cholmeley worked in the Low Countries, but he was certainly known over there. One of his accomplices, Henry Young, at work in Brussels in 1593, was closely questioned by two of the Catholic exiles, Father Holt and Dr Gifford: their purpose, he reports, was 'to sift out what zeal I had for their religion, they hearing that I was seen in England in the company of Cholmeley, who had dealings against them'.

'This cursed Cholmeley' is part of the same shadow-world as Baines and Poley and Skeres, and like them he plays a prominent part in the events of May 1593. Among the documents circulating in that month was an informer's report entitled 'Remembrances of Words & Matter against Ric: Cholmeley'. This contained many allegations about Cholmeley's conduct and opinions, including this one:

> he saith & verily believeth that one Marlowe is able to show more sound reasons for atheism than any divine in England is able to give to prove divinity, & that Marlowe told him he hath read the atheist lecture to Sr Walter Ralegh & others.

This is the only direct reference to Marlowe in the 'Remembrances' but, as we shall see, the whole document is crucial to the case.

The Cholmeley clan – often written 'Cholmondeley', but pronounced 'Chumley' – had extensive family branches in Yorkshire and Cheshire. The one thing we know about Richard Cholmeley the spy is that he had a brother named Hugh, and this seems to assign him to the Cheshire branch. Sir Hugh Cholmeley of Malpas, Cheshire, had a younger, unmarried brother Richard, but as Sir Hugh was born in 1513 this is probably a generation too early. Sir Hugh's sons, by his wife Anne *née* Dorman, were also Hugh and Richard, and the latter is probably our man. The family records do not divulge his dates, but it appears that his elder brother Hugh married in about 1580, and so cannot have been born much after 1560. There were Yorkshire Richard Cholmeleys too. The most prominent of these, Richard Cholmeley of Whitby, is an interesting character, later involved in the Essex Rising, but he was born in 1580 and is too young to be Marlowe's associate.

Sir Hugh Cholmeley, Richard's father, served the government mainly at a local level in Cheshire. In 1584 he reported to Walsingham about a man who had returned from Rome with 'some of the hair of the Virgin and bones of martyrs'. The following year he was part of a team examining a captured seminarist, Thomas Holford. Also on the commission was Sir Rowland Stanley, the father-in-law of Marlowe's coining friend John Poole. In 1588 Sir Hugh was one of the muster-masters recruiting troops in preparation for the Armada invasion. His co-master was Sir John Savage, whose daughter married Lord Strange's friend Thomas Langton, Baron of Walton. In his work as muster-master Sir Hugh came directly under the aegis of Strange, who had overall control of the muster in his capacity as Lord Lieutenant of the county.

Richard Cholmeley grew up in that world of Cheshire and Lancashire gentry – Stanleys and Pooles, Savages and Langtons, Gerards and Heskeths – which gravitated towards the baronial centre of the Earl of Derby and his son, Lord Strange. All these families are touched by the deep tinge of Catholic loyalism in the area. Some, like John Poole, emerge as militant Catholics. Others, like Richard Cholmeley, emerge as pseudo-Catholics, using their origins and connections to entrap Catholics. They are obverse and reverse of the same coin, and both of them come to know Marlowe, perhaps through this shared connection with Lord Strange.

While Sir Hugh Cholmeley was diligently enforcing law and order in Cheshire, young Richard was pursuing a more lurid career down south. In London in 1589 he was present (according to the compiler of those 'Remembrances' against him) at a 'mutiny' in the Strand. This was 'after the Portingale voyage', the ill-fated naval expedition in support of the Portuguese pretender, Don Antonio. It produced only recriminations among its commanders, including the Earl of Essex, and disaffection among its unrewarded participants. It is possible Cholmeley had been involved in the voyage. He was certainly in the thick of the fray in the Strand. And there, so it is reported, he was uttering violent words against Lord Burghley. He was heard by a certain Francis Clerke and 'many other soldiers'. He said that 'he repented him of nothing more than that he had not killed my Lord Treasurer with his own hands, saying he could not have done God better service.'

This kind of angry muttering is typical of what we know of Cholmeley. The 'Remembrances' records his many disparagements of high-ranking government figures:

His manner of proceeding in scorning the Queen's subjects

is first to make slanderous reports of most noble peers and honourable Councillors, as the Lord Treasurer, the Lord Chamberlain, the Lord Admiral, Sir Robt Cecil . . .

he speaketh in general all evil of the Council, saying that they are all atheists & Machiavellians, especially my Lord Admiral . . .

he rails at Mr Topcliffe & hath written another libel jointly against Sir Francis Drake & Justice Young, whom he saith he will couple up together because he hateth them alike . . .

he saith he doth entirely hate the Lord Chamberlain & hath good cause to so do.

The range of Cholmeley's vituperation covers famous military figures (Lord Admiral Howard, Sir Francis Drake), high-ranking politicians (Lord Treasurer Burghley, Lord Chamberlain Hunsdon, Sir Robert Cecil), and noted persecutors of the Catholics (Justice Young and rackmaster Topcliffe). This must not necessarily be taken at face value, however. He is a wild character, but much of his seditious talk seems to be connected to his work as a government agent. His vitriol against the Cecils, for instance, must be weighed up against his known involvement with them in secret matters.

According to the 'Remembrances', Cholmeley was 'employed by some of her Majesty's Privy Council for the apprehension of papists & other dangerous men'. Some of this work can be traced in the official records. It is also reported of him that he abused his position. Sent to arrest suspects, he would 'take money of them, & would let them pass in spite of the Council'. This is in itself unremarkable: taking bribes from Catholics was virtually accepted practice, a spreading of the financial burden of intelligence. More serious are Cholmeley's reported boasts about how he fools his masters on the Council:

He so highly esteemeth his own wit & judgement that he saith that no man are sooner divined and abused than the Council themselves . . .

He can go beyond & cozen them as he list, & that if he make any complaint in behalf of the Queen, he shall not only be privately heard & entertained, but he will so urge the Council for money that without he have what he list, he will do nothing . . .

He saith there be certain men, corrupted by his persuasions, who will be ready at all times & for all causes to swear whatsoever seemeth good to him.

The picture this paints – of an unscrupulous man with a channel right to the heart of government, and to its purse-strings – is the kind of thing that gave the spymasters bad dreams.

Cholmeley's career as an anti-Catholic agent can be traced over a couple of years between 1591 and 1593, before he disappears once more from the record. Much of what emerges bears out the portrait of him in the 'Remembrances'.

The first sighting of him finds him over the borderline, part of the dangerous side, though later proving to be the government's man. On 13 May 1591, a warrant was issued for the arrest of a certain Thomas Drury, and two men who are described as Drury's 'companions'. One of these companions was Richard 'Chomley'. The arresting officer was ordered to search for them in their 'dwelling places', and to bring them 'before their Lordships without delay, all excuses set apart, to answer to such things as shall be objected against them.'

Thomas Drury was indeed brought in. His lodgings were searched for 'papers of State', and on 15 May he was sentenced to be kept in the Marshalsea. He was charged with 'divers fond and great matters'. Cholmeley, however, was not arrested. On the contrary, he was paid for assisting in the arrest of Drury. On 29 July, £6 was issued to 'Burrage and Cholmeley, that apprehended Thomas Drury'. Burrage is Jasper Borage, a known associate of Cholmeley. It looks like Cholmeley and Borage were playing the familiar double game with Drury: they were his companions one day, they turned him in the next.

Cholmeley's routine activities as a hunter of 'papists & other dangerous men' can be gauged from a two-page report compiled in early January 1592. This is endorsed 'Chomley', and its big, pasty handwriting is probably his autograph.

The information it contains is low-grade intelligence about the comings and goings of recusants and priests in London and Sussex. There are many names in it, some familiar, some obscure. Often it is flimsy recusant gossip, but sometimes it is the first-hand observation of a spy. One of the Catholics Cholmeley was reporting on was the Jesuit Robert Southwell. Cholmeley writes: 'There is likewise one Mr Suthwell, a Jesuit, that useth to [i.e. stays at] Mr Cotton's in Fleet Street, and sometimes to Dr Smith's.' At just this time, in December 1591, Southwell was writing a long letter to the news-gatherer Richard Verstegan, in which he complained about the profusion of government snoops among the Catholics in London:

> Their spies, as namely Burden, Baker, Vachel, have pre-tended themselves to be Catholics, and that by the warrantize and advice of their superiors. They have heard Mass, confessed and received [the sacraments], only of purpose to discover Catholics and to entrap them.

Cholmeley is not named by Southwell, but this sums up his role at this time: a phoney Catholic working under the 'warrantize' of the government. In this particular case his information is faulty. He says that Southwell lodges at Mr Cotton's, but in fact 'Cotton' was Southwell's own alias.

According to the 'Remembrances', Cholmeley's work as a phoney Catholic went beyond the taking of mass and confession. It extended to his active involvement in writing Catholic propaganda:

> He made certen libellious verses in commendation of papists and seminary priests, very greatly inveighing

against the State, among which lines this was one: 'Nor may the Prince deny the Papal crown'.

The penning of these 'libellious verses' was obviously part of his pose as a Catholic. He was – or so he claimed – encouraged to write them by the government, particularly by Sir Robert Cecil:

> He had a certain book (as he saith) delivered him by Sir Robert Cecil, of whom he giveth very scandalous report: that he [Cecil] should invite him to consider thereof, & to frame verses & libels in commendation of constant priests & virtuous recusants. This book is in custody, & is called *An Epistle of Comfort*, & is printed at Paris.

Cholmeley is saying here that he has been writing pro-Catholic 'libels' at Cecil's instigation, and that Cecil sent him a copy of a banned Jesuit tract – Robert Southwell's *Epistle of Comfort* – as a handy guide to help him in composing his own pieces. The compiler of the 'Remembrances' finds this a 'scandalous report' against Cecil. It was embarrassing to say the least: the government was extremely sensitive to written propaganda, and Cecil would not wish to be associated with it in this way.

Cholmeley's dealings with Sir Robert Cecil are further revealed in a letter to Cecil from Cholmeley's brother Hugh, dated 19 January 1592. It has been completely missed by the biographers, though it gives a vivid glimpse of him in action.

As so often in this world, it is a querulous letter of self-justification. Hugh is worried about his standing with Cecil. He has endeavoured, he says, to 'effect' Her Majesty's service, but he fears he is under a cloud. Not wishing to be 'laid in oblivion sinisterly', he now writes to clear his name. He is 'loath to find fault' with his brother Richard, but it is on him that the blame rests.

The business is obscure, but the gist of Hugh's complaint is that Richard has used him to gain access to Cecil, and has then tried to exclude him from the rewards that followed. The beginning involved a man called Stronge:

> After my brother had obtained Stronge's consent to these services, he not knowing how to have them so surely & honestly performed as by myself, did acquaint me with the whole secrecy thereof, & told me that my part would be worth £500, further requiring me to write his first & second letters unto Your Honour, the which I did.

I thought for a moment that 'Stronge' was 'Strange', but the name is quite clear. He is presumably Richard Strong whose name is coupled with Cholmeley's in a warrant of March 1593. Who or what he was I do not know. Cholmeley obtained Strong's 'consent' to certain 'services' – it sounds like Strong was Cholmeley's *entrée* into some Catholic circle – and then got brother Hugh to write to Sir Robert Cecil about the project in hand. This Hugh did, and delivered the letters to Cecil in person. Hugh acknowledged Richard as the 'principal' in the matter, and never tried to 'rob him of any credit', but since then Richard has reneged on the 'partnership' between them: 'he seemed therewith nothing at all contented, so would he not endure any man thereof remembered but himself'.

This unspecified project, involving the two Cholmeleys and Richard Strong, went through, but Cecil was not pleased. It was not the project itself that displeased him, but certain breaches of security thereafter, for Hugh speaks of 'Your Honour's misliking of our hasty indiscrete coming, to bring tidings for the accomplishment thereof'. He now apologises for this 'error'. Whatever it was that the Cholmeleys were up to, Cecil wanted it kept at arm's length.

Some time after this, Hugh continues, Richard tried to ditch him completely, claiming this was Cecil's order. He 'did take occasion to bring me word that Your Honour would not have me deal any more in such causes, the which message I know was altogether mistaken, or rather by himself devised.' Hugh says manfully that he chose, for a while, to 'brook the injury' and keep silent. He did this for family reasons, to protect his brother, 'whose oversight I should for very shame conceal, were it not a concealed overthrow unto myself'.

Some confirmation of Hugh's grievance can be found in the Chamber accounts, where 'Richard Cholmley, gent' – but not Hugh – is paid 20 nobles (£6 13s 4d) 'by way of reward for some special service by him done'. This designation is even vaguer than usual, but the date of the payment is 21 December 1591, and it is probably for this enterprise described by Hugh. We know from Hugh's letter that Cholmeley's employer in this was Cecil, but no name is attached to the warrant – Cholmeley is simply paid 'upon ye Council's warrant'. Again this desire to keep Cholmeley at a distance.

Since then, Hugh continues, he and Richard have been 'strangers' to one another – until, that is, 'Monday last' (16 January 1592), when they were both involved in an entrapment operation at the house of William Shelley. William Shelley of Michelgrove, Sussex, was a staunch old Catholic. He had sheltered Father Persons during the first Jesuit mission, and he had suffered years of imprisonment in the Tower. The Cholmeleys now had their hooks into the Shelley family. At the house in Michelgrove, Richard reported about this time, there was a priest named Hurt, and at the Shelleys' London house in Trinity Lane there was 'a private place in a wall, with certain books & papers & writing, with other things I know not what'. At one of these houses, on 16 January, Hugh and Richard Cholmeley brought their surveillance to a climax. Hugh briefly describes the events of that day:

> at Mr Shelley's I played the prologue in the resemblance of a priest, & immediately in another proportion did with my brother Garmond perform the action, first causing my brother Richard Cholmley to confess in friendship that, upon stomach, he had before wronged me unto Your Honour.

This is another of these nasty little pieces of persecutory

theatre. First the 'prologue': Hugh dressed up in costume as a bogus mass-monger. Then the 'action': the arrest of those present by Hugh and 'Garmond' (probably a brother-in-law). And behind the scenes lurks Richard, the unseen director of the operation.

Hugh concludes with some words in favour of brother Richard. He hopes Cecil will 'pardon this ambitious infirmity, in regard of divers other good points that I hope are in him'. He also asks Cecil not to tell Richard about the letter, 'for otherwise his conceit of hatred would grow deeper against me, by the which discord we should the rather hinder Her Highness's further service.'

Richard Cholmeley emerges from this as a squabbling, scheming, impulsive figure, a man of resentment and 'ambitious infirmity'. He acts 'upon stomach'. The stomach, according to popular physiology, was the seat of ambition and arrogance, as in Shakespeare's *Henry VIII*: 'a man of an unbounded stomach, ever ranking himself with princes'.

That Cecil employed him need not surprise us. Nor that Marlowe knew him. He is just one more figure in this story of bad company.

For some months after this Cholmeley's movements are obscure. He returns to the spotlight in March 1593, when a Council warrant was issued ordering his apprehension, along with his accomplice Richard Strong. A couple of months later he is described as 'laid for', or under surveillance. There is little doubt that the report known as the 'Remembrances' is connected with this period of surveillance, though whether as the cause or the product of the government's suspicions is not yet clear. It was certainly written before 30 May, since it refers to Marlowe as alive; other evidence suggests it was compiled in mid-May.

The compiler of these 'Remembrances' against Richard Cholmeley portrays him as a loudmouth and a libeller, as a corrupt and unfaithful government agent, but perhaps most significant in the context of 1593, he portrays him as a militant atheist.

The description of Cholmeley's atheism is particularly significant because it is the opinion of an avowed disciple of Marlowe. Cholmeley is said to have conversed with Marlowe on the subject, and to believe that Marlowe 'is able to show more sound reasons for atheism' than any 'divine' can offer to the contrary. This is confirmed by Richard Baines, who states in his 'Note' on Marlowe that 'one Ric Cholmeley has confessed that he was persuaded by Marlowe's reasons to become an atheist'. It is clear from this (and from other evidence) that Baines knew of the allegations against Cholmeley when he wrote down his own allegations against Marlowe.

This is the only reference to Cholmeley's atheism in the 'Remembrances' itself, but together with the 'Remembrances' there is a letter, written by the same informer to an unnamed official (probably Justice Young). This letter, apparently written a little later than the 'Remembrances' itself, is almost exclusively concerned with Cholmeley's atheism. Cholmeley's 'course', the informer reports, is

to make a jest of the scripture, with these fearful, horrible & damnable speeches: that Jesus Christ was a bastard, St Mary a whore, & the Angel Gabriel a bawd to the Holy Ghost; and that Christ was justly persecuted by the Jews for his own foolishness; that Moses was a juggler & Aaron a cozener, the one for his miracles to Pharaoh to prove there was a God, & the other for taking the ear-rings of the Children of Israel to make a golden calf; with many other blasphemous speeches of the divine essence of God, which I fear to rehearse.

There can be no doubt that these rasping quips are – or at any rate were intended to be – a rehearsal of Marlowe's own views as a scoffer and scorner of the scriptures. This is made crystal clear by comparing this itemisation of Cholmeley's blasphemies with the Baines 'Note'. Every single one of Cholmeley's views is there echoed, and directly attributed to Marlowe:

1 That Jesus Christ was a bastard, St Mary a whore & the Angel Gabriel a bawd to the Holy Ghost. (Cholmeley)
  That Christ was a bastard and his mother dishonest . . . That the Angel Gabriel was bawd to the Holy Ghost. (Marlowe, according to Baines)

2 That Christ was justly persecuted by the Jews for his own foolishness. (Cholmeley)
  That Christ deserved better to die than Barabas and that the Jews made a good choice. (Marlowe/Baines)

3 Moses was a juggler . . . for his miracles to Pharaoh to prove there was a God. (Cholmeley)
  That Moses was but a juggler . . . That it was an easy matter for Moses, being brought up in all the arts of the Egyptians, to abuse the Jews. (Marlowe/Baines)

Cholmeley and Baines intimately corroborate one another on the subject of Marlowe's 'damnable' opinions. On the surface they come at the matter from different angles – Cholmeley is an adherent of Marlowe's views, Baines a denouncer of them – but the effect is the same: a portrayal of Marlowe as a foul-mouthed atheist and, worse, as a propagandist of atheism. The Cholmeley of the 'Remembrances' is a convert, 'persuaded by Marlowe's reasons'. He is a living, breathing example of the dangers of Marlovian atheism.

The informer's letter has more to say on the subject of Cholmeley's atheism, something rather different from this foul-mouthing of Jesus, Mary and Moses. I would call this other aspect 'political atheism'.

One aspect of this is the use of atheism as a critique of the government. This is closely bound up with that other much-vaunted term, 'Machiavellianism'. The premise is that the political masters of the day – for all their pretence of religion, for all their prosecution of religious wars – behave in a calculating, amoral, opportunist way that shows they are not Christians at all, but atheists. This is what Cholmeley is reported as saying: that the members of the Privy Council are 'all atheists & Machiavellians'. He particularly singles out Lord Burghley, Sir Robert Cecil, Lord Admiral Howard and Lord Chamberlain Hunsdon. He says he has 'profound witness' that these men are 'sound atheists', for 'their lives & deeds show that they think their souls do end, vanish, and perish with their bodies'.

This again reflects back on Marlowe, who is closely associated with this kind of Machiavellian perception. From the early *Tamburlaine* to the mature *Edward II*, his plays offer challenging and uncomfortable readings of Christian *realpolitik*:

> Ay, policy! That's their profession,
> And not simplicity, as they suggest.

So says the Jew of the Christians of Malta, and by the end of the play we cannot disagree. Robert Greene, with this sort of line in mind, attributed Marlowe's 'diabolical atheism' to the 'pestilent Machiavellian policy' he had 'studied'.

In this aspect too, Richard Cholmeley is a disciple of Marlowe. When he says that the politicians show by 'their lives & deeds' that they are really 'sound atheists', he is stating baldly what Marlowe says in more subtle form in his plays. Once again, Cholmeley is a kind of embodiment of Marlowe's opinions.

Yet crucially, it is not *just* Cholmeley who embodies these views. He has – according to the government snoop who is reporting on him – a whole 'company' of followers. In his letter the informer warns:

> This cursed Cholmeley hath lx of his company & he is seldom from his fellows, & therefore I beseech your worship have a special care of yourself in apprehending him, for they be resolute murdering minds.

This gang of Cholmeley's is a 'damnable crew', whose intent is 'to draw Her Majesty's subjects to be atheists'. More than that, their practice is, after her Majesty's decease, to make a King among themselves, & live according to their own laws, & this, saith Cholmeley, will be done easily, because there be and shortly will be, by his & his fellows' persuasions, as many of their opinion as of any other religion.

This is an extraordinary description: a gang of sixty men, resolute and violent, pledged to the cause of atheism, and talking in terms of some kind of separatist commune that elects its own king and lives by its own laws. Cholmeley the atheist is a dangerous revolutionary, the head of an Elizabethan Angry Brigade.

This expresses the worst fears of the authorities about the consequences of allowing atheism to prosper: civil disobedience, social breakdown, anarchy. In a constitutional sense, because Church and State were one, atheism was a crime against the State, a form of treason. Cholmeley's 'damnable crew' presses that into political reality. And as all the other aspects of Cholmeley's atheism relate back to Marlowe, it is likely that – in the eyes of the authorities, at least – this one does too. These 'murdering minds' are Cholmeley's followers, 'corrupted by his persuasions'. Cholmeley in turn is a follower of Marlowe, 'persuaded by his reasons'. This is perhaps the most damaging imputation about Marlowe to emerge from the investigation of Richard Cholmeley: that he is not just an atheist, but a whipper-up of sedition and rebellion.

Naturally enough, the government was keen to clap this 'cursed Cholmeley' behind bars. Their informer is set to infiltrate the gang, a dangerous occupation. He has 'soothed the villains with fair words' so that he can 'dive into the secrets of their devilish hearts'. He is fearful that he has been tumbled. Cholmeley has been avoiding him, 'for he doth partly suspect that I will bewray his villainy & his company'. He warns of the dangers of arresting Cholmeley, who moves under the protection of these heavily armed accomplices.

Cholmeley was finally arrested on the evening of 28 June

1593, the very same day that Ingram Frizer was pardoned for killing Marlowe. The following day, Justice Young wrote to the Lord Keeper, the ubiquitous Sir John Puckering:

> These are to advertise your Lordship that yesternight at ix of the clock, Mr Wilbrom came to me, and brought Ric. Chomley with him. He [Cholmeley] did submit himself to him [Wilbrom]. He brought a letter to me written by Mr Doctor Bankar, with a petition that the said Chomley had exhibited to the Lord of Canterbury his Grace, but the effect [of] Mr Doctor's letter was that I should accomplish my Lord's speeches committed to me, that was to commit him the said Chomley to prison, & the rest that should be found of his sect. The which I have done, so that now he is to be examined by such as it shall please your Honours to appoint. And for the rest, I do not doubt but they will submit themselves now one of the principals be apprehended.

According to this letter, Cholmeley had already been patching things up with the ecclesiastical authorities. He had presented some kind of 'petition' to Archbishop Whitgift. A copy of this was now in Justice Young's hands, but with it came a letter urging Young to persevere in arresting Cholmeley, and any other members of his 'sect' he could lay hands on. The letter-writer's name looks (in Young's ill-formed hand) like 'Bankar'. This is almost certainly Dr Richard Bancroft, Canon of Westminster and future Archbishop of Canterbury. He had become Whitgift's private chaplain in 1592, and was his chief agent in the rooting-out of heresy. He is particularly remembered as the orchestrator of the government's counter-attack against the Marprelate pamphlets. In this role he personally commissioned the anti-Marprelate pamphleteers: Nashe, Greene, Munday, Lyly. He is very likely to be involved in the pursuit of a religious renegade like Richard Cholmeley.

Cholmeley was duly hauled off to prison, to be 'examined'. As he was being led away, he shouted: 'I do know the law, and when it comes to pass I can shift well enough.' These are the last words of Richard Cholmeley to be recorded, typical in their bluster and spleen. His ultimate fate is unknown.

Though not primarily concerned with Marlowe, the 'Remembrances' against Richard Cholmeley (in which term I include both the informer's report and the letter which accompanies it) is a key document in the case. I stress again its remarkable similarity to that other key document, the Baines 'Note'. Both documents record the same violently atheistic statements. In the 'Remembrances' they are claimed to be the words of a disciple of Marlowe; in the 'Note' they are claimed to be the words of Marlowe himself. Both documents were written around the same time (though the precise date of the 'Remembrances' is uncertain) and both convey a sense of Marlowe's dangerous influence in religion and politics. Both documents end up on the desk of Sir John Puckering, whose handwriting can also be seen on the back of the 'Remembrances'.

Again we have to pose the simple but ultimately unanswerable question about these documents: do they tell the truth about Marlowe? On the 'Note' I have already ventured an answer, mostly negative: that Baines's track-record as a spy and projector argues strongly against believing him, and that whatever truth is in the 'Note' has been exaggerated and tarnished to the point where it is no longer true. In the case of the 'Remembrances' the question is still more complex, because there are three possible interpretations of the document. The first is that it is true – that it correctly records Cholmeley's militant views, and correctly attributes them to the influence of Marlowe. The second is that it is false, in which case the informer is deliberately incriminating both Cholmeley and Marlowe. And somewhere between these two, in that 'debatable land' of interpretation so frequently arrived at, there is a third possibility, which is that Cholmeley said all these things but did not really mean them; that he was plying his familiar trade of double-dealing. In this scenario Cholmeley would be posing as an atheist revolutionary, just as he had posed as a Catholic, in order to provoke others –

Marlowe, for instance – into criminal utterances. This would tie in with Cholmeley's known career, which belongs precisely in this line of duplicitous role-playing. It might also tie in with that 'petition' which he exhibited to the Archbishop of Canterbury, sometime before his arrest in late June, and which sounds rather like one of those signed certificates or warrants which were so important to the spy, sanctioning what otherwise appeared to be seditious behaviour.

It is possible that the 'Remembrances' is a document of unimpeachable truth, but I doubt it. I suspect there is falsehood, which is the element Cholmeley lives in, but whether it is a falsehood directed against him, or a falsehood perpetrated by him – or whether it is a messy mix of the two: lies built on lies – I cannot yet say.

But if Cholmeley was not *really* an atheist, what about his dastardly 'crew' of followers? Well, what indeed. There are said to be sixty of them, but throughout the investigation, only four are named. Two, Henry Young and Jasper Borage, are named in the 'Remembrances' itself. Two others are listed, along with Young and Borage, in an official docket on the back of the 'Remembrances'. They are described as 'tippinges ii' – in other words, the Tipping brothers, James and John. The interesting thing about all these men is that they appear at one time or another in the rosters of covert intelligence work. Borage was paid along with Cholmeley for apprehending Thomas Drury. Young and the Tippings were all Catholics involved in government intrigue in the Low Countries – James Tipping was one of Michael Moody's correspondents in 1591, and both John Tipping and Harry Young were working as provocateurs, along with Moody, in the Yorke-Williams plot of 1594.

This 'sect' of atheists and revolutionaries turns out, as far as the evidence remains, to consist of a handful of shady government agents and turncoat Catholics: precisely the world out of which Cholmeley comes. Here again we are forced to wonder about the information provided in the 'Remembrances'. It is the only source of evidence about the Cholmeley gang: their number, their violence, their political programme. The informer warns that they are always with Cholmeley, a resolute bodyguard, but when Mr Wilbrom comes to arrest him on 28 June, Cholmeley quietly 'submits' himself. The 'damnable crew' has vanished and is heard of no more.

31

PLACARDS AND FRAGMENTS

THE 'REMEMBRANCES' EMERGES from this underworld of ploys and 'plats' with which we have become wearyingly familiar in the course of this book. A suspicion in one's mind is lit that Marlowe is being set up, either by Cholmeley himself or by the informer who wrote the 'Remembrances'. It is at this stage no more than a suspicion, but it ties in pretty well with our feeling that the Baines 'Note' is also a ploy against Marlowe, and since the 'Note' both mentions and echoes the Cholmeley material, we might further feel that they are part of the *same* ploy. The presence of Lord Keeper Puckering at various stages of the business – the interrogator of Kyd, the annotator of the 'Note', the overseer of Cholmeley's arrest – offers a context of government enforcement in which such a ploy might be attempted. If I am right in the general drift of this argument, we are presented with the idea that both the 'Remembrances' and the 'Note' are, in their different ways, a deliberate smearing of Marlowe as a propagandist of atheism and inciter to sedition.

With this in mind I return to the beginning of Marlowe's troubles: to the first of the 'texts' that concern him. The beginning of the business, as we have seen, was the spate of anti-immigrant 'placards' and 'libels' that appeared in the streets of London in April and May, and in particular the 'Dutch Church libel', affixed to the walls of the Dutch Churchyard on the evening of 5 May. This was the apparent first cause of the investigation of Marlowe. It was the cause in two ways. First, because it is a very Marlovian document in itself: it is signed 'Tamburlaine' and it contains allusions to other Marlowe plays. Second, because it led to the arrest of Thomas Kyd, and so to the discovery of the Arian treatise in Kyd's lodgings, which was said by Kyd to belong to Marlowe.

Until a few years ago, all that was known of the actual text of the Dutch Church libel was the opening four lines:

> You strangers that do inhabit in this land,
> Note this same writing, do it understand.
> Conceive it well, for safeguard of your lives,
> Your goods, your children, & your dearest wives.

This was transcribed from an unidentified manuscript by the antiquary John Strype, and published in his *Annals of the Reformation* (1725–31). The lines catch something of the threatening tone of the libel, but give no clue to other significant features of it. The full fifty-three-line text of the libel only resurfaced in 1971, when it was found among a bundle of 'residual manuscripts' in the collection of Sir Thomas Phillipps. This is not the original document, but a manuscript copy made in about 1600 by a Cambridge man, John Mansell. Mansell's actual heading for the poem is 'A Libel fixed upon the French Church wall in London, *anno* 1593', but this is only an error of a few yards (the French church, St Anthony's, stood next to the Dutch church), and there is no reason to doubt that the Mansell version is an accurate transcript of the fateful Dutch Church libel.

The basis of the libel is crudely racist, but the text has its qualities. Though the author is no poet, he is literate enough to write in iambic pentameters, and he expresses the tradesmen's grievances against the 'strangers' with some force:

> Cutthroat-like in selling, you undo
> Us all, & with our store continually you feast.
> Our poor artificers do starve & die.

He covers all the usual grumbles about foreign merchants –

usury, racking of rents, 'engrossing' (stock-piling in times of scarcity). He also accuses them as underhand subversives – 'intelligencers to the State & Crown' who 'in your hearts do wish an alteration'. Towards the end he enters more dangerous territory, for the libel concludes with a scathing attack on English leaders for protecting the foreigners:

> With Spanish gold you all are infected
> And with that gold our nobles wink at feats.
> Nobles, say I? Nay, men to be rejected,
> Upstarts that enjoy the noblest seats,
> That wound their country's breast for lucre's sake,
> And wrong our gracious Queen and subjects good
> By letting strangers make our hearts to ache.

Part of the Council's anger about this particular libel probably relates to this dangerous criticism, that members of the government were profiteering from their protection of the immigrant merchants.

The fascinating thing revealed by the full transcript of the libel is the author's evident interest in Marlowe. This is signalled most obviously by his pseudonym, 'Tamburlaine', but it is also part of the libeller's discourse. The Dutchman, he says, is a 'Machiavellian merchant', expert in 'counterfeiting religion'. He is 'infected with gold', a predatory usurer 'like the Jews'. These are not perceptions peculiar to Marlowe, of course, but they closely echo the themes of Marlowe's *Jew of Malta*, and it is likely that the echo is intentional. I would say that the *Jew*'s openness to a racist, anti-Semitic reading is being used here. This is not necessarily a good reading of the play, which distributes its charges evenly among Jew, Turk and Christian, but it is a typical one: the success of the play's revival in 1594 was undoubtedly due to the anti-Semitic mood of the country in the wake of the Lopez affair. Here too the libeller annexes Marlowe's play to further his own racist message. Towards the end of the poem, he uses Marlowe's *Massacre at Paris* in much the same way:

We'll cut your throats, in your temples praying,
Not Paris massacre so much blood did spill.

Once again, he is using Marlowe's work as a kind of short-hand. Marlowe's play does not, of course, advocate atrocity, though it does dwell on the subject in lurid detail. The play had premièred at the Rose in January, and was fresh in the minds of the play-going public.

Clearly these Marlovian elements help to explain why Thomas Kyd was arrested a week later under suspicion as the author of the libel. He was a former associate of Marlowe, a fellow playwright, and at some point after 5 May someone put the finger on him, either as the libeller *per se*, or as someone who could throw light on the matter. Marlowe himself was out of town, with Thomas Walsingham at Scadbury.

This explains Kyd's arrest in a broad way, but does not take us very far. Kyd was certainly not the Dutch Church libeller. It is wildly improbable on stylistic grounds, it is convincingly denied by Kyd, and there is in any case no evidence that he was ever actually charged with the offence. Within a few hours of his arrest, in fact, the focus swivels towards Marlowe. The 'vile' Arian treatise is discovered among Kyd's papers, it is identified as belonging to Marlowe, and from then on – judging from Kyd's later depositions – the inter-rogators' interest in him was focused almost entirely on his knowledge of Marlowe and of Marlowe's 'monstruous opinions'. Like the libel itself, the arrest of Kyd leads to Marlowe.

One could say that the author of the Dutch Church libel was an admirer of Marlowe, but in view of the libel's dire conse-quences one must also say he was a causer of considerable trouble to Marlowe. What else, indeed, did he *expect*, when he signed this rabidly illegal document with the pseudonym 'Tamburlaine'?

So who was the author of this troublesome 'placard'? It was not Kyd. Nor was it the scrivener named Shore who was pilloried in June for a libel 'in threating of strangers': Shore's libel was posted up in the Royal Exchange, not the Dutch Churchyard. To my mind, there is one candidate who fits the profile of the mysterious 'Tamburlaine' to a T. He was, or claimed to be, a fervent admirer of Marlowe. He was a known composer of inflammatory libels. He could certainly turn his hand to verse, for one of his productions is described as 'certain libellious verses in commendation of papists'.

On this circumstantial evidence, Richard Cholmeley fits perfectly as the Dutch Church libeller. Documentary evidence is harder to come by: the original libel has disappeared, so no comparison of handwriting is possible (it would probably have been written up by a scrivener anyway). Stylistic comparison is also difficult. We have only one fleeting example of Cholmeley's literary style. In the 'Remembrances', the informer quotes a line from one of his libellous verses. It reads: 'Nor may the Prince deny the Papal Crown.' This is not enough to base a comparison on, but it is worth pointing out that Cholmeley's line is an iambic pentameter, and that this is the verse-form used in the Dutch Church libel (and, of course, in Marlowe's plays).

I cannot at this stage prove the case against Cholmeley, I can only say that he fits – certainly far better than Kyd ever did. And if Cholmeley wrote this libel, he wrote it for a purpose. We know that this was the case with his other libels. Those 'verses in commendation of papists' which he composed were not written out of Catholic belief, but for the opposite reason: to deceive and entrap Catholics. They were written, he claims, at the urging of Sir Robert Cecil, who 'invited' him to use Southwell's recusant prose to help him to compose his verses. It is to be presumed that his other libels – against Topcliffe, Drake, Justice Young – were the same kind of trick. This is Cholmeley's little speciality: the bogus libel.

In Cholmeley's hands the Dutch Church libel takes on an ulterior shape. It is a put-up job. And the particular nature of the put-up is to make it *sound like* it was written by an admirer of Marlowe. The echoes of Marlowe's influence are there as purposeful signposts. They are there to implicate Marlowe, to suggest that he – his plays, his ideas, his message

– is in some way behind this incitement to street violence.

This immediately chimes in with the kind of reading I have suggested for the 'Remembrances': that its presentation of Cholmeley as an atheistic revolutionary is designed to implicate Marlowe, who is specifically named as his atheistic guru. In this way the Dutch Church libel can be seen as the opening move in the smear campaign against Marlowe. The penner of the libel and the ranter of the 'Remembrances' bear the same message: that followers of Christopher Marlowe, those 'persuaded by his reasons', are men bent on political violence. There are lynch-mobs in the street, and there are gangs of malcontents planning to set up communes and 'live according to their own laws', and they are all spouting rhetoric imbibed from Marlowe. The message that is coming out, through these devious means, is that Marlowe is a dangerous man.

There is, furthermore, a specific context for this: the 'commission' set up by the Privy Council to investigate the first wave of anti-alien libelling and rioting. This commission, a five-man team under the lawyer Sir Julius Caesar, was set up on 22 April: this was after the first 'placards' had appeared, and after the civic authorities had signally failed to suppress further ones. The new commission's brief reflects that failure. They are to 'examine by secret means who may be authors of the said libels'. They are to use such 'secret and due means' as they think fit. So at this point there enters this secret police element into the investigation. To use 'secret means' suggests those more covert methods of obtaining information – through infiltration, undercover surveillance, provocation. And among the five commissioners is a man we know well, the former Walsingham henchman Thomas Phelippes, an old hand in the secret theatre, one of the chief contrivers (along with Robert Poley) of the counter-plot against Babington. Another former Walsingham servant, William Waad, was also on the commission. Their presence is precisely a sign that underhand methods are required and expected, that lures are to be cast into these turbid waters. They will also, no doubt, be among the 'commissioners' who examine Thomas Kyd in mid-May, as recalled by Kyd in his letter to Sir John Puckering: 'of my religion & life I have already given some instance to the late commissioners'.

By late April the word is out on the covert grapevine: Phelippes is after the authors of the libels. For a few days there is silence, and then on 5 May there appears a new libel, highly suggestive of a particular author's influence. Cholmeley fits the profile as the composer of this fake libel; if he is, he has written it to draw Marlowe into trouble – that is, more specifically, to draw Marlowe to the attention of Thomas Phelippes, the secret police-chief on the commission of enquiry. In this Cholmeley is unlikely to be working independently. We might suspect Baines's involvement at this earlier stage but have nothing, as yet, to prove it. The crucial role of another – let us call him at this point the Third Man – has also to be investigated. It should also be remembered that Cholmeley was a wanted man. The possibly dangerous role of *agent provocateur* on which he has embarked may have been represented to him as a way to 'do the State some service' by nailing this malcontent Marlowe.

Until now, the biographers have seen the Dutch Church libel as the *chance* cause of Marlowe's troubles in 1593: it led to the arrest of Kyd, which by chance led to Marlowe's heretical Arian tract being found at Kyd's lodgings. The recovery of the full text of the libel has challenged this somewhat, since it shows that the libel had certain connections with Marlowe to begin with. I am now taking this a stage further and saying that the libel was written with the deliberate purpose of drawing Marlowe into trouble. If I am right, this puts the arrest of Kyd in a new and chilling light. The element of chance becomes virtually untenable. The discovery of the Arian manuscript among his papers is not a fortuitous sequel to the Dutch Church libel, but a continuation of its covert purpose: to incriminate Marlowe.

In his letter to Sir John Puckering, written some months later, Kyd describes the discovery of the Arian tract:

When I was first suspected for that libel that concerned the State, amongst those waste and idle papers, which I cared not for & which unasked I did deliver up, were found some fragments of a disputation, touching that opinion affirmed by Marlowe to be his, and shuffled with some of mine, unknown to me, by some occasion of our writing in one chamber two years since.

It is clear from this that Kyd had not actually seen this document before. It was 'unknown' to him. He offers little more than guesswork as to how it came to be in his lodgings: it contains views which he knows to be held by Marlowe; he and Marlowe used to share a chamber together; he can only assume that the document was Marlowe's and had got mixed up with his own clutter of 'waste and idle papers', the bane of every writer's life.

These words were written in the leisure of retrospection. They do not convey the trauma of those first hours of Kyd's arrest on 11 May: the pursuivants at the door, the rifling of chests and shelves, the journey to the jail, the questions, and then this wretched document, this mere 'fragment', being waved in front of his face. The docket on the back of the tract tells its own story. First there is the description of the document: 'Vile heretical conceits denying the deity of Jesus Christ our Saviour, found amongst the papers of Thos Kydd prisoner'. Then there is a pause of some sort before the next phrase is added. The ink colour is different: some who have seen it think it is in a different hand, though to my eye it looks the same. This phrase contains the all-important point: 'which he affirmeth that he had from Marlowe'.

We know that Kyd was tortured while under arrest. He speaks of his 'pains and undeserved tortures'. In that pause, registered in the forensic detail of ink-colour, I hear the sounds of persuasion: the creaking of the rack-ropes, the whistle of the wire whip, or the simple expedient of the 'manacles', still popular in police-states today, where a man's own deadweight, hung from the wrists, inflicts the torture. One remembers that William Waad, another of these

353

'commissioners' who examined Kyd, was later in charge of the interrogation of Guy Fawkes, whose deteriorating signatures bear grim witness to the terrible damage being inflicted on him. The effect of these, or even just the threat of them, is enough to make a man agree to anything. And so Kyd *affirms* that this document, which he has never seen before, belongs to Marlowe.

This is the only evidence that Marlowe had anything to do with this document. The words in it are not his: they are words copied from an old theological text, *The Fall of the Late Arian*. The handwriting is not his: it is a standard scribal italic, and bears no resemblance to Marlowe's hand. That he was interested in the anti-Trinitarian views of the Arianists is plausible, but is not proof that the document was his. That he had shared a chamber with Kyd provides a circumstance, but again proves nothing. The only thing that links Marlowe with the document is Kyd's statement to that effect, probably made under torture.

In this game of black propaganda being directed at Marlowe, there is no room for chance. If the purpose of arresting Kyd was to incriminate Marlowe – and there seems little other reason for this erroneous, puzzling arrest – then the finding of the Arian tract accomplishes that purpose. Was it a lucky find of some bits of paper that had been lying around in Kyd's chamber for two years? Possibly, but more likely, I think, it was a plant. It was copied out of an old book and placed among Kyd's papers during or after the search. Kyd was confronted with it, denied any knowledge of it, and, after whatever prompting or pressure was required, foisted it on to Marlowe. The Arian tract is, in short, another piece of manufactured evidence.

Who might have manufactured it remains to be worked out. It was someone with a modicum of theological expertise, so of the two names that immediately suggest themselves, we might think that Baines the former priest is more likely than Cholmeley the libeller. The logistics of the plant cannot be reconstructed, though easy enough to imagine in the police-raid scenario of Kyd's arrest. One inference of this reading of the Arian tract is that this ploy against Marlowe now has the encouragement of Thomas Phelippes, a man well-seasoned in the theory and practice of forged or interpolated documents. No-one is better placed than Phelippes to introduce this particular document into Kyd's papers, to present it to Kyd during the interrogation of 12 May, and to extract from him, with the technical assistance of Waad, the all-important statement that it had been left in his lodgings by Marlowe. Phelippes has been offered this 'product' of incriminating placards and fragments, and it seems he likes it.

32

THE TARGET

THESE ARE THE texts and documents: the libel written by 'Tamburlaine'; the wild talk of Richard Cholmeley; the heretical Arian fragment; the extracted affirmations of a suspect in prison. And this is my interpretation of them: they were all designed to discredit Marlowe. They precede, and no doubt cause, the summoning of Marlowe by the Privy Council on 18 May; they precede, and apparently prepare for, the delivering of the Baines 'Note' around the end of May. They are the frame of innuendo and manipulated circumstance into which the detailed portrait of the 'Note' is later inserted. It is a classic piece of Elizabethan secret theatre. Marlowe is being given a role to play, the dangerous political atheist, but the words have been written by others. This is not to say he is totally innocent of the charges, but that the particular evidence against him has been fabricated or exaggerated. He has been spotlighted; he has been criminalised; he has been fitted up.

Over the last few chapters I have given my reasons for seeing all this as a ploy against Marlowe, rather than as an accumulation of genuine information about him, but I have not addressed a – perhaps the – central question. *Why* is Marlowe being set up like this? What is the reason for this smear campaign?

One answer relates straight back to the milieu out of which these documents emerge. Spies like Cholmeley and Baines thrived on a diet of sedition – indeed they survived on it: without it their careers ceased to exist – and we know that

Elizabethan spies often created sedition where none, or not enough, existed. To these men, Marlowe as 'danger to the State' was product, and what we are uncovering here, in these documents, is a covert effort to identify and define him as dangerous (precisely Baines's word: 'so dangerous a member'). Lord Keeper Puckering's programme of action against dissenters, and particularly against the published propagandists of dissent, is the context for this. These documents are aimed at Puckering's sphere of interest, and indeed successfully arrive there: his name arises at every stage of this investigation, and his handwriting is found on some of the documents. Here too there might be a need to pump up Marlowe's dangerousness. His plays, though full of trenchant ironies and sub-texts, could hardly be called subversive; as a public utterance on doctrinal matters, *Dr Faustus* is (in the texts that survive) thoroughly orthodox; no evidence survives that any of his plays attracted censure or censorship. Other 'texts' must therefore be produced if Marlowe is to qualify as a propagandist of religious dissent, and thus as a suitable target for prosecution.

In these ways the smearing of Marlowe might have been considered a good thing in itself; elements of personal antagonism (the 'malice' of Baines and perhaps others) may also have played their part. But I suspect there is another reason for this ploy against him: another layer of ulterior meaning. Marlowe is a target, but he is not the only target. There are others who are aimed at, men associated with Marlowe in some way. Some of them are named in these same documents, and some of them become entangled in prosecution as a result, and of these one in particular might be regarded as the chief target or prize in the plotters' minds – Sir Walter Ralegh.

Ralegh's name was and is associated with Marlowe; it would probably be right to call him a patron, but one hesitates to do so because there is no specific evidence of patronage. As we have seen, Marlowe's known association is with Ralegh's friend, the Earl of Northumberland; other poets connected with Marlowe – Watson, Peele, Roydon, Chapman

– also relate to the Earl. The mathematician Thomas Hariot was a salaried retainer of both Ralegh and Northumberland, and a friend to both till death. These men were all part of a definable circle or clique, of which Northumberland was the true centre – both financially and philosophically – and Ralegh the high-profile figurehead. This group is best *not* described as the 'School of Night', which name depends on a shaky interpretation of a line by Shakespeare, and is nowadays chiefly used by historical novelists. It is more soberly called the 'Durham House set', after Ralegh's house on the Strand, but this is not so useful after 1592, when Ralegh ceased to live there, and so one ends up rather lamely calling it the 'Ralegh-Northumberland set'. If the allegations circulating in May 1593 were damaging to Marlowe, they were no less damaging – in the tar-brush mode of Elizabethan police-work – to this little 'set' or coterie of scientists, poets and sceptics of which Marlowe was a part and Ralegh a patron.

Looking a little further back into the events of 1593, and particularly the circumstances leading up to the Dutch Church libel, I think it can be shown quite convincingly that Ralegh was the target of this smear campaign from the very beginning. The context of the Dutch Church libel was the resentment of London traders and artificers against immigrant merchants, particularly the Dutch. One of the focuses of this resentment, the reason for its particular eruption at this time, was that the matter was being debated in parliament. On 21 March, a bill was presented to the House, proposing the extension of various privileges to the immigrant traders. One of the few who opposed it was Ralegh. In the debates that followed (21–24 March) he spoke vehemently against the Dutch merchants and their stranglehold on the economy. 'The nature of the Dutchman,' he said, 'is to fly to no man but for his profit.' The Dutchman is a blood-sucker who 'by his policy hath gotten trading with all the world into his hands.' Ralegh spoke in favour not of 'relieving' them with privileges and concessions, but of expelling them:

Whereas it is pretended that for strangers it is against charity, against honour, against profit to expel them, in my opinion it is no matter of charity to relieve them . . . I see no reason that so much respect should be given unto them . . . In the whole cause I see no matter of honour, no matter of charity, no profit in relieving them.

He was a lone voice of dissent, and the House voted the bill through. Among those who spoke in its favour were Sir Robert Cecil and Sir Moyle Finch, son-in-law of Sir Thomas Heneage.

So Ralegh was known, in public, as an outspoken opponent of the immigrant 'strangers'. Just three weeks later, the first of the anti-immigrant libels appear. They complain about the privileges granted to the strangers, who 'live here in better case and more freedom' than the Queen's own subjects. They demand the expulsion of the strangers 'out of the realm'. These are precisely Ralegh's views expressed in Parliament: the libels echo Ralegh. Already this is damaging to him, for they are pressing his views towards open, rabble-rousing incitement. They threaten 'violence on the strangers'. The 'apprentices will rise', there will be 'many a sore stripe'. For those hostile to Ralegh, and there were many, there is capital to be made of this: Ralegh as the fomenter of street violence, Ralegh as the champion of this hooligan element of libellers and apprentices. On 22 April the Privy Council instructed its special commissioners to investigate the matter of the libels. They were to discover the 'authors of the said libels', but – perhaps more significant – they were urged to discover the 'favourers and abettors' of the libellers.

This was the situation when the libeller calling himself 'Tamburlaine' set to work. His libel, fixed to the Dutch Church wall on 5 May, was the most violent of all. In the Council's words, 'it doth exceed all the others in lewdness'. And if suspicions were already abroad that Ralegh was a 'favourer and abettor' of this anti-Dutch incitement, this libel went a long way to confirm them. For 'Tamburlaine' was clearly a follower of Marlowe, and Marlowe, it was well-known, was a follower of Ralegh.

This is the further purpose of the Dutch Church libel, the point of its Marlowe references. It is forged evidence that this rhetoric of violence and unrest emanates from Ralegh and his circle.

It is a short step from the libels to atheism. The arrest of Kyd accomplishes that step in a matter of hours. With the convenient discovery of the Arian tract among his papers, an investigation about the Dutch Church libel becomes an interrogation about Marlowe's atheism. Cholmeley himself, probably the real author of the libel, provides the government with precisely the same association. As portrayed in the 'Remembrances', he is both a libeller and an atheist. They are all bound up in one simmering malcontent package: disparagements of government figures and debasements of holy scripture. This also leads, through Marlowe, to Ralegh. For it is from Cholmeley, via the 'Remembrances', that the government learns that Marlowe 'hath read the atheist lecture to Sir Walter Ralegh & others'. Once again Ralegh is deliberately brought into focus as the protector of vile atheists like Marlowe. As in the Dutch Church libel the purpose is to taint Ralegh with an involvement in these dangerous currents of political and religious extremism.

The naming of 'Ralegh & others' by Cholmeley is registered as significant by the government investigators. On the back of the 'Remembrances' is an official memorandum. Headed (in Puckering's hand) 'Ye atheism of Cholmeley & others', it lists five names. Four of these are the members of the supposed 'damnable crew': Young, Borage and the two Tippings. The fifth name on the list is 'hariet'. Thomas Hariot is not actually mentioned in the 'Remembrances', so this is a connection supplied from elsewhere. Hariot was, of course, the protégé of Ralegh and Northumberland, the friend of Marlowe, and in the popular imagination the chief 'conjuror' of the Ralegh circle. The investigators have swallowed the hook: Cholmeley's alleged atheism has implicated Hariot, as well as Marlowe, in this game of guilt by association. It was reported a few months later that Hariot had been 'convented before the Lords of the Council for denying the resurrection of the body'. If so, it was probably a direct result of these allegations.

Baines, who follows Cholmeley closely in his description of Marlowe's blasphemies, also follows him in implicating the Ralegh circle. He drags in both Ralegh and Hariot early on in the 'Note' when he reports Marlowe's claim that 'one Heriots [i.e. Hariot], being Sir W Ralegh's man' was a magician far superior to Moses. And he is almost certainly trailing a reference to the Ralegh clique when he says that Marlowe 'hath quoted a number of contrarieties out of the Scripture, which he hath given to some great men, who in convenient time shall be named'. This is a repetition, in a roundabout and cautious manner, of Cholmeley's assertion that Marlowe read the 'atheist letter' to Ralegh. Kyd further cements the connection in his letter to Sir John Puckering, where he names three members of the Ralegh-Northumberland circle – Hariot, Warner and Roydon – as Marlowe's friends and holders of questionable beliefs.

All these sources of information against Marlowe in the early summer of 1593 – Cholmeley, Baines and Kyd – are not only remarkably consistent in their picture of Marlowe as blasphemer and scripture-scorner, but also in their implication of Ralegh and Hariot in this particular kind of atheism.

In the case of the Dutch Church libel, Ralegh's own performance in the parliament of March 1593 provided a jumping-off point. The libel's rabble-rousing rhetoric is an opportunist extension of Ralegh's own anti-Dutch speech. The atheism smear has a similar immediate pretext. Among the bills debated in that parliament was a further harsh enforcement of religious conformity, aimed at both Catholic and Puritan dissenters. Ralegh once again spoke against the official view. He denounced the bill as inquisitorial, an invasion into realms of private opinion and belief that neither could, nor should, be policed:

What danger may grow to ourselves if this law pass, it were fit to be considered. For it is to be feared that men not guilty will be included in it. And the law is hard, that taketh life and sendeth into banishment, where men's intentions shall be judged by a jury, and they [the jury] shall be judges what another means.

Once again there is scope here for those who are hostile to Ralegh. They will say he is arguing against religious enforcement in order to protect his own illicit belief: atheism. His plea for tolerance becomes a weapon to use against him, an instance of his own non-conformity. In fact Ralegh's speech is an almost direct riposte to Sir John Puckering, who undoubtedly supported the bill of conformity. Just a few days previously, in his capacity as Lord Keeper, Puckering had delivered a speech outlining the Queen's views – the official policy – on the strict limits of religious discussion in Parliament or anywhere else. He said:

There will be no good conclusion where every man may speak what he listeth without fit observation of persons, matter, times, places and other needful circumstances . . . For liberty of speech, Her Majesty commandeth me to tell you that . . . [it is] not, as some suppose, to speak there of all causes as him listeth, and to frame a form of religion or a state of government as to their idle brains shall seem meetest.

This is the battle-line in the debate on free speech in 1593, and Ralegh and Puckering are on either side of it.

Of course, the charge of atheism against Ralegh and his friends was nothing new. As mentioned earlier, there was a good deal of gossip and suspicion about what went on in the philosophical circles of the Durham House set. Nashe made a few pointed remarks, without naming names, in *Pierce Penniless*, but the most blatant accusation surfaced in the Catholic broadside generally called *The Advertisement*, circulating in the autumn of 1592. This was an English digest, co-authored by various Catholic exiles in Antwerp, of Father Persons's *Responsio ad Edictum Elizabethae*. It was a lively polemical squib, and it enjoyed much of the same clandestine vogue as *Leicester's Commonwealth*. Its slur on Ralegh was famous:

> Of Sir Walter Rawley's school of atheism, by the way; and of the conjuror that is master thereof; and of the diligence used to get young gentlemen to this school, wherein both Moses and our Saviour, the Old and the New Testament, are jested at, and the scholars taught among other things to spell God backward.

The 'conjuror' referred to is almost certainly Hariot. Hariot himself acknowledged that he was the man intended (though interestingly Dr Dee seems to have believed that *he* was the conjuror referred to).

The terms used by both Cholmeley and Baines about Marlowe tie in quite closely with this rumour of a school of atheism. Cholmeley talks of Marlowe reading an 'atheist lecture'. Baines has him distributing some treatise that lists certain 'contrarieties' – anomalies, contradictions, etc. – in the Bible. All this has the appropriate scholarly overtone. Hariot is the 'master' of this atheist school; Marlowe, it seems, is its lecturer. Cholmeley and Baines also echo the supposed subject-matter of this school – the jesting at Moses, Jesus and the Old and New Testament. All of these are attributed to Marlowe by Cholmeley, Baines or both: that Moses was a 'juggler', that Jesus Christ was a 'bastard', that 'the New Testament is filthily written', and much else in the same vein.

In this sense, many of the charges against Marlowe rehearsed by Cholmeley and Baines are little more than an elaborate reprise of the Persons slur against Ralegh. Their allegations against Marlowe serve to renew these earlier allegations against Ralegh. It is easy to see how this would be desirable to Ralegh's enemies. In its original form the 'school of atheism' jibe was rendered virtually harmless by its provenance. It was a piece of Jesuit black propaganda. *The*

Advertisement in which it appeared was a tissue of similar slurs about other English supremos, notably Lord Burghley. As a charge against Ralegh, it could not be taken seriously: it was titillating, it fuelled gossip and rumour, but it was not finally damaging. So the effect of this new attack on Ralegh is not just to renew the charge, but to legitimise it, to give it substance. The behaviour of Marlowe, as reported by Cholmeley, Baines and Kyd, is presented as living proof of this 'school of atheism'. Here is its lecturer, its propagandist. And here too are some of its political effects: the libels, the riots, the angry brigades.

The aspect of political atheism is also a renewal of the Jesuit charges against Ralegh – not in *The Advertisement*, but in Persons's original Latin text. The corresponding passage there is much longer, and it gets into a whole idea of Ralegh creating an 'atheist commonwealth' in which atheism is the 'law of the land'. Persons asks: what will happen if Ralegh is elected to the Privy Council? We can, he says, confidently expect another edict. This would be similar to the punitive edict of 1591 against the Catholics (the main subject of Persons's book) but it would be an atheist edict. Devised by that 'magian' who is Ralegh's 'praeceptor' (i.e. Hariot), and published in the Queen's name, it would reject all divinity and the immortality of the soul, and would outlaw as disturbers of the realm all those who object in any way to the sweet arguments of 'libertinism' (i.e. free-thinking in the religious sense, though also with the overtone of depravity).

This might be called a propagandist image of 'Ralegh's Commonwealth', in which atheism and 'libertinism' rule as the law of the land.

This is precisely the kind of spectre raised by the 'Remembrances', with its talk of Cholmeley and his crew of followers creating their own little atheistic kingdom. They will 'choose a king' and 'live according to their own laws'. In these ways the texts of May 1593 work over these Jesuit allegations about Ralegh, and seek to give them a new currency.

*

364

All this had its desired effect, though it took a while coming. In March 1594, nearly a year after these events, a special ecclesiastical commission was convened under Viscount Bindon. It met at Cerne Abbas, in Dorset, Ralegh's home town. Its purpose was to investigate the 'atheism or apostasy' of Ralegh and his circle. Though the foreground players were by now dispersed – Marlowe was dead, Kyd would shortly follow him, Cholmeley and Baines had disappeared back into the undergrowth – the allegations that were flying around in May 1593 were still current. The 'interrogatory', to be 'ministered' to those brought before the commission, includes such questions as:

Whom do you know, or have heard, that have argued or spoken against, or as doubting, the being of any God?

Whom do you know, or have heard, that hath spoken against the truth of God His holy word, revealed to us in the scriptures of the Old and New Testament, . . . or have said those scriptures are not to be believed and defended by Her Majesty for doctrine and faith and salvation, but only of policy or civil government?

Whom do you know, or have heard to have . . . spoken against the being or immortality of the soul of man, or that a man's soul should die and become like the soul of a beast?

All of this echoes pretty closely the Marlovian heresies refracted through Cholmeley and Baines – the questioning of 'the divine essence of God', the quoting of 'contrarieties' out of the Scripture, the comments about the political use of religion, and so on. The heresy about the mortality of the soul is referred to by Cholmeley – 'their souls do end, vanish & perish with their bodies' – and this view is further linked to Marlowe by an independent source, Marlowe's young Kentish disciple Thomas Fineux, who believed that 'his soul died with his body, & as we remember nothing before we were born, so we shall remember nothing after we are dead'.

The questions being asked by Bindon's commission in 1594

relate to the allegations against Marlowe, Hariot and Ralegh the previous year. The smear on Ralegh has taken effect. Judging from the commission's findings, it *was* just a smear. They found no evidence whatsoever that Ralegh himself was an atheist: a sceptic, perhaps; a man over-lenient in theology and over-curious in philosophy; but never once a denier of God. They found precious little about his followers either. There was talk of Hariot having 'brought the Godhead in question, and the whole course of the scriptures', but the deponent added that 'of whom he so heard it, he doth not remember'. For light relief there was the behaviour of Ralegh's young friend Thomas Allen, the governor of Portland Castle, who was said to tear pages out of a bible to dry tobacco on, and who one day, angry because the rain had cut short a hawking trip, swore 'that if God were in the bush there, he would pull Him out with His boots'. Allen's servant Oliver was likewise infected, and shocked two local ladies in Lillington by announcing that Moses had a harem of fifty-two concubines.

So the same aura of questioning and scoffing hangs around Ralegh's circle, but it remains at the level of gossip and unsupported allegation, of general atheistic lore being given a local habitation. No charges followed against Ralegh or any other. But gossip sticks, with or without formal charges, and Ralegh's name continued to be associated with atheism. This became particularly serious in 1603, when he was implicated in conspiracy against the new King James: the so-called 'Main' and 'Bye' plots. At his trial, the old rumours resurfaced. He was harangued by the prosecution as a 'damnable atheist', and before passing sentence for high treason, Lord Chief Justice Sir John Popham said to him:

> You have been taxed by the world with the defence of the most heathenish and blasphemous opinions, which I list not to repeat, because Christian ears cannot endure to hear them, nor the authors and maintainers of them be suffered to live in any Christian commonwealth.

Interestingly, it is not just the old rumours that resurface, but the old art of black propaganda, for circulating at the time of the trial was a poem supposedly written by Ralegh. It survives in two MS copies, virtually identical, both bearing the date 1603. The heading given in both copies is 'Certain Hellish Verses devised by that atheist and traitor Ralegh'. These 'hellish verses' are in the old atheist-Machiavellian vein of the early 1590s, and at some points chime in closely with Marlovian attitudes. They describe the origin of religion as a matter of purely secular 'policy':

> Then some sage man among the vulgar,
> Knowing that laws could not in quiet dwell
> Unless they were observed, did first devise
> The name of God, religion, heaven and hell . . .
> Whereas indeed they were mere fictions,
> And if they were not yet I think they were,
> And those religious observations
> Only bugbears to keep the world in fear,
> And make them quietly the yoke to bear.
> So that religion, of itself a fable,
> Was only found to make that peaceable.

This document circulating in 1603 was a blatant forgery. The entire fifty-nine-line poem was lifted out of a speech in an old play, *The Tragical Reign of Selimus*. With a few minor variations – such as changing 'Selim thinks' to 'I think' – the speech is transcribed exactly. The play had been published in 1594; it is usually attributed to Robert Greene.

So here again, ten years after the events concerning Marlowe, we find another of these bogus 'libels' being used against Ralegh. It is less subtle than the smear campaign of 1593, but its purpose is the same: to manufacture evidence of Ralegh's seditious atheism. In the minds of the forgers, one might say, Marlowe is still a weapon to use against Ralegh, for it is thought that *Selimus* was originally written by Greene as a riposte to *Tamburlaine*, and that the arguments advanced by Selimus were intended to be identified with Marlowe's views. Certainly the speech chosen here elaborates a view attributed to Marlowe, who believed (according to Richard Baines) that 'the first beginning of religion was only to keep men in awe', and that we should not be 'afeard of bugbears'.

The 'Hellish Verses' ploy is feeble in the extreme. *Selimus* was available in print, and many must have recognised the lines, and known that they were not really Ralegh's. It is interesting, though, as a reprise of the ploys of 1593. Marlowe's free-thinking views are once again being foisted on Ralegh by means of forgery.

The question arises: who is behind this smear campaign against Marlowe and Ralegh? It is a question I have avoided asking until now, partly because it led me a merry and ultimately unprofitable dance in the first edition, and partly because I am no longer at all sure it is the right question to ask. It is not really obligatory for anyone to be 'behind' it, in the sense of orchestrating it: no courtly intriguer or *éminence grise* pulling strings behind the scenes. We already have a fair-sized cadre. In the foreground there are the spies Richard Cholmeley and Richard Baines: professional incriminators at work. To their names will shortly be added another of the same stamp, a shadowy Third Man whose role in the affair has only recently been uncovered. At a somewhat higher level we discern the unpleasant features of Thomas Phelippes, a minor spymaster now empowered by the Council to use 'secret means' against seditious authors. And at a governmental level, there is Sir John Puckering, with his colleague Lord Buckhurst in frequent attendance, pledged to rid the realm of dangerous religious dissidents. I do not know if this gives us a chain of command; perhaps more precisely it identifies various orbits of interest. It is in the interest of Puckering to receive information about dissident opinions; it is in the interest of Phelippes to ferret out such information; it is in the interest of spooks like Cholmeley and Baines to supply and if necessary invent it. This is a small and unremarkable paradigm of Elizabethan intelligence-gathering – unremarkable except that the intelligence concerns Marlowe and Ralegh.

There are other interests that may be involved in some way. There is, for instance, the Earl of Essex, whom Phelippes has served in intelligence matters since about 1591, working alongside Anthony and Francis Bacon with whom he had cordial relations. There is no evidence of Essex's involvement in this anti-Ralegh move, though he is one of many courtiers who had clashed with Ralegh, temperamentally and politically, and who might have been happy enough to see his reputation tarnished in this way. Ralegh's standing was currently low, since the Queen's discovery of his secret marriage in the summer of 1592, and he was effectively in exile in darkest Dorset. But such rustications often proved temporary, and if Ralegh was famously 'Fortune's tennis ball' (as Sir Robert Naunton called him) he could always bounce back; his combative performances in Parliament showed he was by no means a spent force. Phelippes may have hoped that the exposure of Ralegh as heretic would earn him some credit with Essex, but that is very different from saying he was 'working for' the Earl in this business. His allegiance to the Essex faction is anyway shifting: he also reported to the Cecils from time to time – a report addressed to Lord Burghley is extant, written just a few weeks after these events. The vigilance of the Cecils should never be under-estimated: they had eyes and ears in all corners of the secret world, and if someone was up to something it soon enough touched, and entered, the Cecilian orbit of interest.

Ralegh considered Cecil his friend – which he was, up to a point – and we perhaps get a hint of Ralegh's own awareness of this conspiracy building up against him when he writes to Cecil: 'Every fool knoweth that hatred are the cinders of affection, and therefore to make me a sacrifice shall be thanksworthy.' Now that the Queen hates him, in other words, he has become a suitable target to be attacked, or 'sacrificed'. This was written from Sherborne on 10 May 1593, five days after the posting of the Dutch Church libel, news of which would soon have reached him from London.

33

'BY MY ONLY MEANS SET DOWN'

THE TEXT OF the Dutch Church libel is not the only document related to the Marlowe case which has surfaced in recent years. There is another, a letter, found at Lambeth Palace among the papers of Anthony Bacon, and first published in 1974. It was written from Richmond, 'at the waterside', on 1 August 1593, a couple of months after the events it describes. It is addressed 'to the right worthy Anthony Bacon esquire'. The writer of this letter was a certain Thomas Drury. He is the one I have called the Third Man. He turns out to be closely involved in the case. In fact he actually claims the 'credit' – his own word – for much of what happened.

We have come across Drury's name in passing. He was the man described as a 'companion' of Richard Cholmeley's, in a Council warrant of 1591, and who was later actually arrested by Cholmeley and his henchman Burrage or Borage. That Drury knew Cholmeley is immediately interesting, and becomes even more so when one learns from the text of his letter that he also knew Richard Baines. The Drury letter is an absolute goldmine, in fact. It confirms, circumstantially at least, much of the conspiratorial aspect of the Marlowe affair; it provides new bearings on the involvement of Baines prior to the delivery of his 'Note'; and it brings on to this crowded little stage another player entirely, instantly recognisable as a 'scurvy politician' like the others, but also an individual with his own story. I dealt quite closely with the letter in the first edition, but gave Drury himself rather a cameo role; I have now found out more about him and his activities.

In his letter of August 1593, Drury writes to Anthony Bacon 'to unfold some late accidents which are in my knowledge', and particularly to complain that he has not received due reward for the part he has played in these matters. The tone is aggrieved, the writing hasty, the syntax appalling, but the letter is full of tantalising insights into the events of the previous May.

His account, with some punctuation added for readability, is as follows:

> There was a command laid on me lately to stay one Mr Bayns, which did use to resort unto me, which I did pursue; and in time, although then I did not once so much as imagine where he was, I found him out, and got the desired secret at his hand, for which the City of London promised, as also by proclamation was promised, a hundred crowns, but not a penny performed and a fine evasion made.

> After, there was a libel by my means found out and delivered, a vile book also by my deciphering taken, and a notable villain or two, which are close prisoners and bad matters against them of an exceeding nature, and yet no reward, but all the credit pulled out of my mouth, and I robbed of all.

> Then after all this, there was by my only means set down unto the Lord Keeper and the Lord of Buckhurst the notablest and vildest articles of atheism, that I suppose the like were never known or read of in any age, all which I can show unto you. They were delivered to Her Highness, and command given by herself to prosecute it to the full, but no recompense, no not a penny.

Whatever its obscurities, and possible misrepresentations, this letter is another key document, because it provides an insider's eye-view of the atheism investigation. It gives us, in fact, what we have until now lacked: a chronology. The Drury letter is a narrative.

Let us look at this in detail. Drury's narrative has three episodes, each of them concluding with the petulant chorus of moneys not received. These prove to be three distinct phases of government investigation. First, Drury was commanded to bring in his former acquaintance, Richard Baines, in order to get a certain 'secret' from him. For this secret, Drury says, there was a reward of 100 crowns promised by the City of London. This is undoubtedly an allusion to the Lord Mayor's proclamation of 10 May 1593, which offered 100 crowns in gold for information about the authors of the recent libels, in particular the Dutch Church libel. Drury says that he found Baines, with difficulty, and got the 'desired secret' from him.

The obvious conclusion from this is that the 'secret' which Baines revealed was the information which carried the reward: namely, the identity of the libeller. So this is the first of Drury's revelations: that (as we have suspected) Baines was involved in this business from the outset. Explicitly, sticking with Drury's text, he was sought out as someone who knew something about the Dutch Church libel. It might be expected he would. He was a spy, and he knew Marlowe: he is just the sort of person likely to be sought out by the authorities as they cast around for clues to the authorship of that seemingly Marlovian libel. Unfortunately Drury does not say who 'laid' the command on him to find Baines: it was plausibly Sir John Puckering, whose prior dealings with Drury will be shown later; or indeed Phelippes in his role as commissioner. Nor can we be certain what is meant by 'staying' Baines: not an actual arrest, perhaps, so much as an official summons to give information (though while it was happening to you this distinction would probably be unclear). The command to find Baines would have been issued sometime on or after 6 May (the libel appeared on the night of the 5th), though the divulging of the 'desired secret' appears to have been after the proclamation of 10 May. The hefty reward was no doubt a spur to Baines, and to Drury, to come up with something – or rather, with someone.

So whom did Baines identify as the libeller? The obvious answer is that he named Thomas Kyd. Kyd certainly believed he had been fingered by an informer. In his later letter to Sir John Puckering, restating his innocence concerning 'the libel laid unto my charge', Kyd speaks of 'some outcast Ismael' who had 'incensed your Lordships to suspect me'. This was doubtless done, Kyd says, 'with pretext of duty or religion', though he thinks the informer's true motive was more likely to have been money ('want') or mischief ('his own dispose to lewdness') or ambition ('to reduce himself to that he was not born unto'). All this *could* describe Baines, though the terms are too general to be sure. Later Kyd speaks of more than one informer: 'doubtless your Lordship shall be sure to break open their lewd designs and see into the truth, when but their lives that herein have accused me shall be examined & ripped up effectually'. This clearly expresses Kyd's belief that he was set up ('lewd designs': a precise Elizabethan equivalent of our 'dirty tricks') and he no doubt had some thoughts about who was responsible. On the evidence of the Drury letter, Kyd's accusers were Richard Baines and Thomas Drury, and it seems likely enough he had them in mind when he wrote those words to Puckering.

We should always beware of taking Drury at face value, but this interpretation seems to work. Sometime around 10 May, Baines and Drury reveal the reward-carrying 'secret' about the author of the Dutch Church libel. By 12 May, Kyd is under arrest, 'suspected for that libel that concerned the State'. Kyd later complains of false accusers having 'incensed' these suspicions against him, presumably meaning Baines and Drury. To this fairly straightforward narrative we must add an interesting complication. Kyd was *not* the author of the Dutch Church libel, and it is unlikely that Baines and Drury really thought that he was. The secret they revealed was false. It delivered Kyd up to the Commission, and to torture, and thence by swift degrees to his 'affirmations' about the heretical opinions of his former roommate Marlowe. Their purpose in denouncing Kyd was to arrive, via Kyd's own mouth, at this denunciation of Marlowe. The major evidence against Marlowe was that heretical Arian tract allegedly 'found amongst' Kyd's papers, but in my view planted among them. Baines, who is a scholar and a former priest as well as a spy, had the expertise to produce this document, and his involvement in the framing of Kyd makes it all the more likely that he did indeed compose or concoct it. He may even have owned the copy of Proctour's *Fall of the Late Arian* from which it was taken.

To sum up this line of argument derived from the Drury letter, I would posit a meeting on around 10 or 11 May, in which Drury delivered to Phelippes not so much a 'secret' about the libels as a fairly familiar kind of package. The contents of this package were: a suspect's name ('one Kyd'), a copy of some seditious or heretical writings (the Arian fragment), and a suggestion as to how both might be used to draw other, bigger fish into the net.

The involvement of Richard Baines at this earlier stage makes it yet more likely that he was working in partnership with Richard Cholmeley, whose composition of the fake Marlovian libel in early May set the whole thing in motion. These two dangerous Dicks have hatched up this ploy *together* – an ensnaring of Marlowe, whom they both know and quite possibly dislike, and of the Ralegh 'set' to which he belongs. This is thoroughly opportunist: it arises within a particular climate of government nervousness, and is offered to officials like Phelippes and Puckering who are hungry for a particular kind of information and are not too fussy about whence it comes. According to the narrative of his letter, Thomas Drury arrives a little later on the scene, though as he personally knew both the Dicks it is possible he was *au courant* with their scheme to begin with. His desire to claim the 100 crown reward makes him stress that he 'got' the secret from Baines, but as the secret was deliberate misinformation anyway, we need not take this too literally.

The true 'secret' of the libel, as I have argued, is that it was written by Richard Cholmeley. Baines knew this, and if Drury didn't know it already, he would have soon prised it out of Baines, and having done so he would want to make use of it. With Kyd in prison, sweating out information against

Marlowe, Drury considers his next move. Time now, perhaps, for another name to be fed to the hungry commissioners; another suspect with libels spilling out of his pockets. Cholmeley is about to be hijacked, the projector projected upon. That this was indeed Drury's next move is shown by his letter to Bacon, for the second episode in his little narrative clearly concerns Cholmeley. In this phase of the business – specifically stated to be *after* he got the 'secret' from Baines – Drury claims he was instrumental in a certain libel being 'found out and delivered', and a vile book being 'taken', and a couple of 'notable villains' being imprisoned. Once again he has been unrewarded, and the credit 'pulled out of his mouth'.

This ties in very closely with the 'Remembrances' against Richard Cholmeley. The first specific charge against Cholmeley in the 'Remembrances' concerns a libel he has written. He has 'made certain libellious verses in commendation of papists and seminary priests, very greatly inveighing against the State.' The informer quotes that line from it – 'Nor may the Prince deny the Papal Crown' – which I mentioned earlier. Here is the libel that Drury now describes as having been 'found' by his means.

The next item in the 'Remembrances' concerns a book. Cholmeley 'had a certain book' and was using it 'to frame verses & libels in commendation of constant priests'. The informer knows the title of the book – *An Epistle of Comfort* – and the fact that it was printed in Paris. He says that the book is now 'in custody'. Here, then, is the 'vile book' that was taken through Drury's means.

Finally the two 'notable villains' which Drury refers to, who at the time of his letter (1 August) were in close prison with heavy matters hanging over them. One of these would be Richard Cholmeley himself, arrested by the officers of Justice Young on 28 June, and conveyed to prison 'to be examined'. The other may be Henry Young, who is named as one of Cholmeley's crew, and who is described in the docket of the 'Remembrances' as having been 'taken' and 'made an instrument to take the rest'.

There is little doubt in my mind that Drury is here claiming a leading role in the surveillance and arrest of Richard Cholmeley. We know that Drury and Cholmeley were 'companions' in 1591, and that Cholmeley turned Drury in to the authorities. Here now is Drury's chance to play the same game back at him: to be the same kind of turncoat companion. The result is the 'Remembrances against Ric: Cholmeley', an itemisation of Cholmeley's ill deeds as a libeller, a corrupt government servant and, of course, an atheist. Some of it refers back to events four years ago, other parts are more topical.

Thomas Drury now steps forward as a likely candidate for the informer who compiled the 'Remembrances'. The document as we have it is not in Drury's handwriting, but this is only to be expected, because the extant version is certainly a copy. It is in the same distinctive hand as various government reports of the time, including the Gunson report about John Poole the coiner. In that case too it is a copy: Gunson's handwriting can be seen in a couple of letters to Walsingham, and it is quite different. In all the documents written in this hand, Justice Young is the prosecutor of the matter, and it is most likely that it is the script of one of his officers or clerks.

So Drury writes up this short but explosive account of Cholmeley's scoffs and brags – a document which apparently serves the dual purpose of getting Cholmeley into trouble and further incriminating Marlowe, who is described in it as Cholmeley's instructor in atheism. Marlowe is also said to have 'read the atheist lecture' to 'Ralegh & others'. I have referred to this from time to time as Cholmeley's statement, but it is more precisely a statement attributed to Cholmeley by Drury. Strictly speaking, therefore, this first overt mention of Ralegh's name comes from the pen of Thomas Drury. The 'Remembrances' was doubtless delivered, perhaps via Phelippes, to Sir John Puckering; his handwriting can be seen on the back of it. There is also evidence, which I will look at later, that it was seen by Sir Robert Cecil. The interrogation of Thomas Kyd and the surveillance of Richard Cholmeley are happening at much the same time. Both are on the basis of information supplied by Drury; both throw up the name of Marlowe.

After all these complications the third episode recounted in Drury's letter to Bacon is absolutely clear. It concerns those 'vildest articles of atheism', which were, Drury says, 'set down' for the benefit of Sir John Puckering and Lord Buckhurst, and later delivered to the Queen. There is no doubt at all that Drury is here referring to the Baines 'Note' against Marlowe. According to Drury it was written down at his instigation: 'by my only means set down'. For this fine piece of work, poor Tom Drury has received nothing: 'no, not a penny'.

Drury hasn't finished, however. He has more to offer:

> Sithence that time, there is old hold-and-shove for to get the book that doth maintain this damnable sect, for which book I presume there would be given great sums for, and large promises offered in like manner, but of none of those will I trust. But if I may secretly confer with you, I and one that I have brought with me, a merchant, will give you such light, as I and he can bring you to the man that doth know who did write the book, and they to who it was delivered, and where and when, with divers other such secrets.

This is what has happened since that time – since the delivering of Baines's 'Note'. There has been a great hulla-baloo, Drury says, to find this infamous 'book' which maintains this 'sect'. By this he presumably means the text of the 'atheist lecture' which Marlowe supposedly read to Ralegh. He claims he can find the man 'who did write the book' – since Marlowe was universally said to be the author of it, and is now dead, Drury must be referring to a copyist who prepared it for distribution. He can also identify those to whom the lecture was 'delivered': he doubtless means the Ralegh circle. Whether he had such information is impossible to say. His concern here is to keep the thing on the boil, to hold out the possibility of further product, further prosecution.

*

Thomas Drury emerges as a key player in the tarring of
Marlowe and Ralegh. He is, with Baines, the accuser of
Thomas Kyd; he is, perhaps also with assistance from Baines,
the accuser of Richard Cholmeley. These having laid the
groundwork against Marlowe, he is finally the instigator, or
perhaps the pressuriser, who is standing at Baines's shoulder
as he pens that infamous 'Note', which presents in direct and
digestible form the Marlovian heresies whose existence those
previous accusations had implied. He is the provider of this
material to police-chief Phelippes, who is doubtless aware of
its dodgy provenance; and ultimately to Puckering and
Buckhurst, who may or may not be aware of the scam. It
might be objected that in all this I am taking Drury's letter at
face-value. Might he not be exaggerating his role in the affair
for Bacon's benefit? Certainly the letter has elements of spin
(he did not, for instance, 'get' a secret from Baines so much as
collude with him in a falsehood), but there must be some way
Drury acquired all this specialist and no doubt confidential
knowledge of the events of May, and fortunately this letter is
not the only evidence of his active involvement in them. He
has something more to tell us. This emerges not from the text
of the letter, but from a brief flurry of events immediately
subsequent to it.

When he wrote to Bacon on 1 August, Drury was in
lodgings 'at the waterside' in Richmond, but shortly after this
he was once more in prison. He was arrested on the orders of
the Lord Chamberlain (Henry Carey, 1st Lord Hunsdon).
From prison Drury wrote an anguished letter complaining
about Hunsdon's misunderstanding of his actions. This letter
was addressed to Sir Robert Cecil. Drury writes:

I am committed from my Lord Chamberlain for abusing
him unto you, as also for wicked speeches that I could say
I was able to make any Councillor a traitor. Only this I do
presume, that I told your Honour it was others' practices
and lies also, and not my own; neither did so name it but
that, *exempli gratia*, how it might be so done to all mortal

378

men; and so I presume it will be said by you. If that might deserve imprisonment, let it come with death rather than with favour. If my deserts be thus rewarded it will teach others more wit. Alas, sir, why was I not committed by your own hands, which would have delivered me upon true cause? My Lord Chamberlain is too continually bent against me. His displeasure is everlasting and so is my misery.

This is obscure in the same muddy way of writing as his earlier letter to Bacon, but I think it is clear that Drury's troubles stem from his involvement with Richard Cholmeley, and from the frequent problem which informers had – namely, that they get tarred with the brush that they use to blacken others. They are moving among malcontents one day, and they are informing on them the next, and those not immediately involved tend to blur the distinction between the informer and his target.

I would reconstruct the events leading up to Drury's arrest as follows. In May 1593, Drury submits the report containing his 'Remembrances' of Cholmeley's seditious 'words and matter'. Among these are Cholmeley's abusive words against Lord Hunsdon: he said that 'he doth entirely hate the Lord Chamberlain & hath good cause so to do', and he included Hunsdon among those 'peers and honourable Councillors' who were really, in his opinion, 'sound atheists'. At some point, Hunsdon gets to hear of this document. He hears that he is touched in it, and he hears of the involvement of Thomas Drury in it. He orders Drury's arrest. This is the situation when Drury writes his letter to Cecil. He is accused – as he tells Cecil – of 'abusing' Lord Hunsdon. In other words he is being blamed for comments actually made by Cholmeley. The other charge against Drury is that he bragged he could 'make any Councillor a traitor'. This too is a refraction of Cholmeley's assertions: that 'no man are sooner divined & abused than the Council themselves', that 'he can go beyond & cozen them as he list'.

This now makes sense of Drury's words to Cecil. He

379

complains: 'it was others' practices and lies, not my own'. In other words, he was reporting Cholmeley's 'practices and lies'. He only named the Lord Chamberlain *exempli gratia*, as one example of Cholmeley's wild talk, which could in fact have been applied to 'all mortal men'. In a second letter to Cecil, Drury adds another complaint about Hunsdon's treatment of him: 'if my Lord Chamberlain do detain my writings, I cannot anyway make an end; the stay of my writings has been my utter undoing.' This refers to the same predicament: Drury's papers, seized at his arrest, are being used as evidence against him – evidence that he himself held the opinions contained in these 'writings', though they were actually Cholmeley's opinions which he had written down.

Thomas Drury has been hoist with his own petard. His 'Remembrances' against Cholmeley have been turned around against him: another twist in this game of black propaganda.

Not only does this episode confirm Drury's involvement in the events of May 1593: it also shows that he was in communication with Sir Robert Cecil. He has been accused of abusing the Chamberlain *to* Cecil. He has *told* Cecil about Cholmeley's 'practices and lies'. He 'presumes', or anyway hopes, that Cecil will back him up, and intercede on his behalf. He wishes it had been Cecil, and not Hunsdon, who had committed him, because Cecil would know the 'true cause' of the situation.

All this, one assumes, is the truth. Drury is writing to Cecil himself: he cannot therefore be lying about Cecil's involvement.

Certainly Cecil felt that Drury was owed something. Drury's second letter, dated 17 August, is full of gratitude. Cecil has written to him, in reply to his first letter. He has sent him money: 'only that money I have had by your honourable means is that must be my greatest comfort.' Above all, he has engineered his release from prison. 'In all duty and lowliness of heart,' Drury writes, 'I most humbly thank your Honour for your liberality, as also for my liberty.'

Cecil has also been interceding with the authorities in charge of the atheism investigation. Drury writes: 'it pleased your Honour to speak unto the Lord Keeper' – Sir John

Puckering again – 'that I should sue *in forma pauperis*, which license I would humbly beseech your Honour to procure me.' Here Drury is claiming his poverty, and applying, through Cecil, for the Elizabethan equivalent of legal aid. He also says: 'It hath pleased my Lord of Buckhurst and your Honour that I should be writing acquaint your Honours with my bad and ruinated estate, and not by coming.' Here again is that arm's-length relationship between Cecil and his spies – compare the Cholmeley brothers a year earlier, with their 'hasty indiscrete coming' to Cecil, of which he complained.

At the time of writing this letter Drury was probably still in London – 'this town will consume me, it is so excessively dear' – but he hopes the legalities can be handled, through the good offices of Cecil, Puckering and Buckhurst, 'before my departure'. This sounds like he might be about to leave for the country, or indeed the continent: best, perhaps, to have him out of the way for a while.

We should not jump to conclusions and assume that Cecil's presence connotes some sinister involvement. But we can confidently say that Cecil knew of Drury's dealings with Richard Cholmeley; that he was aware of the information against Cholmeley and Marlowe which Drury compiled; and that he was prepared to deal on Drury's behalf when things went a bit wrong and Drury landed up in prison.

We glimpse Sir Robert Cecil in the background, kept informed by the talkative Drury; and we may also glimpse the Earl of Essex, whose interests Thomas Phelippes has been accustomed to serve. These are, as I have phrased it, orbits of interest: high-up political figures who make it their business to know what is going on (and who particularly like to know something the other does not). They are, like Puckering and Buckhurst, part of the audience for this performance, but there is no evidence of their involvement in the affair, and they are not required to assist in some over-arching courtly conspiracy-theory. My focus now is strictly on the fore-ground: on this trio of projectors – Drury, Baines, Cholmeley – and their contrivances. One can call it a conspiracy against

Marlowe, even an entrapment, but in reality it is just a scrimmage of spies around him, colluding and competing to accomplish some profitable damage. In the foreground there is a suffocating sense of closeness. Drury knows Baines and Cholmeley; Baines and Cholmeley know Marlowe. There is a history of 'malice' between Baines and Marlowe, and probably between Drury and Cholmeley. And out of this little huddle of snoops and counter-snoops there emerges, within the space of a couple of weeks, this barrage of allegations about Marlowe's heretical views, allegations uttered by Baines and Cholmeley, but in each case communicated to the authorities by Thomas Drury. In some cases it is hard to work out who is preying on whom – Cholmeley's allegiances are particularly resistant to interpretation – but this is the nature of these scams. The one constant is that Marlowe is the target.

It takes a long time to tease all this out from its cocoon of pretence, to argue it back into something like the shape it once had, but these actions are not in themselves so complex. This is their métier: fabrications and provocations, 'fictions and knaveries'. The actual workload involved in this stinging of Marlowe and Ralegh is wonderfully light: no more than a few bits of paper – a doggerel poem or placard; a couple of chapters copied from an old book; some 'remembrances'; a 'note'. The real workload is in the head, in the manic ingenuity of it all. I have an inkling that these men are failed or frustrated writers – Baines the author of notes and confessions, written with a certain overheated relish; Cholmeley the penner of doggerel rhymes and thunderous libels; Drury undone because all his 'writings' have been seized. The tools of their trade are pen, paper and inkpot. They relate to Marlowe not just as fellow-spies, but as fellow-scribblers. They hold a mirror up to Marlowe not because of what they say, but because of what they are.

Out of this scrimmage Thomas Drury emerges as something of an orchestrator, an impresario of knaveries, and a letter discovered recently by David Riggs further highlights his involvement, for it shows he has a prior connection with

Lord Keeper Puckering. On 8 November 1592 Lord Buckhurst wrote to Puckering as follows—

> My very good Lord, I did speak to Mr Drury according to your Lordship's desire, and after a long discourse by him to me made of his own misery and hard fortune, I prayed him to set down in writing such matter as might be valuable to the State . . . He was very loath to set down the particularities thereof in writing because it consisted in diverse attempts & industries of his own whereby he meant to hazard his life for the service of Her Majesty and his country. Nevertheless, if he should be urged unto it, he would make it manifest that to the adventure of his life he would do great things . . . I send you also a declaration of his touching the course of his own doings until he was taken. Surely, my Lord, I am persuaded that if he may have liberty & leave to go beyond seas, that to recompense his ill doings past he will adventure himself somewhat to do some service.

It is endorsed on the verso, in Puckering's hand, 'Thom Drury's confession of matters of State'.

As we saw, Drury had been carted off to the Marshalsea in the summer of 1591, having been arrested by his former 'companion', Cholmeley. He was apparently still in prison fifteen months later, for Buckhurst's letter talks of his impending 'liberty'. He has been interviewed there by Buckhurst, at the request of Puckering, who seems to think he has or knows something 'valuable to the State'. He offers a 'declaration' about his 'own doings until he was taken' – in other words, presumably, about what he was up to before he was turned in by Cholmeley in mid-1591. And he appears to be ready – 'if urged unto it' – to 'do some service' to Buckhurst and Puckering, precisely the two men to whom he would deliver, a few months later, those 'articles of atheism' compiled at his instigation by Richard Baines and attributed to the mouth of Marlowe. Knowledge of this earlier dealing with Puckering brings Drury's activities in May 1593 into sharper relief. Dishing the dirt on the atheist Marlowe, and on those like Ralegh who harboured him, seems to be product. It is – at least Drury hopes it is – the kind of 'service' that Buckhurst and Puckering had in mind when they granted him his freedom from the stench of the Marshalsea.

It has seemed, therefore, imperative to track down the slippery Tom Drury, who increasingly takes centre-stage in this game of black propaganda. I gathered a few snippets of his career in the first edition, but did not manage to work out fully who he was (as with Richard Cholmeley there is more than one Thomas Drury around at this time). I have now identified him, and have found in other areas of his life some corroborating episodes which throw light on what might be called his *modus operandi*, and perhaps even some personal motivation for his animus against Marlowe and Ralegh.

For these reasons, and perhaps as some kind of respite from the claustrophobia of these last chapters, I offer now for the first time a brief biography of Thomas Drury, which might be subtitled 'the life and times of an Elizabethan projector'.

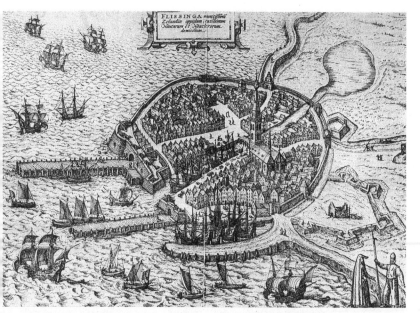

14 THE LOW COUNTRIES. The strategic Dutch port of Vlissingen, or Flushing, from an atlas of 1576.

15 'TAKEN FOR COINAGE'. Official docket relating to Marlowe's deportation from Flushing, 26 January 1592.

S͏ͬ Robert Sidney. & my L.

He sendes over by this bearer his
Auntient one Euan Floyd, and 2 other
Christofher Marly, and Gifford Gilbert.
a goldsmithe taken for coynage. to
be tryed here for ye fact.
There hath bene only one dutch shilling
ottered. the mettall playne peuter.

16 RELUCTANT PRETENDER. Ferdinando Stanley, Lord Strange, a patron of Marlowe's in the early 1590s.

SERO, SED SERIO

17 THE NEW SPYMASTER. Sir Robert Cecil, son of Lord Burghley. A portrait by John de Critz the elder, 1602.

Direction of Lettres to Ro: Poolÿ

Jacob Mymstrale. Italÿano:

Arnolde Molemake Freller:

Direction of Lettres from Ro: Po:

Elÿzabeth Boogarde in den Lylye + den
Augustine strvate: Antwerpen:

Harman vandermÿll Freller op den Dune
Antwerpen:

Coppye of the Grsÿ

A : s. g. 7. h 2.
E : w. z. ~. 5. 5.
J : d. l. 1. o. 3.
O : x. y. v. z. 8.
V : E 3. m. w. o.

B. x. z.
C. y. h.
D. x. n.
F. l. 5.
G. v. 2.
H. p. x.
K. e. s.
L. o. 2.
m. r. s.
n. w. s.
P. g. e.
Q. x. e.
R. f. e.
S. 4. e.
T. w. x.
W. g. o.
X. l. x.
Y. y. n.
Z. s. y.

Pope : x
Emp : 24
Quisitio : y
K : Spa : G
K : Fran : H
K : Scot : o
K : Denma : X
Cardl : Alb : X
L : Teenso : y
E : Essex : X
E : we fins : X
L : Dukers : x
Sr Ro : Cyckl : y
Sr myst : Souly : y
Fa : Pasons : 4
Fa : Halte : 4
Fa : Creiton : L
Qwen : H
Vestegen : Δ
Gal : Joyex : x
Ete : Gregory : x
Poolÿ : 1

England : 4
Spain : 1
France : x
Scotland : 20
Ireland : X
Holland Zeta : 2
Denmark : w
Calles : x
Dunkirke : y
Sr : Owen : x
Antwerp : +
Brabel : x
Lewis : H
messages : Z
Poste : →

18 POLEY'S CODES. Cypher-key and letter-drops for Low Countries
intelligence, c. 1591.

19 THE 'REMEMBRANCES'. Informer's report on Richard Cholmeley, May 1593, implicating both Marlowe (below) and Hariot (right) in atheist propaganda.

ÆTATIS SVÆ
AN 16[...]

[...]OR ET VIRTVTE

20-21 COURTLY RIVALS. The charismatic Robert Devereux, 2nd Earl of
Essex (opposite, in a portrait by William Segar, 1590), and Sir Walter
Ralegh, poet, explorer and reputed atheist (above, a portrait attributed to
the monogrammist 'H', 1588).

22 'VILE HERETICALL CONCEIPTS'. Interrogation of the playwright Thomas Kyd at Bridewell, 12 May 1593.

23 A FAIR COPY? Alterations to the scribal copy of Richard Baines's 'Note' on Marlowe, c. June 1593.

34

DRURY REVEALED

THOMAS DRURY WAS, like others in this story, a younger son of a well-breeched family, thrown onto his wits and cunning to keep himself in the style to which he felt he ought to be accustomed. As certain later events make clear, he was as full of craft in dealing with family matters as he was in these political machinations concerning Marlowe, and in a letter dated c 1599 we find his own nephew describing him as 'that degenerate rogue Tom Drury'.

Thomas Drury was the third son of Robert Drury of Hawstead, Suffolk, and Audrey née Rich, the daughter of Richard, Lord Rich, a former Lord Chancellor. He was born on 8 May 1551; he was thus thirteen years older than Marlowe, and was in his early forties when he became involved in the Marlowe 'affair'. There is a faint literary aspect to Drury's family connections. Through his mother he was a first cousin of Robert, Lord Rich, who in 1581 married Penelope Devereux, sister of the Earl of Essex. She, of course, was the *inamorata* of Sir Philip Sidney, and was the Stella of his famous sonnet sequence *Astrophil and Stella*. This is not a very auspicious connection, however, as cousin Rich is punningly guyed throughout *Astrophil*, and painted as a coarse, heartless booby.

Of Drury's youth, misspent or otherwise, we know a little. He was six years old when his father died. In the will of his grandfather, Sir William Drury, dated 26 December 1557, he is mentioned along with his brothers Henry and Robert as 'sons of my said son Robert Drury deceased'. He receives, with them, a third share of a manorial property in Lincoln-shire, to be held 'in reversion' until their age of majority. The eldest brother William, by contrast, inherits all the Hawstead estates and other Suffolk appurtenances. In 1564, aged thirteen, Thomas Drury was admitted as a 'gentleman pensioner' (a term denoting a well-off student) of Caius College, Cambridge. His brothers William and Robert matriculated there in the same year (his other brother Henry had meanwhile died, at the age of ten, in 1560). We have no further details of his university career, but it is worth noting that he is another Cambridge man, like Baines, Poley and Marlowe, who enters the intelligence business. Caius was also Baines's college, though they were not contemporaries. Even if he was at Cambridge for the full seven years (which is to be doubted given the lack of any BA or MA records) Drury would have left by the time Baines arrived at Caius in 1573. The same is true of John Ballard, the Babington conspirator, who was at Caius in the 1570s. Nonetheless, these later alumni remind us that it was a markedly Catholic college. It is possible Drury was himself a Catholic – other members of his family certainly were. His cousin, Henry Drury of Lawshall, Suffolk, was indicted for recusancy in 1576, and was harbouring a fugitive priest in 1584; another cousin, John, was also presented as a recusant. A younger generation of Catholic relatives included Robert Drury, ordained a Catholic priest in Spain in 1593 and eventually martyred in 1607; and Ambrose Rokewood, the Gunpowder plotter, whose mother Dorothy was of the Suffolk Drurys. Thomas may be another of this story's turncoat Catholics, but this is by no means certain.

We now enter an unknown period of Drury's early career, since he is almost certainly *not* the Thomas Drury who was a 'student in heraldry' in the mid 1560s, and who was later a member of the Inner Temple [see Appendix 2.10]. We must be content with a few interesting fragments. The first is that according to his letter to Anthony Bacon, Drury knew Bacon's father, Sir Nicholas. He speaks of 'the true love I have ever borne to your honorable father, as also to all his house'.

(We also learn from the letter that Drury was 'not gracious in the sight of your brother', Francis Bacon.) This relationship must belong to the 1570s, since Sir Nicholas died in 1579. It may mean that Drury was employed by him, though he does not say so. There was certainly a close connection between the Drurys and the Bacons: a later family tradition claims that the plane trees in the park at Hawstead were grown from seeds sent back by Sir Nicholas from Constantinople. Sir Nicholas's son, also Nicholas (the elder half-brother of Anthony and Francis) later acted as guardian to Drury's nephew, Robert. The latter in turn married his guardian's daughter, Anne Bacon; the marriage took place in January 1592, while Thomas was languishing in the Marshalsea. Thus when Drury wrote to Anthony Bacon in August 1593, there was this particular new family link between them – Bacon's niece had married Drury's nephew.

Drury was himself married, though when he tied the knot is unclear. The Drury family tree states that his wife was the daughter of one Fitzharding, of Ratcliffe, near London, and that they had no children. There is a later reference to his widow, Elizabeth Drury. These may or may not be the same woman.

Another interesting connection comes via the marriage, in the early 1570s, of his older brother, Sir William Drury, to Elizabeth Stafford. She was the sister of Sir Edward Stafford, who later became English ambassador in France. Here is another, hitherto unknown dimension to Thomas Drury: he is a brother-in-law of that most conspiratorial of ambassadors, whose house in Paris was a conduit of spies, agents and conspirators. He is also a brother-in-law of William Stafford, the protagonist of the 'Stafford plot' of 1587, which also involved Michael Moody, himself a former servant of Sir Edward Stafford's in France, and from the late 1580s a close associate of Robert Poley. Of these connections, more later.

Up into his late twenties we might find in Tom Drury a young man of some promise: a student at Cambridge, a satellite of Sir Nicholas Bacon, a brother-in-law to Sir Edward Stafford.

But then we start to hear of another side to his character: a side we will come to know well.

On 27 June 1580, Lord William Burgh filed a bill of complaint against 'one Thomas Drury, gentleman', who is without a doubt our Thomas Drury. In it Burgh alleges that Drury tried to swindle him to the very considerable tune of £300. The story, as presented by Burgh, is as follows. 'Slyly and subtly creeping into the company and familiarity of Thomas and John Burgh, sons of the said Lord Burgh', Drury at length 'insinuated himself' into the acquaintance of Lord Burgh himself, 'pretending great honesty and truth, and such a readiness in every matter to do the said Lord Burgh and his sons pleasure . . . [and] boasting himself to have great sums of money to pleasure his friend'. The upshot was that Drury loaned Burgh £100, but 'subtly devised a bond wherein the said Lord Burgh should stand bound to him in £300' if he failed to repay the debt on time. The due date was 'midsummer day last' – 24 June 1580 – but when Burgh's messengers sought him out on that day, Drury was nowhere to be found. (One of these messengers was the future rackmaster Richard Topcliffe, who was Lord Burgh's nephew.) They arrived at Drury House, the family's London house near the Strand, bearing the £100 that was due. There they met Drury's brother Sir William, but he was unhelpful: he was not 'privy to the matter', he told them. When Topcliffe tried to 'make tender of' the money, Sir William refused to take it, saying he had 'no warrant' to receive it. A couple of days later the charade was repeated. Once again Thomas Drury 'could not be found', and once again Sir William refused the proffered money. Drury was now 'standing upon the extreme forfeiture of the said bond' – i.e. insisting on the full £300 – and Burgh's only recourse was to lodge the bill of complaint of 27 June from which this brief narrative is taken. There had apparently been other deals between them, for in his answer to the complaint Drury claims that the Burgh family owed him a total of £521 10s.

The outcome of the case is not recorded, but this is our earliest hint of Drury as a trickster: we hear of his 'unconscionable dealing', of his 'purpose to entrap'. The episode has a strong whiff of the world of Frizer and Skeres, and their 'evil bargains'. There is separate evidence of Drury as money-lender: in 1593 he claimed to have lent £170 to Sir Edmund Carey and his wife, and once again there was something dodgy about it, for Drury was forced to return 'all his assurances' (i.e. bonds) to Carey.

At about the same time as he was stinging Lord Burgh, we glimpse Drury in the unpredictable company of the Earl of Oxford. Among various accusations laid against Oxford by his former friend Henry Howard was this: 'thus did he proffer all his cutters to Thom Drury to hew my lord Howard in pieces'. Oxford had, in other words, urged Drury to kill Philip Howard, Earl of Arundel, and had placed his 'cutters' – his swordsmen, his goons – at Drury's disposal for this purpose. It is not claimed that Drury had effected any violence, only that Oxford had wanted him to. If this potential hit-man is the same Thomas Drury, and it seems pretty likely it is, this would place him as a minor crony of Oxford's in around 1580 (Howard's deposition is dated 29 December 1580). More importantly, it would place him in the volatile waters of Catholicism and atheism, these being the charges against Oxford at this time. The blasphemous squibs that were attributed to Oxford sound like an early version of the Marlovian blasphemies reported by Baines. Howard reports:

In earnest and with choler he hath stretched out his horrible and most blasphemous voice against the sacred and most glorious Trinity, affirming that . . . the Blessed Virgin (*horresco referens*) made a fault and that Joseph was a wittol [i.e. cuckold], than which words what can be more abominable considering the dainty fruit that sprang of that unspotted root? . . . To the first [chapter] of Matthew, when I vouched it against this beastly paradox, wherein she was affirmed to conceive by the Holy Ghost, he said the Jews of Italy would tell another tale and put both Matthew, Mark and John to silence . . . In divers companies, not for disputation sake but with advisement, he hath sworn that

more plain reasons and examples may be vouched out of
Scripture for defence of bawdry than out of all the books of
Aretinus.

This was the kind of stuff you might hear at Oxford's supper-
table in the late 1570s. 'The Turk himself,' said Howard,
'speaks better both of Christ, of the Virgin, and the canon of
the scriptures'. When it comes to atheism and blasphemy, we
have a sense (as we do with Baines) that Drury has been here
before. When he waxes indignant about Marlowe's blasphemies – the 'vildest articles of atheism that I suppose the like
were never known or read of in any age' – we might counter by
saying that certainly such things had been known before, not
least in that Oxford circle of which Drury, it seems, was a part.

Interestingly, this connection with Oxford would also bring
Drury into apposition with Sir Walter Ralegh, for Ralegh had
also run with the Oxford pack in the late 1570s, before
swiftly switching sides when the capricious Earl's position of
power and influence began to unravel. It has been conjectured
that in befriending Oxford Ralegh had been serving
Walsingham's interests, and it is certainly true that Ralegh's
courtly career began to prosper immediately after this. He and
Oxford became implacable enemies, and in the same
deposition which mentions Drury, Howard also accuses
Oxford of planning to engineer Ralegh's murder:

Thus hath he at this present a practice in Ireland for the
murdering of Denny and Rawley. Thus for a recompense of
Rawley's service, his life should have been latched between
both the walls before his going over, and suits of apparel
given to those that should have killed him for seeking my
Lord of Leicester's favour [i.e. to make it look like Ralegh
had been killed by servants of Leicester].

Whether this would also have involved 'Thom Drury' and my
Lord's 'cutters' is not specified.

The next we hear of Thomas Drury is in the summer of
1585, and he is in the Fleet prison. We do not know why: it

could be something mundane like debt, but what one knows of his subsequent career suggests it may be something more, that 'matters of State' were involved. It is not impossible his imprisonment was connected with his cousin, Henry Drury of Lawshall, who was charged in 1584 with harbouring a Catholic priest. This priest is a mysterious figure: after his capture and confession he was used as a spy by Walsingham, but we know him only by his pseudonyms ('A.B.' or 'Alessandro della Torre').

While in the Fleet Drury was involved with a fellow-prisoner named John Meere or Meeres, a law-student at the Inner Temple, and a man described as 'full of craft'. A bundle of documents concerning Meeres reveals that he had been consorting with a female prisoner, Edetha Best or Beast, and had allegedly used 'sorceries' against her, 'threatening to trouble her with sight of the Devil unless she consented to his desires &c'. On 20 May 1585 Walsingham issued an injunction, or 'obligation', forbidding him further access to her. On 22 June a conversation between Meeres and Drury was overheard and reported as follows:

Drury What a fellow art thou, that will not obey Mr
    Secretary's commandment?
Meeres Why, that Mr Secretary warranted not, for I was
    forbidden to come to Mrs Beast, but she was not
    forbidden to come to me.
Drury Take heed what you say, for Mr Lewcash will say
    what he can against you.
Meeres Why, let Mr Lewcash say what he will, by God I
    will make him speak with a plum-stone in his
    mouth, for by God he hath come to my chamber
    at 11 or 12 o'clock in the night with a candle in
    his hand to call me forth of my bed to come to
    Mrs Beast.
Drury Thou layest with her?
Meeres I? No, that I did not.

We hear Drury verbatim in this brief exchange. This Meeres

is himself a very interesting character. He later became a servant of Ralegh's: an unfaithful servant, as it turned out ('that rogue Meere'; 'so infamous and detested a wretch as Meere' – these are Ralegh's words). He is thus another link between Drury and Ralegh, and it is not impossible he too had a hand in the Marlowe affair: another villain, as if we needed one. On all this see Appendix 2.11.

The next we hear of Drury is in 1587, and his relationship to the Stafford family seems now to be bearing fruit. Sir Edward Stafford was now ambassador in Paris, where he employed a number of dubious 'secretaries' and spies, among them Michael Moody, and where he pursued a cat-and-mouse game of *rapprochement* with Catholic conspirators like Thomas Morgan, Charles Paget, Charles Arundel, etc. In the view of Walsingham, Stafford's relations with the enemy went far beyond the requirements of secret diplomacy, and Conyers Read has marshalled a formidable case against Stafford as a double-agent, who sold more secrets to the Catholics than he ever got from them. It sounds like the perfect milieu for a man of Drury's accomplishments, and he is probably referred to in a letter of 11 September 1587 concerning Stafford's dealings with the Duke of Montpensier, nephew of the Duke of Guise. In this letter the Abbé del Bene, writing in Latin, complains of Montpensier having 'withdrawn from their sworn league' thanks to the 'evil arts of his [Stafford's] secretary, the iniquitous Dewry'. A copy of this letter was sent over to Walsingham on 20 September; a marginal note by Stafford, in French, adds that 'Deury was put with M. de Montpensier by Simier's persuasion'. This is Jean de Simier, well-known in England as the envoy of the Duc d'Anjou during the latter's courtship of the Queen in the late 1570s. It would be fruitless to pursue this into the labyrinth of Parisian politics, but it seems very likely that this 'iniquitous' servant of Stafford's called Dewry is in fact his dodgy brother-in-law Thomas Drury. We thus find Drury mixed up in French affairs – like so many others in this story: Baines, Poley, Thomas Walsingham and, indeed, Marlowe.

*

There is now, when one least wants it, a four year gap. Between September 1587, when he is glimpsed in Stafford's employ in France, and May 1591, when he was imprisoned in the Marshalsea, there is precious little news of him. For some of the time, one may guess, he was watching anxiously as his brother William's career went into freefall. Sir William had an official post in the Exchequer, but whether through mismanagement or dishonesty or both, he ended up with a crippling personal debt to the Queen of £5000. In July 1587 he fled to the Low Countries. He wrote to both Walsingham and Burghley, asking them to intercede with the Queen, but to no avail. He soldiered in the Low Countries for a couple of years, and then in early 1590, en route for France, he fell out with the irascible Sir John Burgh over a 'foolish quarrel about precedency'. (So it was described, though one remembers that William had tangled with the Burgh family ten years earlier, over that bond-business set up by Thomas.) The two men duelled. Drury was badly wounded in the arm. 'Presently he lost his hand with the gangrene,' the report went; 'they therefore cut out his arm, but all that served not.' He died on 8 January 1590. His will survives – the bulk of his estate going to his eldest son, Robert, now fifteen, and a 'remainder to my brother Thomas Drury'. What exactly was entailed in this 'remainder' is not clear, but with at least £3000 still owing to the Queen, it is not likely to have been much. Financial frustration is the refrain of Drury's life.

That Sir John Burgh was the man who killed Thomas Drury's brother may be of some significance, for Burgh was a close associate of both Ralegh and the Earl of Northumberland in the early 1590s. He was the captain of Ralegh's ship the *Roebuck* in 1592, and the captain of a reconnaissance fleet sent out by Ralegh to Trinidad and Guiana in 1593. He dined frequently with Northumberland: the Northumberland household accounts show he was a guest at the Earl's table on nineteen separate occasions in the autumn of 1591. This might be thought to add a personal impetus, in Drury's mind, against the Ralegh set, and thus against Marlowe as a very visible part of it.

This brings us up to the period of Drury's dealings with those involved in the Marlowe investigation. First with Richard Cholmeley, who was his 'companion' in May 1591, and his betrayer. Also perhaps with Richard Baines, who 'did use to resort unto' him – in other words, hung out with him – at some unspecified time before 1593. One is tempted to make Baines another of Drury's companions in mid-1591, and so to find this trio of projectors tuning up together fully two years before their 'plat' against Marlowe. Of Marlowe's whereabouts at the time we know only this: he was sharing a chamber with Thomas Kyd – a situation ascribed by Kyd to mid-1591 ('two years since' in mid-1593), a situation exploited by Baines and Drury in the entrapment of Marlowe. All this is a pipe-dream unsupported by evidence, but it works rather well.

The Council's records do not specify the activities for which Drury was arrested in 1591 – we hear vaguely of 'papers of state' and 'divers fond & great matters' – but we know by now, very well, the sort of thing he was up to. It was some duplicitous, tail-chasing, Machiavellian game of charge and counter-charge: as the cards landed it was Cholmeley who shopped Drury, but it might as easily have been the other way round. A few months later it will be Baines and Marlowe at it together in Flushing, each of them claiming that the other 'had intent to go to the enemy or to Rome'. They are of imagination compact, these four – except that Marlowe has this other dimension, and the texts that remain from his hand are not these low-grade, thumb-stained notes and remembrances, but plays like the *Jew of Malta*, performed at the Rose theatre a few weeks after his return from Flushing: an extraordinary mirroring of this tawdry, convoluted world of which he is a part, this 'secret theatre' in which perhaps he dabbled in search of good copy, and found himself by degrees 'up to the chin'.

There follow the events of 1592–93 which we have looked at already – his meeting with Lord Buckhurst in the Marshalsea prison; his promise of service to Sir John Puckering; his efforts as a projector against Marlowe and Ralegh; his letter to Anthony Bacon indicating that those efforts had been unappreciated; his imprisonment on the orders of Lord Hunsdon; and his release through the good offices of Sir Robert Cecil.

Of Drury's life subsequent to the Marlowe affair I reported a couple of fragments in the first edition, one of which was erroneous and the other interesting. In the early summer of 1595 Drury was in France; he returned to England bearing letters 'on the Queen's service', and received £16 for his pains and charges. The warrant for this payment, dated 14 June 1595, was signed by Lord Burghley. Whatever the success or failure of his project against Marlowe, he is still on the books, posting for the government.

I have now found two further episodes in Drury's career, and though they have no direct bearing on the Marlowe case, they throw a kind of light back on it. They corroborate Drury's type of activity: the way he worked, the kind of man he was. They give us Tom Drury in his element, and it is the same element that we discern in the Marlowe affair – the manipulation of testimony; the exploitation of others' ill-deeds, real or imagined.

The first emerges from a letter written by his nephew Sir Robert Drury (son of the late Sir William) in about 1599. This Drury was a follower of the Earl of Essex; he had been knighted by Essex, at the age of sixteen, during the French campaign of 1591–2 (he may have known Nicholas Skeres in that connection), and he was now serving the Earl in Ireland. The letter is addressed to George Parker, Robert's uncle by marriage and apparently his factotum; the 'Mynne' referred to is Robert's cousin, William Mynne. I have no precise idea what the letter is on about, but whatever 'follies' or indiscretions Mynne had committed, it is clear that Thomas Drury was as ready as ever to exploit them. It is a lengthy letter, so I extract only the parts relative to Thomas:

Uncle Parker, I perceive by your letters how you are crossed by the follies of Mynne and the boys, and that by that degenerate rogue Tom Drury they are published, and by his practices much trouble like to ensue unto you, as also great disgrace to me ... Let Mynne be forewarned of that rogue's company ... I bade Charles [Drury, Sir Robert's younger brother] and all they that were towards me, take heed of him ... I marvel he was not arrested. You shall find that, at one time or another, in his drunken ale-pots his tongue shall walk. You did very ill to spare him. It will rather hurt than otherwise, for if he had spoken upon his arrest any matter it would have received small credit, and you and I know many ways to discredit his testimony ... I perceive there hath been some old sueing and plotting. It seemeth my Lord of Essex is possessed mightly so by some letters, therefore desire mine uncle [Sir Edward] Stafford to write unto his Lordship that it is nothing but Tom Drury's plots that he deviseth to beg and get money with ... I have shown him [Essex] my uncle [Thomas]'s letters and yours; he hath addressed his whole mind to my Lord Chief Justice, which will serve the turn, and seeing it is but matters deposed of others' speeches, and not by the parties themselves, it will not much hurt us.

Let us luxuriate for a moment in these descriptions of Drury's behaviour in 1599. He has 'published' – i.e. made public – something detrimental to Mynne, and also, it seems, to Sir Robert Drury and the Earl of Essex. He is a mischievous tale-bearer making capital out of 'others' speeches'. He is a rogue and a drunkard whose tongue 'walks' when he is 'in his ale-pots'. Above all one notes Sir Robert's weary tone of familiarity: it is 'old sueing and plotting'; it is 'nothing but Tom Drury's plots that he deviseth to get money with'. This is Drury's métier, the letter seems to say. It is precisely the métier I have argued for him in the Marlowe case of 1593 – the manipulator of other mens' misfortunes: 'by his practices much trouble like unto ensue to you'.

The final act in Thomas Drury's spurious career occurs in 1603. I came across this in the course of some research on Sir

Robert Dudley, the illegitimate son of the Earl of Leicester by Lady Douglas Sheffield. Dudley had made various half-hearted efforts to prove his legitimacy, a matter of some delicacy in that his mother was now married to another man – in fact to Sir Edward Stafford, Drury's brother-in-law, which may be how he gets his teeth into the business. The legalities of Dudley's claim boiled down to a single, vital question: had the Earl of Leicester plighted his troth to Lady Sheffield – as she claimed – in a chamber at Esher House in the winter of 1573, or hadn't he? Nobody, it seems, was able or willing to testify to this event, now thirty years past, and the case never prospered. And then in the spring of 1603, up suddenly pops a woman called Magdalen Salisbury, claiming – indeed ready to testify – that in her youth, as Magdalen Frodsham, she had served as Lady Sheffield's 'gentlewoman', and that she had indeed been an eyewitness of the betrothal of Leicester and Lady Sheffield in 1573. Suspicions about this were soon raised. There were those who remembered Magdalen Frodsham, but they were certain she had entered Lady Sheffield's service *after* Robert Dudley's birth in 1574, and not, as she was now claiming, in 1572. These suspicions were well-justified: her account of the supposed betrothal proved contradictory, and it soon became clear that her whole testimony was a sham. A servant named Roose deposed that before she was brought in to testify, she became flustered and distressed, and cried: 'What would they have me to do? I was very young and I cannot remember anything.' It transpired, in fact, that her memory of the event had been coached – had indeed been invented – by someone else: someone who, as a witness drily put it, 'reminded her of many things, which she straight verified and confessed, but did not tell them before'. That someone was our old friend Thomas Drury, and Magdalen Salisbury's sworn statement was another – the last as it turns out – of his concocted texts.

He had somehow got his hooks into her, in late 1602, at the house of one Thomas Ward, where she was living rent-free and apparently in some poverty. He wheedled her into his confidence, offering her 'large promises', presumably of money, if she would depose in court that she had personally witnessed the betrothal. Her statement to this effect was actually taken down in Drury's 'chamber', probably by Drury himself, and was sent by him to Dudley. In a letter dated 8 August 1603, Drury tells Dudley that he has 'made the woman subscribe to the note' and that 'she is very forward to depose, for a further consideration'. The letter ends: 'as I like of your answer and dealing, so I shall proceed; if not pinchingly, I am yours. *Mora trahit periculum* [delay brings danger]'. He was, in short, selling to Sir Robert Dudley the false statements he had extracted from Mrs Salisbury.

Dudley was apparently convinced: it seems to have been largely on the strength of her statement – and that of her brother Henry Frodsham, also suborned by Drury – that he instituted the proceedings to establish legitimacy. The case ground on for nearly two years, before collapsing under the splenetic interrogations of the Attorney-General, Sir Edward Coke, who pronounced the witnesses' statements 'not worth a frieze jerkin'. In the judgement of Star Chamber on 10 May 1605, it was found that Dudley had been the dupe of Thomas Drury, who 'to work his own private gains' had enticed Dudley with these concocted testimonies. Mrs Salisbury was an 'infamous instrument of Drury', and he, in turn, was 'a man of mean condition and notoriously evil character'. It is an apt summary of this troublesome figure; ironic that it comes from the mouth of Attorney-General Coke, whose prosecution of Ralegh for high treason in 1603 had traded on those baseless accusations of atheism fomented by Drury and others ten years previously.

For her part in this charade Mrs Salisbury was fined the considerable sum of £100, as was her brother Henry, but this final unmasking of Thomas Drury's methods and motives had little effect on him, for he had in fact died shortly after his initial dealings with Magdalen, of the plague then rampant in London. The date of his death, as we learn from these documents, was 26 August 1603, at the age of 52. He died at his lodgings in the Swan Inn at Southwark, within earshot, perhaps, of those other fictions performed daily at the Rose and the Globe.

In reality Magdalen Salisbury remembered nothing: she had not been there. But Drury *reminded* her of many things, which she then 'straight verified and confessed': false, non-existent memories of an event she had not really witnessed, 'things she did not tell before' – before, that is, Drury told her to tell them. It is a marvellous little vignette of Thomas Drury in action. In terms of hard evidence it has little real bearing on the Marlowe case: it is a parallel, no more. But it does perhaps tell us this. If Richard Baines did not, in fact, remember Marlowe saying all these dreadful blasphemies – because he never really did say them – then Drury would have been there to *remind* him of them, that is to concoct them with him, and then to persuade him to 'straight verify and confess' them in the form of a signed 'Note'. This last scam of Thomas Drury's brings to mind those same words that Baines himself used in his confession at Rheims – 'dissimulation & fiction' – and is one more pointer to the confected nature of those damaging texts which haunt the last weeks of Marlowe's life.

35

MARLOWE'S LIBERTY

IN EARLY MAY, as the case is building against him – the libel signed 'Tamburlaine', the discovery of the Arian fragment, the reporting of Cholmeley's wild words – Marlowe is down at Scadbury, in the household of his long-time friend Thomas Walsingham, in the glories of the Kentish springtime: 'the meads, the orchards, and the primrose lanes'. Perhaps he is working on *Hero and Leander*, unfinished at his death and later dedicated to Walsingham: a poem about the warm south, and the power of love, and a young man drowning in a storm.

There he breathes, in Edward Blount's poignant phrase, the gentle air of Walsingham's liking. But it is only a matter of time before events in London break into this fragile zone. On 18 May a warrant is issued for Marlowe's apprehension. Henry Maunder, a trusty Messenger of Her Majesty's Chamber, rides down to Scadbury. He is empowered to seek aid 'if it be required', but there seems to be no problem. Marlowe returns with him to London, a man under escort once again, and on 20 May he makes his appearance before the Council.

Now comes a significant fact, the first indication of Marlowe's status in all this. He is not placed under arrest. Instead he is released on bail, and ordered to report daily to the Council. This is important. He has the status of someone who can give information, someone who is required for a purpose, but who is not himself – or not yet – considered criminal. When the arm of the law reached out to Thomas

Kyd, he was searched, imprisoned and tortured. When Richard Cholmeley is brought in to Justice Young a month later, he too will be hauled off to prison, despite his 'petition' of innocence. But Marlowe, the man on whom the investigation centres, the man incriminated by both Kyd and Cholmeley, remains free.

What did the authorities have against him at this stage, on 20 May? There is the general charge, arising from the Dutch Church libel, that his plays have been used for incitements to unrest. There is the charge that the Arian document found in Kyd's lodgings belonged to him. And there are the imputations of the 'Remembrances' against Cholmeley, that he has been broadcasting atheist ideas to Cholmeley and to 'Sir Walter Ralegh & others'.

In the case of the first two charges, Marlowe is in a good position to answer each of them with a denial of any intent on his part. His plays are blameless. They have been passed by Her Majesty's censor, and performed before the Queen at court: it is not his fault if people twist their meanings for malevolent political ends. On the matter of the Arian manuscript, he can plausibly deny that he has anything to do with the document. It is not in his handwriting, he has never seen it before, and anyway the text has been in print, for all to see, since good King Edward's time. In both of these Marlowe's course might be a shrug of non-involvement.

Perhaps the most serious allegation against him by 20 May is contained in the 'Remembrances': that he had 'persuaded' Cholmeley to atheism, and that he had read an 'atheist lecture' to Ralegh and others. These would be harder to shake off. He cannot deny that he knows Cholmeley. He cannot deny that he holds opinions which some would call 'atheist', nor that he has discoursed on such matters within the Ralegh circle. So there is a backdrop of strong circumstantial evidence behind the charges arising from the report on Cholmeley. Nevertheless, it is not considered enough on which to detain him. If Marlowe knows Cholmeley, he knows him for a two-timer, a professional liar, a man of 'ambitious infirmity'. So do some on the Council. On the actual charge of

401

propagandising atheism, it is Marlowe's word against Cholmeley's.

So straight denial is a course open to him when he appears before the Council on 20 May. Yet, in a circumstance as parlous as this, denial would not usually be enough. Marlowe's liberty at this stage seems to demand something more. What it suggests to me is that Marlowe had at this stage some kind of protection. In the realities of Elizabethan politics, it was not innocence that kept a man out of jail, but influence.

Who might this protector be? He has to be a powerful figure, someone with the clout to call off, or anyway delay, the bloodhounds of prosecution. The prosecution of Marlowe, however dubiously initiated, now has the full weight of government behind it – the executive power of Puckering and Buckhurst, the dutiful industry of Phelippes and Waad. I cannot see any of Marlowe's known patrons being in a position to challenge it. Thomas Walsingham does not have the status. Lord Strange would have little to gain, and a lot to lose, and anyway he seems to have severed his connections with Marlowe. Northumberland and Ralegh are out of the question.

A plausible candidate as the protector of Marlowe in May 1593 is Sir Robert Cecil. He too, I have argued, was a kind of patron of Marlowe: not in that poetic, conversational sense of the literary patron, but in the subfusc sphere of political dealings. Marlowe had been used by Cecil. The Flushing episode, though still enigmatic, belongs within the aegis of Cecil's intelligence service, belongs within the ongoing process of the government's surveillance of the presumed Catholic pretender, Lord Strange. The business about Marlowe and the 'K of Scots' suggests that he is still involved, together with his friend Roydon, in this labyrinth of succession politics, in which Cecil was and would continue to be tirelessly active in the interests of the future King James I. Marlowe's involvement in Scottish affairs is mentioned by Kyd as recent ('when I saw him last') and I have argued a connection with the many Scottish journeys made in late 1592 and early 1593 by that other Cecil operative, Robert Poley.

Cecil undoubtedly has the power to keep Marlowe out of prison on 20 May, and the probability that he has employed Marlowe in secret political affairs suggests he might have some particular interest in the case. In fact we have separate evidence of Cecil's interest in the case, in the form of that letter to him from Thomas Drury. This letter, written from prison in August 1593, makes it clear that Cecil had seen Drury's charge-sheet against Cholmeley, otherwise called the 'Remembrances'. Drury's phrasing suggests that he had personally discussed the matter with Cecil – 'I told your Honour' about Cholmeley's 'practices and lies', he writes, 'and so I presume it will be said by you'.

Cholmeley, of course, is another who has been employed by Cecil. We know this from Hugh Cholmeley's letter to Cecil of early 1592, and we know it from the 'Remembrances' itself, where Cholmeley says (or is alleged to have said) that Cecil had supplied him with a Jesuit book, *The Epistle of Comfort*, so he could 'frame verses & libels' in imitation of it: it was 'delivered him by Sir Robert Cecil, of whom he giveth very scandalous report that he [Cecil] should invite him to consider thereof'. If true, this was indeed rather 'scandalous'. It would be embarrassing to Cecil, amid all this rumpus about seditious libelling, if it came out that he had himself encouraged certain seditious libels. If not true, it still pointed up his relationship with the renegade Cholmeley. This potential embarrassment may be the reason why Cecil summoned Drury to discuss the contents of the 'Remembrances', though unfortunately we don't know the date of this meeting.

Some of this is speculative, but it arrives at an interesting conclusion: that there are aspects of this investigation which Cecil might view with some consternation. The problem is a perennial one for spymasters: the friction between the overt and covert sectors of government, and the danger that overt, official enquiries will produce unintended disclosures about covert activities. Already they are searching for Cholmeley; already there is compromising material in the charges against him. And then there is the matter of Marlowe, brought in for questioning on 20 May.

He too has worked for Cecil in these debatable areas of government. He too might know things potentially embarrassing or compromising about the workings of the Burghley spy network. How much, for instance, did he know about Cecil's game-plan against Lord Strange, soon to take shape in the form of the so-called 'Hesketh plot'? It was imperative that nothing should come out about this. The effort of Marlowe's enemies has been to paint him as a dangerous political atheist, but from Cecil's angle he might be dangerous in quite another way: as a potential revealer, under interrogation, of sensitive State matters. In this way, it becomes a priority to protect him; it is a self-serving rather than benevolent protection, as is Cecil's way. At this stage Marlowe is best kept in play, rather than delivered up to the conscience-scraping commissioners, who were empowered to put suspects 'to the torture' and 'draw them to discover their knowledge'.

Two scraps of evidence tend to confirm this possibility. The first is a memorandum, in Cecil's hand, dated 1593. It contains various items of intelligence, including this:

> Typpin is in prison, and writ by Apleby, that seeing Charles Paget was his betrayer, having been employed by Mr Vice-Chamberlain, he would also betray all those persons which carried Charles Paget's letters, which were these: Charles Paget writes to one Adrian de Lange, dwelling in Flushing, and he doth deliver them to one Steven White, who sends them into England.

This is obscure in detail, but the gist is clear enough. The 'Typpin' is James Tipping, the associate of Poley and Moody from Tower days, and since then employed, like them, by the Vice-Chamberlain, Sir Thomas Heneage. 'Apleby' is a certain Thomas Appleby, a low-grade informer. Appleby's intelligence is that Tipping, now in prison, is threatening to disclose information about Paget, de Lange and White. These three men were dealing with Moody, in the Low Countries, at this time. De Lange and White were in fact apprehended early the following year. The interesting point is that Tipping's imprisonment may well be a result of this atheism investigation now under way, for he and his brother ('tippinges ii') are named on the official docket of the 'Remembrances' as members of Richard Cholmeley's 'damnable crew'. Here is a crossover between the atheism investigation and the Cecil intelligence network: an instance of the damage that could be caused when government agents fell foul of the law.

The second point concerns those alterations to the official copy of the Baines 'Note'. One of these is the excising of the entire paragraph concerning Marlowe's acquaintance with John Poole the coiner, and his intention to 'practise' the counterfeiting skills he had learned from him. This item, of course, relates to Marlowe's activity in Flushing, and that activity in turn relates to Cecil's secret dealings against Lord Strange. It seems possible that the suppression of this particular item expresses Cecil's wish to keep the Flushing incident under wraps.

Cecil's involvement in the affair, which we know from Drury, translates into a kind of uneasy vigilance. Marlowe is in this harsh spotlight. He is a problem, a possible security risk. Is it at this stage that the signal goes out to the Netherlands, ordering the return of Robert Poley?

Whatever the reasoning behind Marlowe's release, his continued liberty in the last week of May strikes me as bad news for the plotters against him. He has been accused, he has been apprehended, and yet he remains free. What his antagonists had hoped, I suggest, is that Marlowe would be arrested and tortured, and that – like Kyd – he would then 'affirm' whatever they wanted him to affirm. He would confess to the 'atheist lecture'; he would itemise the torrid blasphemies that were uttered in the private chambers of Durham House; and so they would have their evidence – in this cynical understanding of the word 'evidence' – against Ralegh. But this did not happen according to their plan.

What is needed by the enemies of Marlowe at this stage – by the enemies of Ralegh who wish to blacken him by his association with Marlowe – is something more like hard evidence. The Baines 'Note' and the deposition of Thomas Kyd duly provide that evidence. They are sworn statements, providing an account of specific utterances made by Marlowe. The Baines 'Note' was in circulation on 27 May at the earliest; the Kyd deposition was not written down until after Marlowe's death. So the specific evidence against Marlowe – as opposed to the circumstantial evidence – is laid after he was apprehended, and let out on bail, by the Privy Council. There is a dynamic of accusation and refutation. Marlowe has withstood the first onslaught of innuendo. Now the prosecution takes its next step, principally through the agency of Richard Baines.

The Baines 'Note' is the trump card in the case against Marlowe, which is also a case against Ralegh. But how good is it? Marlowe has so far outplayed his accusers: despite the libel, despite the evidence furnished by Cholmeley and Kyd, he remains at liberty. Can he outplay the Baines 'Note' as well?

The answer partly depends on what we cannot precisely determine: we do not know how much truth there is in what Baines says. Everything about the man, and everything about the circumstances of the 'Note', suggests that it is, at the least, a grotesque distortion of Marlowe's position. It is a piece of propaganda by an experienced practitioner of (in his own words) 'fiction & dissimulation'. And anyway, once again, the truth is only a small part of the matter. What is more important is Marlowe's status – the protection he can call on, the counter-charges he can bring, the claims of state service he can make. He had got out of trouble before: in 1587, when his behaviour was called into question by the Cambridge authorities; in 1592, when he was arrested on the capital charge of coining.

Here is my answer to the question. Of course Marlowe can outplay the Baines 'Note'. He can do so in the way he outplayed those other accusations against him. He can claim that he is not *really* an atheist at all, just as he was not really a defector to Rheims or a Catholic coiner. He is the poet-spy: these damnable opinions are no more than his cover. This is all 'faithful dealing'. I believe that Marlowe's liberty is a result of this specific kind of denial of the charges – really the only kind of denial that could carry weight – and that the protection of warranty that must lie behind his denial comes from Sir Robert Cecil, anxious to shield his former secret operative from the clumsy inquisitions of legal prosecution.

So let us think now of Marlowe's situation, on about 28 May, as the full import of the Baines 'Note' is digested by Sir John Puckering and Lord Buckhurst, to whom it has been delivered the previous day by Thomas Drury. For these men this is the clinching of the case against Marlowe – it is 'proof' – but there is also in their minds a scenario of its possible failure. Perhaps, after all, the 'Note' will prove ineffective; perhaps it will be outplayed by Marlowe's agile political footwork, in the chambers of the Council to which he is reporting daily, and in which he has the discrete but palpable support of Sir Robert Cecil. And so the game will go on, unresolved, and the momentum against the pernicious Ralegh circle will falter. At this point, I would say, Marlowe *himself* has become the major stumbling block. He is a moving target. He is escaping from the confines of the part that has been written for him. But if Marlowe could be removed from the game, silenced in some way, then the 'Note', and all the other accumulated accusations, might be enough to keep the campaign moving towards its desired end, which is the political destruction of Sir Walter Ralegh. According to this twisted Machiavellian logic, it is indeed necessary – as Baines himself says – 'that the mouth of so dangerous a member may be stopped'. I would not say that Puckering and Buckhurst pursued these thoughts to their logical conclusion; but those below them would not scruple to do so.

In the mind of Sir Robert Cecil, meanwhile, there is the danger of the other possibility – the possibility that the Baines 'Note' will succeed in its mission of damage. If prosecutor Puckering does successfully proceed against Marlowe, and has him put to the torture 'to discover his knowledge' of atheism and sedition, there is the danger of other sorts of 'knowledge' being brought to light which would be much better left in the dark. And so an idea plays across Cecil's brain – that complex computer of political profit and loss – that it might after all be safer, and tidier, if Marlowe was out of the way; that this brilliant but troublesome young man has talked enough.

Again one does not expect Cecil to have pursued this thought to the point of action, or even of articulation: *prudens qui patiens* was always his motto. Let such hints as were necessary be discreetly dropped; leave action to others lower and less visible, those servants and agents and 'climbing followers' who make it their business to sniff the shifting winds of political advantage, and to act upon their inter-pretations with or without specific 'warranty' from their superiors. In the back-rooms where men like Drury and Phelippes sit, the interpretation arrived at might be something like this. If an unfortunate accident were at this stage to befall Christopher Marlowe, neither his prosecutor Sir John Puckering nor his protector Sir Robert Cecil would be much displeased. It would serve their turns, and therefore serve ours.

Such thoughts attend the delivery of the Baines 'Note' on Sunday 27 May 1593. Three days later Marlowe lies dead at Deptford.

36

THE RECKONING

WE ARE NOW back at Deptford Strand on the morning of 30 May 1593. At ten o'clock that morning four men met at the house of Eleanor Bull, a bailiff's widow with court connections. They were Ingram Frizer, Nicholas Skeres, Robert Poley and Christopher Marlowe. Their paths have crossed many times in the by-ways of political service. They share an understanding of things. They live on their wits, on their mistrust of one another. The initiator of the meeting, we are told, was Ingram Frizer. He invited Marlowe there for a 'feast'. The four men spent the day together in private. They ate and drank and smoked, they walked in the garden, they came in to supper at six o'clock. Their behaviour during that day is described as 'quiet'. At some point in the evening there was a fight, and Marlowe was stabbed through the eye with Frizer's dagger. According to uncorroborated evidence provided by Skeres and Poley, Marlowe had attacked Frizer during a quarrel about the bill or 'reckoning'. Frizer pleaded self-defence and was acquitted by royal pardon four weeks later.

In the accounts of the killing, Skeres and Poley are shadowy figures. Nothing is said about them in the inquest, except that they were there that day, and that they were positioned either side of Frizer when Marlowe attacked him. Nothing is said of them at all in the independent accounts of Beard, Meres and Vaughan. In all of these, it is a two-hand show: Marlowe and Frizer at odds, for reasons variously described – the bill, a grudge, an affair of the heart. Almost immediately Skeres and

Poley have been written out of the story. Or rather, since they are the principal witnesses on which the story is based, they have written *themselves* out of the story.

This seems entirely convenient for these two 'gentlemen' – as the inquest describes them – for what all these accounts fail to mention is that Nicholas Skeres is a follower of the Earl of Essex, and that Robert Poley is a government agent working under Sir Robert Cecil, and that they are present at this meeting not as boon-companions at a 'feast', but as the particular servants of particular interests.

There is not a shadow of doubt about Skeres's involvement with Essex. He had carried the Earl's letters from Exeter after the Portingale voyage of 1589. He had served under Essex in France in the winter of 1591–2. He will be described as a 'servant' of Essex in 1595, when he is arrested in dangerous company at Edmund Williamson's house in Philip Lane. In the man's own words, given under oath in Star Chamber just a month before the Deptford meeting, the Earl of Essex is his 'Lord and Master'. But this does *not* tell us that Skeres was at this point 'working for' Essex. The latter does not appear to be implicated in this plot against Marlowe and Ralegh, though as I have noted before, he was someone who might stand to gain, personally and politically, by the further demise of Ralegh. What it tells us, rather, is that Skeres would have known Thomas Phelippes, who had been the Earl's *chef de cabinet* in secret affairs since 1591. If Skeres belongs to the Essex retinue, he belongs unequivocally to the shady end of it. He is a man found almost exclusively – apart from his much-protested link with Essex – in the lower strata of London society: among crooked brokers and skinners, and nips and foists. We cannot know his features, but we see his big, ill-formed signature, and we hear the slightly eccentric swagger of his phrasing in his letter to that other Essex crony, Gilly Meyrick. If there is some dirty work afoot, possibly involving bloodshed, then Skeres is the kind of man you called on.

In fact we don't have to guess that Phelippes knew Skeres – he had known him at least since the summer of 1586, when Skeres was to be seen in the company of Anthony Babington and his 'crew', at their lodgings near Bishopsgate, almost certainly as a spy or infiltrator in their company, and therefore a man known to and probably briefed by Phelippes, who was minutely involved in the entrapment of Babington.

This already gives the Deptford meeting a sinister connotation, for a link between Phelippes and Skeres is also a link between the prosecution of Marlowe for atheism, in which Phelippes has been involved, and the killing of Marlowe on 30 May, at which Skeres is physically present. That prosecution, I have argued, has two faces: the visible face of a government obsessed with religious conformity, as represented by Lord Keeper Puckering and Lord Buckhurst; and the hidden face of intrigue and trickery, as represented by the three-headed Cerberus of Drury, Baines and Cholmeley. And between them, at the interface, there is always Master Phelippes: the commissioner, the aparatchik, the interrogator; the secret policeman *par excellence*, peering through his dusty spectacles at those he has selected as victims. Skeres doubtless knew Marlowe personally, but in the precise circumstances of 30 May he walks in through that door as a potential enemy of Marlowe's. Phelippes has not managed to make Marlowe his victim; the prosecution has stalled. There is pressure from above, and there is the pressure of Phelippes's own desire to land other, bigger victims. And so he calls in Skeres to apply a little pressure of his own on this difficult customer Marlowe.

One could see this as one axis of the Deptford meeting: an encounter between Skeres and Marlowe, and thus a privately managed encounter between the forces of prosecution and their intended victim: on the surface of it a 'feast', but in reality a confidential meeting, in a safe house, where matters may be dealt with behind closed doors, or out in the garden where none may overhear. Ingram Frizer is the actual initiator of the meeting, but in this – as in the recent swindling of Drew Woodleff – he is Skeres's accomplice. Frizer has fixed this meeting for Skeres.

Here is another connection never noticed before: the above-named gullible young heir from Aylesbury, Drew Woodleff, into whom Skeres and Frizer had their hooks in the spring of

1593, was a blood relation of Thomas Drury's. Woodleff's mother Anne, who was active in the later Chancery case against Skeres and Frizer, was the daughter of Sir Robert Drury of Hedgerly, and the sister of Sir Drew Drury after whom Drew Woodleff was no doubt named. That Woodleff and Thomas Drury were second cousins is hardly a major connection, though in small tribal London it is not insignificant. It is perhaps just a ghostly reminder of the hundreds of unknown personal connections that intertwine these characters (the conjunction of the names Woodleff and Poley in a property deal of 1597, spotted by the sharp-eyed Dr Urry, is another). But if we were going to speculate – and there is little else we can do now we are back in Deptford – we might say that if Woodleff knew Skeres and Frizer, it is not unlikely that his cousin Tom Drury did too; and that as Drury was himself involved in dodgy money-deals in 1593 – he had to repay £170 to Sir Edmund Carey in August – the likelihood becomes a little stronger. And it would not, after all, be surprising if Drury was found somewhere in the background of the meeting: a man with an interest, like Phelippes, in getting Marlowe to say certain things and do certain things that will further their promising but currently becalmed little project against the heretics of the Ralegh circle.

This is Skeres's role: the bringer of a message, the purveyor of promises and threats on behalf of one or more secret gentlemen who would prefer their names not mentioned at this stage. The Deptford meeting is an exploration of possibilities, a shaking of the dice-box; and indeed the latter – if William Vaughan is right about that game of 'tables' or backgammon – is one of the last sounds Marlowe ever heard.

Poley is perhaps, after all, an unexpected arrival at the meeting. Why, Robin, it was said you were in the Low Countries.

So he had been: he had left England about three weeks previously, bearing the usual 'letters of great importance for Her Majesty's special service'. But now he is back. As I believe, he has been recalled by Sir Robert Cecil, who is anxious that Marlowe's parlous situation might compromise him. Poley himself might share that anxiety. Marlowe is to be questioned: about libels and heresies, about his relations with men like Cholmeley and Baines, about his 'monstruous opinions'. What else might Marlowe explain, under pressure? What else might he reveal in the hope of gaining himself some respite, some leverage, some trade-off? What incriminating knowledge might he have from his dealings in the Low Countries the previous year, done under Cecil's aegis?

No-one better to sift the dangers posed by Marlowe than Robin Poley: a man apprised of the true facts, a specialist in the business of insinuation, and very probably an old acquaintance of Marlowe.

In puzzling over the killing of Marlowe I inevitably find myself thinking of it as a special, even an extraordinary event. In one sense it is, because of Marlowe's uniqueness as a poet, because of what was lost to us by his death at the age of twenty-nine.

In another sense, this meeting was not special at all. It was familiar fare: another conspiratorial gathering in an age of conspiracy, another session among the informers and per-suaders of the Elizabethan police-state. The atmosphere at Mistress Bull's house that day was not so different from that in Poley's garden where Babington and Ballard dined while Walsingham's net closed in around them; or at the lodgings of Thomas Drury, when the mood suddenly changed, and his 'companions' Cholmeley and Borage clapped him on the shoulder and turned him in to the authorities.

So too the 'feast' at Deptford. Its convivialities are but coldly done. Its true configuration is political and factional. The foreground players are Frizer and Marlowe, but as always there is the element of manipulation, the hidden agenda. The key figures are those who appear most faintly in the official story: the two spies, Skeres and Poley. They are at work that day, on confidential business. In the case of Poley this is all but stated in the wording of his warrant of payment in June: 'being on Her Majesty's service all the aforesaid time'.

Skeres and Poley at Deptford Strand are two men in their métier. They have questions to ask, offers to make. They are speaking their familiar language of cajolement, each from their different nook of courtly service. Marlowe is under pressure, but he has his own cards to play, his own ends to serve: he is not so tractable to their lures. In the drowsy afternoon garden, connections become unsure. So much is hidden and held back. Each is uncertain who holds the cards, and what the game is anyway. Wine headaches descend on these men in some rough-cut bower at the back of Mrs Bull's. They have been talking together for eight hours when they come back in from the garden. Time is running out. Persuasion becomes threat, and threat flares up in anger. 'Divers malicious words' are spoken, not about a 'sum of pence', but about matters of life and liberty, truth and betrayal. In the heat of the night, in the irrecoverable fleeting logic of the moment, the situation resolves itself. Someone pulls a knife. There is a brief struggle, and Marlowe is killed by a savage blow to the head.

According to the official story – the story told by Skeres and Poley – it was Marlowe who pulled the knife and Frizer who killed him in self-defence. As for themselves, they were but standers-by, huddlers at the table, close enough for the blood to stain their sleeves, but in no other wise, my Lord, to be touched in the matter. I believe that in this, as in so much else in their careers, Skeres and Poley were lying. They were lying to conceal their involvement – and through them the involvement of ministers of the Crown – in the killing of Christopher Marlowe.

It is true that, whatever cat's cradle of shared secrets and hidden antagonisms binds these four men together, it would still be possible for two of them to have a foolish drunken spat over the bill, and for one of them to die for it. That was the Elizabethan way: no doubt about it. But so was this other kind of episode whose outline I have been trying to recover in this book. These absurdly complex projections and counter-projections were also the Elizabethan way – a way of life, a source of income, and for some a cause of death.

I am not trying to argue that Marlowe's death has to have a meaning. My reading tends only to a more complex kind of meaninglessness than that of a 'tavern brawl'.

The sum of it – my nearest hit at what really happened – is this. Marlowe did not die by mischance, and he was not killed in self-defence. He had become an impediment to this shoddy enterprise against Sir Walter Ralegh which had been promoted by Cholmeley and Baines, manipulated by Drury and Phelippes, and probably winked at – because the end of state security justified the means being used – by Lord Keeper Puckering and, more obliquely, Sir Robert Cecil. The plotters had sought to frame him, to get him imprisoned and tortured; to use him as their 'instrument' against Ralegh. They had tried all this and failed. He had proved elusive, a potential projector against them. His mouth – if it could not be made to say what they wanted it to say – must be 'stopped'. To the plausible Skeres is entrusted this delicate task: to try once more to persuade Marlowe to turn evidence against Ralegh, and failing that, to silence him for good. I do not think the purpose of the meeting was murder. This is not because I underestimate the ruthlessness of the plotters – the treatment of Kyd leaves few illusions on that score – but because if murder had been intended all along, it could have been better accomplished more anonymously. Rather, Marlowe's death was a *decision*. It was a point the day reached, by a process of dwindling options. No-one ordered Marlowe's murder. The killing happens in the hermetic confines of the secret world: a dirty trick, a rogue event, a tragic blunder.

Ingram Frizer may well have struck the fatal blow. It is probable, though not certain, that he did. Even if he did, even if he was in this mechanical sense the murderer, I would still not say he was the true villain of the piece. That distinction I reserve for Nicholas Skeres.

Poley was more truly on the sidelines, where we always find him. As I see it, he is chiefly a manipulator after the event. Whatever his angle at the meeting itself, his priorities become clear the moment the murder is done. The imperative with Poley is discretion. What else would he do, what else could he do – in the interests of the government, in the interests of Sir Robert Cecil, and most particularly in the interests of himself – but close the whole case up as quickly and tightly as possible, and connive with Skeres and Frizer in that exonerating version of the event that was told to Coroner Danby and the jury on the 1st of June 1593?

It was the rule he stuck to – 'I will swear and forswear myself, rather than I will accuse myself to do me any harm.'

We will never know for certain exactly what happened in that room in Deptford in 1593. An event like this, which echoes on through the centuries, takes just a few seconds to happen. Once it has happened, it is gone. Even when there is not deliberate falsification, as there was in this case, there is the inevitable erosion of the truth – all the omissions, distortions, guesses, errors and imaginings that work their way into the record. Thus all events become mysterious. The final truth about Marlowe's death lies hidden under these layers of reconstruction, much as the landscape where it happened lies hidden under the tower-blocks and container-yards of modern Deptford. Only fragments remain: scraps of paper, pieces of jigsaw, the nagging sense of unfinished business.

Putting these fragments together, I conclude that the cause of Marlowe's death was a perception – perhaps a momentary perception – of political necessity. He died in the hands of secret servants: a victim, though not an innocent victim, of the incessant intrigues that flourished in this 'queasy time' of change and succession. It was their interconnections in the world of covert politics that brought those four men to Deptford on that May morning, and kept them there till gone suppertime – kept them there forever, one might say, caught in that web of events whose precise spiderly architecture is too fine-spun to discern. It was not so much conspiracy as a pressing weight of political circumstance, a game of charge and counter-charge in which a man is increasingly boxed and hedged and confined by the constructions of others until there is no way out for him, until he is physically there in that 'little room', with one door out which he does not or cannot take.

As for the story of the 'recknynge', concocted within hours and elaborated over the centuries, it was a lie. It neutralised potential embarrassments. It served to cover up the tracks that led from Mrs Bull's house, through the back-ways of government service, to the doors of Her Majesty's Privy Council. It was just another of these 'fictions and knaveries'.

EPILOGUE

OF THE POLITICAL protagonists of this story, the old campaigners of State matters died peacefully: Sir Thomas Heneage in 1595, Lord Burghley in 1598.

The unfortunate Lord Strange, the Earl of Derby for just a few months, died of a violent and mysterious sickness, at his house at Lathom, in April 1594. He believed he was 'bewitched', but subsequent investigation suggested poison. It is possible that this is some reverberation of the 'Hesketh plot': it is noted that the Hickman brothers, involved suspiciously in the set-up of Hesketh, took horse for the north a few days before Strange's sudden demise.

Sir Walter Ralegh was imprisoned in the Tower in 1603, on treason charges arising from the Bye Plot. The Earl of Northumberland was also sent to the Tower, in 1605, implicated in prior knowledge of the Gunpowder Plot. They passed their days in conversation and experiment. Ralegh wrote *The History of the World*; Northumberland was attended by Marlowe's old friends, Thomas Hariot and Walter Warner. Ralegh was eventually executed in 1618. Northumberland died peacefully, at the age of sixty-eight: a wrinkled, straggle-bearded old scholar.

The Earl of Essex was beheaded at Tower Hill on Ash Wednesday 1601, a month after the *acte gratuit* known as the Essex Rising. Among those executed with him was his stepfather Christopher Blount, the former accomplice of Robert Poley.

Amid all these ructions that attended the last years of

Elizabeth and the first years of James, there is one figure who continued to rise, and to ride the troubled waters of the succession, who was indeed the principal prosecutor of Essex, Ralegh and Northumberland in his role as Mr Secretary. That is, of course, Sir Robert Cecil. On James's accession, he was rewarded for his staunch support of the Jacobean cause. He was created Viscount Cranbourne and in 1605 – the year he successfully unravelled the Gunpowder Plot – 1st Earl of Salisbury. Always sickly, he died shortly before his fiftieth birthday, but he is the one who emerges from these years as the chief manipulator and broker of political power.

Also beneficiaries of James's favours were the Walsinghams, Sir Thomas and Lady Audrey, the latter a great favourite with James's Danish wife, Queen Anne. Marlowe's former patron, who valued 'those parts of reckoning and worth' that were in him, lived to a good age, a respected but somewhat retiring figure compared to his sparky and ambitious wife, and died at Scadbury in 1628.

Among Marlowe's friends and fellow-poets, Thomas Kyd followed him to the grave the next year. His last work, *Cornelia*, is prefaced by a poignant dedication to the Countess of Sussex. We do not know the cause of his death, but the inference that he was broken by the tortures he received in Bridewell is strong.

George Peele died of the 'pox' (it is said) in about 1596. Thomas Nashe, 'sequestered' from his livelihood by the Archbishop's decree against satires, disappears from view in 1600, and is announced as dead the following year, aged about thirty-three: another Elizabethan burn-out.

'Matthew Roydon of Westminster, clerk' is glimpsed in a law-suit in 1599. He seems to have pursued those Scottish associations Kyd hinted at, for in 1604 he was living in the house of James's favourite, William Hamilton, Earl of Haddington. At about this time he wrote a motto in an album preserved at the Huntington Library: 'Unum qui non intelligit, nihil intelligit. Matheus Roydon, Anglus'.

Roydon's friend George Chapman, the continuer of

Marlowe's *Hero*, was truculently prolific for over forty years after Marlowe's death. He turned out tragedies and comedies for the stage – in 1605 he was imprisoned, along with his friend Ben Jonson, for impertinent remarks about King James in their comedy *Eastward Ho* – and he translated the complete works of Homer (*Iliad*, 1611; *Odyssey*, 1616; *Minor Works*, c 1624).

Edward Blount prospered among the booksellers of St Paul's and in 1623 was the publisher and prime mover of Shakespeare's *Works*, the celebrated First Folio.

Thomas Hariot died in 1621, in 'calamitous' pain from cancer of the nose, which ate away his septum and 'held his lips hard and turned upwards'. The gossip Aubrey, in a rather tasteless joke, connects his death with those daring speculations on the Creation that had caused him, and Marlowe, such trouble in 1593:

> He valued not the old story of the Creation . . . He would say *Ex nihilo nihil fit*. But a *nihilum* killed him at last, for in the top of his nose came a little red speck (exceeding small) which grew bigger and bigger, and at last killed him.

Among the enemies and detractors of Marlowe, Thomas Beard became Cromwell's schoolmaster, Francis Meres became a vicar in Rutland, and William Vaughan pursued an eccentric career as a Welsh squire, a minor author, and a part-time political agent. Dr Gabriel Harvey lapsed into silence after the publication of the *Supererogation* and *New Letter* in 1593. Despite the provocations of Nashe, he published nothing thereafter: the absurd 'Gorgon' is thus his last known poem. He retired to his native town, Saffron Walden, lived alone with his books and his memories, and died there in his early eighties: by no means a burn-out, but in many ways another talent tragically wasted.

The spies who have haunted this book fade from view like the ghosts they always were. Michael Moody continued his complex and fruitless conniving in the Low Countries, till a letter of 29 December 1596 casually mentions his recent death. Roger Walton, who crossed swords with Poley in the Netherlands, returned to England after twenty months' imprisonment, to find his wife dead and – judging from his disappearance from the records thereafter – his days of government employment over.

Nothing is heard of Richard Cholmeley after his imprisonment in June 1593. The 'Mr Cholmeley' involved in catering matters at Essex House in 1597 is almost certainly his younger namesake. Thomas Drury's demise, at an inn in Southwark in 1603, has already been noted.

Those who look for some poetic justice in the matter have noted the title of a ballad, which appears in the Stationers' Register on 6 December 1594: 'The Woful Lamentacon of Richard Baynes, executed at Tyborne.' Was this Baines the informer who swung at Tyburn? Court records confirm the case: a Richard Baines was arrested on a charge of murder and robbery, convicted at Newgate Sessions of robbery alone, and sentenced to death at the Gaol Delivery in the first week of December 1594. His crime, it appears, was the theft of a single cup from a tavern. But this is almost certainly not our Baines. The recent discovery that he held the rectory at Waltham in Lincolnshire allows him a more leisuredly career after the conclusion of his business with Marlowe, for he was still rector in 1607. The hanged man was perhaps the other Richard Baines (a Londoner, a student at Oxford and the Middle Temple) who used to be identified with the informer, but is now known to be quite separate.

And so finally to those three who were the last to see Marlowe alive, and the last to know what truly happened.

What we know of Nicholas Skeres subsequent to the killing perhaps, after all, suggests a grim kind of justice. As I have mentioned before, he turns up a couple of years later, at the house of Edmund Williamson, in circumstances suggestive partly of 'brokery' and partly of political surveillance. But this is not the last record of him. On 31 July 1601, a Council warrant instructed the removal of two prisoners from

Newgate. One was named Farmer, the other Nicholas 'Skiers'. They were to be taken to the Bridewell, a political prison, feared as a place of torture and no return. This was a few months after the Essex Rising: perhaps Skeres's minor star fell along with that of his 'Lord and Master'.

Robert Poley – as the Jesuit Southwell once said – 'liveth like himself'. He continues in government service: running agents and despatches in and out of the Netherlands, Scotland and France, employed by Heneage and after Heneage's death, seamlessly, by Sir Robert Cecil. There is one later episode that seems to throw a kind of light back on his relations with Marlowe. In the summer of 1597 the budding young comedian Ben Jonson was imprisoned in the Marshalsea, as co-author (with Nashe) of the 'seditious' comedy *The Isle of Dogs*. Many years later, the Scottish poet William Drummond recorded Jonson's memories of this 'time of his close imprisonment'. Jonson said:

> His judges could get nothing of him to all their demands but Aye and No. They placed two damn'd villains, to catch advantage of him, with him, but he was advertised by his Keeper.

Drummond adds that Jonson wrote an epigram about these two spies. It used to be assumed that he was referring to Jonson's two-line epigram, 'On Spies', but there is another which fits the bill rather better. It is called 'Inviting a Friend to Supper', and it is about the rare pleasure of being able freely to 'speak our minds amidst our meat', and enjoy a cup of Mermaid sack without fear of prying ears in the company. It includes the lines:

> And we will have no Pooly or Parrot by,
> Nor shall our cups make any guilty men.
> But, at our parting, we will be as when
> We innocently met.

'Pooly' and 'Parrot', it is argued, these two men whom Jonson hopes will *not* be in his company at the Mermaid, are the two prison-informers who tried to 'catch advantage' of him in the Marshalsea in 1597. There is a Parrot, or Parrat, found in exactly this role: in Newgate prison, a couple of years later, he is battened on a suspected priest named Barkworth, 'the said Parrat coming unto him every day, and practising for gain'. And there is, of course, a Pooley, who knows the Marshalsea well. The Keeper who tipped Jonson the wink about these two 'villains' was probably Richard Ede, whose path had crossed with Poley's many years earlier, and who described him as a 'very bad fellow' for his dealings with the cutler's wife, Joan Yeomans. All this seems to chime in with the Marlowe case: a writer in political trouble, and Poley close in there, shuffling the cards of innocence and guilt.

The last payment to him in the Chamber Accounts is in 1601. At about this time, 'our well-beloved subject R.P.' was recommended for the post of yeoman-waiter at the Tower of London. This is perhaps Robert Poley, nearing fifty, being put out to grass. The post seems appropriate: a minor official in the enforcement business, comfortably quartered in his old haunt from the days after Babington.

The name of Ingram Frizer is found in a couple of law-suits, and in a series of property-deals in 1603–4, on behalf of Lady Audrey Walsingham. In these he is the fixer, the practical man who attends to the details, and is trusted to do so. He was by then living at Eltham, in Kent, not far from the Walsingham family seat at Scadbury. His life thereafter seems to settle into the parochial mould of a well-to-do Kentish yeoman. He becomes churchwarden in 1605, parish tax-assessor in 1611. He seeks permission to dig a well in the corner of the church close: the water from the well is for brewing ale at his house. He has a daughter named Alice who lives in London; another who married a man called Banks. There is a family servant, Margaret. The 'Mrs Ingeram', buried at Eltham in 1616, was perhaps his wife. A curious record of a payment he made 'for putten forth of Sheeres childe' may indicate his dealing on behalf of a child, or indeed an orphan, of his old accomplice Nicholas Skeres.

Thus the man who killed Christopher Marlowe lived out his days in suburban respectability, and was buried in the churchyard at Eltham on 14 August 1627.

Appendix 1: False Trails

This is a small repository of negative evidence. It contains trails which seemed promising on the subject of Marlowe's political career or his death. Some of them proved to be completely false; others I have abandoned more reluctantly.

1 MORLEY THE MESSENGER

A letter from Robert Ardern to Lord Burghley, dated 2 October 1587, refers to a certain Mr Morley as a messenger for Lord Burghley [PRO SP15/30, f.85]. The letter was written from Utrecht, where Ardern had charge of victualling English troops. This has been taken by at least one biographer to indicate that Marlowe was on government business in the Low Countries in 1587.

The letter itself puts paid to that. The business involving Morley had nothing at all to do with the Low Countries, and it took place a year or two earlier than the date of Ardern's writing. None the less, this is still an interesting trail. The letter is actually about a dispute between Ardern and 'one Felton, an attorney at laws'. Ardern held a lucrative 'patent' to collect crown revenues from former abbey lands in Northumberland, but part of his area – North Shields – had now been granted to Felton. This, Ardern felt, 'sequestered' him from his rightful earnings. It also involved the Earl of Northumberland, whose revenues from the 'anchorage' at Tynemouth were affected. Ardern duly complained to Burghley,

whereupon it then pleased your Honour, after examination

of the cause, to command Mr Morley; Allen King, then the Earl's man; and me (being the messengers from your Honour) to call for the same Felton's patent (being granted during pleasure) and to cancel the same.

This is all we hear about Morley in the letter. It is hard to date his appearance in the business precisely. Felton had been granted the patent 'iii years past' (i.e. 1584), but the intervention by Burghley's envoys seems to have taken place some time in late 1585 or in 1586 (at any rate, before Michaelmas 1586).

This is certainly tantalising. Morley is, as we know, a frequent variant spelling of Marlowe. To find Marlowe in Lord Burghley's service in 1585–6 would tie in with his absences from Cambridge at this time, and with the flush of money that appears on his buttery account. It would also tie in with the later connection with Burghley which lies (so I have argued) behind the debacle at Flushing. Of course, this episode cannot in itself be the 'good service' referred to in the Council certificate of 1587, which has to be something bigger, but it could well be the kind of low-grade, probationary work through which a recruit had to pass before moving on to more politic tasks. There is also the involvement of the Earl of Northumberland. Morley is working alongside one of Northumberland's servants, Allen King. This might be thought to add another hint to the early connection between Marlowe and Northumberland (though only a faint one: there is nothing to suggest the Earl's personal involvement in this routine dispute).

Against these interesting possibilities, there is another Mr Morley, who is involved, on Burghley's behalf, in fiscal business at this time.

In 1586, Archibald Douglas, one of 'the stoutest friends of England at the Scottish court', was promised a 'lease in reversion' worth £200 in recognition of his services. The warrant authorising this is endorsed by Burghley, who dealt closely with Douglas. The administrator of this business was one John Morley. Two letters from Morley to Douglas are among Burghley's papers at Hatfield House [HMC Cecil 3.277, 287]. One of them, dated 5 October 1587, concerns the promised lease. Morley suggests a certain 'manor' fifty miles from London, worth only £80 per annum but with other favourable assets. 'This, I think, will serve your turn.'

John Morley is hard to identify, because the name is a common one. He may be one of the two John Morleys who were members of the Merchant Taylors' company. He is very likely the John Morley who carried confidential despatches from France in 1581. And he is almost certainly the 'Mr Morley of the Exchequer' referred to in a letter to Lord Burghley from the Earl of Essex, 2 November 1587 [PRO SP12/205, no. 3].

He is not precisely identifiable, but I believe that the Mr Morley involved in the case of Ardern v. Felton in c. 1586 was not Christopher Marlowe the poet, but John Morley 'of the Exchequer', who appears in a broadly similar role the following year, administering financial matters on behalf of Lord Burghley.

2   MR MARLIN AT DIEPPE

A letter from Sir Henry Unton to Lord Burghley, 17 March 1592, bears the address: 'To my Lord Treasurer: by Mr Marlin' [PRO SP78/27, f.232]. It concerns complaints by English officers and shipmen of 'Her Majesty's pinnaces', then harbouring at Dieppe. It appears from the letter that this Marlin is their representative, for Unton says: 'this bearer they send, by whom I thought good to write to your Lordship'. 'Marlin' is another known variant of Marlowe, and it has been suggested that this courier was Christopher Marlowe. He was not, however. He was William Marlin or Malin, 'Master of Her Majesty's pinnace called ye Charles'. On 23 March 1592 he was paid 100 shillings, under Burghley's warrant, for bringing 'letters for Her Majesty's affairs' from France [PRO E351/542, f.169]. These doubtless included Unton's despatch. A week or so later he posted back to Dieppe, with letters from Burghley to the English agent there, Otwell Smith. Smith refers to these letters as 'brought by William Mallyne'.

3 MR MORLEY AND ARABELLA STUART

Perhaps the most fascinating trail, and the one I lingered over longest, is opened up in yet another letter to Lord Burghley, this time from the redoubtable Countess of Shrewsbury, popularly known as Bess of Hardwick [BL Lansdowne MS71, art.2]. She had in her charge, for many years, the Queen's young cousin Arabella Stuart, daughter of the Earl of Lennox. This poor girl was cursed, like many others in this story, with a strong blood-claim to the English throne, and she was a virtual prisoner under the Shrewsbury wardship. Among her retinue at Hardwick House was a tutor named Morley, as appears from the following extract from the Countess's letter of 21 September 1592:

One Morley, who hath attended on Arabella and read to her for the space of three year and a half, showed to be much discontented since my return into the country, in saying he had lived in hope of having some annuity granted him by Arabella out her land, or some lease of grounds to the value of £40 a year, alleging that he was so much damnified by leaving of the University . . . I understanding by divers that Morley was so much discontented, and withal of late having some cause to be doubtful of his forwardness in religion (though I cannot charge him with papistry), took occasion to part with him. After he was gone from my house, and his stuff carried from hence, the next day he returned again, very importunate to serve.

In a letter to the *Times Literary Supplement* [27 February 1937] E. St John Brooks broached the possibility that this was Marlowe. His suggestion has been more or less ignored since, but it seemed to me to merit investigation. It certainly sounds like Marlowe in some ways: a university man, 'discontented' and 'importunate' and showing a dangerous 'forwardness' in religion. The business about Morley's university career is obscure, but could just possibly refer to the troubled circumstances of Marlowe's graduation in 1587. The position of tutor was one which attracted writers, then as now. Watson,

Nashe, Samuel Daniel and others held this position in well-to-do families, so why not Marlowe?

On internal evidence it is possible – not convincingly probable, but possible – that Arabella Stuart's tutor, who attended on her and read to her, and whose 'stuff' was carted away in September 1592, was Christopher Marlowe.

What Brooks did not grasp, and what fascinated me about this possibility, was the political undertone. If Morley really was Marlowe, this would place him in a key position in the succession-game. Arabella Stuart was the centre of Catholic intrigue. In 1591, when she was eighteen, plans were afoot to marry her to Rainutio Farnese, son of the Duke of Parma. English agents were busy meddling and projecting in these plans, among them Poley's man Michael Moody. In August 1591, it was reported that Moody 'is busy in getting the picture of Arabella to carry to the Duke of Parma, and has Mr V's letter to aid him therein to Hildyard' [PRO SP12/239, f.164]. Mr V is Vice-Chamberlain Heneage, Poley's boss; Hildyard is the famous miniaturist Nicholas Hilliard. In October Moody wrote to Heneage from Flushing, enquiring if the portrait was ready, for someone is 'very desirous to see it' [HMC Cecil 4, 144–5]. A few months later there was Catholic gossip of an 'intended match' between Arabella and Burghley's grandson, William. The latter was said to be 'prettily instructed in atheism', and 'will not stick openly to scoff at the Bible'. Another rumour connected Arabella with Marlowe's patron, the Earl of Northumberland.

In these ways, Morley the tutor began to seem more and more like Christopher Marlowe the poet-spy: someone placed close to this rather poignant Catholic figurehead, working these cross-currents of intrigue which also involved Poley and Moody, Burghley and Northumberland.

But I cannot call him Marlowe because I want him to be Marlowe. There are too many uncertainties. The main argument against the identification is Marlowe's presence elsewhere. Morley had been tutoring Arabella at Hardwick House 'for the space of three year and a half', i.e. since early 1589. Marlowe was 'lately resident in Norton Folgate' when he fought on Hog Lane in September 1589; was sharing a chamber with Thomas Kyd in mid-1591; was coining in Flushing in January 1592; and was threatening the constables of Shoreditch in May 1592. This is a big question mark against the theory. It is not an insuperable one, because we need not assume Morley was continuously present at Hardwick, but it spreads his presence there pretty thin. (By 13 September 1592 Marlowe was in Canterbury, but this may have been after Morley's dismissal from Hardwick: the Countess does not say how recently this had happened.)

There is also, once again, another Morley flitting around the story. In September 1591, in a newsletter from the Low Countries [PRO SP12/240, no. 19], Charles Paget wrote:

I have seen Morley, that plays on the organ in Paul's. He seemed to be a good Catholic, yet intercepting some letters that Mr Nowell wrote to him I discovered enough to have hanged him, but as he with tears asked forgiveness on his knees, I let him go. I hear that since his coming thither he has played the promoter, and apprehended Catholics.

This was the composer Thomas Morley, organist at St Paul's Cathedral and later Gentleman of the Chapel Royal. What he was up to I do not know, but it is interesting that Paget's letter was addressed to 'Giles Martin', an alias of the English spy Thomas Barnes, who at this time was himself involved in 'matters touching Lady Arabella'. Barnes reported directly to Thomas Phelippes. His reply to Paget's letter, drafted up by Phelippes [ibid, no. 53], includes this:

I have been sought for as the practiser of a marriage between Arabella and the Duke of Parma's son, which is given out to be my errand to England. I marvel at not hearing of these things from you. It is true that Morley the singing man employs himself in that kind of service, and has brought divers into danger.

This is suggestive, and on the basis of it Arabella's

biographer, P.M. Handover, suggests that the tutor at Hardwick was a kinsman of Thomas Morley. (It cannot be Morley himself, who was employed at St Paul's.) This is by no means conclusive. In Phelippes's letter Morley and Arabella are adjacent but not actually connected: 'that kind of service' refers back to Paget's comment about Morley playing the 'promoter'.

The balance is probably against the tutor being Marlowe, but perhaps this trail should be investigated further. In the Talbot Papers at the College of Arms there is a mass of documents about Hardwick House: those that have so far been calendared contain no mention of Morley.

4 MARLOWE'S HOMOSEXUALITY

I count this as a false trail, because it has so often been advanced, in an uncritical way, as a clue to the killing of Marlowe (see for example BBC2's *Christopher Marlowe: An Inquest*, 1986).

Was Marlowe gay? There are really two kinds of evidence. First, the imputation of homosexuality in the Baines 'Note', which reports Marlowe as saying 'all they that love not tobacco and boys were fools'. Baines is a dubious source, but there would be little point in him making the allegation if Marlowe were actually known to be vigorously heterosexual. There is also the remark about Christ and St John being lovers, which is retailed as Marlowe's by both Baines and Kyd. Secondly, his plays show a marked interest in homosexual relations. This ranges from the canoodlings of Jove and Ganymede at the opening of *Dido* (probably his earliest play) to the unexpectedly sympathetic portrait of Henri III in *Massacre at Paris*, and is epitomised in the intense, destructive relationship between Gaveston and Edward in *Edward II*.

But even if one says yes, of course Marlowe was gay, there still remain problems of definition. In his excellent study, *Homosexuality in Renaissance England*, Alan Bray shows how the whole issue is clouded with imponderables. Much of the surviving comment on it is stereotyped and moralistic. The social norms were different. Men 'lay together' because beds were scarce, and kissed because it was the Italian fashion. We do not quite know what it meant to be gay in Elizabethan England.

The idea that Marlowe died because of his homosexuality – a cover-up by Thomas Walsingham, or a *crime passionnel* like the killing of Joe Orton – is entertaining, but is no more than a novelistic convenience.

5 CONSPIRACY THEORIES

Inasfar as my reading of the case is a conspiracy theory, I am bound to include as false trails the other conspiracy theories put forward to explain his death. There are really only two major theories, both following hot on the heels of Hotson's recovery of the inquest. There have been variations on them since, but no complete new theory until now.

The first was advanced by Dr Samual Tannenbaum in 1926, the year after Hotson's find. According to Tannenbaum, Marlowe was murdered at the instigation of Sir Walter Ralegh, in order to prevent him from giving evidence to the Council about Ralegh's 'atheism'. This is improbable because it rests on the premise that Ralegh *really* had something to hide. The historical evidence (primarily the Bindon commission of 1594) suggests the opposite: that there was never any real evidence of Ralegh's 'atheism', only rumour and innuendo. I also suspect the scenario on intuitive grounds: it seems so unlike Ralegh. I believe Tannenbaum made a correct deduction – that Ralegh is a key figure in the case – but then got it entirely the wrong way round. Ralegh was not a perpetrator of these events, but a victim of them; and Marlowe was killed not to conceal a truth about Ralegh, but to protect a lie about him.

A more ingenious theory was set out by Eugénie de Kalb, who was actually on the track of Marlowe's death, by a different route, at the same time as Hotson. She too doubts the inquest, and believes there was a political murder. For her, the *éminence grise* of the murder was Audrey Walsingham, the wife of Marlowe's patron, with whom Frizer's name was associated in certain financial dealings. Noting how Audrey

Walsingham's fortunes blossomed when King James came to the throne in 1603, de Kalb argued that she had been a political intriguer in James's favour while the succession was still in doubt. She links this with Kyd's statement about Marlowe intending to 'go unto' the King of Scots, and with Poley's active role in Scottish intrigue in the early 1590s. The stabbing of Marlowe was in some way a product of this intrigue.

This is far more developed than Tannenbaum's theory, but it has one major flaw: the dates. There is no evidence that Audrey was married to Thomas Walsingham in 1593. The first that is heard of them as a couple is in 1597, when the Queen visited Scadbury and Thomas was knighted. It is generally thought that this celebrated their wedding. The following year, George Chapman dedicated his continuation of *Hero and Leander* to her: clearly he had no inkling of her complicity in the murder of his friend. He writes: 'This poor dedication, in figure of the other unity betwixt Sir Thomas and yourself, hath rejoined you with him, my honoured best friend.' This is obscure, as Chapman tends to be, but seems to suggest that the marriage was recent. Frizer's property-dealings on her behalf are a good deal later: the earliest on record is 1602.

A recent theory (M. J. Trow, *Who Killed Kit Marlowe?*, 2001) hinges on the idea that Richard Cholmeley genuinely had evidence that Lord Burghley and other government figures were 'sound atheists', and that Marlowe was killed as part of a cover-up of this fact. This is highly implausible in itself, and unsatisfactory because it takes Cholmeley's statements (or rather the statements attributed to him in the 'Remembrances') at face value. Though presented as an investigation, the book belongs within a novelistic tradition which depends on the activities of secret sects (typically the so-called 'School of Night') to solve the mystery. At the time of writing, various feature films based on the case are allegedly 'in production'. If any of them ever gets to the screen, it is unlikely to throw light on the case, having invented things which never really happened, and characters who never really existed, in order to fill up the gaps in the story.

Another theory goes something likes this. Marlowe did not

die at Deptford. The affray was a blind: the body that was viewed by the coroner's jury was someone else's. Marlowe was spirited out of the country, and thereafter dedicated his life to writing plays. These plays went out under the *nom de plume* of 'William Shakespeare'. They contain many acrostics and anagrams that prove they are Marlowe's, but people still go on thinking they are by Shakespeare.

This is no kind of trail at all.

Appendix 2: Supplement to the
Second Edition

1. THE FATAL WOUND

Mr J. Thompson Rowling, a general surgeon in Sheffield, offers some additional observations on the 'surgical pathology' of a wound to the orbit, or eye-socket, as described in the inquest [letter, 30 June 1998].

'It is almost certain that the wound was through the orbit and above the eyeball. The orbit is roofed by a thin plate of bone, the superior orbital plate, and terminates posteriorly in the superior orbital fissure. Just posteriorly to the fissure lies the termination of the internal carotid artery where it divides into its two terminal branches, the middle and anterior cerebral arteries. Now, the only condition which would cause rapid death would be intercranial bleeding from a major vessel, and here the coroner's assessment of the depth of the wound is of great importance. He places it at two inches ['*profunditatis duorum pollicium*'], although it might be difficult to assess the depth of such a wound using a probe. Using a skull and calipers the distance between the skin of the eyelid and the internal carotid is almost exactly 2 inches . . . It is therefore perfectly possible and very likely that rapid death was caused by injury to the internal carotid by the point of the dagger. The cause of death would not be from blood loss but from cerebral compression caused by the intracranial haematoma associated with the arterial injury.'

Rowling rejects the possibility of an embolism having caused Marlowe's death. 'It has been suggested that death was due to an air embolus from the circular venous [or cavernous] sinus which surrounds the carotid at this point. However, the normal pressure in the sinus approximates to atmospheric pressure, and with a long narrow wound it is unlikely that such an air embolism could take place.'

In a further letter [10 October 1998] Rowling questions whether Marlowe would have died 'instantly', as claimed in the inquest. 'A lot would depend on whether the artery was severed or merely injured, but I would think he would have lost consciousness in three to four minutes, and be dead in twenty minutes or so. The later account, when he was said to have "died swearing", may well be true. Certainly a dagger wound in the right orbit would be an occasion where a little bad language might be held to be justifiable!'

Gavin Thurston, a coroner in the County of London (Western District), mentions another possible cause of death: 'There is another phenomenon known to opthalmic surgeons as the oculo-cardiac reflex, in which the heart's action is disturbed during operations on the eye. It is rare but could also explain sudden death in an orbital wound' [Thurston, p. 199].

2. FRIZER, DEANE AND CHAMBERLAIN

The conjecture that there were family connections between these men is strengthened by the discovery of another, later Ingram Frizer, and the fact that he lived at Kingsclere in Hampshire, the seat of the Chamberlain family. He died there in the summer of 1639 (twelve years after the death of 'our' Ingram). His will was proved on 3 June. This Ingram is described as the son of 'Peeter Friser'. It seems quite possible that Peter was a brother (or cousin) of Ingram Frizer the poet-killer, and that the junior namesake was therefore Ingram Frizer's nephew (or younger cousin). Peter's wife is identified as Agnes, and may well be the 'Agnes Chamberlyn' of Kingsclere mentioned in a document of 1581. If so, the fulcrum of Frizer's connection with the Chamberlains, and thence with the Deanes, would be his hitherto-unknown relative Peter. It is also to be noted, however, that an earlier generation of the Chamberlain family features an Ingram

Chamberlain; the name is not a common one, so it looks as if the family connections may go further back than this. [Data from the International Genealogical Index at *www.familysearch.com*. I am grateful to Lisa Hopkins of Sheffield University for drawing my attention to this.]

Further material on Deane and Frizer was published by Albert Freeman in 1993 [TLS, 23 June 1993], in the form of a College of Arms list of the mourners at Deane's funeral in May 1608. Ninety-two are named, in marching order, and midway in the vanguard comes 'Mr Frizar'. He was doubtless wearing the cloak of black cloth stipulated in Deane's bequest to him. Freeman notes the presence among the mourners of a certain Paul Bannings or Bayning, a wealthy merchant and grocer, and a London alderman like Deane. He had also, Freeman discovered, served a single term as Sheriff of London in the very year, 1593, when Frizer was charged with homicide. 'So influential an ally, indirect or direct, cannot but have stood the accused in good stead'. If there is anything 'suspicious' about the speed of Frizer's trial and pardon, Freeman suggests, it may be through 'friends and friends-of-friends in high places' – the likes of Bayning and Deane – rather than because of a more political cover-up of the sort alleged by the 'conspiracy theorists'.

3. SKERES AND THE EARL OF ESSEX

The discovery by Paul Hammer of a previously unknown letter by Nicholas Skeres adds to our knowledge of him and his relations with the Essex circle. It was found among the Devereux papers at Longleat, and is addressed 'to my most esteemed friend Gellie Mericke'. Gilly or Gelly Meyrick was a long-term confidant of Essex, and would later die at Tyburn for his part in the Essex Rising; the 'Lord' referred to in Skeres's letter is unquestionably Essex. The letter is autograph but not holograph: only the signature is in Skeres's hand. The poor penmanship of his signature perhaps explains why he got someone else to copy out the letter. The text itself is presumably Skeres's: it provides a unique example of his literary style (though we had already something of his verbal style from the Star Chamber deposition) and has some interesting phrasal quirks.

The letter is undated, but as it refers to 'good Mr Mireke' it must have been written before the summer of 1596, when Meyrick was knighted by Essex for his valour at Cadiz. It may indeed be the Cadiz expedition that Skeres is referring to when he asks Meyrick to 'help me in my present suit to my Lord, which is for some employment and charge in these affairs that are now in hand'. Skeres had already soldiered for Essex in France, and may have been on the Portugal voyage; Meyrick took part in both these ventures. If this is right, the letter would be dateable to spring 1596, when preparations for the Cadiz expedition were visibly 'in hand'. On the other hand, his use of the word 'affairs' does not seem quite right for a military expedition. Given what we know of Skeres's career it may refer to something rather dodgier, such as the labyrinthine political dealings surrounding the 'Lopez affair' of 1593–4, a complex and discreditable episode which ended with the hanging of the Queen's physician Roderigo Lopez, and which certainly involved Essex agents.

The letter both confirms Skeres's long association with the Essex circle – 'Good Mr Mireke, respect my long service and travail' – and suggests that he has in some way fallen out of favour. He hopes his suit to the Earl will not be 'cast off'; its success would, he says, be 'the readiest means for me to recover my umbered blemish'. The refrain that runs through the letter is that he is a reformed man – 'Though I have heretofore forsaken the ways of my good, I am so tired with those walks, as all my labour shall be spent to redress my life'; and again, 'Now I return to myself that have been long a stranger to myself, and do lay upon the love it hath pleased you to bear me.' The sign-off is a positive flourish of abjection – 'Now nothing or worse, but if ever anything, at your commandment'.

One hears in the style something of the man. I particularly like that 'umbered' blemish ('hombred' in Skeres's spelling). The word is given in OED as a participle adjective from the verb 'umber', which in turn has a dual meaning of 'to shadow' [French *ombrer*] and 'to stain or paint with umber'. The general sense is therefore shadowed or darkened, here used figuratively. The earliest use recorded in OED is from Shakespeare's *Henry V* ('each battle sees the other's umbered face'); this is from c.1599, and is thus predated by Skeres. The word was also used in heraldry: Randall Cotgrave's French dictionary of 1611 translates *ombré* as 'umbered or shadowed: a term in Blazon' [i.e. coats of arms]. Another interesting word in the letter is 'avoke': Skeres wishes 'to avoke your thoughts to help me'. One would be tempted to transcribe this as 'evoke', but the word is distinct; it stems from Latin *avocare* as opposed to *evocare*; it is given in OED, though now 'obs'. Its contemporary meaning is given in Henry Cockeram's 1623 dictionary: 'to call from or back again'. It is therefore a very precise use Skeres is making: to call *back* Meyrick's favour which, as the letter makes abundantly clear, Skeres feels has been alienated from him. He once again provides an earlier use than is recorded in OED. These give us a new glimpse of Skeres's intellectual qualities: there is a touch of the showy wordsmith in these usages. His connection with poets like Marlowe, Roydon, Chapman and Lodge has rubbed off on him; he moves here another step closer to Marlowe.

The great unanswered question of the letter, of course, is what exactly is this murky 'blemish' which has in some way blighted Skeres's standing with Meyrick, and by implication with Essex himself. Of known incidents in his career, as Hammer observes, the phrase might point either to his appearance in Star Chamber or to his involvement in the killing of Marlowe. The former seems less likely: loan-sharking is a constant of Skeres's career, and it would be improbably fastidious of Meyrick to withdraw his favour just because of Skeres's appearance in court on minor charges arising from the prosecution of John Wolfall. Could the Marlowe killing be the 'blemish'? One cannot say for certain – it may be some unknown crime Skeres is repenting of; or it may be that the 'blemish' does not, after all, refer to one particular incident – but it is at least a possible inference. This would raise further questions about the 'official story' of the killing, which features Skeres only as a blameless bystander.

[Longleat, Devereux MS 1, fol. 306; P.E.J. Hammer, 'A Reckoning Reframed', *English Literary Renaissance* 26.2, 1996]

4. THE BULLS

Among the other Whitneys mentioned in Blanche Parry's will is one called Eustace [Urry, p. 85]. He is very probably the Eustace Whitney of Whitney, Herefordshire, recorded in the International Genealogical Index. He was born in the mid-1540s, he married Margaret *née* Vaughan, and he died in July 1608. His daughter was called Eleanor. She is certainly too young to be the Eleanor Whitney who became Mrs Bull in 1571. It is entirely plausible, however, that Eustace Whitney was Eleanor Bull's brother, and named his daughter after her. If this is right, Eleanor Bull's father was Robert Whitney, who was born in Icomb, Gloucestershire, in about 1517, and died at Whitney in August 1567; and her mother was Sybill *née* Baskerville of Eardisley, near Hereford. This would add another illustrious family connection: Sir Thomas Baskerville, the veteran military commander described by Marlowe's friend Thomas Nashe as 'one of the most tried soldiers of Christendom', would be Mrs Bull's cousin. One also notes that Eustace Whitney's wife was a Vaughan. The name is common in the Welsh borders, but it is not impossible that William Vaughan of Golden Grove – the author of a very well-informed account of Marlowe's death published in 1600 [see chapter 10] – had some kind of family connection with Mrs Bull.

Richard Bull, husband of Eleanor, can be fleshed out a little more. He was very probably the son of Richard Bull, a 'master shipwright' who was working in Deptford from c 1550, and is last heard of in 1572 [W. Perrin, ed, *The Autobiography of Phineas Pett*, Navy Record Society, 1918, xxi-xiii]. I am grateful to Richard Wilson of Lancaster University for alerting me to this, though I cannot go all the way with his effort to connect Bull with Marlowe, and to place the killing within the context of a giant profiteering scam connected with the Muscovy Company. He nonetheless produces some fascinating background on the Deptford milieu. As a master shipwright, Richard Bull senior would have worked under the Treasurer of the Navy; throughout his known career this was Benjamin Gonson, who held the post from 1549 to 1577. As a bailiff at Sayes Court, Richard Bull junior – Eleanor's husband – worked for the Clerk of the Green Cloth, Christopher Browne, whose wife was Gonson's granddaughter. This at least shows that Eleanor Bull's husband, and presumably Eleanor herself, would have been known to the well-heeled and well-connected Gonson family. It becomes more interesting, for a moment at least, because Benjamin Gonson's nephew was another Deptford businessman, and his name was Anthony Marlowe. This Marlowe was born in London in 1544, and was chief 'agent' of the Muscovy Company from 1576 to 1599; the hub of the Company's activities was Deptford, where the warehouses were crammed with Russian timber, cordage and other imports. The governor of the Company was George Barne, whose daughter was married to another Marlowe, Anthony's first cousin, Walter. George Barne was in turn a brother-in-law of Sir Francis Walsingham, and so the ramifications continue.

Anthony Marlowe has been known about for some time, and unfortunately for Wilson's thesis there is no known connection between him and the Marlowes of Canterbury. The matter was studied carefully by de Kalb [pp. 26–7]: she found that 'the greater part of the London Marlowes had roots in Yorkshire', that Anthony Marlowe's will revealed Yorkshire relatives but not Kentish ones, and that his connection with Kent went no further back than his father (also Anthony), who had purchased the manor at Crayford. Without new evidence to the contrary, there is no evidence that Christopher and Anthony Marlowe shared anything except a surname. As researchers have found to their cost, the name was by no means uncommon. Another interesting figure, Edmund Marlowe – a sea-captain known to Christopher Marlowe's friend Thomas Hariot – has similarly resisted attempts to blood-relate him to the poet. The idea that Anthony Marlowe was the 'cause . . . of the dramatist's fatal connection with the Deptford docks' is not sustainable;

nor is there any evidence for Wilson's further assertion that the Bulls' house in Deptford Strand was some kind of 'customs house' for the Muscovy Company. [R. Wilson, 'Visible Bullets: *Tamberlaine the Great* and Ivan the Terrible', in Grantley and Roberts, pp. 51–69.]

5. NASHE IN NEWGATE

If the religious tone of *Christ's Tears* is in part a reaction to the arrests of Kyd and Marlowe in May 1593, and to the charges of heresy hanging over them, it is perhaps ironic that Nashe's jeremiad resulted in his own arrest and imprisonment, as revealed by two recently discovered documents. In a letter dated 13 November 1593, Sir George Carey wrote to his wife: 'Nashe hath dedicated a book unto you, with promise of a better. Will Cotton will disburse v li [£5] or xx nobles [£6 13s 4d] in your reward to him, and he shall not find my purse shut to relieve him out of prison, there presently in great misery, malicied for writing against the Londoners' [Berkeley Castle, General Series Letters, Bundle 4; Katherine Duncan-Jones, '*Christs Teares*, Nashe's "Forsaken Extremities" ', RES 49. 194 (1998), pp. 167–80]. The offending passage begins: 'London, thou art the seeded garden of sin, the sea that sucks in all the scummy channels of the realm' [Nashe, 2.158–9]; it was substituted with a toned-down version in the second edition of 1594. Carey's comment about Nashe being 'malicied' may refer to the activities of Gabriel Harvey, whom Nashe later describes as 'incensing my L. Mayor . . . to persecute me' (*Have with you*; Nashe, 3.95). He was almost certainly held in Newgate, for on 20 November 'Thomas Nash *generosus*' was bound over to 'appear at the next sessions of Gaol delivery of Newgate . . . to make answer to all such matters as shall be objected against him on her Majesty's behalf' [Repertory for the Court of Aldermen 23, fol 125; Lorna Hutson, 'Thomas Nashe's persecution by the Aldermen', NQ 232 (1987), pp. 199–200]. Carey apparently managed to 'relieve him out of prison', and Nashe was a guest of the family at Carisbrooke Castle, Isle of Wight, over Christmas 1593 'and a great while after' (*Have with you*;

Nashe, 3.96). His *Terrors of the Night* (1594) is full of gratitude for Carey's help in his 'most forsaken extremities', and is dedicated to Carey's teenage daughter Elizabeth.

These events have their own internal consistency: a particular passage of Nasheian invective; a heavy-handed reaction by the London civic authorities; the assistance of friends (the Careys) and the meddling of enemies (Harvey). But they seem also to belong with those other events of mid-1593. A few months after the arrest and torture of Thomas Kyd on charges of libelling, a few months after the apprehension of Marlowe and his violent death at Deptford, another of this troublesome literary crew – one closely associated with Marlowe – is arrested and clapped up in Newgate. One has a suspicion that the passage 'against the Londoners' was something of a pretext for punitive action; that we are witnessing a more general policy of suppression, a clean-up of this element of dissident authorship too bent on pushing the boundaries of 'the liberty of speech'.

6. NICHOLAS FAUNT

Peter Roberts notes: 'The connection between Faunt and Marlowe is closer than hitherto suspected. For Faunt also came from Canterbury and not, as the *Dictionary of National Biography* has it, from Norwich. He was one of the first scholars from Canterbury School to go to Cambridge under the Parker Foundation of 1569 . . . Whether their paths crossed in Canterbury, Cambridge or London, sober history does not relate, but it is legitimate to speculate whether a "Cambridge connection" worked at this level as a route to a covert career in the intelligence service open to the talents of the university wits' ['The "Studious Artizan": Christopher Marlowe, Canterbury and Cambridge', in Grantley and Roberts, 1996, p. 27]. Hasler [2, pp. 109–10] confirms that Faunt was the son of John Faunt of Canterbury, and was – like Marlowe – a pupil at King's, Canterbury. This makes it very plausible that Faunt knew (or knew of) Marlowe, this clever young man some ten years his junior, so precisely following his own aspirant footsteps from Canterbury to Corpus. It does not, of course, prove that Faunt recruited him to government service in c1585, but it provides a strong personal context in which he might have done so. (That Faunt was a close friend of Anthony Bacon raises the possibility of homosexuality as another personal context; that he was a zealous Puritan, and twice married, does not encourage this speculation, though does not quite rule it out.)

And so one looks again at Faunt's political career in the mid-1580s, and particularly at his French activities. His visit to Paris in 1587, which I mention because it coincides with Marlowe's absence from Cambridge, was only one episode in a long involvement with France. We find him in Paris as early as 1572, aged about eighteen; he witnessed the St Bartholomew's Day massacre of Protestants, and was one of the first to bring news of it to England; it is likely he was already employed by Sir Francis Walsingham, then ambassador in Paris, though this is not certain. This could be related to Marlowe's *Massacre at Paris*, with its vivid if bleak reportage of the event. Some of Marlowe's printed sources are identifiable – French histories, newsletters, etc – but there were doubtless oral sources too: among them, perhaps, the eye-witness Faunt.

Among Faunt's French dealings during the years 1585–87 – the likely period in which Marlowe did his 'good service' to the government – are the following.

In early 1586, probably in Paris, he supplies money to the slippery Salomon Aldred, a key player in Walsingham's attempts to turn certain English Catholics in Rheims; some of this money is conveyed to Dr William Gifford – Professor of Theology at Rheims, and a particular target of Walsingham's – and some is used to pay the unnamed messenger who acted as Aldred's courier between Paris and Rheims in the absence of his more regular go-between, John Toper or Tupper [Aldred to Walsingham, 27 March and 14 April 1586, CSP Foreign 1585–6, pp. 710, 725]. It is not impossible that this messenger glimpsed at Rheims in the spring of 1586 was Marlowe.

Early the following year Ambassador Stafford requests Walsingham to send over 'some trusty body' to Paris to debrief an unnamed intelligence source. The latter may be Aldred again, or perhaps the wavering seminarist Edmund

Grately alias Foxley; whoever he is, he knows and trusts
Faunt, and considers him 'honest and discreet', so Faunt is
clearly the man for the job [Stafford to Walsingham, January
1587, CSP Foreign 1586–88, p. 215]. Shortly after this Faunt
is indeed in Paris. While there he learns, from Stafford, about
an assassination plot against the Queen (one of many that
never got past the plotting stage, and may have been largely
imaginary anyway). On 24 March, not long after Faunt's
return to England, Stafford writes to Walsingham about this
would-be assassin: 'Mr Faunt hath seen the man, and
knoweth him very well, and . . . knoweth where he shall haunt
in England, and where to find him out' [ibid, p. 250].

In May 1587 another of Walsingham's Paris agents,
William Waad, writes to him about a certain 'suspected
person', who has been 'accused by some who are not to be
credited'; despite his 'discontentment' he has 'done good
service' in Paris, and would, Waad thinks, 'be a very fit man
to be employed and to perform good and special service'.
Apparently Faunt thinks so too, for he has already 'dealt with'
Walsingham on this man's behalf [Waad to Walsingham,
4 May 1587, ibid p. 288]. It is tempting to think that this
potentially useful malcontent favoured by Faunt is
Christopher Marlowe, and that Waad's assessment of him is
echoed in the phrases of the Privy council certificate issued
just a few weeks later, but the likelihood is that Waad is
referring to William Lilly, a secretary of Stafford's long under
suspicion of double-dealing [cf ibid p. 336]. Faunt's favouring
of him would not be surprising, since Lilly was himself a
Canterbury man; the dramatist John Lilly or Lyly was
probably his brother.

If Marlowe *did* travel to France in Faunt's employ he would
very probably have had dealings with the English embassy in
Paris, and could have mingled with such members of
Ambassador Stafford's retinue as Michael Moody [see
Chapter 27], Samuel Daniel [see Chapter 18], and perhaps
even Thomas Drury, who is almost certainly the 'secretary' of
Stafford's referred to by a French writer as 'Dewry' in a letter
of September 1587 [see Chapter 34]. Despite the persuasive

connection between Faunt and Marlowe, however, it remains the case that there is no discernible mention of the poet amid these fragmentary records of Faunt's French missions.

7. BAINES AT RHEIMS

Further documentation of Richard Baines at Rheims is provided by Roy Kendall ['Richard Baines and Christopher Marlowe's milieu', ELR 24.3, 1994, pp.507–552]. It has been known that Baines made an 'oral confession' while in the town gaol in Rheims; Boas mentions this *en passant* but throws no further light on it. This confession was made earlier than the printed recantation, which was written down a month or so *after* his release. A contemporary transcript or précis of it, in Latin, has now been tracked down by Kendall in the Westminster Diocesan Archives [AAW/A III, No 26, ff. 103–4]. The 'neat hand' of the MS is not actually Baines's (which is known from the 'Baines Note'). It may have been written by one of the two Rheims priests, Thomas Bailey and Laurence Webb, who are named as witnesses of the confession (Cardinal Allen was also present, but it is not in his hand). The document is not entirely in Baines's own words, since it contains some brief interpolations (in which the pronoun switches from 'I' to 'he'), but it is undoubtedly a new window onto his personality.

It might be assumed that the oral confession would be substantially the same as the printed version, but it turns out to contain a number of points and phrases not found in the latter. Here are some interesting extracts (translation by Christopher Upton):

Arrogantly I made examination of the mystical ceremonies [of the Catholic mass] . . . and in secret conversations I said that they were no more than pretty gestures, performing which even a Turk would look holy; and that without them the rest of the mass was nothing but Bale-worship [interpolation: 'a term of scoffing blasphemy'; the reference is to John Bale, a Protestant author much despised by Catholics] . . .

Concerning Purgatory, I said that there was no fire by which souls may be tortured, but it was the worm of conscience. [Interpolation: 'But a witness swore that he said this about Hell'. If the witness spoke true, Baines was voicing something very like Dr Faustus's view that 'hell's a fable'] . . .

I said that the Pope's excommunication was like a braggart's dagger, which he continually brandishes against men for the most trivial reasons . . .

On the Church, I disliked people calling it our mother, being a rotten form of words, and I said that the Church of the Papists was overgrown with age, mould and filth . . .

I laughed at various ceremonies and rites which some use when scourging the tomb of one who had been excommunicated, adding that this stupidity was like Ajax in his madness, beating everyone he met because he believed it to be his enemy, Ulysses.

As Kendall notes, the tone of the oral confession is lighter; it catches a note of scathing wit in the phrasings. The printed confession, done up for public consumption, is shaped into a heartfelt recantation of former heresies; here, the heresies are itemised bluntly and without covering comment. This note of levity makes even more pronounced that closeness of Baines and Marlowe which I discerned on the basis of the printed confession. Thus the idea that the Baines 'Note' of 1593 is the product of a man shocked and scandalised by Marlowe's blasphemies becomes less and less tenable.

A couple of other points from this new text. As in the written confession, Baines mentions having promised his confederate that Walsingham would give them 3000 crowns for their information about the seminary, but here he adds drily that this was 'in order to convince my companion, rather than because I knew it to be true'. He also says that having delivered his information to the English government he 'intended to find employment in the palace and family of some noblewoman, who would raise me to a position of honour'. And I cannot resist noting Baines's comment that Cardinal Allen could be assassinated 'by one bullet from a harquebus which can be fired without making a noise', which furnishes a curiously modern image of the hit-man with silenced gun.

A separate discovery by the Catholic historian Michael Questier ['English Clerical Converts to Protestantism', *Recusant History* 2, 1991, 455–77] offers further insight into Baines's role at the seminary. On 2 May 1582, an unnamed English agent despatched a report from Paris addressed to Walsingham [PRO SP15/27A, f 120]. Among various 'advertisements' is the following brief report: 'Banes has had the strappado and is often tormented'. That Baines was tortured is implied in his own written confession, which refers to the 'bodily afflictions' he had suffered. The date of this report in fact shows that he was under interrogation some weeks prior to Allen's first reference to the case (in his letter to Agazzari, 28 May). More importantly, the phrasing of the bulletin – the lack of any contextual explanation – confirms that Baines was *already* known to Walsingham at that time. One could not be sure about this on the basis of the confessions, where his plans to divulge information to Walsingham need not imply any previous dealing between them; nor was Allen's statement that Baines had communicated 'daily' with the Privy Council throughout his time at the seminary very convincing. The Paris report is convincing precisely because of its casualness; it implies that Walsingham knew precisely who Baines was, and what his situation was.

In the first edition I sought to show that Baines was already known to be Walsingham's man in 1580, and that he was briefly mentioned as such by the spy Charles Sledd in a manuscript of around that date [BL MS 48029, ff. 121–30; CRS 53, pp. 193–225]. Noting the large number of scribal errors in the manuscript (which is a contemporary copy of Sledd's diary) I argued that a certain 'Mr Wanes' whom Sledd met in Paris in April 1580, and whom he describes as a spy 'belonging to' Walsingham, was in reality Baines. On the one hand, his activities seemed to tie in with Baines; on the other hand, I could find no documentary trace of a Walsingham spy called Wanes. As Kendall points out, however, this thesis – which depends on the copyist having mistaken Sledd's capital 'B' for a 'W' – is rather scuppered by a later reference in the MS to the real Baines, in a list of names under the heading 'At Remes'. I have therefore removed the paragraphs advancing my 'Wanes = Baines' theory. Whether Kendall is right in suggesting that 'Wanes' is actually William Wade or Waad (certainly a Walsingham agent but not documented before 1585) I am not sure. The Paris report discovered by Questier re-establishes the link between Baines and Walsingham, visible by early 1582 if not by 1580.

8. 'AT MIDDLEBOROUGH'

Marlowe's presence in the Low Countries in 1591–2 touches on another matter, which I did not pursue in the first edition, suspecting it might be one tangent too many. I put up some ideas on the subject in a paper read at Kent University in 1993 ['At Middleborough', in Grantley and Roberts, 1996, pp. 38–50] and I give here a précis of my argument. It concerns the mysterious first edition of Marlowe's *Elegies* (i.e. his translations of Ovid's *Amores*). These are early works in the canon, often said to have been written at Cambridge; some are very erotic by the standards of the day. The undated first edition contained only ten of them; the full complement (forty-eight) appeared in a later edition of c 1602. In all the early editions Marlowe's elegies appear together with a selection of epigrams by John Davies. The first edition was entitled *Epigrammes and Elegies By I.D. and C.M.*, and according to the title-page it was printed 'at Middleborough'.

This 'Middleborough' is not, of course, the Teesside town of Middlesborough, but the Dutch town of Middelburg, capital of the province of Zeeland, where there was a small but thriving printing industry. Despite the actual existence of Middelburg printers, however, the almost universal view about the provenance of the *Epigrams and Elegies* is that the imprint is a 'decoy', in other words a false imprint designed to conceal an unlicensed printing, in England, of poems too risqué to get past the censors. The use of a false foreign imprint was a common enough ruse for potentially 'objection-able' books, though this usually meant subversive rather than sexy books. (An increasingly popular alternative was the humorous or nonsense locative much used by the Marprelate pamphleteers and their adversaries in the late 1580s.) That the 'Middleborough' imprint is false is the view of leading experts like Roma Gill and Robert Krueger ['The Early Editions of Marlowe's *Elegies*: Sequence and Authority', *The Library* 26.3, 1971], and Fredson Bowers ['The Early Editions of Marlowe's *Ovid's Elegies*', *Studies in Bibliography* 25, 1972].

With the basic premise there can be no quarrel: the *Epigrams and Elegies* was hot stuff by Elizabethan standards. This is demonstrable, for in 1599 a list of banned books was drawn up by the Archbishop of Canterbury's censors, and at the head of this index of 'unseemly' works was the *Epigrams and Elegies*. This was some time after the initial publication, but it shows that the publisher of the first edition (or the authors themselves) had good enough reason for avoiding the legitimate, censored channels of publication. So this is undoubtedly a clandestine printing, but the further deduction – that the 'Middleborough' imprint is false – seems to me shakier. There are many cases of books *actually* being printed abroad (again usually for political reasons), and this is the question raised in my mind by the discovery of the Sidney letter in 1975. As we now know – as Gill and Bowers did not – that Marlowe was present in the Low Countries in the early 1590s, is it not possible that the imprint is, after all, genuine? Middelburg is, in fact, only a few miles from Flushing, where Marlowe had his lodgings in early 1592; today the towns are virtually contiguous, about half an hour's bus-ride from centre to centre. We can now virtually locate Marlowe himself 'at Middleborough', so it seems reasonable to suggest that his Ovidian elegies were printed there, as the title-page says they were.

An interesting addition to this is that Marlowe's co-author,

450

John Davies, also turns out to have been in the Netherlands in 1592. This was discovered by Mark Eccles [*Brief Lives: Tudor and Stuart Authors*, 1982, pp. 36–7]. A student at the Middle Temple, Davies and two others were 'put out of commons' for rowdy behaviour, and in the summer they travelled to the Netherlands and enrolled at the University of Leyden. One of the three, Richard Martin, was admitted on 23 July; Davies himself enrolled on 3 September. A letter of 20 October announces their imminent return to England. It was not a long stay – perhaps about three months – but it places Davies, like Marlowe, in physical proximity to Middelburg in 1592. The date of composition of Davies's epigrams is nebulous, but they were certainly composed before 1594, since there is a manuscript copy of them bearing that date. Three of them ('Ad Musam', 'In Paulum' and 'In Dacum') contain dateable references, all of which point to composition in 1591 or 1592. There appears to be no chronological problem with the idea that Davies's epigrams were already composed by the time he arrived in the Low Countries in about July 1592. Their cynical tone and tart *ad hominem* satire might have been a good reason for him to seek a publisher abroad.

There is no evidence, internal or otherwise, that Marlowe and Davies collaborated on the book. It is assumed it was printed from separate authorial manuscripts (or, less probably, from an intervening manuscript which contained both sets of poems). We can now trace a route by which these manuscripts might have arrived at a printing-house in Middelburg. There is documentary evidence that both authors visited the Netherlands in 1592, and there is a coherent motive, later justified by the suppression of the book in 1599, for them to want these particular poems to be printed abroad. I would say it is circumstantially possible, at the least, that the first edition of the *Epigrams and Elegies* was genuinely produced 'at Middleborough', from manuscripts acquired by a printer during, or as a result of, the authors' presence in the area. If it was, it could have been published, at the earliest, in the last months of 1592.

The only true test of this would be bibliographic: a study of texts printed at Middelburg in the 1590s in comparison with the first edition of *Epigrams and Elegies*, which survives in a unique copy at the Huntington Library in California. (There are two early editions extant, known as the 'Isham' and 'Bindley' texts after their previous owners. They contain only minor variants. Bowers argues convincingly that the 'Isham' copy in the Huntington is the earlier: he shows, for instance, that misprints in 'Bindley' derive from broken type in 'Isham'.) One of the Middelburg printers, Richard Schilders, is quite well-known. He had English connections: in the 1570s he had served apprentice, in London, to the printer Thomas East, and some of the books he printed at Middelburg were in English. These were markedly Puritan works – he was particularly associated with the separatist exile Robert Browne – so he is perhaps unlikely to have printed *Epigrams and Elegies*, but it suggests that other Middelburg printers might be checked out for English-language texts.

A separate point I would like to add, on the general theme of Marlowe in the Low Countries, is that his friend and fellow-poet George Chapman was also there in 1591. It has long been thought that his detailed description of the siege of Nijmegen, in *The Shadow of Night*, suggests his presence at the event itself in July 1591. A spell of soldiering in the Low Countries fits in well enough with a later statement in Star Chamber that he had spent some years abroad ('beyond the seas'). This is mentioned in a lawsuit between Chapman and John Wolfall junior, the son and namesake of Nicholas Skeres's accomplice [see Chapter 3]. A document discovered by Willem Schrickx tends to confirm and extend Chapman's presence, for in a list of English soldiers at the military hospital in Middelburg in October 1586 is one 'Joris Tshampen'. It perhaps needs a small leap of faith to make this into George Chapman, but the Dutch clerk had similar difficulty with Rowland Johnson, also admitted on 20 October, who appears as 'Roelandt Janssen'. Both men were then serving under 'Capt Sidtne', none other than Robert Sidney, the future deporter of Marlowe. [Middelburg

Rijksarchief, Staten 1201; Notes & Queries NS Vol 40.2, June 1993, p.165; I am grateful to Professor Schrickx for drawing my attention to this.]

9. CHOLMELEY & THE EARL OF ESSEX

In the first edition I pursued the idea that the Earl of Essex had certain connections with Richard Cholmeley. I based this on a letter from the Earl, dated 10 November 1593, addressed to three of his political fixers, Richard Bagot, Edward Littleton and Edward Aston. In it Essex thanks them for their work on behalf of his 'servant' Richard Cholmeley, and asks them to continue in their efforts to establish Cholmeley's 'innocency'. Following earlier authorities (Boas, Seaton, etc) I argued that this question of Cholmeley's innocence was related to the charges laid against him in the 'Remembrances', and therefore to his involvement in the Marlowe affair. If so, it seemed Cholmeley's role in the affair was sanctioned by the Earl, who was now trying to extricate him from prosecution.

Paul Hammer places this letter in a very different context ['A Reckoning Reframed', *English Literary Renaissance* 26.2, 1996]. What links the three recipients of the letter, he argues, is that they all 'acted in the capacity of deputy-lieutenants for the county of Staffordshire', for which Essex was himself *de facto* Lord Lieutenant. The likelihood that this letter refers to 'lieutenancy matters in Staffordshire' is strengthened by two further discoveries by Hammer. The first is that in the late summer of 1593, a Richard Cholmeley was one of three men attacked by a gang at Forebridge near Stafford. The date of the affray is not clear, but two of the attackers, William Dudley and William Shaw, were charged with assault and battery on 6 October 1593 [Staffordshire Quarter-sessions, Roll 2, 1590–93; in S. Burne, *Collections for a History of Staffordshire*, 1932, pp. 376–77]. Secondly, Hammer points out that there was a Staffordshire Richard Cholmeley to whom this may well refer. He was the second son of Edward Cholmeley of Coppenhall, near Cuttlestone, a few miles south of Stafford. His elder half-brother Henry was born in c 1557, so he was the right sort of age to be involved in the scuffle at

Forebridge in 1593 (unlike the other Richard Cholmeley I mention in the text, a scion of the Cholmeleys of Whitby, who was only born in c 1580).

On the basis of Hammer's findings, it seems clear that Essex's letter of November 1593 has nothing to do with the activities of Richard Cholmeley as spy and provocateur. It refers to another incident entirely, and very probably to another Cholmeley entirely. This removes a major plank in my case that Marlowe died as a result of machinations by secret operatives of the Essex faction. I am not a great fan of the Earl of Essex – for all his swagger he is a pigmy in comparison to his rival, Ralegh – but I withdraw this libel against him. I have reconsidered my whole approach to the events of May 1593 accordingly.

10. THE OTHER THOMAS DRURY

In a petition dated 5 February 1594 [BL Lansdowne MS 76, art 20] a Mr Thomas Drury asked Lord Burghley to recommend him for a 'herald's place' at the College of Arms. In the first edition I took this to be the same Thomas Drury as was involved in the Marlowe case some months previously, but I am now fairly certain he is distinct (I also stated, wrongly, that the Drury letter to Anthony Bacon and the petition to Lord Burghley had similar signatures. They do not: the similarity is between the signatures on Drury's letter to Bacon and the deposition of 1585 concerning John Meeres, which is certainly by 'our' Drury.)

The petitioner describes himself as 'Thomas Drurye of the Inner Temple'. He is therefore likely to be Thomas Drury of Maids Morton, Buckinghamshire, who was admitted to the Inner Temple in November 1576 [*Students Admitted to the Inner Temple 1571–1625*, 1868, p. 23]. This man is distinct from Thomas Drury of Hawstead though they may well have been distant cousins. I cannot trace him precisely, but he is clearly of the Buckinghamshire Drurys: this branch of the family had been established a couple of generations previously by Sir Robert Drury of Hedgerley, a great-uncle of Thomas Drury of Hawstead.

In his petition he says he had been 'trained up' in heraldry at the College of Arms, 'until the death of Mr Clarenceux Harvey under whom he then served, and missing at that time the hoped reward of his pains and service taken, was enforced to employ his study in some sort otherwise than he at that time expected'. William Harvey, the Clarenceux king-of-arms, died at his home in Thame, Oxfordshire, in February 1567 [DNB]. Drury's spell as his pupil and servant can therefore be dated to the mid-1560s; this in turn suggests a loose birthdate of around 1550. He is probably also the Thomas Drury who matriculated at Jesus College, Cambridge, in 1572 [Venn, 1.2 p. 69]. He would then be rather older than the average freshman, but this might be explicable in terms of the biographical information above; having been 'trained up' in heraldry he was 'enforced' to change the direction of his studies after the death of his master in 1567.

If the petitioner to Burghley is Thomas Drury of Maids Morton, so too is the man who wrote to Burghley from the Fleet prison in June 1586: the handwriting is identical. In that letter [PRO SP12/190, no 12] Drury describes himself as 'having been lately' a servant of the Lord Chancellor, Sir Thomas Bromley. This would figure in that Bromley was a prominent figure at the Inner Temple (he became its Treasurer in 1574). It thus appears that Thomas Drury of Hawstead was in the Fleet prison in 1585, and Thomas Drury of Maids Morton was there in 1586.

In 1590, a Thomas Drury was acting for the current Clarenceux king of arms, Robert Cooke, during a heraldic 'visitation' in Kent. It is recorded that Cooke 'allowed' the Bredgates of Dover a coat of arms 'ex relatione Thomas Drurye' [Roy Kendall, 'Richard Baines & Christopher Marlowe', p. 515; W. B. Bannerman, ed, *Visitations of Kent 1574–92*, Harleian Soc, 1924, p. 84]. This sounds like the same man, though it is odd he does not mention this in his petition to Burghley of 1594.

Thomas Drury of Maids Morton has a fairly cogent biography, and a respectable one too, apart from his spell in the Fleet in 1586. He is not Thomas Drury the plotter against

Marlowe, though they were almost certainly related, they are close in age, and they quite probably knew one another.

There is yet another Thomas Drury knocking around, and as he too is described as 'of the Inner Temple' he is liable to cause confusion [e.g. Kendall, p. 496]. He was Thomas Drury of Rougham, Suffolk. He was of a different generation, however. He was born about 1580, admitted to the Inner Temple in 1599, and called to the bar in 1607. He compiled an early history of the family for which later researchers can be grateful, but he has no connection with the events of 1593.

11. JOHN MEERES

I mentioned John Meeres in the first edition solely because of his fleeting link with Drury in the Fleet prison in 1585. My interest in him was considerably sharpened when I came upon his name, quite unexpectedly, in a court-case dating from some thirty years after this. In a complaint lodged in Star Chamber on 11 February 1615 [PRO STAC 8/260/4], the financier William Sanderson gave the following account of him:

John Meere, being a man of very lewd life and conversation, and such a one as hath been heretofore called in
question for forging and counterfeiting of men's hands, and
was a man about twenty years since that served Sir Walter
Ralegh, and was much employed by him, but for many and
foul misdemeanours and offences, as namely for counterfeiting of the said Sir Walter Ralegh's hand, and other
notorious crimes, was put out of his service.

I soon established that this was indeed the same John Meere or Meeres who had been Drury's companion in the Fleet. I also found that Sanderson's account of Meeres's relations with Ralegh was not quite accurate. He had not entered Ralegh's service in 1595 ('twenty years since') but in 1592. There exists a warrant signed by Ralegh, dated 28 August 1592, authorising 'John Meere, my man' to deal with various matters at Sherborne Castle in his capacity as 'keeper of the said castle' and 'overseer of all my woods and timber' [PRO

SP12/242, No. 124]. Meeres was later called Ralegh's 'bailiff' and his 'steward', and received a small bequest in Ralegh's first will of 1597. His period of service seems to have extended from 1592 to about 1600, when there arose those accusations of forgery to which Sanderson alluded. Ralegh claimed, in a letter of 1602: 'he is so cunning in counterfeiting my hand that he will show my discharges for all actions that I can bring against him . . . I found him myself (coming upon him on the sudden) counterfeiting my hand above a hundred times upon an oiled paper' [Agnes Latham and Joyce Youings, *The Letters of Sir Walter Ralegh*, 1999, p. 230]. A document of January 1609 in which Ralegh (then in the Tower) authorises a lease for Meeres, is described by Joyce Youings as 'almost certainly a forgery' by Meeres.

It seemed piquant to find that as Drury hatched his schemes against Ralegh in 1593, there was a former acquaintance of his actually working as part of Ralegh's household down in Sherborne – and a very dodgy acquaintance at that: a man described by Walsingham as 'full of craft', and by Sanderson and Ralegh as a forger, a counterfeiter and a 'barretor' or trouble-maker.

I have gathered a few snippets of his earlier life. He was born at Sherborne in about 1556; his father was a local 'officer' of the Bishop of Salisbury, from whom Ralegh rented Sherborne Castle. He entered the Inner Temple in November 1580, and according to Ralegh he became a servant of Sir Roger Manwood, the Lord Chief Justice, in the early 1580s. All this is a prelude to his appearance in the Fleet, and his dealings with Thomas Drury. Ralegh mentions this imprisonment – 'he was committed to the Fleet out of Star Chamber about Michaelmas 1584, and there fined at 100 marks' – but does not name his crime: he only says vaguely that Meeres was fined 'for knavery'.

In a letter to the judges of the Western Assizes dated 3 March 1602, Ralegh gave vent to a long denunciation of Meeres's past misdeeds. He has some particularly interesting things to say about Meeres's circumstances in 1592:

About 34 Eliz Regine [i.e. 1591–2] he was condemned at Newgate for clipping of gold, for which the Queen gave him a pardon at the request of the King of Portugal, who used D[octor] Lopez as his instrument therein, by the mediation of one Rawlings, Meeres's brother-in-law, they both being interpreters to the same king, and both of them after hanged at Tyburn for their several villainies.

'Clipping' gold meant removing tiny segments from gold coins, this usually being a prelude to manufacturing counterfeit coins with the gold thus acquired. So we find that Meeres is another coiner in this year 1592: in this respect, at least, the same as Marlowe. And we also find him touched by secret politics: specifically the cloak-and-dagger groups around the *soi-distant* king of Portugal, Don Antonio, out of which emerged the 'Lopez affair' of 1593–4. Dr Lopez ended up, as Ralegh notes, hanged at Tyburn. He was convicted of conspiring to poison the Queen, but the extent of his 'knaveries' remains debatable, and certain spies associated with the Earl of Essex play a dubious role in the affair. In seeking the intercession of Don Antonio, Meeres was apparently drawing on a family connection – his brother-in-law, Rawlings, is an 'interpreter' (i.e. political adviser) to Don Antonio – but one suspects there would be favours required from him in return. All this was happening around the time Ralegh hired him, for in the same letter Ralegh says: 'God hath worthily plagued me for entertaining such a wretch, whom I took eaten with lice out of prison, because it was told me he had all the ancient records of Sherborne, his father having been the Bishop's officer'. Meeres was released, therefore, some time before 28 August 1592, the date of Ralegh's warrant referring to Meeres as 'my man'. Don Antonio was an old enemy of Ralegh's [Nicholl (3), pp. 34–40], and the sub-text of this part of Ralegh's letter may be a suspicion that Meeres's mischief-making was done partly to please Don Antonio.

Among those involved with Don Antonio and Lopez was, unsurprisingly, our old friend Thomas Phelippes. Whether he too had something to do with Meeres's release I cannot say, but it can certainly be demonstrated that Phelippes knew Meeres. The evidence lies, in fact, in that curious little episode at the Fleet prison in 1585 which first brought him to my attention. In that episode, as we have seen, Meeres was accused of importuning a female prisoner, Edetha Best (or occasionally Beast), and was forbidden access to her by an injunction authorised by Sir Francis Walsingham. The puzzling aspect of the story is precisely the involvement of Walsingham. Why should Mr Secretary be bothered with these nocturnal shenanigans at the Fleet prison? Why these injunctions and commandments from on high? The answer is curious, for it emerges that Mrs Best had another admirer – none other than Thomas Phelippes. It was probably he, rather than his boss Walsingham, who was behind the injunction. Meeres himself, examined on 23 June, said he had begun visiting her on Phelippes's behalf: he 'went not to her but as a mean from Mr Phillips, and that upon his request, as others beside had done.' He further claimed that his own relations with Mrs Best were a decoy done for *her* benefit, because she wanted to discourage Phelippes's attentions:

> her purpose was to make Phillips believe that she was so light as that she would be married to any man, to be ridded of him for cc^{li} and l^{li} [£250], which she would give so to be married to one Evans, whom I think she doth yet purpose to marry. This Evans cometh to her by Phillips's means and procurement, notwithstanding the restraint. She did likewise cause her own man to give out to Phillips that she was with child by him. This examinate further saith that she willed him to give out any report against her honesty, to the end that Phillips might be discouraged from pursuing of her, and that she made him a deed of faithment to the end Phillips should believe she would none of him.

There is no space to pursue other spicy aspects of this story. One should not trust Meeres's testimony too far (though one inference of his story – that Phelippes was sexually repulsive to Mrs Best – is surely too good to resist). The interesting point is that Meeres was already involved with Phelippes. He had been one of Phelippes's messengers to Mrs Best; he 'went to her' at Phelippes's 'request'.

In the summer of 1592, the gold-clipper and jailbird John Meeres is released from Newgate and enters the service of Ralegh. He is a man whose connections with Dr Lopez and Don Antonio suggest he is no stranger to secret politics. That he is known personally to both Thomas Phelippes and Thomas Drury does not discourage this suggestion. A couple of months after this, in another London prison, Thomas Drury promises certain 'services' to Sir John Puckering, and the following May both he and Phelippes are involved in a smear campaign designed to deliver Ralegh into Puckering's anti-dissident net. The keynote of this campaign is the production of incriminating texts, and right there in Ralegh's household is that crafty rogue Meeres, whose speciality is the forging and counterfeiting of men's hands – and, particularly, Ralegh's hand.

In the fertile brains of Phelippes and Drury such an opportunity would be hard to miss and harder to ignore. But is there any evidence of it? There is none, certainly, in the extant texts of the Marlowe case: none of the four principal documents – the Dutch church libel, the Arian fragment, the 'Remembrances' and the 'Note' – have any discernible connection with Meeres. None of them, in fact, needed to be *forged* (one could call the Arian fragment a forgery, but it was not one that needed to look like someone else's handwriting). Just possibly, however, there is evidence of Drury's intention to use Meeres's skills. In his letter to Bacon of 1 August 1593 Drury trails a reference to 'the book that doth maintain this damnable sect', which sounds like that 'atheist lecture' which (according to Drury's own 'Remembrances' against Cholmeley) Marlowe had read to 'Ralegh & others'. He does not yet promise a copy of it, but he promises to introduce Bacon 'to the man that doth know who did write the book, and they to who it was delivered, and where and when, with divers other secrets'.

I tentatively suggest that the man Drury had in mind was John Meeres, whose position in Ralegh's household would give his testimony authenticity; whose desire to damage Ralegh is later evident; and whose skills as a forger would doubtless be useful if this part of the ploy prospered and required false documentation, even perhaps – Drury's wildest dream come true – a copy of the 'atheist lecture' in Ralegh's own hand!

This is unprovable, but I would mention two later points. First, the number of unattributed and unsubstantiated rumours about Ralegh's atheism which are recorded in the Bindon enquiry of March 1594. In these too Meeres might be discernible – a stirrer in the background – and the possibility is strengthened by Meeres's known connection with Viscount Bindon (e.g. Ralegh to Cobham, 12 August 1602: 'the Viscount hath so exalted Meeres's suits against me'). The second is a passage in a letter of Ralegh's to Sir Robert Cecil, 25 September 1601 [Latham and Youings, p. 215]. It concerns Meeres's second marriage to a widow named Dorothy, who was 'a kinswoman to my lady of Essex' (i.e. Frances née Walsingham, daughter of Sir Francis, widow of Sir Philip Sidney, and now the widow of the Earl of Essex). Ralegh comments on the marriage as follows:

She [Dorothy] was a poor man's wife of this country . . . and being a broken piece, that I think few or none would have had, this knave [Meeres], hoping thereby to have been upheld by the Earl of Essex, took her. But the Earl did not make show to like Meeres, nor admit him to his presence. But it was thought that secretly he [Essex] meant to have used him for some mischief against me, and if Essex had prevailed he had been used for the counterfeiter, for he writes my hand so perfectly as I cannot any way discern the difference.

We don't know the date, or indeed the truth, of this, but Ralegh's synopsis is broadly the same as the one I have speculated for 1593: that Meeres's counterfeiting skills might be employed by others to cause 'mischief' to Ralegh.

NOTES

All acronyms (PRO, BL, etc) refer to the manuscript collections and calendars listed in Sources/1. Authors' names refer to the books, articles and documents listed in Sources/2.

Introduction: A Torch Turning Downward

p.4   'Was this the face' *Dr Faustus*, V i 1768.

        'Pampered jades' 2 *Tamburlaine*, IV iii 1.

        'High astounding terms' 1 *Tamburlaine*, Prologue.

        'Tobacco & boys' Baines, f 185 verso.

p.5   **The portrait.** Purdon; Hoffman; Wraight, pp. 63–71. Wraight argues that Marlowe is also the subject of the 'Grafton portrait' (1588), now at the John Rylands Library, Manchester. The sitter is the right age, but there is no corroborating evidence, as there is with the Corpus portrait. The visual similarity between the two portraits is debatable.

        A tart's petticoat. Shakespeare, *I Henry IV*, I ii 10: 'a fair hot wench in flame-coloured taffeta'. Taffeta, a thin glossy silk, was associated with prostitutes (e.g. 'your taffety punk', *All's Well That Ends Well*, II ii 21).

p.6   **Thirty shillings.** Thomas Nashe's valuation, in 1592, of a doublet formerly worn by Marlowe's rival, Robert Greene (Nashe, I 288).

        Marlowe's BA. Bakeless, I 69–70. The degree was traditionally awarded on Palm Sunday, which in 1584 fell on 12 April.

p.7   **University dress.** Cooper (1), II 360–1; Nicholl (2), p. 27; Bakeless, I 51–3. The regulations, in a University Statute of 1570, were further enforced by a decree issued 5

November 1585. Stephen Lakes: Cooper (1), II 346. Robert Greene: *The Repentance*, 1592 (Greene, XII 172).

p.8   **'Fill the public schools'** *Dr Faustus*, Ii 117. This notion impressed Marlowe's friend Thomas Nashe, who scribbled the phrase 'Faustus Studie in indian silke' in the margin of a book he was reading: see Kocher (3).

p.9   **'Quod me nutrit'** See Henry Green, *Shakespeare and the Emblem Writers* (1885), pp. 170–5; Daniel, sigs Hvii verso-Hviii. Daniel's book (SR, 26 November 1584) is considered the first English work on emblems. It is mainly a translation from Paolo Giovio, but this passage is from a section of the book 'collected' by Daniel from other sources. The *impresa* of the torch turning downward is illustrated in Symeoni, *Testrastichi Morali* (1561), p. 35; and in George Whitney, *A Choice of Emblems* (1586), p. 183. Shakespeare alludes to the motto twice: in Sonnet 73 ('consum'd with that which it was nourish'd by'); and in *Pericles*, II ii 32–3 ('A burning torch that's turned upside down; / The word, *Quod me alit me extinguit*'). The 'amorous gentleman of Milan' is identified by Symeoni (*Testrastichi*, 1574 edition, p. 200) as 'Monsignior di San Valiere', the father of the Duchess of Valentinois. He fought under Francis I at the Battle of Marignano (1515). Francis's own motto was '*Nutrisco et extinguo*'.

Part One: The Killing

1 Deptford, 1593

p.10   **Elizabethan Deptford.** Bull (2); Urry, pp. 82–3; Hasted, *History of Kent* (ed. H. Drake, 1886). Documents indexed s.v. Deptford in CSP Dom 3 give details of shipbuilding there in the early 1590s.

   Pett & Addy. Peter Pett (d. 1589) was the leading shipwright in Deptford. Much of his timber came from lands in Kent still known at Pett's Wood. His son Joseph, who succeeded him as master-shipwright, was imprisoned in the Marshalsea in 1591 for making 'lewd' comments about Sir John Perrot (PRO SP12/238, No. 58). A plaque on the wall of St Nicholas's, Deptford commemorates Addy's bequest.

Population. Bull (2), pp. 53–4, based on demographic data compiled by Samuel Lysons. The parish registers are extant for burials from 1563, and for baptisms and marriages from 1590. The originals are at the Greater London Record Office.

p.14 **Clerks of the Stores.** Two of the men who held this post in the 1580s, Henry Gillman and Christopher Baker, were sons-in-law of Thomas Morley, a wealthy Deptford resident (d. 1566): PRO SP12/218, Nos 53, 54; de Kalb (3), Appendix 2a. Morley is a frequent variant spelling of Marlowe, and it has been suggested that Marlowe's presence in Deptford may relate to a family connection with the Morleys. See also Appendix 2.4.

'Eating tallow', etc. Nashe, I 171, III 180–1.

'I cannot end my life' Hawkyns to Lord Burghley, 6 July 1589, CSP Dom 2, p. 608.

Rossel, etc. Bull (2), p. 47.

p.15 **Sayes Court.** Urry, pp. 171–3, based on an inventory in uncatalogued Evelyn MSS at Christ Church College, Oxford. John Evelyn bought the house for £3500 and settled there in 1652. It stood on the site of what is now Sayes Court Park.

The slaughter-house. Commissioners for Sewers in Kent to Lord Burghley, 5 December 1593, PRO SP12/246, No. 27.

Drake at Deptford. The reality of the knighting of Drake is obscured under layers of folklore. See Stow (2), p. 808; E.F. Benson, *Sir Francis Drake* (1927), pp. 176–8; John Sugden, *Sir Francis Drake* (1989). Samuel Purchas computed the value of the *Hind*'s cargo as £326,580. Share-holders in Drake's voyage are said to have earned a 4,700 per cent return on their investment. The Queen's speech about the 'use of the sea' is recorded on a plaque at the junction of Foreshore and Deptford Strand.

2 The Official Story

p.18 **The Inquest.** The original (PRO, recently recatalogued to C260/174, no.27) is in Latin, apart from five words, 'le recknynge' and 'nere the bed', which are probably verbatim phrases from the witnesses. The use of the

French definite article for 'recknynge' is puzzling: the word derives from Middle English and has no French associations *per se*. It may just be a scribal contraction for 'the'. The inquest is transcribed and translated by Hotson (pp. 28–34), who discovered it in 1925. See also de Kalb (1).

p.19   **Probable cause of death.** I am grateful to Adrian While, consultant ophthalmic surgeon at the Victoria Eye Hospital, Hereford, for expert advice. See also Thurston, p. 199. Tannenbaum adduces medical evidence that the wound described would not cause instant death, but this does not seem to me a critical point.

'**Brains coming out**' Vaughan, sig C4 verso.

'**Died swearing**' Simon Aldrich, as recorded in the 'commonplace book' of Henry Oxinden, 10 February 1641 (see below, note to p. 244). Aldrich is a good source on Marlowe, but in this case he is only reiterating propagandist accounts of Marlowe's death by Thomas Beard ('together with his breath an oath flew out of his mouth') and others.

p.20   **The coroner and jurors.** Hall, pp. 3–14; Hotson, pp. 38–9; Urry, pp. 92–4.

p.21   '**We think not ourselves discharged**' Marlowe, II 430. Blount's words are widely accepted as a personal recollection of Marlowe's burial. The earliest printed reference to Marlowe's death is the epitaph by George Peele, written some time before 23 June 1593.

The burial entry. Hotson, pp. 17–22. Thomas Macander, a quarrelsome man, was vicar till his death in 1597.

Frizer's pardon. PRO Patent Rolls 1401, 'Regina perdona se defendendo pro Ingramo ffrysar', issued at Kew; Hotson, pp. 34–7.

p.22   **Plague deaths.** My figure is a guesstimate. Nashe (III 87) said that in the summer of 1593 'there died above 1600 a week in London', but he is prone to exaggeration. Stow (Schoenbaum, p. 126) gives a figure of 10,675 Londoners for the whole year, but fatalities were much higher in the summer months.

p.23   **Marlowe's knife-fights.** See below, notes to pp. 103, 210.

3 The Witnesses

p.24   **Woodleff v. Frizer.** PRO Chancery Proceedings, Bundle W25, No. 43; Hotson, pp. 69–73. The bundle contains the Woodleffs' bill of complaint, addressed to the Lord Keeper, and Frizer's answer to it. Neither document is dated, but the writ of *capias utlagatum* against Frizer, arising from the complaint, was issued 16 June 1598. There are gaps in the story where portions of the bundle have rotted away. Urry (p. 87) speculates that Jane Pooley and her son Henry, who owned property in Whitechapel, and Oliver Woodliffe, haberdasher, who leased rooms from them there, were related to Robert Poley and Drew Woodleff.

     Commodities. Nashe, II 95, IV 230; Greene & Lodge, *A Looking Glass for London*, 293f; Marlowe, *Jew of Malta*, II iii 192–5. On 'lute strings and grey paper', see Nashe, III 241: 'I know one . . . that ran in debt, in the space of four or five years, above £14,000 in lute strings and grey paper'.

p.25   **The statute staple.** PRO LC 4/192, f 267.

p.26   **Frizer & Walsingham.** On Thomas (later Sir Thomas) Walsingham, see below, note to p. 138. In 1603 Frizer was an agent for Lady Audrey Walsingham in a land-deal with the Duchy of Lancaster (Hotson, p. 50; de Kalb (3), pp. 92–5). He was by then living at Eltham, Kent, where he remained until his death. This was close to the Walsinghams' seat at Scadbury.

     Marlowe at Scadbury. Privy Council directive to Henry Maunder, 18 May 1593 (APC 24, p. 244).

     Conny-catchers. The wiles of Elizabethan con-men are detailed by Robert Greene in a series of six pamphlets beginning with *The Notable Discovery of Cosenage* (1591) and including the spoof *Defence of Conny-Catching* (1592), probably written with Nashe (see Nicholl (2), pp. 125–30). A 'conny' (i.e. coney or rabbit) is a dupe. Greene's mistress was the sister of a cutpurse, 'Cutting' Ball.

p.27   **Frizer & Deane.** PRO Close Rolls 1339; Hotson, p. 42; Williams.

     Frizer's law suits. Bostock: PRO Exchequer Plea Rolls 381, 396 (Hotson, p. 42). Ballard: ibid, 394 (Hotson, p. 45).

p.28   **Invited for a feast.** Vaughan, sig C4 verso.

      'Ought a grudge' Beard, p. 147 ('ought' is the preterite of 'owe').

      Skeres's birth date. This is here given for the first time, from Skeres's deposition in Star Chamber, 26 April 1593 (Smith v. Skeres, Wolfall et al, PRO STAC 5, Bundle S9/8). The clerk first described him as 'Nycho: Skeyres of the Cytty of London gent, aged xxx yeeres or thereabouts'. The phrase 'or thereabouts' was then changed to '& vj wekes'. This sounds like a fastidious correction by Skeres himself. He was thus born on about 15 March 1563.

      Skeres's family. De Kalb (3), pp. 47–53 and Appendix 2B. *Pace* Urry, there is no doubt this is the right Nicholas Skeres. Despite their father's occupation, neither Jerome nor Nicholas appears on the register of Merchant Taylors' School, though their cousin Ralph Skeres junior studied there from 1564.

p.29   **Skeres as broker's tout.** His dealings with Parradine, Wolfall and Smith are all taken from PRO STAC 5, as above. His dealings with John Smith began with a meeting at St Paul's in the summer of 1588. Further to Smith's accusations Wolfall was convicted of fraud, and sentenced to a £400 fine and two days in the pillory. This case was first mentioned by Mark Eccles during research into the early career of George Chapman (Eccles (5), p. 187.)

p.30   **Skeres & Roydon.** Bond to Henry Banyster, goldsmith, 6 January 1582, PRO Close Rolls 1144/24. See Moore-Smith (2).

      Wolfall & Chapman. Eccles (5), pp. 181–8. Another poet who dealt with Wolfall was Thomas Lodge. He borrowed £30 in about 1584, and was bound by a statute staple for £100. He said that Wolfall abused his 'tender years' to 'entrap' him.

p.31   **Fleetwood's report.** Fleetwood to Lord Burghley, 7 July 1585, BL MS Lansdowne 76, f 115.

p.32   **Skeres & Babington.** Milles to Walsingham, 3 August 1586, CSP Scot 8, pp. 583–4. The name is misread in CSP as 'Ekyeres'. The correct reading, 'Skyeres', was established by Seaton (1), pp. 280–1.

p.33 **Skeres as messenger.** PRO E351/542, f 129. He received £6 13s 4d on a warrant dated 21 July 1589. On Essex and the 'Portingale Voyage', see Lacey (1), pp. 65–70.

p.34 **Essex in France.** Lacey (1), pp. 83–90; W.B. Devereux, *Lives and Letters of the Devereux* (1853), pp. 214–70.

Skeres & Williamson. HMC Cecil 5, pp. 139–42. Skeres's presence in the house suggests his use of 'brokery' as a cover for political surveillance. Nicholas Williamson had been 'apprehended for treason' a few days earlier (ibid, p. 135). He knew, or knew of, another of the Deptford four, Robert Poley. On 7 April 1595, he deposed that 'Pooly' was 'threatened to be apprehended' in the Low Countries (Boas (1), p. 288). He also alleged that Poley had poisoned the Bishop of 'Divelinge' [i.e. Dublin] (see below, note to p. 193). He was a former servant of the Earl of Shrewsbury, and may have been involved in machinations centred on Shrewsbury's royal ward, Arabella Stuart. Poley had dealings in this area in 1591 (see Appendix 1.3).

p.35 **Poley & Babington.** The supper party: Phelippes to Walsingham, 3 August 1586, CSP Scot 8, p. 666. The arrest of Ballard: ibid, pp. 588, 602. Babington's letter: contemporary copies in BL (Lansdowne MS 49, f 25; Add MS 33938, f 22) and Bodleian Library (Rawlinson MS D264, f 1).

p.36 **Poley's career as spy.** He appears frequently in State papers (PRO SP12, SP84, SP106; CSP Scot 8), in the Chamber Accounts (PRO E351/542), and in the Cécil papers (HMC Cecil 4 and 5). Sources are given in detail elsewhere. 'The very genius': Boas (1), p. 293.

The mission of May 1593. PRO E351/542, f 182 verso.

p.37 **Opinions of Poley.** A 'beguiler' and 'bad fellow': deposition of Richard Ede, January 1589, PRO SP12/222, No. 14. A 'notable knave': Francis Milles to Walsingham, 4 August 1586, CSP Scot 8, p. 588. An 'atheist or heretic': Robert Southwell to Richard Verstegan, December 1591, CRS 52 p. 3.

Cutting Poley's throat. CSP Dom 4, p. 423; Seaton (2), pp. 145–6. Wenden, a 'thief and burglar', was servant to Sir John Smythe, the supposed leader of the insurrection. He owed Poley £9.

Poley under interrogation. Statement of William Yeomans concerning 'lewd speeches uttered by Robert Poley against Sec. Walsingham', 7 January 1589, PRO SP12/222, No. 13. Yeomans places this 'about three years ago', i.e. early 1586, but on other evidence (see below, note to p. 157) it took place in the early months of 1585, when the first copies of *Leicester's Commonwealth* were smuggled into England. Of Walsingham's skills in interrogation Fuller wrote (p. 205): 'Marvellous his sagacity in examining suspected persons, either to make them confess the truth, or confound themselves by denying it to their detection'.

p.38   **Poley's arrest in the Netherlands.** Sir Edmund Udall and George Gilpin to Lord Burghley, September 1593, PRO SP84/47, ff 41, 46, 60–1, 62–3; LASP 5, Nos 134–5. On Roger Walton, see below, note to p. 239.

4 Widow Bull

p.40   **Eleanor Bull.** Urry (pp. 83–6) summarises what is known about her (including recent archival discoveries by Jane Apple of Lewisburg, Pennsylvania). His account disperses lingering folklore about her. See also Hall, pp. 14–15; Shield.

Taverns in Deptford. Urry, p. 84, citing a local survey of 1609–10; Hall, pp. 15–18.

Victualling houses. John Marlowe's: Urry, p. 38. The widow of Fleet Street (Hall, p. 15) was called, by coincidence, Ellen or Helen Bull. She was alive in 1600, and cannot be Eleanor. I agree with Urry's conclusion that Eleanor Bull was a 'landlady', and that one of the four men was her 'lodger'. The inquest describes them as 'coming together' [*convenerunt*] at the house that morning, but the term is loose and does not preclude one (or more) of them being already there. Vaughan (sig C4v) says that Frizer 'invited' Marlowe there. Deptford would be a convenient stop-over for Frizer on his journeys between Scadbury and London.

p.41   **The map of Deptford.** The original (Evelyn MSS, Christ Church College, Oxford) differs in some details from the printed version in Hasted's *History of Kent*, Vol I. The latter is reproduced in Hotson, p. 43. Shield and Urry suggest that Mrs Bull's house was on or near Borthwick (formerly Butcher) Street, but this is only a guess.

The Whitneys. *Victoria County History of Herefordshire*, ed. W. Page (1909), s.v. Whitney.

Blanche Parry. She was the daughter of Henry Parry of Bacton. A memorial in St Faith's, Bacton, says that she rocked the Queen in her cradle, and that she died a spinster. Her bequest to Eleanor Bull was first noticed by Shield. Burghley's draft of the will (BL Lansdowne MS 62, f 123) was discovered by Jane Apple.

p.42   **Richard Bull.** Urry, p. 85. Shield suggests he was the brother of the famous musician (and part-time political agent) John Bull, but this must now be discounted. John Bull was born in 1562. His brother Richard was younger than him, and so cannot be the Richard Bull who married Eleanor Whitney in 1571. There may be a connection of some sort, however. John Bull was cathedral organist at Hereford, Eleanor's home city, from 1582 to 1584.

5 Libels and Heresies

p.44   **A 'scholar'.** He is described as such by Sir Robert Sidney in 1592: see below, note to p. 279.

Jibes about his atheism. Most appeared in print after Marlowe's death, but in his lifetime Robert Greene accused him twice of 'atheism', in *Perimedes the Blacksmith* (1588) and the *Groatsworth of Wit* (1592). In both cases the allusion is specific to Marlowe, although he is not named. The same is true of Gabriel Harvey's veiled references to Marlowe in *Four Letters* (1592). Harvey speaks more openly in *Pierce's Supererogation*: 'no religion but precise Marlowism' (Harvey, II 243). This was written before Marlowe's death, but not published until about October 1593.

p.45   **Anti-alien unrest.** The principal narrative source on the riots and libels is Strype, IV Nos 107–8 (pp. 234–6 in the edition of 1824). 'The common people do rage': Richard Verstegan to Robert Persons, 27 May 1593, CRS 52, p. 155.

The stinginess of the strangers. Stow (1), I 208. He cites a 'presentment' listing 150 'households of strangers' in Billingsgate. He also blamed them for the rise in house-rents. In St Botolph's, immigrants were paying £20 per annum for 'a house lately letten for four marks [£1]'.

The Commons vote. D'Ewes, pp. 504f.

p.46   **The first 'placard'.** Council directive to the Mayor of London, 16 April 1593 (APC 24, p. 187).

The commission. APC 24, p. 200. The other two commissioners were Henry Killigrew and Sir Thomas Wilkes.

The 'strict account'. Strype, VI No. 107. A separate survey of foreigners, 'done by the ministers of the French, Dutch and Italian Churches' in the same month, amounted to 3225. The difference between this figure and the 4300 of the 'strict account' presumably indicates those foreigners who were not French, Dutch or Italian (e.g. the Portuguese *marrano* community).

p.47   **The Dutch Church libel.** Strype gives the date as Thursday 5 May 1593, but 5 May fell on a Saturday that year. I have assumed he is right about the date, and wrong about the day. He gives the opening four lines of the 'libel': the full text was only discovered in 1971 (Freeman (2)). On the Dutch Church, also called Austinfriars, see Stow (1), pp. 175–7; Prockter & Taylor, Map 10, ref 4Q.

p.48   **'I come to present the tragedy'** *Jew of Malta*, Prologue, 27–32.

p.49   **Proclamation at the Guildhall.** London Record Office Journals 23, f 191v; Sprott, p. 640.

The Council directive. APC 24, p. 222. It was addressed to Sir Richard Martin, Alderman Buckle and Anthony Ashley, a Clerk of the Council.

p.50   **Kyd's arrest.** Described in Kyd (2), and dated by the docket on the Arian treatise found at his lodgings (BL Harley MS 6848, f 189 verso). It is assumed he was imprisoned in Bridewell, as recommended in the Council directive. This was by no means the only arrest. According to Strype, several apprentices were 'taken', and some were 'carted and whipped' as an example. This is corroborated by a letter of Richard Verstegan (CRS 52, p. 164): 'The apprentices of London have dispersed many libels . . . Some of these libellers are found out and tortured, but the residue hold on still.' The letter, addressed to Fr Persons, is undated, but is itself a copy or digest of an earlier letter, sent to Verstegan from England, probably by the Jesuit Henry Garnet. That letter was dated '26 of May *stylo novo*' [i.e. 16 May in England]. A scrivener named Shore was also arrested for 'writing a libel in threating of strangers'. This was not the Dutch Church libel: it was nailed up on a competitor's door in the Royal Exchange. Shore was pilloried at Cheapside on 1 June 1593 and sentenced to four years in prison and a fine of 5000 marks (Additional MSS of John Stow, BL Harley MS 247, f 217; Seaton (1), p. 274). Kyd was himself the son of a scrivener, and probably eked out an income in the trade. These placards and libels would have been written up by scriveners. It is possible that this contributed to the decision to arrest him.

p.51   'Vile hereticall conceipts' BL Harley MS 6848, ff 187–9. Briggs shows the provenance from the Arian quotations in Proctour. The three folios preserved in MS Harley have been bound in reverse order. On Renaissance Arianism, see Buckley, pp. 54–60.

The copy at King's, Canterbury. Urry (Appendix II) gives a complete catalogue of the library of John Gresshop, headmaster of King's, from an inventory dated February 1579. The *Fall* is valued at 2d. Marlowe entered King's at Christmas 1578.

p.52   **Greene's Groatsworth.** Greene, XII 141–2. According to Henry Chettle, who edited the MS after Greene's death, Marlowe took Greene's words 'offensively'. Chettle also says he suppressed yet more contentious material about Marlowe in the original: 'At the perusing of Greene's book, [I] stroke out what then in conscience I thought he in some displeasure writ; or had it been true, yet to publish it was intolerable' (*Kind Heart's Dream* (1592), ed. G.B. Harrison, pp. 5–6).

Richard Cholmeley. His statements about Marlowe are recorded in 'Remembrances of Wordes and Matter againste Ric: Cholmeley', c. May 1593 (BL Harley MS 6848, f 190).

p.53   **The book 'against the Trinity'.** This is mentioned in contemporary accounts of Marlowe by Beard, Vaughan and Aldrich, and inferred by Nashe. According to Kocher (1), pp. 39–41, the Baines 'Note' is a version of this supposed treatise.

Kyd's charges. Neither of the Kyd documents relating to Marlowe is dated, but both refer to him as dead. The charge-sheet quoted here, Kyd (1), is almost certainly the earlier. It is an itemisation much like the Baines 'Note', and was probably written in prison, at the command of his interrogators, in early June. The letter to Puckering, Kyd (2), is probably a few months later. Kyd died in 1594.

The warrant for Marlowe. APC 24, p. 244.

p.54   **Baines's 'Note'.** There are two copies, one in Baines's hand (BL MS Harley 6848, ff 185–6), and a fair copy for presentation to the Queen (MS Harley 6853, ff 307–8). The latter contains the confusing annotation about the date of the 'Note'.

Part Two: Reactions

6 First Epitaphs

p.59   **Peele's epitaph.** *Honour of the Garter*, lines 57–63 (Peele, I 245f). The 'liberality' to Peele (HMC 6th Report, I 277) was paid by 'Mr Warnour', i.e. Walter Warner, mentioned by Kyd as one of Marlowe's friends. The poem was published by Alice Charlwood some time before the end of 1593 (when she remarried and became Alice Roberts). She also published Nashe's *Christ's Tears* (SR 8 September 1593).

p.00   **Northumberland and Ralegh.** The long friendship between them is not in doubt, but the nature and disposition of their 'circle' is controversial. Muriel Bradbrook (*The School of Night*, 1936) exaggerated its activities, and its cohesiveness, but others have since dismissed it too lightly. There is certainly an identifiable grouping of poets (Marlowe, Roydon, Watson, Peele, Chapman) and scientists (Hariot, Warner), who all knew one another, and who all expressed an allegiance to Northumberland and/or Ralegh. Hariot and Warner (but not the poets) were retained on a salary by the Earl. In 1592, this group was referred to by Jesuit propagandists as Ralegh's 'school of atheism', but whether or not it was referred to by Shakespeare as a 'school of night' (*Love's Labour's Lost*, IV iii 251) is a moot point. Strathmann (2), questions the textual basis of the line. There is certainly topical satire in the play about a nobleman-scholar and his 'little academe', but the allusions seem to point to Lord Strange as its key figure. Strange was also a patron of Marlowe and Roydon, but it is not certain if he was himself connected with the Northumberland-Ralegh set.

p.60 **Marlowe 'well-known' to Northumberland.** As reported by Sir Robert Sidney (see below, note to p. 279).

p.61 **Thomas Edwards.** Bakeless, II 122–3; Eccles (6) pp. 46–7; C.C. Stopes, 'Thomas Edwards', *Modern Language Review* 16 (1921).

p.62 **Nashe's references to Marlowe.** Nashe, II 180, III 131, 195. Nashe's preface to Greene's *Menaphon* (SR 23 August 1589) includes slighting remarks about playwrights who vaunt themselves as 'alchemists of eloquence', and who bombard the listener with the 'spacious volubility of a drumming decasyllabon' (Nashe, III 311–12). Marlowe is not named, but there is little doubt that he is intended, and that this ties in with Greene's attack on Marlowe in *Perimedes* (1588).

'Mice-eyed decipherers' Nashe, III 216–18.

Nashe's veiled allusions. To Kyd: Nashe, III 316. To Chester: I 190–1. Charles Chester is also refracted in the character of Carlo Buffone in Ben Jonson's *Every Man out of his Humour* (1599): see Aubrey, p. 418, Nicholl (2), pp. 103–6.

p.63 **'Aretine' as Marlowe.** Nashe, II 264–6: persuasively interpreted as an elegy on Marlowe by the Feasys (1). The interpretation is accepted by Urry (p. 95) and Rowse (pp. 202–3), though Rowse muddles Nashe's tribute to Aretino with another to the Earl of Surrey. For the corroborating interpretation of Harvey's 'Aretine' (Harvey, I 203, II 270) as also referring to Marlowe, see Feasys (2). 'Hell's a fable': *Dr Faustus* [A Text], Scene 5, line 127. 'Bug-bears & scarecrows': Baines, f 186.

p.65 **De Tribus Impostoribus.** 'The history of this book is wrapped in the greatest obscurity,' says McKerrow in his commentary on this passage (Nashe, IV 279). It was fathered on to various authors besides Aretino, including Machiavelli, Rabelais and Giordano Bruno: see Buckley, pp. 131–2. The earliest known copy is dated 1598, but is thought to be a much later production, perhaps even 18th century. It is questioned whether the book existed at all in the 1590s, except as a rumour.

'Puritans spew forth' A curious excision in the 2nd edition of *The Unfortunate Traveller* makes mincemeat of this passage. The opening sentence of this extract ('Puritans . . . inventions') is omitted, so that the 'you' of the two following sentences appears to refer to Aretino/Marlowe, rather than to the Puritans, and becomes a meaningless attack on him at the end of a tribute to him. There may be interference of some sort here, though it is probably just a printer's error.

The publication of *The Unfortunate Traveller*. Though registered in September 1593 there is textual and bibliographic evidence that it did not appear until c. April 1594: see Nicholl (2), p. 345; C.G. Harlow, 'Nashe's Visit to the Isle of Wight and his Publications of 1592–4', *Review of English Studies* 14 (1963), pp. 234–5.

p.66   'We see great men die' Nashe, II 90. The evils of atheism: ibid, 114–21.

The 'pre-Adamitic' heresy. There is no doubt that the connection between 'men before Adam' and the 'late discovered Indians', made by both Nashe and Baines, also points to Thomas Hariot, the protégé of Ralegh and Northumberland, and the friend of Marlowe. He had studied the mythology of the Algonquian Indians of Virginia in the 1580s, and written on it in his *Brief and True Report of Virginia* (1588). In 1592 Nashe wrote: 'I hear say there be mathematicians abroad that will prove men before Adam, and they are harboured in high places' (I 172). This again suggests Hariot, and Ralegh as his harbourer. Baines refers to 'one Heriots' [i.e. Hariot] in the next item in his 'Note'.

p.67   'I that have poured' Nashe, II 89.

p.68   The lost elegy. Nashe, II 335–7; Thomas Warton, *History of English Poetry* (1774–81), III 435. Osborne was the bookseller who scuffled with Dr Johnson.

7 The 'Goggle-eyed Sonnet'

p.70   'Gorgon' The poem appears on sig D3 of the *New Letter*

(Harvey, I 295–6). It is closely analysed by Moore: my re-reading challenges some but not all of his interpretation. On the composition and publication of the *Supererogation* and the *New Letter* see Nashe, V 95–103, 173–4.

'Like a fart' Nashe, III 133. Harvey's own verdict on the poem (I 269) was that it was 'a trifle for the manner, though the matter be, in my conceit, super-excellent'.

p.72   **The death of Greene.** Harvey, I 170–3; Nashe, I 287–9, III 130; Nicholl (2), pp. 122–4.

p.73   **Harvey *chez* Wolfe.** Nashe, III 87–90; cf H.R. Hoppe, 'John Wolfe, Printer & Publisher', *The Library* (4th series) 14 (1933), pp. 241ff.

  Richard Harvey. He attacked Nashe in *The Lamb of God* (1590) as a 'piperly makeplay or makebate', mainly referring to Nashe's contribution to the Martin Marprelate controversy. He, rather than Gabriel, was the principal target of *Pierce Penniless*, but Gabriel's answer to this, in the third of his *Four Letters*, set up the main contest. One of Richard Harvey's letters to Gabriel, dated 14 June 1592, is printed in his *Philadelphus* (1593), sig C1. It refers to Nashe ('purse penniless') and to another literary enemy, John Lyly ('wild lily').

p.74   **The oddballs.** Monarcho, 'the Italian that wore crowns on his shoes': Nashe, III 76. Old Tooley: Harvey, I 69. Mother Livers, who used pamphlets to 'stop mustard-pots': Nashe, I 274.

  Peter Shakerley. Meres, sigs M2, Aa2; Nashe, I 257, IV 155–6; Harvey, II 325. The allusion to the Shakerley crest is in Nashe's letter to William Cotton, c. August 1596, BL Cotton MS Jul Caes 3, f 280 (Nashe, V 192–6). The entry relating to his burial was spotted by Mark Eccles (Nashe, Supplement p. 19). Another reason for believing that Harvey is not talking about Marlowe's death at all is that Nashe would surely have made capital of such a blunder in *Have with you to Saffron Walden* (1596), where he trawls through the *Supererogation* and the *New Letter* page by page. As it is, he only mentions the 'goggle-eyed sonnet' *en passant* (Nashe, III 133). His references to Harvey's ill-treatment of Marlowe refer not to 'Gorgon' but to Harvey's mentions of Marlowe, by name and as 'Aretine', in the *Supererogation*.

8 Independent Accounts

p.77 **Thomas Beard.** DNB; Hotson, pp. 11–12; Bakeless, I 143–5. He was at Jesus, Cambridge (BA 1588, BD 1602). He is alluded to by John Weever, *Epigrams* (1599), III 13. Weever considered him 'no good divine'. He is not the 'T.B.' whose translation of Pierre de la Primaudaye's *French Academy* (1594) contains remarks vaguely suggestive of Marlowe. This is now identified as Thomas Bowes (Bakeless, I 124–5).

'It so fell out' Beard, Chapter 25, pp. 147–8.

p.78 **'Streets' or 'streete'** Hotson, pp. 38–9.

p.79 **Francis Meres.** DNB; E. Honigmann, *John Weever* (1989), pp. 26ff, 90ff.

Interest at Cambridge. Another instance is the college play, *The Progress from Parnassus*, one of a trio written and performed at St John's, Cambridge, c. 1599–1601. This has a sniffy epitaph: Marlowe was happy in his buskined muse,/Alas, unhappy in his life & end,/Pity it is that wit so ill should dwell,/Wit lent from heaven, but vices sent from hell./(MS version: Nicholl (2), Document 12).

p.80 **On Marlowe's death.** Meres, sig O06. His references to Nashe and Peele occur on the verso.

p.81 **Marlowe's *Hero*.** Copyright was purchased by John Wolfe on 28 September 1593. He must have sold the rights to Blount in a deal unrecorded in SR. Blount's edition appeared in early 1598. On 2 March he transferred the rights to Paul Linley, who published the 2nd edition containing Chapman's sequel. See Marlowe, II 425–9; Greg (2). On the parallel publishing history of Marlowe's *Pharsalia*, see below, note to p. 83.

Sir Thomas Walsingham. Walsingham was knighted in the summer of 1597, when the Queen visited him at Scadbury. The earliest reference to his wife, Audrey *née* Shelton, occurs around this time, and it is thought that the wedding was the occasion of the royal visit. This is a major challenge to de Kalb's theory about the complicity of Lady Walsingham in Marlowe's death (see Wraight, pp. 250–1; Appendix 1.5).

p.82 **Edward Blount.** McKerrow, s.v. Blount. His main claim to fame is as one of the publishers of Shakespeare's *Works*, the celebrated First Folio of 1623. I argue elsewhere that

Blount sheltered Nashe in 1600, when he was an officially banned writer, and that Nashe contributed prefatory material, under the pseudonym of 'Il Pazzissimo', to *The Hospital of Incurable Fools*, published by Blount in 1600 (Nicholl (2), pp. 265–9). This would be part of the same nexus of friendship. The 'stationers in St Paul's': Kyd (2).

Chapman's sequel. Marlowe's poem ends abruptly after two sestiads. Line 818, 'Dang'd down to hell her loathsome carriage', is perhaps the last line he ever wrote. Chapman's sequel in the 2nd edition supplies a further four sestiads. 'Now, swift as time': Sestiad 3, lines 188–90. It is sometimes said that Marlowe had encouraged Chapman to write this sequel, but this is a misreading of Chapman's words. He writes (ibid, lines 195–7): 'Tell it [i.e. Marlowe's soul] how much his late desires I tender / (If yet it know not) and to light surrender / My soul's dark offspring.' But this 'dark offspring' is undoubtedly Chapman's own poem, *The Shadow of Night*, not his continuation of *Hero*. He is saying, in his usual egocentric way, that Marlowe encouraged him to publish the poem, and that he had done so. (It had appeared in 1594, dedicated to Marlowe's friend Matthew Roydon.) There is no reason to suppose, therefore, that Chapman began his sequel to *Hero* in Marlowe's lifetime (nor, as is further inferred, that Marlowe requested this because he knew his life was in danger).

Nashe's version. Nashe, III 195–201. A rough, affectionate, kitchen-sink version of the story, it was in part a riposte to the fustian philosophising of Chapman's sequel.

p.83   **The *Pharsalia*.** Marlowe's fragmentary translation of Lucan's *Pharsalia* is thought to be an early work, perhaps dating from university days. The copyright, like that of *Hero*, was acquired by Wolfe in 1593, then passed at some point to Blount, who in turn passed it to Thomas Thorpe. These transfers are again unrecorded, but in his dedication (Marlowe, II 279) Thorpe refers to Blount's 'old right in it'. In 1609 Thorpe published the first edition of Shakespeare's *Sonnets*. It was he who wrote the prefatory message to 'Mr W. H.', the 'only begetter' of the sonnets, whose identity has so exercised Shakespeare scholars.

The banning of the Elegies. SR 3, p. 67. The early editions of Marlowe's translation, which were published together with the *Epigrams* of John Davies, are undated. They bear a locative, 'At Middleborough' [i.e. Middelburg, Holland], which may or may not be genuine.

9 Touchstone's Riddle

p.85   **The date of** *As You Like It.* See Arden edition (ed. Agnes Latham), pp. xxvi–xxxiv. The entry in SR, 4 August 1600, was one of four 'staying entries', designed to discourage piracy. The play was not published till 1623, in the First Folio.

'**It strikes a man more dead**' *As You Like It*, III iii 9–12. The allusion to Marlowe's death was first noticed, within a few weeks of Hotson's recovery of the inquest, by Oliver Lodge (*Times Literary Supplement*, 14 May 1925). J. Dover Wilson (New Cambridge edition, 1926) concurred, though his backdating of the play to 1593 is unnecessary. Latham (Arden edition, pp. xxxii–xxxiv) sounds some cautionary notes. Touchstone is the first of a series of 'wise fools' that includes Feste in *Twelfth Night* and the Fool in *King Lear*. The parts were created for the actor Robert Armin, who replaced Will Kemp as the Lord Chamberlain's Men's comic in 1599.

'**Infinite riches**' *Jew of Malta*, I i, line 37.

p.86   **Echoes of Marlowe.** 'Hollow pampered jades of Asia': *2 Henry IV*, II iv 161; cf 'Holla, ye pampered jades of Asia', *2 Tamburlaine*, IV iii 1. 'Dead shepherd . . .': *As You Like It*, III v 81–2; cf. *Hero and Leander*, Sestiad I 76. Echoes of *Hero* in *A Midsummer Night's Dream* show that Shakespeare knew the poem in MS.

'**The poor world**' *As You Like It*, IV i 89–103. On the 'pre-Adamitic heresy', see above, note to p. 66.

p.88   '**I must have liberty**' Ibid, II vii 47–51. Latham (p. xxvii) relates this 'discussion on the ethics of satire' to the book-burning of June 1599.

'**I am here with thee and thy goats**' In the same passage as his account of Marlowe's death, Meres compares Nashe's exile in Great Yarmouth to that of Ovid 'among the Getes'. Thus both Meres, Marlowe's disparager, and

Nashe, Marlowe's friend and also a banned author, are subliminally present as we lead up to Touchstone's riddle about Marlowe's death.

p.89　**The bawdy reading.** This is hinted at by Latham (Arden edition, p. xxxiv). On 'death' as a euphemism for orgasm, see Eric Partridge, *Shakespeare's Bawdy* (revised edition, 1968), p. 92. He cites *Much Ado*, V ii 99 ('I will live in thy heart, die in thy lap') and *King Lear*, IV vi 201 ('I will die bravely, like a smug bridegroom'). On 'spirit' as semen, see Alan Brien, 'Afterthought' (*Spectator*, 7 April 1964); Partridge, p. 187. 'The expense of spirit': Shakespeare, *Sonnets*, 129. 'When I died last': Donne, 'The Legacy'. This ambiguous reading of 'death' is central to Donne's poem, *The Ecstasy*.

p.90　**'Now, sir, to you'** MS version of *Massacre at Paris*, corresponding to the printed version at scene xviii, 806–20 (Marlowe, I 390–1). A single page of this MS, almost certainly in Marlowe's hand, is preserved at the Folger Shakespeare Library, Washington, D.C. See J. Q. Adams, 'The *Massacre at Paris* leaf', *The Library* (4th Series) 26 (1934).

10 Vaughan and the Perrots

p.91　**Golden Grove.** Full title is *The Golden Grove Moralized in Three Books*. The three books treat of 'virtue', 'family' and 'civility'. The 'Epistle to the Reader' (sigs A4–A5v) and the dedication to his brother Sir John Vaughan (sigs A2–A4) are both dated 1599. John was knighted by the Earl of Essex on 30 July 1599. The passage on Marlowe occurs in Book I Plant 1 Chapter 3, entitled 'Atheists' (sigs C4v–C5). Some of his comments on atheism are drawn almost verbatim from passages in Nashe's *Christ's Tears*. He returns to the subject in Chapter 7, 'Of the Immortality of the Soul'. Atheists say (he writes) 'that it is not known what becomes of their souls after the death of their bodies, or to what coast they travel, by reason that none returned at any time back from thence to certify them' (sig C8 verso). Could this passage have inspired Hamlet's famous line about death, 'The undiscover'd country from whose bourn no traveller returns'? Shakespeare wrote *Hamlet* in about 1600, the year that the *Golden Grove* was published.

p.92   **'About 7 years ago'** This commendable accuracy is continued in the 2nd edition (1608), where the phrase is
changed to 'about 15 years ago'.

  William Vaughan. See DNB; Shirley (1), pp. 411–13; Yates
(1), p. 93. His schooling at Westminster, not mentioned
in DNB, is referred to on sigs G5v–G6 of *Golden Grove*.
He had a varied career as an author, political agent, and
country squire, and died at Llangyndreyn in 1641.

p.93   **The Perrots.** DNB, s.v. Perrott, Sir John. He served the
Queen in Ireland, but was indicted for treason in 1592,
and died in the Tower that summer. The charges against
him are questionable.

  The marriage of Sir Thomas Perrot. John Strype: *Life of
John Aylmer* (1821), pp. 130, 271–9; Shirley (1). Their
daughter, Penelope, was named after Dorothy's sister,
the 'Stella' of Sir Philip Sidney's *Astrophil and Stella*.

p.94   **Traventi.** This estate came down to Dorothy Perrot's
daughter, Penelope. In c. 1602 she married Sir William
Lower, the friend and correspondent of Thomas Hariot.
Lower's group, the 'Traventane philosophers', took their
name from the estate. One of these was John Protheroe,
who was William Vaughan's brother-in-law. Vaughan
lived nearby (at Torycoed, Llangyndreyn) and was
perhaps part of the group. This is a later ramification of
the Vaughan-Perrot connection.

  James Perrot. Born in 1571, he entered Jesus College in
1586. He wrote a biography of Sir Philip Sidney, which
Anthony Wood knew in MS. He was knighted in 1603,
but was later 'honourably banished' to Ireland. He died
in 1637.

p.95   **Northumberland's marriage to Dorothy Perrot.** Shirley (1),
pp. 225, 391; de Fonblanque, I 203–4. Sir Thomas Perrot
died in 1593: he is described as 'very ill' in a letter from
Essex to Burghley, endorsed '1593', BL Lansdowne MS
76, No. 9. The Queen's favouring of the match was
partly to scotch a rumoured alliance between
Northumberland and Arabella Stuart, also perhaps to
lessen the enmity between the Essex and Ralegh factions
at this time.

  Roydon, Hariot, Warner. All three are mentioned in Kyd

(2) as 'such as he [Marlowe] conversed withal', and are implicitly accused of holding the same 'vile opinion' of atheism.

11 The Questions

p.98 **Seventeenth century versions.** As well as Rudierde (*Thunderbolt*, p. 29) there are redactions of the Beard version in Samuel Clark, *A Mirror or Looking Glass both for Saints and Sinners* (1646), and R.B., *Wonderful Prodigies* (1682). All acknowledge Beard as their source. In *Theatrum Poetarum* (c. 1674) Edward Phillips merely states that Marlowe 'in some riotous fray came to an untimely and violent end'. See Bakeless, I 145–7. The version by Wood is in *Athenae Oxonienses*, I 288–9.

'Francis Archer' See Brereton; Hotson, pp. 17–22.

p.99 **Doubts about the inquest.** First raised by Eugénie de Kalb in her review of Hotson's discovery in TLS (1925), and fully explored in her PhD dissertation (1929). See de Kalb (1) and (3). Questions were also asked by Tannenbaum (1928) and Seaton (1931).

p.101 **Harvey's two hand sword'.** Nashe, I 262, 282.

Spenser & Feake. Bakeless, I 156–7. Spenser was himself killed by his fellow-actor Ben Jonson in a duel on Hoxton Fields in 1598. Aubrey (p. 338) confuses this episode with the killing of Marlowe: 'He [Jonson] killed Mr Marloe the poet, on Bunhill, coming from the Green Curtain playhouse'.

p.102 **The murder of Thomas Arden.** Ralph Holinshed, *Chronicles* (1577), II pp. 1703–8; Keith Sturgess (ed.), *Three Elizabethan Domestic Tragedies* (1969), pp. 297–8. The dramatisation of the story, *Arden of Faversham*, published in 1592, has been attributed to Marlowe (Bakeless, II 285–90.)

The 'privy nip'. George Puttenham, *Art of English Poesy* (1589), III 18; cited in OED, s.v. 'privy', sense 6.

p.103 **The fight with Bradley.** See below, note to p. 210. Bradley was actually killed by Marlowe's friend, Thomas Watson.

Marlowe bound to keep the peace. Middlesex County Records, Session Roll 309, no. 13, 'Christopher Marle his Recognizance', 9 May 1592; Eccles (1), Ch. 5. The complainants were Allen Nicholls, Constable of Holywell Street, Shoreditch, and his sub-constable, or beadle, Nicholas Helliot. Marlowe was bound in the sum of £20 to 'keep the peace' (*ad pacem conservandam*) towards them. He was also required to appear at the next General Sessions, to be held in October. He does not seem to have done so, perhaps because he was then involved in the aftermath of the Corkine affray in Canterbury. The wording of the document is conventional, and gives no idea of how or why Marlowe had threatened the officers.

The fight with Corkine. Urry, pp. 65–8 and Appendix 4. The incident took place on Friday 15 September 1592. Corkine describes himself as having 'suffered loss' and 'incurred damages to the extent of £5' as a result of Marlowe's attack. Corkine's complaint was heard in the Civil Court, 25 September; Marlowe's counter-suit at the Quarter Sessions the following day.

p.104 **'Quite unassailable'.** Urry's assessment (p. 90).

Part Three: The Intelligence Connection

12 Faithful Dealing

p.110 **The Privy Council certificate.** PRO Privy Council Register (Eliz) 6, 381b; APC, 15 p. 141; Hotson, pp. 57–67; Bakeless, I 77–8. The 'other' Christopher Morley entered Trinity in 1578, and commenced MA in 1586 (Venn, III 231). Chaudhuri argues his kinship with the musician Thomas Morley, and his authorship of poems signed 'Infortunatus Ch. M.', sometimes attributed to Marlowe. Another Cambridge man, John Matthew of Trinity College, later used the alias 'Christopher Marlor', but he did not enter Cambridge until 1588 and the earliest reference to the alias is at Valladolid in 1599. He is described by William Vaughan (author of *Golden Grove*) in a letter from Pisa, 4 July 1602, HMC Cecil 12, pp. 211–12. See Bakeless, I 78–81. There is no mention of Cambridge University in the document as we have it (which is a précis of the original), but it was only at Cambridge that the term 'commencement' was used for the MA procedure.

p.111 **Rheims.** On the English College, founded at Douai in 1568 and transferred to Rheims in 1578, see Knox's introduction to *Douai Diaries*; Father Persons's autobiographical MSS (CRS 2); Martin Haile, *An Elizabethan Cardinal* (1914); Eccles (1), pp. 137–44.

p.112 **Berden's 'warranty'.** Letter to Francis Milles, 1586 (Burn, p. 209). Berden had recently been arrested by the recusant-hunting magistrate Richard Young, which explains his nervousness. On Berden, see Read (1), II 316–17. It is often said that Berden was his alias, and Thomas Rogers his real name. It is actually the other way round: he was the son of John Berden, and the step-brother of another Walsingham spy, Salomon Aldred. See Eccles (7), pp. 84, 86.

'If at mine own election' Poley to the Earl of Leicester, spring 1585, PRO SP 78/17, No. 26b. On the misdating of this letter in CSP, see below, note to p. 157. See also Robert Beale, 'Instructions for a Principal Secretary' (1592): 'For dealing with such as the laws of the realm esteemeth traitors . . . see first you have a good warrant to deal in such causes' (Read (1), I 437).

William Parry. Accounts of his chequered and convoluted career are in DNB; Camden's *Annals*; Read (1), II pp. 399–405, 420–1; Hicks (3).

John Edge. The warrant, dated 9 October 1590, is transcribed by Strype (IV, No. 30). The original was in the hand of Lord Burghley, and was signed by 'several of the Lords' of the Privy Council. While on his mission, Edge was to leave the warrant in the custody of Sir Robert Sidney, Governor of Flushing. On 21 January 1591 he was paid £25, under Burghley's warrant, 'for his charges and pains, being lately employed in the Low Countries' (PRO E351/542, f 155). He may be the John Hedge who appears in the Chamber Accounts in 1587 (ibid, f 92 verso).

p.113 **Did Marlowe visit Rheims?** Wraight and Rowse say he did. Hotson, Boas and Bakeless draw more careful conclusions: they do not think he visited Rheims, but allow the possibility of a mission or missions to France. To deduce a trip to Rheims from the wording of the certificate, one would have to take 'was determined to' to mean 'was said to', rather than 'intended to'; and 'had no such intent' to refer only to his remaining there, not to his going there. Alternatively, one could take the Council's denial as a straight-up lie, but this is unlikely. As Grey points out (p. 684), the Council's wording may be deliberately ambiguous. They are sending an instruction to the university authorities, not an explanation.

p.114 **Catholics at Cambridge.** Mullinger, II, 253–62. Donne's sojourn at Cambridge is not documented, but Isaak Walton (*Lives*, 1671, pp. 23–4) says he transferred from Oxford to Cambridge 'in about his fourteenth year' (i.e. in c. 1586), and this is substantially accepted by Bald, pp. 46–7. Henry Constable graduated BA at St John's in 1580, but left before taking his MA, and soon departed for France. See DNB; J.B. Mullinger, *St John's College* (1901), p. 83.

'Plain, simple, sullen' *Satires* III, lines 51–2 (Donne, I 156). On Nashe's detestation of Puritanism at Cambridge, see Nicholl (2), pp. 25–6; and on the evidence of his Catholic sympathies, see pp. 116–18, 158–60, 225–6.

John Marlowe's books. Urry, Appendix 7 ('Inventory of the goods of John Marlowe', 21 February 1605).

p.116 **The Jesuit agent at Cambridge.** See Gray, pp. 688–9; E.L. Taunton, *History of the Jesuits in England*, p. 88; Certificate of Recusants for the County of Cambridge, May 1582 (CRS 53, pp. 1–4).

Robert Sayer. DNB; Cooper (2) II 334–5. He was ejected from Caius, took his BA at Peterhouse, and migrated to Rheims in 1581. He was later a professor at the Benedictine monastery of Monte Cassino.

p.117 **John Ballard.** DNB; Read (1) III 16–17; Venn, *Matriculations and Degrees* (1913), p. 35. He was associated with St Catherine's and King's, as well as Caius. Admitted to Rheims in 1579, and ordained 4 March 1581 (Knox, pp. 158, 177–8), he returned to England a few weeks later, and lived an outlaw life until his apprehension in 1586.

John Fingelow. DNB; Gray, p. 688; CRS 5, p.8. He was executed at York. The name is sometimes written Fingley.

'Invisible' Catholics. Masters at Cambridge to Lord Burghley, 4 February 1592, BL Lansdowne MS 66, No. 46.

The sermon at St Mary's. Cooper (1), II 429.

p.118 **Marlowe's scholarship accounts.** Moore-Smith (1); Boas, pp. 10–15; Bakeless, I 64–77.

The 'buttery books'. Bakeless, I 66f. The exact date of Marlowe's arrival is conjectured as follows. The entries in the buttery book are weekly; the first entry for Marlowe is in the 9th week of the Michaelmas term, 1580; the small amount of 1d suggests he was only present on the last day of that week, i.e. Saturday 10 December.

'Cews'. A 'cew' or cue (written in accounts as 'q') was a ration worth half a farthing. Cf Thomas Middleton, *The Black Book* (1604), sig F2: 'This lamentable cry at the buttery-hatch: Ho Lancelot, a cew of bread and a cew of beer!'

p.119 **Mistress Benchkin's will.** Discovered by Frank Tyler in 1939. See Urry, p. 57 and Appendix 3. Marlowe's uncle was Thomas Arthur; his brother-in-law was John Moore, shoemaker, the husband of his elder sister, Jane.

p.121 **'You must cast the scholar off'** *Edward II*, II i 31ff.

13 The Elizabethan Secret Service

p.122 **Burghley & Leicester.** I reluctantly reject the possibility that the 'Mr Morley' carrying messages for Lord Burghley in c. 1586 was Marlowe (see Appendix 1.1). It cannot be ruled out that Marlowe worked for Burghley in the 1580s, as I believe he did in 1591–2. There is nothing to connect him with the Earl of Leicester.

p.123 **Sir Francis Walsingham.** My account is based, inevitably, on Read's monumental biography, with corrective views from Catholic scholars (e.g. Pollen, Smith, Hicks) and more recent assessments by Burn and Plowden. Alan Haynes and Paul Greengrass have kindly shared their knowledge of Walsingham spycraft with me. The early biographies: Camden, *Annals* (1635 ed.), p. 394; Naunton, p. 59; David Lloyd, *State Worthies* (1670), p. 514. The de Critz portrait is in the National Portrait Gallery, London.

'Books are but dead letters' Read (1), I 19.

Walsingham and Ridolfi. Read (1), I 159–61; Plowden, pp. 14–24. 'He would cherish a plot': Lloyd, *State Worthies*, p. 516.

p.124 **Frances Walsingham.** She married Sidney on 20 September 1583; he died at Zutphen three years later. She later married the Earl of Essex, a clandestine wedding whose date is uncertain (the first of their five children was born in April 1591). See Read (1), III 170; Lacey (1), pp. 79–80. Robert Poley was a servant in her household in late 1585, as a means of access to her father.

Intervention in the Low Countries. Read (1), III 71ff; J.H. Elliott, *Europe Divided* (1968), p. 311. By the Treaty of Nonsuch, 20 August 1585, the Queen promised military aid (5000 foot-soldiers and 1000 horse) to the Dutch, in return for the 'cautionary towns' of Flushing and Brill. The expeditionary force, under Leicester, landed at Flushing in December.

p.125 **Investments in secret service.** Read (1), II 370–1. His figures are from the Signet Book (PRO), which records warrants under the Privy Seal, cross-checked with a list of disbursements to Walsingham from 1585 to 1589, drawn up by Thomas Lake (December 1589, PRO SP12/229. No. 49).

p.126 **The Spanish courier.** CSP Spanish 1580–6, p. 351; Read (1), II 375–6. He was arrested at the border in May 1582, and found with letters from Mendoza, Spanish ambassador in London, to the Earl of Lennox. Plowden (p. 80) suggests he was the Jesuit priest William Watts.

Bisley. Report by Thomas Phelippes, c. 1591, PRO SP12/240, No. 144. On Reinold Bisley (alias Hughes), see CSP Dom 3, index; CRS 52, pp. 75, 77. He was one of many double-agents working in the Low Countries, and was involved there with Poley's accomplice, Michael Moody.

Edmund Yorke. Report by Richard Blundeville, 15 April 1594, PRO SP12/248, No. 69. Yorke also sent letters 'between the linings of doublets'.

Trading code. 'Make them up merchant-wise': Thomas Phelippes to Thomas Barnes, February 1593, PRO SP12/244, No. 35. The cargo of wines: 'Sir Chris. Blount's man' to Sir Robert Cecil, c. November 1591 (ibid 240, No. 77; cf No. 86, where the codes are explained). This agent's code-name for Lord Burghley was 'my landlady'. The brawn, sturgeon and oysters which feature in Moody's despatches to Poley in 1591 are probably trading code also (see below, note to p. 300).

p.127 **The 'sundry foreign places'** DNB, from Burgon, *Life and Times of Sir Thomas Gresham*, I 95n.

Nashe on Bodley. Nashe, III 105–7. Bodley, the founder of the Bodleian Library, was the Queen's agent in the Netherlands, 1589–96.

p.128 **Thomas Phelippes.** Voluminously present in CSP Scot 8 and CSP Dom 2, and in all accounts of the Babington Plot. Mary's portrait of him: letter to Thomas Morgan, 27 July 1586, CSP Scot 8, p. 551. ('Erred' or 'arred' is a Scottish dialect word meaning 'scarred'). Phelippes in Paris: Hicks (1), pp. 111ff. His skills as impressionist: confession of Gilbert Gifford, 14 August 1588 (HMC Cecil 3, pp. 346–9). Morgan hopes to turn him: letter to Gilbert Curle, 5 October 1585 (ibid, p. 111).

p.129 **The gallows on the packet.** Walsingham to Phelippes, 22 July 1586, CSP Scot 8, p. 541.

Arthur Gregory. Fuller, p. 130; HMC Cecil 3, p. 182. He was born in Lyme, and died there 'about the beginning of the reign of King James'. Like Phelippes he received a pension 'out of the exchequer' (cf CSP Scot 8, p. 569). After Walsingham's death he was employed in a similar capacity by Burghley (PRO E351/542, f 157 verso). He was also paid for writing and 'imbrotheringe' certain letters in gold 'for Her Majesty's signature to the Great Turk' (19 June 1590, ibid f 144).

p.130 **Francis Milles.** According to Hicks (1), p. 44, the supposed 'supplication' of the conspirator Francis Throckmorton (1 June 1584, PRO SP12/171, No. 1) is actually in the hand of Milles. He features frequently as Walsingham's 'secretary' in CSP Foreign and CSP Scot 8. He was in charge of the arrest of John Ballard in August 1586.

Nicholas Faunt. See below, note to p. 143.

Robert Beale. DNB; Cooper (2), II 311–13. He was related to Walsingham by marriage (his wife Edith was Lady Walsingham's sister) and was a trusted confidant. He was involved in the racking of Campion but later spoke out against torture. He was a committed Puritan. In a letter to Burghley, 17 March 1593 (Strype, *Life of Whitgift* (1822), II 140–1), Beale attacked Nashe's *Pierce*

Penniless for its anti-Danish sentiment: 'The realm hath otherwise enemies enough, without making any more by such contumelous pamphlets.'

William Waad. Active in secret diplomacy in the 1580s (e.g. as emissary for the Queen in efforts to extradite Thomas Morgan from France, April 1585), he is best known as the torturer of the Jesuit John Gerard and of the Gunpowder plotters.

'There be no trust' Stafford to Walsingham, CSP Foreign, 25 January 1585.

p.131   'He is one in show' Sir Henry Unton to Walsingham, CSP Foreign, 2 June 1583. On Salomon Aldred, see Hicks (2); Read (1), II 421 ff; Eccles (7), p. 84. He died in France in 1592. His widow, Joan, later married the author Thomas Lodge.

p.132   'Money was paid' Edward Englyshe to Henry Maynard, 28 June 1593, PRO SP53/50. No. 76.

Profiteering. Burden: Read, II 330ff. Cholmeley: BL Harley MS 6848, f 190. Topcliffe & Fitzherbert: Burn, p. 209.

p.133   **Torture.** Eustace White to Henry Garnet, 23 November 1591 (Caraman, pp. 235–6). White was executed at Tyburn on 10 December (CRS 5, pp. 206–8). The description of Campion after racking is from Cardinal Allen's biography of him (Caraman, p. 241).

p.134   **Topcliffe & Southwell.** As reported by Fr Henry Garnet to Richard Verstegan, 26 July 1592 (Verstegan to Persons, CRS 52, pp. 67–8).

Topcliffe & the Queen. His letters to her: CRS 5, pp. 209–11. His boasts of intimacy: 'A copy of certain notes written by Mr Portmont', sent by Verstegan to Robert Persons (CRS 52, pp. 97–8). A report by the apostate Catholic James Younger (CRS 5, p. 209) corroborates Verstegan's version. Pormont was executed in February 1592. According to Younger, he was forced to stand 'almost two hours upon the ladder' while Topcliffe 'urged him to deny the words, but he would not'.

p.135   'Be not too credulous' Robert Beale, 'Instructions for a Principal Secretary', MS 1592 (Read (1), I, Appendix). This was written for Sir Edward Wootton, one of the candidates for the post of Secretary after Walsingham's death.

'**Secret theatre**'. John Le Carré, in Sebastian Faulks, 'The Looking-glass Peace' (*Independent Magazine*, 17 June 1989). This aspect of Elizabethan politics is interestingly touched on by Sales (Ch. 2, 'The Theatre of Hell').

14 Thomas Walsingham

p.137 **Thomas Walsingham.** De Kalb (3), pp. 53–62, gives a full account of his employment in intelligence, mostly reconstructed from Chamber accounts and French SP. See also DNB; Webb, *History of Chislehurst*; Bakeless, I 161–6; Wraight, pp. 281–2.

p.138 '**They stopped Walsingham**' CSP Foreign (1581–2), p. 365. Skeggs/Skeres: de Kalb (3), p. 58.

p.139 **Seething Lane.** On Sir Francis's house here, see Stow (1), I 146; Read (2), III 431.

Poley and Thomas Walsingham. Their meeting at Seething Lane is mentioned in Poley's letter to the Earl of Leicester, spring 1585 (see below, note to p. 157). The meeting at Poley's lodgings: Poley's report on the Babington plot, September 1586, CSP Scot 8, p. 602.

p.143 **Nicholas Faunt.** DNB; Cooper (2), II 477, 555. His dealings in France in early 1587 concerned William Lilly, a servant of Stafford's involved with the imprisoned Gilbert Gifford. Another servant of Stafford's, Poley's future accomplice Michael Moody, was also under suspicion, and was 'stayed' by Under-Secretary William Davison in mid-1586.

Paul Ive. Eccles (7), pp. 73–7; Bakeless, I 210–11; CSP Foreign (1585–6), p. 194; PRO E351/542, ff 79, 86. He was not, as Bakeless suggests, a graduate of Corpus Christi, Cambridge: this was a John Ive. Ive later had some connection with the Earl of Northumberland: he dedicated a translation of a Dutch work on fortification to the Earl in 1600 (Batho, p. 249), and he mentions the Earl's brother, Sir Richard Percy, in his will. He died in Ireland in June 1604, requesting that his body 'be buried at Castle Park, so deep that the wolves and dogs do not scrape it up again'.

p.144 '**It must have privy ditches**' 2 *Tamburlaine*, III ii 73ff, cf Paul Ive, *The Practice of Fortification* (1589), Ch. 2, pp. 2–3. Other technical terms in this speech (e.g. 'quinque-angle') are taken from later chapters in Ive's MS.

15 Shaking the Foundation

p.146   'I have shaken the foundation' William Parry to Lord
Burghley, 10 May 1583, BL Lansdowne MS 39, f 21.
Parry was writing from Lyons. It seems he was claiming
to have recruited an infiltrator into the seminary: this
may be Salomon Aldred, who was in Lyons at this time,
or Gilbert Gifford, who reappears at Rheims shortly after
this date.

The epistle to Pope Clement. Caraman, p. 95. It was
originally printed as the preface to A Brief Apologie
(1601).

p.147   Richard Baines. On his university career, see Cooper (2), II
174. The date of his entrance to Rheims is inferred from
Cardinal Allen's letter of 28 May 1582, which says he
had been a spy in the seminary for four years. Kendall
takes the correct date of his enrolment to be 4 July 1579,
when the Douai Diary records that 'Baynes came from
England', but this is more probably a reference to Roger
Baynes, who later became Allen's secretary. There was
another Richard Baines who studied at St John's, Oxford
and the Middle Temple (see Boas (1), pp. 245–50), but
this is not the informer.

The route to Rheims. Examination of John Chapman, 7
August 1582, PRO SP12/155, No. 8.

p.148   Baines at Rheims. Boas (3), based on Douai diaries,
March–October 1581; and on letters of Allen to Agazzari
(28 May, 11 June, 5 August, 20 October 1582, 14 April
1583) in T.F. Knox (ed.), Letters and Memorials of
Cardinal Allen. Quotations from his written 'confession'
of May 1583 are here given from the English text (see
below, note to p. 150).

'Here's a drench' Jew of Malta, III iv 111–12.

p.150   Baines's confession. Allen, pp. 24v–27. On John Nicols, see
DNB; CRS 2 pp. 181–2, 200–4; Morris, pp. 316–18.
Father Persons refuted Nicols's 'spiteful book against the
Jesuits' in A Discovery of John Nicols (1581).

p.153   The rector at Waltham. This episode was discovered by
Connie Kuriyama: see her article in Sources/2. William
Ballard sued Baines for repayment of £20 in 1592. The

connection with John Ballard was suggested to me by
Alan Haynes. It must remain tentative: Ballard's father
was named William, but the family home was at
Wratting, Cambridgeshire. The living at Waltham was
valued at £15 10s 10d per annum.

p.154 **Gilbert Gifford.** See DNB; Read (1), II 429–31, III 1f; Pollen
& Butler; and all accounts of the Babington Plot. He
features frequently in SP Domestic and Scottish (under
such aliases as 'Pietro', 'Jacques Colerdin' and 'Mr
Cornelius'). The physical description of him is by the
French ambassador Chateauneuf (Labanoff, VII 209).
The earliest firm evidence of his dealing with
Walsingham dates from December 1585, but it is
generally supposed that they were *au courant* before this
(see above, note to p. 146).

'He can hide nothing from me' Gifford to Walsingham, 11
July 1586, BL Harley MS 286, f 136.

16 Robert Poley

p.157 **Poley at Cambridge.** Venn, III 380; Seaton (2), p. 147. It is
possible he was a chorister at King's College in 1564.

'But a poor gentleman' Thomas Morgan to Mary, 18
January 1586 (CSP Scot 8, p. 197); Boas, p. 120.

'Pooley' & Lord North. In *Leicester's Commonwealth* (p.
86) this Pooley is described as a 'trusty' of Lord North's,
who repeated certain words of North's to Sir Robert
Jermyn in c. 1578. Both North and Jermyn were satellites
of the Earl of Leicester, and both zealous Puritans. Boas
suggested that this was Robert Poley (Boas (1), p. 123),
but it is more likely to be either Sir John Poley of Badley,
or his son Edmund. Sir John (d 1590) was a wealthy East
Anglian landowner (as were North and Jermyn); his son
Edmund was a local MP (as were North and Jermyn); his
nephew Christopher Blount was a rising star in the
Leicester retinue. There was also Thomas Poley of
Icklingham, a JP in Suffolk in the 1570s, and 'active in
the Puritan interest with Sir Robert Jermyn': he too is a
candidate. See Hasler, s.v. Poley, Jermyn, Blount.
Though there was no Robert among the Badley Poleys
(BL Add MS 12507), there was one in another Suffolk
family. He was the nephew of William Pooley of Boxted,

near Cavendish, and he was alive in 1587 (Hall, p. 22). This could be our man.

Poley's early career. There are two major sources for Poley's circumstances in the early 1580s. 1) The collection of depositions gathered in January 1589 further to complaints against him by William Yeomans (PRO SP 12/222, Nos 4, 13, 14). 2) His undated letter to the Earl of Leicester (PRO SP 78/17, No. 26b). In CSP this is catalogued as early 1587, and those biographers of Marlowe who mention it have followed this date. I entirely agree with Leo Hicks (see Hicks (1), pp. 247–9) that the session of Parliament referred to by Poley is not that of 1587, but 1584–5; and that the correct date of the letter is c. March 1585. The reference to Richard Norris as one of the priests who were 'last sent over' also indicates this date, referring to the mass-exile of priests, Norris included, in January 1585. This redating affords new perspectives on Poley's apprenticeship in state matters.

p.158 **Catholic tracts.** The tailor is said by Yeomans to have distributed the 'Execution of Justice' and the 'Treatise of Schism'. The first is presumably a confused reference to Dr Allen's *True Sincere and Modest Defence of English Catholics* (1584), which was written in answer to the pro-government *Execution of Justice in England* (c. 1583), attributed to Lord Burghley. The second is Nicholas Sanders, *De Origine Schismatis Anglicanae* (1585), a work which earned the author the nickname of 'Slanders'. On these books see J.W. Allen, *A History of Political Thought in the Sixteenth Century* (1928), pp. 203–6.

Poley's child. Anne, 'a daughter of Robert Pollye', was baptised 22 August 1583: *Registers of St Helen's, Bishopsgate* (Harleian Society), p. 3; de Kalb (2), p. 42.

p.159 **Prisoners at the Marshalsea.** Prison list, 8 April 1584 (PRO SP12/170, Nos 8–15; CRS 2, pp. 235–6). The 'mass-hearers' were reported to Lord Burghley, 24 August 1582 (PRO SP12/155, No. 27; CRS 2, pp. 221–2).

p.160 **Maliverny Catlin.** Read (1), II 327–30. His request for transfer to the Marshalsea is dated 25 June 1586 (PRO SP12/190, No. 51).

'**Loath to lay himself open**' Walsingham to Phelippes, 3 August 1586 (Smith, p. 184, from original in BL Cotton Appendix 1, 140).

Richard Norris. Knox, pp. 206, 230; CRS 5, pp. 51–5. His banishment was authorised 15 January 1585 (PRO SP12/176, No. 9), but he was back in England by the end of May. He died in Spain in 1590.

Anthony Hall. CRS 5, p. 104; 53, p. 19; Strype, IV No. 106.

p.161　**Arrest of Silvester Norris.** PRO SP12/172, No. 33.

p.162　**Poley and Leicester's Commonwealth.** The new dating of Poley's letter to Leicester, which mentions his 'late examination' by Mr Secretary, shows that this took place in early 1585. On *Leicester's Commonwealth* see the critical edition by Hyder Rollins; Hicks (4). In the summer of 1586, Poley was 'bound with two sureties to appear every 20 days at court', and asked Babington for £40 or £50 'to make means for my discharge' (CSP Scot 8, p. 596). This may be a lingering effect of his dealings with the 'Greencoat'.

p.164　**Thomas Morgan.** See DNB, Hicks (1), and all accounts of Mary Stuart and the Babington Plot. Opinions are divided about his true allegiances. Persons deeply mistrusted him, and he had few friends among the Catholics after the execution of Mary. Hicks contends that he and Charles Paget were English agents from the start. His communications with Walsingham and Phelippes are not *per se* evidence against him, since they could have been part of a genuine pro-Marian initiative. If he was not a double-agent he was certainly a bungler: all the key English projectors used against Mary in 1585–6 – Phelippes, Gifford, Blount, Poley – were personally recommended to her by Morgan.

p.165　**Christopher Blount.** The best account of his career is Hasler, s.v. He was not, as Boas believed, the brother of Sir Charles Blount, later Lord Mountjoy, but the son of Thomas Blount of Kidderminster and Margery *née* Poley.

p.166　**Morgan's imprisonment.** Full accounts are given by Charles Paget (CSP Scot 7, p. 627) and Thomas Throckmorton (ibid, p. 636)

Poley's mission to Paris. Letters from Morgan and Paget to Mary, July 1585 (CSP Scot 8, pp. 11, 18, 20, 23–6). A copy of Morgan's letter of 10 July is in HMC Cecil 3, pp. 101–3, miscalendared to 1586.

p.169 **The 'beer-keg' post.** See below, note to p. 181.

Poley at the French embassy. Morgan to Mary, 18 January 1586 (CSP Scot 8, p. 197). Poley's report to Walsingham (ibid, p. 20) is calendared July 1585, but is more probably c. October–November. Chateauneuf did not take up his post at the embassy until early October. See Hicks (1), pp. 209–10.

Poley & Sir Philip Sidney. The earliest reference to this is in Morgan's letter to Mary, 18 January 1586 (as above). See also Morgan to Mary, 21 March 1586 (CSP Scot 8, p. 274); Paget to Mary, 31 March 1586 (ibid, p. 292); Boas (1), pp. 120–2. In conversation with Babington in July 1586 Poley speaks of having dealt with Walsingham 'in some business of my master, Sir Philip Sidney' (CSP Scot 7, p. 597), though what kind of business this was is unclear. Sidney left England for the Netherlands on 16 November 1585, and remained there until his death on 17 October 1586.

p.170 **Morgan & Paget's instructions to Poley.** 'Particulars of two letters from Morgan and Paget', endorsed 'Poley' in Phelippes's hand, 6 January 1586 (CSP Scot 8, pp. 178–9; Hicks (1), pp. 206–9.) The 'practice' against Leicester: Poley reported in September 1586 (ibid. p. 600) that he had received letters 'out of France four or five months since' (i.e. April or May), and that he replied, on Leicester's instruction, 'above six weeks since' (i.e. late July).

p.171 **Poley at Tutbury.** Morgan to Mary, 18 January 1586 (as above; HMC Cecil 3 pp. 129–30.) I agree with Hicks that Poley was involved in the experimental letter-run of December 1585, but do not agree that he was the actual messenger, who is described by Chateauneuf as a 'small, fair man' named Motin, who 'served Lord Stafford'. I believe this may be Michael Moody (or Mody), Poley's future accomplice in Low Countries espionage. He was indeed a servant of Stafford's, and it is plausible for a Frenchman to hear the name as 'Motin'. (A year later, however, Chateauneuf knows Moody's name, and spells it 'Mode', in his deposition concerning the Stafford plot:

see below, note to p. 194.) It is possible that Poley turned up at Chartley as well. In March 1586, Morgan received letters from him: he 'writeth me he hath been in the parts where Your Majesty remaineth' (CSP Scot 8, p. 273). This appears to mean Chartley, though may only be a delayed or muddled recap of Poley's presence at Tutbury a few months previously. Mary herself (letter to Morgan, 27 July 1586, ibid, p. 550) gives no indication that she personally knew Poley. She knows of him from the 'assurances' of Morgan and Paget, and she has received an anonymous letter which she 'guesses' is from him, though the handwriting is 'unknown' to her.

Poley's knowledge of Scotland. Morgan to Mary, 18 January 1586 (ibid, p. 197); Phelippes to Walsingham, 19 March 1586, (ibid, p. 253).

17 The Babington Plot

p.173 **The plot.** The original documents are in PRO (State Papers, especially SP53 and SP12) and BL (Yelverton and Lansdowne MSS). They are conveniently collected in Pollen (3) and Labanoff. There are contemporary Catholic accounts by Fr William Weston (Morris, pp. 181–9) and Fr Robert Southwell, *A Humble Supplication* (1591), pp. 17ff. Camden gives a semi-official version of events in his *Annals*. Modern accounts vary according to the sympathy of the author: the best are Read (1), III 1ff, and Smith.

Davis the priest. Challoner, *Memoirs of Missionary Priests* (1741), I p. 214; CRS 52, p. 19.

The meeting at the Plough. Babington's confession of 2 September 1586 (Pollen (3), p. 95); Smith, pp. 3–7. The description of Barnwell: Francis Milles to Walsingham, 22 July 1586, CSP Scot 8, p. 539. On Henry Dunne's relation to John Donne: Bald, p. 23.

p.175 **Barnard Maude.** See Smith, pp. 114–5; Pollen (3), p. clii. Maude had (like Thomas Morgan) served Dr Sandys, Archbishop of York, and was imprisoned in the Fleet for trying to blackmail him (cf PRO SP12/155, No. 102). Camden (p. 302) describes him as 'a notable crafty dissembler who had engregiously deceived the unwary priest [i.e. Ballard]'. He was also named by a minor conspirator, Edward Windsor, as a government projector: 'a chief persuader with me for going forward in those causes' (Read (1), III 19).

Ballard's mission to France. Paget to Mary, 19 May 1586 (CSP Scot 8, pp. 385–6). According to the government indictment, Ballard's meeting with Mendoza took place on 26 April. Mendoza (letter to Philip II, 2 May 1586; Smith, p. 255) says that Ballard spoke of 'four men of position' in England who had 'discussed for three months their intention of killing her [Elizabeth]'. The invasion force was a continuous, largely chimerical threat, which attached itself to various plots. The meeting at Hern's Rents is described in Babington's first confession (Pollen (3), pp. 52–4.)

p.176   **John Savage.** He served with the Spanish in the Low Countries, enrolling at Rheims in May 1583. On the 'vow' he swore there in 1585, under the persuasion of the Giffords, see his confessions (CSP Scot 8, p. 611; Read (1) III 26). It is not certain when Gifford further urged him to 'execute what he had vowed'. Gifford 'came unto' Savage in person, presumably in London, and thus before the end of April 1586, when Gifford left England for France. He also wrote to Savage, as did Dr William Gifford.

p.177   **Poley and Babington.** The only substantial source is Poley's own report, written in September 1586 (CSP Scot 8, pp. 595–602), cross-checked where possible with Babington's confessions and Walsingham's letters to Phelippes. Tindall, the intermediary between them, is probably Thomas Tindall or Tyndale of Eastwood Park, Thornbury, who is mentioned in connection with the 'Stafford plot', which involved Poley's associate Michael Moody (see letter of Henry Smith, 26 January 1587, PRO SP78/30, No. 9). His son, Thomas junior, later married William Stafford's daughter.

p.178   **The meetings with Walsingham.** Poley's account may be sanitised, but it is broadly confirmed by Fr William Weston (Morris, pp. 184–6). Weston warned Babington about dealing with Walsingham: 'I cannot tell you in what manner you can escape out of his snares: if you yield, you give up your religion; if you renounce him and decline his offers, you surrender yourself inevitably to the peril of death.'

p.180   **George Blake.** As described by Charles Wheeler, BBC TV, 20 September 1990.

       Babington's letter to Mary. PRO SP53/19, No. 12 (CSP Scot 8, pp. 573–4). This is one of various contemporary copies: the original is not extant. Babington's confirms its major points in his confessions (Pollen (3), pp. 61–4). His vagueness about 'the six': ibid, p. 75.

p.181   **The 'beer keg' post.** Read (1), III 8–13, 65–70; Smith, pp. 104–15. This is probably Walsingham's most famous operation (the story was recently used in an advertising campaign for Burton Ales). Among those involved in the couriering was a mysterious 'Barnaby'. Read challenges the assumption that this was Thomas Barnes, a cousin of Gifford's who later became a regular government agent. I wonder if it is Michael Moody again. Among Moody's aliases in the Low Countries in the 1590s was 'Bar: Riche'.

       'Pooley said it was convenient' Babington's version of this conversation (Pollen (3), p. 60) contrasts with Poley's (CSP Scot 8, pp. 600–1), where it is presented as a more abstract discussion about the lawfulness of assassination: 'I told him that was the old question, so long and often debated', and so on. Poley says it was Babington who brought up the subject first: 'he told me of a practice . . . for killing my Lord of Leicester'.

p.182   **Babington's doubts about Poley.** Babington to Nau, undated, BL Cotton MS Caligula 9, f328; CSP Scot 8, p. 492. Nau's reply: ibid, p. 521.

       'Poley may yet last' Phelippes to Walsingham, 7 July 1586, CSP Scot 8, p. 510.

p.183   **'How is it'** Dialogue reconstructed from Poley's reported speech (ibid, p. 597). This conversation was after Babington's third meeting with Walsingham.

       Mary's reply to Babington. Ibid, pp. 525–6; cf Phelippes to Walsingham, 19 July 1586 (ibid, p. 531). It is possible that the document Babington received was entirely composed and cyphered by Phelippes: Babington would not expect to recognise the handwriting. Black (p. 381) cites a letter from Walsingham to Leicester, dated 9 July, in which the spymaster 'appears to know *in advance* that her [Mary's] answer to Babington's letter will "break the neck of all conspiracies"'. A certain Thomas Harrison later claimed that he had 'assisted Thomas Phelippes in all the letters which implicated Mary in the conspiracy' (CSP Scot 9, p. 530; Read (1) I 409). Read considers this a 'preposterous lie'.

p.184 **Poley with the conspirators.** At the Three Tuns: confession of John Charnock (CSP Scot 8, p. 690). At the Castle Inn: report of Francis Milles (ibid, p. 569). The Rose: deposition of William Leigh (ibid, p. 604). 'Poley's garden': the house Poley used was perhaps outside Bishopsgate, where there were many 'garden-houses' or 'summer-houses for pleasure'. The messenger, John Furriar, speaks of walking 'over the fields' (i.e. Moorfields?) towards the house. The owner of the house, Anthony Hall, was later employed to guard Claude de Nau, Mary's secretary, 'I only lying on a pallet in a chamber, until he had delivered all the truth he knew' (Hall to Lord Burghley, 12 February 1593; Strype, IV No. 106).

p.186 **Arrest of Ballard.** Milles to Walsingham, 4 August; Poley's report (CSP Scot 8, pp. 588, 602).

p.187 **Babington's letter to Poley.** On the various copies see above, note to p. 35. The diamond sounds like a previous gift to Poley, but is more probably the 'pendant jewel' which Babington had pawned to a London goldsmith, Peter Blake, and which he now wished to redeem. Blake still had the jewel when he was examined on 11 August (ibid, pp. 613–14). He said 'that there was no time appointed for the redeeming of the said diamond, but that Mr Babington said he would call for it as he passed by'.

Flight & arrest. Smith, pp. 85–9, based principally on Camden's *Annals*, Babington's 2nd confession (Pollen (3), pp. 70–1), and testimony at trial by John Charnock. On the Bellamys, see also Morris, pp. 45–66. The legal proceedings are recorded in *State Trials* (1804), I pp. 1127–62.

p.189 **Execution.** Smith, pp. 239–42. Camden's account in *Annals* is probably first-hand. See also G.W., *The Censure of a Loyal Subject* (1587): the author of this diatribe may have been George Whetstone.

Arrest of Poley. The date and circumstance of his arrest is unknown. His report ends abruptly at 4 August, after his last meeting with Babington. His servant, Nicholas Dalton, was committed to the Wood Street Counter on 6 August (CRS 2, p. 269). His arrival at the Tower, 18 August, is recorded in the Lieutenant of the Tower's quarterly accounts (PRO E407/56, No. 44; de Kalb (2).)

p.190 **'A notable knave'** Milles to Walsingham, 4 August 1586 (CSP Scot 8, p. 588).

p.191 **Catlin's report.** 'II' to Walsingham, 19 September 1586, (PRO SP12/193, No. 52).

Southwell's view. CRS 52 pp. 3–4, 19–21. He wrote two broadly similar accounts, in a letter to Richard Verstegan, early December 1591, and in *A Humble Supplication*, written at this time but not printed until later. (The earliest known edition is dated 1595, the year of Southwell's execution, but on bibliographic grounds it is assigned to 1600.)

p.192 **Poley in the Tower.** His presence there can be traced in prison lists for 1586–8 (CRS 2, pp. 257ff), and in the quarterly accounts or 'Tower bills' in de Kalb (2). Only three such bills for Poley are extant (18 August to 30 September 1586; 25 December 1587 to 25 March 1588; 24 June to 29 September 1588). De Kalb infers that he was out of the Tower during the other quarters, and she is followed by Boas and Bakeless. I believe this is untenable. The prison lists show he was there in November 1586, and letters to Walsingham (see below) show he was there in November 1587: neither of these periods is covered by the bills. These supposed periods of freedom were partly conjectured to account for Poley's movements as described in his letter to Leicester: now that this is dated to 1585, rather than 1587, this is unnecessary. It is more plausible that Poley remained in the Tower continuously, and that there is some other, more fortuitous explanation for the absence of some of the bills.

p.193 **Poley's letters to Walsingham.** The first is lost, but is referred to in a subsequent letter, 25 November 1587 (PRO SP12/205, No. 49). The subject of the letter (whose name Poley writes only as 'And^s') may be the Richard Andrews described in a prison-list of 1588 as 'reconciled' [i.e. a convert to Catholicism]. Poley was wheedling information from him, and urged his continuance in the Tower: 'hear me speak, ere you discharge him'.

Poley as poisoner. Southwell's accusation: CRS 52, p. 3. Williamson (deposition of 7 April 1595; Boas, p. 288) was actually repeating charges against Poley made by 'Creighton' (presumably the Jesuit intriguer, William Crighton). Thus both these strands of rumour trace back to Jesuit propagandists. Nicholas Williamson was the brother of Edmund Williamson, at whose house Nicholas Skeres was arrested in March 1595.

p.194 **George Gifford.** DNB; Pollen (2) Pt 5, pp. 607f; Nicholl (3), pp. 70–74. He had a chequered and partly criminal career. Among his early associates was a highwayman called Nix. In 1583 he was posing as an assassin of the Queen, and in 1586 Babington named him to Walsingham as a 'practiser' against her. He was perhaps placed in the Tower as a plant among the imprisoned conspirators. He was later a member of Ralegh's expedition in search of El Dorado.

The Stafford plot. PRO SP12/197, Nos 4, 6, 7, 10, 15–18; Read (1), III pp. 60–4. The plot takes its name from William Stafford, a younger brother of the ambassador in France, Sir Edward Stafford. It was he who first 'revealed' the plot, and everything points to him as the provoker of it, on Walsingham's behalf.

Michael Moody. His political career can be traced in CSP Dom 2 and 3, LASP 3, HMC Cecil 3–5, etc. He is sometimes indexed under an alias (John Bristow, Robert Cranston, Bar. Rich). On his dealings in the Low Countries, see below, notes to pp. 300–06.

James Tipping. On this shadowy but ubiquitous figure, see Seaton (1) and prison lists in CRS 2. In 1586 he was implicated by Ballard, arraigned at Newgate, and whipped at Bridewell. He was later associated with another spy in this story, Cholmeley; It is possible he knew Marlowe.

Poley's release. Yeomans's dating ('about Michaelmas') is corroborated by the Tower bills, which have no reference to Poley after 29 September 1588.

p.195　**Official missions.** Of the thirty known missions of Poley, twenty-six are listed in the Chamber accounts (PRO E351/542; de Kalb (3)), and three are listed on the verso of one of Poley's cypher-keys (PRO SP106; see below, note to p. 299). There is no record of payment for his mission to the Netherlands in September 1593, which we know about from diplomatic despatches (PRO SP84/47, ff 41 et seq). The 'Poole' spotted in Denmark in 1587 was not Robert Poley, who was then in the Tower.

'I am of a mind to use the Devil' Stafford to Walsingham, 27 October 1583, PRO SP78/10, f 65.

Part Four: *Poets and Spies*

18 'Our Best for Plotting'

p.200　**'Kind Kit Marlowe'.** J.M., *The New Metamorphosis* (c. 1600–15), BL Add MS 14824 Vol I f 39; Bakeless I p. 187.

'Serious farce' T.S. Eliot, 'Notes on the Blank Verse of Christopher Marlowe', in *The Sacred Wood* (1920), p. 92. Eliot uses Barabas's sardonic comment about fornication – 'That was in another country, And besides the wench is dead' (*Jew of Malta*, IV i 43–4) – as the epigraph for his poem, 'Portrait of A Lady'.

Massacre at Paris. Weil, Ch. 5 ('Mirrors for Foolish Princes'), finds that the play's 'anti-Catholic farce' is tempered with the 'darker suggestion' of Protestant bankruptcy. On Marlowe's sources for the play, see Bakeless II 73–89; Kocher (2). He used political commentators like de Serres and Hotman, and propagandist news pamphlets like the pro-Guise *Martire des Deux Frères* (1589). The lines concerning Rheims (xix, 1030–32)—Did he not draw a sort of English priests/ From Douai to the seminary at Rheims,/To hatch forth treason gainst their natural Queen?

— are sometimes cited to support the idea that Marlowe had himself been there, but there is nothing in them to suggest first-hand knowledge.

p.201　**Matters of State.** There are possible political undercurrents in *The Jew*, connected with the *marranos*. There was a powerful community of *marranos* (Christianised Jews from Portugal) in Elizabethan London, among them Hector Nuñez and Dr Roderigo Lopez. Nuñez, who is actually mentioned in the play ('Nones of Portugal'), was an intelligencer for both Walsingham and Burghley. Lopez was the Queen's physician, executed in 1594 for plotting to poison the Queen. I have followed this trail some way: I think it likely that Marlowe's play, written in about 1591, contains traces of secret political manoeuvrings around the Portuguese pretender, Don Antonio, but I cannot translate this into any practical idea of how Marlowe might have been involved in it. (Note, however, that two of his associates, Nicholas Skeres and Richard Cholmeley, appear in connection with the 'Portingale voyage' of 1589). This trail links to David Passi, the Turkish-born Jew who is strongly argued as a prototype for Marlowe's Barabas (see Tucker-Brooke (2), Bakeless I 336–43). He was active in Don Antonio's cause.

p.202 **Payments to authors.** According to 'Cuthbert Conny-catcher' [?Thomas Nashe], Greene received 20 nobles from the Queen's Men for *Orlando Furioso*, and when they were on tour 'sold the same play to the Lord Admiral's Men for as much more' (Greene, XI pp. 175–6). Henslowe's diary suggests that £4 was a more standard rate for a play. 'Forty shillings & an odd pottle': anon, *The Return from Parnassus* (c. 1601), line 344. See Edwin Miller, *The Professional Writer in Elizabethan England* (1959); Phoebe Sheavyn, *The Literary Profession in the Elizabethan Age* (1967).

p.203 **Spenser as courier.** Cooper (2) II 258. He had matriculated as a sizar scholar at Pembroke Hall the previous May.

George Gascoigne. See biography by C.T. Prouty (1942). He is described as a 'spy' and an 'atheist' in contemporary documents. In the Low Countries in 1573 he was working with Rowland Yorke, who later betrayed Deventer to the Spanish; and William Herle, a veteran English spy. Extracts from *The Spoil of Antwerp* are in Roger Pooley (ed.), *The Green Knight* (1982), pp. 131–6.

Samuel Daniel. His early career is pieced together by Eccles

(6). His letters to Walsingham (March and May 1586) are PRO SP78/13, No. 87b; and 78/15, No. 140. His payment is PRO E351/542, f 82. Gaymer and Renney: BL Lansdowne MS 48, No. 70.

p.205 **Anthony Munday.** Eccles (7) pp. 98–100; Burn, pp. 212–15; Anthony Kenny, 'Antony Mundy in Rome', *Recusant History* 56 (1959). The 'broils' at Rome are described by Fr Persons in CRS 2. Munday's diatribe against Campion was answered by Thomas Alfield's *True Report*: one of the printers of this was Richard Rowlands, who later reverted to his Dutch family-name, Verstegan, and became the Catholics' chief intelligence gatherer in the Netherlands.

p.206 **Munday and Haddock.** See the 'relation' of Haddock's execution 'sent to Fr Robert Southwell' (CRS V, pp. 57–61). Among those indicted with Haddock (or Haydock) in February 1584 was Poley's target, the priest Richard Norris.

p.207 **Munday and 'Marprelate'.** Nicholl (2), pp. 67–9; 'Martin senior', *The Just Censure* (1589), sig A2 verso; J. Dover Wilson, 'Anthony Munday' (*Modern Language Review* 4 (1909), p. 484).

19 Thomas Watson

p.209 **Thomas Watson.** There is no full biography of Watson. See DNB; Eccles (1), pp. 32–68, 114–71, and (7), p. 130. The dedication by 'C.M.' (Marlowe, II 538–9) was first attributed to Marlowe by Eccles. Shakespeare is called 'Watson's heir' by William Covell, *Polimanteia* (1595), sig R3. Watson's only extant play is in Latin: a translation of Sophocles's *Antigone* (1581). He is prized as a dramatist by Meres and Nashe. 'Twenty fictions': see below, note to p. 223.

p.210 **Nashe on Watson.** Nashe, III 126–7. Watson died within a few weeks of Robert Greene. His funeral, 26 September 1592, was at St Bartholomew the Less.

Elizabethan Shoreditch. Stow (1), II 74–5, 369; APC 23, p. 230; Eccles (1), pp. 122–6. Theatrical inhabitants of Shoreditch included the Burbages, the Beestons, the comic Richard Tarlton and Gabriel Spenser. Greene's mistress, surnamed Ball, lived on Holywell Street; their son Fortunatus was buried in Shoreditch in 1593. Robert Poley was another inhabitant, certainly by 1592 (PRO SP12/238, No. 140). In 1593 he was an executor of the will of a Shoreditch widow, Rose Crayford; and in 1597 he wrote to Cecil from 'Hoggesden' (i.e. Hoxton), where Spenser was killed in a sword fight with Ben Jonson.

Hog Lane incident. PRO Chancery Misc, Bundle 68, file 12/362; Eccles (1), pp. 9–101. This bundle, containing the coroner's inquest on the death of Bradley, and gaol delivery documents concerning Watson and Marlowe, was discovered by Mark Eccles in the early 1930s. One fragment of the case – Marlowe's bond for release, 1 October 1589 – had been turned up some years earlier (Sidney Lee, *Athenaeum*, 18 August 1894) but misdated to 1588. William Bradley's father kept the Bishop Inn on Gray's Inn Lane. His dispute with Watson (but not, apparently, with Marlowe) can be traced back a couple of years.

p.212 **Marlowe's sureties.** Eccles (1), Ch. 4: Urry, p. 64. Eccles suggests that Humphrey Rowland may have been related to Richard Rowlands, alias Verstegan (see above, note to p. 205).

Watson's pardon. PRO Patent Rolls 32 Eliz (Pt 4), C66/1340.

'Muses so mutinous' Nashe, III 321.

Watson at Winchester. Eccles (7) p. 130; DNB, s.v. Garnett. The Thomas Watson of Bishopsgate, born c. 1556, is distinct from the Thomas Watson of Evesham, born c. 1563, who also studied at Winchester.

p.213 **Watson's continental travels.** The exact dating is not certain. Three sets of data have to be reconciled: a) he spent 7½ years in Europe (preface to *Antigone*); b) he returned to England in August 1577 (*Douai Diaries*); c) he studied at Oxford some time before 1579, and knew a 'preacher' named William Beale there (evidence re Mrs Burnell). Eccles says he was at Oxford in 1571, but this does not seem possible: his return to England in mid-1577 suggests he had left the country by early 1570. He must have studied at Oxford before he left England, since his friend William Beale was only there until 1572. Beale supplicated as Bachelor of Divinity, and became rector of

West Horsley in that year. (He is more likely to be the 'preacher' Beale than a later William Beale at Oxford, who took his BA in 1574 and seems to have left the university in 1575: see Eccles (1), pp. 159–60.) My conclusion is that Watson attended Oxford in c. 1569, aged about thirteen – young but not unusually so – though he may also have resumed his studies after his return to England in 1577. He signs himself 'Thomas Watson, Oxon' in the preface to Greene's *Ciceronis Amor* (1589), but elsewhere as 'Thomas Watson, *i.u. studiosus*' (a 'student of both laws', i.e. canon and civil law).

p.214 **Philip Howard.** See CRS 21. There was no clue to his future blessedness at the time of Watson's dedication – he had recently been accused of seducing Mercy Harvey of Saffron Walden, sister of Dr Gabriel Harvey – but (*pace* Eccles) this does not lessen the Catholic overtone of the dedication.

'Strangers that go not to church' BL Lansdowne MS 33, No. 59.

The Watsons of Bishopsgate. Benjamin Beard to Sir John Puckering, 11 May 1594 (CSP Dom 3, p. 504). That the priest was William Watson is conjecture, but I can find no other ordained Watson in 1594. He was born in Durham, but may have been related to the Bishopsgate Watsons. His pamphlets against Persons (*Quodlibets*, 1598; *The Sparing Discovery*, 1599) have great panache. Persons caricatures him in *A Manifestation of Great Folly* (Caraman, pp. 131–2).

p.215 **'Watson's daughter'.** Yeomans versus Poley, PRO SP12/222, Nos 13, 14; de Kalb (2), p. 42. She is of the same generation as Thomas, and unless there were two distinct dynasties of Catholic Watsons in the parish of St Helen's, she was either a sister or a cousin.

p.216 **Watson and Thomas Walsingham.** Watson published two versions of his elegy: *Meliboeus* in Latin, and *An Eglogue* in English. There are first editions of both in the British Library. On Thomas Walsingham's career as courier in France, see above, note to p. 138.

Burghley's diary. HMC Cecil 13, p. 200. The reference to Watson has not been noticed before. Another Watson, mentioned sometimes as a 'servant' of Walsingham, is John Watson, the Keeper of St Katherine's Tower. But there is no evidence he ever went to France.

p.217 **Watson's jests.** Anon, *Ulysses upon Ajax* (1596), p. 15. Eccles speculates that the author heard Watson's jests on the stage, and that 'in Paris' means at the Paris Gardens on Bankside. This seems unnecessary given Watson's own reminiscence of his days in Paris. A separate edition of *Ulysses* has 'John Watson'. This is probably a misprint: it is unlikely that the author was referring to the Bishop of Winchester.

20 Fictions and Knaveries

p.219 **The King of Spain's daughter.** 'Examinations taken by Mr Dalton, touching one Mrs Burnell', April 1587, BL Lansdowne MS 53, No. 79 (ff 162–3). The case was discovered by Hotson and is fully investigated in Eccles (1), pp. 145–61. Edward Burnell was released from the Tower in 1579 (APC 11, p. 102) and was probably the 'Mr Burnell' imprisoned there in September 1586 (CRS 2, p. 257).

p.222 **The whipping of Mrs Burnell.** Decreed by Privy Council, 10 December 1592 (London Guildhall Records 23, f. 153; Eccles (1) p. 156), and described in Stow (2), p. 764. The ballad was registered on 18 December (SR 2, p. 624).

p.223 **Watson & the Cornwallises.** My account is based on Hall, who discovered the documents (PRO Tower Misc Rolls, 458; STAC 5, Bundle 33, No. 38); and on Eccles (1), pp. 60–1.

21 The Wizard Earl

p.228 **'His spies waited'** David Lloyd, *State Worthies* (ed. 1766) I 400.

Watson & Northumberland. Eccles (1), p. 160–1. The unique surviving copy of *Helenae Raptus* is at Cambridge University Library. 'Concerning Waters' was one of the Northumberland MSS from Petworth House sold at Sotheby's, 23–4 April 1928, and is now in the Bodleian.

p.229 **The literary grouping.** While not necessarily a cohesive 'set' of writers, the connections among them are numerous.

Roydon's praise of 'deep-searching Northumberland' is quoted by Chapman, in the dedication of *The Shadow of Night*, registered 31 December 1593. The wording of this dedication does not suggest that Chapman was already a part of the group, though the tone of *The Shadow* is intended to appeal to the Earl's occultist interests. He later wrote in praise of Ralegh (*De Guiana*, 1598), and dedicated *Achilles Shield* (1598) to his 'admired and soul-loved friend, Mr Harriots'.

Marlowe's translation of *Helenae Raptus*. Bakeless, II 293–4. Coxeter died in 1747. His assertion was known to Thomas Warton (*History of English Poetry*, 1781, III 433) and to Malone, though neither of them saw the work in question.

p.230 **Henry Percy.** There is no full biography of this attractive, complex man, whose career touches so many interesting areas of Elizabethan life. The best account of him is in Shirley (2). See also Brenan; Batho (1) and (2); Edward de Fonblanque, *Annals of the House of Percy*, 2 Vols (1887); and the anonymous essay on Northumberland's 'character', written for Sir Francis Vere, c. 1603 (BL Hargrave MS 226, ff 241–3), which also says of him: 'he bears himself so as to seem not the man who gives, but receives, all the honour of the meeting'.

'Hawks, hounds' This account of his 'conversion' from fun to scholarship is from his undated MS essay (PRO SP14/11, No. 9, assigned to c. 1604 in CSP Dom). This is printed in Yates (1), Appendix 3.

p.231 **The Earl's library.** Batho (2), Gatti. Walter Warner was the Earl's librarian. Dr Dee's library was larger but less eclectic: see his autograph catalogue, 6 September 1583, in BL Harley MS 1879, ff 20–108.

Thomas Hariot. He was employed by Ralegh in the 1580s, as his tutor in mathematics and as the 'discoverer' [i.e. surveyor] on the Virginia expeditions (1584–5). He received a gift of £24 from Northumberland in 1593, and was a 'pensioner' in his retinue from 1598 until his death in 1621.

Walter Warner. DNB; Shirley (2), pp. 367–71; Jacquot (1). He entered the Earl's service in the 1580s, and was a retainer (at £20 per annum) from 1591. According to

Aubrey, he believed his theories on blood-circulation had been communicated to Harvey by 'Mr Protheroe' (presumably John Protheroe, the brother-in-law of William Vaughan: see above, note to p. 94). He died in 1640.

p.232 **Dr Dee.** See Peter French, *John Dee: The World of an Elizabethan Magus* (1972); Yates (3). Dee was patronised by Ralegh and Sir Humphrey Gilbert (Ralegh's half-brother), and he believed he was the target of Catholic slanders about Ralegh's 'conjuror' (though this was actually Hariot). See Strathmann (4). There are records of meetings between Dee and Hariot in August 1592 and March 1594 (Shirley (2), p. 180), and it is possible that Hariot is the 'philosopher' who met with Dee and the coiner Thomas Webbe on 28 August 1593.

Sir Walter Ralegh. On his relations with Northumberland, see Shirley (2), pp. 168–70, and (3); Lacey (2), pp. 123–6, 202, 214. 'Say to the court': 'The Lie', verse 2. The poem is attributed to Ralegh in the miscellany, *A Poetical Rhapsody* (2nd ed., 1608), though doubts have been raised as to his authorship.

Marlowe and Ralegh. This poetic exchange between them (Marlowe, II 519–33, 536–7; Bakeless, II 149–60) is not proof that they knew one another personally; nor is Cholmeley's assertion (BL Harley MS 6848, f 190) which has ulterior motives. What these do show is an instinctive contemporary linking of the two men, which adds to circumstantial links (via Northumberland and Hariot) between them. There is a tenuous link via Thomas Walsingham. In an inventory of Scadbury House (1727) are included seventeen paintings which hung on the 'White Staircase'. These are undoubtedly the famous watercolours by John White, now at the British Museum, depicting scenes of life among the natives of Virginia. White was a colleague of Hariot on the Virginia expeditions, and an employee of Ralegh's. It is plausible (but not provable) that these paintings were purchased by Thomas Walsingham himself. See Wraight, pp. 257–8.

p.233 **'In those dark times'** Aubrey, p. 167.

p.234 **The 'school of atheism'.** On the provenance of this smear, see below, note to p. 362.

Catholic hopes for Northumberland. In Paris with Paget: CSP Foreign, pp. 512, 552; CSP Dom Add, pp. 52ff. See also Hicks (1), pp. 9–12; and the examination of Northumberland's father (CRS 21, p. 120), where he recalls that Burghley or Walsingham 'told him of Her Majesty's misliking that the L. Percy should frequent the company of Paget'. On the Throckmorton plot, see Read (1), II 381–6. On Northumberland's pedigree and royal claim, see de Fonblanque, *Annals*, II 584. He was at one time mooted by Catholic propagandists as a match for Arabella Stuart (daughter of the Duke of Lennox and cousin of the Queen), and it is said that the Queen pressed for his marriage to Dorothy Perrot to scotch this possibility (Shirley (2), pp. 224–5).

p.236   **Catlin and Jackson.** 'Secret advertisement from Catlyn in ye Marshalsey', BL Harley MS 286, f266. The report is undated, but can be assigned to July 1586. On 25 June Catlin wrote from Portsmouth jail, requesting a transfer to the Marshalsea (PRO SP12/190, No. 51). He cannot have been there much before 1 July. Some time in August he suggested to Walsingham: 'My liberty about a se'ennight hence may do more good than imprisonment' (ibid 192, No. 20), and by 30 August he was reporting from the North of England (ibid, No. 57). 'Piercing into the mind' of a leading nobleman: ibid 195, No. 38. See Read (1) II 330.

p.238   **Northumberland's retinue.** I use the term loosely. His actual 'retinue' (i.e. those retained on a salary) was relatively small by Elizabethan standards. An analysis of wage-lists and check-rolls shows a complement of about fifty in the late 1580s and early 1590s, rising to seventy in 1603 (see Batho (1), pp. xxi). These household officials and servants were entitled to wear the Earl's livery: 'azure blue cloth with a cognizance of silver bearing the Percy moon'.

p.239   **Thomas Hole.** Named by Roger Walton, c. March 1588, PRO SP12/209, No. 57.

      Roger Walton. He is described by Verstegan (CRS 52, p. 204) as 'sometime page unto the Earl of Northumberland that was slain in the Tower'. By 1588 he was in France reporting to Walsingham. He appears frequently in the

Chamber Accounts between 1588 and 1593, when he was imprisoned in the Hague after a clash with Robert Poley. The visual description is by Sir Edward Stafford (letter to Walsingham, 10 July 1588, BL Harley MS 288 f 218; Read II 420). Stafford thought him 'little above twenty', but he was in fact born in about 1562 (HMC Cecil 5, p. 341).

22 The 'Priest of the Sun'

p.241 *Tamburlaine.* The date of the staging of *Tamburlaine 1* is inferred from that of *Tamburlaine 2*, which in turn depends on the incident described in Gawdy's letter of November 1587 (*Letters of Philip Gawdy*, ed. I.H. Jeayes (1906), p. 23). This was first connected to *Tamburlaine* by Sir Edmund Chambers (*Times Literary Supplement*, 28 August 1930). See Bakeless, I 198–200. It must anyway have been on-stage before Greene wrote his preface to *Perimedes* (1588). Both parts were printed, without Marlowe's name, in 1590 (registered 14 August, SR 2, p. 262). It was his only play, as far as we know, to be printed during his lifetime.

Edward Alleyn. Nashe, I 215. The coat and breeches are mentioned in an inventory of play-goods of 1598. Alleyn also played the title-roles of the *Jew* and *Dr Faustus*. He may also have performed as the Duke of Guise in the *Massacre*, though in Henslowe's later accounts William Birde (or Borne) is associated with this role.

p.242 **Greene's attack.** Preface to *Perimedes* (Greene, VII 8), closely analysed by Ribner. Nashe furthers this controversy in his preface to Greene's *Menaphon* (1589), but refrains from particularising Marlowe. Greene and Marlowe's university careers intersect for a couple of years only (Greene commenced MA in 1583), but Cambridge seems formative in this quarrelsome literary sub-group of Greene, Nashe, Harvey and Marlowe.

p.243 *Selimus.* The play's polemical link to *Tamburlaine* is argued by Ribner. The date of the play (c. 1591?) and the attribution to Greene are uncertain, however. One 'atheistic' speech spoken by Selimus is of interest because its wording is close to one of the items in Baines's report on Marlowe. Malicious efforts were made, in 1603, to attribute the lines to Ralegh, as an instance of his 'atheism' (see below, note to p. 367).

Oxinden and Aldrich. Material on Marlowe appears in two of Oxinden's commonplace-books (BL Add MS 28012, f514; Folger Shakespeare Library, Washington, MS 750/1). These are copies made by Oxinden from an original annotation in the fly-leaf of his copy of *Hero and Leander*. This, the 'Heber *Hero*', was last seen in 1914. See Eccles (2), pp. 39–41; Marlowe, II 534–5. On Aldrich, see also Urry, pp. 60, 75.

p.244 **Thomas Fineux.** Urry, pp. 26, 60–1. Another opinion attributed to Fineux – that the soul 'died with the body' and 'so shall we remember nothing after we are dead' – could be linked to Marlowe's reputed interest in Arianism. Arians and 'Socinians' (followers of the updated Arianism of Sozzini) held this heresy of oblivion, rather than damnation, as the reward of sin. A similar view is expressed by another of Marlowe's 'atheist' associates, Richard Cholmeley, who spoke of souls that 'end, vanish and perish with their bodies.' In *Faustus and the Censor*, William Empson argues that this heresy may have been expressed in certain lost passages from *Dr Faustus*.

p.245 'Come show me demonstrations' *Dr Faustus*, I i 177.

p.246 'His looks do menace' 2 *Tamburlaine* I ii 157.

Giordano Bruno. The literature on this hectic, fascinating Italian is vast. On his years in England I have drawn primarily on Yates (2) and (4). John Mebane expands on some of her findings in *Renaissance Magic and the Return of the Golden Age* (1989), pp. 78–89. Her general interpretation of Bruno's 'mission' has been challenged by Wiener, and more recently by Bossy, who opens up a new political dimension to Bruno's activities in 1583–5.

'Behold now standing' *Cena de le Ceneri*, in Bruno, *Opere Italiane*, ed. Gentile (1925–7), I p. 26.

'That Italian didapper' George Abbot, *The Reasons of Dr Hill for the Upholding of Papistry* (1604), pp. 88–9; Robert McNulty, 'Bruno at Oxford', *Renaissance News* 13 (1960) pp. 300–5. 'Didapper' is an archaic word for that small, swift river-bird, the dipper. Another who probably saw Bruno dispute at Oxford was Samuel Daniel. Bruno is referred to, not entirely respectfully, by the unidentified 'N.W.', who wrote the preface to Daniel's *Paulus Iovius* (1585).

p.248 **Bruno and *Dr Faustus*.** See Eriksen; Nicholl (4).

p.249 **'I that have with subtle syllogisms'** *Dr Faustus*, I i 139ff. Eriksen points out that Bruno's *Oratio Valedictoria*, published at Wittenberg in 1588, is 'patterned on' the mythological 'Choice of Paris', and that this links with Faustus's famous apostrophe to Helen. Bruno equates Helen with 'Sophia', mystical wisdom, so there is this emblematic level to Faustus's vision played off against the element of peep-show eroticism. As the recent production by Barry Kyle (Swan Theatre, Stratford, 1989) reminds us, Helen would have been played by a boy. The 'Saxon Bruno' episode could be topical to mid-1592 (when Bruno was arrested by the Venetian inquisition) and the scene may therefore be Marlowe's.

p.251 **Northumberland & Bruno.** The general Brunian tendency of the Northumberland circle was first examined by Yates in relation to *Love's Labour's Lost* (see Yates (1), pp. 89–101). See Gatti's analysis of the Earl's annotated Bruno texts. In view of the Earl's admiration of Bruno, Bossy's theory that 'Fagot' was really Bruno has a curious twist: the information laid by 'Fagot' was a key factor in the arrest of Francis Throckmorton in 1583, which in turn led to the arrest and death of Northumberland's own father.

p.252 **'Heroical'** The word was a favourite of Bruno's, and occurs also in the *Cena*, where the followers of 'our Pythagorean school' are described as 'god-like in theology and heroic in every way [*in tutti efetti eroici*]' (*Opere Italiane*, ed. Gentile, I, 34).

p.253 **Hariot & Bruno.** See Yates (1), pp. 92–4; Jacquot (2).

p.255 **'Doctor Jordano Bruno'** Cobham to Walsingham, March 1583 (CSP Foreign, cited in Yates (2), p. 204).

p.256 **Watson's *Compendium*.** Yates, *The Art of Memory*, p. 274 and note 64; Bossy, p. 213. The Scotsman Alexander Dixon, who appears as 'Dicsono' in some of Bruno's dialogues, also published a work on memory, *De Umbra Rationis* (1583). This was dedicated to the Earl of

Leicester (Yates (2), p. 199). Dixon also had connections with the intelligence service: see the forthcoming study of him by Peter Beal. Watson's dedicatee Henry Noel is among those listed by 'Fagot' as resorting to the French embassy.

Part Five: The Low Countries

23 New Masters

p.263 **Death of Walsingham.** Read, III 445–8; Camden, *Annals* (1635), p. 394; Robert Southwell to Richard Verstegan, December 1591, CRS 52 p. 16. Southwell's account appears verbatim in Verstegan's *Declaration of the True Causes* (1592), p. 54.

p.264 **Sir Robert Cecil.** The best modern biographies are by Handover and Haynes. 'Bossive Robin': a humorous epithet applied by James I (*Works*, 1616, p. 513). The word is an archaic formation from 'boss', meaning a knob or swelling (cf French *bossu*, 'hunch-backed'). The Queen also called him 'pygmy'.

p.265 **Sir Thomas Heneage.** See DNB; Hasler; Cooper (2), II 192, 548. In 1591, Roger Watson was travelling in France under Heneage's passport. Poley's earliest connection with him dates back to late 1588, when he had William Yeomans committed for 'disregarding a warrant of Mr Vice-Chamberlain'. Poley is described as Heneage's 'man' in an unsigned letter to 'Peter Hallins' [i.e. Robert Cecil], 2 December 1594 (HMC Cecil 5, p. 26). The text actually has 'Pistol's man', with a marginal decipher that 'Pistol' is Mr Vice-Chamberlain and his 'man' is Poley. The nickname is curious, but has no connection with the Pistol of Shakespeare's *Henry IV* (c. 1596).

Anthony Bacon. See DNB, Du Maurier. Bacon's papers are in Lambeth Palace Library, London (MSS 647–62). A number of them were transcribed by Birch in the late eighteenth century. Birch Vol I is perhaps the best narrative source on the formation of Essex's intelligence service. See also studies of the Lopez conspiracy (e.g. M.A. Hume, *Treason and Plot*). The 'unmasking' of Lopez was Essex's most noted intelligence success.

p.266 **Phelippes as an Essex operator.** Francis Bacon and William

Sterrell to Phelippes, c. April 1591, PRO SP12/238, Nos 137, 138; Anthony Bacon to Phelippes, 1594, LP MS 650, ff 233, 259, 302, 316–18. Another letter of Francis Bacon to Phelippes, 15 September 1592 (PRO SP12/243, No. 13) is obviously on intelligence matters: Bacon refers to Phelippes's 'Mercury', and says both the Queen and 'my Lord' [i.e. Essex] are privy to 'Mercury's coming over' [probably from the Low Countries]. These factions are palpable but not rigid. On occasions Phelippes reported to Burghley (e.g. in June 1593, ibid/245, No. 27).

p.267 **Low Countries.** On secret politics there, see Motley, Wernham (1), Loomie, and Petti's edition of Verstegan's letters (CRS 52). The State Papers Foreign for the 1590s are still being calendared.

24 Lord Strange

p.268 **Marlowe & Strange.** The 'Lord' referred to by Kyd has been interpreted as Robert Ratcliffe, 5th Earl of Sussex, since Kyd dedicated his last work, *Cornelia* (1594), to the Countess of Sussex. The Earl did have a company of players, but neither Kyd nor Marlowe is known to have written for them. There are three troupes associated with Marlowe's plays: Lord Admiral's Men (*Tamburlaine*); Lord Strange's Men (*Jew of Malta* and *Massacre at Paris*); and the Earl of Pembroke's Men (*Edward II*). Of these Lord Strange always seemed the most probable as Marlowe's patron in c. 1591, and the matter was put beyond reasonable doubt by the discovery of the Sidney letter (see below, note to p. 278) which records Marlowe's statement that he was personally 'known' to Strange. None of Marlowe's other patrons – Thomas Walsingham, Northumberland, Ralegh – had a company of players.

Strange as literary patron. See Nicholl (2), pp. 87–8; Nashe, I 242–5, III 403–15; George Chapman, *Shadow of Night* (1594); George Peele, *Polyhymnia* (1590); Edmund Spenser, *The Ruins of Time* (1591) and *Colin Clout's Come Home Again* (1595). In the latter, Spenser alludes to Strange under the pastoral name of 'Amyntas', as Nashe had done in *Pierce Penniless*. (According to DNB,

Spenser's 'Amyntas' was Thomas Watson. It is true that Watson was also known by this name, as in the epitaphs by Peele and Edwards, but both Nashe and Spenser are referring to a patron, not a colleague.) Alice, Lady Strange was the daughter of Sir John Spenser of Althorpe; the sister of Lady Elizabeth Carey, to whom Nashe dedicated *Christ's Tears* (1593); and a distant forebear of the late Princess of Wales. Strange is named in the list of contributors to *Belvedere*, but the poems are not individually identified.

p.270 **The Stanleys.** Documentary material on the family is in the Derby 'household books' (ed. Raines). Edward Stanley is cited for recusancy: HMC Cecil 4, p. 240. Thomas Langton: Hasler s.v., HMC Cecil 4, p. 428. There is excellent research on the Catholic families of the area in E.A.J. Honigmann, *Shakespeare: The 'Lost Years'* (1985) and *John Weever* (1987). Another Catholic in the Stanley retinue was the brother of the Jesuit William Holt, one of Owen's associates in Brussels (Raines, p. 180).

p.271 **Catholicism in Lancashire.** See A.L. Rowse, *The England of Elizabeth*, pp. 84–90.

'Lords Strange and Percy': Examination of 'George Dingley' [i.e. James Younger], 14 September 1592, PRO SP12/243, No. 11.

John Cycell. See DNB; CRS 5, pp. 198–9. His name is often written 'Cecil': I have used the variant spelling to avoid confusion with Sir Robert Cecil. In CSP, references to him are also indexed under 'John Snowdon', one of his aliases. The letter brought by Cycell and Fixer (HMC Cecil 4, p. 104) is questioned as a forgery by Devlin (pp. 34–5). See also 'Snowdon' to Burghley (21 May 1591, PRO SP12/238, No. 160); and to Cecil (3 July 1591, ibid 239, No. 78), which reiterate the 'matter of Lord Strange'.

p.273 **The Gerards.** John Gerard of Bryn is described by Topcliffe (Caraman, p. 130). He was captured in 1594, but escaped. He was later implicated in the Gunpowder Plot. His *Autobiography* (ed. Caraman) describes his torture by William Waad. Lord Strange was a particular friend of his brother, Thomas Gerard, who is described by Fixer as one of Strange's 'familiars' (PRO SP12/238, No. 163).

p.274   **Sir William Stanley.** See DNB; Loomie, pp. 129–81; Hicks, 'Allen and Deventer, 1587' (*The Month*, 1934, pp. 507–17).

    Short Admonition. The printer Jones used the same wood-cut of a soldier in armour for this book and for Marlowe's *Tamburlaine*. He also printed the first edition of Nashe's *Pierce Penniless*. Dr Allen's defence of Stanley is *The Yeelding up of the City of Daventrie* (Antwerp, 1587). The foreword, signed 'R.A.', is by Roger Ashton, one of Stanley's lieutenants, later executed in London.

    Iacomo Francisci. CRS 5, p. 252; Loomie, pp. 151–5. Born in Antwerp, of Venetian extraction, Francisci (also known as 'Jacques Francesco' or 'Captain Jacques') was an agent of Sir Christopher Hatton's in the 1580s. He was lieutenant-colonel in Stanley's regiment from 1590 to 1596, and a constant intriguer with English projectors in the Low Countries. His brother, Tommaso, also appears in the regiment.

p.275   **Hugh Owen.** Loomie, pp. 52–93. His intelligence network in France and Spain is described in a report of August 1590 (PRO SP12/233, No. 32). At least one of his 'intelligencers' mentioned there, Anthony Rolston, was actually an English spy. The confessions of the Jesuit Walpole (CRS 5) provide further details of Owen's operations.

    Stanley's hopes for Lord Strange. Confession of Henry Walpole, 13 June 1594 (CRS 5, pp. 255–6); confession of Edmund Yorke, 12 August 1594 (PRO SP12/249, No. 63). See also the report on the 'traitorous speech' of Philip Woodward, 11 July 1593 (HMC Cecil 4, p. 335). A Capt William Morgan later claimed he had given 'warning that the late Lord Strange should be dealt with for practices against the State' (CSP Dom 4, pp. 19–20). He was possibly the Captain Morgan, 'a tall man with one eye', who had once served in Stanley's regiment (HMC Cecil 4, p. 500).

p.276   **'Foolish speeches'** Nicholas Williamson to Attorney General Coke, 21 June 1595 (HMC Cecil 5, p. 253), reporting the opinion of his mistress, the Countess of Shrewsbury. (Williamson knew Poley, and his brother Edmund knew Nicholas Skeres.) The quarrel between

Strange and Essex is presumably that which occasioned the letters between them in HMC Talbot 2, pp. 180–1. Strange wrote to Essex on 14 December 1593, complaining about the conduct of certain Essex followers, some of them 'fugitives' from his own family's service. Essex replied on 17 January 1594. It was, he thought, 'lawful for any gentleman born a freeman to make his own choice of a master'.

25 The Dutch Shilling

p.278   **Arrest as coiner.** Sir Robert Sidney to Lord Burghley, 26 January 1592, PRO SP 84/44, f 60 (calendared in LASP Foreign 3, No. 81). See Wernham (2); Schrickx. The episode is mentioned by Rowse and Urry but neither has much of interest to say about it.

  Flushing. Vlissingen was ceded to England, along with Brill, under the terms of the Anglo-Dutch treaty of 1585. The garrison was a constant target for Catholic saboteurs. Events there can be traced in detail in LASP Foreign 3. On Sir Robert Sidney, see DNB, and his letters in PRO SP84 and HMC Sidney 2. According to Catholic gossip he hovered on the brink of nervous breakdown, and sometimes stepped over. '[He] hath of late been distracted of his wits, and hath burnt almost all his books, and still cried out that he was damned': Verstegan, 29 October 1592 (CRS 52, p. 86). On the English church there, see Coert Peter Krabbe, 'De Middelkerk te Vlissingen' (*Kunstlicht* 2–3, 1988).

p.280   **The archives.** I am grateful to the archivist, Adrian Meerman, for his help in tracing material at the Gemeente Archief, Vlissingen. Unfortunately, 'ninety per cent' of the town's records were destroyed in the nineteenth century, as a result of bombardment by the English navy. Roger Walton can be traced, further to his clash with Poley in September 1593, in documents at the Rijksarchief, Middelburg (*Resolutien der Staten General* (1593–5), p. 153; *Raad van State* 12 (Res), 17 November 1593). There is also material on Adrian de Lange, a contact of Michael Moody and a courier for Charles Paget (see *Notulen van de Staeten van Zeelandt* (1594), p. 168).

p.281   **Bartholomew Gilbert.** See HMC Cecil 4, p. 549; Haynes, pp. 28–9. Gilbert was arrested further to the theft of a large uncut diamond, said to be worth £500, from the booty of the Portuguese carrack, *Madre de Deus*. Among those involved in the matter were Sir Robert Cecil, who was investigating the theft; Sir Walter Ralegh, whose ship the *Roebuck* captured the carrack in August 1592; and Sir John Burgh (a close friend of the Earl of Northumberland) who was captain of the *Roebuck*. It is possible, therefore, to argue a tenuous link, via the Ralegh-Northumberland circle, between Marlowe and Bartholomew Gilbert. Perhaps 'Gifford' Gilbert *is* Bartholomew Gilbert: a coiner in Flushing in 1592; a fence for the *Madre de Deus* diamond in 1593. This is pure conjecture on the present evidence.

    The 'uttered' shilling. Contemporary usage of 'utter' in this commercial sense – to issue goods or money on to the open market – is recorded in OED. The vocal or verbal sense of 'utter' appears to be a transference from this.

p.282   **Sir Thomas Markenfield.** The manner of his death is described often by Verstegan (CRS 52, pp. 72, 96, 100). It seems, curiously, to have shocked him more than the hangings and tortures he relates elsewhere. The poverty of the Catholic exiles was axiomatic. Cholmeley's associate Henry Young pawned his cloak and sword in Brussels to further his cover as a distressed Catholic.

    Evan Fludd. He is 'Flud' in Sidney's letter, but 'Lloyd' in the docket. The 'Mr Flood' who served under Stanley had been captured in October 1591, but escaped the following month. He had apparently killed the brother of George Gifford (see above, note to p. 194) in a quarrel. He had previously served with Essex in France. See PRO SP84/43, ff 78, 191.

p.283   **Coining.** A coining session, using a 'little fire in a fire-shovel', is described in PRO SP12/71, No. 63. See W.H. Hart, 'Observations on some Documents relating to Magic in the Reign of Queen Elizabeth', *Archaeologia* 40, p. 389 (1866); Nicholl (1), pp. 10–14. The exploits of the coiner Frank Quicksilver in Jonson, Chapman and Marston's *Eastward Ho* (1605) provide a useful introduction to the tricks of the trade.

'**When other subtle shifts**' Thomas Lodge, *Fig for Momus* (1595), sig I2 verso.

p.284 **Examination of Dawbney.** Sir Edmund Udall to Lord Burghley, 5 January 1593 (LASP Foreign 4, p. 107); Verstegan to Persons, 1 April 1593 (CRS 52, p. 115).

p.285 **Marlowe in the Chamber accounts.** Payment to David Lloyd, 3 March 1592, PRO E351/542, f 169 verso.

26 Marlowe and Poole

p.286 **John Poole.** Eccles (2); Anderton; Ormerod, *History of Chester* (1882), II 422–4. His birth date is not given. Anderton's information that he was married before 1561 may be faulty, since his father (1531–1613) was then only twenty-nine. He lived at Capenhurst, near Chester. He was imprisoned on 'suspicion of coining' some time before 25 July 1587 (the date of Gunson's report) and was still there in October 1590 (APC 20, p. 28). He died in 1601.

p.287 **Gunson's report.** PRO SP12/273. No. 103 (miscalendared under 1599). On the handwriting, which is not Gunson's own, see below, note to p. 376.

Poole and 'Potter'. On Geoffrey Poole, see CRS 5, p. 189. The Pormont (or Portman) he assisted in Flushing was the same who reported Topcliffe's erotic reverie about the Queen (see above, note to p. 134). On Stransham (or Transom) alias 'Potter', see Anderton; Morris, pp. 155, 231, 266; CRS 22, 128. His career is easily confused with that of Edward Stransham (alias 'Barber'), who was martyred in 1586.

p.289 **Sir Edward Fitton.** Fitton was kin to the Pooles: his aunt, Susan, married John Poole senior (though she was not apparently the mother of John Poole junior). In 1586, Fitton, Sir Rowland Stanley and both the John Pooles were involved together in a scheme for colonising ('peopling') Munster: Eccles (2), citing CSP Irish. A document dated 3 April 1591 (PRO SP 15/32 No. 8) describes Fitton as 'with the now Countess of Northumberland' (i.e. the 9th Earl's mother). He was the father of Mary or Mal Fitton, whose beauty infatuated Sir Francis Knollys and led him (it is argued) to be caricatured as Malvolio ('I want Mal') in Shakespeare's *Twelfth Night*.

Pooles and Stanleys. See Eccles (2); letter of Sir William Stanley, c. 1580, HMC Cecil 13, p. 186; Raines, p. 41.

p.290 **Later investigations of Poole.** The letter of October 1590 demanding his examination (APC 20, p. 28) was signed by Burghley and Heneage, among others. It appears that Gunson was only one of Poole's accusers at this point. 'Captain Poole' at Erith: HMC Cecil 4, 458.

p.291 **Edward Bushell.** He is described as a 'servant' of Lord Strange in c 1591 (i.e. at the time of the Winchester robbery) and of Lady Strange in 1594 (PRO SP12/249, Nos 64, 103). I am grateful to Betty Gilbert of Leicester for further information about him. He was the son of Thomas Bushell and Elizabeth *née* Winter. His brother, Thomas Bushell jr, was the publisher of the *Epigrams* of John Weever, whose own connections with Lord Strange's circle are shown by Honigmann in *John Weever* (1987); and of the first known edition of Marlowe's *Dr Faustus* (1604). He may or may not be the Edward Bushell trading in Turkey in 1594 (LASP Foreign 5, Nos 692 etc). He was later 'gentleman usher' to the Earl of Essex, and was knighted by him in 1601. After the Essex rebellion he was imprisoned in the Marshalsea. In 1605 he was present at a meeting of the 'Gunpowder Plot' conspirators at a tavern called The Irish Boy.

The Winchester robbery. PRO SP12/249, Nos 64, 87, 103. The documents date from mid-1594, but the robbery seems to have taken place in c. 1591. The ringleader, Williams, states (ibid, No. 70) that he 'went into France' with Essex [i.e. in summer 1591] and that this was after the robbery. Given the involvement of Sir Griffin Markham in the coining operation, it is interesting that a kinsman of his, Francis Markham, was in Flushing in December 1591. He was in communication with Sir Robert Sidney there, and was 'considerably treated' by him (HMC Talbot 2, p. 205). There may be a cross-over between the Winchester robbery and the Poole-Marlowe connection. In March 1594, this Markham was under suspicion, and was examined by Lord Keeper Puckering (ibid, p. 183).

p.292 **Henry Duffield.** Crushe to Burghley, c. March 1591 (PRO SP12/241, No. 112); Burghley to Ralegh, 23 May 1592

(HMC Cecil 4, p. 200). Duffield was presumably one of the crew of Burgh's ship, the *Roebuck*, which took the *Madre de Deus*, and is thus another possible link between Marlowe and Bartholomew Gilbert (see above, note to p. 281). On Burgh and Northumberland: Shirley (1), p. 204. The informer against Duffield, Paul Crushe, seems to have had access to Northumberland, since he reports that one Pigott has urged him to 'reduce' [i.e. persuade] the Earl to the 'see of Rome'. In late 1593 Duffield was in the Tower dealing with, and informing on, the priest John Bost (HMC Cecil 13, pp. 494ff).

p.293 **Richard Williams.** Extensive reports and confessions in PRO SP12/248 and 249. He is on a list of 'pensioners' of Stanley's regiment in 1593 (Loomie, p. 263). In early 1594, it was reported that he swore to kill the Queen 'by poisoned arrow, pistol or rapier'. He said he 'wished the deed were done, and they on their horses again'. Among his fellow-conspirators was Henry Young, a former accomplice of Marlowe's acquaintance Richard Cholmeley. Also involved were Michael Moody and the Tipping brothers. On the scaffold in February 1595, Williams claimed he had never intended to kill the Queen, but 'through the great extremity of torture they made him say the contrary' (Verstegan to Persons, 25 May 1595, CRS 52 pp. 238–9).

Captain Dyer. Probably Robert Dyer, who features in the rosters of Stanley's regiment in 1593 and 1596, and who in March 1597 requested a tax exemption for his family, now settled in Brabant (Loomie, p. 248).

p.295 **Ralph Birkenshaw.** LASP Foreign 4, Nos 85, 87. Udall's letter to Sir Robert Sidney, 16 December 1592 (HMC Sidney 2, p. 129) refers to the same affair (though this is not immediately apparent, due to Udall's spelling of Birkenshaw as 'Borchensho'.)

The Hesketh plot. Letters, reports and confessions relating to the plot are collected in HMC Cecil 4, September–November 1593. The key documents are itemised in Nicholl (2), p. 311. There are some later memoranda in Burghley's hand (HMC Cecil 5, pp. 58–9) and contemporary accounts by Verstegan (CRS 52, p. 203), and by Camden. Devlin's investigation is pro-Catholic but convincing in its findings concerning Cecil's involvement. Hesketh's innocence partly depends on accepting his own testimony (1st Confession, HMC Cecil 4, p. 409) on what he thought the fatal letter contained. Petti (CRS 52, p. 200) supports Devlin's conclusion: Hesketh 'played his part unwittingly' and delivered the letter 'at the instigation of Burghley and others'. Hesketh was related to Sir Thomas Hesketh of Rufford, in whose company of players in 1581 was a certain 'Shakeshaft', believed by some to be the teenage William Shakespeare. He was also kin to Cardinal Allen.

p.297   'It seemeth that they are afraid' Hopkins to Allen, 25 December 1593 (Devlin, pp. 159–60). According to Verstegan (13 January 1594) there were rumours that Strange himself had been arrested. Hesketh was, he writes, 'sent with some message to the present Earl of Derby, but whether he were by him detected or not is uncertain, for some report that the Earl is deprived of his liberty' (CRS 52, p. 203). The whole affair seems to have been kept as quiet as possible. Six weeks after Hesketh's execution Verstegan knows only vague rumours. The same is true of the Jesuit Holt, who mentions news of Hesketh's death in a letter to Fr Persons, 6 January 1594, but adds: 'whether it be true or no, in short time we shall understand' (Strype, IV No. 96).

27 Poley's Network

p.299   **Poley to Brussels.** He left Whitehall on 1 March 1592, and was back four days later (PRO E351/542, f169). This is the only occasion on record when his payment was authorised by Burghley.

    Poley's cyphers. PRO SP106/2, Nos 73B, 73C, 73D, 105, 105A, 105B. First examined and analysed by Ethel Seaton in 1931: see Seaton (2). No. 105, in Poley's hand, is the cypher of c. 1591 discussed here. It is endorsed as 'found with French papers of 1590', but its area of interest is the Netherlands, and as it lists Cecil as Sir Robert it must have been written after May 1591, when he was knighted. No. 73B (in Poley's hand) and No. 105B (in clerk's hand, headed 'Another cypher for Ro: Pooley') are an identical key. On 73B the endorsement reads 'Martin's cypher'. I agree with Seaton that this cannot be made to read 'Marlin's [i.e. Marlowe's] cypher'. 'Giles Martin' was one of the aliases used by the intelligencer Thomas Barnes in 1591: it is possible that this is Poley's key to Barnes's correspondence with Phelippes. There is no firm date for this key: the mention of Sir Thomas Heneage gives a *terminus ad quem* of 17 October 1595, the date of Heneage's death. The latest of the cypher-keys is No. 105A, duplicated with minor variations in Nos 73C and 73D. This is after February 1596 (reference to Duke Alberti as 'Cardinal Governor' of Flanders) and has memoranda of payments to Poley in 1596-7 on the verso.

p.300 **Rutkin's statement** PRO SP12/238, No. 140. In CSP it is assigned to c. April 1591, but there is no evidence that Moody was in the Low Countries before the end of May. A more likely date is May 1592, when Burghley was investigating a 'bundle' sent by Moody, and wished to know 'who that Rutkyn is' (see below, note to p. 305). In this case, Rutkin's mention of Poley visiting the Low Countries 'about a year past' would perhaps refer to his mission to Ostend in December 1590 (PRO E351/542, f 154 verso). Rutkin and Poley later appear together in the Chamber accounts. Both had been in Antwerp, and both were paid, under Heneage's warrant, on 3 September 1592 (ibid, f 171 verso).

p.301 **Moody's despatches to Poley.** The earliest is a brief note from Flushing, 2 October 1591 (HMC Cecil 4, p. 142). Moody's other letters to Heneage of October 1591 (ibid, pp. 144-5, 147) are incorrectly calendared as being to the Earl of Essex. The addressee is identified only by a symbol, but it is not hard to discern 'T.H.' in the symbol, and it is anyway clear from Poley's reply (summarised in his memorandum: ibid, p. 156) that they were to Heneage. A letter from 'John Brystowe' to 'Mr Robyn' (19 June 1594, ibid p. 550) is also from Moody to Poley.

p.302 **Tipping and Moody.** On James Tipping, see above, note to p. 194. Moody wrote to him from Flushing, 2 October 1591 (ibid, pp. 141-2), asking him to tell Lady Jane Percy that her mother, the old Countess of Northumberland, was dead, and that a legacy was due to her. Charles Paget wrote on the same subject to 'Giles

Martin' [i.e. Thomas Barnes] a few days earlier (PRO SP12/240, No. 19).

Moody's recruitment. Moody to Heneage, 18 December 1590 (HMC Cecil 4, p. 77); Moody to Burghley, 18 and 27 May 1591 (PRO SP12/238, Nos 155, 185); Burghley's warrant for payment to Moody, 'for carrying of letters beyond the seas, and for other service to be done there', 27 May 1591 (PRO E351/542, f 156 verso).

Moody's first mission. See anonymous newsletter, 8 August 1591 (PRO SP101/1, f 173); the reports of Moody's companion, John Ricroft, August 1591 (PRO SP12/239, Nos 128, 132, 139, etc); the intercepted letters (HMC Cecil 4, pp. 270–1). The latter is miscalendared to 1587: references to the Siege of Noyou point to the summer of 1591. The abstracts of Ricroft's reports in CSP are confused and lack the important identification of 'Mr V' (Mr Vice-Chamberlain, i.e. Heneage).

Moody and Sidney. This episode is reconstructed from Sidney's letters to Burghley (October 1591 to January 1592, PRO SP84/43 and 44; LASP 3, Nos 72, 76, 79); Burghley to Heneage, 12 October 1591, HMC Cecil 4, p. 147; Poley's 'particulars' of his letter to Moody (ibid, p. 156). Ricroft accused Moody of colluding with Owen and Cosmo (secretary to the Duke of Parma) and of 'feigning' the letters he claimed to have intercepted. 'Notes of Moody's bad proceedings': PRO SP12/239, No. 140).

p.303 **Owen's ulterior ends.** Another shady operator in Flushing at this time, Patrick Sedgrave, was dealing with Sidney on Owen's behalf. 'Mr Owen told me', confessed Henry Walpole (CRS 5, p. 245), 'that there had been an Irishman, one Segrave, with the Governor of Vlissing, to deal with him about the town.' Sedgrave's dealings are traced in detail in LASP Foreign 3. He reappears in Flushing in 1595 under the alias 'Fitzjames' (HMC Cecil 5, pp. 415, 450–4).

p.305 **The 'bundle' at Sandwich.** Cecil to Heneage, 23 May 1592 (HMC Cecil 4, pp. 199–200) and 25 May 1592 (PRO SP12/242, No. 25).

p.307 **Who is keeping an eye on whom?** That it was the job of an English spy to spy on other English spies is a truism of the time. Cecil despatched one John Mowbray to Flushing in July 1591 for just that purpose: 'he will tell the Queen who are the intelligencers from England and to England, all which is double viewed by them there, and so we fed with fraud' (PRO SP12/240, No. 25). Mowbray was tumbled by Father Holt and interrogated by Secretary Cosmo. He was back in England by mid-September. Some time shortly after this, Marlowe posts to Flushing. It is possible that one of his tasks was to spy out Moody, whom Cecil suspected of duplicity and 'fraud'. Baines may have been there on a similar brief, though who he might have been working for (if anyone) is not known.

28 Roydon and the King of Scots

p.308 **Matthew Roydon.** There is no biography of him, and little remains of his work. See Eccles (7), pp. 117–18; Peele, I 67; Grey, p. 696. His 'Friend's Passion' was first published in the *Phoenix Nest* (1593), but was known to Nashe in MS in 1589. In his edition of the enigmatic *Willobie His Avisa* (1594), G.B. Harrison argues Roydon's authorship, but this is not generally accepted. On Roydon and Skeres see above, note to p. 30.

'Comic inventions' Nashe, III 323.

p.309 **Sir Edward Kelley.** See Dee's *Diary*; Elias Ashmole, *Theatrum Chemicum Britannicum* (1652); Nicholl (1), pp. 19–22. His first seance with Dee is recorded in BL Sloane MS 3188, f 9. Kelley is loftily treated by Dee's biographers: they underestimate his political role in Bohemia. I examine his early connections with Lancashire, and possibly with Lord Strange, in Nicholl (2), pp. 192–4. There are possible allusions to Kelley in Nashe's burlesque of the 'cunning man' in *Terrors of the Night* (Nashe, I 363–7), which was dedicated to Strange's niece, Elizabeth Carey.

p.310 **Hesketh and Dee.** Dee's *Diary*, 12 August 1581; Devlin, pp. 29–30. Cf Verstegan on Hesketh (CRS 52, p. 203): 'He had been sometime a merchant, but was fallen into decay by dealing with alchemists.'

Kelley and Burghley. Letters between them are in State Papers (Germany States and Hamburg); and Strype, Vols III and IV. See Sargent, pp. 97–122. Kelley reported the intended treasons of Christopher Parkins, a former schoolfellow of Thomas Watson, in 1589 (Strype, IV No. 1). Sir Edward Dyer is best known for his poem 'My Mind To Me A Kingdom Is'. Details remain of his alchemical experiments, under Kelley's tuition (Bodleian, Ashmole MS 1420, 1426 etc; Sargent, pp. 112f). Thomas Webbe as coiner: HMC Cecil 4, pp. 490, 537. Like Marlowe, he was accused of inducing a goldsmith (Abel Feckman) to the act; and like Marlowe he escaped serious punishment (PRO SP12/239, No. 20: 'Pardon for Thomas Webbe, convicted of coining and uttering Elizabeth shillings', 1 July 1594). He was despatched thereafter to the Low Countries.

'I have good cause' Burghley to Kelley, May 1591 (Strype IV, No. 2).

p.314   **Poley in Scotland.** PRO E351/542, ff 156 verso, 167 verso, 170 verso, 180, 180 verso, 181 verso.

Part Six: The Frame

29 Texts of Atheism

p.319   **'Get these glass eyes'.** *King Lear*, IV v 166–8. The pejorative definition of 'politician' is OED Sense 1: 'a politic person, chiefly in a sinister sense; a shrewd schemer, a crafty plotter'. This is styled obsolete (the latest citation is from 1764) though the modern, blander usage (Sense 2: 'one versed in the theory or science of government') carries instinctive vestiges of the earlier sense. The usage of 'policy' has a parallel evolution. As used by Marlowe and his contemporaries it conveys an idea of cynical political political exediency, or *realpolitik*. Cf Shakespeare, *1 Henry IV*, I iii 108: 'Never did base and rotten policy/Colour her working with such deadly wounds', where 'colour' is intelligence jargon for to cover or disguise. These senses of 'politician' and 'policy' were intimately associated with the theories of Machiavelli (cf Greene's comment about Marlowe and 'Machiavellian policy' in the *Groatsworth*, 1592; Greene xii 141–2).

p.320   **Nineteen allegations.** As itemised by Baines there are eighteen allegations, each beginning with the legalistic 'that ...' (i.e. 'Marlowe said and believed that ...'). The concluding paragraph contains a nineteenth: 'he saith loikewise that he hath quoted a number of contrarieties out of the Scripture which he hath given to some great men'.

p.321 **The vexed question.** Kocher hailed the 'Note' as 'the master-key to the mind of Marlowe' and 'an extraordinary document in the history of free thought' (Kocher (1), p. 33) but he was unaware of Baines's own mentality. It can be argued that some of its squibs have a serious intellectual position somewhere behind them (e.g. Christ as a 'bastard' and homosexual is a tarnished version of the Arian belief in the humanity of Christ; the quip about taking communion in a tobacco pipe echoes controversies about the symbolic nature of the sacrament; and so on) but this does not resolve whether Marlowe or Baines was responsible for the scurrilous form they take in the 'Note'.

p.323 **Sir John Puckering.** See DNB; W. J. Jones, *The Elizabethan Court of Chancery* (1967); David Lloyd, *State Worthies*, pp. 607–8; biographical notes by Bishop Kennett (BL, Lansdowne MS 982, f 246). Born in Yorkshire in 1544 and trained as lawyer, he was named Queen's Sergeant in 1586. On 28 April 1592 he succeeded Sir Christopher Hatton as Lord Keeper of the Great Seal and was knighted. He entertained the Queen at his country house at Kew. That Puckering was the anotator of the Baines 'Note' is shown by the endorsement on a letter he received from Lord Buckhurst, 8 November 1592 (see below, note to p. 383); the handwriting of this endorsement is certainly the same as that found on the 'Note', and the use of the personal pronoun ('matters concerning me . . . wch he sendeth me') shows it was Puckering himself, rather than one of his clerks, who wrote it.

Lord Buckhurst. Thomas Sackville, Baron Buckhurst (1536–1608) held the post of Lord High Butler, and was a Commissioner for Eclesiastical Causes. He was blood-related to the Queen: the Earl of Leicester said of him and Lord Hunsdon that 'they were *noli me tangere*', that is 'they were not to be contested with, for they were indeed of the Queen's near kindred' (Naunton, pp. 41–2). His name is coupled with Puckering's in documents relating to the Marlowe case but there is no specific indication of his role. Jones (*Elizabethan Court of Chancery*, p. 46) cites a contemporary manuscript to the effect that 'the Lord Keeper was a tool of Buckhurst and others'. Ironically Buckhurst had himself been a playwright: he was co-author with Thomas Norton of the early blank verse drama *Gorboduc* (performed 1561, published 1565).

Puckering's papers. BL Harley MS 7042 (transcripts by Baker), Stowe MS 166 (letters on behalf of Privy Council), Lansdowne MS 32, 47 (various).

p.324 **Barrow and Greenwood.** See DNB; J.W. Allen, *History of Political Thought in the Sixteenth Century*, pp. 220–28; various histories of Congregationalism. Greenwood was briefly contemporary with Marlowe at Corpus Christi, Cambridge: he graduated BA there in 1581. Penry's last weeks are vividly recorded in A. Peel (ed), *The Notebook of John Penry 1593* (Camden Soc., 1944). On the 'Mareprelate' controversy, see Nicholl (2), pp. 62–79.

Silencing dissidents. It was specifically as writers that Barrow and Greenwood were sentenced to death: they were arraigned under the elastically suppressive statute of 23 Eliz (1580–1) which made it a felony to 'write print, set forth or circulate . . . any book, rhyme, ballad, letter or writing . . . to the defamation of the Queen's Majesty or to the stirring up of insurrection'. Among their works, smuggled in 'slips and fragments' out of prison and printed in the Netherlands, were *The Brief Discourse of the False Church* (1590), and *Mr Barrow's Platform* (1593). Puckering's interest in seditious writings is evident in a warrant despatched by him and Sir Thomas Heneage on 29 May 1593, concerning 'certain books & writings . . . dangerous to Her Majesty & the State' found in the house of one Thomas Denton; investigators were ordered to 'privately search & peruse' the seized books, and 'take into their custody as many as they shall think fit' (CSP Dom Add 1580–1625, p. 351). He was also active in the prosecution of the Puritan author John Udall. On the silencing of authors at this time see also Appendix 2.5, 'Nashe in Newgate'.

p.326 **Cholmeley arrested.** BL Harley MS 7002, f. 10.

30 The Damnable Crew

p.328 **William Cholmeley.** He was 'clerk of the munition' at Flushing, at least from October 1592 and perhaps earlier (LASP Foreign 5, no 79; HMC Sidney 2, p. 174). He attended on Sir Robert Sidney during the latter's visit to England in 1593 (ibid, p. 145). Another possible Cholmeley-Marlowe connection is that John Cholmeley, a citizen-grocer of London, was part owner, with Philip Henslowe, of the Rose theatre, where Marlowe's *Jew of Malta* was performed by Strange's Men in 1592. However, there is no known connection between either of these men and Richard Cholmeley. Prof. Ernst Honigmann, who is expert on theatrical wills of the period, tells me John Cholmeley's will has not been discovered. He was possibly son of William Cholmeley (d. 1554) author of *The Request and Suit of a True-hearted Englishman* (1553), who was also a London grocer.

Young in Brussels. Confession of Henry Young, 30 July 1594 (PRO) SP12/249, No. 41). Young was named as an accomplice of Cholmeley's in the 'Remembrances' against Cholmeley (BL Harley MS 6848, ff. 190–1).

p.329 **The Cholmeley clan.** A genealogy of the Cholmeleys of Malpas is in *The Visitation of Cheshire 1580*, ed J.P. Rylands (London, 1882), pp. 63–4; this is based on manuscripts prepared by Robert Glover, Somerset Herald (BL Harley MSS 1424, 1505). The brief account of the family in DNB (sv Cholmondeley, Sir Hugh and Lady Mary) is apparently erroneous: the Lady Mary in question (née Holford) was not the wife of Sir Hugh Cholmeley senior (b. 1513), but of Hugh Cholmeley junior, who became Sir Hugh after his father's death in 1596. The confusion arises because Sir Hugh senior's second wife was also Mary (née Griffith). The IGI gives a birthdate for Richard Cholmeley jr of c 1556, but IGI's approximations are to be treated with caution. Richard's aunt Ursula was married to Thomas Stanley, a cousin of Lord Strange.

Yorkshire Cholmeleys. On Richard Cholmeley of Whitby, see Lacey (1) p. 273. He was involved in a scuffle at the Blackfriars theatre in 1603 (Gurr, pp. 69–70). He may be the 'Mr Cholmeley' concerned with catering matters at Essex House in 1597 (HMC Sidney 2, pp. 235–6), though this could be the Staffordshire Richard Cholmeley discovered by Hammer (see Appendix 2.9). Bakeless notes a Richard Cholmeley of Ingleton, Yorks, ordered to 'give bond' before the Privy Council in October 1591, but nothing further is heard of him. And David Riggs has found yet another candidate, Richard Cholmeley of Lewisham, Yorkshire, accused in Star Chamber of having forcibly entered the house of one Battersby, causing his wife to have a miscarriage. The case (PRO, STAC B13/18 II 39 *et al*) was mostly heard during 31 Eliz (i.e. between November 1588 and November 1589).

Sir Hugh Cholmeley. Writes to Walsingham, 25 September 1584 (PRO SP12/173, No. 26); investigates Holford, 18 May 1585 (CRS 5, pp. 109 ff); musters Cheshire troops, April 1588 (PRO SP12/209, No. 96). In 1593, he was considered 'fit to be a Treasurer at War' (HMC Cecil 4, p. 461).

p.330 **Francis Clerke.** This informer against Cholmeley in c. 1589 may be the same as the Francis Clercke who was involved in privateering ventures at this time (K. R. Andrews, *English Privateering Voyages to the West Indies, 1588–95* (1959), pp. 81, 345, 362, 374), and who may in turn be related to Ralegh's sea captain John Clarke, on whom see Nicholl (3), pp. 77, 369.

p.332 **Cholmeley and Drury.** APC 21, pp. 119, 291, 354; PRO E351/542, f 157 verso.

p.333 **Report by 'Chomley'.** PRO SP12/241, No. 35. Cholmeley's material about Southwell ('Suthwell') is not indexed in CSP, where the name is mistranscribed as 'Cuthwell'. Southwell on spies: CRS 52, p. 17. Burden is the veteran Nicholas Berden; Vachel may be the John Vachel described in a prison-list of 1593 as 'reconciled [i.e. converted] in the Marshalsea' (Strype, IV No. 109). I cannot identify Baker: it may be an alias. In the first edition I suggested that Cholmeley was referred to by Walsingham's former secretary Robert Beale in his 'Instructions for a Principal Secretary' (Read (1), I 437): 'for dealing with such as the laws of the realm esteemeth traitors . . . see first you have a good warrant to deal in such cases, as Montague and Chomley had, saving themselves by especial pardons'. This was written in c.

1592, but Beale was in fact looking back some forty years, to the involvement of Sir James Montague and Sir Roger Cholmeley in events surrounding the 'nine day reign' of Lady Jane Grey in 1553.

p.334 **Hugh Cholmeley's letter.** PRO SP12/241, No. 22. Warrant for Cholmeley and Richard Strong: APC 24, p. 130.

p.336 **Payment to Cholmeley.** PRO E351/542, f 167 verso.

The Shelleys. William Shelley was imprisoned in the Tower in 1583, further to the Throckmorton revelations. In 1588 he was the oldest prisoner in the Tower. His wife Jane, a native of Sutton, Herefordshire, had local connections with the family of Blanche Parry, who was the 'cousin' of Eleanor Bull (letter of James Parry, 11 November 1593, HMC Cecil 4, p. 413).

p.338 **The letter.** Seaton assumes the letter was an enclosure *with* the 'Remembrances'. It is certainly bound next to it in the Harley MSS, but that is to be expected whether it was contemporary with it or not. I suspect it was a later communiqué from the informer. I infer that it was addressed to Young because it was he who took charge of Cholmeley's apprehension in June, and because the handwriting is found in other reports connected with him (see below, note to p. 376). The form of address used, 'Your worship', suggests that the recipient was neither a knight ('Your honour') nor a nobleman ('Your lordship'). This rules out all the senior government figures, but is appropriate for Justice Young.

p.340 **'Ay, policy!'** *Jew of Malta*, I ii 160–1.

p.341 **'Live according to their own laws'** This echoes the professed aim of the sect called the 'Family of Love', an off-shoot of the Anabaptists. Founded in Holland by Henry Nicolas, it 'enjoyed considerable success with the lower classes in England' in the late sixteenth century. Anti-Familist propaganda claimed that 'they were libertines and lay with one another's wives; that they desired to have all men's goods in common; that they accounted whoredom, murder, poisoning, etc., to be no sin'. See Buckley, pp. 48–50; Strype, I p. 564. The sect is satirised in Thomas Middleton's *Family of Love* (1607).

p.342 **Cholmeley's arrest.** Young to Puckering, 29 June 1593, BL Harley MS 7002, f 10. I have regularised the spelling of

'Chomley' though Young often writes it 'Chamley'. The endorsement, in another hand, reads 'Mr Yong that Cholmeley is taken'. Wilbrom may be the same as the 'Mr Wilbram' who was involved in the prosecution of Nashe and Jonson after the staging of *The Isle of Dogs* in 1597 (APC 27, p. 338). Young features regularly in enforcement matters, and is typically mentioned in the same breath as Topcliffe. He had recently been authorised by Essex 'to deliver and receive letters'. These letters concerned intelligence matters, since they used cover-names devised by Phelippes (Essex to Phelippes, ?June 1593, PRO SP12/245, No. 41).

'**Bankar**' I am not certain of this reading, but fairly certain that Bancroft is referred to. On his role as propagandist and ecclesiastical spymaster, see Burn, pp. 149–80; Albert Peele (ed.), *Tracts Ascribed to Richard Bancroft* (1953); and commentators on the 'Marprelate' controversy.

p.344 **Henry Young.** He was 'Harry Young, son and heir of Mr Young of Kent, worth £60 a year' (PRO SP12/248, No. 69). On the docket he is said to have been 'taken & made an instrument to take the rest'. He had, in other words, been used against Cholmeley in or shortly after May 1593: another turncoat. Later that year he travelled to the Low Countries, where he is described as Captain Edmund Yorke's 'man', and as 'very good in making poison'. He played the projector with Yorke and Williams, but was imprisoned along with them in summer 1594. He doubtless knew Michael Moody, who also dogged this group. Of Jasper Borage nothing is known except the word 'dangerous' written beside his name on the docket.

'**Tippinges ii**' On James Tipping, see above, notes to pp. 194, 302. John Tipping seems to have been based largely in the Low Countries. It is probably he, rather than James, who is named (along with Moody) as a potential assassin of the Queen. See Seaton (1), pp. 276–9. In 1601, John is described as 'late lieutenant to Captain Stanley' (probably Sir William's brother, Edward Stanley). Sir Robert Cecil is warned that he is 'a dangerous fellow, coming over for your patronage' (CSP Dom 1601–3, pp. 37–8).

31 Placards and Fragments

p.346 **Dutch Church libel.** For sources, see above, notes to pp. 47–49.

p.350 **The bogus libel.** The penning of bogus Catholic propaganda has a dual purpose for the anti-Catholic agent: it serves as his cover; and it provides a useful source of false evidence against Catholic suspects.

p.351 **The Commission.** APC 24, p. 200. Sir John Puckering was present at the Privy Council meeting of 22 April, when the Commission was set up, and at the other two Council meetings about the libels (16 April, 11 May).

p.353 **'When I was first suspected'** As with many Elizabethans, Kyd's sentences are heavy on commas. It is conventional to prune these for modern readability, but here this involves an editorial decision. I have removed the comma between 'opinion' and 'affirmed', because I interpret Kyd to be saying that the opinion of Arianism, and not the document itself, had been 'affirmed by Marlowe to be his'. This is the natural reading, both from the syntax and the context.

32 The Target

p.358 **The aliens bill.** D'Ewes, p. 504; Lacey (2), pp. 210–11.

p.361 **Hariot 'convented' before the Council.** Deposition of Nicholas Jefferys, vicar of Wyke Regis, to the Bindon Commission, March 1594. Jefferys qualifies this as hearsay. Similarly, John Jessop, minister of Gillingham, deposed that 'he hath heard that one Herryott, of Sir Walter Rawleigh his house, hath brought the godhead in question, and the whole course of the Scriptures, but of whom he so heard it, he doth not remember'.

p.362 **Puckering's speech.** Black, p. 218.

The _Advertisement_. See Philopater, p. 18. This pamphlet, loosely attributed to Persons, seems mainly to have been the work of Richard Verstegan (CRS 52, p. xli), with contributions by Sir Francis Englefield and Henry Walpole. Walpole says it was 'begun to be translated and augmented' by Englefield, who them 'gave me the residue to prosecute, which I did, following too much his [i.e. Persons's] humour and style' (CRS 5, p. 265). Its full title is _An Advertisement Written to a Secretary of My L._

Treasurer of England by an English Intelligencer, concerning another book newly written in Latin against Her Majesty's Late Proclamation (i.e. it professes to be a Catholic interception of a government spy's report about Persons's book). See Strathmann (1), pp. 25 ff, and (2); Shirley (1), pp. 179–80.

p.365 **The Bindon commission.** 'Examinations Taken at Cearne [i.e. Cerne Abbas]', 21–8 March 1594, BL Harley MS 6849, ff 183–90. See Lacey (2) pp. 215–23; Shirley (1), 189–200; Buckley, pp. 137–52.

p.367 **The 'Hellish' verses.** HMC Marquis of Bath 2, pp. 52–3; BL Add MS 32092, f 201; Jacquot (1). The verses correspond to *Selimus* (1594), ii 305–67. The involvement of Sir Robert Cecil is suspected.

p.369 **Phelippes and Essex.** See above, note to p. 266.

Ralegh's exile. See Nicholl (3), pp. 41–8; A. L. Rowse, *Ralegh and the Throckmortons* (1962). 'Fortune's tennis ball': Naunton, p. 71.

Phelippes and Ralegh. This may not be the first time that Phelippes had been involved in a ploy against Ralegh. In February 1592 he despatched the following instructions to one of his agents, William Sterrell, who was about to return to the Low Countries. He should 'lay the ill success of the last employment on the Italian, S. Angelo, who cast so many difficulties that the executioner could not be brought in by him, and could not attend your return to Calais and the letters procured from Sir Walter Ralegh to the executioner, according to his desire' (Phelippes to 'Mr Saintman' [i.e. Sterrell], PRO SP12/241, No. 44). This is typically obscure, but from the general drift of the letter it appears that yet another 'sham plot' was underway, fomented by Phelippes and Sterrell; and that those letters from Ralegh to the 'executioner' (i.e. sham assassin) were intended to cause him problems by associating him with the plot. How Sterrell 'procured' these letters from Ralegh does not appear: some deception or forgery may be assumed.

Phelippes to Burghley. PRO SP12/245, No. 27, endorsed 'June 1593'.

'Every fool knoweth'. HMC Cecil 4, pp. 310–11.

33 'By My Only Means Set Down'

p.370 **Drury's letter.** LP MS 649, f 246; Bill, p. 29; first published and analysed by Sprott. The endorsement reads 'Lettre [not, as Sprott reads, 'Leave'] A Monr de Monr Thomas Dreury'. Sprott infers that Drury 'may have been in France', but the phrasing is that of Bacon's secretary (who frequently endorses Bacon's correspondence in French) not of Drury himself.

p.372 **The Lord Mayor's proclamation.** Sprott, citing London Records Office, Journal 23, f 191 verso.

p.375 **Notable villains.** Cholmeley and Young are the most likely candidates, though there is also a reference to one of the Tipping brothers, probably John, being in prison at some unspecified point in 1593: see below, note to p. 404.

p.376 **Handwriting of the 'Remembrances'.** Documents in the same hand are in BL Harley MS 6848, ff 32–36, 43–43 verso, 85. They are all examinations of religious suspects, by Young and others. The script, with its huge scooping back-formations, is rather unpleasant. Gunson's handwriting: letters to Walsingham from Newgate prison, 1586, ibid 286, ff 58–60.

p.378 **Drury imprisoned.** His first letter to Cecil from prison (HMC Cecil 4, pp. 366–7) is undated, but it must be some time between 1 August, when he wrote to Bacon from Richmond, and 17 August, when he wrote a further letter to Cecil (ibid. pp. 357–8), thanking him for his release.

p.383 **Buckhurst's letter.** BL Harley MS 6995, f 137. The letter is dated 8 November 1592, but endorsed by Puckering as 6 November. In a further letter, 12 November (ibid, ff 142–3), Buckhurst adds: 'Mr Drury longeth to receive your Lo[rdship's] answer, but more for your liberality for I see he is in great need, & some relief I have supplied towards him'. Puckering duly notes on the verso: 'My L of Buckhurst . . . for some money to Tho Drury.' See Kendall (2), pp. 524–7.

34 Drury Revealed

p.385 **The Drurys of Hawstead.** A detailed geneaology is in BL Add MS 19127. See also Arthur Campling, *History of the family of Drury* (London, 1937), especially chap 5, 'Drury of Hawstead', in which Thomas is fleetingly mentioned; Hasler, s.v. Drury, Sir William; Bald, pp. 237–46. Roy Kendall has made some important inroads into Drury's biography (Kendall (2), pp. 486 ff) but failed to work out which of the Thomas Drurys on record he was (cf Appendix 2.10 above). The more famous Elizabethan Drurys – Sir William, governor of Ireland in the late 1570's; and Sir Drew – were of the Buckinghamshire branch; their father, Sir Robert of Hedgerley, Bucks, was Thomas's great-uncle.

p.386 **Drury at Caius.** Venn I, 2, p. 69.

p.388 **Drury and Lord Burgh.** PRO, C2 Eliz I/B19/7/1; Kendall (2), pp. 498–505.

p.389 **Drury and Carey.** Drury to Sir Robert Cecil, 17 August 1593 (HMC Cecil 4, pp. 357–8). The £170 was partly owed to him (he claimed) on account of 'velvets and other silks' he had purchased for Carey and his wife. Sir Edmund Carey was the second son of the Lord Chamberlain, Baron Hunsdon.

    Drury and Oxford. Henry Howard to Queen Elizabeth, c. 29 December 1580 (BL, Cotton MS Titus C6, ff. 7–8). I am grateful to Alan Nelson, who is writing a biography of Oxford, for alerting me to this episode. On Ralegh's ambivalent relations with Oxford, see B.M. Ward, *Seventeenth Earl of Oxford* (1928), pp. 207–24; Lacey (2), pp. 34–7.

p.391 **Drury in the Fleet.** PRO SP12/178, No. 62, (injunction against John Meere, 20 May 1585); ibid/179, Nos 29 (Meere's deposition, 23 June), 42 (Drury's deposition, 26 June), etc. It is not clear when Drury was released: the Thomas Drury who was in the Fleet in the summer of 1586, and who wrote thence to Lord Burghley (ibid/190, No. 12), is the 'other' Thomas Drury (of Maids Morton), on whom see Appendix 2.10.

p.392 **Stafford and 'Dewry'.** Del Bene to de Buzenval, 11 September 1587, CSP Foreign 1586–88, pp. 374–80; Kendall (2), pp. 511–12. On Stafford as double agent, see Read (2).

p.393 **Sir William Drury.** On his debts and death, see Hasler, sv; Campling, Chap 5, citing accounts by Lord Willoughby and William-Lilly.

    Sir John Burgh. Tensions between Burgh and Sir William's son Robert are still evident in mid-1591, when Burgh requests an audience with the Queen now that 'young Mr Drury' has 'gone to France' (Burgh to Burghley, 12 August 1591, PRO SP12/239, f. 133). On Burgh and Ralegh, see Nicholl (3), pp. 49–50; K. R. Andrews, *English Privateering Voyages to the West Indies* (1959), pp. 225–35. On Burgh and Northumberland, see Shirley (1), p. 204. Burgh was himself killed in a duel, in early 1594, by Ralegh's nephew John Gilbert.

p.395 **Drury in France.** PRO E351/542, f. 208 verso.

Sir Robert Drury. His letter relating to Thomas Drury and William Mynne, c. 1599, is transcribed by Campling from an unidentified source in the Cecil MSS. Later letters from Sir Robert Drury to Cecil (19 and 20 December 1600; HMC Cecil 10, pp. 423, 425) refer to 'malicious reports' against him by certain 'villains' who 'hoped, by putting him in fear of their accusations, to make him relieve their wants'. This perhaps refers to Thomas. Sir Robert was later the patron of John Donne; the early death of his daughter Elizabeth (Thomas Drury's great-niece) in 1610 occasioned two of Donne's finest late poems, *The Progress of the Soul* and *An Anatomy of the World*.

p.397 **Drury and Dudley.** See A. Gould Lee, *The Son of Leicester* (1964), pp. 100–116; G. F. Warner (ed), *The Voyage of Robert Dudley to the West Indies* (1899), pp. xxxviii–xlvii; HMC Penshurst 3, pp. 142–7; Longleat, Dudley Papers 4, No. 88, and 6–8 *passim*. Among the deponents in the case was Elizabeth Drury, widow of Thomas.

35 Marlowe's Liberty

p.404 **'Typpin is in prison'** HMC Cecil 13, p. 502. 'Writ by Appleby' is ambiguous: it may mean that Appleby wrote *to* Tipping or that Appleby wrote *about* Tipping. A report by Thomas Appleby, dated 9 May 1593 (PRO SP85/1, f 156) contains the same information about Paget, de Lang, and White, but does not mention Tipping.

p.408 **'Climbing followers'.** Jew of Malta, Prologue spoken by 'Machiavel', l. 13.

SOURCES

1 Manuscript Collections and Calendars
(Acronyms used in the notes refer to the following sources)

APC   *Acts of the Privy Council, 1542–1604*, ed. J.R. Dasent, 32 vols (1890–1907).

BL   British Library, London; especially the Harley, Lansdowne, Cotton, Sloane and Additional collections in the Department of Manuscripts.

CRS   Catholic Record Society publications; especially:
Vol 2: *Miscellanea*, ed. J.H. Pollen, 1906.
Vol 5: *Unpublished Documents relating to the English Martyrs, 1584–1603*, ed. J.H. Pollen, 1908.
Vol 52: *The Letters & Despatches of Richard Verstegan*, ed. Anthony G. Petti, 1959.
Vol 53: *Miscellanea*, ed. Clare Talbot, 1961.

CSP   Calendar of State Papers; especially Domestic, Domestic Additional, Scottish and Foreign.

HMC   Historical Manuscripts Commission calendars and reports; especially:
Cecil: *Calendar of the Manuscripts of the Marquis of Salisbury at Hatfield House*, ed. various, 23 Vols (1883–1973).
Sidney: *Report on the Manuscripts of Lord de L'Isle at Penshurst Place*, ed. C.L. Kingsford et al, 4 Vols (1929–35).
Talbot: *A Calendar of the Shrewsbury and Talbot Papers at the College of Arms*, ed. G.R. Batho, 2 Vols (1969–71).

LASP   List and Analysis of State Papers; a continuation of CSP Foreign, currently up to December 1594.

LP   Lambeth Palace Library, London; especially the Bacon collection.

PRO   Public Record Office, London; especially Exchequer records (E), State papers (SP12, Domestic; SP15, Domestic Additional; SP53, Scottish; SP78, France; SP84, Holland) and Star Chamber proceedings (STAC).

SR   *A Transcript of the Registers of the Company of Stationers of London*, ed. Edward Arber, 5 Vols (London, 1875–94).

2 Individual Texts

(Authors' names in the notes refer to the following books, articles or documents)

Allen, William (ed.): *A True Report of the Late Apprehension of John Nicols* (Rheims, 1583).

Anderton, H. Ince: 'Marlowe in Newgate' (*Times Literary Supplement*, 13 September 1934).

Aubrey, John: *Brief Lives*, ed. Oliver Lawson Dick (Harmondsworth, 1972).

Bakeless, John: *The Tragicall History of Christopher Marlowe*, 2 vols (Cambridge, Massachusetts, 1942).

Baines, Richard: 'A Note Containing the Opinion of one Christopher Marly concerning his Damnable Judgement of Religion' (BL Harley MS 6848 ff 185–6 [original text], 6853 ff 307–8 [copy], 1593).

Bald, R. C.: *John Donne: A Life* (Oxford, 1970).

Batho, G. R.: (1) *The Household Papers of Henry Percy, 9th Earl of Northumberland* (London, 1962)

Batho, G. R.: (2) 'The Library of the Wizard Earl, Henry Percy, 9th Earl of Northumberland' (*The Library*, 5th Series, 15, 1960).

Bawcutt, N. W.: 'Machiavelli and Marlowe's *Jew of Malta*' (*Renaissance Drama* 3, 1970).

Beard, Thomas: *The Theatre of God's Judgements* (London, 1597).

Bill, E. G. W.: *Index to the Papers of Anthony Bacon in Lambeth Palace Library* (London, 1974).

Birch, Thomas: *Memoirs of the Reign of Queen Elizabeth*, 3 Vols (London, 1754).

Black, J. B.: *The Reign of Elizabeth* (Oxford, 1959).

Boas, F. S.: (1) *Christopher Marlowe* (Oxford, 1940).

Boas, F. S.: (2) 'Robert Poley: An Associate of Marlowe' (*Nineteenth Century and After*, October 1928).

Boas, F. S.: (3) 'Informer against Marlowe' (*Times Literary Supplement*, 16 September 1949).

Bossy, John: *Giordano Bruno and the Embassy Affair* (London, 1991).

Bray, Alan: *Homosexuality in Renaissance England* (London, 1982).

Brenan, G.: *History of the House of Percy* (London, 1902).

Brereton, J. Le Gay: 'The Case of Francis Ingram' (*Sydney University Publications 5*, 1905).

Briggs, William Dinsmore: 'On a Document Concerning Christopher Marlowe' (*Studies in Philology* 20, 1923).

Brooke, C.F. Tucker: (1) *Life of Marlowe* (London, 1930).

Brooke, C.F. Tucker: (2) 'The prototype of Marlowe's Jew of Malta' (*Times Literary Supplement*, 8 June 1922).

Brooks, E. St John: 'Marlowe in 1589–92?' (*Times Literary Supplement*, 27 February 1937).

Buckley, George T.: *Atheism in the English Renaissance* (Chicago, 1932).

Bull, G. B. G.: (1) 'John Evelyn & his Deptford' (*Transactions of the Lewisham Local History Society*, 1966).

Bull, G. B. G.: (2) 'Elizabethan Deptford' (*Transactions of the Lewisham Local History Society*, 1968).

Burn, Michael: *The Debatable Land* (London, 1970).

Byrne, Muriel St Clare: *Elizabethan Life in Town and Country* (London, 1925).

Caraman, Philip: *The Other Face: Catholic Life Under Elizabeth I* (London, 1960).

Chaudhuri, Sukanta: 'Marlowe, Madrigals & a New Elizabethan Poet' (*Review of English Studies* 39, 1989).

Clark, Eleanor Grace: *Ralegh and Marlowe: A Study in Elizabethan Fustian* (New York, 1941).

Cooper, Charles Henry: (1) *Annals of Cambridge*, 5 vols (Cambridge, 1842–1908).

Cooper, Charles Henry & Thompson: (2) *Athenae Cantabrigienses*, 2 vols (Cambridge, 1858–61).

Cunnington, C. Willett & Phillis: *Handbook of English Costume in the Sixteenth Century* (London, 1970).

Daniel, Samuel: *A Worthy Tract of Paulus Iovius, containing a Discourse of Imprese* (London, 1585).

Deacon, Richard: (1) *John Dee* (London, 1968).

Deacon, Richard: (2) *A History of the British Secret Service* (London, 1969).

Devlin, Christopher: 'The Earl and the Alchemist', 3 pts (*The*

Month, 1959).

Donne, John: *Poetical Works*, ed. H. J. C. Grearson, 2 vols (Oxford, 1912).

Eccles, Mark: (1) *Christopher Marlowe in London* (Cambridge, Massachusetts, 1934).

Eccles, Mark: (2) 'Marlowe in Newgate' (*Times Literary Supplement*, 6 September 1934).

Eccles, Mark: (3) 'Marlowe in Kentish Tradition' (*Notes & Queries*, 13, 20, 27 July 1935).

Eccles, Mark: (4) 'Jonson & the Spies' (*Review of English Studies* 13, 1937).

Eccles, Mark: (5) 'Samuel Daniel in France & Italy' (*Studies in Philology* 34, 1937).

Eccles, Mark: (6) 'Chapman's Early Years' (*Studies in Philology* 43, 1946).

Eccles, Mark: (7) 'Brief Lives: Tudor and Stuart Authors' (*Studies in Philology* 79, 1982).

Empson, William: *Faustus and the Censor* (Oxford, 1987).

Eriksen, Roy T.: 'Giordano Bruno & Marlowe's *Dr Faustus*' (*Notes & Queries*, December 1985).

d'Ewes, Sir Simonds: *Journal of the House of Commons* (London, 1693).

Feasy, Lynette & Eveline: (1) 'Nashe's *The Unfortunate Traveller*: Some Marlovian Echoes' (*English* 7, No. 39, 1948).

Feasy, Lynette & Eveline: (2) 'The Validity of the Baines Note' (*Notes & Queries*, 26 November 1949).

Fraser, Antonia: *Mary Queen of Scots* (London, 1969).

Freeman, Arthur: (1) *Thomas Kyd: Facts and Problems* (Oxford, 1968).

Freeman, Arthur: (2) 'Marlowe, Kyd & the Dutch Church Libel' (*English Literary Renaissance* 3, 1973).

French, Peter, J.: *John Dee: The World of an Elizabethan Magus* (London, 1972).

Friedenreich, Kenneth; Gill, Roma; Kuriyama, Constance (eds): '*A Poet and a Filthy Play-maker': New Essays on Christopher Marlowe* (New York, 1988).

Fuller, Thomas: *The History of the Worthies of England* (1662), ed. Richard Barber (London, 1989).

Gatti, Hilary: 'Giordano Bruno: The Texts in the Library of the Ninth Earl of Northumberland' (*Journal of the Warburg and Courtauld Institutes* 46, 1983).

Grantley, Darryll, and Roberts, Peter (eds): *Christopher Marlowe and English Renaissance Culture* (Aldershot, 1996).

Gray, Austin K.: 'Some Observations on Christopher Marlowe, Government Agent' (*Publications of the Modern Language Association of America* 43, 1928).

Greg, W. W.: (1) *Marlowe's 'Dr Faustus', 1604–16* (London, 1950).

Greg, W. W.: (2) 'The Copyright of *Hero and Leander*' (*The Library*, 4th Series, 24, 1944).

Greene, Robert: *Complete Works in Prose and Verse*, ed. Alexander B. Grosart, 15 vols (London, 1881–6).

Gurr, Andrew: *Playgoing in Shakespeare's London* (Cambridge, 1987).

Hall, E. Vine: 'Marlowe's Death at Deptford Strand' (*Testamentary Papers* 3, 1937).

Hall, Hubert: 'An Elizabethan Poet and his Relations' (*Athenaeum*, 23 August 1890).

Handover, P. M.: *Arabella Stuart* (London, 1957).

Harvey, Gabriel: *Works*, ed. Alexander B. Grosart, 3 vols (London, 1884–5).

Hasler, P. W.: *The House of Commons, 1558–1603*, 3 vols (London, 1981).

Haynes, Alan: (1) *Robert Cecil, 1st Earl of Salisbury* (London, 1989).

Haynes, Alan: (2) *Invisible Power: the Elizabethan Secret Service 1570–1603* (Stroud, 1992)

Henslowe, Philip: *Diary*, ed. R. A. Foakes and R. T. Rickert (Cambridge, 1961).

Hicks, Leo: (1) *An Elizabethan Problem: the Careers of Two Exile-Adventurers* (London, 1964).

Hicks, Leo: (2) 'An Elizabethan Propagandist: The Career of Solomon Aldred' (*The Month*, May-June 1945).

Hicks, Leo: (3) 'The Strange Case of William Parry' (*Studies*, Dublin, September 1949).

Hicks, Leo: (4) 'The Growth of a Myth: Father Robert Persons and *Leicester's Commonwealth* (*Studies*, Dublin, Spring 1957).

Hoffman, Calvin: *The Murder of the Man Who Was Shakespeare* (London, 1955).

Hotson, J. Leslie: *The Death of Christopher Marlowe* (Cambridge, Massachusetts, 1925).

Jacquot, Jean (1): 'Ralegh's "Hellish Verses" and the *Tragicall Raigne of Selimus*' (*Modern Language Review* 48, 1953).

Jacquot, Jean: (2) 'Harriot, Hill, Warner and the New Philosophy' (in Shirley (2) , pp. 107ff).

Kalb, Eugénie de: (1) 'The Death of Marlowe' (*Times Literary Supplement*, 21 May 1925).

Kalb, Eugénie de: (2) 'Robert Poley's Tower Bills' (*Nineteenth Century & After*, November 1928).

Kalb, Eugénie de: (3) 'An Elucidation of the Death of Christopher Marlowe' (Ph.D. Dissertation, Cambridge University Library, 1929).

Kalb, Eugénie de: (4) 'Robert Poley's Movements as a Messenger of the Court, 1588–1601' (*Review of English Studies* 9, 1933).

Kendall, Roy: (1) 'Richard Baines and Christopher Marlowe's milieu' (*English Literary Renaissance* 24.3, 1994).

Kendall, Roy: (2) 'Richard Baines and Christopher Marlowe: A Symbiotic relationship' (Ph.D. dissertation, University of Birmingham, 1998).

Knox, T. F.: *The First and Second Diaries of the English College, Douai* (London, 1878).

Kocher, Paul: (1) *Christopher Marlowe: A Study in his Thought, Learning and Character* (Chapel Hill, 1946).

Kocher, Paul: (2) 'François Hotman and Marlowe's *Massacre at Paris*' (*Publications of the Modern Language Association* 56, 1941).

Kocher, Paul: (3) 'Some Nashe marginalia concerning Marlowe' (*Modern Language Notes* 57, 1942).

Kuriyama, Constance: 'Marlowe, Shakespeare, and the Nature of Biographical Evidence' (*University of Hartford Studies in Literature* 20, No. 1, 1988).

Kyd, Thomas: (1) 'Touching Marlowe's Monstruous Opinions' (BL Harley MS 6848, f 154, 1593).

Kyd, Thomas: (2) Letter to Sir John Puckering (BL Harley MS 6849, ff 218–218 verso, 1593).

Labanoff, Prince A.: *Lettres de Marie Stuart*, 7 vols (London, 1844).

Lacey, Robert: (1) *Robert, Earl of Essex: An Elizabethan Icarus* (London, 1971).

Lacey, Robert: (2) *Sir Walter Ralegh* (London, 1973).

Loomie, Albert: *The Spanish Elizabethans* (London, 1965).

Marlowe, Christopher: *Complete Works*, ed. Fredson Bowers, 2 Vols (Cambridge, 1981).

du Maurier, Daphne: *Golden Lads: A Study of Anthony Bacon* (London, 1975).

McKerrow, R. B.: *A Dictionary of Printers and Booksellers in England, 1557–1640* (London, 1910).

Meres, Francis: *Palladis Tamia, or Wit's Treasury* (London, 1598).

More, Hale: 'Gabriel Harvey's References to Marlowe' (*Studies in Philology* 23, 1926).

Morris, John: *The Troubles of our Catholic Forefathers* (London, 1875).

Moore-Smith, G. C.: (1) 'Marlowe at Cambridge' (*Modern Language Review* 4, 1909).

Moore-Smith, G. C.: (2) 'Matthew Roydon' (*Modern Language Review* 9, 1914).

Motley, John Lothrop: *History of the United Netherlands*, 4 Vols (London, 1867).

Nashe, Thomas: *Works*, ed. R. B. McKerrow and F. P. Wilson, 5 vols (Oxford, 1958).

Naunton, Sir Robert: *Fragmenta Regalia* (1641), ed. John S. Cerovski (Washington D. C., 1985).

Nicholl, Charles: (1) *The Chemical Theatre* (London, 1980).

Nicholl, Charles: (2) *A Cup of News: the Life of Thomas Nashe* (London, 1984).

Nicholl, Charles: (3) *The Creature in the Map: A Journey to El Dorado* (London, 1995).

Nicholl, Charles: (4) '*Dr Faustus* and the Politics of Magic' (*London Review of Books*, 8 March 1990).

Peters, C. H. J.: *Flushing Throughout the Ages* (Vlissingen, n.d.).

Petti, Anthony G.: See CRS in Sources/1.

'Philopater, Andreas': *An Advertisement written to a Secretary of My L. Treasurer* (Antwerp, 1592).

Plowden, Alison: *The Elizabethan Secret Service* (London, 1991).

Pollen, J. H.: See CRS in Sources/1.

Pollen, J. H.: (1) *The English Catholics in the Reign of Queen Elizabeth* (London, 1920).

Pollen, J. H.: (2) 'The Politics of the English Catholics during the Reign of Queen Elizabeth' (*The Month*, March–August 1902).

Pollen, J. H.: (3) 'Mary Queen of Scots and the Babington Plot' (Scottish History Society, 1922).

Pollen, J. H., and Butler, E. C.: 'Dr William Gifford in 1586' (*The Month*, March–April 1904).

Prokter, Adrian, and Taylor, Robert: *The A–Z of Elizabethan London* (London Topographical Society, 1979).

Purdon, Noel: 'Quod me Nutrit' (*Cambridge Review*, 1967).

Raines, F. R. (ed.): *The Household Books of Edward and Henry, 3rd and 4th Earls of Derby* (Manchester, 1853).

Read, Conyers: (1) *Mr Secretary Walsingham and the Policy of Queen Elizabeth*, 3 Vols (Oxford, 1925).

Read, Conyers: (2) 'The Fame of Sir Edward Stafford' (*American Historical Review* 20, 1915).

Ribner, Irving: 'Greene's attack on Marlowe: Some Light on *Alphonsus and Selimus*' (*Studies in Philology* 52, 1955).

Riggs, David: (1) 'Marlowe's Quarrel with God' in White, pp. 15–38.

Riggs, David: (2) 'The Killing of Christopher Marlowe' (*Stamford Humanities Review* 8.1, 2000)

Sales, Roger: *Christopher Marlowe* (London, 1991).

Sahel, Pierre: 'Les Prisons Politiques chez Marlowe et Shakespeare' (*Société Française Shakespeare*, Paris, 1981).

Sargent, Ralph: *At the Court of Queen Elizabeth: The Life & Lyrics of Sir Edward Dyer* (London, 1935).

Schoenbaum, S.: *William Shakespeare: A Documentary Life* (Oxford, 1975).

Schrickx, Willem: 'Christopher Marlowe in Vlissingen' (*Documenta* 1, No. 3, 1983).

Seaton, Ethel: (1) 'Marlowe, Robert Poley & the Tippings' (*Review of English Studies* 5, 1929).

Seaton, Ethel: (2) 'Robert Poley's Ciphers' (*Review of English Studies* 7, 1931).

Shakespeare, William: *The Works* (Arden edition, ed. various, 1889 onwards).

Shepherd, Simon: *Marlowe and the Politics of Elizabethan Theatre* (Brighton, 1986).

Shield, H. A.: 'The Death of Marlowe' (*Notes & Queries*, March 1957).

Shirley, John W. (ed.): (1) *Thomas Harriot: Renaissance Scientist* (Oxford, 1974).

Shirley, John W.: (2) *Thomas Harriot: A Biography* (Oxford, 1974).

Shirley, John W.: (3) 'The Scientific Experiments of Sir Walter Ralegh, the Wizard Earl, and the Three Magi in the Tower, 1603–17' (*Ambix* 4, 1948).

Smith, Alan Gordon: *The Babington Plot* (London, 1936).

Southern, A. C.: *Elizabethan Recusant Prose* (London, 1950).

Sprott, S. E.: 'Drury & Marlowe' (*Times Literary Supplement*, 2 August 1974).

Stow, John: (1) *A Survay of London* (1603), ed. C. H. Kingsford, 2 Vols (Oxford, 1908).

Stow, John: (2) *Annales, or General Chronicle of England* (London, 1631).

Strathmann, Ernest A.: (1) *Sir Walter Ralegh: A Study in Elizabethan Scepticism* (New York, 1951).

Strathmann, Ernest A.: (2) 'The Textual Evidence for "The School of Night"' (*Modern Language Notes* 56, 1941).

Strathmann, Ernest A.: (3) 'Ralegh and the Catholic Polemists' (*Huntington Library Quarterly* 4, 1945).

Strathmann, Ernest A.: (4) 'John Dee as Ralegh's "Conjuror" (*Huntington Library Quarterly* 10, 1947).

Strype, John, *Annals of the Reformation*, 4 Vols (Oxford, 1824).

Talbot, Clare: See CRS in Sources/1.

Tannenbaum, Samuel: *The Assassination of Christopher Marlowe* (Hartford, 1926).

Thomson, H. W., and Padover, S. E.: *Secret Diplomacy: A Record of Espionage and Double Dealing, 1500–1815* (London, 1937).

Thurston, Gavin: 'Christopher Marlowe's Death' (*Contemporary Review*, March–April 1964).

Urry, William: *Christopher Marlowe and Canterbury* (London, 1988).

Vaughan, William: *The Golden Grove Moralized* (London, 1600).

Venn, John and J. A.: *Alumni Cantabrigienses*, 4 vols (Cambridge, 1922–7).

Watson, Thomas: *Compendium Memoriae Localis* (London, *c.* 1585).

Weil, Judith: *Christopher Marlowe: Merlin's Prophet* (Cambridge, 1977).

Weiner, Andrew D.: 'Expelling the Beast: Bruno's Adventures in England' (*Modern Philology*, August 1980).

Wernham, R. B.: (1) *After the Armada* (Oxford, 1948).

Wernham, R. B.: (2) 'Christopher Marlowe at Flushing in 1592' (*English Historical Review*, April 1976).

White, Paul Whitfield (ed): *Marlowe, History and Sexuality: New Critical Essays on Christopher Marlowe* (New York, 1998).

Williams, F. B. jun.: 'Ingram Frizer' (*Times Literary Supplement*, 15 August 1935).

Wraight, A. D.: *In Search of Christopher Marlowe* (London, 1965).

Yates, Frances: (1) *A Study of 'Love's Labour's Lost'* (London, 1936).

Yates, Frances: (2) *Giordano Bruno and the Hermetic Tradition* (London, 1964).

Yates, Frances: (3) *The Occult Philosophy in the Elizabethan Age* (London, 1979).

Yates, Frances: (4) 'Essays on Giordano Bruno in England' (*Collected Works*, Vol. 1, 1982).

3 Illustrations

Bodleian Library, Oxford – pl. 6; British Library – pls. 4, 5, 7, 8, 19, 22, 23; Centre for Kentish Studies, Maidstone – pl. 2 (signature of Christopher Marlowe); Christ Church College, Oxford, courtesy of the Evelyn Trustees – endpapers, pl. 3; The Master and Fellows of Corpus Christi College, Cambridge – frontispiece (supposed portrait of Christopher Marlowe); The Earl of Derby – pl. 16; Gemeente Archief, Vlissingen – pl. 14; National Gallery of Ireland – pl. 20; National Portrait Gallery, London – pls. 10, 17, 21; Public Record Office – pls. 1, 2 (signatures of Ingram Frizer, Nicholas Skeres, and Robert Poley), 11, 12, 15, 18: Crown Copyright material in the Public Record Office is reproduced by permission of the Controller of Her Majesty's Stationery Office; Rijksmuseum, Amsterdam – pl. 13; The President and Fellows of Trinity College, Oxford – pl. 9.

INDEX

Abingdon, Edward 177, 180, 189
Acheley, Thomas 213
Acquaviva, Claudius 116
Addey, John 13
Advertisement, The (pamphlet) 362-4
Agazzari, Alfonso 149
agents provocateurs 135-6
Agrippa, Cornelius 248
Alderney, Channel Islands 275
Aldred, Salomon 115, 130-1, 204, 205, 443, 490
Aldrich, Henry 244
Aldrich, Simon 244-5, 464
Aldrich, Thomas 244
Allde, John 205
Allen, Thomas (mathematician) 233
Allen, Thomas (governor of Portland Castle) 366
Allen, Dr (*later* Cardinal) William 145, 274; and Baines 146, 148, 149, 153, 445, 447; and Cycell 271, 273; and Hesketh 297, 522; and Northumberland 235; *A True Report of the . . . Imprisonment of John Nicols* 150

Alleyn, Edward 241, 268
Anger, Henry 42
Anjou, François, Duke of 16, 124, 139, 216, 392
Antonio, Don (Portuguese pretender) 33, 170, 330, 457
Appleby, Thomas 404
Archer, Francis *see* Frizer, Ingram
Arden, Thomas 101-2
Ardern, Robert: letter to Lord Burghley 425-6
Areopagus, the (literary group) 213
Aretino, Pietro 63, 64, 65, 390
Arian treatise 50-1, 53, 347, 352-5, 349, 360, 373-4, 401
Arianism 51, 66
Arundel, Charles 392; *Leicester's Commonwealth* 37-8, 162, 288
Arundel, Philip Howard, Earl of 214, 389
Assheton, Reverend John 51
Aston, Edward: Essex's letter to 452
Aubrey, John 232, 233, 420

Babington, Anthony 173, 174, 176, 177, 192; and Poley

35-6, 177, 178-80, 181-3, 184-5, 186, 187, 189-90; and Skeres 32-3, 35, 141; trial and execution 188-9

'Babington Plot' 32, 117, 129, 132, 140-1, 153-4, 160-1, 173-95, 261-2

Bacon, Anthony 265-6, 369, 443; Drury's letter to 370-4, 375, 377, 378, 386-7, 395, 459

Bacon, Francis 265, 266, 369, 387

Bacon, Sir Nicholas 386, 387

Bacon, Nicholas 387

Bagot, Richard: Essex's letter to 452

Bailey, Thomas 445

Baines, Richard 147, 386, 421; and Cholmeley 374; and Drury 370; 371, 372, 394, 399, 407; at English College, Rheims 146-7, 148-53, 155, 205, 321-2, 445-8; frames Kyd as libeller 372-3, 374; and Marlowe 109, 155, 199, 279, 280, 281, 282, 284, 291, 318, 322, 368, 381-2; 'Note' on Marlowe 54-5, 66-7, 69, 87-8, 115, 152-3, 286, 319, 320-7, 338-9, 343, 346, 356, 357, 361, 363, 377, 378, 405, 406-7, 408, 431, 446; as rector of Waltham 153-4

Baldwin, Robert 20, 42

Ballard, John 117, 173, 386; and Baines 147, 153-4; role in 'Babington Plot' 117, 140-1, 161, 174-6, 177, 179, 186, 190; trial and execution 188-9

Ballard, William 153

Bancroft, Richard, Archbishop of Canterbury 342

Bannings (Bayning), Paul 436

'Barasino' see Throckmorton, Thomas Barkworth (priest) 423

Barne, George 440

Barnes, Thomas ('Giles Martin') 115, 430-1, 523, 524

Barnwell, Robert 174, 177, 188, 189

Barrow, Henry 324

Bartholomew's Eve massacre 48, 124, 200, 443

Basingstoke: Angel Inn 27

Baskerville, Sir Thomas 439

Beale, Robert, 130, 135, 531

Beard, Dr Thomas 77, 327, 420; account of Marlowe's death (in The Theatre of God's Judgements) 77-9, 80, 84, 92, 97-8, 104, 105, 409

Beaton, James, Archbishop of Glasgow 140, 164, 168, 217

Bellamy, Bartholomew 188

Bellamy, Jeremy 188

Belvedere (anthology) 269

Benchkin, Mistress 119

Bene, Abbé del 392

Berden, Nicholas 112, 115, 130, 132, 186, 190, 288, 333, 531

Best (Beast), Edetha 391-2, 458-9

Bickley, Ralph 132

Bindon Commission 365-6, 460

Birde, William 250

Birkenshaw, Ralph 295
Blount, (Sir) Christopher 157, 164-6, 167, 168-9, 170, 193, 400; execution 165, 418
Blount, Edward 21, 83, 142, 200, 420; preface to *Hero and Leander* 21, 26, 69, 81-2, 138
Blount, Lettice 165
Boas, F. S. 149, 445
Bodley, Thomas 127
Borage, Jasper 332-3, 344, 360, 370, 533
Borough (Burgh), Sir John 292, 393-4, 518
Bossy, John 254
Bostock, Thomas 27
Bowers, Fredson 449, 451
Bradley, William 103, 210-12
Bradshaw, Elizabeth 221
Brandon, Eleanor 271
Bray (ship) 290
Bray, Alan: *Homosexuality in Renaissance England* 431-2
Bridewell prison 49, 135, 419, 422
Bridgeman, Jacob 120
Bridgwater, John: *Concertatio Ecclesiae Catholicae in Anglia* 149
Bromley, Sir Thomas 388, 454
Brooke, Christopher 61
Brooks, E. St John 428, 429
Broughton, James 98
Browne, Christopher 15
Browne, Mrs 161-2
Browne, Robert 451
Bruce, Robert, of Binnie 130, 313
Bruno, Giordano 246-50, 253-7; *Cena de le Ceneri* 246,

247, 248, 249; *De Gli Eroici Furori* 246, 251-3; *De Umbris Idearum* 256; *Spaccio della Bestia Trionfante* 246, 253, 254
Buc, George 213
Buckhurst, Lord 323, 368, 407; and Drury 377, 378, 381, 383, 395
Buckle, Sir Cuthbert 46
Bull, Eleanor (*née* Whitney) 41-3, 439, 440; Deptford Strand house 18, 20, 40-1, 43, 100, 199, 156, 314, 409, 413, 441
Bull, George 43
Bull, Richard, Sr 439-40
Bull, Richard 42, 439, 440
Burgh, Sir John *see* Borough, Sir John
Burgh, Lord William 388-9
Burghley, William Cecil, Lord 31, 42, 117, 222, 418; abused by Cholmeley 331, 340; and Drury 393, 395, 453-4; involvement in intelligence service 122, 264, 265, 266, 299, 313, 369; and Edward Kelley 310-11; and Marlowe 110, 279, 282, 284-5, 295, 299; and Moody 303, 304, 305; and Poley 299, 303; Sir Robert Sidney's letter to 279-80, 281, 293, 293, 294; surveillance of Lord Strange 272, 277, 292, 294, 314; and Francis Walsingham 123, 216, 264
Burnell, Anne (*née* Kirkall) 219-22, 256
Burnell, Edward 219, 220-1

Bushell, Edward 291-2, 293
'Bye Plot' 215, 366, 418

Caesar, Dr Julius 46, 351
Caldecott, Thomas 116
Cambridge University 77, 114-
 16, 203, 261, 288; Caius
 116-17, 147, 154, 386;
 Christ's 147; Clare 157;
 Corpus Christi 6-7, 8, 9, 62,
 110, 113, 118-21, 143, 244,
 442; Jesus 454; Pembroke
 79; St John's 62; Trinity 7
Camden, William 213; *Annals
 of England* 123, 192, 263,
 265, 296, 302
Campion, Edmund 116, 133-4,
 206, 271
Carey, Sir Edmund 389, 412
Carey, Sir George 308, 441-2
Catlin, Maliverny 159-60, 191,
 236, 237-8, 239
Cecil, Sir Robert 126, 264,
 265, 299, 359, 369, 419; and
 Cholmeley 328, 331, 334-7,
 340, 350, 376, 379-80, 381,
 403; Drury's letters to 378-
 81, 403; and 'Hesketh plot'
 296, 297; and Marlowe 294,
 299, 306-7, 402-5, 407-8,
 415; and Moody 303, 305,
 307, 314; and Poley 265,
 299, 305, 306-7, 413, 416,
 422; portrait 7; and Ralegh
 369; surveillance of Lord
 Strange 272-3, 277, 294
Cecil, William *see* Burghley,
 Lord Cecil, William
 (Burghley's grandson) 429
Chalkhill, Mr (coroner) 211
Chamberlain, Agnes 435

Chamberlain, Andrew 27
Chamberlain, Ingram 435-6
Chamberlain, Margery (*née*
 Deane) 27
Chapman, George 30, 227,
 229, 357, 420, 451; sequel to
 Hero and Leander 82, 433;
 The Shadow of the Night 30,
 308-9, 451
Chapman, John 147
Chateauneuf, Guillaume de
 l'Aubespine, baron de 169,
 171-2, 194, 491
Chester, Charles 62-3
Chettle, Henry 85, 471
Chislehurst, Kent: St Nicholas's
 73; *see also* Scadbury House
Cholmeley, Lade Anne (*née*
 Dorman) 329
Cholmeley, Edward 452
Cholmeley, Henry 453
Cholmeley, Sir Hugh 329-30
Cholmeley, Hugh 329, 334-7
Cholmeley, Richard 52, 328,
 329, 330; accuses Marlowe
 of atheism 52-3, 60, 233,
 234, 319, 329, 338-9, 340,
 341, 343, 360, 363, 364;
 arrested 326, 341-3, 345,
 375, 401; and Baines 374,
 378; as Dutch Church libeller
 350-2; and Essex 452-3; in
 intelligence service 52, 55,
 109, 132-3, 265, 328, 332-3
 (*see also under* Cecil, Sir
 Robert); and Marlowe 328,
 381-2, 401-2; *see also* Drury,
 Thomas
Cholmeley, William 328
Citolino, Paolo 139
Clement, VIII, Pope 146

Clerke, Francis 330
Cobham, Sir Henry 139, 140, 217, 234-5, 255
Coke, Sir Edward 231, 398
Constable, Henry 114
Cooke, Robert 454
Copernicus, Nicolas 247
Corkine (tailor) 103
Corkine, William 103
Cornwallis, Frances 223-4, 227
Cornwallis, William, Sr 223, 224-5, 227
Cornwallis, William 223, 224, 225, 227
Corpus Christi College *see* Cambridge University
Cosmo (Duke of Parma's secretary) 524, 525
Coxeter, Thomas 229
Creagh, Richard, Archbishop of Armagh 193
Crighton, William 313, 500
Critiz, John de: *Sir Francis Walsingham* 123
Crofts, Sir James 110
Cromwell, Oliver 77, 420
Crushe, Paul 292
Curll, Gilbert 184
Curry, William 20
Cycell, John 271-3, 277, 294, 313

Dabyns, Henry 20
Dalton, James 221
Damnable Life of Dr John Faustus, The ('P.F.') 250
Danby, William (coroner) 20, 21, 22, 45
Daniel, Samuel 203-5, 209, 227, 251, 444; *Delia* 203;

The Worthy Tract of Paulus Jovius 9-10
Davies, John 449-50; *Epigrammes and Elegies By I.D. and C.M.* 448-51
Dawbney, Thomas 284
De Tribus Impostoribus Mundi (anon.) 65
Deane, James 27, 435, 436
Dee, Dr John 42, 231, 232, 233-4, 248, 252, 310, 363
Defoe, Daniel 202
Deptford 13-17; docks 440; *see also* Sayes Court
Deptford Green: St Nicholas's 20-1, 42, 98
Deptford Strand 13, 20, 40-1; *see also* Bull, Eleanor
Derby, Ferdinando Stanley, 5th Earl of *see* Strange, Lord 270, 290
Derby, Henry Stanley, 4th Earl of 2, 70, 290
Deventer, battle of 274, 276, 289
Devlin, Christopher 297
Digges, Alice 222
Digges, Thomas 247
Donne, John 61, 89, 114, 174
Douai, France 301; English College 145, 213, 214
Douglas, Archibald 426
Drake, Sir Francis 15-17, 221, 331
Drummond, William 422
Drury, Anne (*née* Bacon) 387
Drury, Audrey (*née* Rich) 385
Drury, Charles 396
Drury, Sir Drew 412
Drury, Elizabeth (*née* Fitzharding) 387

Drury, Elizabeth (née Stafford) 387

Drury, Henry (Thomas's brother) 385, 386

Drury, Henry (Thomas's cousin) 391

Drury, John 386

Drury, Sir Robert (Thomas's nephew) 387, 393; letter to George Parker 395-6

Drury, Sir Robert, of Hedgerly 412

Drury, Robert (Thomas's father) 385

Drury, Robert (Thomas's brother) 385

Drury, Robert (martyr) 386

Drury, Thomas 384, 385-6, 387-90, 392-3, 395-6, 398-9, 411-2, 421; arrested 332-3, 344, 378, 383, 394, 444; as author of 'Remembrances. . . against Cholmeley. . .' 376 (see under Cholmeley, Richard); and Baines 370, 371, 372, 394, 399, 407; and Cholmeley 332-3, 370, 374-6, 378, 379-80, 381, 383, 394, see also 'Remembrances' (below); and Kyd 373-4; letter to Anthony Bacon 370-4, 375, 377, 378, 386-7, 395, 459; letter to Sir Robert Cecil 378-81, 403; and Marlowe 381-2, 390, 394, 412; marriage 387; and Meeres 391-2, 459-60; and Magdalen Salisbury and Robert Dudley's legitimacy 397-9; and Puckering see

under Puckering, Sir John; and Ralegh 390-1, 392, 393-4 'Remembrances of Words & Matter against Ric: Cholmeley' (and informant's letter) 52-3, 60, 233, 234, 319, 328-9, 330-2, 333-4, 337-41, 343-5, 346, 350, 351, 360, 363, 364, 375, 376, 377, 379, 380, 401, 403, 405

Drury, Thomas (of Maids Morton) 453-5

Drury, Thomas (of Rougham) 455

Drury, Sir William (Thomas's grandfather) 385

Drury, Sir William (Thomas's brother) 386, 387, 388, 393

Dudley, Sir Robert 397, 398

Dudley, William 452

Duffield, Henry 292

Dunne, Henry (Harry) 32, 174, 177, 188

'Durham House Set' 60, 358, 362-4, 377, 405

'Dutch Church libel' 47-9, 50, 346-52, 358, 359-60, 361, 372-3, 374

Dyer, Sir Edward 213, 310

Dyer, Captain (?Robert) 293

East, Thomas 451

Eccles, Mark 450

Ede, Richard 195, 423, 467

Edge, John 112-3

Edwards, Thomas 61; Narcissus (epitaph to Marlowe) 61, 225

Eliot, T. S. 200

Elizabeth I 14, 15, 21, 41, 46, 61, 122, 136, 236, 263, 304; and British foreign policy 124-5, 255; and Lord Burghley 42, 122, 123, 264; conspiracies against 123-4, 154, 166, 293, 444 (*see also* 'Babington Plot'; 'Lopez Affair'; 'Stafford Plot'); and Dorothy Devereux's marriages 93, 95; and Essex 33, 34; knights Drake 15-6, and Thomas Walsingham 433; marriage negotiations 124, 139, 216, 392; and Ralegh 369; and Sir William Stafford 393; and Topcliffe 134

Englefield, Sir Francis 354

English Colleges *see* Douai; Rheims; Rome

Epigrammes and Elegies By I. D. and C. M. 448-51

Epistle of Comfort, An see Southwell, Robert

Essex, Robert Devereux, 2nd Earl of 92, 94, 330; and Christopher Blount 165; and Cholmeley 452-3; and Drury 395, 396; and Elizabeth I 33, 34, 93, 95; execution 418, 419; French expedition 33-4, 293; intelligence network 129, 264, 265, 266, 299, 369, 381, 532; and Meres 460; rivalry with Ralegh 95, 232, 369, 410; and Skeres 33-4, 293, 318, 410, 436-8

Essex, Walter Devereux, 1st Earl of 287

Evelyn, John 41

Fall of the Late Arian, The see Proctour, John

Farnese, Rainutio 429

Faunt, Nicholas 130, 142-3, 144, 442-5

Faust, Georg 248

Fawkes, Guy 275, 354

Field, Richard: Blackfriars shop 87

Finch, Sir Moyle 359

Fineux, Thomas Sr 365

Fineux, Thomas 244-5

Fingelow, John 117, 147

Fitton, Sir Edward 174, 177, 289

Fitzherbert, Thomas 133

Fixer, John 272

Fleetwood, William 31

Florio, John 246

Flud, Evan 279, 282-3

Flushing, Netherlands 278, 289; Marlowe's arrest 278-80, 281-5; Marlowe as spy 293-5, 297, 299, 306, 307, 318, 402, 405; Moody in 302-4, 306, 307; White in 304, 404-5

Foxe, John 7

'Foxley' *see* Grately, Edmund

Francisci, Iacomo ('Captain Jacques') 274-5, 293

Freeman, Albert 436

Frizer, Ingram 26-8, 423, 435-6; confusion over names 21, 98-9; and Marlowe's murder 18-20, 21, 22, 23, 26, 28, 80-1, 92, 96, 100-1, 409, 414, 415; and Skeres 22, 26, 100, 101, 411, 423-4; and Lady Walsingham 433; and Thomas Walsingham 78, 81,

109, 138, 141; and Woodleff 24-6, 411-2
Frizer, Peter 435
Frodsham, Henry 398
Furnival's Inn of Chancery, Holborn 30, 61
Furriar, John 216

Gallop, George 213
Garnett, Henry 212-3
Gascoigne, George 203, 209; *The Spoil of Antwerp* 203
Gawdy, Philip 242
Gaymer, Henry 204
Gerard, John 273, 276, 488
Gerard, Sir Thomas 273
Gifford, George 194
Gifford, Gilbert 115, 131, 169, 199, 204, 205, 288; and 'Babington Plot' 154, 156, 176, 179, 188; death 199
Gifford, Dr William 154, 328, 443
Gilbert, Bartholomew 281
Gilbert, Gifford 279, 281, 282, 283-4
Gill, Roma 449
Gilpin, George 127
Globe Theatre, London 85, 90
Golden Hind 15-6
Gonson, Benjamin 440
Googe, Barnaby 219
Grately, Edmund 443-4
Greene, Robert 7-8, 31, 62, 202, 229, 247-8, 342, 504; accuses Marlowe of atheism 52, 242-3, 245-6, 250, 251, 253, 262-3, 340, 469; death 66, 72-3; pamphlets: *Ciceronis Amor* 210; *Greene's Groatsworth* ...

52, 469; *Perimedes the Blacksmith* 242-3, 245, 469; plays: *Alphonsus, King of Aragon* 243; (with Lodge) *A Looking Glass for London* 25; *The Tragical Reign of Selimus* 243, 367-8
Greenwich Palace 14, 15, 20, 161, 178, 314
Greenwood, John 324
Gregory XIII, Pope 146
Gregory, Arthur 129
Greville, Fulke 246
Guise, Henri, Duke of 124, 145, 146, 176, 200, 392
Guise, Marie of 164
'Gunpowder Plot' 313, 386, 418, 419, 488
Gunson (Gunstone), Humphrey 287, 288, 290, 376

Haddington, William Hamilton, Earl of 419
Haddock, George 206-7
Halfpenny, George 20
Hall, Anthony 160-1, 185, 206
Hammer, Paul 436, 452, 453
Handover, P. M.: *Arabella Stuart* 431
Harington, Sir John: *Metamorphosis of Ajax* 217
Hariot, Thomas 253, 420, 474; accused of atheism 360-1, 363, 364, 420; and Marlowe 95, 360, 361; and Northumberland 95, 231, 232, 253, 262, 358, 360, 418, 440
Harvey, Dr Gabriel 62, 127, 210, 213, 420; account of Marlowe's death (in

'Gorgon') 70-2, 73-4, 75-6, 77; attacks Nashe and Marlowe 63-4, 65, 71-2, 441; gloats over Greene's death 72-3
Harvey, Reverend Richard 62, 73
Harvey, William 454
Hastings, Sir Francis 277
Hatton, Sir Christopher 110, 188
Hawkyns, Sir John 14
Heneage, Sir Thomas 131, 224, 227-8, 265, 359, 404; death 418, 523; and Moody 300, 301, 302, 303, 305, 429; and Poley 36, 228, 265, 300-1, 302, 303, 422
Henri III, of France 146, 254
Henri IV, of France (Henri of Navarre) 34, 200, 201
Henry VIII, of England 41, 63, 93, 271, 337
Hesketh, Richard 'Hesketh plot' 295-7, 309, 310, 311, 404, 418, 522
Hesketh, Sir Thomas 522
'Hickman, Mr' 296
Hickman brothers 418
Hilliard, Nicholas 429
Hoffman, Calvin 6
Hog Lane: Marlowe's fight with Bradley 103, 210-12, 287
Holder (W.) & Sons 6, 9
Hole, Thomas 238-9
Holford, Thomas 329
Hollford, Agnes 161, 162
Holt, William 313, 328, 522, 525
Hopkins, Richard 297

Hopton, Sir Owen 193, 211
Hotson, Leslie 99
Howard, Charles, 2nd Baron Howard of Effingham 14, 42, 331, 340
Howard, Sir George 42
Howard, Henry 389-90
Howard, Philip see Arundel, Earl of Howard, Thomas see Norfolk, Duke of
Huddlestone family 116
Hues, Robert 232
Hunsdon, Henry Carey, 1st lord 110, 331, 340, 378, 370, 380
Huntingdon, Earl of 277
Huntingdon Grammar School 77

Isam, Mrs 72
Ive (Ivy), Paul 143-4; The Practice of Fortification 144

Jackson, Edward 160, 236-7
'Jacques, Captain' see Francisci, I acomo
James I, of England (James VI, of Scotland) 312-3, 314, 366, 402, 419, 420, 433
Jefferys, Reverend Nicholas 534
Jeffries, Thomas 127
Jermyn, Sir Robert 491, 492
Jessop, Reverend John 534
Johnson, Richard 116
Johnson, Rowland 451
Jones, Reverend 98
Jones, Richard 274
Jonson, Ben 202, 205, 420, 422, 481; The Case is Altered 208; Eastwood Ho

420; 'Inviting a Friend to Supper' 422-3; (with Nashe) *The Isle of Dogs* 79, 422, 532

Kalb, Eugénie de 432-3, 440
Kelley, Sir Edward 309-11
Kemp, Will 268
Kendall, Roy 445, 446, 448
King, Allen 426
Kitchen, Richard 212
Krueger, Robert 449
Kyd, Thomas 49-50, 54, 82, 232, 268, 374-5, 376, 400-1, 402, 419; accused of Dutch Church libel 50, 347, 349, 351-2, 372-3; accuses Marlowe of atheism 53, 54, 309, 319, 323, 406; accuses Marlowe of violence 102-3, 199-200; found with Arian treatise 50-1, 347, 349, 352-5, 360, 373-4, 401; on Marlowe and Roydon 309, 311-2, 313-4, 361, 419; on Marlowe and Lord Strange 269, 277, 297-8

Lakes, Stephen 7
Lambe, John 234
Lange, Adrian de 404-5
Langton, Thomas, 'Baron of Walton' 271, 309, 330
Lawson, Tom 266
Leicester, Robert Dudley, Earl of 122, 124, 274, 287-8, 390, 397; and Christopher Blount 165, 169, 170, 193; and Bruno 254, 255; and Poley 158, 160, 163, 164, 171

Leicester's Commonwealth 37-8, 162, 288
Lewknor, Samuel 296
Lilly, William 444
Littleton, Edward: Essex's letter to 452
Lloyd, David (author) 123, 124
Lloyd, David (ensign) 279, 283, 285
Lodge, Thomas 466; *A Fig for Momus* 283; (with Greene) *A Looking Glass for London* 25
'Lopez Affair' 348, 437, 457, 502
Lord Admiral's Men 241, 268
Lord Chamberlain's Men 268
Lord Strange's Men 49, 87, 268
Lower, Sir William 253
Lucan: *Pharsalia* (Marlowe's translation) 83, 201
Lumley, Lord 231, 283
Lyly (Lilly), John 210, 213, 227, 342, 444

Macander, Reverend Thomas 21
Machiavelli, Niccolò/Machiavellianism 47-8, 63, 331, 339-40
'Main Plot' 366
Mansell, John 347
Manwood, Sir Roger 456
Markenfield, Sir Thomas 282
Markham, Sir Griffin 291
Markham, Jervis 200
Marlin, William 427
Marlowe, Anthony 440
Marlowe, Christopher 3-5; accused of atheism 44, 50-3,

65, 66-7, 243-5, 318-9, *see
also* Baines, Richard ('Note'),
Cholmeley, Richard, Greene,
Robert, Kyd, Thomas;
accused of violence 102-3,
199-200; as 'Aretine' 63-4,
65, 70; Bruno's influence
248-50, 251, 253-4; burial
20-1; at Cambridge 6, 7, 10,
62, 110-11, 114-5, 118-21,
143, 244, 442; and George
Chapman 30, 82, 229, 357;
as counterfeiter 278-85, 293-
5, 402; death and inquest 18-
23, 26, 37, 39, 44-5, 59, 97,
98, 100-1, 102, 104-5, *see
also* Beard, Thomas, Frizer,
Ingram, Harvey, Dr Gabriel
Meres, Francis, Skeres,
Nicholas, Vaughan, William;
and Drury 381-2, 390, 394,
412; epitaphs *see* Edwards,
Thomas, Peele, George; fight
with Bradley 103, 210-2,
287; and Hariot 95, 360,
361; homosexuality 431-2;
involvement in intelligence
work 4-5, 110-3, 199-200,
122, 130, 137, 138, 155,
156, 163, 257, 261-2, 294-5,
299, 402-3, 404, 405, 407;
and Moody 194, 302, 306,
429, 444; and Nashe 61, 62-
3, 64-9, 82-3; in Newgate
211, 212, 287; as poet and
playwright 4, 44, 63, 122,
200-2, *see Works* (*below*);
portrait 5-10, 119, 120-1;
and Roydon 30, 309, 311-
14, 402; and Francis
Walsingham 122, 156, 257,
261, *see also* Baines,
Richard; Cecil, Sir Robert;
Northumberland, 9th Earl
of; Poley, Robert; Ralegh, Sir
Walter; Strange, Lord;
Walsingham, Thomas;
Watson, Thomas *Works*:
'Come Live With Me' 103,
233; *Dido, Queen of
Carthage* 68, 201, 431; *Dr
Faustus* 4, 64, 201, 202,
229-30, 243, 245, 248-50,
251, 252, 257, 357, 446;
Edward II 121, 201, 340,
431; *Hero and Leander* 21,
26, 61, 81, 83, 85, 86-7,
400, *see also* Blount,
Edward, Chapman, George;
Jew of Malta 4, 47-8, 86,
148, 201, 268, 270, 340,
348, 394; Lucan's *Pharsalia*
(translation) 83, 201; *The
Massacre at Paris* 48, 89-90,
200-1, 268, 270, 348-9, 431,
433; Ovid's *Elegies*
(translation) 83, 201, 448,
449; *Tamburlaine the Great*
47, 120, 201, 241, 243, 274,
340, 367; *Tamburlaine,
Second Part . . .* 144, 241-2,
246
Marlowe, Edmund 440
Marlowe, John 40, 114
Marlowe, Katherine (*née*
Arthur) 244
Marlowe, Walter 440
Marprelate pamphlets 207,
342, 449
Marshalsea, the 133, 135,
159- 60, 224, 236, 288, 422;
Drury in 332, 393; Poley in

36, 37, 158-60, 195, 215, 423

Marston, John 200

'Martin, Giles' *see* Barnes, Thomas

Martin, Gregory 214

Martin, Sir Richard 34, 35

Martin, Richard 450

Marvell, Andrew 202

Mary I (Mary Tudor) 123, 136

Mary Queen of Scots (Mary Stuart) 123, 128, 140, 194, 214, 236; and 'Babington Plot' 32, 129, 155, 173, 174, 180-1, 183-4, 185, 261; and Morgan 128-9, 161, 164, 165-7, 168, 169-71; and Poley 171

Maude, Barnard 175, 176, 179, 188

Maunder, Henry 53-4, 206, 400

Mauvissière, Michel de Castelnau, Sieur de la 251, 254

Medici, Catherine de' 216

Meeres, Dorothy 460

Meeres, John 391-2, 453, 455-60

Mendoza, Don Bernadino de 168, 175

Meres, Francis 79, 420; account of Marlowe's death 80-1, 84, 85, 87, 97-8, 104, 105, 409; *Palladis Tamia* 74, 79-81, 208, 210

Meyrick, Gilly (Gelly): Skeres' letter to 436-9

Middleton, Thomas 250

Milles, Francis 32, 130, 131, 138, 186, 190

Mondoucet, Monsieur de 16

Montague, Dean James 41-2

Montpensier, Duke of 392

Moody, Michael 115, 265, 300-6, 392, 421; and Marlowe 194, 302, 306, 429, 444; and Poley 301, 302, 303, 305, 307, 387; and 'Stafford Plot' 194, 301, 387; and Sir Robert Sidney 302-4; and the Tippings 302, 344, 404-5

More, Sir Thomas 7

Morgan, Thomas 128-9, 164, 174, 175, 204, 217, 267, 392; and Poley 161, 162, 164-72, 217, 314

Morley (tutor) 428-30

Morley, John 426-7

Morley, Thomas 430-1

Mowbray, John 525

Munday, Anthony 85, 205-8, 342; *Discovery of Edmund Campion* 206; *The English Romayne Life* 206

Muscovy Company 439, 440, 441

Mynne, William 395-6

Nashe, Thomas 24, 62, 83, 114, 208, 229, 342, 419, 532; 'exiled' 79, 82; and Greene 52, 62; and Dr Gabriel Harvey 62, 63-5, 74-5, 127, 441; on Harvey's 'Gorgon' 71-2, 76; and Marlowe 61, 62-3, 64-9, 82-3; in Newgate 441-2; in praise of Alleyn 241, Roydon 308, and Watson 210; and Lord Strange 268-9, 526;

Works: Carmine Elegiaco. . .
68, 77; *The Choice of
Valentines* 269; *Christ's
Tears over Jerusalem* 66-7,
88, 441; (with Jonson) *The
Isle of Dogs* 79, 422, 532;
Lenten Stuff 82; *Pierce
Penniless* 63, 70, 268-9, 362;
Strange News 74-5; *Terrors
of the Night* 441-2, 526; *The
Unfortunate Traveller* 61,
63-6, 67
Natridge, Dente 14
Nau, Claude 182, 184
Naunton, Sir Robert 123, 369
Newgate prison: Marlowe in
211, 212, 287; Nashe in
441-2; John Poole in 286-7,
290, 291; Skeres in 422
Nicols, John 150
Noel, Henry 256
Norfolk, Thomas Howard, 3rd
Duke of 123, 214
Norris, Sir Henry 216
Norris, Richard 160-1, 162,
217
Norris, Silvester 161
North, Roger, Lord 157
Northumberland, Countess of
(*formerly* Dorothy Perrot)
93-5, 97
Northumberland, Henry Percy,
8th Earl of 234, 235-6, 239
Northumberland, Henry Percy,
9th Earl of 59, 230-2, 234-7,
292, 393-4, 418, 429; and
Bruno 251-3, 255-6; literary
circle 60, 233, 238, 251,
252, 253, 255-6, 309, 357-8,
360, 361; and Marlowe 60,
95, 232, 239-40, 251, 253,
257, 262-3, 360, 361; and
Ralegh 60, 95, 231, 232-3,
292, 358, 393, 418; and
Lord Strange 270-1, 276,
293, 308; and Watson 228-
30, 238-9, 256
Northumberland, Thomas
Percy, 7th Earl of 234

Ocland, Christopher 214
Ovid 88-9; *Elegies* (Marlowe's
translation) 83, 201, 448,
449
Owen, Hugh 275, 277, 281,
299, 302-4, 313
Oxford, Francis de Vere, Earl
of 227, 389-90
Oxinden, Henry 243-5, 464

Paget, Charles 164, 175, 217,
299, 392, 493; corres-
pondence with Thomas
Barnes 430-1; and Moody
304, 404-5; and Morgan
164, 167, 168, 170, 175; and
the Northumberlands 234-5,
236, 237; and Poley 167,
168, 170, 182
Paracelsus 248
Parker, George: Sir Robert
Drury's letter to 395-6
Parker, Archbishop Matthew 7
Parkins, Christopher 213, 526
Parma, Alessandro Farnese,
Duke of 112, 176, 267, 275,
303, 429
Parpoynt *see* Pierrepoint,
Gervaise
Parradine, Richard 28
Parrat (prison-informer) 423
Parris, Ferdinando 116

Parry, Blanche 41, 42, 531; will 439

Parry, William 112, 166, 264

Paule, Stephen 127

Paulet, Sir Amias 128, 181

Peele, George 52, 80, 269, 419; *The Honour of the Garter* (first epitaph to Marlowe) 59-60, 69, 95, 225, 252-3; and Northumberland 59, 60, 95, 229, 262, 357; and Watson 210, 213, 229

Pembroke, Mary Herbert, Countess of 204-5, 209, 227, 251

Penry, John 324

Percy, Harry 266

Percy, Lord Henry *see* Northumberland, 9th Earl of

Percy, Sir Thomas 234

Perrot, Lady Dorothy (*née* Devereux) *see* Northumberland, Countess of

Perrot, James 93, 94; *The Consideration of Human Condition* 94; *A Discovery of Discontented Minds* 94

Perrot, Sir John 93

Perrot, Sir Thomas 93, 94-5

Perrot, William 93

Persons, Robert 116, 117, 162, 164, 235, 267, 299, 336; and Lord Strange intrigue 272-4, 275, 277; *Responsio ad Edictum Elizabethae* 363, 364

Pett, Peter 13

Phelippes, Thomas 128; and 'Babington Plot' 128-9, 160, 181, 182, 183-4, 186, 411;

and the Bacons 266, 267; and Burghley 266; and Drury 374, 378; in Essex's network 129, 266, 267, 369, 381, 410; and Kyd's Arian treatise 355, 374; on libel commission 351, 352, 372; and Marlowe's incrimination 352, 355, 368, 411; and Meeres 457-9; and Morgan 128-9, 217; and Poley 170, 171-2, 182; and Ralegh 368, 369; and Skeres 410-1; on Stransham 288; and Lady Arabella Stuart and Thomas Morley 430-1; in Walsingham's intelligence service 46, 126, 128, 129, 131, 132, 138, and Thomas Walsingham 140

Philip II, of Spain 274, 275; *see also* Burnell, Anne

Philipps, Sir Thomas 347

Pickering, Sir William 265

Pierrepoint (Parpoynt), Gervaise 160

Pole, Cardinal Reginald 288

Poley, Sir John 157, 165

Poley (Pooley), Robert 36-8, 157-9, 161-2, 199, 215, 504; and 'Babington Plot' 35-6, 124, 140-1, 160-1, 173, 177-80, 181-3, 184-7, 189-95; and Christopher Blount 157, 164-5, 166, 167, 168, 169; in intelligence service 36-7, 109, 112, 115, 163, 265, 267, 299-301, 314, 412-14, 422-3 (*see also under* Moody, Michael; Morgan, Thomas; Walsingham, Sir

Francis); letter to Leicester 163, 164; and Marlowe 306-7, 314, 318, 403, 405, 412, 413-4; and Marlowe's death 18, 19, 20, 22-3, 100-1, 156, 409-10, 414, 415-6; and Norris 160-1, 217; and Thomas Walsingham 140-1, 142, 152, 161, 186, 262, 306; and Watson 215, 217, 218

Poole, Geoffrey 288

Poole, John, Sr 286, 289, 290

Poole, John 286-91, 293, 306, 310, 330, 405

Poole, Mary (née Stanley) 289

Pooley, Robert see Poley, Robert

Popham, Sir John 366

Pormont, Thomas 134, 288

Porta, Giovanni Battista della: De Furtivis Literarum Notis 126

'Portingale voyage' 33, 330, 410

Prague: pro-Strange conspiracy 277, 295-7, 309, 310, 311, 314, 404

Privy Council 14; abused in 'Remembrances . . . against . . . Cholmeley' 331-2, 339-41, 379-80; Baines working for 54-5, 148, 149, 150-1; and Drury 370, 372, 379-80; and libels 46-7, 48-9, 348, 351-2, 359, 372; Kyd charged by 50-1, 373; Marlowe summonsed by 44, 51, 52, 53-4, 318-9, 400-2; Marlowe working for 110-13, 118, 130, 132, 239, 261,

262, 294, 295, 317-8; Poole investigated by 290; reaction to Rheims English College 146

Proctour, John: The Fall of the Late Arian 51, 354, 374

Puckering, Sir John 323-4, 342, 346, 357, 362, 368, 407, 408; annotations to Baines' 'Note' 323, 324-7; and Drury 372, 376, 377, 378, 380-1, 382-4, 395, 407, 459; Kyd's letter to 50, 268, 312, 323, 352-3, 361, 373

Puttenham: Art of English Poesy 102

Rackwood, John 116

Ralegh, Sir Walter: accused of atheism 52, 233, 360, 361-4, 365-9, 398, 432; as author and poet 232-3, 418; and Essex 95, 232, 369, 410; and Marlowe 52, 60, 233, 262, 357; Marlowe used in campaign against 359-64, 367-8, 405-6, 407, 415; and Meeres 392, 455-6, 457, 459, 460; and Northumberland 60, 95, 231, 232-3, 292, 358, 393, 418, 518; and Oxford 390; Poole attacks 290; against privileges for foreigners 45, 358-9; trial and execution 366-7, 398, 418

Read, Conyers 392

Renat/Renato (Italian assassin) 204

Rheims English College 111, 145-6, 147-8, 159, 204, 209;

alumni: Baines 146-7, 148-53, 155, 321-2, 445-8; Cambridge students 116-7, 145, Cycell 271-2, Gilbert Gifford 154, Morgan 164, Munday 206, Norris 160, John Savage 154, Stransham 288, William Watson 214; Marlowe associated with 110, 111, 113-4, 116, 117-8, 145, 155

Rich, Penelope, Lady (*née* Devereux) 385

Rich, Robert, Lord 385

Ricroft, John 303, 524

Ridolfi plot 123

Riggs, David 382

Roberts, Peter 442

Roebuck (ship) 393, 518

Rokewood, Ambrose 386

Rokewood, Dorothy (*née* Drury) 386

Rome: English College 111, 117, 150, 154, 159, 205, 206

Rose Theatre, London 4, 27, 48, 85, 87, 268, 394

Rossel, Pierre 14

Rowland, Humphrey 212

Rowley, Samuel 249-50

Rowling, J. Thompson 434-5

Royce, Wenfayd 14

Roydon, Matthew 308, 419-20; Chapman's *Shadow of the Night* dedicated to 309; and Kelley 309, 210-11; and Marlowe 30, 309, 311-4, 402; member of Northumberland circle 95, 229, 262, 308, 309, 357; and Skeres 30, 308; and Lord

Strange 269, 270, 308; and Watson 210, 213, 229, 308; writes elegy for Sir Philip Sidney 308

Rudierde, Edward: *Thunder-bolt of God's Wrath* 98

Rudolf II, Emperor 295, 310

Rutkin, Robert 300-1, 302, 305

Sadler, Sir Ralph 227

Salisbury, Magdalen (*née* Frodsham) 397-9

Salisbury, Robert Cecil, 1st Earl of *see* Cecil, Sir Robert

Salisbury, Thomas 174, 177, 180, 188

Sanderson, William 455, 456

Savage, Sir John 330

Savage, John: and Babington plot 154, 173, 176, 179, 180, 184; trial and execution 187, 188, 189

Sayer, Robert 116-7, 147

Sayes Court, Deptford 15, 41, 42, 440

Scadbury House, Kent 26, 28, 49, 73, 142

Schilders, Richard 451

'School of Night' *see* 'Durham House set'

Schrickx, Professor Willem 451, 452

Sedgrave, Patrick 525

Shakerley, Peter 72, 74-6

Shakespeare, William 209, 227, 268, 420, 433, 462, 522; *As You Like It* 85-90, 97; *Henry IV* 86; *Henry V* 438; *Henry VI* 87, 268; *Henry VIII* 337; *King Lear* 319; *Love's*

Labour's Lost 60, 270; *Love's Labour's Won* 79; *The Merchant of Venice* 86; *Titus Andronicus* 268; *Venus and Adonis* 87

Shaw, William 452

Sheffield, Lady Douglas 397

Shelley, William 159, 336

Shore (scrivener) 349-50

Short Admonition Upon the Detestable Treason, A (pamphlet) 274

Shrewsbury, Elizabeth Talbot, Countess of 276-7; letter to Lord Burghley 428, 430

Shrewsbury, George Talbot, Earl of 174

Sidney, Lady Frances (*née* Walsingham, *later* Countess of Essex) 124, 170, 177, 460

Sidney, Sir Philip 124, 169, 170, 213, 246, 254, 274, 279, 308; *Astrophel and Stella* 251, 385

Sidney, Sir Robert 279, 282, 284, 302-4, 451-2; letter to Lord Burghley 279-80, 281, 283, 293, 294

Simier, Jean de 392

Skeres, Jerome 30

Skeres, Nicholas 28, 30-1, 421-2, 423-4; and 'Babington Plot' 32, 33, 35, 141, 185, 411; and Drury 395, 412; and Essex 33-4, 266, 318, 395, 410, 436-9; involvement in intelligence work 32-3, 109, 266, 318; and Marlowe's murder 18, 19, 20, 22-3, 100, 101, 409-10, 411, 413-15; money-lending

activities 24, 25-6, 38-40; and Phelippes 410-11; and Poley 35, 410, 414, 416; and Roydon 30, 308, 311, 312; Star Chamber deposition 29-30, 312, 410; and Thomas Walsingham 139, 141, 142; and Woodleff extortion case 24, 25-6, 34, 411-2

Sledd, Charles 205, 206, 447

Smith, John 29

Smith, Otwell 427

Southampton, Henry Wriothesley, Earl of 227

Southwell, Robert 37, 129, 134, 191-2, 193, 333, 422; *An Epistle of Comfort* 334, 375, 403

Spenser, Edmund 203, 213, 269

Spenser, Gabriel 101

Stafford, Sir Edward 130, 143, 195, 204, 387, 392, 393, 397, 443-4

'Stafford Plot' 194, 301, 387

Stanley, Sir Edward 271

Stanley, Sir Rowland 271, 289, 329

Stanley, Sir William 126, 274-5, 281, 291, 293, 299; and Poole 289-90; and Lord Strange 271, 273-4, 275-6, 277, 293, 296

Stow, John 45, 222

Strange, Alice, Lady (*née* Spenser) 269, 292

Strange, Lord (Ferdinando Stanley, later 5th Earl of Derby) 268-77, 290, 293, 330; death 269-70, 418; and Marlowe 268, 269, 270,

277, 297-8, 314, 404; and
Northumberland 270-1, 276,
293, 308; and Prague
plotters 277, 295-7, 309,
310, 311, 314, 404; and
Roydon 308, 311, 314;
target of intrigue 271-4, 276-
7, 313, 402, 405
Stransham, George ('Potter')
288
Strong, Richard 335, 337
Strype, John: *Annals of the
Reformation* 347
Stuart, Arabella 428, 429, 430-
1
Sussex, Countess of 419
Swift, Hugh 223-4
Swift, Thomas 223, 224, 225

Tankard, Richard 311
Tannebaum, Dr Samuel: *The
Assassination of Christopher
Marlowe* 432
Tanner, Bishop Thomas 68
Theatre, The (Shoreditch) 4,
210, 250
Thomson, Sir George 6
Thorpe, Thomas (publisher) 83
Throckmorton, Francis
'Throckmorton Plot' 235,
254
Throckmorton, Thomas 164,
166-7
Thurston, Gavin 434, 435
Tichbourne, Chidiock 174,
177, 180, 187, 188, 189
Tilney, Charles 177, 180, 187,
189
Tipping, James 194, 302, 344,
360, 404, 405
Tipping, John 344, 360

Topcliffe, Richard 133-5, 331,
388; on Munday 206, 208;
on the Stanleys 276
Toper (Tupper), John 443
'Torre, Alessandro della' 391
Trappes, Leonard des 194

Udall, Sir Edmund 295
Udall, John 529
Ulysses upon Ajax (anon.)
216-7
Unitarianism 51
University Wits (literary set)
214
Unton, Sir Henry: letter to Lord
Burghley 427
Urry, Dr William 412

Vachel, John 333, 531
Vaughan, Sir John 94
Vaughan, Letitia (Lettice) (*née*
Perrot) 93-4
Vaughan, Walter 92, 93
Vaughan, William 92-3, 94,
420, 439; account of
Marlowe's death (in *The
Golden Grove*) 91-2, 94-6,
97-8, 104, 109, 409, 412
Verstegan, Richard 284, 333,
470-1, 522, 534
Vlissingen *see* Flushing

Waad, William 46, 130, 166,
351, 353-4, 355, 444, 448
Walpole, Henry 275, 276, 525,
534
Walsingham, Lady Audrey 26,
82, 419, 423, 432-3
Walsingham, Sir Francis 26,
123-4, 440; and 'Babington
Plot' 32, 33, 35, 124, 160,

173, 175, 177, 178-9, 180-1, 182, 183-4, 185-7, 190, 192; and Baines 146-7, 153, 154, 446, 447-8; and Bruno 254-5; death 216, 273, 419; and Faunt 443-4; intelligence service of 115-6, 122-3, 124-8, 129-33, 135-6, 138, 203, 228, 257, 263; and Marlowe 122; and Meeres 391, 458; and Northumberland 234, 236, 255-6; and Poley 37, 124, 158, 160, 161, 162, 169-72, 190, 191, 193, 195, 217; portrait 123; and Ralegh 390; Rheims English College infiltrated 145, 146-7; and Sir Edward Stafford 194, 204, 392, 443-4; and Thomas Walsingham 26, 109, 139, 140, 216; and Watson 216, 218

Walsingham, Guldeford 139

Walsingham, Thomas 73, 138-42, 262, 419, 433; *Hero and Leander* dedicated to 21, 81-2; as Marlowe's patron 26, 28, 49, 73, 138, 142, 144, 349, 400, 402; and Poley 140-1, 142, 152, 161, 186, 262, 306; and Francis Walsingham 26, 109, 139, 140, 216; and Watson 216-7, 238

Walton, Baron of *see* Langton, Thomas

Walton, Roger 38, 239, 265, 266, 280, 421

Warner, Walter 95, 231-2, 262, 418, 472

Warton, Thomas 68

Watson, Anne (*née* Swift) 223, 227

Watson, Thomas 209-10, 212-4; and Bruno 256-7; and Anne Burnell 219-22; defrauds the Cornwallises 223-4; friendship with Marlowe 60, 61, 210, 211-2, 225-6, 256-7; marriage 223; and Northumberland 357-8; Peele's tribute to 60, 61; and Poley 215, 217, 218; and the Walsinghams 215-8; *works: Amintae Gaudia* 209; *Amintas* 209, 256; *Antigone* 213, 214; *Compendium Memoriae Localis* 256, 257; *Ekatompathia* 209, 210, 308; *Helenae Raptus* 228, 229, 238; *Meliboeus* 216, 217

Watson, William 214-5

Webb, Laurence 445

Webbe, Thomas 310, 526

Wenden, Thomas 37

Wernham, Professor Robert B. 279

White (priest) 133

White, Stephen 304, 404-5

Whitgift, John, Archbishop of Canterbury 36, 83, 110, 342, 344

Whitney, Eleanor *see* Bull, Eleanor

Whitney, Eustace 439

Whitney, James 41

Whitney, John 42

Whitney, Robert 439

Whitney, Sybill (*née* Baskerville) 439

Whitworth, Geoffrey 212

Wiggington, Reverend Giles 207

Wilbrom, Mr 342

William of Orange 124, 203

Williams, Richard 275, 292-3, 344

Williams, Sir Roger 34

Williamson, Edmund 34, 35, 410, 421, 500

Williamson, James 35

Williamson, Nicholas 34, 193-4, 500, 517

Wilson, Richard 439, 441

Winchester Cathedral robbery 291-3

Winchester School 212-3

Wolfall, John 28-9, 30, 31-2, 33, 308, 311, 438

Wolfall, John, Jr 451

Wolfe, John (publisher) 61, 70, 73, 75

Wolley, Sir John 61

Wood, Anthony à: *Athenae Oxonienses* 98

Woodcock, Thomas (publisher) 68

Woodleff, Anne (*née* Drury) 24, 412

Woodleff, Drew 24, 25-6, 34, 411-2

Wyld, Stephen 211

Yates, Frances 247, 254

Yeomans, Joan 158-9, 161, 193, 215, 423

Yeomans, William 37-8, 158, 159, 193, 194-5, 513

Yorke, Edmund 126, 276, 344, 533

Yorke, Sir Rowland 274, 276, 503

Young, Henry (Harry) 328, 344, 360, 375, 518, 521

Young, Justice Richard 290, 326, 331, 338, 342, 375, 376, 401

Younger, James 271

Also available from Vintage

Charles Nicholl

THE FRUIT PALACE

'Evokes that vague, sleepy enchantment which comes from dreaming of "somewhere else"...there are echoes of Chandler, of Burroughs, of Baudelaire and even of Eliot"
Sunday Times

Charles Nicholl is on a quest for 'The Great Cocaine Story'. The time is the early eighties and the place – Colombia. The Fruit Palace is a little whitewashed café and juice-shop a couple of blocks off the Caribbean Sea, but it is also a meeting place for a variety of black-market activities and the place where Nicholl unwittingly begins his quest.

Nicholl relates his story with irrepressible energy and vividness as he careens from shantytowns and waterfront barrios to steamy jungle villages and slaughterhouses. He survives fever, earthquake and discovery by a dealer who threatens to 'check his oil' with a knife. And he emerges with a triumphant piece of travel writing which is also a comic extravaganza.

'One of the most absorbing travel books I have read...No book I know gives a more perceptive glimpse of the life of the urban poor who are the majority of South Americans. A brilliant book, informative, well-written and fun to read'
New York Times Book Review

VINTAGE BOOKS
London